CYCLING USA WEST COAST

Marisa Gierlich
Gregor Clark
Neil Irvine
Tullan Spitz
Katherine Widing

LONELY PLANET PUBLICATIONS
Melbourne • Oakland • London • Paris

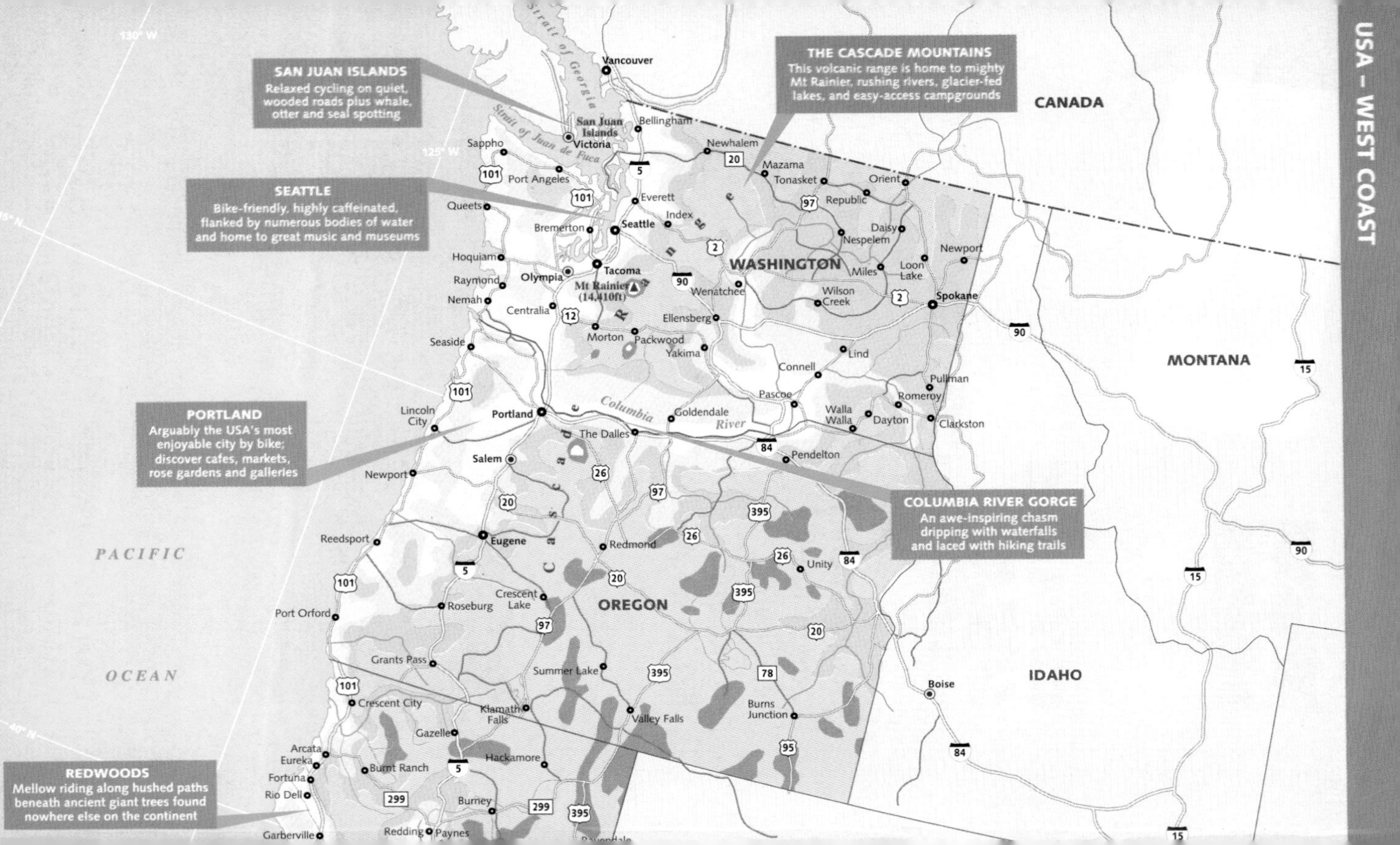
USA – WEST COAST
SAN JUAN ISLANDS
Relaxed cycling on quiet, wooded roads plus whale, otter and seal spotting
THE CASCADE MOUNTAINS
This volcanic range is home to mighty Mt Rainier, rushing rivers, glacier-fed lakes, and easy-access campgrounds
SEATTLE
Bike-friendly, highly caffeinated, flanked by numerous bodies of water and home to great music and museums
PORTLAND
Arguably the USA's most enjoyable city by bike; discover cafes, markets, rose gardens and galleries
COLUMBIA RIVER GORGE
An awe-inspiring chasm dripping with waterfalls and laced with hiking trails
REDWOODS
Mellow riding along hushed paths beneath ancient giant trees found nowhere else on the continent
CANADA
MONTANA
IDAHO
WASHINGTON
OREGON
PACIFIC
OCEAN
Strait of Georgia
Strait of Juan de Fuca
Columbia River
Vancouver
San Juan Islands
Victoria
Bellingham
Sappho
Port Angeles
Everett
Queets
Seattle
Index
Bremerton
Hoquiam
Tacoma
Olympia
Raymond
Mt Rainier (14,410ft)
Nemah
Centralia
Wenatchee
Ellensberg
Morton
Packwood
Yakima
Seaside
Newhalem
Mazama
Tonasket
Republic
Orient
Daisy
Nespelem
Newport
Miles
Loon Lake
Wilson Creek
Spokane
Lind
Connell
Pullman
Romeroy
Pascoe
Walla Walla
Dayton
Clarkston
Lincoln City
Portland
Goldendale
The Dalles
Pendelton
Salem
Newport
Reedsport
Eugene
Redmond
Unity
Crescent Lake
Roseburg
Port Orford
Grants Pass
Summer Lake
Crescent City
Klamath Falls
Valley Falls
Burns Junction
Boise
Gazelle
Arcata
Eureka
Hackamore
Burnt Ranch
Fortuna
Rio Dell
Burney
Garberville
Redding
Paynes
130° W
125° W
45° N
40° N

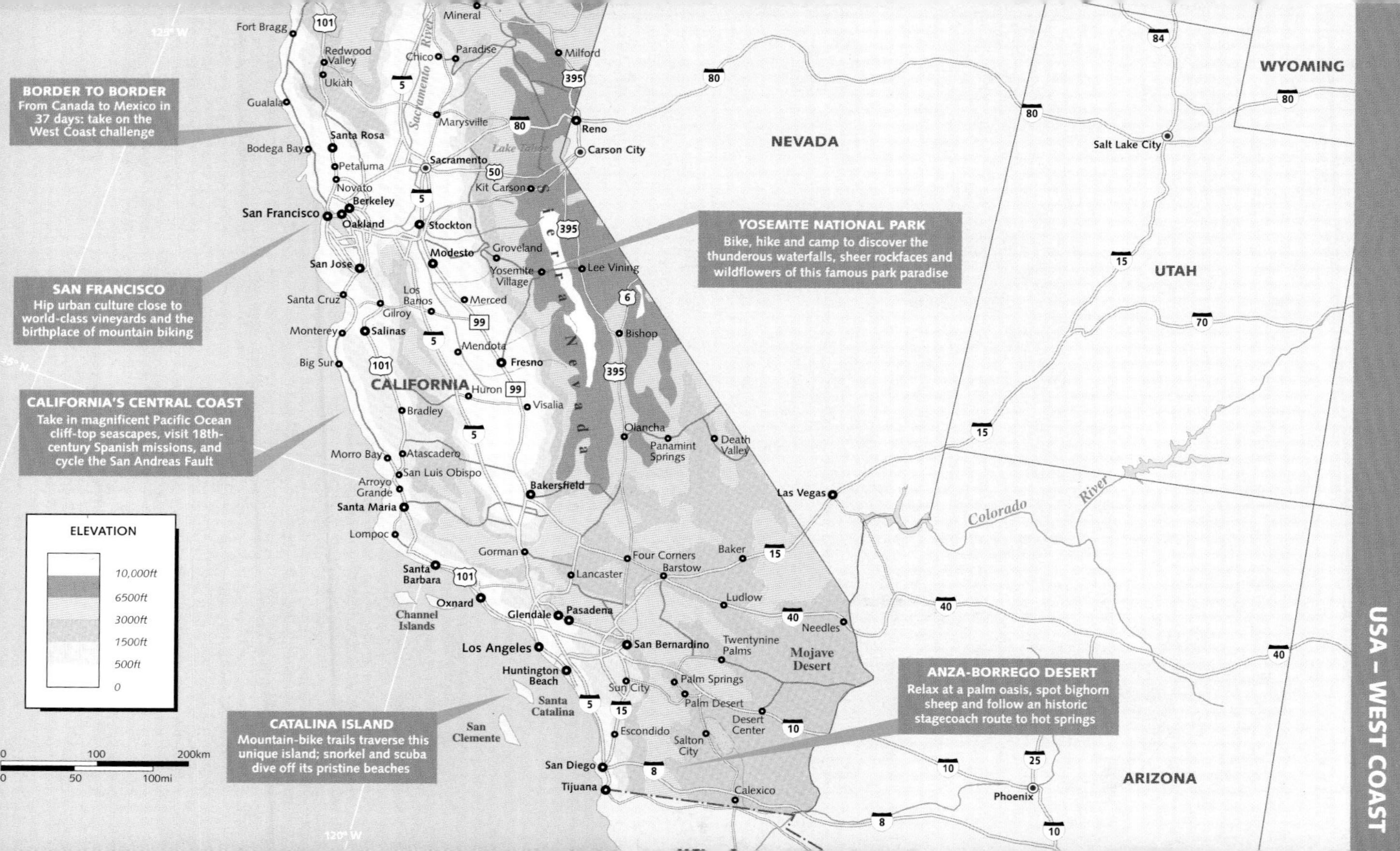

BORDER TO BORDER
From Canada to Mexico in 37 days: take on the West Coast challenge
SAN FRANCISCO
Hip urban culture close to world-class vineyards and the birthplace of mountain biking
CALIFORNIA'S CENTRAL COAST
Take in magnificent Pacific Ocean cliff-top seascapes, visit 18th-century Spanish missions, and cycle the San Andreas Fault
YOSEMITE NATIONAL PARK
Bike, hike and camp to discover the thunderous waterfalls, sheer rockfaces and wildflowers of this famous park paradise
CATALINA ISLAND
Mountain-bike trails traverse this unique island; snorkel and scuba dive off its pristine beaches
ANZA-BORREGO DESERT
Relax at a palm oasis, spot bighorn sheep and follow an historic stagecoach route to hot springs
ELEVATION
10,000ft
6500ft
3000ft
1500ft
500ft
0
0
100
200km
0
50
100mi
125° W
120° W
35° N
NEVADA
UTAH
WYOMING
ARIZONA
CALIFORNIA
Sierra Nevada
Mojave Desert
Colorado River
Sacramento River
Lake Tahoe
Channel Islands
Santa Catalina
San Clemente
Fort Bragg
Redwood Valley
Ukiah
Mineral
Chico
Paradise
Milford
Gualala
Marysville
Reno
Carson City
Santa Rosa
Bodega Bay
Petaluma
Novato
Sacramento
Kit Carson
Berkeley
San Francisco
Oakland
Stockton
Modesto
Groveland
Yosemite Village
Lee Vining
San Jose
Santa Cruz
Los Banos
Gilroy
Merced
Bishop
Monterey
Salinas
Mendota
Fresno
Big Sur
Huron
Visalia
Bradley
Olancha
Panamint Springs
Death Valley
Morro Bay
Atascadero
San Luis Obispo
Arroyo Grande
Bakersfield
Santa Maria
Las Vegas
Lompoc
Gorman
Four Corners
Baker
Barstow
Santa Barbara
Lancaster
Ludlow
Oxnard
Glendale
Pasadena
Needles
Los Angeles
San Bernardino
Twentynine Palms
Huntington Beach
Sun City
Palm Springs
Palm Desert
Desert Center
Escondido
Salton City
San Diego
Tijuana
Calexico
Salt Lake City
Phoenix
101
5
395
80
50
6
99
15
40
10
8
25
70
84

Cycling USA – West Coast
1st edition – May 2002

Published by
Lonely Planet Publications Pty Ltd ABN 36 005 607 983
90 Maribyrnong St, Footscray, Victoria 3011, Australia

Lonely Planet Offices
Australia Locked Bag 1, Footscray, Victoria 3011
USA 150 Linden St, Oakland, CA 94607
UK 10a Spring Place, London NW5 3BH
France 1 rue du Dahomey, 75011 Paris

Photographs
Many of the images inside are available for licensing from Lonely Planet Images.
e lpi@lonelyplanet.com.au
w www.lonelyplanetimages.com

Main front cover photograph
Cycle in the company of giants on Northern California's forest roads. (Craig Aurness, APL/Westlight)

Small front cover photograph
See San Francisco's famed Golden Gate Bridge by bike. (Ben Davidson)

ISBN 1 86450 324 6

Printed by SNP SPrint (M) Sdn Bhd
Printed in Malaysia

Contents

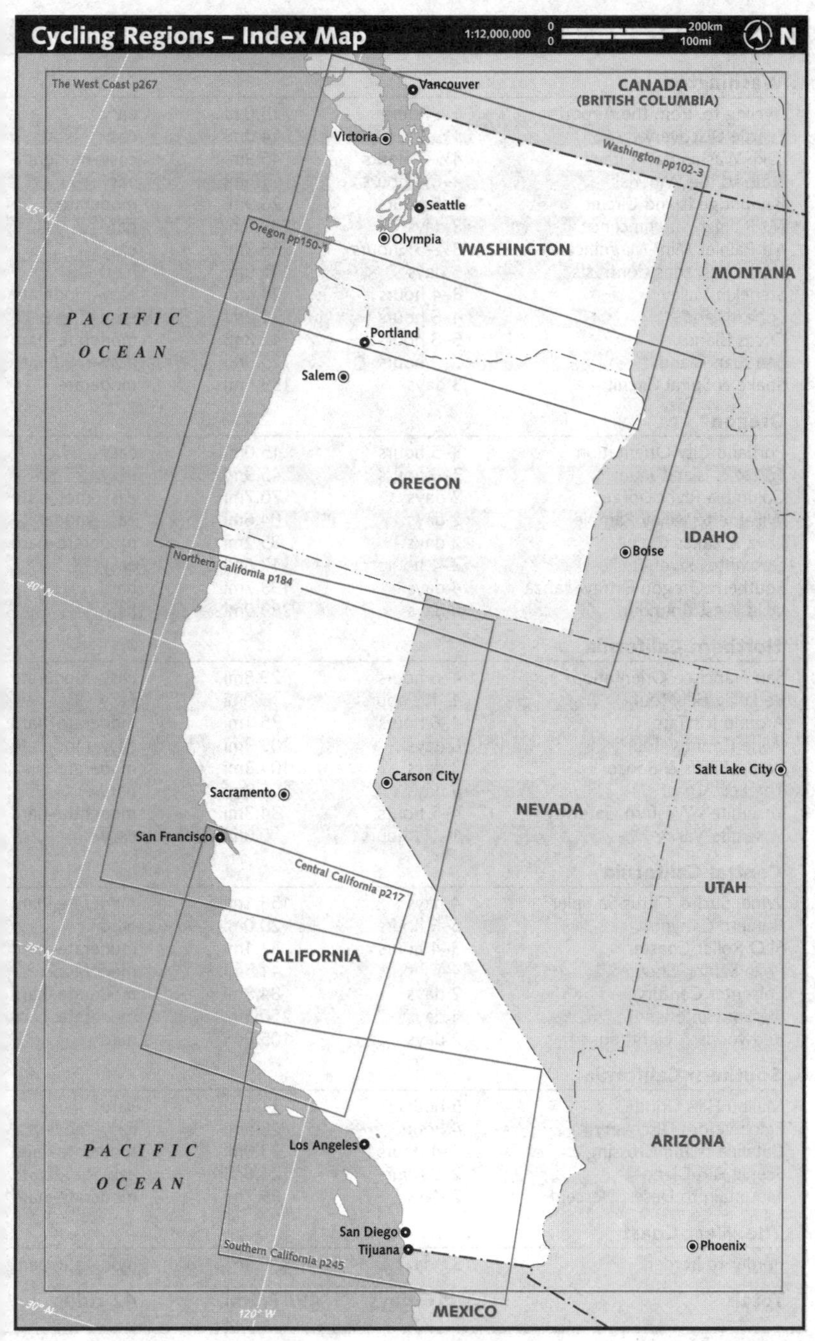
Cycling Regions – Index Map
1:12,000,000
0 200km
0 100mi
N
The West Coast p267
Vancouver
CANADA
(BRITISH COLUMBIA)
Victoria
Washington pp102-3
Seattle
Olympia
Oregon pp150-1
WASHINGTON
MONTANA
PACIFIC
OCEAN
Portland
Salem
OREGON
IDAHO
Boise
Northern California p184
Salt Lake City
Carson City
Sacramento
NEVADA
San Francisco
Central California p217
UTAH
CALIFORNIA
PACIFIC
OCEAN
Los Angeles
ARIZONA
San Diego
Tijuana
Phoenix
Southern California p245
MEXICO
45° N
40° N
35° N
30° N
120° W

The Rides	Duration	Distance	Difficulty
Washington			
Cycling to/from the Airport	1½ hours	15.0mi	easy
Seattle Discovery	1½–2½ hours	14.0mi	easy
Lake Washington Circuit	4½–7 hours	45.9mi	easy–moderate
Trails to the Wineries	4–6½ hours	51.4mi	easy
Bainbridge Island Circuit	3–5 hours	26.9mi	moderate
Mt Rainier Magnificence	3 days	173.0mi	hard
Mt Rainier Mini-Magnificence	3½–5½hours	35.3mi	easy
North Cascades Contrasts	5 days	247.0mi	hard
Stehekin Valley	3–4 hours	24.4mi	easy–moderate
Lopez Island	4–6 hours	31.2mi	easy
Orcas Island	5–8 hours	42.8mi	moderate–hard
San Juan Island	3–5 hours	25.9mi	easy–moderate
Snake & Spiral Circuit	3 days	139.5mi	moderate
Oregon			
Portland City Orientation	3–5 hours	15.0mi	easy
Forest & Island Jaunt	3–6 hours	45.9mi	easy
Columbia River Gorge	2 days	70.7mi	easy–moderate
Willamette Valley Ramble	2 days	104.6mi	easy–moderate
Lava & Lakes Circuit	2 days	85.2mi	moderate–hard
Deschutes River Trail	2–4 hours	17.6mi	easy
Southern Oregon Extravaganza	4 days	193.7mi	hard
Wild West Roundup	6 days	289.0mi	hard
Northern California			
San Francisco Orientation	4–6 hours	29.8mi	easy–moderate
Berkeley Hills Tour	1–1½ hours	9.0mi	easy
Around Mt Tam	4–6 hours	35.1mi	moderate–hard
Wine Country Tour	6 days	209.9mi	easy–moderate
Baths, Barns & Booze	3 days	104.3mi	moderate
The Lost Coast	3 days	106.3mi	hard
Yosemite's Western Gateway	4–5 hours	34.3mi	moderate–hard
Yosemite Valley	1–1½ hours	8.0mi	easy
Central California			
Wine, Surf & Citrus Sampler	4 days	158.1mi	moderate–hard
Romero Canyon	5–6 hours	20.0mi	hard
SLO Roller Coaster	3–4 hours	31.1mi	moderate–hard
Pozo Saloon Stagger	4–5 hours	41.5mi	moderate
Epicenter Century	2 days	84.8mi	moderate–hard
Big Sur Hinterland	5 days	250.3mi	moderate–hard
Redwoods & Lighthouse	2 days	105.8mi	hard
Southern California			
Malibu Hills Grind	5 hours	31.1mi	hard
Palos Verdes Discovery	4 hours	28.5mi	easy–moderate
Catalina Island Crossing	3–4 hours	23.0mi	moderate–hard
Scenic San Diego	2–3 hours	24.6mi	easy–moderate
Mountain to Desert Descent	2 days	89.7mi	moderate–hard
The West Coast			
Border to Border	37 days	1838.3mi	moderate–hard
Totals	**116 days**	**4957.5mi**	**42 rides**

The Authors

Marisa Gierlich

When Marisa wasn't skateboarding or surfing, she was riding her bike along the shores of Hermosa Beach, California, where she grew up. Weekend bike rides with Mom and Dad began at the age of five.

Her real passion for cycle touring developed when she began working for Backroads, leading tours of Yellowstone National Park and France's Loire Valley. Continually inspired by co-leaders' tales of cycling across the USA or from Fairbanks, Alaska, to Tierra del Fuego, Argentina, she decided to check out self-supported touring and immediately fell in love with it.

Most of her rides these days are with her husband, Paul, in the Berkeley Hills, although Rajasthan and a return to the Loire Valley are on this year's touring agenda. She finds no better way to get around, whether the distance is two or 200mi.

Marisa is also author of Lonely Planet's *Rocky Mountains*, *California & Nevada*, *California Condensed* and *Hiking in the USA*.

Gregor Clark

Gregor Clark started his cycling career with a bang, when at age six he hurtled down a steep New York City street on training wheels and collided with a trash can just short of Broadway. The experience made a lasting impression, and he has been fond of life on two wheels ever since.

A 20-year California resident, Gregor has traveled virtually every back road in the state and has also cycle toured in New England, the US and Canadian Rockies, Austria, France, Italy, Cuba and Bali. With a degree in Romance Languages, Gregor has visited over 50 countries and worked as a bilingual teacher, European bike tour leader, youth hostel travel store manager, and translation rights manager for a computer publishing company. Since 9 September 1999 he has enjoyed sharing his lifelong passion for languages, travel and the natural world with his mischievous daughter, Maggie.

Neil Irvine

Despite an abject failure to establish a career as a racing cyclist like his hero, the late Sir Hubert Opperman, Neil's determination to earn a living as a professional cyclist has not abated.

His first job at 15, as a telegram messenger (like Hubert), took him by bicycle to the far-flung corners of his New South Wales (Australia) home town. Later, as a cycling journalist and editor of *Push On* and *Australian Cyclist* magazines, he was able to cycle to the far-flung regions of Australia.

Now, with Lonely Planet, he is able to experience the world on two wheels and attempts to share the joy of discovery with a worldwide audience. He reckons it's a lot easier and much more fun than chasing Lance Armstrong up a mountain.

With his very supportive wife, Alethea, he has shared a love of cycling long distances and in mountains, in combination where possible. Lately their riding has been more gentle, with a child seat or trailer on the back, as they introduce their young children, Alexander and Laura, to cycling's pleasures.

Tullan Spitz

Tullan is a native of Cincinnati, Ohio, where at five or six years of age she insisted on learning to ride a bicycle. Due to her single-mindedness – and thanks to the patience and encouragement of her father – she succeeded. Following an inexplicable hiatus, she rediscovered the joy of cycling in her mid-20s while living in San Francisco, pursuing a former bike messenger whom she later married. Together they have been on many cycling adventures, and share a passion for lugged steel frames, leather saddles and woolies. Formerly an editor in Lonely Planet's Oakland office, Tullan lives in Portland, Oregon, and works for Oregon Public Broadcasting.

Katherine Widing

Katherine began cycling when she was five years old, riding her bike to school in Melbourne, Australia. France is the country that inspired her to take up international bicycle touring, and the country of her first Lonely Planet title, *Cycling France*. Addicted to cycle touring, she finds it allows her to travel at a pace she enjoys, observing, meeting people, inhaling sights, sounds and smells, plus it allows her to feel less guilty about copious chocolate consumption (her other addiction).

She has cycle toured in several European countries, the USA and her homeland, Australia. Her first book, *Cycling the Netherlands, Belgium & Luxembourg* was co-authored with husband, Jerry. She is a travel writer and has been the travel book editor for *Transitions Abroad* magazine since 1991. After a dozen years cycling the roads and bikepaths of Seattle and rural Washington she recently moved to northern California where more glorious cycling adventures await.

FROM THE AUTHORS

Marisa Gierlich Thanks to my Mom for always riding a little bit faster than me – even when I was 20 and you were 63! You instilled the 'just get out there and do it!' bug in me at an early age, which has taken me through so many great adventures. And thanks to my dad for his unquestioning support in all things.

Research wouldn't have been nearly as fun without the assistance of apple-eating, star-gazing Amy K. Thanks sweet thing! Paul pedaled me up the Ink Grade and made the best 'camping' partner at Harbin. He also makes the best life partner this wandering soul could ever imagine. The Lost Coast was more enjoyably found after conversations with brother Kurt, a night's rest with Kitty Rohrs and family visits with Aunt Martha. Thanks to the family!

John and Kim provided great material for the Wine Country and Sierra Nevada rides, while Jill and Eric Smith gave me shelter from no-storms. Last but never least go thanks to the Home Team, without whom writing books wouldn't be nearly as fun: Marla, Britt, the Mocks, Sara, Kelley, Paige, David, Kim, Bill and Sarah, Sharron, Baty, Kathleen and Steiner the cat.

Gregor Clark A huge thank you to Darren Elder, Marisa Gierlich, and Neil Irvine for making my first book project such a rewarding experience. Thanks also to Bernhard Schmidt, Roslyn Bullas, and John Spriggs at Lonely Planet.

An endless list of southern and central Californians offered their expertise and hospitality, helping this confirmed San Franciscan discover the beauty of the Golden State's 'other' half. Karen Hammer, Cory Irimes, Dennis Beltram, Elaine Simer, Dale Combs, Kathy Keehan, George Morrison, and the wonderful folks at the Parkfield Cafe deserve special mention.

I gratefully tip my helmet to all the cycling companions who have shared and fueled my enthusiasm for this wonderful way of seeing the world – especially Oliver Miller, Jim Bruce, Dawn Stephens, Monica Serrano, Peter Martin, Bob Gramberg, Carole St-Laurent, Jimbo Norrena, and Aideen O'Rourke – and to the friends and family members who have encouraged me to write over the years, among them, Julee Short, Ted Nace, Nancy Wartik, and my parents, Henry and Lyn Clark.

Thanks April, Jim, and Gabriel for lending the bike trailer to baby Maggie. Thanks Janida, Kristi, Jake, Ian, Luke, Jessica, Margo, Neil, Orlando, Emma, Ted, and Carl for watching the baby while I pedaled and for putting a roof over our vagabond heads.

Most of all, loving thanks to my wife Gaen Murphree and daughter Meigan Quetzal Clark, constant supporters and traveling companions, for making me smile and helping me live my dreams.

Neil Irvine Working on this book was made so much more enjoyable by the greater-than-usual interaction with other authors, since I was pedaling through (invading?) each one's territory. (You didn't seem to mind, guys.) Thanks particularly to Katherine and Gregor for successfully tracking me down and sharing some time on the road. Sorry to Tullan and Marisa that the schedules just didn't mesh – we'll hope for better luck next time.

Thanks also to cyclists met on the road for companionship, opinions, information and hospitality – Eric from West Virginia, Suzanne and Lloyd from San Francisco, Martin from Germany, the whole Halliwell family from New Zealand, Tony Parry from Newport Beach, and many others whose names I failed to catch.

Huge appreciation goes to the patient staff of various visitor centers for sharing their enthusiasm and helpful insights. My boundless gratitude and apologies also go to those left at home, carrying the burden during my absence. I wish you could have been with me to do the coast in the right direction this time.

Tullan Spitz Cycle touring can be an exhausting, solitary way to travel. People who offer directions, help, food – or merely a kind word – along the way make a significant difference in the quality of the journey. For their hospitality (and great pizza) I thank Julia and Alan Mendenhall in Baker City. For the lift from Elgin to La Grande that surely prevented a case of frostbite, I thank Joe Estes and little Misty. Thanks to Suk and Amit for sharing their home in Portland and to Patty, Bill, Oliver and Ruby for dinner in the garden.

I am grateful to my mother, father and sister for listening and generously providing advice and support; to Nicholas, my stepson, for reminding me to have fun; and to Felicity for laughing with me when that was what I needed most. Julie, having your kitchen and friendship to return to got me up the big hills. That brings me to Andrew, without whom this chapter would not have been conceived, pedaled, mapped or written, and with whom I look forward to spending all subsequent chapters in life.

Katherine Widing Thanks to all the friendly people and cyclists in Washington State, and particularly tourist office and National Park staff for their invaluable assistance. Thanks to bike shops and clubs for your cherished cycling camaraderie, information and advice.

Many thanks to Neil Irvine, Tullan Spitz, and Gregor Clark, a great team of authors, and to co-ordinating author, Marisa Gierlich. Locally, there are tons of people to thank, such as Julie Salathé of the Cascade Bicycle Club, Betty Widing, Don Strathy, Deborah Carlson, Hildur Lovel, Mike Seamans, Shirli Axelrod, Frauke Rynd and David 'Mac' Shelton. Huge smiles and gratitude to Mary Schafer, Lizza Demsetz and Leslie Anderson for enthusiastic pedaling.

To my husband Jerry, a Seattle native who introduced me to this diverse and spectacular state, thanks for your unfailing encouragement and support, and for being a great cycling companion.

WARNING & REQUEST

Things change – prices go up; schedules change; bad dirt roads get paved and decent ones get washed out; good places go bad and bad places go bankrupt – nothing stays the same. So, if you find things better or worse, recently opened or long since closed, please tell us and help make the next edition even more accurate and useful. We genuinely value all the feedback we receive. A well-traveled team reads and acknowledges every letter, postcard and email and ensures that every morsel of information finds its way to the appropriate authors, editors and cartographers for verification.

Everyone who writes to us will find their name in the next edition of the appropriate guidebook. They will also receive the latest issue of *Planet Talk*, our quarterly printed newsletter, or *Comet*, our monthly email newsletter. Subscriptions to both newsletters are free. The very best contributions will be rewarded with a free guidebook.

We may edit, reproduce and incorporate your comments in all Lonely Planet products, such as guidebooks, Web sites and digital products, so let us know if you don't want your comments reproduced or your name acknowledged.

Send all correspondence to the Lonely Planet office closest to you:

Australia: Locked Bag 1, Footscray, Victoria 3011
USA: 150 Linden St, Oakland, CA 94607
UK: 10a Spring Place, London NW5 3BH
France: 1 rue du Dahomey, 75011 Paris

Or email us at: e talk2us@lonelyplanet.com.au

For news, views and updates see our Web site: w www.lonelyplanet.com

Maps & Profiles

Most rides in this book have an accompanying map outlining the route and the services provided in towns en route (along with side trips, depending on the map scale). For greater detail, we also recommend the best commercial map available. The Border to Border feature ride is mapped for on-the-road use. You'll find a detailed map for every day of riding, showing the route, towns, services, attractions (look for the star symbol) and side trips. These maps are oriented left to right in the direction of travel; a north point is located in the top right corner of each map. The maps are intended to stand alone but could also be used with a commercial map.

We provide an elevation profile when there is a significant level of climbing and/or descending on a day's ride. These are found at the back of the book with the cue sheets, except for the Border to Border ride, where the profile and cues are placed on the map for that day.

FOLD&GO

The Border to Border ride maps are oriented in the direction of travel, so you can fold the book in half and slip it into your handlebar-mounted map case for easy reference on the road.

MAP LEGEND

Note: not all symbols displayed below appear in this book

MAP SYMBOLS

[ON RIDE MAPS]

Airport
Bike Shop/Repairer
Campground
Cafe or Takeaway
Grocery Store
Hostel
Hotel
Information
Place to Eat
Point of Interest, Other
Point of Interest in Town
Viewpoint (Lookout)

[ON CITY MAPS]

Bike Shop/Repairer
Information
Other Services
Place to Eat
Place to Stay
Point of Interest
Post Office
Transport

POPULATION

CAPITAL .... National Capital
CAPITAL .... State Capital
LARGE Medium .... City
Town .... Town
Town .... Start/End Town
Urban Area

ROUTES & TRANSPORT

Freeway
Primary Road
Secondary Road
Tertiary Road
Unsealed Road
Bikepath/Track
4WD/ATV Track
Train Line, Train Station
Tramway
Ferry

HYDROGRAPHIC FEATURES

Coastline, River, Creek
Lake

GEOGRAPHIC FEATURES

Mountain
Pass, Saddle

AREA FEATURES

Building
Park

CUE SHEET SYMBOLS

Continue Straight
Turn Right
Veer Right
Turn Left
Veer Left
Return Trip
Point of Interest
Mountain/Hill Climb
Alternative Route
Caution or Hazard
Traffic Lights
Traffic Circle (Roundabout)
Side Trip

CYCLING ROUTES

Main Route
Alternative Route
Side Trip
Previous/Next Day/Other Ride
Route Direction

ROUTE SHIELDS

33 .... US Highway
33 .... Interstate Highway
88 .... State Highway

BOUNDARIES

International
State

Cue Sheets

Route directions are given in a series of brief 'cues', which tell you at what mileage point to change direction and point out features en route. The cues are in a section at the back of the book, with the elevation profiles. These pages could be photocopied or cut out for on-the-road reference and used with a recommended map. (On the Border to Border ride, the cues and profiles are on the corresponding map.) The only other thing you need is a cycle computer.

To make the cue sheets as brief and simple to understand as possible, we've developed a series of symbols (see the Map Legend on p10) and the following rule:

Once your route is following a particular road, continue on that road until the cue sheet tells you otherwise.

Follow the road first mentioned in the cues even though it may cross a highway, shrink to a lane, change name (we generally only include the first name, and sometimes the last), wind, duck and climb its way across the country. Rely on us to tell you when to turn off it.

Because the cue sheets rely on an accurate odometer reading we suggest you disconnect your cycle computer (pop it out of the housing or turn the magnet away from the fork-mounted sensor) whenever you deviate from the main route.

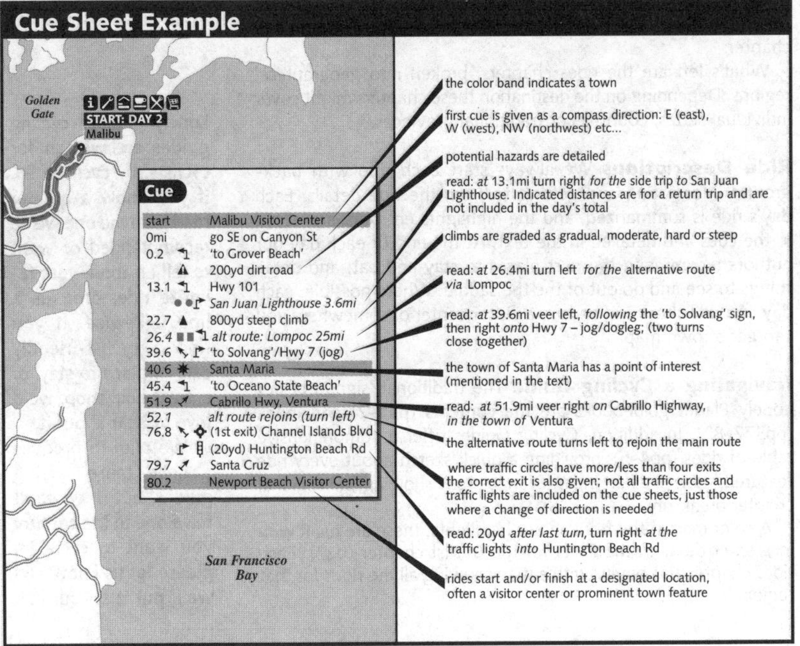

Cue Sheet Example
Golden Gate
START: DAY 2
Malibu
San Francisco Bay
Cue
start Malibu Visitor Center
0mi go SE on Canyon St
0.2 'to Grover Beach'
200yd dirt road
13.1 Hwy 101
San Juan Lighthouse 3.6mi
22.7 800yd steep climb
26.4 alt route: Lompoc 25mi
39.6 'to Solvang'/Hwy 7 (jog)
40.6 Santa Maria
45.4 'to Oceano State Beach'
51.9 Cabrillo Hwy, Ventura
52.1 alt route rejoins (turn left)
76.8 (1st exit) Channel Islands Blvd
(20yd) Huntington Beach Rd
79.7 Santa Cruz
80.2 Newport Beach Visitor Center
the color band indicates a town
first cue is given as a compass direction: E (east), W (west), NW (northwest) etc...
potential hazards are detailed
read: at 13.1mi turn right for the side trip to San Juan Lighthouse. Indicated distances are for a return trip and are not included in the day's total
climbs are graded as gradual, moderate, hard or steep
read: at 26.4mi turn left for the alternative route via Lompoc
read: at 39.6mi veer left, following the 'to Solvang' sign, then right onto Hwy 7 – jog/dogleg; (two turns close together)
the town of Santa Maria has a point of interest (mentioned in the text)
read: at 51.9mi veer right on Cabrillo Highway, in the town of Ventura
the alternative route turns left to rejoin the main route
where traffic circles have more/less than four exits the correct exit is also given; not all traffic circles and traffic lights are included on the cue sheets, just those where a change of direction is needed
read: 20yd after last turn, turn right at the traffic lights into Huntington Beach Rd
rides start and/or finish at a designated location, often a visitor center or prominent town feature

Foreword

HOW TO USE A LONELY PLANET CYCLING GUIDE

The best way to use this Cycling Guide is any way you choose. Some people might link a few days of one ride with a few days of another; others might feel most comfortable following the cue sheets to the letter for an entire tour; or you might use the guide simply to gather ideas on the areas you'd like to explore by bike. Keep in mind that the most memorable travel experiences are often those that are unexpected, and the finest discoveries are those you make yourself.

Our approach is to detail the 'best' rides in each destination, not all possible rides, so if you intend touring for several months you should consider also packing our *Pacific Northwest* and *California* guidebooks.

What's Inside Cycling Guides follow roughly the same format as regular Lonely Planet guidebooks. The Facts about the Destination chapters give background information ranging from the history of cycle touring to weather. Facts for the Cyclist deals with the cycle-touring practicalities – it answers planning questions and suggests itineraries. Health & Safety covers medical advice and road rules, while basic maintenance is addressed in Your Bicycle. The Getting There & Away and Getting Around chapters will help you make your travel plans and also give handy hints on packing your bicycle. In countries where English is not the main language, we include a cyclist-specific language chapter.

What's left are the rides chapters, broken into geographical regions. Depending on the destination these chapters might cover individual states, countries or traditional provinces.

Ride Descriptions We always start each ride with background information and getting to/from the ride details. Each day's ride is summarized, and the highlights en route are noted in the cues and detailed in the text. At the end of each day our authors recommend the best places to stay and eat, and detail things to see and do out of the the saddle. Where possible, each day of a ride starts and ends at a visitor center or somewhere you can get a town map.

Navigating a Cycling Guide The traditional 'signposts' for Lonely Planet guidebooks are the contents (pp1–2) and index (pp377–82). In addition, Cycling Guides offer a comprehensive table of rides (pp4–5), providing a quick sketch about every ride featured, as well as an index of maps (p3) showing the regional chapter break-up.

A color map at the front shows highlights; these are dealt with in greater detail in the Facts for the Cyclist chapter (p27). Each rides chapter also begins with a map showing all the rides for that region.

Lonely Planet's cycling guides are written for cyclists, by cyclists. So, if you know a quieter road than the one we've recommended or want to tell us about your favorite ride, drop us a line. Likewise, if you find a cyclist-friendly cafe or place to stay, or a great bike shop, we'd love to hear about it.

We plan to produce a heap more cycling guides, but if we don't have one to the country you want to cycle in, please let us know and we'll put it on our list.

Introduction

Why decide between the mountains, the desert, the ocean or the city when you can spend a week on the US West Coast and get a taste of each? Diversity is undoubtedly the most unique thing the West Coast has to offer. From redwood forests to movie-star–covered beaches to snow-capped volcanic peaks to vast desert skyscapes, there are limitless possibilities for the explorer on two wheels.

Though they share the common Americanisms of McDonald's, Coca-Cola and 'Have a nice day!', Washington, Oregon and California offer varied attractions. Around Washington's Puget Sound you'll see tree-covered islands plunging into blue water, cut by the occasional breach of whales. Oregon's Columbia River Gorge offers moss-covered canyons and rushing rivers, while its eastern reaches give you the Wild West. California brings its own unique 'Californication' culture; with the famous palm-studded south, as well as tiny fishing villages along the wind-sculpted north coast and Native American settlements in the eastern deserts.

Surround yourself with museums, galleries and urban attractions on a ride through Seattle or San Francisco, or traverse rural Catalina Island. Riding the length of the coast, from the Canadian to the Mexican border, may not take in the scope of the West Coast, but it is a classic ride.

While the the public transport system lacks breadth, the region is easy to get around. Roads are well kept and easy to navigate with a map. Finding accommodations – from five-star to camping – is easy, as is satisfying almost every cultural and gastronomic whim.

We have mapped and detailed a selection of the best rides, ranging from a few hours to 37 days, to suit all ability levels. We offer a wealth of suggestions to smooth your trip: tips on bike transport; the best places to stay and tastiest food en route; plus advice on fixing your bike and staying healthy on tour.

The biggest drawback to cycle touring here is that you must first decide where to begin. That, and what follows, is what this book is all about.

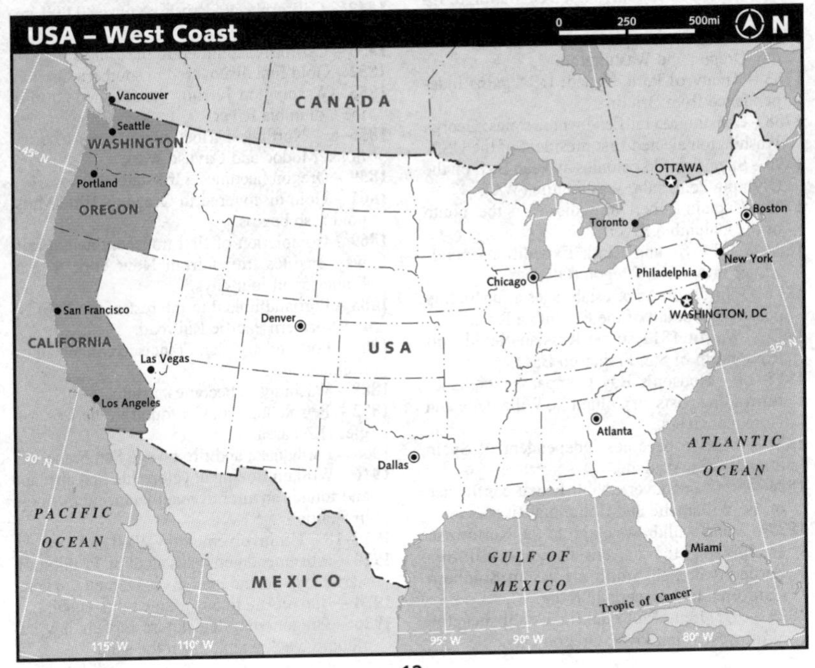

Facts about the USA – West Coast

HISTORY

Before 10,000 BC – nomadic hunters from East Asia migrate to North America across Bering Strait.

9000 BC –Native Americans make stone butchering tools in Clovis, New Mexico.

1000 BC – Chumash tribe makes earliest rock art in California (CA).

1492 – Columbus 'discovers America', making landfall in the Bahamas.

1539 – Francisco de Ulloa discovers that Spanish settlements on the southern tip of California are not on an island but on a peninsula.

1540 – Expedition led by Francisco de Coronado wanders through the Southwest.

1542 – Juan Rodríguez de Cabrillo's ships enter San Diego harbor while charting the West Coast and the Channel Islands. As colonists explore and settle the West, Native Americans are forced off their land and exposed to diseases resulting in severe population loss.

1579 – Sir Francis Drake lands on northern California coast and claims land for England.

1592 – Greek explorer Juan de Fuca plies the coast of Washington.

1769 – Padre Junípero Serra establishes California's first mission in San Diego.

1776 – American colonies sign Declaration of Independence on July 4.

1778 – James Cook explores the coast of present-day Oregon and Washington.

1783 – Treaty of Paris signed; USA gains independence from Britain.

1788 – Constitution ratified by nine states; George Washington elected first president of the USA.

1790 – Spanish build colonies at Neah Bay, on the Olympic Peninsula, Washington (WA).

1792 – Captain Robert Gray discovers the mouth of the Columbia River.

1804–6 – Lewis and Clark Expedition spends winter in Astoria, Oregon (OR).

1811 – John Jacob Astor establishes a fur-trading post at the mouth of the Columbia River.

1812 – War of 1812 starts; Russians build Fort Ross, north of San Francisco Bay.

1812–18 – Hudson's Bay Company establishes fur-trading posts on Columbia, Willamette and Umpqua Rivers.

1821 – Mexico becomes independent of Spain after 10-year struggle.

1824 – Fort Vancouver established at confluence of the Willamette and Columbia Rivers.

1827 – Spain withdraws claim to the Northwest, establishing the current Oregon-California border. Jedediah Smith arrives in Southern California by an overland route.

1829 – Dr John McLoughlin establishes the Northwest's first town: Oregon City.

1830 – Indian Removal Act begins final forced exodus of Native Americans from eastern states.

1833–5 – California's missions secularized and the land divided into *ranchos* (small ranches/farms).

1834 – Oregon's first Methodist mission founded, north of Salem.

1839 – First recorded instance of women crossing the Oregon Trail.

1841 – First wagons follow new immigrant trails to California.

1843 – Vote at Champoeg replaces authority of Hudson's Bay Company with a provisional government.

1843–60 – 53,000 settlers come across the Oregon Trail to the Northwest.

1846 – Oregon territory acquired from Britain; USA declares war on Mexico.

1847 – Whitman Massacre occurs near Walla Walla, WA, where Native Americans kill 14 missionaries, believing they had introduced measles to decimate the local population. Thousands of Native Americans also die in subsequent famous battles such as Big Hole (1877) and Wounded Knee (1890).

1848 – Treaty of Guadalupe Hidalgo cedes present-day California, Arizona, Nevada and New Mexico and parts of Wyoming, Utah and Colorado to the USA. Oregon becomes a US territory.

1849 – California gold rush begins; 80,000 immigrants arrive.

1850 – California admitted to the Union.

1852 – Gold first discovered in southern Oregon.

1853 – Washington Territory established north of the Columbia River.

1855–6 – Northwest tribes forced onto reservations; Modoc and Cayuse Wars.

1859 – Oregon becomes 33rd state.

1861 – Gold discovered in Oregon's Blue Mtns; gold rush begins.

1869 – Completion of first transcontinental railway enables travel from New York to San Francisco in four days.

1883 – Portland linked to the rest of the USA by the Northern Pacific Railroad.

1886 – Portland and San Francisco connected by train.

1889 – Washington becomes a state.

1892 – Petroleum deposits found in the Los Angles (LA) area.

1906 – Earthquake and fire ravage San Francisco.

1916 – William Boeing develops his first airplane and founds an aircraft manufacturing business in Seattle.

1917–18 – US involvement in WWI.

1920 – 18th amendment bans alcohol, Prohibition starts; 19th amendment gives women the vote.

1924 – Native Americans granted citizenship.

1926 – Oregon state legislature repeals law excluding black people from the state.

1929 – Stock market crash starts the Great Depression.
1932 – Olympic Games held in LA.
1933 – Franklin D Roosevelt introduces New Deal economic initiatives; Prohibition ends.
1937 – Golden Gate Bridge opens in San Francisco. Bonneville Dam completed.
1941 – Pearl Harbor bombed; USA enters WWII.
1945 – WWII ends.
1950 – Korean War starts.
1950 – Stanford University leases land to high-tech companies for 99 years, spurring the development of Silicon Valley.
1955 – Disneyland opens.
1961 – First US forces go to Vietnam.
1963 – President John F Kennedy assassinated in Dallas.
1963 – California becomes the most populous state in the USA.
1965 – Race riots occur in LA; 34 killed.
1967 – 'Summer of Love': the hippie movement blossoms in San Francisco.
1968 – Martin Luther King Jr assassinated in Memphis.
1968 – Robert Kennedy assassinated in LA.
1973 – Last US forces leave Vietnam.
1974 – Nixon resigns over Watergate.
1975 – Paul Allen and Bill Gates found Microsoft.
1979–80 – US hostages held in Iran.
1984 – Olympic Games held in LA.
1986 – Space shuttle *Challenger* explodes.
1989 – Exxon Valdez oil spill.
1992 – Race riots in LA triggered by 'not guilty' verdict in Rodney King court case; 50 die.
1994 – California votes to deny illegal immigrants access to state government services.
1998 – President Bill Clinton impeached in Monica Lewinsky scandal.
1999 – Anti–World Trade Organization riots occur in Seattle.
2000 – George W Bush defeats Al Gore for the presidency after a month of no result, despite Gore's majority of popular votes.
2001 – USA leads 'War on Terror' following attacks on the World Trade Center, New York, and the Pentagon, Washington, DC.

The Lewis & Clark Expedition

When President Thomas Jefferson made the decision in 1801 to explore the uncharted western part of North America to find a waterway to the Pacific, he enlisted his young protégé and personal secretary, Meriwether Lewis, to lead an expedition. Lewis, 27, had no expertise in botany, cartography or Indian languages, and was known to have bouts of 'hypochondriac affections' (a euphemism for schizophrenia) but couldn't resist the opportunity. He in turn asked his good friend William Clark, 33, already an experienced frontiersman and army veteran, to join him. In 1804, they left St Louis, Missouri, and headed west with an entourage of 40.

They traveled 8000mi in about two years, documenting everything they came across with such bad spelling that it must have taken historians a few extra years just to sort out what they wrote. In an almost biblical fashion they named 120 animals and 170 plants, including the grizzly bear and prairie dog. While Clark's entries are the more scientific, Lewis was known to explore alone and write pensive, almost romantic, accounts of the journey.

Despite hostilities shown to them, the Corps of Discovery (their official name) fared quite well and Lewis and Clark returned to a heroes' welcome in St Louis in 1806.

Bill McRae

History of Cycling

Bicycles were introduced to the USA by aristocratic Europeans not long after Baron von Drais patented his 'Draisienne' in 1817. The Draisienne was also called a 'hobby horse' because it was essentially a wooden hobby horse affixed with wheels. The rider powered it by pushing off with their feet. Velocipedes, which had pedals, were the first machines known to be manufactured in the USA, around 1868.

Early Developments In 1876, the first ordinary, better known as a 'high wheeler', was displayed in USA, at the Continental Exposition in Philadelphia. A year later, manufacturing began on the East Coast and in 1879 the first ordinaries arrived in San Francisco and Seattle.

Modeled after Britain's Good Roads Society, the League of American Wheelmen (now the League of American Bicyclists) was founded in 1880 to lobby for road improvements and bring riding into the public consciousness. In 1884, Thomas Stevens became the first person to pedal across the USA, from Oakland, CA, to Boston, Massachusetts. This same year, JK Starley invented the 'safety bicycle' with two wheels of equal diameter and on which the rider sat 'approximately a leg's length from the ground'. The Tacoma Wheelmen (the first bicycling club in Washington) were exceptionally active during this period, with an 1897 membership of 2750 (the town's population was 42,000) of which 500 were women.

More significant changes came in 1888: Dr Dunlop put pneumatic tires on a tricycle for his son; the first all-women cycling club was formed in Washington, DC; a six-day race exclusively for women finished in New York's Madison Square Garden; and the Rhode Island Supreme Court upheld the conviction of a wagon driver who failed to move aside to let a cyclist pass, establishing the rights of bicycles as equal to those of other vehicles.

Golden Age The 1890s brought the golden age of bicycles, when mass-produced safety bicycles became wildly popular for both transportation and pleasure. This is when Ignaz Schwinn emigrated from Germany to Chicago and, with his partner, established Arnold, Schwinn & Co. By 1885 they were producing 25,000 bicycles per year and Chicago's mailmen began using Schwinns to deliver mail.

Women rode regularly by now and the bicycle became a source of liberation. The bustle and corset were tossed out in favor of 'rational dress' that allowed more comfort and mobility. In 1895, Annie Londonderry returned from a one-year ride around the world and Margaret Valentine Le Long rode from Chicago to San Francisco. Susan B Anthony, leader of the woman's suffrage movement in the USA, is quoted as saying:

> Let me tell you what I think of bicycling. I think it has done more to emancipate women than anything else in history…It gives woman a feeling of freedom and self expression.

New Markets In 1896, Henry Ford invented the automobile. At first this didn't affect the bicycle's popularity. In fact, in 1900 there were two patent offices in the USA: one for bicycle-related items, and one for everything else. Around this time, Seattle's Mayor George Cotterill engineered and developed 25mi of designated bicycle routes, among the first in the USA.

But by 1909, automobiles were affordable, electric trolleys ran in most major cities and the bicycle became passé. Entrepreneurial sorts found new uses for bikes: James Casey and Claude Ryan started the American Messenger Service (now United Parcel Service), delivering parcels and messages by bike in Seattle. Manufacturers thus turned their attention to producing bikes as children's toys, fortified to withstand rough treatment and outfitted with bells and snazzy colors.

The Great Depression of the 1930s had various effects on bicycle use: many people gave up their cars and resorted to less costly transportation, while others couldn't afford shoes, let alone a bicycle. A lasting legacy from that era is the Redmond, WA, Bike Derby, the nation's oldest road race, which started as a fundraiser for Christmas decorations and school athletic equipment in 1939.

DILLON-HINES COLLECTION

The golden age of bicycles: rest and refreshments at a cycling clubhouse make for a fine day out in 1896.

During WWI and WWII, most bicycle manufacturers were involved in producing plane parts, ammunition and guns. Bicycles became important for transport again, especially when fuel was rationed after the USA became directly involved in WWII (1941).

After the war, companies blended the aesthetics of children's bicycles, which reflected post-war exuberance, with wartime technology. From the 1920s to 1965, companies such as JP Higgins, Monark-Silver King Co, Iver Johnson and Mercury produced heavyweight, art-deco influenced bicycles (now called Classics) with electric horns, shock-absorbing handlebars, speedometers and headlights. Using heavy ornamentation and stylized design became a uniquely American approach to bike building. These beauties have a quite a following and can now fetch more than $10,000.

A hearty resurgence of interest in cycling came in 1962, when the president's Council of Physical Fitness extolled the importance of regular exercise. The 10-speed derailleur was introduced in 1970, and two years later bicycles outsold cars 13 million to 11 million. Oil embargoes in 1973 and 1978 shifted the relative price of transport options and increased awareness of bicycles.

Mountain Bikes Some contend that the mountain bike first appeared in France, when Jean Duda and other members of the Velo Cross Club Parisienne combined motorbike components with standard racing bikes. It is more widely accepted, however, that modern mountain bikes were invented by Gary Fisher, Tom Ritchey and friends at Mt Tamalpais, in Marin, just north of San Francisco (see the boxed text 'Mountain Biking in the USA', p42). In either case, the Specialized Stumpjumper became the first mass-produced mountain bike in 1981. Mountain biking debuted as an internationally bona fide sport 15 years later at the 1996 Olympic Games in Atlanta, Georgia.

International Strength American racers were world-famous in the 1890s; Minnesota cyclist JS Johnson held, at one time or another, all of the world's records for distances up to 5mi between 1893 and 1896, including the 'flying mile' record of 1 min, 46 seconds.

US cyclists again gained prestige in the 1980s, with gold-medal performances in the 1984 Olympics and Greg Lemond's first-ever American victory in the Tour de France (1986). His subsequent wins in 1989 and 1990 solidified the American presence. Finally, Lance Armstrong's highly publicized battle with cancer followed by back-to-back wins of the Tour (1999, 2000, 2001) has probably done more for the USA's cycling ego than any other event.

DILLON-HINES COLLECTION

US cycling champ JS Johnson (R) and team, 1896.

GEOGRAPHY

Oregon and Washington comprise two major geographical regions: the islands, mountains and valleys of the Pacific coastline and the Cascade Range; and the plateaus east of the Cascades, which stretch to the Rocky Mtns. Linking these two regions is the mighty Columbia River, which drains a 295,000-sq-mi area, including nearly all of Oregon and Washington.

California stretches south from the Oregon border to Mexico, with 700mi of Pacific coast on its western edge and Nevada and Arizona in the east – an area roughly the size of Sweden.

Rising from the Pacific shore are coastal mountains – in California and Oregon the Coast Range, in Washington the Olympic Mtns. The southern third of California is the least rugged, and most inhabited, part of the coast. The Sierra Nevada stretches 400mi along California's eastern border and joins the southern end of the Cascade Range, just north of Lake Tahoe. While the two ranges appear to form an almost continuous line, they contain very different geology: the Sierra Nevada is a westward-tilted fault block with glacier-carved valleys, while the Cascade Range is a chain of volcanic peaks.

Between the coastal mountains and the Sierra Nevada and Cascade Ranges are fertile agricultural valleys. California's Central Valley leads the country in the production of cotton, peaches, almonds, walnuts, grapes, apricots, plums, oranges and olives. In Oregon and southern Washington, farms, dairies, plant nurseries, orchards and vineyards thrive. The region east of the Cascades is underlain by huge flows of lava, some of the largest in the world. These vast steppe-like uplands are now devoted to dry-land farming and ranching.

GEOLOGY

About 200 million years ago the North American continent wrenched loose from Europe and Africa. As it drifted westward (an inch or two a year, over millions of years), the heavier rocks of the sea floor dove under the lighter rocks of the continent and melted into the earth's mantle, forming magma. Some magma eventually rose to the surface through volcanoes. Along the eastern edge of present-day California, the magma cooled into granite and, over 80 million years, uplifted to form the Sierra Nevada.

As North America continued to move westward it occasionally encountered offshore land masses that (because they were too light to be forced beneath the continental land mass) became embedded along the coast, adding mountain ranges to eastern and southern Oregon (the Klamaths, Wallowas, Ochocos and Blues) and to northern Washington (the Okanogans and North Cascades).

About 60 million years ago a large chunk of continental crust docked onto the edge to form today's Olympic Mtns and Coast Range. Three intense periods of volcanism followed: first, a line of volcanoes shot up through the newly arrived landmass about 40 million years ago; then, 20 million years ago, the volcanic scene shifted eastward and lava oozed out of the earth, flooding central Oregon and Washington with molten rock; the last great volcanic era began four million years ago, when the Cascade Range began to rise, and continues to this day (Mt Rainier, Mt Hood and Mt Baker are still considered volcanically active).

The Oregon coast is near the Cascadia Subduction Zone, one of North America's largest active faults and a source of some of the many tsunamis (so-called 'tidal waves') which strike the Oregon coast.

California is divided by the San Andreas Fault Zone along a line from Point Arena, north of San Francisco, to LA. The land west of the fault, part of a separate crustal plate, moves northwest relative to the rest of continental USA in a series of jumps accompanied by devastating earthquakes. One of these destroyed San Francisco in 1906.

CLIMATE

Climatic conditions change greatly between the north and south of the West Coast, but a common thread is dry summers and wetter winters. Rainfall increases through fall, generally peaking in December or January.

The Pacific Coast is divided into two climatic zones by the National Climate Data Center (NCDC): Oregon and Washington belongs to the Northwest and California to the West.

The Northwest has two distinct weather patterns: east and west of the Cascade Mtns. West of the Cascades the weather is dominated by the marine currents of the Pacific Ocean. Winds blow in from the west and circulate towards the equator, blowing from north to south. They range from gentle breezes to occasional gales during winter storms. Winter temperatures are moderate, except at higher elevations where they can fall below freezing. Summers are mild, with days that rarely reach above 90°F and nights that almost always require a jacket. Spring tends to be warm and rainy, while September to mid-November is generally dry and mild. Beautiful Indian summers can last well into October. Rainfall ramps up markedly in November in the Northwest where many places receive more than 100 inches annually and marine clouds and fog are prevalent. Gray and damp weather prevails in winter and early spring. Marine fog is prevalent year-round, but especially in winter and spring.

The Cascades halt any moist or cloudy Pacific air, allowing a continental weather pattern to prevail in the east. Rainfall patterns vary throughout the region, but there is much less precipitation overall and most of that in the mountainous regions falls as snow. Sunshine is the norm in both winter and summer, but temperatures fluctuate from above 100°F (common in summer) to occasionally below 0°F.

California has its own plethora of microclimates that get milder the farther south you go. Three-quarters of the way down the state the Transverse Range joins the Sierra Nevada to the Coast Range. From here south

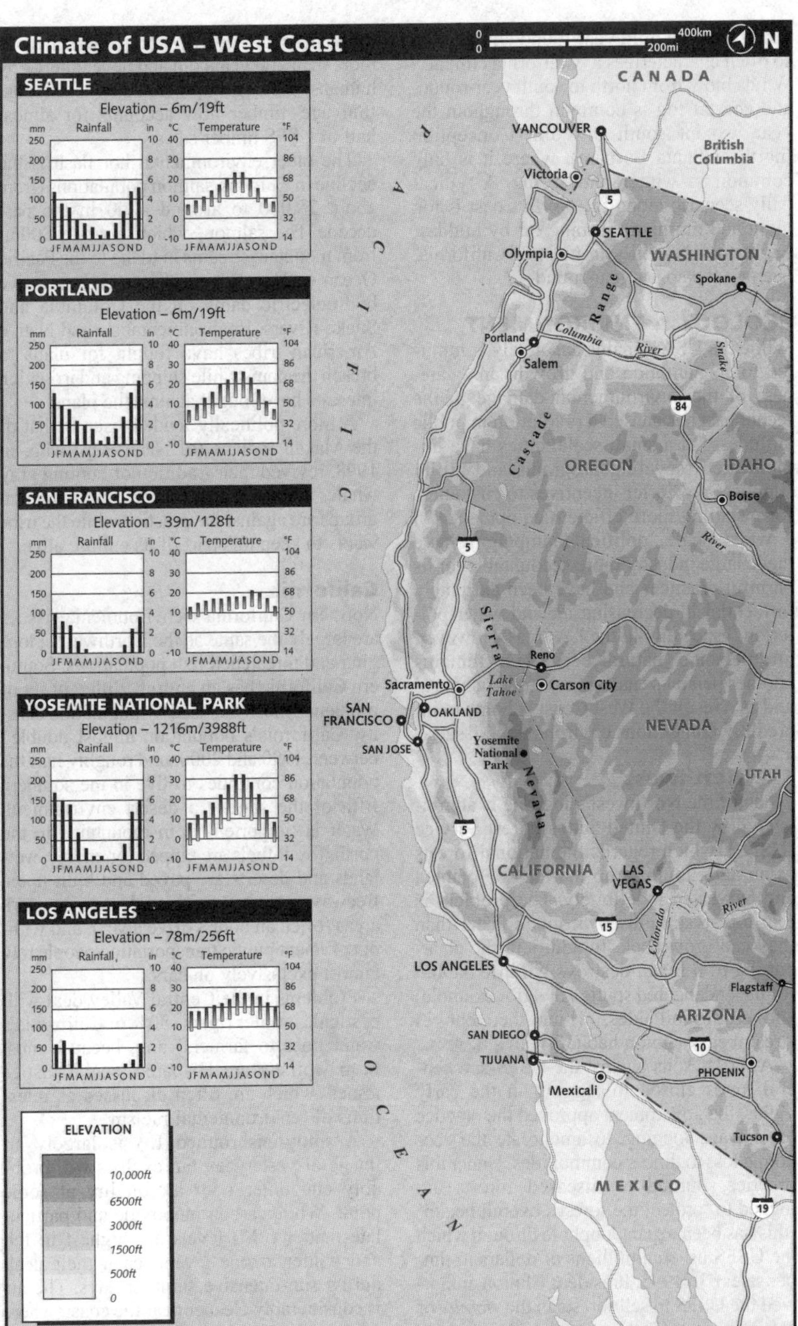
Climate of USA – West Coast
0 400km
0 200mi
N
SEATTLE
Elevation – 6m/19ft
Rainfall
Temperature
JFMAMJJASOND
PORTLAND
Elevation – 6m/19ft
SAN FRANCISCO
Elevation – 39m/128ft
YOSEMITE NATIONAL PARK
Elevation – 1216m/3988ft
LOS ANGELES
Elevation – 78m/256ft
ELEVATION
10,000ft
6500ft
3000ft
1500ft
500ft
0
CANADA
VANCOUVER
British Columbia
Victoria
SEATTLE
WASHINGTON
Olympia
Spokane
Portland
Salem
Columbia River
Snake
OREGON
IDAHO
Boise
Cascade Range
Sierra Nevada
Reno
Carson City
Sacramento
Lake Tahoe
SAN FRANCISCO
OAKLAND
SAN JOSE
NEVADA
UTAH
Yosemite National Park
CALIFORNIA
LAS VEGAS
Colorado River
LOS ANGELES
Flagstaff
ARIZONA
SAN DIEGO
TIJUANA
PHOENIX
Mexicali
Tucson
MEXICO
PACIFIC OCEAN

you'll find the mild year-round climate that so often characterizes a 'California climate'. Winds blow from north to south year-round, and coastal fog is common throughout the year, except south of Point Conception (north of Santa Barbara), where it is only common in winter and spring. A typical daily scenario along the North Coast is fog night and morning, burning off by midday. Nights can be chilly in most of California, even on the coast, year-round.

ECOLOGY & ENVIRONMENT

While the USA remains absolutely committed to consumption and growth, an awareness of the environmental damage of the recent past has caused a revolution in public attitudes. On a small scale, cities have implemented recycling programs and utility suppliers now offer incentives to customers for installing more efficient equipment. On a wider scale, political campaigns have made large industry more accountable for its harmful practices and have been extremely influential in decreasing air and water pollution (especially in the LA area). However, one person's 'natural ecosystem' remains another person's 'natural resource bonanza' and as a result the West Coast is home to incredibly contentious environmental issues.

The Northwest

Much of the Northwest's logging is administered by the United States Forest Service (USFS), which regards the national forests as an agricultural crop that can be planted and harvested indefinitely. The problem is that forests are cut down much faster than they can grow back. In addition, the clear-cutting of a forest destroys wildlife habitat (of the endangered spotted owl, for example) and erodes hillsides, which then chokes streambeds (salmon habitat) with silt.

After lawsuits against the USFS saw federal lands closed to logging in the early 1990s, the government approved the practice of 'salvage logging' to ameliorate the economic loss to timber communities. Under this practice, burned or diseased forests are logged to 'protect the forest's overall health' (this has been a giant loophole through which the USFS ushered millions of dollars in timber sales). In 1995, President Clinton authorized the USFS to sell forests in the *vicinity* of any salvage area, thus opening the doors to logging of old-growth forests (defined as more than 200 years old and never altered by humans) previously protected by legislation. 'Salvage' timber now accounts for almost half of USFS timber sales.

The other environmental hot flash is the decline in Chinook salmon populations (from about 28,000 to around 4000 in the past decade The salmon, which migrate 800mi from mountain streams in Idaho to the Pacific Ocean each spring, must face eight massive hydroelectric dams on the Columbia and Snake Rivers. Environmentalists and Native American tribes have fought for plans to breach the dams while shipping and irrigation interests have fought against the plans.

A more politically loaded issue is that of the Makah Indians (of Neah Bay) who, in 1998, revived their tradition of hunting gray whales after a 70 year hiatus. Environmental groups are against the practice while the tribe wants to keep this part of its culture alive.

California

Northern California's environmental issues are largely the same as the Northwest's: logging and threatened fish populations. Southern California has an entirely different set of problems, mostly caused by population density. California's population almost doubled between 1990 and 2000, and roughly half the population continues to live in the southern fifth of the state – a desert environment. Water is 'imported' from mountains in the north, fossil fuels are tapped for energy, wetlands and deserts are paved and built upon, freeways connect residential areas to work areas (often an hour's drive apart), and without efficient public transportation people rely almost exclusively on cars.

Problems in the Central Valley deal with pesticides, water rights (80% of California's water goes to farmers) and, because most farm workers are Hispanic, social justice issues, which are often discussed as questions of 'environmental racism'.

A smog-enshrouded LA is largely an image of yesteryear, but cyclists will probably encounter poor air quality at some point. While carbon monoxide and particulate matter (PM) levels are highest in fall and winter, ozone levels reach their peak during sun-intensive summer days. The air is considerably cleaner near the coast, where offshore breezes blow the gunk eastward.

GOVERNMENT & POLITICS

The USA has a federal system with a president and a bicameral Congress, consisting of the 100-member Senate and the 435-member House of Representatives. Each of the 50 states has two senators and a number of representatives in proportion to its population: Oregon has five, Washington nine and California a whopping 52.

The US Constitution, passed in 1789 and amended 26 times since, provides the laws for the running of the national government and the relations between the national and state governments. The three branches of federal government are: the legislature branch, which makes the laws; the executive branch, which carries them out; and the judiciary branch, which studies and interprets both the Constitution and the laws. The president is chosen by an Electoral College consisting of electors (chosen by voters) from each state equivalent to its number of senators and representatives combined. These electors vote in accordance with the popular vote within their state. To be elected, the president must obtain a majority of 270 of the total 538 electoral votes (the District of Columbia has no voting representatives in Congress, but nevertheless has three electoral votes). The president may serve only two four-year terms.

The head of state government is the governor, who presides over a bicameral legislature consisting of a senate and a house delegation. Smaller administrative districts within the states are divided into counties and cities.

The two main political parties are the Republicans (called the GOP for Grand Old Party) and the Democrats. The Green Party shook this bipartisan structure in 2000 when Ralph Nader secured 3% of the vote. This same year brought such a narrow margin between the Democratic (Al Gore) and Republican (George W Bush) candidates that the nation waited over a month for a result, while ballots were recounted and numerous electoral practices were contested. Al Gore won the popular vote, but George W Bush became president because he won the electoral vote.

ECONOMY

Whole areas of the USA are wealthier than others and within a city the standard of living can vary considerably from neighborhood to neighborhood. The lowest 20% of the population receives only 4.4% of the national income distribution, while the top 5% receives 17.6%.

The Northwest's economy has traditionally been tied to lumber and wood products. However, between the federal government's restrictions on logging public lands and state laws that have prohibited exportation of raw lumber from state-owned lands, the forest-product industry is a fraction of what it once was. Cyclists may feel that the clear-cuts in Washington along Hwy 1 go on forever, only to arrive in a small town where locals who once relied on logging are now dependent on welfare.

The Northwest's new economy is international: Seattle is home to Boeing, the world's largest aircraft manufacturer; Microsoft; Amazon.com and Starbucks; while Portland is the primary grain shipment point on the West Coast and home to high-tech giants Intel and Techtronix.

Agriculture is important throughout the West Coast – from the dairy farms along the Oregon coast, to the orchards of peaches, pears, apples and cherries produced for international markets along the Columbia and Okanogan Rivers, and to the highly mechanized corporate 'agribusiness' of California's Central Valley.

Even before the growth of Silicon Valley, California was the largest economy in the USA and had the economic power to stand as the world's seventh richest nation (if it were one). The high-tech industry, real estate, agriculture and all things surrounding Hollywood are its biggest sources of income.

POPULATION & PEOPLE

The current population of Washington and Oregon combined is just under nine million. Add California's population and that of the West Coast rises to 42 million! Although California is the largest of the three states, its population is disproportionately larger: there are 34.5 people per sq mi in Oregon and 86.5 people per sq mi in Washington, while California has 212.5 people per sq mi.

Population is concentrated in metropolitan areas. Between 1990 and 1999, all three states had a rise in per capita income and a decline in the percentage of population below the poverty level.

The populations of Washington and Oregon have traditionally been overwhelmingly

Flora & Fauna of the West Coast

Bristlecone Pine

According to botanists, ornithologists and zoologists, North America belongs in the Nearctic – new north – Zoogeographical Realm which encircles the northern part of the globe. Plants and wildlife found here are thus similar to those in parts of Europe and China. Further similarities are due to the migration of species across the Bering Strait and Central American isthmus, both of which have been passable intermittently over the past several million years.

Flora

Because the West Coast is so long, it has almost every combination of latitude, elevation, precipitation and soil composition. Of special note are the northern hemisphere's only temperate rain forest (in Washington) and the superlative trees of California which include the world's tallest (coast redwood), largest (sequoia) and oldest (bristlecone pine).

Coastal ecosystems range from very wet in the north to very dry in the south. In coastal forests you'll find Douglas fir (which can grow to 300ft high), Sitka spruce, western hemlock, maples, oaks, red cedar and, in southern Oregon and northern California, coast redwoods. South of San Francisco are Monterey cypress and the windswept-looking Monterey pine. The last mainland stands of Torrey pine, a species adapted to sparse rainfall and sandy soil, are in San Diego.

Forests of the Cascades and Sierra Nevada are dominated by ponderosa and lodgepole pines. East of the Cascades and in the deserts of southeastern California is an abundance of low-growing juniper trees whose small, round, purplish-blue cones (resembling blueberries) are used for flavoring gin.

Fauna

Development of the USA's natural landscape has had drastic effects on some species (see Endangered Species) while benefiting others such as pocket gophers, prairie dogs, raccoons and skunks. In some areas, housing developments are causing wildlife habitats to dwindle so much that deer and mountain lions are becoming part of the urban landscape. Most campers will see mule deer and elk in the early morning and around sunset, and may be serenaded by coyotes at night.

Two furry critters that may be foreign to international visitors are raccoons and skunks. Raccoons are nocturnal animals, usually the size of a small dog, known for making midnight forays into trash cans (or anywhere food is stored). They have long, ringed tails, dexterous hands, small black eyes, a pointed nose and a black mask that befits their love of thievery.

Skunks are black-and-white, housecat-sized creatures known for the strong-smelling secretion they emit when excited or threatened; it's said that soaking in tomato juice is the best way to erase the smell.

Crested, blue-bodied Stellar's jays are noisy and common in forests, as are enormous crows and ravens. Sharp eyes may spot rufous hummingbirds and a keen ear can detect woodpeckers.

Notable streamside birds include blue herons, belted kingfishers and loons. Along the coast, gulls are ubiquitous, and you can also spot (less frequently) other sea birds such as cormorants, puffins and pelicans. From the coast you may also see seals, sea lions, sea otters and, from fall to spring, gray whales migrating to or from warm waters in Mexico.

Bottle-nosed dolphins and porpoises swim quite close to shore. They can be seen year-round from Morro Bay to Mexico. One of the oddest creatures off the coast are flying fish, often seen between

Flora & Fauna of the West Coast

the southern coast and Catalina Island. At low tide look for sea anemones, starfish, mussels and hermit crabs in tide pools.

Endangered Species

In 1973 Congress passed the Endangered Species Act, which has been instrumental in bringing several species – such as the peregrine falcon and American crocodile – back from the brink of extinction. Other native species, such as passenger pigeons and ivory-billed woodpeckers, were not as lucky.

Since the mid-1980s serious efforts have been made to protect the 3000 to 5000 pairs of northern spotted owls remaining in the wild.

Peregrine falcons, bald eagles and whooping cranes suffered drastically from poisoning by DDT used during WWII to treat lice and other pests brought in from war zones and, later, in wetlands for mosquito control. Bald eagles were the focus of several aggressive restoration campaigns; by 1995 populations were estimated to have risen to between 80,000 and 110,000, so the majestic national bird was 'downlisted' from endangered to threatened.

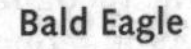

HUGH D'ANDRADE

Bald Eagle

One bird near extinction is the California Condor, largest of North America's birds with a wing span of 9ft, able to fly to 15,000ft in elevation. There are 100 condors in captivity and 36 others have been released since 1995.

No story of the USA's endangered species is complete without discussion of the American bison or buffalo, which outnumbered people in North America until less than 200 years ago. In the 1820s there were an estimated 60 million bison roaming the prairies and woodlands. By the mid-1880s, the population was down to 800 beasts. They were killed for their hide, for sport and as part of the military's Indian suppression strategy. In 1902 a herd of 41 was placed under government protection in Yellowstone National Park. Currently 2000 or so still survive in Yellowstone, and another 28,000 are on private and public reserves.

National Parks & Reserves

The US Congress created the world's first national park, Yellowstone, in 1872, and in 1916 the National Park Service (NPS; W www.nps.gov) was established.

This book covers the Olympic, North Cascades and Mt Rainier National Parks in Washington; Crater Lakes National Parks in Oregon; and, in California, Redwood and Yosemite National Parks and Golden Gate National Recreation Area.

For cyclists, the real riches are the many state parks and wildlife refuges that generally provide more intimate contact with nature. Oregon has 224 state parks (the most in the nation). Washington has more than 200 and California isn't far behind. Each state has its own system of state parks, wildlife areas and reserves. While generally smaller than those in the federal system these contain some surprisingly beautiful scenery and fine camping.

National forests are less protected than parks, being managed by the US Forest Service (USFS) under the concept of 'multiple use', which includes timber cutting, watershed management and recreations.

HAYDEN FOELL

Sea Lion

white but, according to the 1999 census, Hispanic populations in both states have risen over 75% since 1990 and Asian populations have risen over 50%.

California's racial mix continues to change. Hispanic and Asian communities are increasing while whites are the only group actually posting a decline.

Native Americans

The federal government recognizes 50 tribes in the Northwest, which are closely tied to Alaskan tribes, and 100 in California, which are more akin to tribes in Mexico.

Federally recognized tribes have reservations or trust lands set aside for them and receive government assistance for tribal schools and cultural centers. There are a number of Native American groups without federal recognition (usually due to an insufficient concentration of members, or land issues that compete with other interests), which makes it difficult to maintain cultural identity and nearly impossible to obtain government aid.

ARTS

The West Coast is home to four of the USA's most dynamic arts scenes, in LA, San Francisco, Seattle and Portland. But while there are identifiable West Coast trends in music, literature, and visual arts they are a part of national and global trends. LA and San Francisco, especially, look for artistic association (in prestige if not in aesthetics) with New York or Europe rather than with their West Coast brethren.

That said, there is a West Coast sensibility (especially visible in works from LA) and a consistent level of invention and creativity coming from West Coast artists in general. New trends take root quickly, and the warm, overridingly liberal environment attracts people with a willingness to experiment. Don't hesitate to duck into galleries or go to local music or theater productions in out-of-the-way places: you'll often find a high level of sophistication and quality in the work of artists who've left the 'rat race' behind.

In summer lots of music and theater is performed outdoors. Jazz festivals in the San Juan Islands, weekend concerts in southern California's city parks and open-air theater festivals in the Portland and San Francisco Bay areas are worth seeking out.

Music

The urban centers mentioned earlier offer a variety of live music, from jazz to Celtic to reggae to punk. Club scenes – where trance, house and hip-hop are the trends *du jour* – thrive in Seattle and San Francisco. The best place to find a list of current happenings is in free, regional newspapers *(LA Weekly, SF Weekly* or *Seattle Weekly)*.

Seattle deserves special mention as the birthplace of 'grunge', a guitar- and angst-driven derivative of punk rock that reached it's apex in the early 1990s. Nirvana was among the most popular of many Northwest bands, including Pearl Jam and Soundgarden, that exemplified the sound. Seattle was also home of Jimi Hendrix, who is paid highest respects in Paul Allen's EMP (see the boxed text 'Jimi Hendrix Is Alive & Well…& Playing in Seattle', p104).

In the classical realm, the LA Philharmonic, conducted by Esa-Pekka Salonen, and San Francisco Symphony, under the hand of Michael Tilson Thomas, rival each other for 'best of the West'. The Seattle Symphony is also regarded as world-class.

Literature

A good start to Northwestern literature is *Undaunted Courage*, by Stephen Ambrose, which tells the real-life adventure story of Lewis and Clark, (see the boxed text 'The Lewis & Clark Expedition', p15). Native American tales and myths are covered in Jarold Ramsey's *Coyote Was Going There* while Annie Dillard's *The Living* is a minutely researched tale of 19th-century white settlement.

Prominent Northwestern authors include poet and short story writer Raymond Carver, Native American novelist Sherman Alexie and David Guterson (author of the best-selling *Snow Falling on Cedars*).

California has been chronicled by thousands of writers; from Mark Twain's sketch of silver-mining life, *Roughing It* to *Martin Eden* by Jack London. *My First Summer in the Sierra*, and any other book by John Muir, reveals his talent for lighthearted, poetic writing and passion for the outdoors.

John Steinbeck's classic novels *The Grapes of Wrath*, *Cannery Row* and *East of Eden* paint evocative portraits of a California now hidden beneath subdivisions and tourist enclaves.

The narrators of Jack Kerouac's *On the Road* chased enlightenment in San Francisco and other California locales, while Beat movement writers found their second home (after New York) in San Francisco.

Visitors to California might consider picking up the modern novels of Ishmael Reed, Amy Tan, Alice Walker or Kathy Acker.

Theater & Film

Seattle has one of the most vibrant live theater scenes in the USA. San Francisco's is more developed but tends to be a bit more traditional. San Diego is making inroads with consistent productions of irreverent comedies.

Hollywood and 'the Industry' not only create California's most conspicuous export, they define the state's self-image and international identity. For a taste, try the movies *Citizen Kane*, *American Graffiti*, *Chinatown*, *LA Story*, *Swingers* or *LA Confidential*. Seattle's notable films include *It Happened at the World's Fair*, *The Fabulous Baker Boys*, *Singles* and *Sleepless in Seattle*.

Shakespeare fans can see excellent productions year-round at San Diego's Old Globe Theater. The annual Shakespeare Festival in Ashland, Oregon, gets international acclaim.

Visual Arts

Portland and Seattle both have a '1% for Art' program that requires 1.33% of their capital improvement funds to go toward public artwork. This has brought sculpture, temporary installations and lunchtime concert series to the streets.

The gorgeous Seattle Art Museum is probably the best place to see Native American art. Downtown Seattle also has a good number of galleries dedicated to Native American traditions. Glass blowing is a specialty of the Puget Sound region. You'll see works by Dale Chihuly in public places around the state.

A good deal of Oregon's new art comes from the Oregon College of Arts and Crafts, near Portland. Their student gallery has an excellent collection. College towns such as Eugene and Corvallis have smaller arts scenes. Joseph, in eastern Oregon, has a reputation as an artists' haven, though it's about as far away from the Louvre figuratively as it is literally.

LA brought California onto the national art canvas when Man Ray moved there and brought surrealism and dadaism with him. The rebellious, off-the-wall lifestyle of California, coupled with its Pacific-washed light, spurred artists to experiment and attracted such greats as Sam Francis, James Turrell and Robert Irwin. The LA County Museum of Art, LA Museum of Contemporary Art (MOCA), Geffen Contemporary and UCLA's Armand Hammer Museum are excellent venues.

San Francisco is where David Park led the movement away from abstract expressionism in the 1950s. Elmer Bischoff and Richard Diebenkorn are among the notables that followed, giving birth to the Bay Area Figurative Movement. Pop Art traces its roots to San Francisco as well. San Francisco Museum of Modern Art (SFMOMA) and California Palace of the Legion of Honor have world-class shows. San Francisco's South of Market (SoMA) district is good places to see a variety of contemporary work.

Unique to San Diego is its proximity to the vibrant arts scene of Tijuana, Mexico. Every two years, the Museum of Contemporary Art, San Diego hosts a tri-national (Canada, USA, Mexico) exhibition in which artists build installations throughout the San Diego–Tijuana region.

SOCIETY & CONDUCT

Visiting cyclists are likely to find the West Coast a friendly, easy-going place. People tend to be very informal: dressing up and putting on airs is not a big part of life, especially in rural areas.

The West Coast shares the 'general' US and Canadian culture. The interesting twists lie in eastern Oregon and Washington and northeastern California, where Old West culture is still very much alive. The same can be said of California's Central Valley, but it's the Mexican laborers who live the cowboy's life more than their wealthy, agribusiness employers. Fishing towns along the coast, especially north of Fort Bragg, California, have a distinctive and often gritty sensibility that comes from making a living on the stormy and dangerous Pacific Ocean. Urban dwellers get out of town on weekends to ski, hike, climb or windsurf. It's fair to say that the natural environment is an overriding and cherished part of life for most people in this region (LA may be the exception). Large cities and university towns tend to be more accepting and a bit less wary of outsiders than rural areas, where people may seem a bit more reserved.

Traditional Culture

Native American communities are based on reservation lands governed by federal and tribal law. Each tribe is independent and what is permitted on one reservation may be banned on another. Visitors to reservations are generally welcome, but should behave in an appropriately courteous and respectful manner. Many tribes ban all forms of recording – photography, videotaping, audiotaping or drawing. Others permit these activities in certain areas only if you pay a fee. Obtain permission before you photograph anyone on a reservation, including children – a tip is usually expected.

The rip-off of Native American arts has become a lucrative business, with imitations from China or Taiwan often passed off as authentic. The Pacific Northwest has managed to avoid this to a large extent, partly because of the stewardship of non-Native Northwesterners and partly because many related tribes (in Alaska and the Aleutian Islands) are still practicing traditional lifestyles. If you're considering purchasing Native American art, find a legitimate shop and either look for authenticating labels or find out who the artist is.

Dos & Don'ts

The USA is a very well-ordered society and, generally speaking, people stand in line, obey the rules and follow the instructions. Talking loudly, discarding litter on the ground, smoking in the presence of non-smokers, trampling vegetation (to put up a tent, or otherwise), disregarding permit or fee payments and taking more than your portion of a campsite are practices that are frowned upon. In towns and national park centers, shirt and shoes are required to enter most stores and all restaurants.

When passing someone on route, try to give them advanced notice, and be prepared to make a bit of small talk. When entering someone's house, a B&B or a museum, remove your cleats or change out of your bike shoes. Cycling shorts are OK in most establishments (even for dinner), though you may get curious sideward glances.

American English

In the 18th century, Ben Franklin, by trade a printer, sought to rationalize and standardize the disordered spelling of the English language. Although his plans weren't adopted at the time, he did influence Noah Webster, who published the *American Dictionary of the English Language* in 1828. It was Webster who popularized the change in spellings of such words as *theatre* to *theater*, *colour* to *color* and *organise* to *organize*.

But it's not the spelling that makes American English so distinctive – it's the wealth of new words and expressions that it has brought to the language. Several Native American words have come into English, including *moccasin*, *moose*, *toboggan* and *kayak*. Many more words have come from European languages via immigrants to America, such as *loafer* from German, *schmuck* from Yiddish, *prairie* from French and *canyon* from Spanish.

Nevertheless, the vast majority of Americanisms come from America itself. American inventiveness produces not only new products, but new words to describe them and a new vocabulary to market them. So there's not just *soda pop*, *root beer* and *sarsaparilla* (all American inventions), but the brand names *Coca-Cola*, *Coke* and *Pepsi* are also in the language, along with advertising slogans like 'the Pepsi Generation', and imaginative new concepts like Coca-Colonization. American business, technology, cars, movies, military forces and especially sports have all contributed words that are so familiar that it's easy to forget they're American.

LANGUAGE

There are regional differences in accent, idiom and use of vocabulary, but American English is relatively uniform when compared to, say, the varieties of English spoken in Britain. Most foreign visitors will be familiar with American English through the mass media. (See also the boxed text 'American English'.)

Facts for the Cyclist

HIGHLIGHTS

See the Table of Rides (pp4–5) for the page numbers of the rides below.

Best Mountain Scenery On the North Cascades Contrasts ride, keeping your eyes on the road is a constant battle, as stunning peaks appear around every corner.

The Wild West Roundup ride offers stunning views of the Wallowas (the 'Switzerland of America'), soaring to 9000ft and the magnificent Elkhorn Range etched on the horizon.

The Yosemite Valley ride provides spectacular views of sheer granite walls, waterfalls and pine-covered slopes.

Score views of both the Olympic and Cascades mountains (without having to climb them) from Port Townsend, Day 3 on the Border to Border ride.

Best Mountain Biking Whoop-de-do hills and lava flows punctuate the Deschutes River Trail.

The Around Mt Tam ride doesn't offer the most remote, single-track experience but it's still as fun as it was when Gary Fisher and Tom Ritchey were experimenting with the first mountain bikes here.

Best Coastal Scenery Evergreen-edged shorelines, windswept peninsulas and stunning views from Mt Constitution make San Juan Islands–hopping a must.

For sea stacks, wilderness and wildlife, the Big Sur Hinterland ride is hard to beat; the coast is also visited on Day 28 of the Border to Border ride.

Best Descent Do the lush and spectacular North Cascades Contrasts ride, with a 16mi, 3200ft plunge to the Methow Valley.

After climbing to 5280ft on Day 4 of the Southern Oregon Extravaganza, make a steep 12mi descent with the Siskiyou Mtns unfolding like ripples in a giant velvet quilt.

On The Lost Coast ride, the descent from Panther Gap curves down a remarkable grade towards the coast.

For mesmerizing views and sheer thrills, try the 40mi drop from Mt Laguna to the Anza-Borrego Desert on the Mountain to Desert Descent ride.

The Big Sur Hinterland ride sends you swooping down to the coastline through open hills and fragrant redwood canyons, with the sea glittering on the horizon the whole way.

Best Ascent Slithering up the canyon wall above the Snake and Clearwater rivers, the Snake & Spiral Circuit is a challenge.

Magnificent views of Mt Rainier dominate as the road wriggles up to Paradise (5400ft) on the Mt Rainier Magnificence ride; old-growth forests blanket the lower slopes, where you pass waterfalls and enormous glaciers.

On the Southern Oregon Extravaganza, climb above 7000ft to the rim of Crater Lake, deepest in the USA and arguably the bluest in the world.

Leggett Hill (Day 21 on the Border to Border ride) gets lots of bad press but it's much easier than everyone thinks – the downside is that *after* the downside there's another, steeper climb.

Most Remote Set deep in the Cascades, Stehekin Valley is only accessible by boat, plane or foot. Cut through forests, following the fast-flowing Stehekin River beneath towering peaks.

It's all in a name on The Lost Coast ride. Deep, deep, deep you go into the redwood forest, finally emerging where land meets sea, and sheep and cattle outnumber people.

Only two hours from LA, dodge buffalo and wander isolated beaches on the Catalina Island Crossing ride.

The Big Sur Hinterland ride winds through sleepy towns and valleys reminiscent of the 19th century, traverses condor and mountain lion habitat, ending with a tour of the landslide-riddled coast.

On the Epicenter Century ride, overnight in Parkfield, population 37, and follow the San Andreas Fault without a town in sight.

Best Deviation On Lopez Island, hike through Shark Reef Sanctuary, emerging from the trees to expansive water views. Walk five minutes more to watch seals basking in the sun.

The Columbia River Gorge National Scenic Area requires exploration on foot: the wet path through Oneonta Gorge is so narrow you'll have to hop stones and logs to get to the spectacular falls at its end.

Three (out of six) days of the Wine Country Tour could be considered deviations in themselves: stop for a tasting at every winery and you'll be deviated in no time!

For rock 'n' roll riders, Seattle's Experience Music Project is well worth a detour. In the natural world, the Jedediah Smith Redwoods State Park, near Crescent City, is simply awe-inspiring. Both are easily accessible from the Border to Border ride.

PLANNING

When to Ride

The West Coast is a year-round cycling destination. Though the sun may shine more from May to September, there are few regions (mountains excepted) in this book that cannot be cycled in winter. For more information, see Climate, pp18–20. Also read the When to Ride sections in the ride chapters.

Suggested Itineraries

Build your itinerary by linking rides together, depending on how much time you have. Remember to schedule in transport, rest and sightseeing time. See the Cycling Regions Index Map (p3) for an overview of cycling areas in this guide.

One Week

Use your time wisely: limit your cycling adventures to one state.

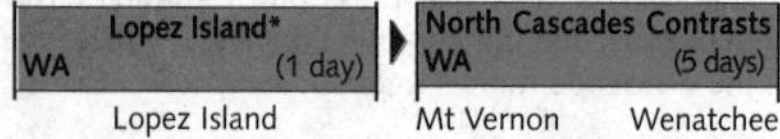

*Or choose any of the three San Juan Islands for an offshore jaunt.

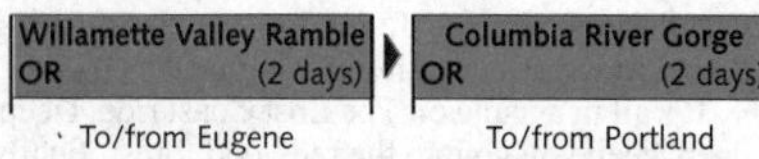

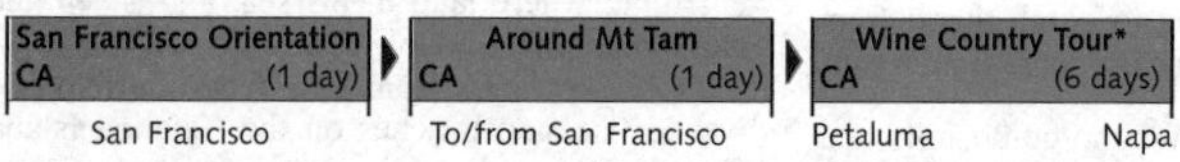

*Choose the first or last three days of the Wine Country Tour.

Two Weeks

This gives you time to explore the remote reaches of one state, or even to combine states.

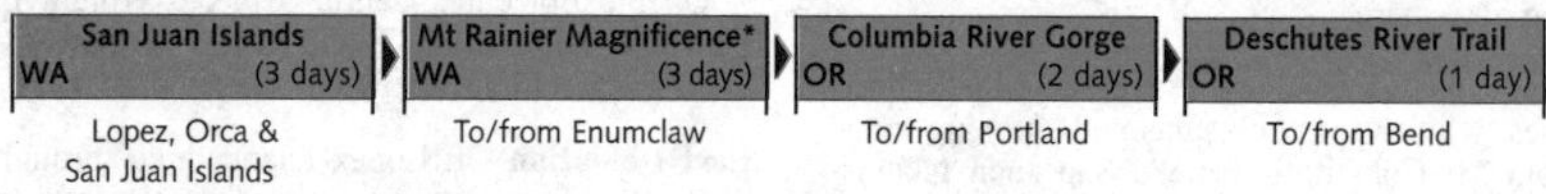

*You may decide to follow the Mt Rainier Magnificence ride with Northern California's Lost Coast ride (3 days), or the Around Mt Tam ride (1 day) plus the San Francisco Orientation ride (1 day).

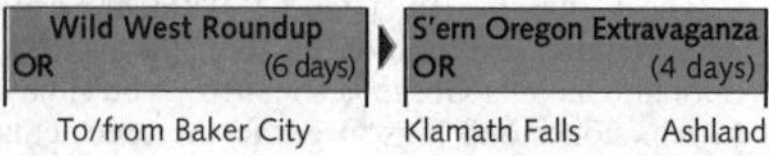

You could spend a week in California's South, as per the third 'One Week' option, plus;

*Or follow the Wine Country Tour with the Redwoods & Lighthouse ride (2 days), or head west to the Yosemite's Western Gateway ride (1 day).

One Month

A month would allow a stop in every major city: Seattle, Portland, San Francisco, LA and San Diego. Alternatively you could base yourself in one of those cities and do the majority of rides in that region, possibly venturing into the neighbouring state for a ride or two.

For a two-month itinerary see the boxed text 'Long-distance Touring', p270.

If you plan to cover much territory, think about when you'll be starting: in spring, start south and work north; in the fall, start north and head south to warmer climates.

If one month had to be picked as the best for the entire West Coast, it would probably be September. The climate is stable, it's wine and apple season, and the school holidays are over.

The official start and end of summer is Memorial Day weekend (the last of May) and Labor Day weekend (the first of September). School holidays are from mid-June to early September, with an additional two weeks from mid-December to early January and usually another week in April. It's most noticeable that 'school's out' in small tourist towns and national parks. Destinations for business travelers (Seattle, Portland, San Francisco) and areas with year-round tourism (most of Southern California) are less likely to be impacted in such a concentrated way.

Maps

For general planning you can't beat Bartholomew's World Travel Map, *Western USA* (1:2,500,000; about $10). It covers the West Coast and inland states of Montana, Wyoming, Colorado and New Mexico.

Adventure Cycling Association (formerly Bikecentennial; ☎ 406-721-1776 or ☎ 800-721-8719, W www.adv-cycling.org), PO Box 8308, Missoula, MT 59807, makes the USA's best bicycle-touring maps. Each costs around $12 (mail order only) and includes route notes, elevation and temperature charts, and recreation information.

The American Automobile Association (AAA; ☎ 800-922-8228, W www.aaa.com) produces free maps of varying scale (available at local branch offices to members only). There is reciprocity between AAA and automobile associations in other countries; bring your membership card.

Maps by Rand McNally and Compass are widely available. These vary in scale and appropriateness to cycling but both are well-respected publishers.

Trails Illustrated publishes excellent national parks maps (around $6 for paper; $9–11 waterproof) available from visitor centers, outdoors stores and bookstores.

Two atlas series', the DeLorme's *Atlas & Gazetteer* (around $17) and Benchmark's *Road & Recreation Atlas* (around $20) cover each state, with clear maps, park recreational information, campgrounds and activities. Although weighty and unwieldy they are handy for planning, and relevant pages can be extracted.

The Border to Border ride is comprehensively mapped day by day in this book. The other rides are mapped at a smaller scale and additional maps are recommended in the Planning sections of the rides. To source these maps before you leave home, contact a specialty map store such as:

Australia Map Land (☎ 03-9670 4383, W www.mapland.com.au) 372 Little Bourke St, Melbourne, Victoria 3000

Europe Geographic Bookshop Jacob van Wijngaarden (☎ 020-612 19 01, W www.jvw.nl) Overtoom 97, 1054 HD, Amsterdam, Netherlands

UK Stanfords (☎ 020-7836 1321, W www.stanfords.co.uk) 12–14 Long Acre, Covent Garden, London WC2E 9LP

USA Easy Going (☎ 510-843-3533 or ☎ 800-675-5500, W www.easygoing.com) 1385 Shattuck Ave, Berkeley, CA 94709

What to Bring

Think light. Think dry. Bring only the essentials. Practically anything you overlook can be purchased on the West Coast.

While few places on the rides are so remote that you couldn't find shelter in a weather emergency, exposure to the elements can be a serious hazard in any environment. Waterproof gear (especially clothing) will minimize danger and potential discomfort.

Clothing When considering comfort, bike shorts (knicks) may be the most important equipment a cyclist owns. With a chamois-padded crotch these make hours in the saddle bearable. They are designed to be worn without underwear. If Lycra isn't your look, get 'baggies' – ordinary looking shorts with sewn-in padding.

In cooler weather, put a pair of tights or long pants (preferably with a gusset crotch) over your bike shorts, or buy a pair of cycling 'longs' (tights with sewn-in padding). Another option is to get a pair of leg warmers, usually made of Lycra, that zip at the ankle and hug the thigh with elastic. Arm warmers work the same way and both can be shed as temperatures rise.

If it's really cold consider full-finger gloves (either thin polypropylene gloves to wear with cycling gloves or more wind/rain-resistant ones), thermal socks, Neoprene booties (which go over your shoes) and a close-fitting cap under your helmet.

Layering is the best way of keeping your core temperature where it needs to be. Start with a lightweight synthetic (CoolMax, polypropylene or Capilene are good choices) or silk top, followed by a warmer insulating layer such as a thin synthetic fleece, then a waterproof jacket and pants. A vest is highly recommended as it can go over the base layer or the insulating layer, and can be worn off the bike.

Avoid cotton for all cycling purposes – when it gets wet it stays wet (and cold).

Equipment Check List

This list is a general guide to the things you might take on a bike tour. Your list will vary depending on the kind of cycling you want to do, whether you're roughing it in a tent or using hotels, and on the time of year. Don't forget to take on board enough water and food to see you safely between towns.

Bike Clothing

- ☐ cycling gloves
- ☐ cycling shoes and socks
- ☐ cycling tights or leg warmers
- ☐ helmet and visor
- ☐ long-sleeved shirt or cycling jersey
- ☐ padded cycling shorts (knicks)
- ☐ sunglasses
- ☐ thermal undershirt and arm warmers
- ☐ T-shirt or short-sleeved cycling jersey
- ☐ visibility vest
- ☐ waterproof jacket & pants
- ☐ windproof jacket or vest

Off-Bike Clothing

- ☐ change of clothing
- ☐ spare shoes or sandals
- ☐ swimming costume
- ☐ sunhat
- ☐ fleece jacket
- ☐ thermal underwear
- ☐ underwear and spare socks
- ☐ warm hat and gloves

Equipment

- ☐ bike lights (rear and front) with spare batteries (see flashlight)
- ☐ elastic cord
- ☐ camera and spare film
- ☐ cycle computer
- ☐ day-pack
- ☐ medical kit* and toiletries
- ☐ sewing/mending kit (for everything)
- ☐ panniers and waterproof liners
- ☐ pocket knife (with corkscrew)
- ☐ sleeping sheet
- ☐ small handlebar bag and/or map case
- ☐ small towel
- ☐ tool kit, pump and spares*
- ☐ flashlight (torch) with spare batteries and globe – some double as (front) bike lights
- ☐ water containers
- ☐ water purification tablets, iodine or filter

Camping

- ☐ cooking, eating and drinking utensils
- ☐ clothesline and dishwasing items
- ☐ portable stove and fuel
- ☐ insulating mat
- ☐ matches or lighter and candle
- ☐ rope for hanging food in bear country
- ☐ sleeping bag
- ☐ tent
- ☐ toilet paper and toilet trowel

* see the boxed texts 'First-Aid Kit' (p51) and 'Spares & Tool Kit' (p73).

Gosh! Lots of luggage. Where's your bike?
In there... somewhere!
Hatcher/99
DON HATCHER

Consider carrying a non-synthetic piece of clothing to put on at the end of the day.

There are some excellent breathable water-and-windproof jackets on the market. Those made with Gore-Tex fabric are probably the best known and respected. REI and Patagonia also manufacture their own versions. Cheaper water-resistant jackets are less effective.

Bright or light-colored clothing is cooler and maximizes visibility. For added safety, wear a reflective vest or safety triangle, and reflective straps around your ankles.

The padded palms of fingerless cycling gloves reduce the impact of jarring on your hands, which can lead to nerve damage; gloves also prevent sunburn and protect your hands in case of a fall.

Cycling shoes increase the efficiency of your stroke but stiff-soled ordinary shoes work well as an alternative. Avoid spongy-soled joggers; stiff soles transfer the power from your pedal stroke directly to the pedal.

Sunglasses are essential cycling wear, not only to minimize exposure to UV radiation but to shield your eyes from insects and prevent them from drying out in the wind. A helmet visor provides some sun protection and a bandanna is useful for soaking up sweat and protecting your neck from sun.

Bicycle No rides in this book, other than mountain-bike rides (for which the hiring possibilities are listed), require knobby tires or upright handlebars. A 21- or 24-speed derailleur might make some of the climbs more manageable but an 18-speed will probably be just fine.

Equipment See Bicycle Equipment (p63) for mandatory cycling equipment and helmet advice.

Panniers are of course essential. If you don't want to spend the extra money on the waterproof variety, buy some heavy-duty trash bags to line them. A handlebar bag is good for light items (wallet, maps, sunglasses, this book) but can be dangerous to the steering system if packed too heavily.

Personal hydration systems help eliminate the risk of dehydration and can be refilled along the way. People with neck problems should test one before heading out.

If you're planning to camp, you'll also need a lightweight tent, sleeping pad, sleeping bag and flashlight (torch), or preferably a headlamp. Cooking equipment is optional – for hot oatmeal and tea on a cold morning.

Fuel cannot be carried on aircraft but is readily available. White gas, methylated spirits and kerosene are available at gas stations. Gas cartridges can be found at outdoors stores or hardware stores in small towns.

Buying & Hiring Locally When buying big-ticket items, be aware of relevant sales tax (see Taxes, p36).

The USA has some excellent bicycle manufacturers, including Trek, Cannondale, GT, Litespeed and Gary Fisher. Expect to pay $800 and up for a decent touring bicycle and $1000 and up for a quality mountain bike. Good panniers – by Madden Mountaineering, Overland or Mountainsmith, for example – cost $30 to $65, plus $25 for a rack. A good helmet – Giro or Bell – will be around $50. A combination tool, pump and patch kit, lock and chain lube will be another $80. Add $150 if bike shorts, a cycling top, sunglasses and a hydration system are on the list.

The largest outdoor gear retailer on the West Coast is Recreation Equipment Inc (REI; ☎ 253-891-2500 or ☎ 800-426-4840, w www.REI.com), founded in Seattle in 1938. Call them or access the Web site to find the store nearest you. Most of their stores carry a good supply of bicycles and gear, and rent tents, stoves, lanterns etc.

Bike hire is widely available in large cities and near mountain-biking areas. Shops are often recommended in the rides chapters.

Buying Online Many people swear by the gear they buy online or from catalogs. Many mail-order companies, which are prolific in the US outdoors scene, do not maintain retail space, so can offer tremendous bargains.

Bicycle and outdoors equipment traders include:

Performance Bicycle (☎ 800-727-4177, w www.performancebike.com) Sells top-quality, name-brand products ranging from altimeters to panniers to fleece gloves.

Campmor Inc (☎ 800-525-4784, w www.campmor.com) PO Box 700-BC97, Saddle River, NJ 07458-0700

Sierra Trading Post (☎ 800-713-4534, fax 800-378-8946, w www.sierratradingpost.com) 5025 Campstool Rd, Cheyenne, WY 82007-1898

TOURIST OFFICES

Local Tourist Offices

Every state has a tourist office, which will send out a swag of promotional materials:

California Division of Tourism (☎ 916-323-9882 or ☎ 800-462-2543, fax 322-3402, W www.gocalif.ca.gov) 801 K St, Suite 1600, Sacramento, CA 95814

Oregon Tourism Commission (☎ 503-986-0000 or ☎ 800-547-7842, fax 986 0001, W www.traveloregon.com) 775 Summer St NE, Salem, OR 97310

Washington State Tourism (☎ 360-725-5059 or ☎ 800-544-1800, W www.experiencewashington.com) 210 11th Avenue SW, Suite 101, Olympia, WA 98504-2500

Many cities also have an official Convention & Visitors Bureau (CVB) whose main function is to attract the conference trade. Most aren't set up to assist individuals but some are helpful.

In smaller towns, the local chamber of commerce, an organization of local businesses that promotes the town and the commercial interests of its members, will often maintain a list of hotels, motels, restaurants and services. The list will mention only chamber of commerce members and may not include camping options.

A visitor center may serve either of these functions (or both) but is usually open on the weekend when CVBs and chambers of commerce close. Where possible rides start and/or end at visitor centers. Here, cyclists can find a bathroom, drinking fountain, maps and accommodations listings. National or state park visitor centers serve a similar purpose, as do local libraries.

State parks information is available at W www.parks.wa.gov, W www.prd.state.or.us and W www.cal-parks.ca.gov. National park information is sorted by park on a central Web site, W www.nps.gov/parks.html.

Tourist Offices Abroad

There is no national tourist office promoting US tourism in other countries, though some states may have an office or agent in a prime market.

VISAS & DOCUMENTS

Passport & Visas

All foreign visitors (other than Canadians) must bring their passports. Your passport should be valid for at least six months longer than your intended stay in the USA. Canadians must have proof of citizenship, such as a citizenship card.

Under the Visa Waiver Program, citizens of Andorra, Argentina, Australia, Austria, Belgium, Brunei, Denmark, Finland, France, Germany, Iceland, Ireland, Italy, Japan, Liechtenstein, Luxembourg, Monaco, the Netherlands, New Zealand, Norway, San Marino, Slovenia, Spain, Sweden, Switzerland and the UK may enter the USA without a visa for stays of up to 90 days. You *must* have a roundtrip or onward ticket that is nonrefundable in the USA, and you may be required to show evidence of adequate funds.

Those not entering under the Visa Waiver Program, need to obtain a visa from a US consulate or embassy (pp33–4). Evidence of sufficient funds, a return or onward ticket and/or guarantees from a US resident are sometimes required, particularly for those from developing countries. The relevant authority is the US Immigration & Naturalization Service (INS), a body not noted for its easygoing attitude. For detailed information about visas and immigration, check the US State Department Web site W travel.state.gov/visa_services.html.

A visitors visa is good for one or five years with multiple entries. It specifically prohibits the visitor from taking paid employment in the USA. The validity period depends on your country of origin. The length of time you'll be allowed to stay is determined by the INS when you enter.

It's a good idea to be able to show an itinerary, and that you have $300 or $400 for each week of your intended stay. A couple of major credit cards will go a long way toward establishing 'sufficient funds'.

If you want, need or hope to stay in the USA longer than the date stamped on your passport, go to the local INS office (call ☎ 800-755-0777 or look in the White Pages under US Government) to apply for an extension *before* your visa expires.

Onward Tickets

A roundtrip or onward ticket is a requirement only for the Visa Waiver Program. If you have a visitors visa, a ticket out of the country may help persuade the INS that you don't intend to stay permanently but it's not a formal requirement.

National Park Entry Permits

Entry to a national park ranges from $5 to $20 per vehicle, and free to $10 for pedestrians and cyclists.

The National Parks Pass ($50) is available online at W www.nationalparks.org or by mail from National Parks Pass, 27540 Avenue Mentry, Valencia, CA 91355. If you're going to several national fee areas (including national parks, monuments, historic sites, recreation areas and national wildlife refuges), it pays to upgrade and buy a Golden Eagle hologram. This costs an additional $15 and is available at National Park Service, Fish and Wildlife Service and Bureau of Land Management fee stations.

See Senior Cyclists (p41) for information about The Golden Age Passport.

Travel Insurance

It is highly advisable to take out travel insurance that covers you for medical expenses, hospital treatment and an emergency flight home.

You may prefer a policy that pays doctors or hospitals directly rather than requiring you to pay on the spot and claim later. If you have to claim later, make sure you keep all documentation. Some policies ask you to call back (collect) to a center in your home country where an immediate assessment of your problem is made.

Be sure to read the fine print, as many policies do not cover emergency evacuation or injuries incurred while engaged in 'sporting activities' (which can including cycling). If insurance that does cover such activities seems expensive, it's still nowhere near the cost of a medical emergency in the USA.

A good option for cyclists who travel frequently is an annual policy, offered in the USA. These policies cost around $150 per year and, while they do not cover trip cancellation or interruption, they provide up to $50,000 in medical-evacuation costs and usually have no prohibitive clauses for adventurous types. Two established providers are Access America (☎ 800-284-8300, W www.accessamerica.com), PO Box 90315 Richmond, VA 23286; and Travelex (☎ 888-407-5404, W www.travelex-insurance.com), 11717 Burt St, Suite 202, Omaha, NE 68154.

Cover for luggage theft or loss, cancellations, delayed travel arrangements and ticket loss is also advisable, as is coverage against civil liability (sadly, the USA is a very litigious society, and if you accidentally cause someone loss or damage you may be sued for millions).

Other Documents

All visitors should bring their home driving license and any health- or travel-insurance cards. To buy alcohol, you'll need photo identification to show that you are over 21 years of age.

Most visitors can legally drive in the USA for up to a year with their home driving license. An International Driving Permit (IDP; available from your local road authority) is useful if taking a car over an international border.

If you are a student, bring your school identification to take advantage of the available discounts. Unless you plan on visiting quite a few sights or attending movies and performances, an ISIC (International Student Identity Card) is not necessary.

The IYTC (International Youth Travel Card), issued to those aged 25 and under, can help you get a reduced rate on airfare, car rental and other costs. People over the age of 60 often receive discounts on presentation of proof of age.

Copies

Keep photocopies of your essential documents such as passport and airline tickets separately from the originals (in a waterproof bag stashed in a pannier, for example). If you're staying at the same hotel before and after a ride, leave valuable documents with them. Also leave a copy at home – it can make it easier to obtain replacements. You can store details of your documents in Lonely Planet's free online Travel Vault; create your own password at W www.ekno.lonelyplanet.com.

EMBASSIES & CONSULATES

US Embassies & Consulates

Listed below are the details of embassies, plus cities that have consulates.

Australia (☎ 02-6214 5600) 21 Moonah Place, Yarralumla, ACT 2600
Consulates: Melbourne, Perth, Sydney

Canada (☎ 613-238-5335) 490 Sussex Dr, Ottawa, Ontario K1N 1G8
Consulates: Calgary, Halifax, Montreal, Quebec, Toronto, Vancouver

France (☎ 01 43 12 22 22) 2 ave Gabriel, 75008 Paris
Consulates: Marseille, Strasbourg
Germany (☎ 030-238 51 74) Neustädtische Kirchstrasse 4–5, 10117 Berlin
Consulates: Düsseldorf, Frankfurt, Hamburg, Leipzig, Munich
Ireland (☎ 01-668 7122) 42 Elgin Rd, Dublin 4
Japan (☎ 03-3224 5000) 1-10-5 Akasaka, Minato-ku, Tokyo
Consulates: Fukuoka, Nagoya, Naha, Osaka, Sapporo
Mexico (☎ 01-5080-2000) Paseo de la Reforma 305, Colonia Cuauhtémoc 06500, Mexico City
Consulates: Ciudad Juarez, Guadalájara, Hermosillo, Matamoros, Merida, Monterrey, Nogales, Nuevo Laredo, Tijuana
Netherlands (☎ 70-310 9209) Lange Voorhout 102, 2514 EJ The Hague
Consulate: Amsterdam
New Zealand (☎ 04-462 6000) 29 Fitzherbert Terrace, Thorndon, Wellington
Consulate: Auckland
South Africa (☎ 12-342 1048) 877 Pretorius St, PO Box 9536, Pretoria 0001
UK (☎ 020-7499 9000) 24 Grosvenor Square, London W1A 1AE
Consulates: Belfast, Edinburgh

Embassies & Consulates in the USA

Just about every country in the world has an embassy in Washington, DC. Call ☎ 202-555-1212 for phone numbers or check W www.embassy.org/embassies for information. Many countries also have consulates in other large cities such as Seattle, San Francisco and LA – look under 'Consulates' in the Yellow Pages.

Australia (☎ 202-797-3000, W www.austemb.org) 1601 Massachusetts Ave NW, Washington DC 20036
Canada (☎ 202-682-1740, W www.canadianembassy.org) 501 Pennsylvania Ave NW, Washington DC 20001
Consulates: LA, Seattle
France (☎ 202-944-6000, W www.info-france-usa.org) 4101 Reservoir Rd NW, Washington DC 20007
Germany (☎ 202-298-4000, W www.germany-info.org) 4645 Reservoir Rd NW, Washington DC 20007-1998
Japan (☎ 202-238-6700, W www.embjapan.org) 2520 Massachusetts Ave NW, Washington DC 20008-2869
Consulates: LA, Portland, San Francisco, Seattle
Mexico (☎ 202-728-1600, W 207.224.13.65/english) 1911 Pennsylvania Ave NW, Washington DC 20006
Consulates: LA, Portland, San Diego, San Francisco, Seattle
Netherlands (☎ 202-244-5300, W www.netherlands-embassy.org) 4200 Linnean Ave NW, Washington DC 20008
New Zealand (☎ 202-328-4800, W www.nzemb.org) 37 Observatory Circle, Washington DC 20008
South Africa (☎ 202-232-4400, W www.usaembassy.southafrica.net) 3051 Massachusetts Ave NW, Washington DC 20008
UK (☎ 202-588-6500, W www.britainusa.com/consular/embassy/embassy.asp) 3100 Massachusetts Ave NW, Washington DC, 20008
Consulates: LA, San Francisco, Seattle

CUSTOMS

US Customs allows each person to bring in 1L of liquor (provided you are at least 21 years old) and 50 (non-Cuban) cigars or 200 cigarettes duty free. US citizens may import duty-free gifts to the value of $400 while non-US citizens are allowed to import $100 worth.

US law permits you to bring in, or take out, as much as $10,000 in US or foreign currency, traveler's checks or letters of credit without formality. Any larger amount of any or all of the above must be declared.

Prohibited Imports

There are heavy penalties for attempting to import illegal drugs. It's also forbidden to import chocolate liqueurs, pornography, lottery tickets, items with fake brand names, and goods made in Cuba, Iran, Iraq, Libya, North Korea or Sudan. Any fruit, vegetables, or other food or plant material must be declared or left in the bins in the arrival area. Most food items are prohibited to prevent the introduction of pests or diseases.

The USA is a signatory to CITES, the Convention on International Trade in Endangered Species. The import and export of products made from species that may be endangered in any part of the world is prohibited. This includes ivory, tortoise shell, coral, and many fur, skin and feather products. If you want to bring a fur coat, snakeskin belt or bone carving with you, you may have to show a certificate that it was not made from an endangered species. The easiest option is not to bring anything even remotely suspect. CITES restrictions also apply to what you take home. Alligator-skin cowboy boots might be a great souvenir but be ready to convince customs authorities that they're not made from endangered 'gators.

MONEY

Currency

The US dollar is divided into 100 cents (c). Coins come in denominations of 1c (penny), 5c (nickel), 10c (dime), 25c (quarter) and the seldom-seen 50c (half-dollar). It's handy to have a stash of quarters, the coins most commonly used in vending machines, telephones and campground showers. Notes, usually called bills, come in $1, $2, $5, $10, $20, $50 and $100 denominations.

There is a $1 coin that the government has tried unsuccessfully to bring into mass circulation; you may get one as change from ticket and stamp machines. Be aware that it looks similar to a quarter.

Exchange Rates

At time of printing, exchange rates were:

country	unit	US dollar
Australia	A$1	$0.51
Canada	C$1	$0.63
France	FF10	$1.36
Germany	DM1	$0.46
Hong Kong	HK$10	$1.28
Japan	Y100	$0.79
Netherlands	NF1	$0.56
New Zealand	NZ$1	$0.42
UK	UK£1	$1.43
Euro	€1	$0.89

Exchanging Money

You can rely on credit/debit cards instead of bringing cash into the USA. Just bring some small notes and coins and/or traveler's checks to use on arrival.

Cash & Traveler's Checks Banks in cities will exchange cash or traveler's checks in major foreign currencies; however, banks in outlying areas may not, or may take some time to do so. Thomas Cook and American Express offices and exchange counters at airports and international borders will also exchange foreign currencies, though you'll probably get a better rate at a bank.

American Express and Thomas Cook traveler's checks are widely accepted and have efficient replacement policies if you have a record of the check numbers (keep it separately from the checks). Buy checks in US dollars as foreign currency checks can only be changed at a bank or at exchange counters in large cities.

ATMs Almost every bank, as well as shopping centers, grocery stores and airports has ATMs (automated teller machines) available 24 hours a day. You can withdraw cash from an ATM using a credit card, which will usually incur a fee. Most ATMs are linked with one or more of the main ATM networks (Plus, Cirrus, Exchange, Accel), and you can use them to withdraw funds from an overseas bank account if you have an affiliated card. This is usually cheaper than a credit transaction and has a good exchange rate. Check with your bank or credit card company about using its cards at ATMs in the USA.

Credit & Debit Cards Major credit cards are accepted at hotels, restaurants, gas stations and shops throughout the USA. It's almost impossible to make phone reservations without one. If you're relying primarily upon credit cards, bring more than one and include a Visa or MasterCard in your deck.

Also widely accepted (phone reservations included), a debit card deducts payment directly from your bank account, and charges a small fee for the transaction. Check with your bank to confirm that your debit card will be accepted in the USA; you may need to change your PIN (Personal Identification Number) to four digits.

International Transfers When instructing your bank back home to send you a draft, specify the city, bank and branch where you want the money directed. It is easier if you've authorized someone back home to access your account.

Money sent by telegraphic transfer should reach you within a week; by mail, allow at least two weeks. When it arrives, it will most likely be converted into US dollars.

You can also transfer money by American Express, Thomas Cook or Western Union. These services are expensive.

Security

While the West Coast is, overall, a safe place to travel, it's a good idea to divide your money and credit cards and stash them in several places. Keep an extra bit of cash somewhere off your bike: a hotel that you'll return to or know you can trust to forward the money; a friend's house; or in a letter that you send to yourself (c/o General Delivery) in the town of your final destination.

Stash Your Cash

I pay for supplies, most food and accommodations with a credit card, and keep cash on hand for snacks, souvenirs and campground fees. As a further safety measure (and I'm *not* the paranoid type), I stash $20 (all taped up so that it's really hard to get to) in a pannier, for emergencies.

Marisa Gierlich

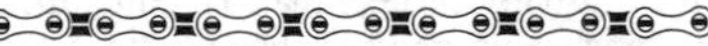

Costs

The main expenses between rides are transportation, accommodations, food, sightseeing and entertainment. Cyclists traveling alone will pay a bit more, on average, for accommodations and supplies. National park entry and campsite fees are per person for cyclists. Typical expenditures are:

Item	Cost
budget motel room	$36/45 single/double
hostel bed	$15–21 per person
campground fee	$3/21 public/private
budget restaurant meal	$6 per person
glass of wine/beer	$3.50
brick of cheese	$2.50
loaf of bread	$2
instant noodle soup	$1
quality bike tube	$4
local phone call	$0.35

Tipping

People waiting tables in restaurants are paid minimal wages and rely upon tips for their livelihoods. Tip 15% unless the service is terrible or up to 20% if the service is great.

Baggage carriers should be tipped $1 for one bag and $0.50 for each additional bag. Taxi drivers expect you to round up the fare and tip an additional $2 on shorter rides, $5 on long rides.

Taxes

Oregon has no sales tax; the base rate in Washington is 6.5%; and in California it can be up to 8.25%. In addition, there may be county and city sales taxes (maybe an extra 5%) and sometimes other separate taxes, such as a 'bed tax' (usually 4%) on lodging or a special tax on car rentals.

When inquiring about accommodations rates, be sure to ask whether taxes are included. Unless otherwise stated, the prices in this book don't include taxes. In stores, sales tax is added at the register.

POST & COMMUNICATIONS

Post

The US Postal Service (USPS; ☎ 800-275-8777, Ⓦ www.usps.com) is reliable and relatively inexpensive.

Post offices in main towns are usually open 8am to 5pm Monday to Friday and 8am to noon on Saturday. General delivery mail (ie, poste restante) can be sent to you c/o General Delivery at any post office that has its own zip code. Mail is held for 10 days before it's returned to the sender; request your correspondents write 'Hold for Arrival' on their letters. You'll need picture identification to collect your mail.

Telephone

All phone numbers within the USA consist of a three-digit area code followed by a seven-digit local number. For all long-distance and toll-free numbers, dial ☎ 1 first. The most common toll-free numbers start with ☎ 800 and ☎ 888. The ☎ 900 prefix is for premium-rate calls – phone sex, horoscopes, jokes etc.

Phone Cards Phone cards are now almost essential for travelers in the USA. There are two main types. A phone credit card bills calls to your home number. Some cards issued by foreign phone companies work in the USA – inquire at home.

A phone debit card is a good alternative and is widely available from vending machines in airports, bus stations and hotel lobbies in big cities. To call, you access the company through a toll-free number, key in your PIN and follow voice prompts. The cost of calls is immediately debited from the value of the card. A unit is good for a call of

Useful Phone Numbers

Directory assistance	☎ 411
Emergency (police, ambulance & fire)	☎ 911
International direct dial access code	☎ 011
Long-distance & toll-free prefix	☎ 1
Operator (local and national)	☎ 0
USA country code	☎ 1

one minute within the USA, half a minute or less to overseas. Some phone debit cards allow you to add extra value by billing an additional amount to your regular credit card.

Long-Distance Calls Long-distance charges vary depending on the destination and the telephone company – call the operator (☎ 0) for rate information but don't ask to be connected; operator-assisted calls are much more expensive than direct-dial calls.

For assistance outside your area code, dial ☎ 1, plus the three-digit area code of the place you want to call, plus ☎ 555-1212. This is charged as a long-distance call.

Generally, nights (11pm–8am), all day Saturday, and Sunday (8am–5pm) are the cheapest times to call. Evenings (5–11pm, Sun–Fri) are mid-priced. Day calls (8am–5pm, Mon–Fri) are full-price.

International Calls To make an international call dial ☎ 011, then the country code, followed by the area code and phone number. International country codes (as well as American and Canadian area codes) are listed in the front of most phone books.

Hotel Phones Many hotels and motels add a service charge ($0.50–$1) for local calls. They also have hefty surcharges for long-distance calls, and even charge you for calling ☎ 800 numbers. Ask if they offer free calls before picking up the phone.

Fax

Fax machines are easy to find at shipping companies such as Mail Boxes Etc, photocopy services and hotel business service centers. Be prepared to pay more than $1 a page.

Email & Internet Access

Most public libraries have free Internet access. Other options are Internet cafes, copy centers or hotels catering to business travelers. Many hostels offer inexpensive Internet access to their guests.

eKno Communication Service

Lonely Planet's eKno Communication Card provides budget international calls, a range of messaging services, free email and travel information. Check the eKno Web site (W www.ekno.lonelyplanet.com) for joining, new features and access numbers.

DIGITAL RESOURCES

The Internet is a good place to start planning: search for cheap airfares, book a flight, check the weather, get travel advisories or find the current exchange rate.

There's no better place to start your explorations than the Lonely Planet Web site (W www.lonelyplanet.com). Here you'll find succinct summaries on traveling to most places on earth, postcards from travelers and the Thorn Tree bulletin board, which has a cycling branch, where you can ask questions or disperse advice. You can also find travel news and updates to many of our most popular guidebooks, and the subWWWay section has links to the most useful travel resources elsewhere on the Web.

There is a wealth of information on the Internet about the USA, including:

CNN's Travel Guide (W www.cnn.com/travel) Travel advisories and links to city profiles, including weather, accommodations and transport information.

Excite Travel on North America (W directory.excite.com/travel) The best starting place for airfares, maps and accommodations.

US Federal Government (W www.firstgov.gov) Well-organized and succinct information about federal policies, statistics and current events.

Cycling-specific Web sites include:

Bike Lane (W www.bikelane.com) A comprehensive list of links to international and regional clubs and manufacturers etc.

Bike Ride Online (W www.bikeride.com) Books, events, newsgroups and links to organizations in the Pacific Northwest.

League of American Bicyclists (W www.bikeleague.org) Site of the USA's oldest bicycle advocacy group, with ride itineraries, events and national bike news.

Velo News (W www.velonews.com) An excellent online bicycle magazine, it has a ride calendar, training tips, plus national and international bicycle news.

BOOKS

The West Coast is divided into Pacific Northwest (Washington and Oregon) and California by many books. West Coast literature is discussed in Arts, p24.

Lonely Planet

Lonely Planet's *USA* and *USA phrasebook* are indispensable tools for a cross-country journey. A more playful look into travel in the USA is Sean Condon's *Drive Thru America*, in the Journeys travel literature series. *Hiking in the USA* would be an excellent companion for cyclists who want to get out of the saddle.

More information can be found in Lonely Planet's *Pacific Northwest* and *California* guides. See the rides chapters for details of city guides.

Cycling

Bicycling Magazine publishes a series of books that are comprehensive, easy to read and well illustrated; titles include the *Complete Book of Road Cycling Skills*, the *Ultimate Ride Guide for Road & Mountain Biking* and the *Complete Guide to Bicycle Maintenance & Repair*.

Mountain bikers swear by Leonard Zinn's *Zinn and the Art of Mountain Bike Maintenance*, a fun, instructive read.

Steve Butterman's *Bicycle Touring: How to Prepare for Long Rides* covers planning and equipment strategies that make any trip seem feasible.

Further inspiration may come from the first-person account of Thomas Stevens, who rode a high-wheeler around the world in 1884. *Around the World on a Bicycle* was first published in 1887 and recently re-released in paperback.

To find out what the US offers from a cyclist's point of view read *Roll Around Heaven All Day: A Piecemeal Journey Across America by Bicycle*, by Stan Purdum.

Regional cycling and mountain-bike guides are detailed in the relevant ride chapters.

General

There's a long history of foreigners and Americans traveling around the USA, trying to make sense of it. They include Alexis de Tocqueville in 1835–40, with *Democracy in America*; Charles Dickens, who wrote *American Notes* in 1842; Oscar Wilde, with *Impressions of America* (1883); and GK Chesterton, who described his visit in *What I Saw in America* (1923).

Cadillac Desert: The American West and its Disappearing Water, by Marc Reisner, is an altogether fascinating environmental history of the West and its quest for water. *The Good Rain: Across Time and Terrain in the Pacific Northwest*, by Timothy Egan, is an insightful discussion of the Northwest and its people.

Peterson Field Guides (published by Houghton-Mifflin) are the definitive birding books in the USA, and are also good for just about every outdoors subject – from trees to caterpillars.

NEWSPAPERS & MAGAZINES

National newspapers such as the *The Wall Street Journal*, *The New York Times* and *USA Today* are widely available.

Best for regional coverage are the big city dailies, which circulate well outside the city limits. Seattle's two dailies are the *Seattle Post-Intelligencer* and *The Seattle Times*; Oregon relies on Portland's *The Oregonian*; Californians read the *San Francisco Chronicle* and *Los Angeles Times*.

Travelers will also find local newspapers keeping tabs on events and political issues from a hip, primarily liberal perspective.

Bicycling Magazine, *Bicycle Magazine* and *Mountain Bike Magazine* are the titles you'll find in airports, supermarkets and most bike shops. Less glossy are *Dirt Rag*, a favorite of many hardcore mountain bikers, and *Velo News* – both available from bookstores and, occasionally, bike shops.

WEATHER INFORMATION

In the front section of the White and Yellow Pages, listed under Weather in the US Government section, is a local number you can call for updated weather information.

The National Climactic Data Center (W lwf.ncdc.noaa.gov/oa/ncdc.html) handles forecasts and marine warnings. A quicker and easier Web site is the University of Michigan's WeatherNet (W cirrus.sprl.umich.edu/wxnet), which covers weather, forecasts and warnings for even the most remote areas.

Weather for Your Ears

Radio hounds can pick up a National Weather Radio receiver for $25 to $100 at electronics stores throughout the USA. With the receiver you can access 24-hour weather news, warnings and forecasts on the public band between 162.400 and 162.550 MHz. For a current list of frequencies and transceiver locations, visit W www.nws.noaa.gov/nwr.

RADIO & TV

Most radio stations have a range of less than 100mi, with scores of stations in and near major cities crowding the airwaves with a wide variety of music and entertainment. In rural areas, be prepared for country and western music, local news and talk radio. News-oriented National Public Radio (NPR) can usually be found in the lower numbers of the radio band. Many public stations also carry the BBC World Service, a good source for foreign news.

All the major TV networks have affiliated stations on the West Coast. Most hotels have cable (subscriber) channels, including news stations such as ESPN and The Weather Channel. Smaller motels may charge a fee for cable.

PHOTOGRAPHY & VIDEO

Stock up on film in your gateway city, as selection is limited and prices are high in small towns and national park centers.

Invest in a good waterproof camera bag, or bring a heavy-duty, sealable plastic bag for wet conditions (a Gore-Tex stuff sack also works well).

Airport X-ray machines in the USA don't jeopardize most film. If you have high-speed film (1600 ASA and above), then you may want to carry your film spools loose (in a clear plastic container) and ask the X-ray inspector to manually check the film.

The standard video type is VHS. Video film and equipment is widely available. The only filming restrictions you're likely to face are at museums, recording studios and crime scenes.

TIME

All of Washington and California, and most of Oregon, are on Pacific Standard Time (PST), which is eight hours behind Greenwich Mean Time (GMT), three hours behind New York City on Eastern Standard Time (EST) and 17 hours behind Tokyo. The West Coast is 19 hours behind Sydney and eight hours behind London. A small sliver of easternmost Oregon is on mountain standard time (MST), one hour ahead of PST.

The West Coast observes the switch to daylight saving time; clocks are set forward one hour on the first Sunday in April and back one hour on the last Sunday in October.

ELECTRICITY

The nationwide voltage is 110V. Plugs have two flat pins, sometimes with an extra round one. Adapters are easy to buy at hardware stores and drugstores.

WEIGHTS & MEASURES

Distances are in feet, yards and miles. Dry weights are in ounces (oz), pounds (lbs) and tons. Liquid measures differ from dry measures. One pint equals 16 fluid oz; 2 pints equal 1 quart – a common measure for liquids. US pints and quarts are 20% less than Imperial ones. Gasoline is dispensed by the US gallon, which is also about 20% less than the Imperial gallon. See the conversion table on the inside back cover.

LAUNDRY

There are self-service, coin-operated laundry facilities in most towns of any size and at better campgrounds. Washing a load costs about $1.50 and drying, another $1. Some laundries have attendants who will wash, dry and fold your clothes for an additional charge.

A favorite environmentally friendly washing product (for teeth, pots and pans, hair and clothes) is Dr Bronner's, available at outdoors stores and natural food stores.

WOMEN CYCLISTS

In most cycling circles gender equality is highly valued. There is a general sense that *any* person in pursuit of fresh air and wide-open roads is as good as any other. This female author, and others on this book, did the majority of research alone, without any undue hassle.

That said, women potentially face more challenging situations when cycling alone than men do. If you're unaccustomed to cycling solo, stick to well-traveled routes and consider staying indoors instead of camping.

Safety Precautions

In towns and cities, be aware of unsafe areas, particularly after dark. Ask at your hotel or telephone the tourist office or women's center for advice on what parts of a city to avoid.

In rural areas a woman traveling alone may be viewed with disapproval. If a backwoods character scoffs at a woman in cycling clothes try not to take active offense. Don't take an adversarial role in a situation that is unlikely to change and could get ugly if words are exchanged.

To deal with potential dangers, many women protect themselves with a whistle, Mace, cayenne-pepper spray or self-defense training. If you are assaulted, call the police (☎ 911). Larger towns and cities usually have rape crisis centers.

Resources & Organizations

For an all-women bike tour, check in with Woman Tours (☎ 800-247-1444, W www.womantours.com).

National Organization for Women (NOW; ☎ 202-331-0066; W www.now.org/), 1000 16th St NW, Suite 700, Washington, DC 20036, is a good resource for women-related information. NOW can refer you to local branches.

A Journey of One's Own, by Thalia Zepatos (Eighth Mountain Press), contains travel tips, anecdotes and a long list of sources and resources for the independent female traveler. *Adventures in Good Company*, also by Thalia Zepatos, covers a huge range of adventure, outdoors and special interest tours and activities for women.

GAY & LESBIAN CYCLISTS

While the West Coast is probably the easiest region in the USA in which to be openly homosexual, gay and lesbian travelers should be careful – *especially* in conservative rural areas, where holding hands could get you bashed.

San Francisco and LA are, by a wide margin, the most openly gay-friendly cities on the West Coast. Seattle and Portland are liberal-minded but much of the Northwest (and parts of northeastern California) is far more conservative. The Oregon Citizens Alliance (OCA) is notorious for attempting to limit gay civil rights.

Resources & Organizations

Damron Women's Traveler with listings for lesbians and *Damron Address Book* for men are both published by Damron Company, out of San Francisco. Ferrari's *Places for Women* and *Places for Men* are also useful. These are out of print but may still be found at good bookstores.

The *Gay Yellow Pages*, published by Village Station (New York), has national and regional editions.

Touring with Children

Children can travel by bicycle from the time they can support their head and a helmet, at around eight months. There are some small, lightweight, cute helmets around, such as the L'il Bell Shell.

To carry an infant or toddler requires a child seat or trailer. Child seats are more common for everyday riding and are cheaper, easier to move as a unit with the bike and let you touch and talk to your child while moving. Disadvantages, especially over long distances, can include exposure to weather, the tendency of a sleeping child to loll, and losing luggage capacity at the rear. The best makes, such as the Rhode Gear Limo, include extra moulding to protect the child in case of a fall, have footrests and restraints, recline to let the child sleep and fit very securely and conveniently onto a bike rack.

With a capacity of up to 110lb (versus around 39lb for a child seat), trailers can accommodate two bigger children and luggage. They give good, though not always total, protection from sun and rain and let children sleep comfortably. It's also handy to be able to swap the trailer between adults' bikes. Look for a trailer that is lightweight, foldable, brightly coloured with a flag, and that tracks and handles well.

Be sure that the bike to which you attach a child seat or trailer is sturdy and low-geared to withstand – and help you withstand – the extra weight and stresses. Seats and trailers are treated as additional luggage items when flying.

DON HATCHER

Alyson Adventures (☎ 800-825-9766, W www.alysonadventures.com), PO Box 180179, Boston, MA 02118, organizes gay and lesbian bike trips around the world.

CYCLISTS WITH A DISABILITY

Public buildings (including hotels, restaurants, theaters and museums) are required by law to have accessible restroom facilities. Public transportation services must also be made accessible for all, including those in wheelchairs. Telephone companies are required to provide relay operators for the hearing impaired. Many banks provide ATM instructions in Braille and you will find audible crossing signals as well as dropped curbs at busier intersections.

Larger private and chain hotels have suites for guests with a disability. Amtrak and Greyhound frequently sell two-for-one packages when attendants are required.

Access-Able Travel Source (W www.access-able.com) has an excellent Web site with many links. Useful cycling contacts include the US Handcycling Federation (W www.ushf.org) and the American Cycling Network (W www.americancycling.net).

SENIOR CYCLISTS

Travelers aged over 60 can expect to receive cut rates and benefits at many hotels, campgrounds, chain restaurants (Denny's, Perko's, Carrows), theaters and museums.

The Golden Age Passport ($10) gives free admission to national parks, plus a 50% reduction on camping and other visitor fees. It is available to US citizens and permanent residents aged 62 years or older (with proof of age). The Passport is available at a federal area where an entrance fee is charged.

These Web sites may also be helpful:

American Association of Retired Persons (AARP; ☎ 800-424-3410, W www.aarp.org) An advocacy group for US citizens aged 50 and older, and a good source for travel bargains.

Elderhostel (☎ 877-426-8056, W www.elderhostel.org) A not-for-profit organization offering academic tours and adventures to people aged 55 years and older.

CYCLING WITH CHILDREN

A great information source is Lonely Planet's *Travel With Children*.

Children's discounts are widely available for everything from museum admissions to

Touring with Children

From the age of about four, children can move on to a 'trailer-bike' (effectively a child's bike, minus a front wheel, which hitches to an adult's bike) or to a tandem (initially as 'stoker' – the rider at the back – with 'kiddy cranks', or crank extensions) – this lets them help pedal. The tandem can be a long-term solution, keeping you and your child together and letting you compensate if the child tires.

Be careful of children rushing into touring on a solo bike before they can sustain the effort and concentration required. Once they are ready and keen to ride solo, at about age 10 to 12, they will need a good quality touring bike, properly fitted (US$250 and up).

Bike touring with children requires a new attitude as well as new equipment. Be sensitive to their needs – especially when they're too young to communicate them fully. In a seat or trailer, they're not expending energy and need to be dressed accordingly. Keep them dry, at the right temperature and protected from the sun. Keep their energy and interest up. When you stop, a child traveling in a seat or trailer will be ready for action, so always reserve some energy for parenting. This means more stops, including at places for children to play. Older children will have their own interests and should be involved in planning a tour. Before setting off on a major journey, try some day trips to check your set-up and introduce your child to cycling.

Children need to be taken into account in deciding each day's route – traffic and distances need to be moderate and facilities and points of interest adequate. Given the extra weight of children and their daily needs, you may find it easier to opt for day trips from a base. The very fit and adventurous may not need to compromise to ride with children, but those who do will still find it worthwhile.

As with other activities, children bring a new perspective and pleasure to cycle touring. They tend to love it.

Alethea Morison

bus fares and motel stays. The age definition of a child varies – anything from under six to under 18.

Many hotels and motels allow children to share a room with their parents for free or for a modest fee, though B&Bs rarely do and some don't allow children at all. Larger hotels often have a baby-sitting service or can help you make arrangements. Alternatively, look in the Yellow Pages for local agencies.

Most car-rental firms have children's safety seats for hire at a nominal cost; book them in advance. The same goes for highchairs and cots (cribs); they're common in many restaurants and hotels but numbers are limited. There is a great choice of baby food in supermarkets. Diaper-changing stations can be found in many public toilets in malls, department stores and family restaurants.

MOUNTAIN BIKING

With its mild climate and proliferation of mountainous landscapes, the West Coast is great for mountain biking. The Cascade and Sierra Nevada ranges offer classic, high-altitude riding in summer, much of it on single-track and within the boundaries of a national or state park. The area around San Francisco is the supposed birthplace of the sport, with epic, accessible rides year-round.

Mountain Biking in the USA

The bottom of Repack Fire Rd in Fairfax, California is a tranquil place these days. A little stream, a nice footbridge; no monument or plaque, nothing distinguishing. No evidence that 25 years ago a handful of local road racers riding modified Schwinn Excelsior bicycles and wearing jeans, T-shirts and hiking boots skidded sideways to a stop here and catalyzed an $8 billion worldwide industry.

On the morning of 21 October 1976, the first 'official' mountain-bike race ended here. The course begins 2.1mi above at the confluence with San Geronimo Ridge and drops 1300ft over a route that is unrelentingly loose, rocky, deeply rutted and off-camber

The Schwinns were called 'clunkers', 'beaters' or 'ballooners', owing to their appearance and big 26 by 2¼ inch tires. The bikes weighed about 60lb, had one gear and a single rear coaster brake. Braking through the descent generated enough heat to vaporize the lube in the rear hub. After each race the hub was repacked with grease, and thus the road was named.

Over nine years 24 races were held at Repack. The names of the original participants constitute a masthead of the sport's history: Otis Guy, Joe Breeze, Gary Fisher, Charlie Kelly and Wende Cragg.

Gary Fisher holds the record of 4 minutes, 22 seconds. Today it takes me about 15 minutes to gingerly descend Repack. My bicycle has 27 gears, knobby tires, front and rear suspension, disk brakes, weighs less than 30lb, and I will not have to repack my hubs anytime soon.

In 1976 there were only a few dozen mountain bikers. Last year 24 million Americans rode mountain bikes, and the US retail market for mountain bikes pushed four billion dollars. Two thirds of the bikes sold in the USA last year were mountain bikes.

Here in Marin County there are over 200mi of trails and fire roads. Trail access is hotly contested, and the vast majority of single-track trails remain off-limits to bicycles. Hiking groups like the Sierra Club are a powerful and well-funded force behind the segregation. The issue has escalated to a degree of near-silliness betrayed in the signs posted at each trailhead: 'It is illegal to ride, carry, or walk bicycles on this trail'. What about skipping? Can you skip with your bike on this trail?

Cyclists riding illegally on Marin trails now risk a $500 fine, and could even receive a six-month jail sentence if the judge is so inclined.

Similar trail access concerns exist nationwide. Organizations like the Bicycle Trails Council of Marin (W www.btcmarin.org) and the International Mountain Biking Association (W www.imba.com) serve as advocates for the mountain-biking community. Since their inception in 1988 the IMBA and affiliated clubs have donated more than one million volunteer hours of trailwork and built more than 5000mi of new trails.

Those first riders on Repack had no idea what they were starting. Like all the best movements this one started with people who had no intention of starting a movement – they were just passionate.

Jim Kravets

The mountain biking is also excellent in many other areas covered in this book.

The local bike shop will inevitably be the best place to scope out a ride. For a general look at the US mountain-biking scene, pick up an issue of *Mountain Bike* magazine. Visit **W** www.mtbreview.com for reviews of biking areas, trails and gear.

Mountain-bike rides described in this book recommend a local bike shop for hire and further information. Mountain bikers should try these rides:

Catalina Island Crossing (pp253–6)
Deschutes River Trail (p168)
Romero Canyon (p226)
Stehekin Valley (pp128–9)

USEFUL ORGANIZATIONS

Cycling Organizations

While the local bike shop will be your best resource on the road, these contacts are great for planning:

Adventure Cycling Association (☎ 406-721-1776 or ☎ 800-755-2453, **W** www.adv-cycling.org) PO Box 8308, Missoula, MT 59807. The USA's best resource for all things bike-touring: advocacy, bicycle and gear reviews, organized rides and mapped bicycle routes.

USA Cycling (☎ 719-578-4581, **W** www.usacycling.org) 1 Olympic Plaza, Colorado Springs, CO 80909. The umbrella organization for the US Cycling Federation, National Off-Road Bicycle Association, US Professional Racing Organization and National Bicycle League. It oversees just about all issues concerning the sport in the USA.

Local cycling clubs are generally the best source of regional information (many are mentioned in the Information sections of ride chapters) and often have weekly rides open to non-members.

Conservation Organizations

For conservation information and activities, these organizations are active and accessible:

Earth First! (**W** www.efmedia.org) PO Box 324, Redway, CA 95560. Founded in 1979, Earth First! takes a direct action approach, from grassroots organizing and legal action to civil disobedience and monkeywrenching.

National Audubon Society (☎ 212-979-3000, **W** www.audubon.org) 700 Broadway, New York, NY 10003. One of the USA's biggest conservation organizations, the society was founded in 1905 to conserve and restore natural ecosystems. Local chapters hold hikes and clean-up initiatives.

Sierra Club (☎ 415-977-5500, **W** www.sierraclub.org) 85 Second St, 2nd Floor, San Francisco, CA 94105-3441. Since its founding in 1892, with John Muir as its first president and the defeat of a proposed reduction in the boundaries of Yosemite National Park as its first conservation effort, the Sierra Club has grown to a large (some say cumbersome) body of political influence. Local chapters run hiking, backpacking, biking and ski trips.

LEGAL MATTERS

If you are stopped by the police for any reason, bear in mind that there is no system of paying fines on the spot. Attempting to pay the fine to the officer is frowned upon and may lead to a charge of bribery.

If you are arrested for more serious offenses, you are allowed to remain silent and are presumed innocent until proven guilty. There is no legal reason to speak to a police officer if you don't wish. All persons who are arrested are legally allowed (and given) the right to make one phone call. If you don't have a lawyer or family member to help you, call your embassy. The police will give you the number upon request.

BUSINESS HOURS

Regular business hours are from 9am to 5pm, but there are no hard and fast rules. In any large city, a few supermarkets, restaurants and the main post office are open 24 hours.

Shops (Including Bike Shops) Usually open from 9 or 10am to 5 or 6pm (often until 9pm in shopping malls), except Sunday, when hours are noon to 5pm (often later in malls).

Post Offices Open weekdays 8am to 4 or 5:30pm; some open 8am to noon Saturday.

Banks Usually open from 9 or 10am to 5 or 6pm weekdays; a few banks also open until 1 or 2pm on Saturday.

National Park Visitor Centers and Ranger Stations Generally open daily from 8 or 9am to 6 or 7pm from Memorial Day (late May) to Labor Day (1 Sept); in the busiest parks they may open until 8pm. After Labor Day they open later, close earlier and may close for an hour for lunch. In winter, many open weekends only.

PUBLIC HOLIDAYS & SPECIAL EVENTS

National public holidays are celebrated throughout the USA. Banks, schools and government offices (including post offices) are closed and transportation, museums and other services operate on a Sunday schedule. Many stores, however, maintain regular business hours. Holidays falling on a weekend are usually observed the following Monday.

Regional cycling events are listed at the beginning of each ride chapter.

US public holidays are:

New Year's Day 1 January
Martin Luther King Jr Day 3rd Monday in January
Presidents' Day 3rd Monday in February
Memorial Day Last Monday in May
Independence Day 4 July
Labor Day 1st Monday in September
Columbus Day 2nd Monday in October
Veterans Day 11 November
Thanksgiving 4th Thursday in November
Christmas Day 25 December

Some of the most widely celebrated events are:

Chinese New Year (late Jan/early Feb) – a two-week festival kicked off with parades, firecrackers, fireworks and lots of food.
Valentine's Day (14 Feb)
St Patrick's Day (17 Mar) – the patron saint of Ireland is honored by those who feel the Irish in their blood, and those who want to feel Irish beer in their blood. Everyone wears green (if you don't, you can be pinched).
Easter (Mar/Apr)
Mothers Day (second Sunday, May)
Fathers Day (third Sunday, Jun)
Halloween (31 Oct) – kids and adults dress in costumes; the kids go 'trick-or-treating' for candy while the adults go to parties to act out their alter egos.
Day of the Dead (2 Dec) – in Mexican communities, families honor deceased relatives and make breads and sweets resembling skeletons and skulls.
Thanksgiving (third Thursday, Nov) – people eat a 'traditional' dinner of turkey, mashed potatoes, cranberry relish and pumpkin pie, in remembrance of how thankful the first pilgrims were that the Native Americans they encountered were friendly.
Chanukah (Dec) – an eight-day Jewish holiday (also called Hanukkah or the Feast of Lights) commemorating the victory of the Maccabees over the armies of Syria.
Kwanzaa (26–31 Dec) – this African American celebration is a time to give thanks for the harvest.
New Year's Eve (31 Dec)

CYCLING ROUTES

This guide aims to cover the 'best of' cycling in Washington, Oregon and California. For that purpose, we've agreed that the 'best' rides are scenic, pass through interesting towns or historic areas, are lightly used by cars and easy (as much as possible in this car-dependent country) to reach by public transport.

Cyclists can use this book as an introduction and planning tool, as well as on the road. We hope that once cyclists become familiar with local conditions they start planning their own routes, too.

Route Descriptions

Rides are designed to be feasible for a visitor with limited time and to link easily, ensuring continuity for extended trips (of course, if you really want an extended tour, do the 37-day Border to Border ride, pp269–353).

Cycling for a Cause

The biggest cycling events in the USA have more to do with fundraising than with sport: since 1994 the AIDSRide (☎ 800-825-1000, W www.aidsride.org) has raised more than $69 million for HIV-related causes.

The AIDSRides, which last three to seven days, attract thousands of cyclists, many of whom have never ridden more than 10mi. At least half of the riders have a loved one, or have lost a loved one, with HIV. The camaraderie and emotion of the event is profound.

The ride must qualify as one of the best organized events in the USA. At the end of each day, riders are greeted by mobile cities where tents, showers, hot meals, entertainment and massages await. Water and snack stops are plentiful and the volunteers who staff the ride are as enthusiastic a support team as a bonked cyclist can handle.

Other fundraising rides include:

- American Lung Association's Big Ride Across America (W www.bigride.com/gateway.html), which has raised around $4 million per year with its cross-country event;
- Breast Cancer Foundation's Ride for Life (W www.abcride.org); and
- One Voice Foundation's Ride Against Childhood Cancer (W www.onevoiceusa.org), which may only attract 100 cyclists but can raise upwards of $10,000.

Various transport options for getting to and from each ride are discussed.

Each ride is broken into days, with accommodations and food options available at each day's end. Side trips are suggested for many of the rides.

Ride Difficulty

Each ride is graded according to its difficulty in terms of distance, terrain, road surface and navigation. The grade appears in the Table of Rides (pp4–5) and in the introduction to each ride.

Grading is unavoidably subjective and is intended as a guide only; the degree of difficulty may vary according to the weather, the weight in your panniers or how hungry and tired you are. Many rides also involve easy and hard days, which are weighed up to create an overall grading.

Easy These rides involve no more than a few hours riding each day, over *mostly* flat terrain with good, sealed road surfaces. Navigationally, they are very straightforward.

Moderate These rides present a moderate challenge to someone of average fitness; they are likely to include some hills, two to six hours riding each day and may involve some unsealed roads and/or navigation.

Hard These are for fit riders who want a challenge; they involve long daily distances and/or challenging climbs, may require negotiation of rough and remote roads and present navigational challenges.

Times & Distances

Each ride is divided into stages and we've suggested a day be spent on each stage. In some cases the distance for, and duration of, a particular stage is relatively short, but other attractions in the region warrant spending extra time – distance junkies may decide to condense two stages into one day.

A suggested riding time has been given for each day. Because individual speed varies widely, these should be used as a guide only. They only take into account the actual riding time – not time taken for rest stops, taking photographs or eating – and are generally based on an average riding speed of between 6 and 11mi/h (sometimes lower, depending on the terrain or road surface).

Cues & Elevation Profiles

Navigational directions for each stage are given as a series of cues, based on the distance (in miles) from the start point. Elevation profiles are given for days with significant changes in altitude. Information about terrain is also included in the ride description and cues. A ride with no elevation profile is not necessarily *flat* but it won't involve major climbing.

Cues and elevation profiles are located in a 'tear-out' section at the back of this book, so you can use them on the road with the recommended maps. In The West Coast feature chapter, the cues and elevation profiles are located with that chapter's more detailed standalone maps. See pp10–11 for more on how to read cues and elevation profiles.

ACTIVITIES

If cycling isn't enough activity for you try these options.

Hiking

Besides cycle touring, there is perhaps no better way to appreciate the beauty of the West Coast than on foot. Taking a few days (or a few hours) break from the saddle to explore the backcountry gives cyclists a heightened appreciation of scenery beyond the roadside.

Cyclists with little hiking experience will appreciate the well-marked and well-maintained trails in national parks, often with restroom facilities and interpretive displays. These trails (generally no longer than 2mi) give access to the parks' natural features, and are usually shown on NPS (National Parks Service) maps as nature trails or self-guided interpretive trails.

Hikers seeking true wilderness away from heavy foot traffic should avoid national parks and try less-celebrated national forests, especially wilderness areas. Yosemite National Park has a route of High Sierra Camps for people who enjoy backpacking without carrying a heavy load.

See Best Deviation (p27) for some hiking suggestions in this book; or pick up a copy of Lonely Planet's *Hiking in the USA* or *Hiking in the Sierra Nevada* for in-depth coverage.

Climbing & Mountaineering

The granite monoliths and glacial peaks of the Sierra Nevada and singular volcanic domes of the Cascades entice the world's best climbers and mountaineers. El Capitan and Half Dome in Yosemite National Park are both legendary climbs up the face of sheer granite walls. The peaks of Washington's Mt Rainier, Oregon's Mt Hood and California's Mt Shasta (all above 13,000ft) are impressive destinations; Mt Whitney (CA) is the highest in the USA at 14,497ft.

Some recommended climbing outfits are Alpine Ascents International (☎ 206-378-1927, W www.alpineascents.com), Seattle; Alpine Skills International (☎ 530-426-9108, W www.alpineskills.com), in the Sierra Nevada near Lake Tahoe; and Yosemite Mountaineering School (☎ 209-372-8344 Sept–May, ☎ 209-372-8435 Jun–Aug), in Yosemite National Park.

Rafting

Mighty rivers that pour into the Pacific Ocean make this one of the top whitewater destinations in the USA. A number of outfitters organize trips, from half-day floats (around $50 per person) to three and four-day expeditions (around $100 per person per day). Most outfitters also rent whitewater kayaks and canoes, which require more skill; instruction is usually provided.

Rivers are rated from I (flat water) to VI ('...rarely run except by highly experienced kayakers under ideal conditions. The likelihood of serious injury is high.'). Popular rivers in Washington are the Skagitt, Yakima and Wenatchee; Oregon offers the Deschutes and the Rogue; and California's favored destination is the south fork of the American River (between Sacramento and Lake Tahoe).

Sea Kayaking

This quiet, unobtrusive sport allows you to visit unexplored islands and stretches of coast, and view marine life at close range. Sea kayaks, which hold one or two people, are larger and more stable than whitewater boats, making them safer and easier to navigate. They also have storage capacity so you can do overnight or even week-long trips.

Good areas to do a bit of sea kayaking include Washington's Puget Sound (notably Port Townsend); California's Central Coast (especially Monterey and Santa Barbara); and Catalina Island.

Surfing

California's 'big three' surf spots are Rincon, Malibu and Trestles, all of them point breaks (where swells peak up into steep waves as they encounter a shelf-like point). Beginner and intermediate surfers should stick to beach breaks or long, shallow bays where waves are small and rolling such as San Onofre and San Diego's Pacific Beach.

The Pacific Crest Trail

A truly amazing thing about the West Coast is that you can walk from Mexico to Canada, across the entire expanse of California, Oregon and Washington, almost without ever leaving national park or national forest lands. Simply follow the Pacific Crest Trail (PCT). This 2638mi trail passes through 24 national forests, seven national parks, 33 designated wilderness areas and six state parks, always following as closely as possible the crest of the Sierra Mtns in California and the Cascade Range in Oregon and Washington, at an average elevation of 5000ft.

To hike the trail in its entirety, at a good clip of 15mi a day, would take nearly half a year; the Oregon and Washington portions can each feasibly be hiked in one month. But you don't have to undertake such a dramatic, cross-state trek to take advantage of the PCT. Day or weekend hikers can plan short trips along any stretch of the trail.

Many of the West Coast's most spectacular wilderness sites are traversed by the PCT, including Yosemite and Sequoia National Parks in California, Crater Lake National Park, Three Sisters Wilderness and Mt Hood in Oregon, and Mt Rainier and North Cascades National Parks in Washington.

The Pacific Crest Trail Association (☎ 888-728-7245 or ☎ 916-349-2109, W www.pcta.org), 5325 Elkhorn Blvd, PMB#256, Sacramento, CA 95842-2526, provides detailed information, as well as addresses for regional USFS (United States Forest Service) and Wilderness Areas offices. Also contact the association for tips on long- and short-distance backpacking trips, weather conditions and wilderness permit information.

Bill McRae

The north coast has its own surf scene, with colder water, bigger waves and an abundance of sharks. Mavericks (near Half Moon Bay) has waves to rival Hawaii. Humboldt County grows its own crop of big-wave surfers right along with its marijuana plants. Only hearty, thick-skinned souls do much surfing in Oregon and Washington. When they do, it's usually at Oregon's Otter Cove, Sunset Beach or Smuggler's Cove.

ACCOMMODATIONS

Accommodations on the West Coast cover the spectrum from primitive campsites to ultra-luxurious resorts. Seasonal price fluctuations are quite common, with rates leaping up in summer in most places. High-season prices are quoted in this guide. Rates are also high – and availability low – around major holidays such as Labor Day, Thanksgiving and Christmas.

Room rates vary more by number of beds than number of people. The price difference between single and double occupancy is usually nonexistent or small.

Accommodations listed in this book have a place to keep bicycles (sometimes it's outside). As a courtesy, it's good to mention you are traveling by bicycle (especially if you insist on keeping your trusty steed inside).

Local visitor centers are often very helpful in finding accommodations and may even call around to find a room for you. AAA (p97) publishes an annual guide to accommodations across the USA.

Camping

Basic national forest and state park campsites usually have toilets, fire pits, picnic benches and drinking water. Hiker/biker campsites are generally reserved until 7pm, but then given to cars if needed. Cyclists usually pay \$3 to \$5 per person for a site where cars pay \$7 to \$11 per vehicle.

Hiker/biker sites cannot be reserved; it's first-come, first-served but cyclists will not be turned away. Even in peak times, there's always room for one more small tent! However, if you're cycling in a large group (eight or more), we advise you to 'attempt' to book (especially at peak times) or get there early. For Oregon and Washington sites call ☎ 800-452-5687. The service costs \$7. For California state park campsites call ☎ 800-444-7275; from overseas call ☎ 916-638-5883.

Facilities at the majority of private campgrounds include hot showers, coin laundry and often a swimming pool, games area, playground and convenience store. Tent sites run from around \$14 for two people, plus \$1 to \$3 for each extra person. A national network of private campgrounds is Kampgrounds of America (KOA; ☎ 406-248-7444, **w** www.koa.com) with sites usually ranging from \$17 to \$22. RV parks generally look like paved parking lots but some have grassy sites for tents.

Hostels

The US hostel network is less widespread than in Canada, the UK, Europe and Australia. You'll find hostels in most gateway cities and at points along the coast. Bike storage can be an issue when a hostel is full but most are accommodating if you call ahead.

Hostelling International The 'official' youth hostels in the USA are affiliated with Hostelling International-American Youth Hostels (HI-AYH; ☎ 202-783-6161, **w** www.hiayh.org), 733 15th St NW, Suite 840, Washington, DC 20005. Beds cost \$7 to \$24 for members, and usually \$3 more for nonmembers. Memberships cost \$25 per year, are free for those under 18 and \$15 if over 55; they're available at most hostels, Council Travel agencies and regional offices.

Facilities include gender-segregated dorm (private rooms are sometimes available); shared single-sex bathrooms; kitchens; and a common room with TV, games and reading material. Most hostels close during the day and some have a curfew, though these rules vary.

Independent Hostels The quality of these hostels varies but bathrooms are usually shared and most have a kitchen, laundry and TV. Sometimes a light breakfast is included. They don't usually have curfews and dorms tend to be mixed. Dorm beds cost about \$10 to \$16. A private room costs from \$30 for two people. Jim Williams' *The Hostel Handbook for the USA and Canada*, available at most hostels and from the author (☎ 212-926-7030; **e** editor@aol.com; 722 St Nicholas Ave, New York, NY 10031) lists independent and HI-AYH hostels. The Internet Guide to Hostelling (**w** www.hostels.com) lists hostels throughout the world.

Often independent hostels say they only accept international travelers, to keep out destitute locals. In fact they will usually take Americans who look like they will fit in with the other guests.

B&Bs

For people who want a comfortable, atmospheric alternative to motel rooms, B&Bs are ideal. Typically they are restored older houses where a room and substantial breakfast for two costs $60 to $120. B&B owners prefer advance reservations, though some will happily oblige a drop-in. Look for the *Complete Guide to American Bed & Breakfasts* or guides concentrating on the areas you fancy.

Hotels & Motels

Motel and hotel prices vary tremendously from season to season; prices quoted in this book are for the high season, unless otherwise noted. Simply asking about 'specials' can often get you a discount.

The cheapest motels are usually smaller independent establishments with prices as low as $20. They offer small rooms, normally with private shower, toilet and TV, some have kitchen facilities.

Downtown hotels tend to be either very expensive or very seedy. Old hotels, often near the train or bus station, sometimes double as transient rooming houses. If you have doubts ask to see the room before you commit.

Chain motels usually fall in the mid-range price category and maintain a consistent level of quality and style (sterile and sterile). The cheapest national chain is Motel 6, which charges from $28 for a single in smaller towns, from $40 in larger towns, plus $6 for each additional person. Motel chains in the next price level (Super 8, Days Inn, Econo Lodge) have firmer beds and cable TV. Stepping up to the $80 range (Best Western, Holiday Inn, Comfort Inn,) you'll find noticeably nicer rooms; on-site or adjacent cafes, restaurants and/or bars; and perhaps an indoor swimming pool, spa or exercise room. At the highest end (Hilton, Hyatt, Radisson, Sheraton) are rooms for $100 plus, with gourmet restaurants and in-room spas.

FOOD

The West Coast food scene is wonderfully diverse, incorporating a wide variety of flavors and ingredients into a year-round palate of fresh produce. Foodies will want to spend an extra day in each of the major gateway cities, just to check out their restaurants and ethnic markets.

'Pan-Asian' and 'Pacific Rim' cooking, which relies heavily on Japanese, Chinese, Vietnamese and Thai ingredients, is popular in Seattle. Portland is something of a rising star on the US culinary horizon, with creative new restaurants of all varieties sprouting. San Francisco has everything from Cambodian to Eritrean to Sicilian food, at all price ranges and in every ambience imaginable. LA isn't far behind but has a focus on Japanese and Mexican food.

Seafood is widely available; it would be a shame to leave the West Coast without trying salmon from the Northwest, oysters from Fanny Bay and clam chowder from a San Francisco sourdough bread bowl. You'll also find exceptional sushi from border to border.

Dairy products are an important part of Oregon and Northern California's economy, with milk and cheese the staple stars. Eastern Washington is known for its apples, while Oregon's Willamette and Columbia River valleys grow a variety of stone fruits and grapes.

For healthy eating on the road, see Nutrition (p54).

Local Food

Cafes specializing in coffee and pastries can be terrific for an affordable (and tasty) lunch of salads, sandwiches and soups.

Brewpubs (or breweries) offer homemade libations (usually including root beer and lemonade) as well as hearty appetizers that easily make a meal.

For a stereotypically American meal, head to a diner or coffee shop. Breakfast

> **Decisions, Decisions**
>
> Americans love choices, and for every meal you'll have to answer a deluge of questions to complete your order: 'How do you want your eggs?', 'What kind of bread: white, wheat, rye or sourdough?', 'French fries, coleslaw, baked potato, potato salad, cottage cheese or sliced tomatoes with your sandwich?', 'Soup or salad?', 'What kind of salad dressing: Italian, blue cheese, thousand island, ranch or honey-mustard?'. And these are just the basics.

(under $5) consists of pancakes, hearty omelettes or bacon and eggs. Lunch ($4–7) is along the lines of a hamburger or chef's salad (with sliced ham, cheese and hard-boiled egg). Dinner ($6–11) might be chicken-fried steak (steak breaded – crumbed – and pan-fried), spaghetti with meat sauce or roast beef and mashed potatoes with gravy.

Even in small towns, you'll often find a Mexican, Chinese and Italian restaurant on the same block. These offer alternative flavors at a reasonable price.

Fast Food Gourmet grocery and natural food stores often have a deli section where you'll find sandwiches, salads, hot soups, coffee and the occasional (microwaved) burrito. Chain-owned Wild Oats and Whole Foods are reliable sources that often have a salad bar. Big supermarkets (Albertson's, Ralphs, Safeway) offer similar, if less healthy, set ups.

Fast-food chains (McDonald's, Burger King, Taco Bell, Pizza Hut, KFC) are cheap standbys for just about any meal (and will usually have clean bathrooms). The health-conscious might try Subway, which makes hot and cold sandwiches and salads, or 360°, which has a variety of wraps. Family restaurants such as Sizzler or Denny's often have big servings of good-quality but unspectacular food.

Ice-cream lovers will want to try a dipped cone at Foster's Freeze and a 'Blizzard' (like a thick milk shake spiked with M&Ms, peanut butter cups or chocolate cookies) at the local DQ (Dairy Queen). True aficionados, however, should tap into Ben & Jerry's.

Self-Catering

Large and medium-sized towns have big supermarkets (Vons, Lucky, Ralph's, Safeway and Albertson's) with an overwhelming range. Even smaller markets in smaller towns have a large variety.

For breakfast, pick up instant oatmeal, which comes in individual servings or in bulk. Besides cutting down on packaging, buying bulk oatmeal lets you add a bunch of goodies. Try powdered milk, cinnamon, brown sugar, raisins, dried apples and nuts.

Lunch can be crackers, bagels, rye bread, peanut butter, canned tuna, jerky, dried fruit, deli meats, cheese, pretzels, granola or cereal bars.

Energy bars, such as Clif, Balance Bar, MetRx, 40-30-30 and PowerBar, usually have more vitamins and minerals than regular candy bars, plus they don't melt.

Easy camping dinners include ramen (noodle soup), quick-cooking macaroni and cheese, 'instant' rice, pasta, chili beans and a variety of 'instant' soups. Salsa is good on everything from rice to potatoes. A small armada of spices (including powdered garlic), bouillon cubes and olive oil in your panniers can do wonders for a camp meal.

Tea, coffee and cocoa are reviving. Powdered drinks are another option.

DRINKS

Nonalcoholic drinks

Firstly, it's safe to drink tap water; in Berkeley, CA, for example, the quality is excellent. See Hydration (p53) for advice on staying watered on tour.

Odwalla and Naked Juice are the biggest and best fresh-juice suppliers. Find their juice, smoothies and protein drinks in the refrigerated section of a market.

Coffee is notoriously good and strong in Seattle (birthplace of the Starbucks chain) and the San Francisco Bay Area (home to Peet's Coffee & Tea, Starbucks' prime competitor). In rural towns and diners you may have to settle for 'truck-stop' coffee, which looks weak but packs a zing. Espresso can be found everywhere.

Sports Drinks There are a mind-boggling number of sports drinks on the market, many of them with no nutritional value beyond glucose (unless food coloring counts). Gatorade is widely available and does have enough salts to make it worth drinking. ERG, Cytomax and Ultima Replenisher are available in powder form from outdoors stores and bike shops. These have a good balance of easy-to-absorb glucose and electrolytes, and come in a variety of flavors.

Alcoholic Drinks

If your identification says you're over 21 years of age, you can enjoy some of the best and cheapest booze in the world. Even in dry counties, some restaurants let you bring your own wine or beer.

Microbreweries, or brewpubs, offer beers brewed on the premises, and you can get a dozen different types on tap. Supermarkets and liquor stores stock a bewildering variety of imported and local beers. If you're fond of Fosters, Heineken or Moosehead at home, you may be disappointed to find that it has been wimped down for the American market – beer sold in the USA has a lower alcohol content than in most other countries.

California is America's leading wine producer but there are plenty of wineries in Washington and Oregon, too. A reasonable bottle of California red or white costs $6 to $10 at a supermarket or liquor store, much more in restaurants.

All bars have a big range of hard liquor (spirits) invariably served with lots of ice (on the rocks) unless you ask for it straight up. If you ask for whiskey, you'll get American whiskey; called bourbon if it's made in Kentucky (eg, Jim Beam) or whiskey if it's not (eg, Jack Daniels). If you want Scotch whisky, ask for Scotch. The American taste for cocktails originated during Prohibition, when lots of flavorful mixers were used to disguise the taste of bathtub gin. Many bars will have their own special concoction, usually with a fancy or a funny name.

Health & Safety

Keeping healthy on your travels depends on your predeparture preparations, your daily health care and diet while on the road, and how you handle any medical problem that develops. Few touring cyclists experience anything more than a bit of soreness, fatigue and chafing, although there is potential for more serious problems. The sections that follow aren't intended to alarm, but they are worth reading before you go.

Before You Go

HEALTH INSURANCE

Make sure that you have adequate health insurance – some hospitals will refuse care without evidence of insurance. See Travel Insurance (p33).

IMMUNIZATIONS

You don't need any vaccinations to visit the USA, though cholera and yellow fever vaccinations may be necessary if you've come from an area with a history of those diseases. It's always wise to keep up-to-date with routine vaccinations such as diphtheria, polio and tetanus – boosters are necessary every 10 years and are highly recommended.

FIRST AID

It's a good idea at any time to know the appropriate responses in the event of a major accident or illness, and it's especially important if you plan to ride offroad in a remote area. Consider learning basic first aid through a recognized course before you go, and carrying a first-aid manual and small medical kit.

Although detailed first-aid instruction is outside the scope of this guide, some basic points are listed under Traumatic Injuries (p61–2). Undoubtedly the best advice is to avoid an accident in the first place. Safety on the Ride (p63–6) contains tips for safe onroad and offroad riding, as well as information on how to summon help.

PHYSICAL FITNESS

Most of the rides in this book are designed for someone with a moderate degree of cycling fitness. As a general rule, however, the fitter

First-Aid Kit

A possible kit could include:

First-Aid Supplies

- ☐ **sticking plasters (Band Aids)**
- ☐ **bandages (including elastic) & safety pins**
- ☐ **elastic support bandage** for knees, ankles etc
- ☐ **gauze swabs**
- ☐ **nonadhesive dressings**
- ☐ **small pair of scissors**
- ☐ **sterile alcohol wipes**
- ☐ **butterfly closure strips**
- ☐ **latex gloves**
- ☐ **syringes & needles** – for removing gravel from road-rash wounds
- ☐ **thermometer** (note that mercury thermometers are prohibited by airlines)
- ☐ **tweezers**

Medications

- ☐ **antidiarrhea, antinausea drugs** and **oral rehydration salts**
- ☐ **antifungal cream** or **powder** – for fungal skin infections and thrush
- ☐ **antihistamines** – for allergies, eg, hay fever; to ease the itch from insect bites or stings; and to prevent motion sickness
- ☐ **antiseptic powder** or **solution** (eg, povidone-iodine) and **antiseptic wipes** for cuts and grazes
- ☐ **diaper rash (nappy rash) cream**
- ☐ **calamine lotion**, **sting-relief spray** or **aloe vera** – to ease irritation from sunburn and insect bites or stings
- ☐ **cold** and **flu tablets**, **throat lozenges** and **nasal decongestant**
- ☐ **painkillers** (eg, aspirin or paracetamol/ acetaminophen in the USA) – for pain and fever
- ☐ **laxatives**

Miscellaneous

- ☐ **insect repellent**, **sunscreen**, **lip balm** and **eye drops**
- ☐ **water purification tablets** or **iodine**

Getting Fit for Touring

Ideally, a training program should be tailored to your objectives, specific needs, fitness level and health. However, if you have no idea how to prepare for your cycling holiday these guidelines will help you get the fitness you need to enjoy it more. Things to think about include:

Foundation You will need general miles in your legs before you start to expose them to any intensive cycling. Always start out with easy rides – even a few miles to the shops – and give yourself plenty of time to build towards your objective.

Tailoring Once you have the general condition to start preparing for your trip, work out how to tailor your training rides to the type of tour you are planning. Someone preparing for a three-week ride will require a different approach than someone building fitness for a one-day or weekend ride. Some aspects to think about are the ride length (distance and days), terrain, climate and weight to be carried in panniers. If your trip involves carrying 45lb in panniers, incorporate this weight into some training rides, especially some of the longer ones. If you are going to be touring in mountainous areas, choose a hilly training route.

Recovery You usually adapt to a training program during recovery time, so it's important to do the right things between rides. Recovery can take many forms, but the simple ones are best. These include getting quality sleep, eating an adequate diet to refuel the system, doing recovery rides between hard days (using low gears to avoid pushing yourself), stretching and enjoying a relaxing bath. Other forms include recovery massage, spas and yoga.

If you have no cycling background this program will help you get fit for your cycling holiday. If you are doing an easy ride (each ride in this book is rated; see Cycling Routes, pp44–5), aim to at least complete Week 4; for moderate rides, complete Week 6; and complete the program if you are doing a hard ride. Experienced cycle tourers may start at Week 3, while those who regularly ride up to four days a week could start at Week 5.

Don't treat this as a punishing training schedule: try cycling to work or to the shops, join a local touring club or get a group of friends together to turn weekend rides into social events.

	Monday	Tuesday	Wednesday	Thursday	Friday	Saturday	Sunday
Week 1	6mi*	–	6mi*	–	6mi*	–	6mi*
Week 2	–	9mi*	–	9mi*	–	12mi*	–
Week 3	12mi*	–	12mi†	15mi*	–	15mi*	15mi†
Week 4	–	19mi*	–	22mi*	19mi†	19mi*	–
Week 5	19mi*	–	25mi†	–	22mi*	–	25mi†
Week 6	19mi*	–	25mi†	–	–	37mi*	25mi†
Week 7	19mi*	–	25mi†	–	19mi†	43mi*	19mi*
Week 8	–	37mi*	19mi†	–	25mi†	–	56mi*

* steady pace (allows you to carry out a conversation without losing your breath) on flat or undulating terrain
† solid pace (allows you to talk in short sentences only) on undulating roads with some longer hills

The training program shown here is only a guide. Ultimately it is important to listen to your body and slow down if the ride is getting too hard. Take extra recovery days and cut back distances when you feel this way. Don't panic if you don't complete every ride, every week; the most important thing is to ride regularly and gradually increase the length of your rides as you get fitter.

For those with no exercise background, be sure to see your doctor and get a clearance to begin exercising at these rates. This is especially important for those over 35 years of age with no exercise history and those with a cardiac or respiratory condition of any nature.

Kevin Tabotta

you are, the more you'll enjoy riding. It pays to spend time preparing yourself physically before you set out, rather than let a sore backside and aching muscles draw your attention from some of the world's finest cycle-touring countryside.

Depending on your existing level of fitness, you should start training a couple of months before your trip. Try to ride at least three times a week, starting with easy rides (even 3mi to work, if you're not already cycling regularly) and gradually building up to longer distances. Once you have a good base of regular riding behind you, include hills in your training and familiarize yourself with the gearing on your bike. Before you go you should have done at least one 40mi to 45mi ride with loaded panniers.

As you train, you'll discover how to adjust your bike to increase your comfort – as well as deal with any mechanical problems.

Staying Healthy

The best way to have a lousy holiday (especially if you're relying on self-propulsion) is to become ill. Heed the following advice and the only thing you're likely to suffer from is that rewarding tiredness at the end of a full day.

Reduce the chances of falling ill by washing your hands frequently, particularly after working on your bike or going to the toilet and before handling or eating food.

HYDRATION

You may not notice how much water you're losing as you ride, because it evaporates in the breeze. However, don't underestimate the amount of fluid you need to replace – particularly in warm weather. The magic figure is supposedly around one quart per hour, though many cyclists have trouble consuming this much – remembering to drink enough can be harder than it sounds. Sipping little and often is the key; try to drink a mouthful every 10 minutes or so and don't wait until you get thirsty. Water 'backpacks' can be great for fluid regulation since virtually no physical or mental effort is required to drink. Keep drinking before and after the day's ride to replenish fluid.

Use the color of your urine as a rough guide to whether you are drinking enough. Small amounts of dark urine suggest you need to increase your fluid intake. Passing reasonable quantities of light yellow urine indicates that you've got the balance about right. Other signs of dehydration include headache and fatigue. For more information on the effects of dehydration, see Dehydration & Heat Exhaustion (p58).

Water

With few exceptions, tap water in the USA is safe to drink. It may taste bad because it's been treated with chlorine and/or fluoride.

Always beware of natural sources of water. A gurgling creek may look clear but the risk of infection from human or animal sources is real. For information on giardiasis, see Infectious Diseases (p59).

The simplest way of purifying water is to boil it thoroughly. Vigorous boiling for five minutes should do the job. Simple filtering will not remove all dangerous organisms, so if you can't boil water treat it chemically. Chlorine tablets will kill many pathogens, but not *Giardia lamblia*. Iodine is very effective in purifying water and is available in tablet and liquid form, but follow the directions carefully and remember that too much iodine can be harmful. Flavored powder will disguise the taste of treated water and is a good thing to carry if you are spending time away from town water supplies.

Sports Drinks

Commercial sports drinks such as ERG Gookinade, Gatorade and PowerAde are an excellent way to satisfy your hydration needs, electrolyte replacement and energy demands in one. On endurance rides, especially, it can be difficult to keep eating solid fuels day in, day out. Sports drinks can supplement these energy demands and allow you to vary your solid fuel intake a little. The bonus is that those all-important body salts lost through perspiration get restocked.

Drink plenty of water as well; if you have two water bottles on your bike (and you should), it's a good idea to fill one with sports drink and the other with plain water.

If using a powdered sports drink, don't mix it too strong (follow the instructions) because, in addition to being too sweet, too many carbohydrates can actually impair your body's ability to absorb the water and carbohydrates properly.

NUTRITION

One of the great things about bike touring is that it requires lots of energy, which means you can eat more. Depending on your activity levels, it's not hard to put away huge servings of food and be hungry a few hours after.

Because you're putting such demands on your body, it's important to eat well – not just lots. As usual, you should eat a balanced diet from a wide variety of foods.

The main part of your diet should be carbohydrates rather than proteins or fats. A general guideline is to eat 50% carbohydrates, 27% proteins and 23% fats while in the saddle. While some protein (for tissue maintenance and repair) and fat (for vitamins, long-term energy and warmth) is essential, carbohydrates provide the most efficient fuel. They are easily digested into simple sugars, which are then used in energy production. Less-refined foods such as pasta, rice, bread, fruit and vegetables are all high in carbohydrates.

Eating simple carbohydrates (sugars, such as candy or sweets) gives you almost immediate energy – great for when you need a top-up (see the boxed text 'Avoiding the Bonk'); however, because they are quickly metabolized, you may get a sugar 'high' followed by a 'low'. For cycling it is far better to base your diet around complex carbohydrates, which take longer to process and provide 'slow-release' energy over a longer period.

Avoiding the Bonk

The bonk, in a cycling context, is not a pleasant experience; it's that light-headed, can't-put-power-to-the-pedals weak feeling that engulfs you (usually quite quickly) when your body runs out of fuel.

If you experience it the best move is to stop and refuel immediately. It can be quite serious and risky to your health if it's not addressed as soon as symptoms occur. It won't take long before you are ready to get going again (although most likely at a slower pace), but you'll also be more tired the next day so try to avoid it.

The best way to do this is to maintain your fuel intake while riding. Cycling for hours burns considerable body energy, and replacing it is something that needs to be tailored to each individual's tastes. The touring cyclist needs to target foods that have a high carbohydrate content. Foods that contain some fat are not a problem occasionally, as cycling at low intensity (when you're able to ride and talk without losing your breath) will usually trigger the body to draw on fat stores before stored carbohydrates.

Good cycle-touring foods include:

- bananas (in particular) and other fruits
- bread with jam, jelly or honey
- breakfast and muesli bars
- rice-based snacks
- muffins
- prepackaged high-carbohydrate sports bars (eg, PowerBar)
- sports drinks

During lunch stops (or for breakfast) you can try such things as spaghetti, cereal, pancakes, baked beans, sandwiches and rolls.

It's important not to get uptight about the food you eat. As a rule of thumb, base all your meals around carbohydrates (eg, pasta, rice, bread and potatoes) of some sort, but don't be afraid to also indulge in local culinary delights.

The book *High-Performance Bicycling Nutrition*, by Richard Rafoth, is a useful reference for nutrition and health advice for all cyclists.

Day-to-Day Needs

Eat a substantial breakfast – whole-wheat cereal or bread is ideal, with fruit or juice for vitamins. If you like cooked breakfasts, try to include carbohydrates (porridge, toast or potatoes) and avoid high-fat foods (greasy bacon and eggs), which take longer to digest.

Bread is the easiest food for lunch, topped with ingredients such as cheese, peanut butter, salami and fresh salad vegetables. If you're in a town, salad rolls or focaccias make for a satisfying meal (chips or pizza will feel like a lump in your stomach if you continue straight away).

Keep topping up your energy during the ride. See the boxed text 'Avoiding the Bonk' for tips. Try to eat a high-carbohydrate meal in the evening. If you're eating out, Italian or Asian restaurants tend to offer more carbo-based meals.

Rice, pasta and potatoes are good staples for self-caterers. Team them with fresh vegetables and ingredients such as instant soup, canned beans, fish or bacon. Remember that even though you're limited in terms of what you can carry on a bike, it's possible – with some imagination and preparation – to eat delicious as well as nutritious camp meals.

The authors of this book claim their favorite snacks are dried fruit (especially cherries, apricots and figs), fig bars, tamari roasted almonds, hard candies and chocolate (especially chocolate-covered licorice).

AVOIDING CYCLING AILMENTS

Saddle Sores & Blisters

While you're more likely to get a sore butt if you're out of condition, riding long distances does take its toll on your behind. To minimize the impact, always wear clean, preferably padded, bike shorts (also known as 'knicks'). Brief, unfitted shorts can chafe, as can underwear (see Clothing, p29–31). Shower as soon as you stop and put on clean, preferably nonsynthetic clothes. Moisturizing or baby diaper rash (nappy rash) creams also guard against chafing – apply liberally around the crotch area before riding. For information on adjusting your bike seat, see Saddle Height & Position (pp70–71).

If you do suffer from chafing, wash and dry the area and carefully apply a barrier (moisturizing) cream.

You probably won't get blisters unless you do a very long ride with no physical preparation. Wearing gloves and correctly fitted shoes will reduce the likelihood of blisters. If you know you're susceptible to blisters in a particular spot, cover the area with medical adhesive tape before riding.

Knee Pain

Knee pain is common among cyclists who pedal in too high a gear. While it may *seem* that you'll go faster by turning the pedals slowly in a high gear, it's actually more efficient (and better for your knees) to 'spin' the pedals – that is, use a low enough gear so you can pedal quickly with little resistance. For touring, the ideal cadence (the number of pedal strokes per minute) ranges from 70 to 90. Try to maintain this cadence even when you're climbing.

It's a good idea to stretch before and after riding, and to go easy at the start of each day. This reduces the chance of injury and helps your muscles work more efficiently.

You can also get sore knees if your saddle is too low, or if your shoe cleats (for use with clipless pedals) are incorrectly positioned. Both are discussed in greater detail in the Your Bicycle chapter (pp67–86).

Numbness & Backache

Pain in the hands, neck and shoulders is a common complaint, particularly on longer riding days. It's generally caused by leaning too much on your hands. Apart from discomfort, you can temporarily damage the nerves and experience numbness or mild paralysis of the hands. Prevent it by wearing padded gloves, cycling with less weight on your hands and changing your hand position frequently (if you have flat handlebars, fit bar ends to provide more hand positions).

When seated your weight should be fairly evenly distributed through your hands and seat. If you're carrying too much weight on your hands there are two ways of adjusting your bike to rectify this: either by raising your handlebars or, if you are stretched out too much, fitting a smaller stem (talk to your local bike shop). For more guidance on adjusting your bicycle for greater comfort, see the Your Bicycle chapter (pp67–86).

Stretching

Stretching is important when stepping up your exercise levels: it improves muscle flexibility, which allows freer movement in the joints; and prevents the rigidity developing in muscles that occurs through prolonged cycling activity.

Ideally, you should stretch for 10 minutes before and after riding and for longer periods (15 to 30 minutes) every second day. Stretching prepares muscles for the task ahead and limits the stress on muscles and joints during exercise. It can reduce post-exercise stiffness (decreasing the recovery time between rides) and reduce the chance of injury during cycling.

You should follow a few basic guidelines:

- before stretching, warm up for five to 10 minutes by going for a gentle bike ride, jog or brisk walk
- ensure you follow correct technique for each stretch
- hold a stretch for 15 to 30 seconds
- stretch to the point of discomfort, not pain
- breathe freely (ie, don't hold your breath) and try to relax your body whenever you are stretching
- don't 'bounce' the stretch; gradually ease into a full stretch
- repeat each stretch three times (on both sides, when required)

Do not stretch when you have an injury to a muscle, ligament or tendon (allow it to heal fully), as it can lead to further injury and/or hinder recovery. Warming up the muscles increases blood flow to the area, making it easier to stretch and reducing the likelihood of injury.

The main muscle groups for the cyclist to stretch are: quadriceps, calves, hamstrings, lower back and neck. Use the following stretches as a starting point, adding extra stretches that are already part of your routine or if you feel 'tight' in other areas (eg, add shoulder rolls if your shoulders feel sore after a day's cycling).

Quadriceps

Facing a wall with your feet slightly apart, grip one foot with your hand and pull it towards the buttocks. Ensure the back and hips are square. To get a better stretch, push the hip forward. You should never feel pain at the knee joint. Hold the stretch, before lowering the leg and repeating the stretch with the other leg.

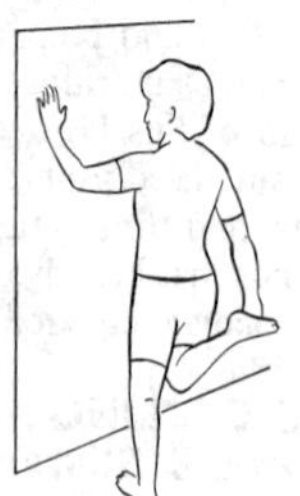

Calf

Stand facing a wall, placing one foot about 1ft in front of the other. Keep the heels flat on the ground and bend the front leg slowly toward the wall – the stretch should be in the upper-calf area of the back leg. Keep the back straight and bend your elbows to allow your body to move forward during the stretch. Hold the stretch; relax and repeat with the other leg.

Stretching

Hamstrings

Sit with one leg extended and the other leg bent with the bottom of the foot against the inside of the extended leg. Slide your arms down the extended leg – bending from the waist – until you feel a pull in the hamstring area. Hold for 15 seconds, before returning to the start position. Keep the toes pointed up; avoid hunching the back.

Lower-Back Roll

Lie on your back (on a towel or sleeping mat) and bring both knees up towards the shoulders until you feel a stretch in the lower back. Hold the stretch for 30 seconds; relax.

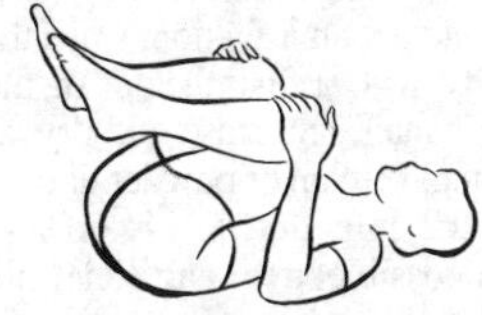

'Cat Stretch' Hunch

Another stretch for the lower back. Move to the ground on all fours (hands shoulder-width apart; legs slightly apart), lift the hips and lower back towards the sky until you feel a stretch. Hold for 15 seconds; return to start position.

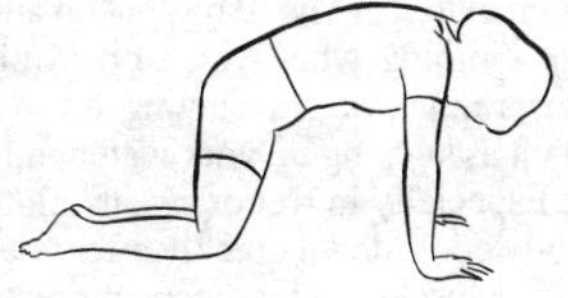

'Cat Stretch' Arch

One more stretch for the lower back. With hands and knees in the same position as for the Cat Stretch above, roll the hips and lower back toward the ground until you feel a stretch. Hold for 15 seconds; return to start position.

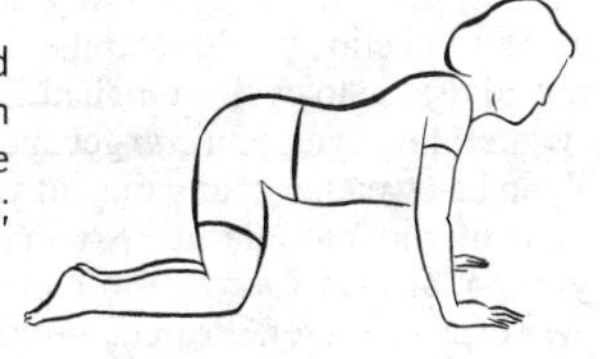

Neck

Gently and smoothly stretch your neck each of the four ways: forward, back and side to side. Do each stretch separately. (Do not rotate the head in a full circle.) For the side stretches, use your hand to pull the head very gently in the direction of the stretch.

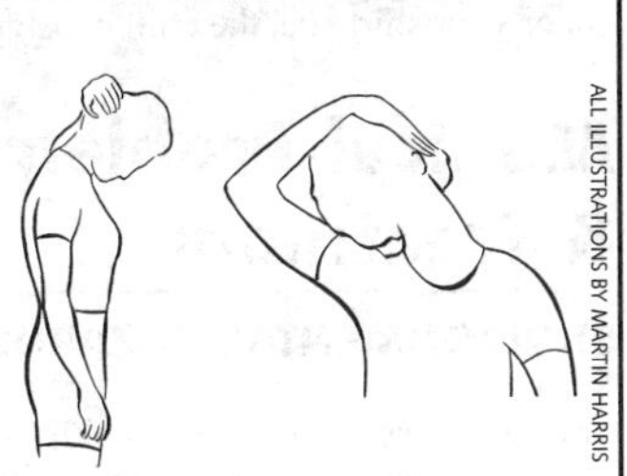

ALL ILLUSTRATIONS BY MARTIN HARRIS

Fungal Infections

Warm, sweaty bodies are ideal environments for fungal growth; physical activity, combined with inadequate washing of your body and/or clothes, can lead to fungal infections. The most common are athlete's foot (tinea) between the toes or fingers, and infections on the scalp, in the groin or on the body (ringworm). You can get ringworm (which is a fungal infection, not a worm) from infected animals or other people.

To prevent fungal infections, wash frequently and dry yourself carefully. Change out of sweaty bike clothes as soon as possible.

If you do get an infection, wash the area at least daily with a disinfectant or medicated soap and water, and rinse and dry well. Use an antifungal cream or powder like tolnaftate. Expose the infection to air or sunlight as much as possible; avoid artificial fibers; and wash all towels and underwear in hot water, change them often and dry them in the sun.

Staying Warm

Except on extremely hot days, put on another layer of clothing when you stop cycling – even for a quick break. Staying warm is as important as keeping up your water and food intake. Especially in wet or sweaty clothing, your body cools down quickly after you stop working. Muscle strains occur more easily when your body is chilled and hypothermia can result from prolonged exposure (see Hypothermia, p59). Dressing warmly helps prevent chest infections, colds and the flu.

It's not advisable to cycle at high altitude during winter; however, you *can* get caught suddenly in bad weather at any time of year, especially in the mountains. No matter when you go, always carry warm clothing and a waterproof layer. Protect yourself from the wind on long downhill stretches – even stuffing a few sheets of newspaper under your shirt cuts the chill considerably.

Medical Problems & Treatment

ENVIRONMENTAL HAZARDS

Sun

You can get sunburnt quite quickly, even on cool or cloudy days, and especially when riding on shadeless roads.

Take sun protection seriously – unless you want to be fried and increase your chances of heatstroke and skin cancer:

- Cover up wherever possible: wear a long-sleeved top with a collar, and a peaked helmet cover – you may want to go the extra step and add a 'legionnaire's flap' to your helmet to protect the back of your neck and ears. Make sure your shirt is sunproof: very thin or loosely woven fabrics still let sun through. Some fabrics are designed to offer high sun protection.
- Use high-protection sunscreen (30+). Choose a water-resistant 'sports' sunscreen and reapply every few hours as you sweat it off. Don't forget to protect your neck, ears, hands, and feet if wearing sandals. Zinc cream is good for sensitive noses, lips and ears.
- Wear good sunglasses; they will also protect you from wind, dust and insects and are essential protection against sticks and flying objects if you're mountain biking.
- Sit in the shade during rest breaks.
- Wear a wide-brimmed hat when off the bike.

Mild sunburn can be treated with calamine lotion, aloe vera or sting-relief spray.

Heat

Treat heat with respect. California, in particular, can get extremely hot, so don't set a demanding touring schedule as soon as you arrive; take things easy until you acclimatize.

Dehydration & Heat Exhaustion Dehydration is a potentially dangerous and easily preventable condition caused by excessive fluid loss. Sweating and inadequate fluid intake are common causes of dehydration in cyclists, but others include diarrhea, vomiting and fever – see Diarrhea (p59–60) for the appropriate treatment in these circumstances.

The first symptoms are weakness, thirst and passing small amounts of very concentrated urine. This may progress to drowsiness, dizziness or fainting when standing up and, finally, coma.

It's easy to forget how much fluid you are losing via perspiration while cycling, especially if a strong breeze is drying your skin quickly. Make sure you drink sufficient liquids (see Hydration, p53). Refrain from drinking too many caffeinated drinks (including some soft drinks). They act as a diuretic, causing you to lose water through urination; don't drink them for rehydration.

Dehydration and salt deficiency can cause heat exhaustion. Salt deficiency is characterized by fatigue, lethargy, headaches, giddiness and muscle cramps; salt tablets may help, but adding extra salt to your food is probably sufficient.

If one of your party suffers from heat exhaustion, lie the casualty down in a shady spot and encourage them to drink slowly but frequently. If possible, seek medical advice.

Heatstroke This serious and occasionally fatal condition can occur if the body's heat-regulating mechanism breaks down and the body temperature rises to dangerous levels. Continuous periods of exposure to high temperatures and insufficient fluids can leave you vulnerable to heatstroke.

The symptoms are feeling unwell, not sweating very much (or at all) and a high body temperature (102–106°F or 39–41°C). Where sweating has ceased, the skin becomes flushed and red. Severe, throbbing headaches and lack of coordination will also occur, and the sufferer may be confused or aggressive, eventually becoming delirious or convulsing.

Hospitalization is essential; in the interim get the casualty out of the sun, remove their clothing, cover them with a wet sheet or towel and then fan continuously. Give them plenty of fluids (cool water), if conscious.

Cold

Hypothermia This occurs when the body loses heat faster than it can produce it and the body's core temperature falls. It is surprisingly easy to progress from very cold to dangerously cold because of a combination of wind, wet clothing, fatigue and hunger, even if the air temperature is above freezing.

Symptoms of hypothermia are exhaustion, numb skin (particularly toes and fingers), shivering, slurred speech, irrational or violent behavior, lethargy, stumbling, dizzy spells, muscle cramps and powerful bursts of energy. Irrationality may take the form of sufferers claiming they are warm and trying to take off their clothes.

To prevent hypothermia, dress in layers (see Clothing, pp29–31). A strong, waterproof outer layer is essential. Protect yourself against wind, particularly for long descents. Eat plenty of high-energy food when it's cold; it's important to keep drinking too – even though you may not feel like it.

To treat mild hypothermia, first get the person out of the wind and/or rain, remove wet clothing and replace it with dry, warm clothing. Give them hot liquids – not alcohol – and some high-kilojoule, easily digestible food. Do not rub victims but allow them to slowly warm themselves. This should be enough to treat the early stages of hypothermia; however, medical treatment should still be sought, urgently if the hypothermia is severe. Early recognition and treatment of mild hypothermia is the only way to prevent severe hypothermia, a critical condition.

INFECTIOUS DISEASES

Diarrhea

Simple things like a change of water, food or climate can cause a mild bout of diarrhea but a few rushed toilet trips with no other symptoms do not indicate a major problem. Serious diarrhea is caused by infectious agents transmitted by fecal contamination of food or water, by using contaminated utensils, or directly from one person's hand to another. Paying particular attention to personal hygiene, drinking purified water and taking care of what you eat are important measures to take to avoid getting diarrhea while touring.

Dehydration is the main danger with any diarrhea, particularly in children or the elderly, as it can occur quickly. Under all circumstances, the most important thing is to replace fluids (at least equal to the volume being lost). Urine is the best guide to this – if you have small amounts of dark urine, you need to drink more. Weak black tea with a little sugar, soda water, or soft drinks allowed to go flat and diluted 50% with clean water are good. With severe diarrhea it's better to use a rehydrating solution to replace lost minerals and salts. Commercially available oral rehydration salts should be added to boiled or bottled water. In an emergency, make a solution of six teaspoons of sugar and a half teaspoon of salt in one quart of boiled or bottled water. Drink small amounts often. Stick to a bland diet as you recover.

Gut-paralyzing drugs such as diphenoxylate or loperamide can bring relief from the symptoms, although they don't cure the problem. Only use these drugs if you do not have access to toilets, that is, if you *must* travel. These drugs are not recommended for children under 12 years of age, or if you have a high fever or are severely dehydrated.

Seek medical advice if you pass blood or mucus, are feverish or suffer persistent or severe diarrhea. Another cause of persistent diarrhea in travelers is giardiasis.

Giardiasis

An intestinal disorder contracted by drinking water contaminated with the *Giardia lamblia* parasite, giardiasis' symptoms are stomach cramps, nausea, a bloated stomach, watery and foul-smelling diarrhea, and frequent gas. It can appear several weeks after exposure. The symptoms may disappear for a few days and then return; this can go on for several weeks. Seek medical advice if you think you have giardiasis but, where this is not possible, tinidazole or metronidazole are the recommended drugs. Treatment is a 2g single dose of tinidazole or 250mg of metronidazole three times daily for five to 10 days.

Tetanus

This disease is caused by a germ that lives in soil and in the feces of horses and other animals. It enters the body via breaks in the skin. The first symptom may be discomfort in swallowing or stiffening of the jaw and neck; this is followed by painful convulsions of the jaw and whole body. The disease can be fatal but can be prevented by vaccination.

HIV & AIDS

Infection with the human immunodeficiency virus (HIV) may lead to acquired immune deficiency syndrome (AIDS), which is a fatal disease. Any exposure to blood, blood products or body fluids may put you at risk. The disease is often transmitted through sexual contact or dirty needles – vaccinations, acupuncture, tattooing and body piercing can be potentially as dangerous as intravenous drug use. The blood supply in the USA is well screened, so blood transfusions are an unlikely source of infection. The US Center for Disease Control has a helpful AIDS hotline (☎ 800-342-2437) and support groups are listed in the front of phone books.

INSECT-BORNE DISEASES

Lyme Disease

This is a tick-transmitted infection that may be acquired throughout North America. The illness usually begins with a spreading rash at the site of the tick bite and is accompanied by fever, headache, extreme fatigue, aching joints and muscles, and mild neck stiffness. If untreated, these symptoms usually resolve over several weeks but over subsequent weeks or months disorders of the nervous system, heart and joints may develop. Treatment works best early in the illness. Medical help should be sought.

BITES & STINGS

Bees & Wasps

These are usually painful rather than dangerous. However, anyone allergic to these can suffer severe breathing difficulties and will need medical care. Calamine lotion or a commercial sting-relief spray will ease discomfort, and ice packs will reduce the pain and swelling. Antihistamines can also help.

Snakes & Scorpions

There are several varieties of venomous snakes in the USA but they do not cause instantaneous death and antivenins are available. First aid is to place a light, constricting bandage above the bite, keep the wounded part below the level of the heart and move it as little as possible. Administer CPR if breathing stops. Stay calm and get to a medical facility as soon as possible. Bring the dead snake for identification if you can but don't risk being bitten again. The use of tourniquets and sucking out the poison are now comprehensively discredited.

To minimize the risk of being bitten, wear boots, socks and long trousers when walking through undergrowth where snakes may be. Don't put your hands into holes and crevices and be careful when collecting firewood.

In the Southwest and other dry regions, both rattlesnakes and scorpions may be an issue. Rattlesnakes usually give warning of their presence and backing away from them (slowly!) usually prevents confrontation. Remember that their bites are seldom fatal and that only one in three adult rattlers actually injects venom when it bites (younger ones are more prone to inject venom, as they haven't learned self discipline).

Scorpions are not aggressive, but will sting if you sit or step on them. Always check your shoes before putting them on; shaking out your sleeping bag isn't overly cautious either.

Spiders

Black widow spiders are found throughout the USA. Their bites are toxic but they inject a small amount of venom. Bites are rarely fatal, but can cause localized and sometimes systemic inflammation – again, stay calm and seek medical help immediately.

Ticks

Ticks can cause skin infections and more serious diseases, such as Lyme disease, so always check all over your body if you have been walking or camping in a potentially tick-infested area.

To remove a tick, press down around its head with tweezers, grab the head and gently pull upwards. Avoid pulling the rear of the body as this may squeeze the tick's gut contents through the attached mouth parts into your skin, increasing the risk of infection. Pulling a tick off and leaving the head in the skin can also lead to infection. Smearing chemicals on, or burning, the tick is no longer recommended. After removing the tick, clean the wound and apply an antiseptic solution such as povidone-iodine.

WOMEN'S HEALTH

Cycle touring is not hazardous to your health, but women's health issues are relevant wherever you go, and can be a bit more tricky to cope with when you are on the road.

If you experience low energy and/or abdominal or back pain during menstruation, it may be best to undertake less strenuous rides or schedule a rest day or two at this time.

Gynecological Problems

If you have a vaginal discharge that is not normal for you with or without any other symptoms, you've probably got an infection.

- If you've had thrush (vaginal candidiasis) before and think you have it again, it's worth self-treating for this (see the following section).
- If not, get medical advice, as you will need a test and an appropriate course of treatment.
- It's best not to self-medicate with antibiotics; there are many causes of vaginal discharge, which can only be differentiated with tests.

Thrush (Vaginal Candidiasis) Symptoms of this common yeast infection are itching and discomfort in the genital area, often with thick white vaginal discharge (said to resemble cottage cheese). Many factors, including diet, pregnancy, medications and hot climatic conditions can trigger thrush.

You can help prevent it by wearing cotton underwear off the bike and loose-fitting bicycle shorts; maintaining good personal hygiene is particularly important when wearing cycling knicks. It's a good idea to wash regularly but don't use soap, which can increase the chance of thrush occurring. Washing gently with a solution of one teaspoon of salt in a quart of warm water can relieve the itching. A single dose of an antifungal pessary (vaginal tablet) such as 500mg of clotrimazole is an effective treatment. Alternatively, you can use an antifungal cream inserted high in the vagina (on a tampon if you don't have an applicator). A vaginal acidifying gel may help prevent recurrences.

If you're stuck in a remote area without medication, you could use natural yogurt (applied directly to the vulva or on a tampon inserted in the vagina) to soothe and restore the normal balance of organisms in the vagina.

It may also help to avoid yeast products like bread and beer, and eat yogurt with acidophilus culture.

Urinary Tract Infection

Cystitis, or inflammation of the bladder, is a common condition in women. Symptoms include burning when urinating and having to urinate urgently and frequently. Blood can sometimes be passed in urine.

If you think you have cystitis:

- Drink plenty of fluids to help flush the infection out; citrus fruit juice or cranberry juice can help relieve symptoms.
- Take a nonprescription cystitis remedy to help relieve the discomfort. Alternatively, add a teaspoon of bicarbonate of soda to one glass of water when symptoms first appear.
- If there's no improvement after 24 hours despite these measures, seek medical advice because a course of antibiotics may be needed.

TRAUMATIC INJURIES

Although we give guidance on basic first-aid procedures here remember that, unless you're an experienced first aider and confident in what you're doing, it's possible to do more harm than good. Always seek medical help if it is available, but if you are far from any help, follow these guidelines.

Cuts & Other Wounds

Here's what to do if you suffer a fall while riding and end up with road-rash (grazes) and a few minor cuts. If you're riding in a hot, humid climate or intend continuing on your way, there's likely to be a high risk of infection, so the wound needs to be cleaned and dressed. Carry a few antiseptic wipes in your first-aid kit to use straight away, especially if no clean water is available. Small wounds can be cleaned with an antiseptic wipe (only wipe across the wound once with each). Deep or dirty wounds need to be cleaned thoroughly.

- Clean your hands before you start.
- Wear gloves if you are cleaning somebody else's wound.
- Use bottled or boiled water (allowed to cool) or an antiseptic solution like povidone-iodine.
- Use plenty of water – pour it on the wound from a container.
- Embedded dirt and other particles can be removed with tweezers or flushed out using a syringe to squirt water (you can get more pressure if you use a needle as well) – this is especially effective for removing gravel.
- Dry wounds heal best, so avoid using antiseptic creams that keep the wound moist; instead apply antiseptic powder or spray.
- Dry the wound with clean gauze before applying a dressing (use any clean material that's not fluffy).

Bleeding Wounds

Most cuts will stop bleeding on their own, but if a blood vessel of any size has been cut it may bleed for some time. Wounds to the head, hands and at joint creases tend to be particularly bloody.

To stop bleeding from a wound:

- Wear gloves if you are dealing with a wound on another person.
- Lie the casualty down if possible.
- Raise the injured limb above the level of the casualty's heart.
- Use your fingers or the palm of your hand to apply direct pressure to the wound, preferably over a sterile dressing or clean pad.
- Apply steady pressure for at least five minutes before looking to see if the bleeding has stopped.
- Put a sterile dressing over the original pad (don't move this) and bandage it in place.
- Check the bandage regularly in case bleeding restarts.

Never use a tourniquet to stop bleeding as this may cause gangrene – the only situation in which this may be appropriate is if the limb has been amputated.

Cuts and wounds make you vulnerable to tetanus infection – if you didn't have a tetanus injection before you went on tour, get one now.

A dressing will protect the wound from dirt, dust and flies. Alternatively, if the wound is small and you are confident you can keep it clean, leave it uncovered. Change the dressing regularly (once a day to start with), especially if the wound is oozing, and watch for signs of infection.

If you have any swelling around the wound, raising the affected limb can help the swelling settle and the wound to heal.

It's best to seek medical advice for any wound that fails to heal after a week or so.

Major Accident

Crashing or being hit by an inattentive driver in a motor vehicle is always possible when cycling. When a major accident does occur what you do is determined to some extent by the circumstances you are in and how readily available medical care is. Be prepared to do at least an initial assessment and to ensure the casualty comes to no further harm.

First of all, check for danger to yourself. If the casualty is on the road ensure oncoming traffic is stopped or diverted. A basic plan of action is:

- Keep calm and think through what you need to do and when.
- Get medical help urgently; send someone to phone ☎ 911.
- Carefully look over the casualty in the position in which you found them (unless this is hazardous for some reason, eg, on a cliff edge).
- Call to the casualty to see if there is a response.
- Check for pulse (at the wrist or on the side of the neck), breathing and major blood loss.
- If necessary (ie, no breathing or no pulse), and you know how, start resuscitation.
- Check the casualty for injuries, moving them as little as possible; ask them where they have pain if they are conscious.
- Don't move the casualty if a spinal injury is possible.
- Take immediate steps to control any obvious bleeding by applying direct pressure to the wound.
- Make the casualty as comfortable as possible and reassure them.
- Keep the casualty warm by insulating them from cold or wet ground (use whatever you have to hand, such as a sleeping bag).

Safety on the Ride

ROAD RULES

There are few national road rules for bicycles in the USA but state codes are fairly universal. Bikes are expected to act as cars and obey road signs and traffic signals. For road rules publications see under Car, p96. Riding on the sidewalk is not illegal but frowned upon without a good reason. Letting people know before passing is a safety courtesy.

All states on the West Coast require cyclists to be as close as practicable to the right-hand curb (or edge of the road), except when avoiding a hazardous condition or passing. Cyclists must use bike lanes when provided, and use standard hand signals (left arm extended straight means left, left arm extended upwards at a right angle means right) when turning.

California enforces the same drug and alcohol laws for cyclists as for motorists: if you are found to have a blood alcohol concentration of 0.08% or more (0.01% if you are under 21 years old), you can serve 48 hours to six months in jail and pay up to $1000 in fines. Violation of most other bicycle laws results in a $25 fine.

BICYCLE EQUIPMENT

State laws along the West Coast require a bicycle to have a white light visible for 500ft in front and a rear reflector visible for 600ft in back. In California, your pedal reflectors have to be visible from 200ft. A mountable light powered by the energy of your wheel is a good investment, since you won't have to keep replacing batteries (which tend to wear out quickly with most bike lights).

Helmets & Visible Clothing

Washington does not have any helmet requirements while Oregon requires a helmet for all riders under 16 years and California requires a helmet for riders under 18 years. In keeping with its liberalism, however, Oregon law states that,'A person is exempt from the requirements...if wearing the headgear would violate a religious belief or practice of the person'.

We recommend that you wear a helmet. Make sure it fits squarely on your head with the front low on your brow to protect your forehead. It should be snug, but not tight, once it has been fastened, and there should be no slack in the straps. If it has been in a crash, replace it.

Whether it is day or night, it is always a good idea to wear brightly colored clothing, and at night, garments with reflective strips.

RIDING OFFROAD

Trail etiquette requires mountain bikes to yield to hikers and equestrians. But it's more important just to use common courtesy while on the trail. Bike paths are often shared with pedestrians; ring your bell or give a holler before passing on the left.

The Off Road Cyclist's Code recommends you minimize impact by carrying out all human-made elements that you bring into a wilderness area; stay on trails and take care to avoid soil erosion (muddy trails are more vulnerable); never scare animals; control your speed; and wear a helmet at all times.

Although most rides are not far from civilization, always remember one of the first rules about offroading: never go alone. It's not uncommon for people to go missing, either through injury or after losing their way. It's best to go in a small group – four is usually considered the minimum. This way, if there's an accident, one person can stay with the casualty and the others can go for help.

Always tell someone where you are going and when you intend to be back – and make sure they know that you're back! Take warm clothing, matches and enough food and water in case of emergency. Carry enough tools so you can undertake any emergency repairs. (See the 'Spares & Tool Kit' boxed text, p73, for advice on a basic tool kit.)

Carry a map and take note of the surroundings as you ride. If you get really lost, stay calm and stop. Try to work out where you are or how to retrace your route. If you can't, or it's getting dark, find a nearby open area, put on warm clothes and find or make a shelter. Light a fire and help searchers by making some obvious signs (eg, creating smoke, displaying brightly colored items or making symbols out of wood or rocks).

TOURING DANGERS & ANNOYANCES

Bears

Black bears and (rarely) grizzly bears are found in the mountainous areas of the region, and can be attracted to campgrounds for food.

Tips for Better Cycling

These tips on riding technique are designed to help you ride more safely, comfortably and efficiently:

- Ride in bike lanes if they exist.
- Ride about 3ft from the edge of the curb or from parked cars; riding too close to the road edge makes you less visible and more vulnerable to rough surfaces or car doors being opened without warning.
- Stay alert: especially on busy, narrow, winding and hilly roads it's essential to constantly scan ahead and anticipate the movements of other vehicles, cyclists, pedestrians or animals. Watch for potholes and other hazards as well.
- Keep your upper body relaxed, even when you are climbing.
- Ride a straight line and don't weave across the road when reaching for water bottles or climbing.
- To negotiate rough surfaces and bumps, take your weight off the saddle and let your legs absorb the shock, with the pedals level (in the three and nine o'clock positions).

At Night

- Only ride at night if your bike is equipped with a front and rear light; consider also using a reflective vest and/or reflective ankle bands.

Braking

- Apply front and rear brakes evenly.
- When your bike is fully loaded you'll find that you can apply the front brake quite hard and the extra weight will prevent you doing an 'endo' (flipping over the handlebars).
- In wet weather gently apply the brakes occasionally to dry the brake pads.

Cable Car & Train Tracks

- Hit these as near to 90 degrees as possible to avoid getting your wheel stuck in the gap. In the wet, the metal rails are especially slippery and dangerous; take special care.

Climbing

- Change down to your low gears to keep your legs 'spinning'.
- When climbing out of the saddle, keep the bike steady; try not to rock the handlebars from side to side.

Cornering

- Loaded bikes are prone to sliding on corners; approach corners slowly and don't lean into the corner as hard as you normally would.
- If traffic permits, take a straight path across corners; hit the corner wide, cut across the apex and ride out of it wide – but never cross the dividing line on the road.
- Apply the brakes before the corner, not while cornering (especially if it's wet).

Corrugations (Ruts)

- For short sections, stand up out of the seat and let the bike rock beneath you. On longer sections, look for the least corrugated area (often the edges or middle of the road), grin and bear it.

Descending

- Stay relaxed, don't cramp up: let your body go with the bike.
- A loaded bike is more likely to wobble and be harder to control at speed, so take it easy.
- Pump the brakes to shed speed rather than applying constant pressure; this avoids overheating the rims, which can cause your tire to blow.

Tips for Better Cycling

Gravel Roads

- Avoid patches of deep gravel (often on the road's edge); if you can't, ride hard, as you do if driving a car through mud.
- Look ahead to plan your course; avoid sudden turning and take it slowly on descents.
- Brake in a straight line using your rear brake and place your weight over the front wheel if you need to use that brake.
- On loose gravel, loosen toe-clip straps or clipless pedals so you can put your foot down quickly.

Group Riding

- If you're riding in a group, keep your actions predictable and let others know, with a hand signal or shout, before you brake, turn, dodge potholes etc.
- Ride beside, in front or behind fellow cyclists. Don't overlap wheels; if either of you moves sideways suddenly it's likely both of you will fall.
- Ride in single file on busy, narrow or winding roads.

In Traffic

- Obey the rules of the road, and signal if you are turning.
- Look at the wheels to see if a car at a T-junction or joining the road is actually moving or not.
- Scan for trouble: look inside the back windows of parked cars for movement – the person inside may open the door on you.
- Look drivers in the eye; make sure they've seen you.
- Learn to bunny hop your bike (yes, it can be done with a loaded touring bike; just not as well) – it'll save you hitting potholes and other hazards.

In the Wet

- Be aware that you'll take longer to slow down with wet rims; exercise appropriate caution.
- When descending apply the brakes lightly to keep the rims free of grit/water etc and allow for quicker stopping.
- Don't climb out of the saddle (unless you want a change); shift down a gear or two and climb seated.

Why don't you just change down?
Don Hatcher 97

DON HATCHER

On Bikepaths

- Use a bell or call out to warn of your approach.

Pick-a-Plank Bridges

- Timber bridges with planks running parallel to the road should be approached with caution.
- Unless you have wide tires, look carefully at the gaps between the planks and decide whether you can safely ride across the bridge without your wheels falling into a gap; otherwise, walk. To ride, pick a line and stick to it by looking ahead rather than straight down.

In the USA, most bears have encountered human activity, so people are generally in little danger of being attacked. Still, every year there are several maulings. How to avoid this?

- Let them know you're coming! Bears are less likely to feel threatened if they have time to flee. Make noise or use bear bells when in densely forested areas.
- Heed the warnings about not keeping food or anything scented (including soap, toothpaste and lotion) in your tent. Be extremely diligent about this. Put all smelly things in a bag and hoist it up in a tree or a 'bear pole'.
- In regions where hanging is known to be ineffective, use a bear-proof container (available from outdoors suppliers) set 50ft from camp, or take advantage of the metal bear-boxes provided.
- Have designated cooking clothes that you put in the 'smelly things' bag, and never let these clothes into your tent.
- Keep an immaculate camp, particularly regarding food scraps and washing up.
- If you do encounter a bear, stay still and slowly raise your arms above your head. If the bear attacks, *do not run*! Drop to the ground in the fetal position and clasp your hands behind your neck to protect your spinal cord. *Do not fight back*! Play dead until the bear leaves.
- Don't try to get closer to a bear to take its photograph. Be particularly careful if you encounter a mother with cubs.
- Remember that bears hibernate all winter. In the spring they are hungry and active, in the fall they are becoming sleepy and slow.

Mountain Lions

Also called pumas or cougars, mountain lions are most common in the lower western Sierra and the mountains and forests east of LA and San Diego. Attacks are rare. Rangers recommend staying calm if you meet a lion. Hold your ground, try to appear large by raising your arms or grabbing a stick. If the lion attacks, fight back, shout and throw objects at it.

Earthquake

In California, there are dozens of harmless earthquakes every week. In the unlikely event of a serious quake, remember this advice:

- Indoors: take cover under a table or, failing that, a doorway. Stay clear of windows or anything that might fall. Don't use elevators.
- Outdoors: get to an open area away from buildings, trees and power lines. If cycling, pull over to the side of the road away from bridges, overpasses and power lines.
- If you are outdoors near buildings, duck into a doorway to protect yourself from falling debris.

Emergency Number

Throughout the USA, dial ☎ 911 for emergency service of any kind; the number can be called free from any phone.

Hunting

Hunting is permitted in national forests and cyclists should take precautions on back roads during hunting season (usually Oct–Mar; check the latest at the USFS Web site: W www.fs.fed.us).

EMERGENCY PROCEDURES

If you or one of your group has an accident (even a minor one), or falls ill during your travels, you'll need to decide on the best course of action, which isn't always easy. Obviously, you will need to consider your individual circumstances, including where you are and whether you have some means of direct communication with emergency services, such as a cell phone (mobile phone). Some basic guidelines are:

- Use your first-aid knowledge and experience, as well as the information in this guide if necessary, to make a medical assessment of the situation.
- For groups of several people, the accepted procedure is to leave one person with the casualty, with as much equipment, food and water as you can sensibly spare, and for the rest of the group to go for help.
- If there are only two of you, the situation is more tricky; you will have to make an individual judgement of the best course of action.
- If you leave someone, mark their position carefully on the map (take it with you). Also make sure they can be easily found by marking the position with something conspicuous, such as bright clothing or a large stone cross on the ground. Leave them with warm clothes, shelter, food, water, matches and a flashlight (torch).
- Try attracting attention by using a whistle or flashlight, lighting a smoky fire (use damp wood or green leaves) or waving bright clothing; shouting is tiring and not very effective.

The uncertainties associated with emergency rescue in remote wilderness areas should make it clear how important careful planning and safety precautions are, especially if you are traveling in a small group.

YOUR BICYCLE

ALL PHOTOS BY JEFF CROW

Fundamental to any cycle tour you plan is the bicycle. In this chapter we look at choosing a bicycle and accessories, setting it up for your needs, learning basic maintenance, and loading and carrying your gear. In short, everything you need to gear up and get going.

CHOOSING & SETTING UP A BICYCLE

The ideal bike for cycle touring is (strangely enough) a touring bike. These bikes look similar to road bikes but generally have relaxed frame geometry for comfort and predictable steering; fittings (eyelets and brazed-on bosses) to mount panniers and mudguards; wider rims and tires; strong wheels (at least 36 spokes) to carry the extra load; and gearing capable of riding up a wall (triple chainrings and a wide-range freewheel to match). If you want to buy a touring bike, most tend to be custom-built these days, but Cannondale (W www.cannondale.com) and Trek (W www.trekbikes.com) both offer a range of models.

Of course you can tour on any bike you choose, but few will match the advantages of the workhorse touring bike.

Mountain bikes are a slight compromise by comparison, but are very popular for touring. A mountain bike already has the gearing needed for touring and offers a more upright, comfortable position on the bike. And with a change of tires (to those with semi-slick tread) you'll be able to reduce the rolling resistance and travel at higher speeds with less effort.

Hybrid, or cross, bikes are similar to mountain bikes (and therefore offer similar advantages and disadvantages), although they typically already come equipped with semi-slick tires.

Racing bikes are less appropriate: their tighter frame geometry is less comfortable on rough roads and long rides. It is also difficult to fit wider tires, mudguards, racks and panniers to a road bike. Perhaps more significantly, most racing bikes have a distinct lack of low gears.

Tires Unless you know you'll be on good, sealed roads the whole time, it's probably safest to choose a tire with some tread. If you have 700c or 27-inch wheels, opt for a tire that's 28–35mm wide. If touring on a mountain bike, the first thing to do is get rid of the knobby tires – too much rolling resistance. Instead, fit 1–1½ inch semi-slick tires or, if riding unpaved roads or off-road occasionally, a combination pattern tire (slick centre and knobs on the outside).

To protect your tubes, consider buying tires reinforced with Kevlar, a tightly woven synthetic fiber very resistant to sharp objects. Although more expensive, Kevlar-belted tires are worth it.

Pedals Cycling efficiency is vastly improved by using toe clips, and even more so with clipless pedals and cleated shoes. Mountain bike or touring shoes are best – the cleats are recessed and the soles are flexible enough to comfortably walk in.

Fold & Go Bikes

Another option is a folding bike. Manufacturers include: Bike Friday (W www.bikefriday.com), Brompton (W www.bromptonbike.co.uk), Birdy (W www.foldsoc.co.uk), Moulton (W www.alexmoulton.co.uk) and Slingshot (W www.slingshotbikes.com). All make high-quality touring bikes that fold up to allow hassle-free train, plane or bus transfers. The Moulton, Birdy, Brompton and Slingshot come with suspension and the Bike Friday's case doubles as a trailer for your luggage when touring.

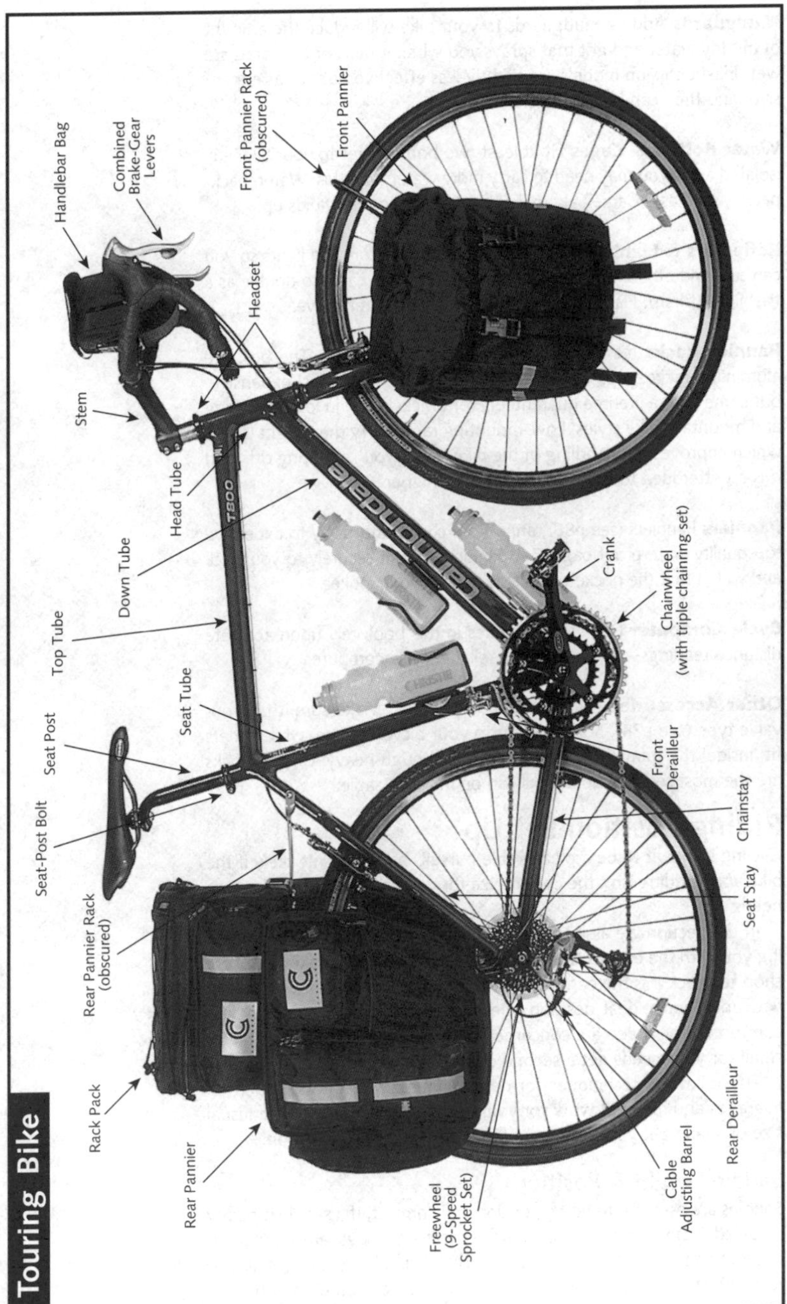
Touring Bike
Rack Pack
Rear Pannier
Rear Pannier Rack (obscured)
Seat-Post Bolt
Seat Post
Seat Tube
Top Tube
Down Tube
Head Tube
Stem
Headset
Handlebar Bag
Combined Brake-Gear Levers
Front Pannier Rack (obscured)
Front Pannier
Crank
Chainwheel (with triple chainring set)
Front Derailleur
Chainstay
Seat Stay
Rear Derailleur
Cable Adjusting Barrel
Freewheel (9-Speed Sprocket Set)

Mudguards Adding mudguards to your bike will reduce the amount of muddy water and grit that sprays you when it rains or the roads are wet. Plastic clip-on models are slightly less effective but not as expensive, and they can be less hassle.

Water Bottles & Cages Fit at least two bottle cages to your bike – in isolated areas you may need to carry more water than this. Water 'backpacks', such as a Camelbak, make it easy to keep your fluids up.

Reflectors & Lights If riding at night, add reflectors and lights so you can see, and others can see you. A small headlight can also double as a flashlight (torch). Flashing tail-lights are cheap and effective.

Pannier Racks It's worth buying good pannier racks. The best are aluminium racks made by Blackburn. They're also the most expensive, but come with a lifetime guarantee. Front racks come in low-mounting and mountain-bike styles. Low-mounting racks carry the weight lower, which improves the handling of the bike, but if you're touring off-road it is a better idea to carry your gear a bit higher.

Panniers Panniers (see p86) range from cheap-and-nasty to expensive top-quality waterproof bags. Get panniers that fit securely to your rack and watch that the pockets don't swing into your spokes.

Cycle Computer Directions for rides in this book rely upon accurate distance readings, so you'll need a reliable cycle computer.

Other Accessories A good pump is essential. Make sure it fits your valve type (see p74). Some clip on to your bicycle frame, while others fit 'inside' the frame. Also carry a lock. Although heavy, U- or D-locks are the most secure; cable locks can be more versatile.

Riding Position Set Up

Cycling is meant to be a pleasurable pursuit, but that isn't likely if the bike you're riding isn't the correct size for you and isn't set up for your needs.

In this section we assume your bike shop did a good job of providing you with the correct size bike (if you're borrowing a bike get a bike shop to check it is the correct size for you) and concentrate on setting you up in your ideal position and showing you how to tweak the comfort factor. If you are concerned that your bike frame is too big or small for your needs get a second opinion from another bike shop.

The following techniques for determining correct fit are based on averages and may not work for your body type. If you are an unusual size or shape get your bike shop to create your riding position.

Saddle Height & Position

Saddles are essential to riding position and comfort. If a saddle is poorly adjusted it can be a royal pain in the derriere – and legs, arms and back. In addition to saddle height, it is also possible to alter a saddle's tilt and its fore/aft position – each affects your riding position differently.

Saddle Tilt Saddles are designed to be level to the ground, taking most of the weight off your arms and back. However, since triathletes started dropping the nose of their saddles in the mid-1980s many other cyclists have followed suit without knowing why. For some body types, a slight tilt of the nose might be necessary. Be aware, however, that forward tilt will place extra strain on your arms and back. If it is tilted too far forward, chances are your saddle is too high.

Fore/Aft Position The default setting for fore/aft saddle position will allow you to run a plumb bob from the centre of your forward pedal axle to the protrusion of your knee (that bit of bone just under your knee cap).

Fore/Aft Position: To check it, sit on your bike with the pedals in the three and nine o'clock positions. Check the alignment with a plumb bob (a weight on the end of a piece of string).

Saddle Height The simplest method of roughly determining the correct saddle height is the straight leg method. Sit on your bike wearing your cycling shoes. Line one crank up with the seat-tube and place your heel on the pedal. Adjust the saddle height until your leg is almost straight, but not straining. When you've fixed the height of your saddle pedal the cranks backwards (do it next to a wall so you can balance yourself). If you are rocking from side to side, lower the saddle slightly. Otherwise keep raising the saddle (slightly) until on the verge of rocking.

The most accurate way of determining saddle height is the Hodges Method. Developed by US cycling coach Mark Hodges after studying the position of dozens of racing cyclists, the method is also applicable to touring cyclists.

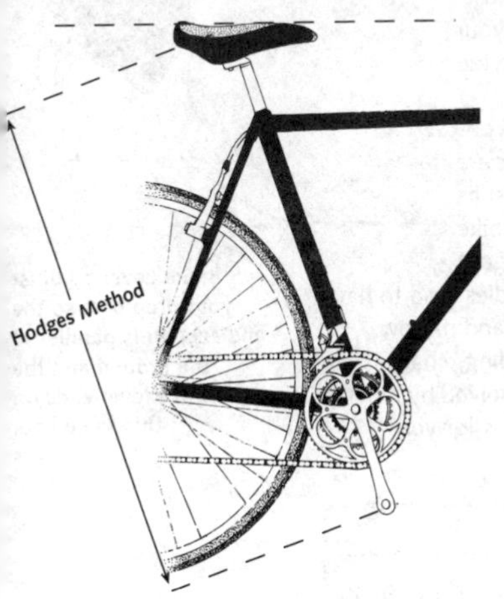

Standing barefoot with your back against a wall and your feet 15cm apart, get a friend to measure from the greater trochanter (the bump of your hip) to the floor passing over your knee and ankle joints. Measure each leg (in mm) three times and average the figure. Multiply the average figure by 0.96.

Now add the thickness of your shoe sole and your cleats (if they aren't recessed). This total is the distance you need from the center of your pedal axle to the top of your saddle. It is the optimum position for your body to pedal efficiently and should not be exceeded; however, people with small feet for their size should lower the saddle height slightly. The inverse applies for people with disproportionately large feet.

If you need to raise your saddle significantly do it over a few weeks so your muscles can adapt gradually. (Never raise your saddle above the maximum extension line marked on your seat post.)

Handlebars & Brake Levers

Racing cyclists lower their handlebars to cheat the wind and get a better aerodynamic position. While this might be tempting on windy days it doesn't make for comfortable touring. Ideally, the bars should be no higher than the saddle (even on mountain bikes) and certainly no lower than 75mm below it.

Pedals

For comfort and the best transference of power, the ball of your foot should be aligned over the center of the pedal axle (see right).

If using clipless pedals consider the amount of lateral movement available. Our feet have a natural angle that they prefer when we walk, run or cycle. If they are unable to achieve this position the knee joint's alignment will be affected and serious injury may result. Most clipless pedal systems now have some rotational freedom (called 'float') built in to allow for this, but it is still important to adjust the cleats to each foot's natural angle.

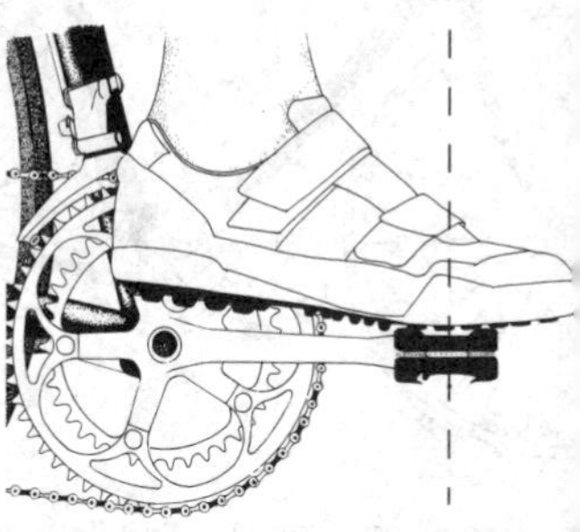

Pedal Alignment: The ball of your foot should be over the center of the pedal axle for comfort and the best transfer of power.

Comfort Considerations

Now that you have your optimum position on the bike, there are several components that you can adjust to increase the comfort factor.

Handlebars come in a variety of types and sizes. People with small hands may find shallow drop bars more comfortable. Handlebars also come in a variety of widths, so if they're too wide or narrow change them.

With mountain bike handlebars you really only have one hand position, so add a pair of bar-ends. On drop bars the ends should be parallel to the ground. If they're pointed up it probably means you need a longer stem; pointed down probably means you need a shorter stem.

On mountain bikes the **brake levers** should be adjusted to ensure your wrist is straight – it's the position your hand naturally sits in. For drop bars the bottom of the lever should end on the same line as the end section.

Getting the right **saddle** for you is one of the key considerations for enjoyable cycling. Everybody's sit bones are shaped and spaced differently, meaning a saddle that suits your best friend might be agony for you. A good bike shop will allow you to keep changing a new (undamaged) saddle until you get one that's perfect. Women's saddles tend to have a shorter nose and a wider seat, and men's are long and narrow.

If you feel too stretched out or cramped when riding, chances are you need a different length **stem** – the problem isn't solved by moving your saddle forward/aft. Get a bike shop to assess this for you.

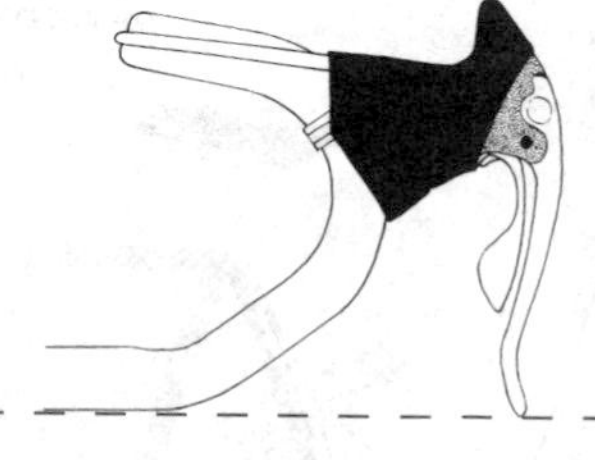

Brake Levers: Adjust your drop bars so the end section is parallel to the ground and the brake lever ends on this same line.

Record Your Position

When you've created your ideal position, mark each part's position (scratch a line with a sharp tool like a scribe or use tape) and record it, so you can recreate it if hiring a bike or when reassembling your bike after travel. The inside back cover of this book has a place to record all this vital data.

MAINTAINING YOUR BICYCLE

If you're new to cycling or haven't previously maintained your bike, this section is for you. It won't teach you how to be a top-notch mechanic, but it will help you maintain your bike in good working order and show you how to fix the most common touring problems.

If you go mountain biking it is crucial you carry spares and a tool kit and know how to maintain your bike, because if anything goes wrong it's likely you'll be miles from anywhere when trouble strikes and face a long walk home.

If you want to know more about maintaining your bike there are dozens of books available (*Richard's 21st-Century Bicycle Book*, by Richard Ballantine, is a classic; if you want to know absolutely everything get *Sutherland's Handbook for Bicycle Mechanics*) or inquire at your bike shop about courses in your area.

Predeparture & Daily Inspections

Before going on tour get your bike serviced by a bike shop or do it yourself. On tour, check over your bike every day or so (see the boxed text 'Predeparture & Post-Ride Checks' on p77).

Spares & Tool Kit

Touring cyclists need to be self-sufficient and should carry some spares and, at least, a basic tool kit. How many spares/tools you will need depends on the country you are touring in – in countries where bike shops aren't common and the towns are further spread out you may want to add to the following.

Multi-tools (see right) are very handy and a great way to save space and weight, and there are dozens of different ones on the market. Before you buy a multi-tool though, check each of the tools is usable – a chain breaker, for example, needs to have a good handle for leverage otherwise it is useless.

Adjustable wrenches are often handy, but the trade-off is that they can easily burr bolts if not used correctly – be careful when using them.

The bare minimum:

- ☐ pump – ensure it has the correct valve fitting for your tires
- ☐ water bottles (2)
- ☐ spare tubes (2)
- ☐ tire levers (2)
- ☐ chain lube and a rag
- ☐ puncture repair kit (check the glue is OK)
- ☐ Allen wrenches to fit your bike
- ☐ small Phillips screwdriver
- ☐ small flat screwdriver
- ☐ spare brake pads
- ☐ spare screws and bolts (for pannier racks, seat post etc) and chain links (2)

For those who know what they're doing:

- ☐ spoke key
- ☐ spare spokes and nipples (8)
- ☐ tools to remove freewheel
- ☐ chain breaker
- ☐ pliers
- ☐ spare chain links (HyperGlide chain rivet if you have a Shimano chain)
- ☐ spare rear brake and rear gear cables

Always handy to take along:

- ☐ roll of electrical/gaffer tape
- ☐ nylon ties (10) – various lengths/sizes
- ☐ hand cleaner (store it in a film canister)

Fixing a Flat

Flats happen. And if you're a believer in Murphy's Law then the likely scenario is that you'll suffer a flat just as you're rushing to the next town to catch a train or beat the setting sun.

Don't worry – this isn't a big drama. If you're prepared and know what you're doing you can be up and on your way in five minutes flat.

Being prepared means carrying a spare tube, a pump and at least two tire levers. If you're not carrying a spare tube, of course, you can stop and fix the puncture then and there, but it's unlikely you'll catch that train and you could end up doing all this in the dark. There will be days when you have the time to fix a puncture on the side of the road, but not always. Carry at least two spare tubes.

1 Take the wheel off the bike. Remove the valve cap and unscrew the locknut (hex nut at base; see Valve Types) on Presta valves. Deflate the tire completely, if it isn't already.

2 Make sure the tire and tube are loose on the rim – moisture and the pressure of the inflated tube often makes the tire and tube fuse with the rim.

3 If the tire is really loose you should be able to remove it with your hands. Otherwise you'll need to lift one side of the tire over the rim with the tire levers. Pushing the tire away from the lever as you insert it should ensure you don't pinch the tube and puncture it again.

4 When you have one side of the tire off, you'll be able to remove the tube. Before inserting the replacement tube, carefully inspect the tire (inside and out); you're looking for what caused the puncture. If you find anything embedded in the tire, remove it. Also check that the rim tape is still in

Valve Types

The two most common valve types are Presta (sometimes called French) and Schraeder (American). To inflate a Presta valve, first unscrew the round nut at the top (and do it up again after you're done); depress it to deflate. To deflate Schraeder valves depress the pin (inside the top). Ensure your pump is set up for the valve type on your bike.

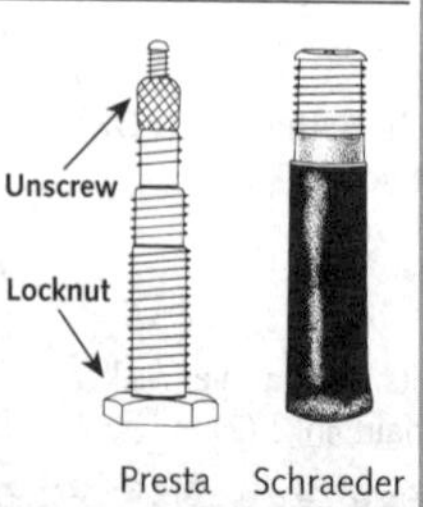

place and no spoke nipples (see pp82–3) protrude through it.

5 Time to put the new tube in. Start by partially pumping up the tube (this helps prevent it twisting or being pinched) and insert the valve in the hole in the rim. Tuck the rest of the tube in under the tire, making sure you don't twist it. Make sure the valve is straight – most Presta valves come with a locknut to help achieve this.

6 Work the tire back onto the rim with your fingers. If this isn't possible, and again, according to Murphy's Law, it frequently isn't, you might need to use your tire levers for the last 20–30cm. If you need to use the levers, make sure you don't pinch the new tube, otherwise it's back to Step 1. All you need to do now is pump up the tire and put the wheel back on the bike. Don't forget to fix the puncture that night.

Fixing the Puncture

To fix the puncture you'll need a repair kit, which usually comes with glue, patches, sandpaper and, sometimes, chalk. (Always check the glue in your puncture repair kit hasn't dried up before heading off on tour.) The only other thing you'll need is clean hands.

1. The first step is to find the puncture. Inflate the tube and hold it up to your ear. If you can hear the puncture, mark it with the chalk; otherwise immerse it in water and watch for air bubbles. Once you find the puncture, mark it, cover it with your finger and continue looking – just in case there are more.

2. Dry the tube and lightly roughen the area around the hole with the sandpaper. Sand an area larger than the patch.

3. Follow the instructions for the glue you have. Generally you spread an even layer of glue over the area of the tube to be patched and allow it to dry until it is tacky.

4. Patches also come with their own instructions – some will be just a piece of rubber and others will come lined with foil (remove the foil on the underside but don't touch the exposed area). Press the patch firmly onto the area over the hole and hold it for two to three minutes. If you want, remove the excess glue from around the patch or dust it with chalk or simply let it dry.

5. Leave the glue to set for 10–20 minutes. Inflate the tube and check the patch has worked.

Chains

Chains are dirty, greasy and all too often the most neglected piece of equipment on a bike. There are about 120 or so links in a chain and each has a simple but precise arrangement of bushes, bearings and plates. Over time all chains stretch, but if dirt gets between the bushes and bearings this 'aging' will happen prematurely and will likely damage the teeth of your chainrings, sprockets and derailleur guide pulleys.

To prevent this, chains should be cleaned and lubed frequently (see your bike shop for the best products to use).

No matter how well you look after a chain it should be replaced regularly – about every 3000–5000mi. Seek the advice of a bike shop to ensure you are buying the correct type for your drivetrain (the moving parts that combine to drive the bicycle: chain, freewheel, derailleurs, chainwheel and bottom bracket).

If you do enough cycling you'll need to replace a chain (or fix a broken chain), so here's how to use that funky-looking tool, the chain breaker.

1 Remove the chain from the chainrings – it'll make the whole process easier. Place the chain in the chain breaker (on the outer slots; it braces the link plates as the rivet is driven out) and line the pin of the chain breaker up with the rivet.

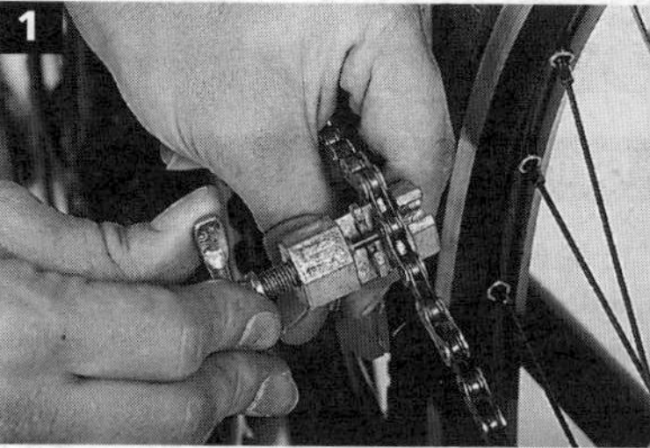

2 Wind the handle until the rivet is clear of the inner link but still held by the outer link plate.

3 Flex the chain to 'break' it. If it won't, you'll need to push the rivet out some more, but not completely – if you push it all the way out, you'll have to remove two links and replace them with two spare links. If you're removing links, you'll need to remove a male and female link (ie, two links).

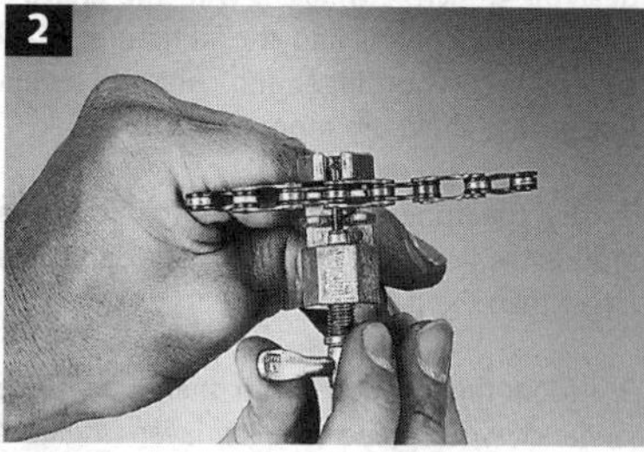

4 Rejoining the chain is the reverse. If you turn the chain around when putting it on you will still have the rivet facing you. Otherwise it will be facing away from you and you'll need to change to the other side of the bike and work through the spokes.

Join the chain up by hand and place it in the breaker. Now drive the rivet in firmly, making sure it is properly lined up with the hole of the outer link plate. Stop when the rivet is almost in place.

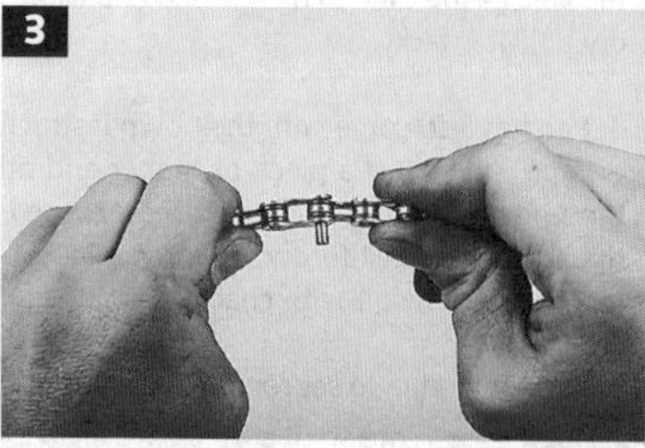

5 Move the chain to the spreaders (inner slots) of the chain breaker. Finish by winding the rivet into position carefully (check that the head of the rivet is raised the same distance above the link plate as the rivets beside it). If you've managed to get it in perfectly and the link isn't 'stiff', well done!

5

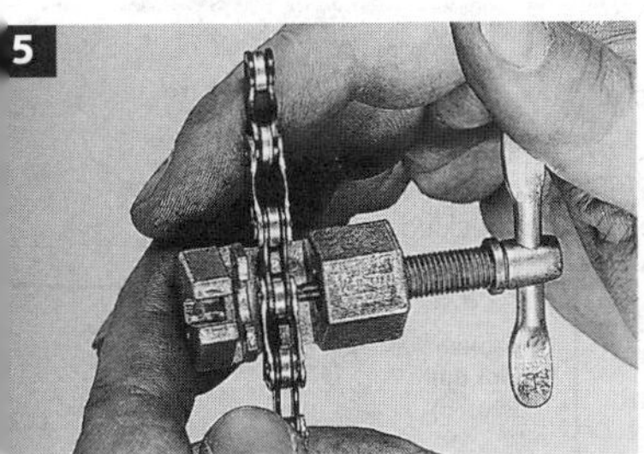

Otherwise, move the chain to the spreaders on the chain breaker and gently work the chain laterally until the link is no longer stiff.

If this doesn't work (and with some chain breakers it won't), take the chain out of the tool and place a screwdriver or Allen wrench between the outer plates of the stiff link and carefully lever the plates both ways. If you're too forceful you'll really break the chain, but if you're subtle it will free the link up and you'll be on your way.

Chain Options

Check your chain; if you have a Shimano HyperGlide chain you'll need a special HyperGlide chain rivet to rejoin the chain. This will be supplied with your new chain, but carry a spare.

Another option is to fit a universal link to your chain. This link uses a special clip to join the chain – like the chains of old. You'll still need a chain breaker to fix a broken chain or take out spare links.

Predeparture & Post-Ride Checks

Each day before you get on your bike and each evening after you've stopped riding, give your bike a quick once-over. Following these checks will ensure you're properly maintaining your bike and will help identify any problems before they become disasters. Go to the nearest bike shop if you don't know how to fix any problem.

Predeparture Check List

- ☐ brakes – are they stopping you? If not, adjust them.
- ☐ chain – if it was squeaking yesterday, it needs lube.
- ☐ panniers – are they all secured and fastened?
- ☐ cycle computer – reset your trip distance at the start.
- ☐ gears – are they changing properly? If not, adjust them.
- ☐ tires – check your tire pressure is correct (see the tire's side wall for the maximum psi); inflate, if necessary.

Post-Ride Check List

- ☐ pannier racks – check all bolts/screws are tightened; do a visual check of each rack (the welds, in particular) looking for small cracks.
- ☐ headset – when stationary, apply the front brake and rock the bike gently; if there is any movement or noise, chances are the headset is loose.
- ☐ wheels – visually check the tires for sidewall cuts/wear and any embedded objects; check the wheels are still true and no spokes are broken.
- ☐ wrench test – wrench (pull) on the saddle (if it moves, tighten the seat-post bolt and/or the seat-clamp bolt, underneath); wrench laterally on a crank (if it moves, check the bottom bracket).

Brakes

Adjusting the brakes of your bike is not complicated and even though your bike shop will use several tools to do the job, all you really need is a pair of pliers, a wrench or Allen wrench, and (sometimes) a friend.

Check three things before you start: the wheels are true (not buckled), the braking surface of the rims is smooth (no dirt, dents or rough patches) and the cables are not frayed.

Begin by checking that the pads strike the rim correctly: flush on the braking surface of the rim (see right and p79) and parallel to the ground.

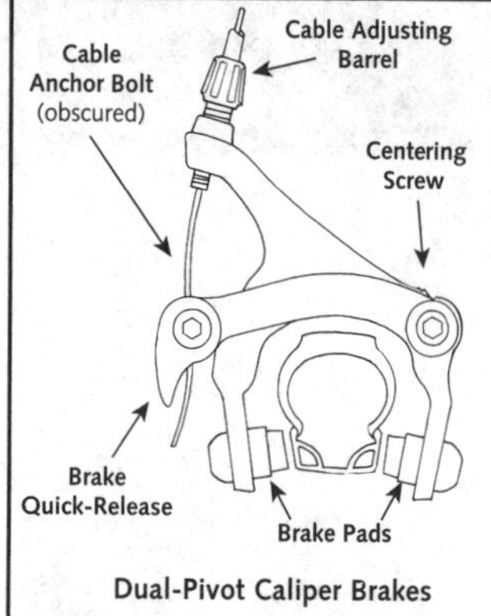

Dual-Pivot Caliper Brakes

Caliper Brakes

It's likely that you'll be able to make any minor adjustments to caliper brakes by winding the cable adjusting barrel out. If it doesn't allow enough movement you'll need to adjust the cable anchor bolt:

1 Undo the cable anchor bolt – not completely, just so the cable is free to move – and turn the cable adjusting barrel all the way in.

2 Get your friend to hold the calipers in the desired position, about 2–3mm away from the rim. Using a pair of pliers, pull the cable through until it is taut.

3 Before you tighten the cable anchor bolt again, check to see if the brake lever is in its normal position (not slack as if somebody was applying it) – sometimes they jam open. Also, ensure the brake quick-release (use it when you're removing your wheel or in an emergency to open the calipers if your wheel is badly buckled) is closed.

4 Tighten the cable anchor bolt again. Make any fine-tuning to the brakes by winding the cable adjusting barrel out.

Brake Cables

If your brakes are particularly hard to apply, you may need to replace the cables. Moisture can cause the cable and housing (outer casing) to bond or stick. If this happens it's often possible to prolong the life of a cable by removing it from the housing and applying a coating of grease (or chain lube) to it.

If you do need to replace the cable, take your bike to a bike shop and get the staff to fit and/or supply the new cable. Cables come in two sizes – rear (long) and front (short) – various thicknesses and with different types of nipples.

Cantilever Brakes

These days most touring bikes have cantilever rather than caliper brakes. The newest generation of cantilever brakes (V-brakes) are more powerful and better suited to stopping bikes with heavy loads.

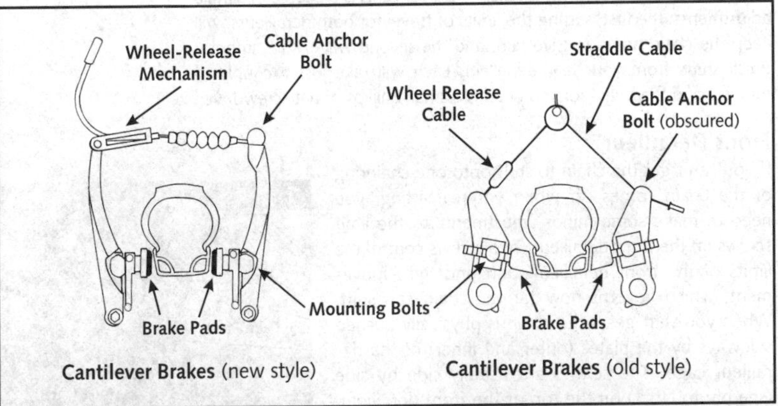

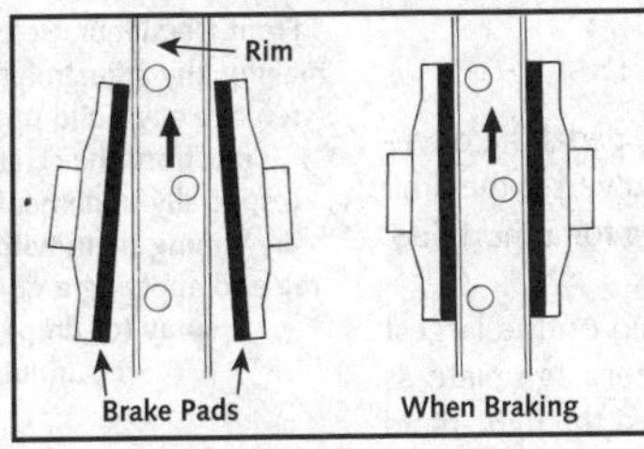

Cantilever Brake Toe-In: This is how the brake pads should strike the rim (from above) with correct toe-in.

On cantilever brakes ensure the leading edge of the brake pad hits the rim first (see left). This is called toe-in; it makes the brakes more efficient and prevents squealing. To adjust the toe-in on cantilever brakes, loosen the brake pad's mounting bolt (using a 10mm wrench and 5mm Allen wrench). Wiggle the brake pad into position and tighten the bolt again.

If you only need to make a minor adjustment to the distance of the pads from the rim, chances are you will be able to do it by winding the cable adjusting barrel out (located near the brake lever on mountain bikes and hybrids). If this won't do you'll need to adjust the cable anchor bolt:

1 Undo the cable anchor bolt (not completely, just so the cable is free to move) and turn the cable adjusting barrel all the way in. Depending on the style of your brakes, you may need a 10mm wrench (older bikes) or a 5mm Allen wrench.

2 Hold the cantilevers in the desired position (get assistance from a friend if you need to), positioning the brake pads 2–3mm away from the rim. Using a pair of pliers, pull the cable through until it is taut.

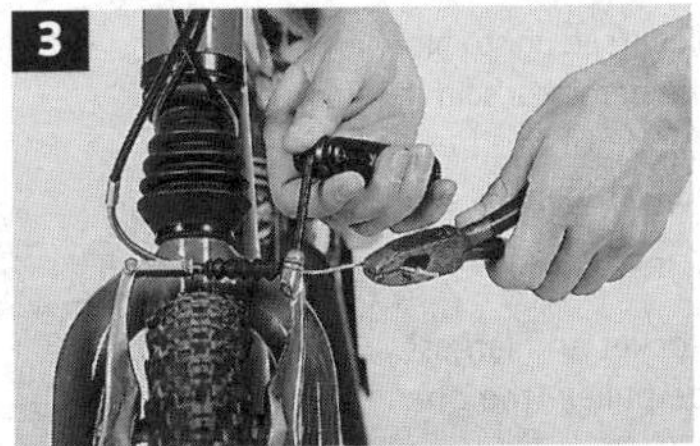

3 Before you tighten the cable anchor bolt again, check to see if the brake lever is in its normal position (not slack as if somebody was applying it) – sometimes they jam open.

4 Tighten the cable anchor bolt again. Make any fine-tuning to the brakes by winding the cable adjusting barrel out.

Gears

If the gears on your bike start playing up – the chain falls off the chainrings, it shifts slowly or not at all – it's bound to cause frustration and could damage your bike. All it takes to prevent this is a couple of simple adjustments: the first, setting the limits of travel for both derailleurs, will keep the chain on your drivetrain, and the second will ensure smooth, quick shifts from your rear derailleur. Each will take just a couple of minutes and the only tool you need is a small Phillips or flat screwdriver.

Front Derailleur

If you can't get the chain to shift onto one chainring or the chain comes off when you're shifting, you need to make some minor adjustments to the limit screws on the front derailleur. Two screws control the limits of the front derailleur's left and right movement, which governs how far the chain can shift. When you shift gears the chain is physically pushed sideways by the plates (outer and inner) of the derailleur cage. The screws are usually side by side (see photo No 1) on the top of the front derailleur. The left-hand screw (as you sit on the bike) adjusts the inside limit and the one on the right adjusts the outside limit.

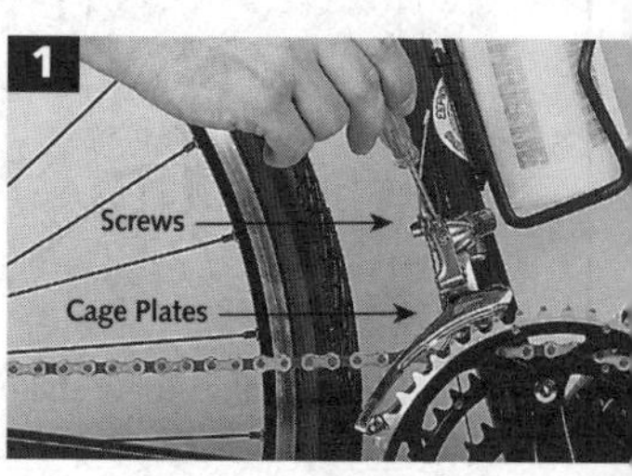

Front Derailleur: Before making any adjustments, remove any build up of grit from the screws (especially underneath) by wiping them with a rag and applying a quick spray (or drop) of chain lube.

After you make each of the following adjustments, pedal the drivetrain with your hand and change gears to ensure you've set the limit correctly. If you're satisfied, test it under strain by going for a short ride.

Outer Limits Change the gears to position the chain on the largest chainring and the smallest rear sprocket. Set the outer cage plate as close to the chain as you can without it touching. Adjust the right-hand limit screw to achieve this.

Inner Limits Position the chain on the smallest chainring and the largest rear sprocket. For chainwheels with three chainrings, position the inner cage plate between 1–2mm from the chain. If you have a chainwheel with two chainrings, position the inner cage plate as close to the chain as you can without it touching.

Rear Derailleur

If the limit screws aren't set correctly on the rear derailleur the consequences can be dire. If the chain slips off the largest sprocket it can jam between the sprocket and the spokes and could then snap the chain, break or damage spokes or even break the frame.

The limit screws are located at the back of the derailleur (see photo No 2). The top screw (marked 'H' on the derailleur) sets the derailleur's limit of travel on the smallest sprocket's (the highest gear) side of the freewheel. The bottom screw ('L') adjusts the derailleur's travel towards the largest sprocket (lowest gear).

Outer Limits Position the chain on the smallest sprocket and largest chainring (see photo No 3). The derailleur's top guide pulley (the one

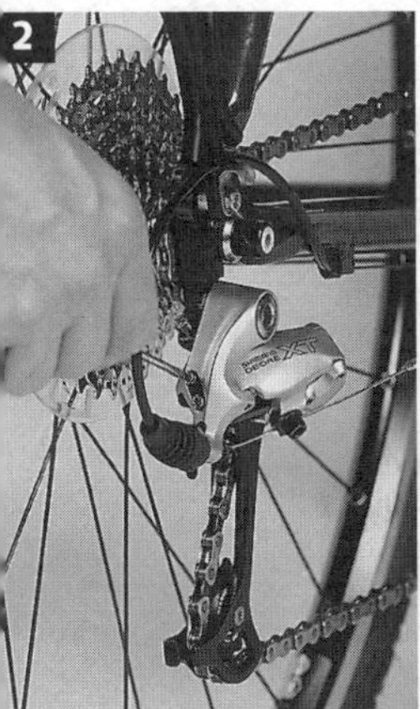

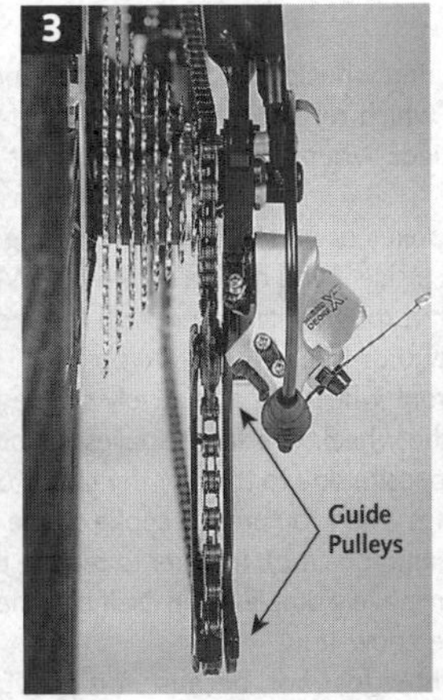

closest to the sprockets) should be in line with the smallest sprocket; adjust the top screw ('H') to ensure it is.

Inner Limits Position the chain on the largest rear sprocket and the smallest chainring (see photo No 4). This time the guide pulley needs to be lined up with the largest sprocket; do this by adjusting the bottom screw ('L'). Make sure the chain can't move any further towards the wheel than the largest sprocket.

Cable Adjusting Barrel

If your gears are bouncing up and down your freewheel in a constant click and chatter, you need to adjust the tension of the cable to the rear derailleur. This can be achieved in a variety of ways, depending on your gear system.

The main cable adjusting barrel is on your rear derailleur (see photo No 5). Secondary cable adjusting barrels can also be found near the gear levers (newer Shimano combined brake-gear STI levers) or on the downtube of your frame (older Shimano STI levers and Campagnolo Ergopower gear systems) of some bikes. Intended for racing cyclists, they allow for fine tuning of the gears' operation while on the move.

Raise the rear wheel off the ground – have a friend hold it up by the saddle, hang it from a tree or turn the bike upside down – so you can pedal the drivetrain with your hand.

To reset your derailleur, shift gears to position the chain on the second smallest sprocket and middle chainring (see photo No 6). As you turn the crank with your hand, tighten the cable by winding the rear derailleur's cable adjusting barrel counterclockwise. Just before the chain starts to make a noise as if to shift onto the third sprocket, stop winding.

Now pedal the drivetrain and change the gears up and down the freewheel. If things still aren't right you may find that you need to tweak the cable tension slightly: turn the cable adjusting barrel counterclockwise if shifts to larger sprockets are slow, and clockwise if shifts to smaller sprockets hesitate.

Replacing a Spoke

Even the best purpose-made touring wheels occasionally break spokes. When this happens the wheel, which relies on the even pull of each spoke, is likely to become buckled. When it is not buckled, it is considered true.

If you've forgotten to pack spokes or you grabbed the wrong size, you can still get yourself out of a pickle if you have a spoke key. Wheels are very flexible and you can get it roughly true – enough to take you to the next bike shop – even if two or three spokes are broken.

If you break a spoke on the front wheel it is a relatively simple thing to replace the spoke and retrue the wheel. The same applies if a broken spoke is on the non-drive side (opposite side to the rear derailleur) of the rear wheel. The complication comes when you break a spoke on the drive side of the rear wheel (the most common case). In order to replace it you need to remove the freewheel, a relatively simple job in itself but one that requires a few more tools and the know-how.

If you don't have that know-how fear not, because it is possible to retrue the wheel without replacing that spoke *and* without damaging the wheel – see Truing a Wheel (below).

1 Remove the wheel from the bike. It's probably a good idea to remove the tire and tube as well (though not essential), just to make sure the nipple is seated properly in the rim and not likely to cause a puncture.

2 Remove the broken spoke but leave the nipple in the rim (if you think it's not damaged; otherwise replace it). Now you need to thread the new spoke. Start by threading it through the vacant hole on the hub flange. Next lace the new spoke through the other spokes. Spokes are offset on the rim; every second one is on the same side and, generally, every fourth is laced through the other spokes the same way.

3 With the spoke key, tighten the nipple until the spoke is about as taut as the other spokes on this side of the rim. Spoke nipples have four flat sides – to adjust them you'll need the correct size spoke key. Spoke keys come in two types: those made to fit one spoke gauge or several. If you have the latter, trial each size on a nipple until you find the perfect fit.

Truing a Wheel

Truing a wheel is an art form and, like all art forms, it is not something mastered overnight. If you can, practise with an old wheel before leaving home. If that's not possible – and you're on the side of the road as you read this – following these guidelines will get you back in the saddle until you can get to the next bike shop.

1 Start by turning the bike upside-down, so the wheels can turn freely. Check the tension of all the spokes on the wheel: do this by

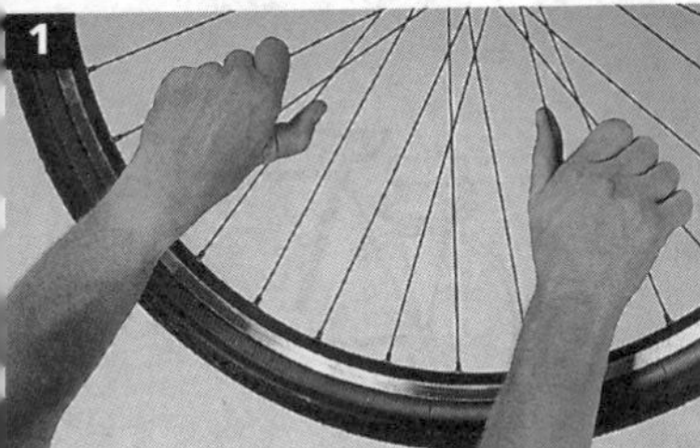

squeezing each pair of spokes on each side. Tighten those spokes that seem loose and loosen those that seem too tight. Note, though, the spokes on the drive side of the rear wheel (on the same side as the freewheel) are deliberately tighter than the non-drive side.

2 Rotate the wheel a couple of times to get an idea of the job at hand. If the wheel won't rotate, let the brakes off (see pp78–9).

3 Using the chalk from your puncture repair kit, mark all the 'bumps'. Keep the chalk in the same position (brace the chalk against the pannier rack or bike's frame) and let the bumps in the wheel 'hit' the chalk.

4 In order to get the bumps out you'll need a constant point of reference – to gauge if the bumps are being removed. Often, if it is not a severe buckle, you can use a brake pad. Position the brake pad about 2–3mm from the rim (on the side with the biggest buckle).

5 With your spoke key, loosen those spokes on the same side as the bump within the longest chalked area, and tighten those on the opposite side of the rim. The spokes at the start and the finish of the chalked area should only be tightened/loosened by a quarter-turn; apply a half-turn to those in between.

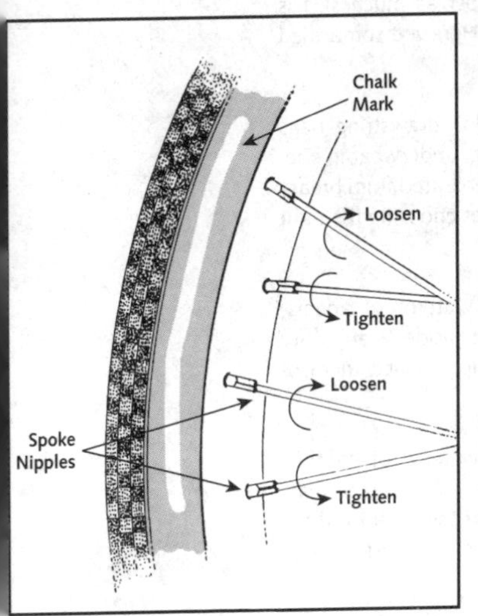

6 Rotate the wheel again; if you're doing it correctly the buckle should not be as great. Continue this process of tightening and loosening spokes until the bump is as near to gone as you can get it – as the bump is removed turn the nipples less (one-eighth of a turn on the ends and a quarter-turn in between). Experienced exponents can remove buckles entirely, but if you can get it almost out (1mm here or there) you've done well.

7 If the wheel has more than one bump, move onto the second-longest chalk mark next. As each bump is removed you might find it affects the previous bump slightly. In this case, remove the previous chalk mark and repeat Steps 4–6. Continue to do this until all the buckles are removed.

Don't forget to readjust the brakes.

If you've trued the wheel without replacing the broken spokes, have them replaced at the next bike shop.

Loading Your Bicycle

If you've ever been to Asia and seen a bike loaded with boxes piled 6ft high or carrying four, five or six people, plus a chicken or two, you'll realize that there are more ways to carry your gear than would otherwise seem. More realistic options for you come from a combination of front and rear panniers, a handlebar bag or trailer.

'Credit-card tourists', who are intent on traveling lighter, further and faster and who are happy to stay in hotels or hostels, can get by with a handlebar bag and rack pack or rear panniers (see top right). The downside to this configuration is poor bike-handling; the steering feels particularly 'airy'. It's possible to adopt the 'lighter, further, faster' principle and still camp, but it means frugal packing.

If you want to be more self-sufficient or you're carrying 45lb or more, you'll probably find it easier (and your bike will handle better) with front and rear panniers. The tried-and-tested configuration that works best for a touring bike is to use four panniers: two low-mounting front panniers with two high-mounting rear panniers (see bottom right). The only other thing you might want to add is a small handlebar bag for this book, snacks, sunblock, money, camera etc.

Pannier Configurations: the four pannier system is the best way of carrying your gear and having a bike that handles well; packing light saves weight but the compromise is poor bike handling.

This combination, with a few light but bulky items on the rear rack (eg, tent, sleeping mat etc), allows you to carry a large load and still have predictable and manageable bike handling.

If you're riding a mountain bike and riding off-road you'll probably want high-mounting front panniers to give you more clearance.

Packing Your Gear

It's frequently said that, in packing for a cycle tour, you should lay out everything you need to take and then leave half of it behind. The skill is in knowing which half to leave behind. Almost as much skill is needed in organizing the gear in your panniers. Here are some tried and tested tips.

Compartmentalize Pack similar items into nylon drawstring bags (stuff sacks), to make them easier to find again (eg, underwear in one, cycling clothes in another, and even dinner food separated from breakfast food). Using different colored stuff sacks makes choosing the right one easier.

Waterproof Even if your panniers are completely waterproof, and especially if they're not, it pays to put everything inside heavy-duty plastic bags. Check bags for holes during the trip; replace them or patch the holes with tape.

Reduce Flood Damage If your panniers are not waterproof and they pool water, you can reduce problems by putting things that are unaffected by water, say a pair of flip-flops (thongs), at the bottom of the bag. This keeps the other stuff above 'flood level'. Try using seam sealant on the bags' seams beforehand, too.

Load Consistently Put things in the same place each time you pack to avoid having to unpack every bag just to find one item.

Balance the Load Distribute weight evenly – generally around 60% in the rear and 40% in the front panniers – and keep it as low as possible by using low-mounting front panniers and packing heavy items first. Side-to-side balancing is just as critical.

Group Gear Pack things used at the same time in the same pannier. Night/camp things like your mat, sleeping bag and pajamas, which you don't need during the day, could all be in the bag most difficult to access – likely to be on the same side as the side of the road you are riding on, since you will probably lean that side of the bike against a tree, pole or roadside barrier.

Put all clothing in one pannier, if possible, sorted into separate bags of cycling clothes, 'civilian' clothes, underwear, wet weather gear and dirty clothes. Keep a windproof jacket handy on top for descents.

In the Front Food and eating utensils are convenient to have in a front pannier along with a camping stove. Toiletry items, towel, first-aid kit, reading material, flashlight and sundry items can go in the other front bag.

In the Pockets or Bar Bag Easily accessible pockets on panniers or on your cycling shirt are useful for items likely to be needed frequently or urgently during the day, such as snacks, tool kit, sun hat or sunscreen. A handlebar bag is good for these items if your panniers don't have pockets, but remember that weight on the handlebars upsets a bike's handling.

Keep Space Spare Remember to leave some spare space for food and, if using a Camping Gaz stove or the like, for the fuel canister. Be mindful when packing foods that are squashable or sensitive to heat

Another Option – Trailers

Luggage trailers are gaining in popularity and some innovative designs are now on the market. By spreading the load onto more wheels they relieve the bike and can improve rolling resistance. Their extra capacity is a boon for traveling on a tandem or with a young family. They can be combined with racks and panniers, but the hitch (the point where it connects with the bike) of some trailers may interfere with your panniers, so check first.

PETER HINES

Two-wheeled trailers are free standing and can take very heavy loads, including babies and toddlers. Often brightly colored, they give a strong signal to car drivers who tend to give you a wide berth. However, their relatively wide track can catch a lot of wind and makes them ungainly on rough, narrow roads or trails.

Single-wheeled trailers such as the BOB Yak share the load with the bike's rear wheel. They track well and can be used on very rough trails and may be the easiest option for full-suspension bikes. The load capacity of these units is somewhere between that of a bike with a rear rack only and a fully loaded (four panniers plus rack-top luggage) touring bike.

and protect or insulate them – unless you're working on a gourmet pasta sauce recipe that includes socks.

Prevent 'Internal Bleeding' Act on the premise that anything that can spill will, and transfer it to a reliable container, preferably within a watertight bag. Take care, too, in packing hard or sharp objects (tools, utensils or anything with hooks) that could rub or puncture other items, including the panniers. Knives or tools with folding working parts are desirable.

Fragile Goods Valuables and delicate equipment like cameras are best carried in a handlebar bag, which can be easily removed when you stop. Alternatively, carry these items in a fanny pack (bum bag) which will accompany you automatically.

Rack Top Strap your tent lengthways on top of the rear rack with elastic cord looped diagonally across from front to rear and back again, and maybe a third short one across to anchor the rear end. Be sure the cords are well-tensioned and secure – deny their kamikaze impulses to plunge into the back wheel, jamming the freewheel mechanism, or worse.

What to Look for in Panniers

Panniers remain the popular choice for touring luggage. They offer flexibility, in that one, two or four can be used depending on the load to be carried, and they allow luggage to be arranged for easy access.

Many people buy a rear rack and panniers initially, and it is wise to buy the best quality you can afford at this stage. These bags will accompany you on all of your tours as well as day-to-day shopping and commuting trips for years to come.

The attachment system should be secure, but simple to operate. That big bump you hit at 30mph can launch a poorly designed pannier and your precious luggage.

The stiffness of the pannier backing is another concern – if it can flex far enough to reach the spokes of the wheel the result can be catastrophic. Good rack design can also help avoid this.

The fabric of the panniers should be strong and abrasion- and water-resistant. You can now buy roll-top panniers, made from laminated fabrics, that are completely waterproof. Bear in mind that these bags are only waterproof until they develop even the smallest hole, so be prepared to check them and apply patches occasionally. Canvas bags shed water well, but should be used in conjunction with a liner bag to keep things dry. Cordura is a heavy nylon fabric with excellent abrasion resistance. The fabric itself is initially waterproof, but water tends to find the seams, so using a liner bag is a good idea once again.

Pockets and compartments can help to organize your load, but the multitude of seams increase the challenge of keeping the contents dry in the wet. A couple of exterior pockets are great for sunblock, snacks and loose change that you need throughout the day. Carrying front panniers as well as rear ones allows more opportunities to divide and organize gear.

When fitting rear panniers check for heel strike. Long feet, long cranks and short chainstays will all make it harder to get the bags and your body to fit.

Getting There & Away

AIR

Whether coming from elsewhere in the USA or from abroad, the fastest way to get to the West Coast is by air. US domestic airfares vary tremendously depending on the season, the day of the week, the length of your stay and the flexibility of the ticket. Nothing determines fares more than demand, and when things are slow, regardless of the season, airlines will lower their fares to fill empty seats. There's a lot of competition, and any airline could offer the cheapest fare. Expect less fluctuation with international fares.

Airports & Airlines

The region's main gateway airports for domestic and international flights are Seattle-Tacoma (Sea-Tac), San Francisco (SFO) and Los Angeles (LAX). Vancouver International Airport (YVR) is an international gateway to the Northwest, best for cyclists doing the Border to Border ride or heading to the Seattle region. Portland (PDX) and San Diego (SAN) both have an increasing number of international flights, but they are rarely the cheapest choices.

Buying Tickets

You may be able to finance an extra week of cycle-touring with the money saved by shopping around for an airline ticket. Start your research early – the cheapest tickets must be bought months ahead of time and popular flights sell out early.

You can use the Internet to hunt for low fares. Services recommended by travelers include Cheap Tickets (W www.cheaptickets.com), Travelocity (W www.travelocity.com) and Lowest Fare (W www.lowestfare.com). While some find this a convenient way to purchase budget tickets, others have reported long waits, or have found that the online services can't always match travel agencies or airlines. Many major airlines, including United (W www.ual.com), Delta (W www.delta.com) and Southwest (W www.southwest.com), offer substantial discounts for tickets purchased through their Web sites. United Airlines releases discount tickets for selected routes and dates each Wednesday, but you must first register and sign up for their Mileage Plus program (☎ 800-421-4655).

Warning

The information in this chapter is particularly vulnerable to change: prices for international travel are volatile, routes are introduced and canceled, schedules change, special deals come and go, and rules and visa requirements are amended. You should check directly with the airline or a travel agent to make sure you understand how a fare (and ticket you may buy) works.

The upshot of this is that you should get opinions, quotes and advice from as many airlines and travel agents as possible before you part with your hard-earned cash. The details given in this chapter should be regarded as pointers and are not a substitute for your own careful, up-to-date research.

Baggage Restrictions

The 2001 terrorist attacks on the USA mean airlines worldwide now impose tight restrictions on carry-on baggage. No sharp implements of any kind are allowed onto the plane – this means cyclists need to pack items such as bicycle tools, pocket knives, camping cutlery and first-aid kits into their checked luggage.

If you're planning to pack your bike at the airport, remember to disassemble it before you check your luggage – and tools!

Cyclists carrying a camping stove should remember that airlines also ban fuels (unleaded gasoline, white spirits or any flammable liquid) and gas cartridges from all baggage, both check through and carry on. Empty all fuel bottles and buy what you need at your destination.

The USA's high season is mid-June to mid-September and the weeks around Thanksgiving and Christmas holidays. The best rates are found November through March.

Cheaper tickets are available in two categories: official and unofficial. Official ones have a variety of names, including advance-purchase fares, budget fares, Apex and super-Apex. Unofficial tickets are released by the airlines through selected travel agents. The cheapest tickets are often nonrefundable; many are also nonchangeable or charge a heavy penalty for changing your flight.

Packing for Air Travel

We've all heard the horror stories about smashed/lost luggage when flying, but a more real threat to cycle tourists is arriving in a country for a two-week tour and finding their bike with broken wheels or in little bits spread out around the baggage carousel. Fixing a damaged bike could take days, and the delay and frustration could ruin your holiday.

How do you avoid this? Err on the side of caution and box your bike. Trust airline baggage handlers if you want (we're told some people actually do) and give your bike to them 'as is' – turn the handlebars 90°, remove the pedals, cover the chain with a rag or bag (to protect other people's baggage) and deflate your tyres (partially, not all the way) – but is it worth the risk? If you want to take that sort of risk do it on your homeward flight, when you can get your favorite bike shop to fix any damage.

Some airlines sell bike boxes at the airport, but most bike shops give them away. Fitting your bike into a box requires a few simple steps and only takes about 15 minutes:

1 Loosen the stem bolt and turn the handlebars 90°; loosen the clamp bolt(s) and twist the handlebars as pictured.

2 Remove the pedals (use a 15mm wrench, turning each the opposite way to how you pedal), wheels and seat post and saddle (don't forget to mark its height before removing it).

3 Undo the rear derailleur bolt and tape it to the inside of the chainstay. There's no need to undo the derailleur cable. You can remove the chain (it will make reassembly easier) but it isn't necessary.

4 Cut up some spare cardboard and tape it beneath the chainwheel to prevent the teeth from penetrating the floor of the box and being damaged.

5 Remove the quick-release skewers from the wheels and wrap a rag (or two) around the cluster so it won't get damaged or damage anything else.

If you run your tires at very high pressure (above 100psi), you should partially deflate them – on most bikes this won't be necessary.

6 Place the frame in the box, so it rests on the chainwheel and forks – you might want to place another couple of layers of cardboard underneath the forks.

Most boxes will be too short to allow the front pannier racks to remain on the bike; if so, remove them. The rear rack should fit while still on the bike, but may require the seat stay bolts to be undone and pushed forward.

Packing for Air Travel

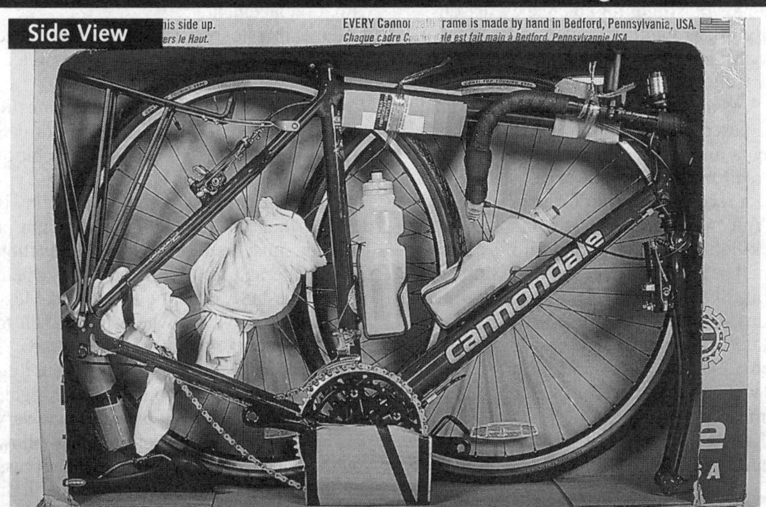

ALL PHOTOS BY JEFF CROW

7 Place the wheels beside the frame, on the side opposite the chainwheel. Keep the wheels and frame separate by inserting a piece of cardboard between them and tying the wheels to the frame (to stop them moving around and scratching the frame).

8 Slot the saddle and seat post, your helmet, tools and any other bits and pieces (eg, tent, sleeping bag) into the vacant areas. Wrap the skewers, chain and other loose bike bits in newspaper and place them in the box. Add cardboard or newspaper packing to any areas where metal is resting on metal.

9 Seal the box with tape and write your name, address and flight details on several sides.

Now all you need to do is strap your panniers together and check them in. If you don't have room to pack your helmet, take it as carry-on.

Bike Bags

If you're planning on traveling between regions via train, plane or bus then consider taking a bike bag. The simplest form of zippered bike bag has no padding built into it, is made of Cordura or nylon, and can be rolled up and put on your rear pannier rack and unfurled when you need to travel again.

Some of the smaller ones require you to remove both wheels, the front pannier racks, pedals and seat post to fit inside the bag. However, these make for (relatively) easy and inconspicuous train, plane or bus transfers so the extra effort is worthwhile.

Insurance may cover this loss if you have to change your flight for emergency reasons.

Return (roundtrip) tickets usually work out cheaper than two one-way fares – often *much* cheaper. Use the fares quoted in this book as a guide only. They are approximate and based on the rates advertised by travel agents and airlines at the time of writing. Quoted airfares do not necessarily constitute a recommendation for the carrier.

You may decide to pay more than the rock-bottom fare by opting for the safety of a better known travel agent. Established firms like STA Travel (W www.sta-travel.com), Council Travel (W www.counciltravel.com), Travel CUTS (W www.travelcuts.com) in Canada and Flight Centre (W www.flightcentre.com) offer good prices to most destinations.

Keep a photocopy of your ticket in a safe place (separate from your ticket). If the ticket is lost or stolen, this will help you with a replacement.

Remember to buy travel insurance (see Travel Insurance, p33) as early as possible.

Do the Bump

How do you receive free lodging at a five-star hotel, an $800 travel voucher and upgrade to first class on an international flight just for spending an extra 12 hours in Las Vegas?

Airlines routinely overbook and count on some passengers canceling. Occasionally, almost everybody does show, and then passengers must be 'bumped' onto another flight. Getting bumped can be a nuisance if you have a tight schedule but you can work the bump to your advantage.

When you check in, ask if the flight is full. If there is a need for 'bump' volunteers, get your name on the list. Depending on how oversold the flight is, compensation may range from a discount voucher toward your next flight to a fully paid roundtrip ticket or even cash. If you have to spend the night, airlines frequently foot the hotel bill, transportation to/from the hotel and all meals for their bumpees. You don't have to accept the airline's first offer and can haggle for a better deal (nicer hotel, car rental instead of taxi fare).

When being bumped, try to confirm a later flight so you don't get stuck on standby. During bad weather or strikes, this may be easier to negotiate by calling the airline first. The confirmation number you receive should get you a seat.

Marisa Gierlich

Visit USA Passes Almost all domestic carriers offer Visit USA passes to non-US citizens. The passes are actually a book of coupons – each coupon equals a flight. Typically, the minimum number of coupons is three or four and the maximum is eight or 10. They must be purchased in conjunction with an international airline ticket anywhere outside the USA except Canada and Mexico. Coupons cost anywhere from $100 to $160, depending on how many you buy.

Most airlines require you to plan your itinerary in advance and to complete your flights within 60 days of arrival, but rules may vary between airlines. A few airlines may allow you to use coupons on standby, in which case call the airline a day or two before the flight and make a standby reservation. This gives you priority over all other standby travelers.

Round-the-World Tickets Round-the-world (RTW) tickets can work out the same price or cheaper than an ordinary roundtrip ticket. Prices start at about UK£850, A$1800 or US$1100. These are for 'short' routes such as LA, New York, London, Bangkok, Honolulu, LA. As soon as you start adding stops south of the equator, fares can go up to the US$1600 to US$2500 range.

All the major airlines offer RTW tickets in conjunction with other international airlines and permit you to fly anywhere on their route systems as long as you don't backtrack. You may have to book the first sector in advance; cancellation penalties apply. Tickets are usually valid from 90 days up to a year. An alternative type of RTW ticket is one put together by a travel agent using a combination of discounted tickets.

Most airlines restrict the number of sectors that can be flown within the USA and Canada to four, and some airlines black out a few heavily traveled routes (like Honolulu to Tokyo), though stopovers are otherwise generally unlimited. In most cases a 14-day advance purchase is required. After the ticket is purchased, dates can be changed without penalty and tickets can be rewritten to add or delete stops for around $50 each.

Circle Pacific Tickets The tickets use several airlines to circle the Pacific – combining Australia, New Zealand, North America and Asia. These tickets allow you to swing through a variety of destinations as long as you don't backtrack. Fares, generally a little cheaper than RTW tickets, include four stopovers with the option of adding stops at $50 each. There's a 14-day advance purchase requirement, a 25% cancellation penalty and a maximum stay of six months.

Cyclists with Special Needs

If you have special needs of any sort – a broken leg, dietary restrictions, a wheelchair, a baby, fear of flying – let the airline know as soon as possible. Remind them when you reconfirm your booking (at least 72 hours before departure) and again when you check in at the airport. It may also be worth ringing around the airlines to find out how they can handle your particular needs.

With advance warning, airports and airlines can be surprisingly helpful. Most international airports can provide escorts from check-in desk to plane, and there should be ramps, lifts and accessible toilets and phones. Aircraft toilets, however, could present a problem; travelers should discuss this early with the airline.

Guide dogs often have to travel in a specially pressurized baggage compartment with other animals, away from their owners, though smaller guide dogs may be admitted to the cabin. Guide dogs are not subject to quarantine as long as they have proof of vaccination against rabies.

Deaf travelers can ask for airport and inflight announcements to be written down.

Children under two travel for 10% of the standard fare (or free, on some airlines), as long as they don't occupy a seat. (They don't get a baggage allowance.) 'Skycots' should be provided by the airline if requested in advance; these will take a child weighing up to about 22lbs. Children aged between two and 12 can usually occupy a seat for half to two-thirds of the full fare and do get a baggage allowance. Strollers can often be taken on as hand luggage.

Within the USA

There are hundreds of air routes making it possible to fly almost anywhere within the

Cycle-Friendly Airlines

Not too many airlines will carry a bike free of charge these days – at least according to their official policy. Most airlines regard the bike as part of your checked luggage. Carriers working the routes to the USA from Europe, Asia and the Pacific usually allow 44 lbs (20kg) of checked luggage (excluding carry-on), so the weight of your bike and bags shouldn't exceed this. If you're over the limit, technically you're liable for excess-baggage charges.

Carriers flying within or through North America use a different system. Passengers are generally allowed two pieces of luggage, each of which must not exceed 70lb (32kg). Excess baggage fees are charged for additional pieces, rather than for excess weight. Some airlines may count a bike as one of your two pieces; others charge a set fee for carrying a bike, which may then be carried in addition to your two other pieces. Check whether these fees are paid for the whole journey, each way or per leg.

Some airlines require you to box your bike, while others accept soft covers, or just ask that you turn the handlebars, remove the pedals and cover the chain. Check this policy before getting to the airport; only a few airlines sell sturdy boxes at the check-in counter.

When we looked into the policies of different carriers, we found that not only does the story sometimes change depending on who you talk to – and how familiar they are with the company's policy – but the official line is not necessarily adhered to at the check-in counter. If a company representative or agent reassures you that your bike travels for free, ask them to annotate your passenger file to that effect. If your flight is not too crowded, the check-in staff are often lenient with the excess charges, particularly with items such as bikes.

The times when you are most likely to incur excess baggage charges are on full flights and, of course, if you inconvenience the check-in staff. If you suspect you may be over the limit, increase your chances of avoiding charges by checking in early and being well organized, friendly and polite – a smile and a 'Thankyou' can go a long way!

USA. Often the most competitive ticket prices are on the major 'air highways', especially between San Francisco or LA and major East Coast cities such as New York and Washington, DC. Flights to Chicago and Miami are also fairly competitive, but those to smaller cities, eg, in the South or Midwest, are often expensive and rarely nonstop. Flights between West Coast cities are generally very affordable. Southwest Airlines has some of the best fares, especially between San Diego, Oakland, CA and Seattle.

Check the weekly travel sections of major newspapers such as *The New York Times*, *Los Angeles Times* and *San Francisco Chronicle* for fares. Council Travel (☎ 800-226-8624, 🅦 www.counciltravel.com) and STA (☎ 800-781-4040, 🅦 www.sta-travel.com) have offices in major cities nationwide. The magazine *Travel Unlimited*, PO Box 1058, Allston, MA 02134, publishes details of the cheapest airfares and courier possibilities.

Nonstop flights between the coasts take about 4½ hours eastbound and 5½ hours westbound (prevailing winds make the difference).

Domestic Sample Fares

These fares give an approximate idea of what a roundtrip ticket to the West Coast from major gateways around the USA might cost.

City	Fare
To Los Angeles from:	
Chicago	$389
New York City	$550
Seattle	$210
San Francisco	$119
To Seattle from:	
Chicago	$431
New York City	$536
Los Angeles	$201
San Francisco	$137
To Portland from:	
Chicago	$358
New York City	$394
Los Angeles	$196
San Francisco	$124

Canada

Travel CUTS (☎ 866-246-9762 or ☎ 416-977-2185 in Toronto, 🅦 www.travelcuts.com) has offices in all major cities. The Toronto *Globe and Mail* and *Vancouver Sun* carry travel agents' ads. Canada 3000 (☎ 888-300-069), one of the first discount airlines to operate in Canada, offers flights to Vancouver from other major Canadian cities. A US discounter, Reno Air, flies to Vancouver from California and the US Southwest.

There are daily flights to San Francisco and LA from Vancouver and Toronto, and other Canadian cities have connections as well. Flights between LA and Vancouver cost about US$250 to US$300 roundtrip.

Eating Well at 30,000ft

Bringing your own food was once the only way to ensure a satisfying airplane meal, but these days the choice is astonishing. When making a reservation or confirming a flight (at least 72 hours in advance) you can now specify special meals. These are meant for people with dietary restrictions, but are used by many travelers. Generally, a specially prepared meal is a bit fresher and more flavorful than the standard. Meals offered include: vegetarian, low fat, kosher, low sodium, Asian, macrobiotic and combinations thereof (low-fat kosher vegetarian, for example).

The UK

The primary airlines serving Seattle, San Francisco and LA from London are British Air, SAS, Delta and United. Air Canada and Canadian Airlines both have direct flights to Vancouver from London. Check the ads in *Time Out*, the *London Evening Standard*, *TNT* and other publications, including the freebies usually available outside railway and major tube stations in London.

Most British travel agents are registered with Air Travel Organisers' Licensing (ATOL). If your ATOL-registered agent goes out of business and you have paid for your flight, ATOL will guarantee a refund or an alternative.

London is arguably the world's headquarters for bucket shops; they're well-advertised and can usually beat published airline fares. Many such firms are honest and solvent, but there are a few rogues who will take your money and disappear. If you feel suspicious don't hand over all the money at once – leave a deposit and pay the balance on receiving the ticket. If they insist on cash in advance, go elsewhere. Once you have the ticket, ring the airline to confirm that you are actually booked on the flight.

Good, reliable agents for cheap tickets in the UK include Trailfinders (☎ 020-7937 5400), 194 Kensington High St, London, W8 7RG; Council Travel (☎ 020-7730 7285), 52 Grosvenor Gardens, London SW1W, and STA Travel (☎ 020-7581 4132), 86 Old Brompton Rd, London SW7 3LQ.

Australia & New Zealand

All flights to North America from Australia and New Zealand are routed through California. Qantas flies to LA from Sydney, Melbourne (via Sydney or Auckland) and Cairns. United flies to San Francisco from Sydney and Melbourne (via Sydney) and to LA from Sydney and Auckland.

The Saturday editions of major daily newspapers often advertise cheap fares. STA Travel (in Australia ☎ 1300-733 035, in New Zealand ☎ 05-0878 2872, w www.statravel.com) and Flight Centres International (in Australia ☎ 133 133, in New Zealand ☎ 0800-243 544, w www.flightcentre.com) are major dealers in cheap airfares, with special deals for students and travelers aged under 30. The cheapest tickets have a 21-day advance-purchase requirement, a minimum stay of seven days and a maximum stay of 60 days. Flying with Air New Zealand is slightly cheaper, and both Qantas and Air New Zealand offer more expensive tickets with longer stays or stopovers.

Continental Europe

Many airlines, including KLM (Amsterdam), Air France (Paris), Swissair (Zurich), Lufthansa (Frankfurt) and Iberia (Madrid), have direct flights to LA or San Francisco. Seattle receives nonstop flights from Copenhagen and Amsterdam. Vancouver has direct links to Frankfurt, Zurich and Amsterdam. Many other international and US airlines arrive via a stop in a gateway city (usually Chicago or Miami) and continue on domestic flights. The direct flight (London to LA) takes about 11 hours westbound and nine or 10 hours eastbound, due to prevailing winds.

In Amsterdam Kilroy Travels (☎ 50-524 5100, w www.kilroytravels.com) is at Singel 413–15. In Paris, USIT Connect (☎ 01 42 34 56 90), 6 rue de Vaugirard, has great student fares. At the same address is Council Travel (☎ 01 43 29 69 50), which also has two offices in Germany: in Düsseldorf at

International Sample Fares

These fares give an approximate idea of what a roundtrip ticket to the West Coast from outside the USA might cost.

City	US$ Fare
Auckland to:	
Los Angeles	$885
Seattle	$1100
Portland	$1150
Frankfurt to:	
Los Angeles	$450
Seattle	$450
Portland	$545
Johannesburg to:	
Los Angeles	$850
Seattle	$895
Portland	$1000
London to:	
Los Angeles	$320
Seattle	$450
Portland	$550
Sydney to:	
Los Angeles	$1000
Seattle	$1100
Portland	$1100
Tokyo to:	
Los Angeles	$450
Seattle	$620
Portland	$650
Vancouver to:	
Los Angeles	$240
Seattle	$130
Portland	$185

Graf-Adolf-Strasse 64 (☎ 0211-17 93 86 40) and in Munich at Adalbertstrasse 32 (☎ 089-38 83 89 70). STA has an office in Frankfurt at Bergerstrasse 118 (☎ 069-43 01 91).

South Africa

The cheapest tickets from South Africa are via New York City, typically from Johannesburg on South African Airways. The price (around $1250) is about the same as a RTW fare. STA Travel (W www.sta-travel.com) has offices in Johannesburg, at Wits University and Capetown. Flight Centre (☎ 0860-400 747, W www.flightcentre.com) has offices in Johannesburg, and other discount agencies are appearing.

Asia

United Airlines has three flights a day to Honolulu from Tokyo with connections to West Coast cities. Delta Air Lines has daily nonstop flights to Portland from Tokyo and Seoul. Northwest and Japan Air Lines also have daily flights to the West Coast from the Pacific Rim.

Bangkok and Singapore, which have a number of bucket shops, are the best places to get cheap fares. Ask the advice of other travelers before buying a ticket. STA Travel has branches in Hong Kong, Tokyo, Singapore, Bangkok and Kuala Lumpur.

LAND

Bus

Bargain airfares can often undercut bus fares on long-distance routes. It can sometimes be cheaper to rent a car than to ride the bus. However, long-distance bus trips are often available at bargain prices if you buy or reserve tickets three days in advance.

Greyhound (☎ 800-229-9424, W www.greyhound.com) runs cross-country buses between New York and the West Coast for around $130 one-way ($109 with seven-day advance purchase). The passes they offer may be a good deal if you plan on seeing a lot of the USA and Canada in a short period. Passes are valid for a continuous period starting on the first day of use. You can stop over in any city for as long as you like within the validity period of the pass. The best part about these is that they are valid on most local carriers covering small towns that Greyhound does not. The Domestic Ameripass, good for travel within the USA, costs $185 for seven days and up to $509 for 60 days; the Domestic North America CanAm Pass, good for all of the USA and Canada, costs $399 for 15 days, $639 for 60 days; the Domestic Western CanAm Pass, good for travel in the Western USA, Western Canada and Tijuana, Mexico, costs $299 for 15 days, $399 for 30 days. For details of travel within the West Coast, including restrictions/requirements for bicycles, see Bus (p95) in the Getting Around chapter.

Train

Amtrak (☎ 800-872-7245, W www.amtrak.com), the national carrier, is a scenic, but slow and not exceptionally cheap way to travel. The *California Zephyr* travels from Chicago to San Francisco; the *Empire Builder* from Chicago to Seattle/Portland (it divides in Spokane, WA, with separate trains to Portland and Seattle); the *Southwest Chief* from Chicago to LA, via Albuquerque; and the *Sunset Limited* from Orlando to LA, via San Antonio and New Orleans. Prices vary according to route and season, but a ticket from Chicago to the West Coast is around $140 to $190. The North America Rail Pass costs $674/471 high season/low season, for 30 days of unlimited travel throughout the USA and Canada.

Reserving a sleeper costs around $300 for a cross-country ticket and includes three meals each day. Advance booking is recommended, especially during the peak season. For details of travel within the West Coast, including restrictions/requirements for bicycles, see Train (p96) in the Getting Around chapter.

Car

If you're driving into the USA from Canada or Mexico, don't forget the vehicle's registration papers, liability insurance and your home driving license. Obtaining an international driving permit (before you leave home, from your local road authority) is a good idea if you are taking a car over an international border. A vehicle rented in the USA can usually be driven into Canada, but very few rental companies will let you take a car into Mexico.

Getting Around

For a country as civilized as the USA, its public-transport system is nothing short of barbaric. The country, especially its western reaches, developed mostly after the automobile was invented, and the transport infrastructure reflects this. For this reason, there is not one 'best' mode of transport for getting around the West Coast. You'll probably need to use planes, trains and buses, depending on where and for how long you travel.

AIR

If you're covering long distances flying is the most convenient, and often cheapest, way to go. A number of routes have especially frequent and convenient service, with airplanes taking off every 45 minutes to 1½ hours; these routes include Seattle–LA, Seattle–San Francisco and San Francisco–LA. Southwest Airlines offers exceptionally cheap fares between Oakland (just outside San Francisco) and LA/San Diego/Portland. A number of smaller airports will be convenient for particular rides, including Wenatchee (Washington), Eugene (Oregon) and Santa Barbara (California).

It's possible to just show up at the airport, buy your ticket and hop on, though you will only be guaranteed a seat by buying your ticket in advance. You will also usually get a lower fare. For more about advance purchase and discount fares, see Buying Tickets (pp87–90). If you're only flying around the West Coast, passes such as Visit USA (p90) may not be as cheap as individual discount tickets. It pays to do a little research before you leave home.

Carrying Your Bicycle

All airlines require bikes to be boxed or bagged, with the pedals removed and handle bars turned sideways. You'll have to check the bicycle as a piece of luggage, so allow time to stand in the baggage check-in line. If you don't have a box, you can buy one from most baggage counters for $10 to $20.

Here are some of the main airlines serving the West Coast, plus their one-way charges for checking a bicycle:

Alaska Airlines (☎ 800-252-7522, Ⓦ www.alaskaair.com) $50

American Airlines (☎ 800-433-7300, Ⓦ www.aa.com) $75

Delta Air Lines (☎ 800-221-1212, Ⓦ www.delta.com) $75

Horizon Air (☎ 800-547-9308, Ⓦ www.horizonair.com) $50

Southwest Airlines (☎ 800-435-9792, Ⓦ www.southwest.com) $40

United Airlines (☎ 800-241-6522, Ⓦ www.ual.com) $50

Baggage Restrictions

For details of airline restrictions for both carry-on and checked baggage, see the Warning boxed text on p87.

BUS

As Americans rely so much on cars and usually fly when traveling longer distances, bus transport has become rather limited, though good deals are still available. You may not want to travel between regions by bus, but may not have a choice when getting to the start of a ride.

Greyhound requires that you box your bike, while local and regional buses often have a rack that can hold bikes (excluding those with front pannier racks) for no charge. Hang your bike on the rack before boarding and remind the driver that you must retrieve it as you're getting off.

Information on local bus operators can be found in the ride chapters.

Greyhound

The nation's largest carrier, Greyhound (☎ 800-229-9424, Ⓦ www.greyhound.com) has extensive scheduled routes and its own terminal in most cities. Buses are comfortable, the company has an exceptional safety record and buses are more or less on time.

In many small towns it no longer maintains terminals, but merely stops at a given location, such as fast-food restaurants. In these unlikely terminals, boarding passengers usually pay the driver with exact change. Tickets can be bought over the phone or on the Web site by credit card. Greyhound terminals accept American Express, traveler's checks and cash.

Bicycles must be boxed and can be checked for free if they are one of your two allowed pieces of baggage; any additional baggage costs $15 per piece. All buses are nonsmoking.

For information about Greyhound's discount passes, see Bus (p94) in the Getting There & Away chapter.

TRAIN

Amtrak (☎ 800-872-7245, W www.amtrak.com) fares vary greatly, depending on promotions and destinations. Reservations can be made anytime from 11 months in advance to the day of departure. It's a good idea to reserve as early as possible, as space is limited and you'll have a better chance of getting a discount fare.

Besides the long-distance routes that reach the West Coast from across the USA (see Train, p94, in the Getting There & Away chapter), several routes operate along the West Coast. The *Coast Starlight* goes from LA to Seattle ($121, 36 hours), stopping in Sacramento and Portland. A branch of the *Empire Builder*, which hails from Chicago, leaves Portland, crosses to Vancouver, Washington and runs up the north side of the Columbia Gorge to meet the eastbound train in Spokane. It is a truly spectacular trip. The *Cascades* routes connect Seattle to Portland; Eugene; and Vancouver, British Columbia.

In California, the *San Joaquins* route travels from Oakland/Emeryville to LA; the *Pacific Surfliner* goes from San Luis Obispo to San Diego, while the *Capitol Corridor* connects Auburn to San Jose, via Sacramento and San Francisco.

In some areas, especially California, Amtrak rails do not run continuously, so you'll have to transfer to a bus midway through the trip. San Francisco, for example, can only be reached by bus from Amtrak stations in Martinez or Emeryville. When purchasing a ticket, the bus ride is incorporated into the schedule and ticket price and will be indicated by a bus icon on the ticket.

Fares

Rail travel in the US is not cheap, but you can cut costs by purchasing special fares in advance. A variety of one-way, roundtrip and promotional fares are available, with discounts for seniors aged 62 and over, children aged between two and 15, military personnel and disabled travelers. Fares vary according to type of seating, which include coach seats or various types of sleeping compartments. Special fares are available year-round, but are more likely between mid-October and May.

Besides the North America Rail Pass (see Train, p94), there are passes for travel within California: the statewide 7-in-21 day pass allows seven days of travel within a 21-day period ($160); the Northern or Southern California 5-in-7 day pass allows five days of travel within Northern or Southern California within one week ($99).

Note that most small train stations don't sell tickets; you have to book them with a travel agent or Amtrak directly. Trains may only stop at certain small stations if you have bought a ticket in advance.

Carrying Your Bicycle

Amtrak's bicycle transport policy is a point of contention for many cyclists, mostly because it's unclear and unreliable: one agent will charge $15 for a boxed bike while another will charge $5. In either case, on long-distance routes such as the *Coast Starlight* or *Empire Builder*, a bike must be boxed or bagged and can be checked as a regular piece of luggage (a box costs $10).

Some routes, such as the *Pacific Surf liner* and *Cascades*, have bicycle racks in the baggage car. If so, hand over your bike to the conductor in the baggage car before boarding, then retrieve it from the same car when you disembark. Rack space is available on a first-come, first-served basis, so if the first baggage car is full, you must go to the next one. In some stations, this requires you to climb a set of stairs and walk across to the next platform.

Before transferring to an Amtrak bus your bike must be put in a box. There is never a guarantee that there will be room for the bike in the luggage compartment, though it is rarely full. If there is no room, you'll have to wait for the next bus with available space (you can't bring the bike on board).

CAR

Driving is certainly the easiest, and can be the cheapest, way to get around the West Coast – if you don't want to travel entirely by bike. For road rules, access these publications, available free on the Web sites:

California Driver Handbook; W www.dmv.ca.gov
Oregon Driver Manual; W www.odot.state.or.us/dmv
Washington Driver Guide; W www.wa.gov/dol

Drive-Aways

Drive-aways are cars whose owners need them driven somewhere. For example, if somebody moves from LA to Chicago, they may elect to fly and leave their car with a drive-away agency. The agency will find a driver and take care of all necessary insurance and permits. If you happen to want to drive from LA to Chicago, have a valid driving license and a clean driving record, you can apply to be that driver. Normally, you have to pay a refundable deposit and gas (though sometimes a gas allowance is given). You are allowed a set number of days to deliver the car – usually based on driving eight hours a day. You are also allowed a limited number of miles, based on the best route (as decided by the agency) and allowing for reasonable side trips, so you can't zigzag all over the country. This is a cheap way to get around if you like long-distance driving.

Drive-away companies often advertise in the classified sections of newspapers under Travel. They are also listed in the Yellow Pages under Automobile Transporters & Drive-away Companies.

You need to be flexible about dates and destinations; if going to a popular area, you could leave within two days, or have to wait more than a week before a car becomes available. The most common routes available are coast to coast.

Rental

Rental companies require that you have a major credit card, that you be at least 25 years old (21 in some cases), and that you have a valid driving license (your home license will do).

Prices vary widely so shop around for the best rate – discounts may be offered on weekends; for three-day or week-long rentals; or even for driving a car to another city. Car rental is cheaper in big cities, especially LA. The major nationwide rental car companies are:

Alamo	☎ 800-465-5266
Avis	☎ 800-230-4898
Budget	☎ 800-527-0700
Dollar	☎ 800-800-3665
Enterprise	☎ 800-736-8222
Hertz	☎ 800-654-3131
National	☎ 800-227-7368
Thrifty	☎ 800-847-4389

Rent-A-Wreck (☎ 800-421-7253) offers older vehicles at cheaper prices. There are also thousands of smaller local companies, which are sometimes less expensive. RVs can also be rented; check the Yellow Pages under Recreational Vehicles – Renting & Leasing.

Purchase

If you're spending several months in the USA, purchasing a car is worth considering but it can be complicated and require some research.

Cars bought at a dealer cost more but may come with warranties and/or financing options. Buying from an individual is usually cheaper; look in the newspaper classifieds or special trade publications. If you buy from a dealer, the dealer will submit the required forms to the Department of Motor Vehicles (DMV) for the car's registration to be transferred into your name. If you buy privately, you must register the vehicle with the DMV within 10 days of purchase. To do this you need the bill of sale, the title to the car (the 'pink slip'), proof of insurance or other financial responsibility, and a state smog certificate.

Insurance

Californian law specifies a fixed minimum amount of liability insurance to protect the health and property of others in case of an accident. If you are involved in any type of accident, regardless of fault, and you don't have insurance, penalties are severe. In addition to financial penalties, your driving license will be suspended for one year.

In order to get insurance, some states request that you have a US driving license and that you have been licensed for at least 18 months. Also make sure you're insured before hiring a car.

American Automobile Association

If you'll be doing much driving in any car, membership in the American Automobile Association (AAA, called 'triple A'; ☎ 800-874-7532, W www.aaa.com) is worthwhile. Only US and Canadian residents can join but members of foreign AAA affiliates, such as the Automobile Association in the UK or the ADAC in Germany, are entitled to the same services if they bring their membership cards.

Carrying Your Bicycle

A cheap but solid bike rack will cost around $80, which may be more economical than renting a car large enough to hold your bikes. The cheapest place to find a rack will be at a superstore such as Target, Wal-Mart or K-Mart. Large outdoors stores such as REI, Sportsmart or Big 5 will also have a good selection at reasonable prices. Smaller bike shops usually only carry one or two models. Obtain your car first, then shop around for the rack.

ORGANIZED RIDES

Joining an organized cycle tour can be great if you're short on time or like the idea of traveling in a group. Most companies offer a variety of itineraries, and provide meals, van support and accommodations, ranging from a tent to a five-star hotel. You are usually free to go at your own pace without the burden of luggage, which the company hauls for you. Generally you bring your own bike or pay an extra $150 for hire.

The Internet is a good place to look for tour operators. If an organization isn't well established, try to speak with one of its past guests before signing up for a trip. Some of the USA's most respected tour companies are:

Backroads (☎ 800-462-2848, W www.backroads.com) Based in Berkeley, CA, this is an extremely well-run outfit offering tours of the Puget Sound, California Wine Country and places around the globe. Excellent meals, support and outstanding leadership is part of both camping and inn trips. Prices start at $2500.

Classic Adventures (☎ 800-777-8090, W www.classicadventures.com) Based in New York, this company focuses its itineraries in the eastern part of the USA, mostly northern New York/Canada and Mississippi.

Crossroads Cycling Adventure (☎ 800-971-2453, W www.crossroadscycling.com) Organizes fully supported long-distance tours, including a 50-day ride from Boston to Seattle ($5095). Food and van support are provided, but you supply your own tent.

Cycle America (☎ 800-245-3263, W www.cycleamerica.com) Offers affordable rates ($500 to $700 per week) for tours of the Oregon coast, California coast and several national parks. Prices include meals and camping fees.

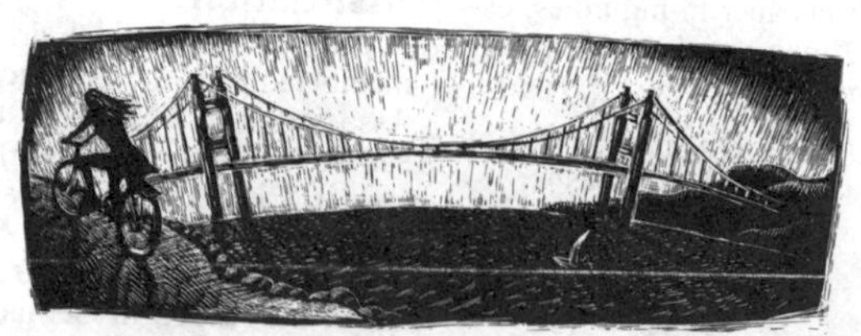

WASHINGTON

Highlights

- imposing Mt Rainier – vistas, forests & wildflowers
- superb San Juan Islands seascapes
- magnificent mountain scenery in the Cascades
- the rolling hills of the Palouse Range

Special Events

- Opening Day of the Boating Season (first Sat in May)
- Northwest Folklife Festival (Memorial Day weekend, May) Seattle
- Seafair (early Jul–early Aug) Seattle; parades, sporting events & fun races
- Bite of Seattle (mid-Jul) food, wine, beer, coffee & more
- Bumbershoot (Labor Day weekend, Sept) Seattle; music, crafts & food

Cycling Events

- Chilly Hilly (last Sun in Feb) Bainbridge Island
- Daffodil Classic (late Apr) near Mt Rainier
- RAMROD (late Jul) Ride Around Mt Rainier in One Day
- Seattle to Portland Bicycle Classic (early Jul)
- Ride Around Washington (mid-Aug)

Food & Drink Specialties

- salmon, oysters, mussels, clams and Ivar's clam chowder
- world-famous red delicious apples from central Washington
- Washington wines
- Seattle's crazy coffee culture

ANN CECIL

Washington

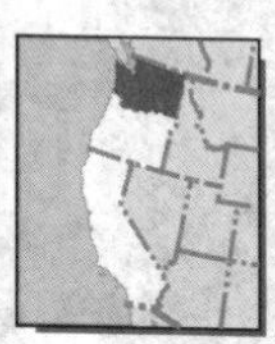

Tucked away in the northwest corner of the United States, Washington sits unobtrusively, offering visitors diverse and magnificent land- and seascapes.

Western Washington is like a stage, with a curtain of clouds, but when the curtain is lifted, the audience is presented with some of the most fabulous scenery imaginable. The choices for cyclists are vast: the mountains of the Cascade range; serene river valleys; dense evergreen forests; tranquil islands; and Seattle, one of North America's most bicycle-friendly cities.

Eastern Washington's curtain is open for about 300 days a year. Draped with sunshine, the arid landscape lends itself to interesting cycling, boasting mighty river valleys, orchards and vineyards, rolling hills and expansive plains.

Scattered throughout the state are reminders of bygone days: rivers and trails of exploration; towns steeped in history. Combine these with the great outdoors, and Washington is a cyclist's playground.

HISTORY

Washington's first inhabitants were Native Americans. Coastal tribes owed their survival to fishing. Further inland, the tribes existed by salmon fishing in rivers during summer, and hunting deer and elk in winter.

The first European exploration of Washington was by sea. In 1592 a Greek explorer, Juan de Fuca, made his way towards Puget Sound. James Cook explored the coast in 1778, followed in 1792 by George Vancouver, another Brit. Also in 1792, American Robert Gray discovered the mouth of the Columbia River. The most significant piece of exploration in the Pacific Northwest is the 1804–6 overland expedition by Lewis and Clark (see the boxed text, p15).

In 1845, Washington's first European settlement was a mill town, Tumwater. It soon needed a port, and to its north, Olympia, later to become the state's capital, was founded in 1846. The logging centers of Seattle and Port Townsend were established in 1851.

The US Congress voted to create the Washington Territory in 1853; Isaac Stevens was the first governor. The mid-1800s saw Native American unrest in the eastern part of the region, later spreading west. In 1889 Washington became a state.

Western Washington thrived in the late 1800s, based on dairy farming, fishing and logging. Shipping was the major transport; port cities boomed. A rail link came to Tacoma in 1887, and Seattle in 1893.

Washington prospered into the 20th century embracing massive hydroelectric and irrigation schemes. The naval yards at Bremerton were the Northwest's major ship-building facility during WWI and WWII, and William Boeing built planes for the military south of Seattle.

Both Seattle and Spokane hosted world's fairs with futuristic themes, in 1962 and 1974 respectively. Microsoft, Seattle native Bill Gates' software company, located in the environs of Seattle, has set the city its place in computer history.

NATURAL HISTORY

The Cascade Range forms the backbone of Washington. The massive volcanoes of Mt Rainier and Mt St Helens dominate the southern horizon, while Mt Baker stands tall in the area known as the North Cascades.

The Cascades effectively block the eastward flow of moist Pacific air, most rain falling on the western slopes. The wet, western slopes sustain fern-covered floors and thick evergreen forests while sparser pines thrive on the drier eastern slopes. The Columbia River cuts through the desert basin of south-central Washington, and the far east of the state rises toward the Rocky Mtns.

The Olympic Peninsula lies across Puget Sound from Seattle. The peninsula's mountains, the Olympics, also block moist marine air, the precipitation creating North America's only temperate rain forests. Puget Sound and the Strait of Juan de Fuca are home to hundreds of islands.

On the coast watch for seals, sea otters, sea lions and migrating orcas. Deer and squirrels are ubiquitous but spotting a marmot, elk or coyote takes more patience (or luck). Black bears and cougars are found in Washington.

Bird life is abundant, including Stellar's jays, woodpeckers, hummingbirds, blue herons, belted kingfishers, seagulls and bald eagles.

CLIMATE

Washington's climate is wet in the west and dry in the east. The Pacific Ocean and the Cascade Range determine this pattern, the coast receiving moist, marine air. Seattle and the area west of the Cascades often suffer from gray days and a misty drizzle (summer months are the driest), while eastern Washington receives little rain.

Temperatures in western Washington are rarely above 80°F in summer and seldom below 25°F in winter. Eastern Washington sees summer highs of around 100°F, and harsher winters, with the average January temperature below 20°F. Seattle rarely sees snow but, to the Cascades, Olympics and eastern Washington, snows can come as early as mid-October. Snow can close mountain passes until late May or early June.

Westerly winds prevail in Washington. Summer brings northwest winds to western Washington, changing to southwest in the winter. March is the windiest month and the lightest winds are in summer. Eastern Washington's prevailing winds are westerly in the summer, turning easterly in the winter.

INFORMATION

Maps

The free *Washington State Highway Map*, a great planning tool, is available at most visitor centers, the Washington State Department of Tourism (see Information Sources) and the Department of Transportation (W www.wsdot.wa.gov). Free from the Department of Transportation, the *Washington State Traffic Data for Bicyclists Map* provides information on traffic flow on major roads, cycling restrictions on highways and basic ferry information. Information for obtaining this and other Washington state cycling maps is at W www.wsdot.wa.gov/hlrd/Bicycle-Pages/List-Bike-Maps.htm.

Two atlases, the DeLorme *Washington Atlas & Gazetteer* (1:150,000; $16.95) and Benchmark's *Washington Road & Recreation Atlas* (1:200,000; $19.95) provide clear maps, plus recreational information on parks, campgrounds and activities. Carry only the pages you need.

Books

For more detail on longer stays use Lonely Planet's *Pacific Northwest* and *Seattle*.

For mountain biking around Seattle, check out John Zilly's *Kissing the Trail: Greater Seattle Mountain Bike Adventures* ($14.95). For statewide mountain biking, pick up *Mountain Bike America: Washington* ($17.95), by Amy & Mark Poffenbarger.

History buffs should look for *Exploring Washington's Past: A Road Guide to History*, by Ruth Kirk & Carmela Alexander (University of Washington Press; $27.95).

Information Sources

For statewide information, contact the Washington State Department of Tourism (☎ 360-586-2088 or ☎ 800-544-1800, W www.experiencewashington.com), PO Box 42500, Olympia, WA 98504-2500.

Washington State Parks (☎ 800-233-0321, W www.parks.wa.gov) can make reservations at 100 campgrounds in Washington and Oregon through Reservations Northwest (☎ 800-452-5687). There is a $7 nonrefundable fee.

Washington has several bicycle clubs, organizations and publications:

Bicycle Alliance of Washington (W www.bicyclealliance.org) A statewide lobbying organization.

The Bicycle Paper (W www.bicyclepaper.com) A regional tabloid covering all things bicycle – touring, club activities, events in the Pacific Northwest. Available at bike shops or online.

Cascade Bicycle Club (☎ 206-522-3222, W www.cascade.org) 6310 NE 74th St, Building 30, Seattle. With 5500 members, it's the largest cycling club in the USA. The club runs several major event rides, notably the Seattle to Portland (STP). With maps and other resources, the office is near the Burke-Gilman Trail.

Other Clubs: Seattle Bicycle Club (W www.seattlebike.org) and, for mountain bike enthusiasts, the BBTC (Backcountry Bicycle Trails Club; W www.bbtc.org). For other clubs in the state, go to W www.cascade.org/clubs.

Tour de Morte

Attention all cycling witches and warlocks: looking for Halloween cycling fun? Don a costume and join Cascade Bicycle Club's (W www.cascade.org) annual 35mi Tour de Morte. Pedal to 13 cemeteries and other ghoulish sites. When else but 31 October (or close to it).

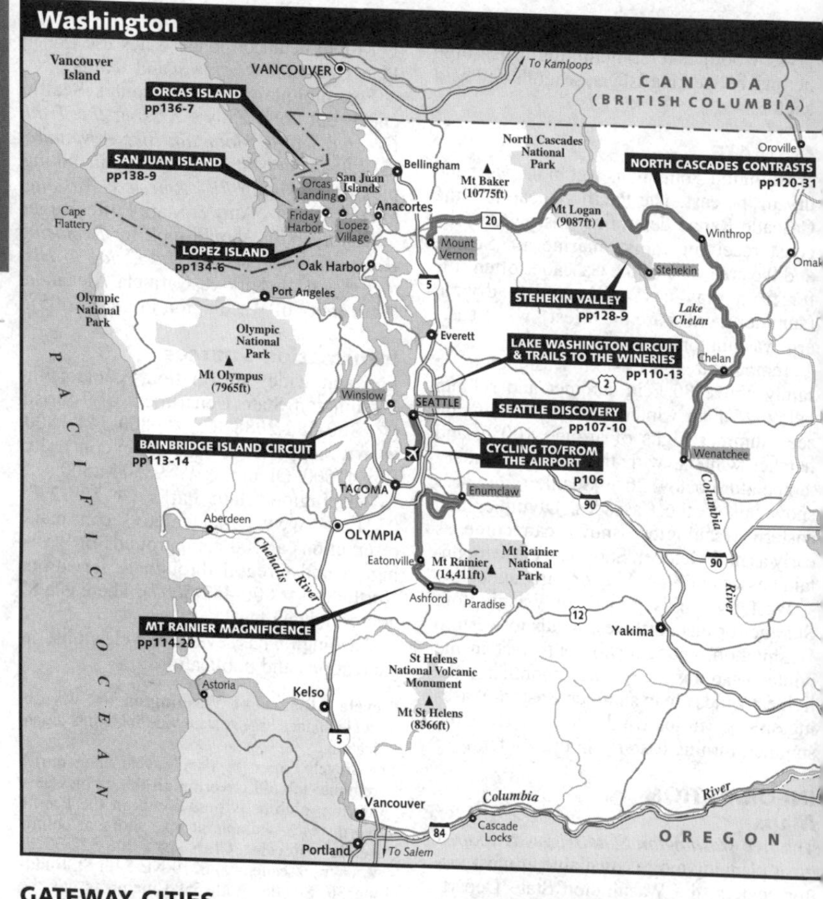

GATEWAY CITIES

Seattle

☎ 206

Seattle is a vibrant and diverse city. It has become known for the coffee craze, grunge music and microbrews, and is the headquarters of Microsoft, Boeing, REI, amazon.com and Starbucks.

One of the country's most livable cities, Seattle occupies a gorgeous setting on Puget Sound, surrounded by the Olympic and Cascade Mtns. Water plays a huge role in the city's character, ferries plow Puget Sound to outlying islands, and lakes, linked by rivers and canals, dot the landscape.

Seattle, despite its reputation for rain, is full of outdoor enthusiasts. The city is hilly and incredibly scenic, has an excellent network of bikepaths and every public bus is equipped with bike racks. It is home to the largest cycling club in the nation and a police bike force.

Information Seattle–King County visitor center (☎ 461-5840, W www.seeseattle.org), 800 Convention Place, is in the Washington State Convention Center.

Most major banks have offices in the downtown area and branches throughout the Puget Sound area.

For maps and travel books, Metsker Maps (☎ 623-4787 or ☎ 800-727-4430, W www.metskers.com), 702 1st Ave, is downtown in Pioneer Square, and in Wallingford, Wide World Books & Maps (☎ 206-634-3453 or ☎ 888-534-3453,

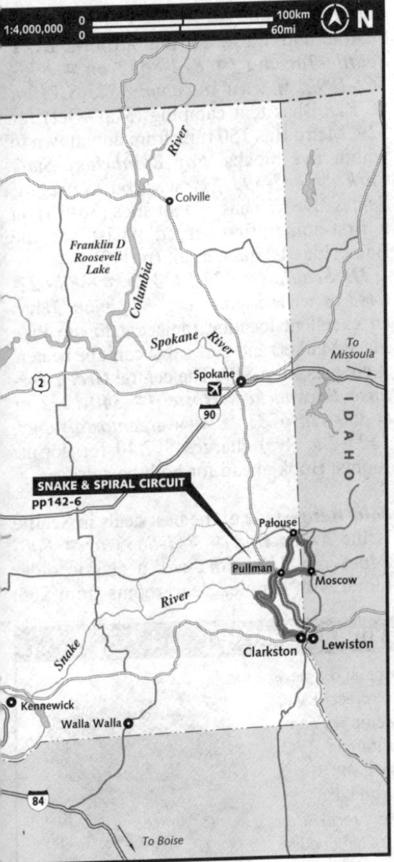

www.travelbooksandmaps.com) is at 4411A Wallingford Ave N.

The American Automobile Association (AAA; ☎ 206-448-5353) at 330 6th Ave N has maps and other travel information.

A must for any cyclist in the area are two free maps: *Seattle Bicycling Guide Map* (☎ 684-7583, W www.pan.ci.seattle.wa.us), 600 4th Ave, 7th Floor; and the *King County Bicycling Guidemap* (King County Department of Transportation). These maps are available at the visitor center, Metsker Maps, REI, Cascade Bicycle Club and bike shops.

Internet access is available at public libraries, Speakeasy Cafe (☎ 971-5100), 2304 2nd Ave, and Online Coffee (☎ 381-1911), 1111 1st Ave.

Seattle has a multitude of bike shops:

Blazing Saddles (☎ 341-9994, W www.blazingsaddles.com) 1230 Western Ave. Rents bikes and can do basic repairs.

Elliott Bay Bicycles (☎ 441-8144) 2116 Western Ave. A full-service bike shop.

Gregg's Aurora Cycles (☎ 783-1000) 7401 Aurora Ave N. Specializes in tandems.

Gregg's Greenlake Cycles (☎ 523-1822, W www.greggscycles.com) 7007 Woodlawn Ave E. One of Seattle's largest bike shops. It offers repairs, sells bike gear, and rents bikes and inline skates.

REI (☎ 223-1944, W www.rei.com) 222 Yale Ave N. Has a bicycle department and a maintenance section.

Things to See & Do Established in 1907 as a farmers market, today the **Pike Place Market** (W www.pikeplacemarket.org) is one of Seattle's most popular attractions. As well as an extensive selection of shops, you'll find some of the most entertaining fishmongers in the world. (Watch out for flying fish!)

The **Waterfront** is a combination of shops, restaurants, and port and tourist activities. At Pier 59, visit the **Seattle Aquarium** (☎ 386-4320, W www.seattleaquarium.org) or the **IMAX Dome** (☎ 622-1868), a 180-degree domed-screen theater. The 100-year-old **Ye Olde Curiosity Shop** (☎ 682-5844), Pier 54, is a cross between a museum and a souvenir shop. From Pier 52, take a ferry to enjoy some of the best views Seattle has to offer, or do the Bainbridge Island Circuit (pp113–4).

Pioneer Square is where Seattle began. This old downtown district boasts historic buildings, tree-lined streets, art galleries, book shops and restaurants. The **Underground Tour** (☎ 682-4646) is an hour-long subterranean hike beneath Pioneer Square. Guides introduce local history in a lighthearted, irreverent style. Tours leave from Doc Maynard's Public House, 608 1st Ave S.

Hammering Man, a four-story action sculpture, welcomes visitors to the **Seattle Art Museum** (☎ 654-3100, W www.seattleartmuseum.org), corner University and 1st Sts. The museum has permanent displays of Asian, African and Native American art, plus pieces by European and American artists. Traveling shows can be seen in the Special Exhibits Gallery.

Seattle's landmark is the 'Jetsonesque' **Space Needle** (☎ 443-2111, W www.spaceneedle.com), centerpiece of the **Seattle Center**, site of the 1962 World's Fair. The 360-degree views from the top are fabulous on a clear day. Also on the site, **Pacific Science Center** (☎ 443-2001, Ⓦ www.pacsci.org) features exhibits (many hands on) and houses the **IMAX Theater** and a **planetarium**.

Adjacent to the Seattle Center is the **Experience Music Project** (EMP), don't miss it; see the boxed text below.

A shop may seem odd in this section, but not when it's **REI**, the largest purveyor of sporting and recreational gear in the nation. With its origins in Seattle, the huge flagship store (☎ 206-223-1944), 222 Yale Ave N, is a must-see for any outdoor enthusiast.

More Seattle attractions – such as the **Hiram M Chittenden Locks**, **Discovery Park**, **Washington Park Arboretum** and Seattle area **wineries** – can be seen on the rides in and around Seattle.

Places to Stay Seattle has lots of festivals and events. If accommodations are tight, turn to the ***Seattle Hotel Hotline*** *(☎ 461-5882 or ☎ 800-535-7071)* for assistance. .

Camping & Budget About 15mi south of Seattle and close to the airport, ***KOA Seattle-Tacoma*** *(☎ 872-8652 or ☎ 800-562-1892;* Ⓦ *www.koa.com; 5801 S 212th St, Kent)* has tent camping (May–Oct) for $29. Metro Bus 150 runs from downtown to within five blocks. ***Fay Bainbridge State Park*** *(☎ 842-3931,* Ⓦ *www.parks.wa.gov, Sunrise Dr NE)* has 39 tent sites ($6–13) on a first-come, first-served basis; see the Bainbridge Island Circuit (pp113–14).

HI Seattle *(☎ 622-5443 or ☎ 888-622-5443,* Ⓦ *www.hiseattle.org, 84 Union St)* has an excellent location (adjacent to the Pike Place Market) and views that can't be beaten. It charges from $17. The central ***Green Tortoise Backpackers Hostel*** *(☎ 340-1222 or ☎ 800-424-6783,* Ⓦ *www.greentortoise.net, 1525 2nd Ave)* charges $17/40 for dorms/rooms. Book ahead for both hostels.

Mid-Range One of the best deals in Seattle is the ***Kings Inn*** *(☎ 441-8833 or ☎ 800-546-4760, 2106 5th Ave)*, a classic older motel with simple, clean rooms from $65.

Jimi Hendrix Is Alive & Well…& Playing in Seattle

Hometown boy Jimi Hendrix left a big mark on Seattle and a new museum dedicated to him, the **Experience Music Project** (EMP; ☎ 206-367-5483 or ☎ 877-367-5483; Ⓦ www.emplive.com) makes sure no one will forget. Opened with great fanfare in 2000, three decades after the legendary guitarist's death, EMP is in a building inspired by the swooping lines of an electric guitar.

From downtown, take the monorail. Inside, visitors receive an electronic MEG (Museum Exhibit Guide) and a brief training course in its use before being turned loose in the dark and cavernous exhibition halls.

Officially EMP 'celebrates and explores creativity and innovation expressed through popular music' – but it's fun, honestly! Interactive exhibits take visitors through the history of rock and roll from its roots to rap and grunge – and show how a fair bit of it happened right here in town. Photographs, memorabilia (including pieces of guitars smashed, burned and otherwise destroyed in performances by Hendrix) and videos pay tribute to many of the colorful characters of counter-culture – Diddley, Waters, Dylan, Joplin, Winwood, Clapton, Beck and Cobain are all here. One gallery tells the design story of the electric guitar, featuring models from all eras, including the classic Fender Stratocaster.

Experiencing EMP could easily consume a whole day, so allow plenty of time. It can also be crowded, so try to get there before 11am or stay after 6pm on the weekend (open 10am–6pm Sun–Thurs, 10am–11pm Fri & Sat).

Neil Irvine

HAYDEN FOELL

Near the Seattle Center, the ***Loyal Inn Best Western*** *(☎ 682-0200 or ☎ 800-528-1234, W www.bestwestern.com, 2301 8th Ave)* has rooms from $110, including continental breakfast.

B&Bs Lovingly remodeled ***Pensione Nichols B&B*** *(☎ 441-7125 or ☎ 800-440-7125, W www.seattle-bed-breakfast.com, 1923 1st Ave)* offers singles/doubles for $90/110 (shared bathroom), including a generous continental breakfast. ***Wall Street Inn B&B*** *(☎ 448-0125 or ☎ 800-624-1117, W www.wallstreetinn.com, 2507 1st Ave)* used to be a residence for sailors. Many of the refurbished rooms have kitchenettes and Murphy beds. Rooms cost between $139 and $179, with a bountiful breakfast.

Near the University of Washington and close to the Burke-Gilman Trail, the ***Chambered Nautilus B&B Inn*** *(☎ 522-2536 or ☎ 800-545-8459, W www.chamberednautilus.com, 5005 22nd Ave NE)* is a Georgian colonial home. Rooms cost from $99, including gourmet breakfast. Next door, the B&B also has four apartments from $114.

Top End Built in the 1920s, the attractively restored ***WestCoast Vance Hotel*** *(☎ 441-4200 or ☎ 800-426-0670, W www.westcoasthotels.com, 620 Stewart St)* has rooms from $140. The ***Inn at the Market*** *(☎ 443-3600 or ☎ 800-446-4484, W www.innatthemarket.com, 86 Pine St)* is in the midst of market activity. The 70-room boutique hotel costs from $190/250 for city/waterfront views. The sundeck has a panorama across Elliot Bay and the Olympics.

Places to Eat Don't drink too many lattes and find yourself 'sleepless in Seattle'. Seattle's coffee culture is everywhere, from Seattle-based coffee chains Starbucks, Seattle's Best Coffee (SBC) and Tully's to numerous individual coffee shops.

Pike Place Market Look no further for edibles. Here you'll find fresh produce stands, baked goods at the ***Three Girls Bakery***, food stalls such as ***Mee Sum Pastries***, and ***DeLaurenti's***, a grocery reminiscent of Italy. For breakfast, lunch or dinner, try interesting seasonal and French-inspired offerings at ***Cafe Campagne*** *(☎ 728-2233, 1600 Post Alley)*. Excellent seafood is served at ***Etta's*** *(☎ 443-6000, 2020 Western Ave)*, where innovative mains cost around $20. To browse the market's selection, go to W www.pikeplacemarket.org/dine/dining.

Downtown For a quick bite, head to the food court in the ***Westlake Center*** *(cnr 4th Ave & Pine St)*. The ***Dahlia Lounge*** *(☎ 682-4143, 2001 4th Ave)* boasts some of Seattle's most creative Northwest cuisine. Reservations are essential, and you'll have to change out of your cycling shorts for this fine dining experience.

International District The place for cheap eats. Chinese and Vietnamese restaurants line ***Jackson St*** between 6th and 12th Aves. Lunch will cost around $5, and you'll easily fill up for under $10 at dinner. Don't miss ***Uwajimaya*** *(519 6th Ave)*, one of the best Asian supermarkets in the country.

Capitol Hill There's plenty of good, inexpensive eating here. For Thai food, ***Siam on Broadway*** *(☎ 324-0892, 616 Broadway Ave E)* is popular. For Mediterranean flavors, try ***El Greco*** *(☎ 328-4604, 219 Broadway Ave E)*. The ***Deluxe Bar & Grill*** *(☎ 324-9697, 625 Broadway Ave E)* is the place for burgers. Save room for a delectable sweet treat at ***Pacific Dessert Co*** *(516 Broadway Ave E)*. The menu at the ***Coastal Kitchen*** *(☎ 206-322-1145, 429 15th Ave E)* changes every couple of months, inspired by a different world cuisine.

Ballard The Seattle Discovery ride (pp107–10) passes through Ballard. ***Lombardi's Cucina*** *(☎ 783-0055, 2200 NW Market)* serves Italian meals. ***Burk's Cafe – Creole and Cajun*** *(☎ 782-0091, 5411 Ballard Ave NW)* does spicy food. ***Ballard Ave*** is home to lots of pubs and clubs. The side trip to Golden Gardens passes ***Ray's Boathouse*** *(☎ 789-3770)* and ***Anthony's Home Port*** *(☎ 783-0780)*, both on the water with views of the Olympic Mtns, both known for great seafood.

Fremont Start or end the Lake Washington Circuit with a meal. For breakfast, try the ***Longshoreman's Daughter*** *(☎ 633-5169, 3510 Fremont Place N)*. For a big, fat $5 burrito or $2 tacos, try ***Taco del Mar*** *(3526 Fremont Place N)*. The ***Fremont Noodle House*** *(☎ 547-1550, 3411 Fremont Ave N)*

Cycling to/from the Airport

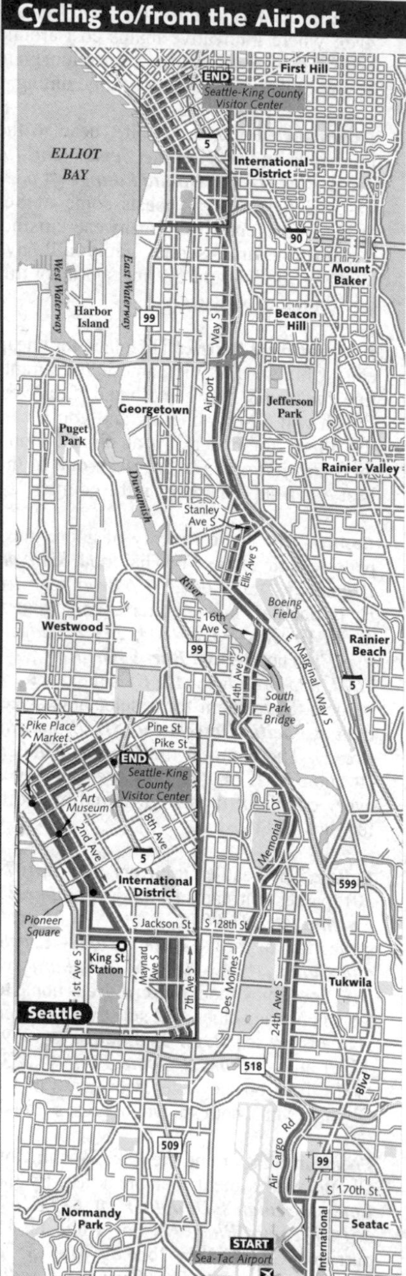

Sea-Tac airport is 15mi south of downtown Seattle. This route is straightforward and, apart from some easy hills at the start, mostly flat, making this a good option for cyclists arriving in Seattle.

Planning

The *Seattle Bicycling Guide Map* (see Information, pp102–3) makes an excellent companion. Most of the route is covered on the map, which also includes an airport access insert.

The Ride

1½ hours, 15mi

From the baggage claim area, take the terminal's south exit. A sidewalk leads to International Blvd (Hwy 99), where you go north (left). Turning left onto S 170th St, on a clear day spectacular Mt Rainier will tower over your left shoulder. Once on Des Moines Dr/Memorial Dr, coast downhill for 2mi with views of the Cascades on your right.

At 6.6mi continue straight on the busy overpass following the sign to 14th Ave S. Negotiate the South Park Bridge and at 7.8mi turn left onto busy E Marginal Way S. The buildings on the right are part of the Boeing aircraft plant.

Turn right at Ellis Ave S, left onto Stanley Ave S, and left again onto Airport Way S. Continue straight for nearly 4mi, veering right onto 7th Ave S. Turn left onto S Jackson St (12.8mi) and enter Seattle's International District. A right at 1st Ave S leads into the historic Pioneer Square district. After 0.5mi, you can't miss the Seattle Art Museum. Across from the famous Pike Place Market, turn right and continue to the Convention Center and Seattle–King County visitor center.

Returning to the airport, one-way streets alter the start of the route. From the Convention Center entrance on Pike St, head northwest down 8th Ave, then turn left onto Pine St and left again onto 2nd Ave. Turn left onto S Jackson St, right onto Maynard Ave S, then veer left onto Airport Way S.

serves great Asian-influenced noodle dishes. There are several other offerings, including cafes, pubs and ethnic restaurants.

Getting There & Away One of the nation's most bicycle-friendly cities, Seattle is also well serviced by public transport.

Air Seattle's airport, known as Sea-Tac (☎ 800-544-1965), has daily flights to Europe, Asia, Canada and several US destinations on many national and regional carriers, as well as small regional commuter airlines.

The airport is 15mi south of the city; see the boxed text, 'Cycling to/from the Airport'. Metro bus 194 (express) and bus 174 run a downtown–Sea-Tac service about every 30 minutes. Fares are $2 (peak) and $1.25 (off-peak); bikes are free.

Bus Greyhound (☎ 628-5530 or ☎ 800-229-9424, Ⓦ www.greyhound.com) is at 811 Stewart St. Fares to New York start from $109 (70 hours); Los Angeles (LA) $59 (25 hours); Vancouver, $28 (four hours).

Quick Shuttle (☎ 800-665-2122, Ⓦ www.quickcoach.com) makes five daily express runs between Sea-Tac/Seattle downtown and Vancouver ($38, bikes are free but must be boxed or bagged).

Train King St Station is at 303 S Jackson St. Amtrak (☎ 800-872-7245, Ⓦ www.amtrak.com) leaves for Chicago (from $189, 46 hours) and destinations en route daily. There is a daily service to/from LA (from $104, 35 hours) and points en route. Bikes cost $5 and must be boxed.

Amtrak Cascades travels between Eugene, Oregon and Vancouver with several stops. Seattle to Portland costs $30 (three per day, 3½ hours), and to Vancouver is $28 (daily, four hours). Bikes cost $5, and are carried in the bicycle section of the baggage car. No boxing is required, however, due to limited space, advance reservations must be made.

Boat The *Victoria Clipper* (☎ 448-5000 or ☎ 800-888-2535, Ⓦ www.victoriaclipper.com), a high-speed passenger boat, operates to/from Victoria, BC daily (2½ hours, $66). Bikes cost $10 each way – book ahead. The boat leaves from Pier 69. Washington State Ferries (☎ 464-6400 or ☎ 800-843-3779, Ⓦ www.wsdot.wa.gov/ferries) operate ferries throughout Puget Sound (Bainbridge Island, Bremerton and Vashon Island), also connecting the San Juan Islands with Vancouver Island, BC. Puget Sound ferries leave downtown from Pier 52. Passenger fares vary according to destination; bikes cost $0.70.

Local Transport Metro Transit (☎ 553-3000 or ☎ 800-542-7876, Ⓦ transit.metrokc.gov) has bike-racks on all buses. Downtown, buses travel on surface streets or through the bus tunnel. Cyclists can only access two of the five tunnel stops, Convention Place and International District. Exact change is required for fares: $1.50 (peak), $1.25 (off-peak). Bikes are free.

Seattle Discovery

Duration ....1½–2½ hours
Distance 14mi
Difficulty ....easy
Start/End ....Pier 52 ferry terminal

Discover some of the best water and mountain views in Seattle, plus historic locks, an Indian Cultural Center, beaches and wild urban parks. An ideal time to ride is early evening, when sunset views across Puget Sound, with an Olympic Mtns backdrop, are incredible. Allow plenty of time to take in the side trips. Cues are not needed for this ride as it can be navigated using the map supplied.

THE RIDE (See Map, p108)

From the ferry terminal, cycle alongside Seattle's lively waterfront. For part of the route along Alaskan Way, there is a bikepath on the east side of the trolley tracks. Leave the bustling city behind and enter Seattle's twin **waterfront parks**, Myrtle Edwards Park and adjacent Elliott Bay Park. The **Elliott Bay bikepath** leads past the **rose garden**. Pause here for a moment, not just to smell the roses, but to look back at Mt Rainier, to the south across Elliott Bay. At 2.1mi, pass the huge **grain elevator** at Pier 86 Grain Terminal.

Link to the **Terminal 91 bikepath**, a fenced path through the railway yards, developed by the Port of Seattle (open 6am–9pm in summer, 6am–7pm winter).

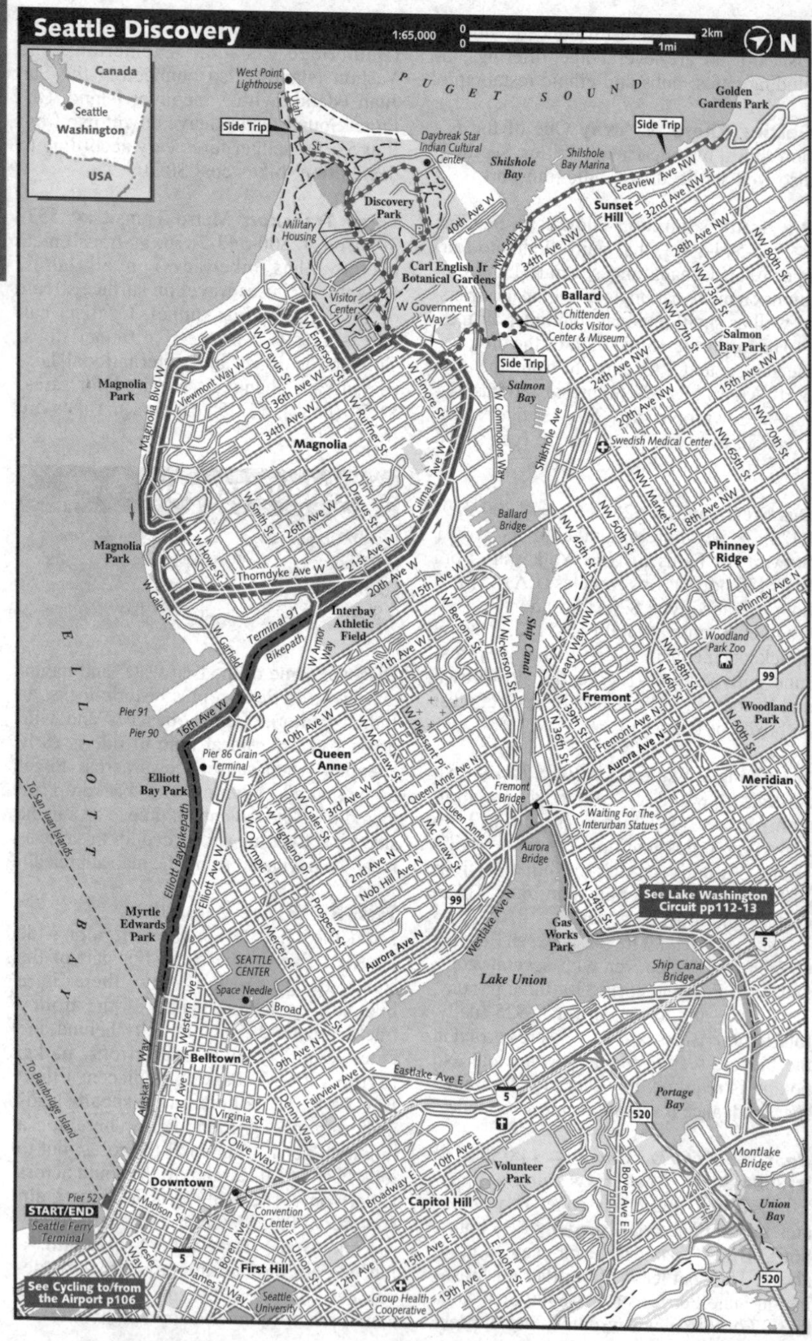
Seattle Discovery
1:65,000
0
0
2km
1mi
N
Canada
Seattle
Washington
USA
West Point Lighthouse
Utah
St
Side Trip
PUGET SOUND
Daybreak Star Indian Cultural Center
Shilshole Bay
Shilshole Bay Marina
Golden Gardens Park
Side Trip
Seaview Ave NW
Sunset Hill
32nd Ave NW
28th Ave NW
NW 80th St
Discovery Park
Military Housing
40th Ave W
NW 54th St
34th Ave NW
Carl English Jr Botanical Gardens
Ballard
NW 73rd St
NW 67th St
Visitor Center
W Government Way
Chittenden Locks Visitor Center & Museum
Salmon Bay Park
Side Trip
24th Ave NW
15th Ave NW
Magnolia Park
Magnolia Blvd W
Viewmont Way W
W Dravus St
W Emerson St
36th Ave W
W Elmore St
Salmon Bay
34th Ave W
W Ruffner St
W Commodore Way
Shilshole Ave
20th Ave NW
NW 70th St
Magnolia
Swedish Medical Center
NW 65th St
W Dravus St
Gilman Ave W
W Smith St
26th Ave W
NW Market St
8th Ave NW
Ballard Bridge
NW 50th St
NW 45th St
Magnolia Park
W Howe St
21st Ave W
Phinney Ridge
Thorndyke Ave W
20th Ave W
15th Ave W
W Galer St
W Bertona St
Phinney Ave N
Terminal 91
Interbay Athletic Field
Ship Canal
W Nickerson St
ELLIOTT BAY
W Garfield
Bikepath
W Armor Way
11th Ave W
Leary Way NW
Woodland Park Zoo
NW 48th St
99
Pier 91
St
Fremont
N 46th St
Woodland Park
Pier 90
16th Ave W
10th Ave W
W Pleasant Pl
N 39th St
N 36th St
Fremont Ave N
N 50th St
Pier 86 Grain Terminal
Queen Anne
W Mc Graw St
Queen Anne Ave N
Aurora Ave N
Meridian
Elliott Bay Park
3rd Ave W
Fremont Bridge
Queen Anne Dr
To San Juan Islands
W Galer St
Waiting For The Interurban Statues
W Highland Dr
Mc Graw St
Aurora Bridge
Elliott Ave W
W Olympic Pl
2nd Ave N
Nob Hill Ave N
Elliott Bay Bikepath
99
N 34th St
See Lake Washington Circuit pp112-13
Westlake Ave N
Myrtle Edwards Park
Prospect St
Gas Works Park
5
Mercer St
Aurora Ave N
SEATTLE CENTER
Lake Union
Ship Canal Bridge
Space Needle
Broad St
Western Ave
Belltown
9th Ave N
Alaskan Way
Eastlake Ave E
2nd Ave
Fairview Ave
5
Portage Bay
To Bainbridge Island
Virginia St
Denny Way
520
Olive Way
10th Ave E
Volunteer Park
Montlake Bridge
Downtown
Broadway E
Boyer Ave E
Pier 52
Capitol Hill
Union Bay
START/END
Seattle Ferry Terminal
Madison St
Convention Center
E Union St
5
Boren Ave
15th Ave E
E Aloha St
E Yesler Way
First Hill
12th Ave
19th Ave E
520
James
Way
Seattle University
Group Health Cooperative
See Cycling to/from the Airport p106

At 5.5mi is the start of the side trips to the **Chittenden Locks** and **Golden Gardens Park** (See Side Trips 1 & 2). Further on is the turnoff to **Discovery Park** (see Side Trip 3).

Back on the main route, cycle through the prestigious suburb of Magnolia. With Puget Sound and the Olympics to the northwest, Seattle and Mt Rainier to the southeast, this quiet stretch along Magnolia bluff has views to die for.

It's downhill back to the Terminal 91 bikepath. If it's a clear day and Mt Rainier is 'out', its magnificence dominates the horizon as you return to the ferry terminal.

Side Trip 1: Chittenden Locks

1mi return

To see these historic locks (see the boxed text 'Locks & Ladders'), leave the route at 5.5mi, following the bike route sign to the locks. After 0.1mi, veer right over railway tracks on a pedestrian/bike bridge, and through tiny 33rd Ave W. Cross W Commodore Way to Commodore Park, from where you look down at the **locks** and **Salmon Bay**. From here you must walk your bike as cycling is not allowed on the locks or in the adjacent **Carl English Jr Botanical Gardens**.

Side Trip 2: Golden Gardens

4.8mi return

Golden Gardens Park has a beach, picnic facilities and hiking trails on the wooded hillside abutting the shorefront. The park is a further 1.7mi beyond the lock's north entrance. Turn left onto NW 54th St, veering left onto Seaview Ave NW. Pass several notable seafood restaurants on Shilshole Bay, such as ***Anthony's Home Port*** and ***Ray's Boathouse*** (see Places to Eat, p105). Posh boats line the **Shilshole Bay Marina**.

Side Trip 3: Discovery Park

2.5mi return

This is Seattle's largest park. Originally Fort Lawton Army Base, today it is 534 acres of urban wilderness with 7mi of hiking trails, an extensive shoreline and a sanctuary for wildlife.

The side trip loops through the park, detouring to West Point Lighthouse. Enter the park and take the first left to the **visitor center** (☎ 206-386-4236), where park maps cost $1. Begin on the signed bike route with a short climb, then follow the sign to Daybreak Star Indian Cultural Center. At the bottom of the hill, follow the parking lot left (in the direction of the one-way sign) and continue to the **Daybreak Star Indian Cultural Center**, on

Locks & Ladders

The higher-elevation freshwater of Lake Washington and Lake Union meets the saltwater of Puget Sound in the 8mi-long Lake Washington Ship Canal. In 1911, under the direction of Hiram Chittenden, the unification of the waters began: a channel between the two lakes lowered Lake Washington by 9ft, then the canal was cut through to Puget Sound, and two locks were installed in 1917.

Up to 100,000 boats a year pass through the canal and the Chittenden Locks (also known as the Ballard Locks). With the adjacent fish ladder and the peaceful seven-acre Carl English Jr Botanic Gardens, this is a must-see for any visitor.

It's fascinating to watch the boats pass through the locks. Walkways offer a good look at the workings of these water elevators.

On the south side of the locks, the fish ladder allows salmon to fight their way to their spawning grounds. View the salmon close-up through underwater glass-sided tanks, or from above.

Inside the **visitor center** (☎ 783-7059), a **museum** and **film** document the locks' history. Free tours run from May to September.

The Mountain is Out!

Garrison Keilor, host of the popular radio show *Prairie Home Companion*, while doing a special show from Seattle, was making fun of Seattle's drizzly, gray weather. He joked that some people in Seattle reach puberty without sighting Mt Rainier. This is somewhat exaggerated but it is true to say that days, sometimes weeks, can go by when Mt Rainier hides mysteriously behind a misty shroud, and can't be seen, even on a clear day.

But on days when Mt Rainier is visible, words can't describe the awesome sight. On those days, locals will affectionately refer to this phenomenon by saying 'The Mountain is out!'.

the right. To reach it, take the path marked 'Serpent Mound' and 'Reflecting Pools'. This is a community center for Native Americans and has a small art gallery. The **views** here are spectacular.

Pedal up a short, steep hill to Utah St. To add to the side trip, making it 4.3mi return, turn right and ride 0.9mi to the still operational **West Point Lighthouse**, established in 1881. It's a great glide down – and a steep climb back!

Back on the side trip loop, a signed bike route climbs past former officers' quarters. Sweeping views of **Puget Sound** and the **Olympics** will impress, before the return to the visitor center. Turn left towards the gate and Washington Ave, and soon turn right onto the bike route, veering left after 0.1mi. Pass the visitor center, then turn right back to the park entrance.

Lake Washington Circuit

Duration	4½–7 hours
Distance	45.9mi
Difficulty	easy–moderate
Start/End	*W.F.T.I* statues, Fremont
Cues & Elevation Profile	p356

This ride showcases Seattle's natural beauty: panoramic mountain and lake vistas, secluded coves and forested hills. Start at the *Waiting for the Interurban* statues, corner N 34th St and Fremont Ave N, before traveling the Burke-Gilman Trail, Seattle's premier rail trail. You'll also visit prestigious lakeside suburbs and their waterfront parks, and pass over a floating bridge and through the Washington Park Arboretum.

GETTING TO/FROM THE RIDE

Bus

Metro Bus 28 leaves downtown twice an hour for the 20-minute ride to the statues. After 7pm and on Sunday, take Bus 26. The corner of Union St and 4th Ave is a central spot to catch it.

Bicycle

It's 3mi from the Seattle visitor center to the statues. From the Convention Center entrance on Pike St, head down 8th St, then turn left onto Pine St. Turn right at 6th Ave and after about 0.3mi, turn right onto Blanchard St and left onto 7th Ave. After 0.1mi veer right onto Dexter Ave N and continue for 2mi. Cross the Fremont Bridge. The statues are on the right.

Due to downtown Seattle's one-way streets, the return route is slightly different. Go south over the Fremont Bridge and continue on Dexter Ave N, which turns into 7th Ave. After one block turn right into Bell St. At the monorail tracks, turn left onto 5th Ave, then right onto Pike St. The Convention Center is a further 0.2mi.

THE RIDE (See Map, pp112–13)

Waiting for the Interurban, a group of statues of commuters huddled under a bus shelter, is probably Seattle's best-loved piece of public art. Decorating the statues is common, so don't be surprised if they're decked out in birthday garb or football team outfits.

Don't miss the side trip at 0.1mi. The short, steep climb ends at another fabulous piece of public art, the **Fremont Troll**. The 18ft-high troll keeps a watchful eye over Fremont from under the Aurora Bridge.

At 0.3mi, be sure to get on the bikepath, which looks like the sidewalk. Off to the right is **Gas Works Park** (0.7mi), site of a former gas-processing plant. Occupying one of the best viewpoints of the Seattle skyline, urban planners redefined the plant into an attractive, if somewhat unusual, park.

Gas Works Park marks the start of the **Burke-Gilman Trail**, a 12.5mi converted railway bed. Cruise along the trail beside **Lake Union**, through the **University of Washington** campus (2.2mi), along **Lake Washington**, with Cascade Mtn views to the right, to Tracy Owen Station Park. The route also runs near the Cascade Bicycle Club office (see Information Sources, p101).

The trail connects to the Sammamish River Trail; to add a side trip to the wineries, follow the Trails to the Wineries ride (p111) from 13.4mi.

Turn off the Burke-Gilman Trail (at 13.5mi, don't go under the underpass) and prepare for an extended climb. Enjoy a delicious descent to the lake and **OO Denny Park**. For the next 20mi, the route undulates alongside the lake, offering grand views. Pass through the vibrant town of **Kirkland**, filled with cafes and restaurants. Lakeside parks include Houghton Beach Park (24.1mi), with **kayaks** for rent (May–Sept).

At 25.2mi, don't be discouraged by the dead-end sign; bikes can squeeze though the gap at 25.8mi. It's a little trickier finding the start of the **Points Loop Trail**. Turn right onto NE 33rd, then look for the trail to the left of the dead-end sign. This lovely trail comes as quite a surprise, running parallel to Hwy 520.

Continue through quiet lakeside suburbs into Bellevue (30.1mi), enjoying stunning views of **Meydenbauer Bay** and the I-90 floating bridge. At 36mi, go downhill onto the **floating bridge** and glide along almost at water level for 1.5mi. It's hard to keep your eyes ahead, as outstanding views of Mt Rainier beg you to turn your head left.

From the 41.1mi mark, it's idyllic cycling through the **Washington Park Arboretum**, 200 acres of mature forest. Paths trace through a variety of gardens, a waterfront nature trail and a formal Japanese garden. In spring, Azalea Way is a dizzying display of color. The visitor center, at the north end of Arboretum Dr E (42mi), has maps.

A quick change to the left lane is needed immediately after the turn onto Lake Washington Blvd E (42.3mi), then continue on Lake Washington Blvd E for 0.4mi.

At 42.9mi, the **Museum of History & Industry**, showcasing Seattle and Puget Sound history, is on the right.

At busy Montlake Blvd, use the sidewalk – local cyclists do! This will take you back to the Burke-Gilman Trail for the last few miles to Fremont.

Trails to the Wineries

Duration	4–6½ hours
Distance	51.4mi
Difficulty	easy
Start/End	*W.F.T.I* statues, Fremont

This is an easy ride on bikepaths. Begin on the Burke-Gilman Trail (see the Lake Washington Circuit, pp110–11) and continue on the Sammamish River Trail to the Woodinville wineries and Marymoor Park. This ride can be a side trip on the Lake Washington Circuit, cues are not needed as it can be navigated using the map supplied.

THE RIDE (See Map, pp112–13)

Follow the Lake Washington Circuit until 13.4mi. Continue straight, using the underpass to access the **Sammamish River Trail**, which follows the Sammamish River through a mix of residential and pastoral areas, 12.3mi to Marymoor Park, at the north end of Lake Sammamish.

At 15.4mi use the underpass; when you emerge, veer left onto the trail (don't cross the bridge). Follow 'trail' signs over the second bridge. At Brackett's Park, the trail continues on the other side of Woodinville Dr.

At 20.2mi, turn right to the Woodinville wineries (see Side Trip). The Sammamish River Trail continues a further 5.5mi to **Marymoor Park**. Maps of the 642-acre park are available from the Recreation Office, 0.3mi after you enter the park, on the right in Willowmoor Meadow. Of interest is the **velodrome** (☎ 206-675-1424, W www.marymoor.velodrome.org), the only one in the Pacific Northwest, 0.8mi from the park's entrance. Races are held from May to September (7pm Wed & Fri) and track classes are offered.

Side Trip: Woodinville Wineries

0.6mi return

The striking Victorian-style building of **Columbia Winery** (☎ 425-488-2776, W www.columbiawinery.com), Washington State's oldest producer of premium wines, is on the right at 0.3mi. Across the road, **Chateau Ste Michelle** (☎ 425-488-1133, W www.ste-michelle.com) is one of Washington's first wineries. The centerpiece, a building reminiscent of a French chateau, is surrounded by 87-acre grounds and makes a lovely picnic spot.

Don't look for acres of vineyards here. Both wineries are production facilities, using grapes from eastern Washington. Basic picnic supplies are available from both wineries.

About 200 yards before the wineries is **Redhook Ale Brewery** (☎ 425-483-3232, W www.redhook.com), one of Washington's first microbreweries. Their original home is 200 yards from the start of this ride in Fremont (3400 Phinney Ave N). Meals and brews are served at their ***Forecaster's Public House***.

Contact the wineries/brewery for tours and tasting details.

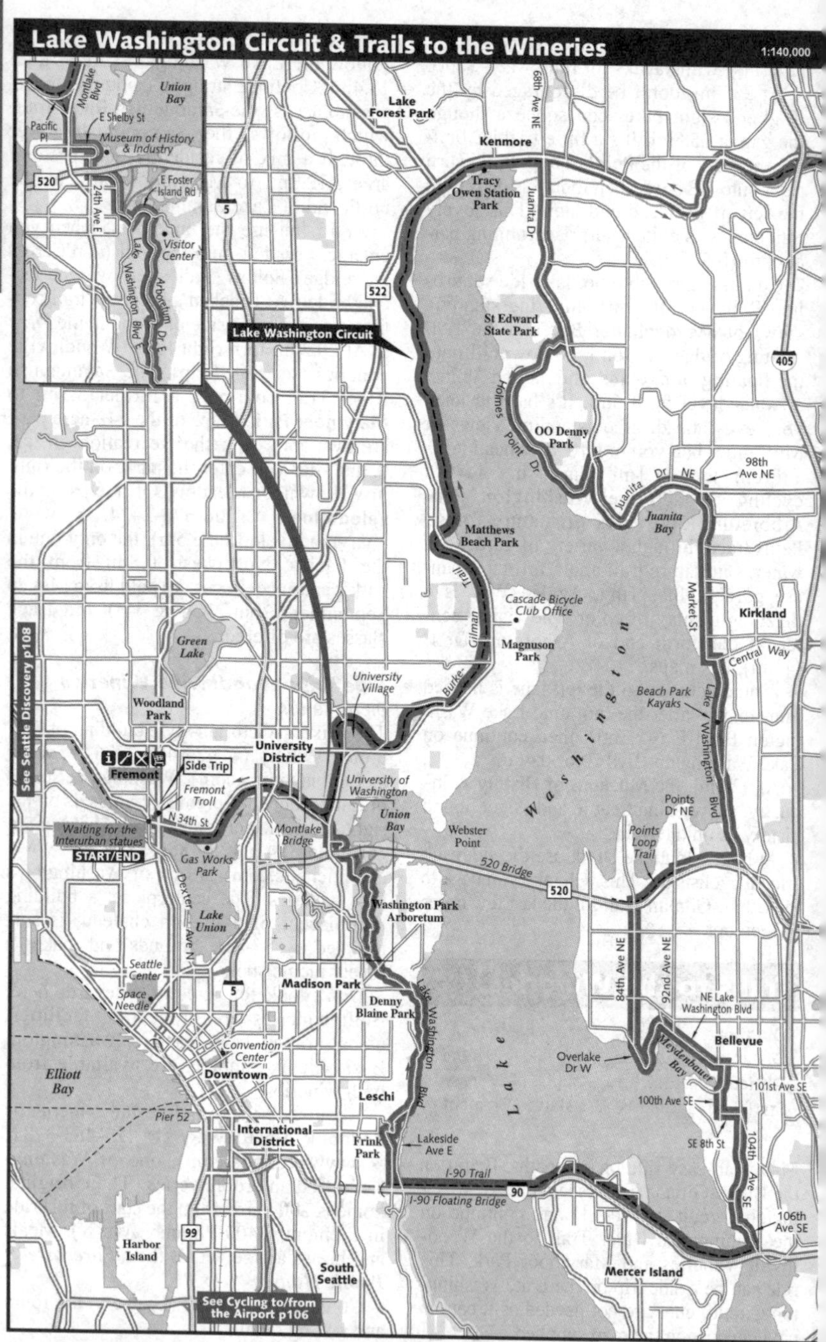
Lake Washington Circuit & Trails to the Wineries
1:140,000
Montlake Blvd
Union Bay
Pacific Pl
E Shelby St
Museum of History & Industry
520
24th Ave E
E Foster Island Rd
Visitor Center
Lake Washington Blvd E
Arboretum Dr E
Lake Forest Park
68th Ave NE
Kenmore
Tracy Owen Station Park
Juanita Dr
5
522
St Edward State Park
Lake Washington Circuit
405
Holmes Point Dr
OO Denny Park
98th Ave NE
Juanita Dr NE
Juanita Bay
Matthews Beach Park
Burke-Gilman Trail
Cascade Bicycle Club Office
Market St
Kirkland
Magnuson Park
Central Way
Green Lake
Woodland Park
University Village
Beach Park Kayaks
Lake Washington Blvd
University District
Side Trip
Fremont
Fremont Troll
University of Washington
N 34th St
Waiting for the Interurban statues
START/END
Union Bay
Webster Point
Points Dr NE
Points Loop Trail
Montlake Bridge
Gas Works Park
520 Bridge
Dexter Ave N
Washington Park Arboretum
Lake Union
84th Ave NE
92nd Ave NE
Seattle Center
Madison Park
Space Needle
Denny Blaine Park
NE Lake Washington Blvd
Bellevue
Convention Center
Downtown
Overlake Dr W
Meydenbauer Bay
101st Ave SE
Elliott Bay
Leschi
100th Ave SE
Pier 52
Lake Washington
International District
Frink Park
Lakeside Ave E
SE 8th St
104th Ave SE
I-90 Trail
90
I-90 Floating Bridge
106th Ave SE
99
Harbor Island
South Seattle
Mercer Island

See Seattle Discovery p108

See Cycling to/from the Airport p106

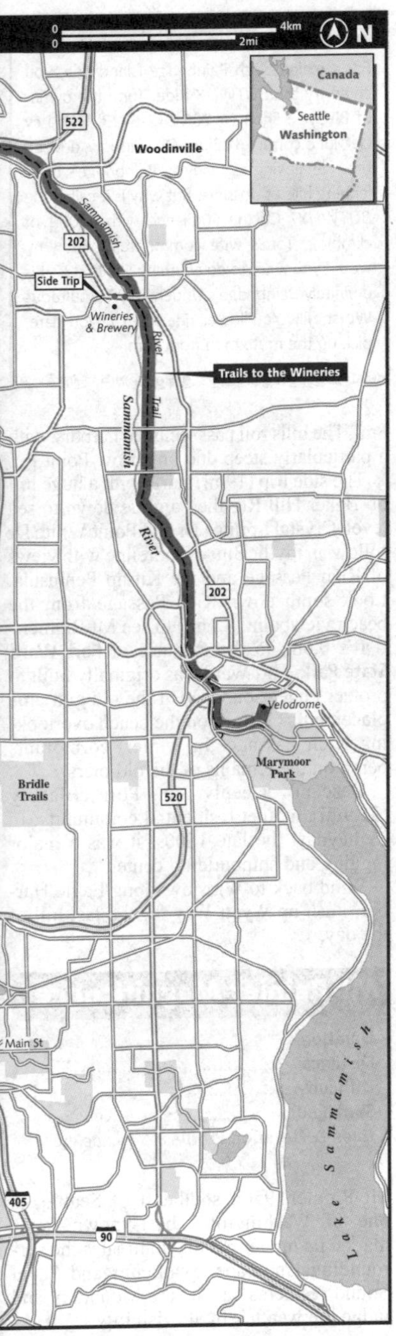

Bainbridge Island Circuit

Duration	3–5 hours
Distance	26.9mi
Difficulty	moderate
Start/End	Chamber of Commerce
Cues & Elevation Profile	p356

It's hard to believe this rural haven is only 10mi from Seattle. The 35-minute ferry ride across Puget Sound – a sightseeing extravaganza – is worth the trip alone. Hilly and challenging, the ride winds through the island on quiet roads flanked by ivy-clad firs and cedars, beside shorelines and snug harbors. The icing? Unsurpassed views of Seattle and the Cascades.

PLANNING

With more than a dozen B&Bs, a motel and a campground, the island is an alternative to staying in Seattle. The ferry docks in Winslow, the island's commercial center, which has accommodations, and interesting shops and galleries. For information, head to the Bainbridge Island Chamber of Commerce (☎ 206-842-3700, W www.bainbridgechamber.com), 590 Winslow Way E; it's a short 0.3mi ride up Olympic Dr from the ferry.

When to Ride

This ride can be done year-round. It is not unusual to see people cycling Bainbridge in winter, to prepare for the Chilly Hilly ride.

Maps

Both AAA's *Bremerton/Kitsap County Map* ($3) or Rand McNally's *Kitsap County Map* ($4) cover Bainbridge Island at 1:40 000.

GETTING TO/FROM THE RIDE

Washington State Ferries operates hourly ferries from Seattle's Pier 52 to Winslow on Bainbridge Island (35 minutes, $3.70, $0.70 for bikes).

THE RIDE (See Map, p114)

Bainbridge is hilly! On the last Sunday in February, Bainbridge Island hosts the ride that kicks off the Northwest cycling season, the aptly named **Chilly Hilly**. Considered by *Bicycling Magazine* to be one of the four classic rides in the nation, the *Chilly Hilly* attracts more than 2000 stalwart cyclists each year. Contact the Cascade Bicycle Club (see p101). This ride follows a similar route to the Chilly Hilly, following quiet roads counterclockwise around the island.

Leaving Winslow, the road is sprinkled with a mix of Victorian and contemporary houses. After a couple of miles of primer hills, the road curves around **Murden Cove** with its unobstructed views of Seattle and the Cascades. Disregard the 'Do Not Enter' sign (3.3mi), which is for cars only, and continue on the right-hand side on the pedestrian/cycle path.

At the island's northeast corner (6.7mi), **Fay Bainbridge State Park** has picnic and camping facilities, a sandy driftwood-covered beach and more views. **Frog Rock**, two 'cute' painted boulders, greets you at 8mi. The hills roll past secluded harbors, with a particularly steep duo on Arrow Point Rd.

The side trip (19mi) starts with a huge hill on Baker Hill Rd, then a glide down to sea level. Crystal Springs Dr and Point White Dr follow an idyllic 3mi of shoreline with views of Rich Passage and the Kitsap Peninsula. Look south down Rich Passage from the beach viewpoint (4.1mi) to see Mt Rainier.

It's 0.6mi to the entrance of **Fort Ward State Park**. Fort Ward was originally built to protect Puget Sound. Visit the old **gun emplacements** (1.3mi), on the beach overlooking Rich Passage. In winter, cormorants perch on the remains of the old piers.

Descend steeply to Port Blakely (21.9mi), a quiet residential community. In its heyday, the late 1800s, it was a major logging and shipbuilding center.

Wind back to Winslow along Eagle Harbor. Push up Wyatt Way for the last hill of the day.

But Why?

For a really tough Bainbridge Island ride, you could try the *BUTWHY* Ride. Tom, the owner of BI Cycle Shop (☎ 206-842-6413, e b-i-cycle@juno.com), 162 Bjune Dr, Winslow, devised the ride, linking as many of Bainbridge's challenging hills as possible. But why is it called the *BUTWHY*? Of the 50mi ride with 4200ft of climbing, Tom's wife commented, 'But why would you want to do anything like that?'. It is definitely **B**ainbridge's **U**ndeniably **T**umultuous **W**orst **H**ills **Y**ou'll ever ride Ride! If you dare, pick up the route map from Tom.

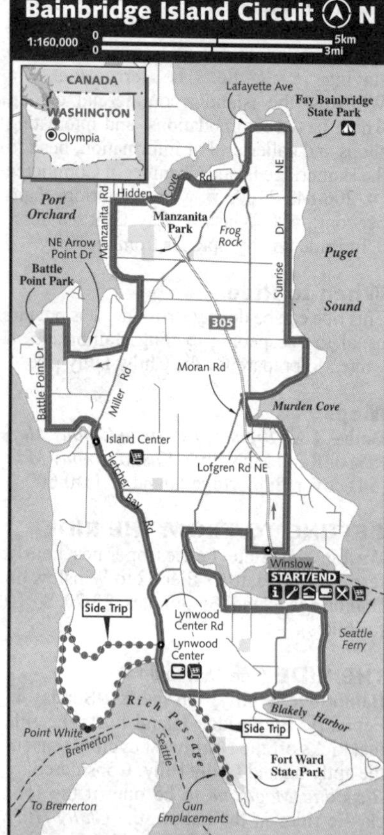

Mt Rainier Magnificence

Duration	3 days
Distance	173mi
Difficulty	hard
Start/End	Enumclaw
Cues & Elevation Profiles	pp356–7

Mt Rainier, 95mi southeast of Seattle, is one of Washington's best-known landmarks. Its immense bulk dominates the surrounding landscape. Seattleites and Puget Sound residents call it 'the Mountain' and judge the weather by its visibility.

The highlight of this ride is 'the Mountain', which appears right from the start, then plays hide and seek as the ride weaves through valleys and rural towns. The forests open up during the ascent to Paradise, revealing Mt Rainier's enormity.

Mt Rainier begs the cyclist to don a daypack and walking shoes, whether for a few hours or a few days. The park's trails offer a wonderland of old-growth forests, wildflower meadows, waterfalls and glaciers.

Sections of the route between Orting and Ohop Lake are parts of the Tacoma Wheelmen Bicycle Club's Daffodil Classic ride. Most of Day 1 features in Redmond Bicycle Club's Ramrod ride.

HISTORY

Well before Europeans laid eyes on this mighty mountain, Native Americans knew this volcanic peak as Tahoma, translated as 'great snowy peak'. They visited the foothills to hunt, fish and pick huckleberries, but were uneasy about climbing the mountain, believing it was the dwelling place of an ill-tempered god.

In 1792 British captain George Vancouver spotted the peak from Puget Sound, and named it for his friend Rear Admiral Peter Rainier. The first documented ascent to the summit was in 1870, by Hazard Stevens and Philemon van Trump. Commercial tourism began in the 1880s when James Longmire built a mineral hot springs lodge where Longmire stands today. He established a trail up the mountain to Paradise, allowing access for mountain climbers.

Mount Rainier was declared the fifth national park in the USA in 1899. In 1890, Fay Fuller, a Puget Sound schoolteacher, became the first woman to climb Mt Rainier.

NATURAL HISTORY

Mt Rainier (14,411ft) is the highest peak in the Cascades. With 25 glaciers, it is the USA's most heavily glaciated peak outside Alaska.

Geologically, the Cascade peaks are very young. About a million years ago, Mt Rainier was created by repeated volcanic eruptions. Its height was about 16,000ft, when some 5800 years ago it 'blew its top'. Another blast occurred about 2500 years ago, and the last notable eruption was about 150 years ago. Although quiet, it is believed that the volcano is not extinct.

Mt Rainier Mini-Magnificence

If you don't have time for the three-day ride around Mt Rainier, this year-round day ride offers spectacular views as it winds through rural farmlands on quiet back roads and along the Foothills Trail.

The Ride

3½–5½ hours, 35.3mi

Begin in Enumclaw, following the first 19.2mi of Day 1 of the Mt Rainier Magnificence ride to Orting. Return from Orting to Enumclaw, following the Day 3 route from 48.2mi.

Mt Rainier is known for its alpine wildflowers. Forests of Douglas fir, Western hemlock and Western red cedar dominate the lower elevations while mountain hemlock and subalpine fir are found above 4000ft. Black-tailed deer, mountain goats, hoary marmots, Douglas squirrels, pikas, black bears and cougars inhabit the park as well as a variety of birds such as eagles, thrushes, wrens and Stellar's jays.

PLANNING

When to Ride

Depending on snow levels, it is possible to ride from June to mid-October – check road conditions (☎ 360-569-2211). Trails are usually snow-free by July, when wildflowers bloom. Huckleberries are ripe in August, and September sees fiery fall colors dot the mountainside. Avoid cycling Day 2 of this ride on weekends, due to heavy tourist traffic. The least crowded months are June, September and early October.

Maps & Books

The Pierce County Transportation Division (☎ 253-798-7250), 2401 S 35th St, Tacoma, WA 98409, produces the free *Pierce County Bicycle Guide Map*. The Benchmark and the DeLorme atlases also cover the ride area. Trails Illustrated *Mount Rainier National Park* (1:50,000; $8.95) shows the park and hiking trails in good detail.

Lonely Planet's *Hiking in the USA* has a section on the park. Ira Spring & Harvey Manning's *50 Hikes in Mount Rainier National Park* ($14.95) has more hikes. For interesting reading, pick up Betty Filley's *The Big Fact Book about Mount Rainier* ($17.95).

Information Sources

Contact Mt Rainier National Park, Tahoma Woods, Star Route, Ashford, WA 98304 (☎ 360-569-2211 or ☎ 569-4453, **W** www.nps.gov/mora) for permits and information. Request the *Tahoma News* and park map (both are also free at the Nisqually entrance). A permit is required for backcountry hiking, which can also be picked up (up to 24 hours in advance) from the Longmire Wilderness Information Center or Paradise visitor center.

What to Bring

Weather is very changeable on and near all the Cascade peaks, so pack warm clothes and rain gear. On Day 2 temperatures can vary by at least 10°F from the lower elevations to Paradise.

GETTING TO/FROM THE RIDE

Enumclaw

Bus Metro buses serve Enumclaw via Auburn. Bus 150 leaves downtown for Auburn every half-hour, connecting to Bus 915 to Enumclaw only once an hour (5am–6pm). Each-way fare is $1.75 (ask for a transfer to the second bus); bikes are free. Plan carefully, as the connection from Auburn to Enumclaw only operates on weekdays. The Auburn–Enumclaw ride is about 11mi, mostly on Hwy 164, which is quite busy around Auburn.

Bicycle The basic route of the 43mi ride from Seattle to Enumclaw is outlined on the *King County Bicycling Guidemap*. Carrying the *Seattle Bicycling Guide Map* for the portion to Renton and a detailed Seattle map is advised. Most of the route is pleasant but there are sections with heavy traffic, such as Rainier Ave S and parts of Hwy 169.

From downtown Seattle make your way to the I-90 bikepath. Just before the I-90 floating bridge turn south turn onto Lake Washington Blvd, which becomes Seward Ave S at Seward Park. There are turns on Rainier Ave S, 57th Ave S, Waters Ave S and Holyoke Way S en route to Rainier Ave S. At the southern end of Lake Washington, 8mi after Seward Park, turn left onto Airport Way, then at Logan Ave turn left and access the Cedar River Trail, a paved bikepath which continues 7mi almost to Maple Valley. The bikepath begins as a park-like stretch along the Cedar River, then passes through Cedar River Park. It continues alongside Renton–Maple Valley Rd (Hwy 169) until the paving ends after 7mi. Go left on Cedar Mountain Place to Jones Rd and continue on busy Hwy 169, through Maple Valley and Black Diamond to Enumclaw.

THE RIDE

Enumclaw

☎ 360

Enumclaw proudly calls itself the 'Gateway to Mt Rainier'. Enumclaw, meaning 'thundering mountain', was named after a mountain northeast of town, where local Native Americans were frightened by a thundering noise within the mountain. The town was planned in 1885 after the arrival of the railroad, and is now surrounded by farmlands. Its historic center has an old-world charm.

Information Enumclaw Chamber of Commerce (☎ 825-7666, **W** chamber.enumclaw.wa.us) is at 1421 Cole St (closed Sunday). Locally, Mt Rainier information is available from the Snoqualmie Ranger District Office (☎ 825-6585), 857 Roosevelt Ave E, where there is a National Parks representative (open weekdays & Sat between Memorial Day and Labor Day).

Key Bank, Bank of America and Wells Fargo are all on Cole St.

Enumclaw Cyclery (☎ 825-4461) is at 1456 Cole St Enumclaw Ski & Mountain Company (☎ 825-6910 or ☎ 800-766-9297, **W** www.tx3.com/~enumski), 240 Roosevelt Ave E hires mountain bikes. These are the only bike shops on the ride.

Things to See & Do Pick up the **Enumclaw Historical Walking Tour** from the Chamber. The tour winds through the town's streets, indicating century-old buildings and houses of historical interest.

MacRae's Indian Books, 1605 Cole St, houses a huge collection of books on Native Americans, and is reputed to be the largest bookstore of its kind in the USA. The friendly owner is a well of information.

The King County Fairgrounds (see Places to Stay) hosts the **King County Fair**, a week-long, old-fashioned county fair (third week in Jul). It's followed by the **Pacific Northwest Highland Games**, a Scottish Festival (last weekend in Jul).

The **Mutual of Enumclaw Stage Race** (mid-May) consists of three stages, a time trial, criterium and road race. The sponsor is TiCycles, a bicycle shop in Seattle (☎ 206-522-7602, 🆆 www.ticycles.com).

Places to Stay The ***King County Fairgrounds*** *(☎ 825-7777 or ☎ 206-296-8888, 45224 284th Ave SE)*, 1.3mi from the town center, is also the local campground (open April–Nov). Reservations are essential (call weekdays 9am–4.30pm), as they don't cater to walk-ins. The cost is $12 per tent.

Adjacent to the fairgrounds, bicycle-friendly ***King's Motel*** *(☎ 825-1626, 🆆 www.kingsmotel.com)* has singles/doubles from $55/65 and an outdoor pool.

A stately 1922 Colonial mansion houses the ***White Rose Inn B&B*** *(☎ 825-7194 or ☎ 800-404-7194, 🆆 www.whiteroseinnbb.com, 1610 Griffin St)*. The inn has four rooms from $85, including breakfast. The owners are cyclists.

Places to Eat Self-caterers can go to the ***QFC supermarket*** *(cnr Monroe St & Roosevelt Ave E)*.

Mel's Cuppa Joe & Deli *(☎ 825-3384, 1236 Griffin Ave)* offers the requisite coffee choices plus soups, sandwiches and baked goods. Across the road is the ***Back Door Bake Shop*** *(☎ 825-2823)*. A few doors away, ***Cynthia's Pony Express Cafe*** *(☎ 825-2055)* has good-value, home-style meals ($5–13).

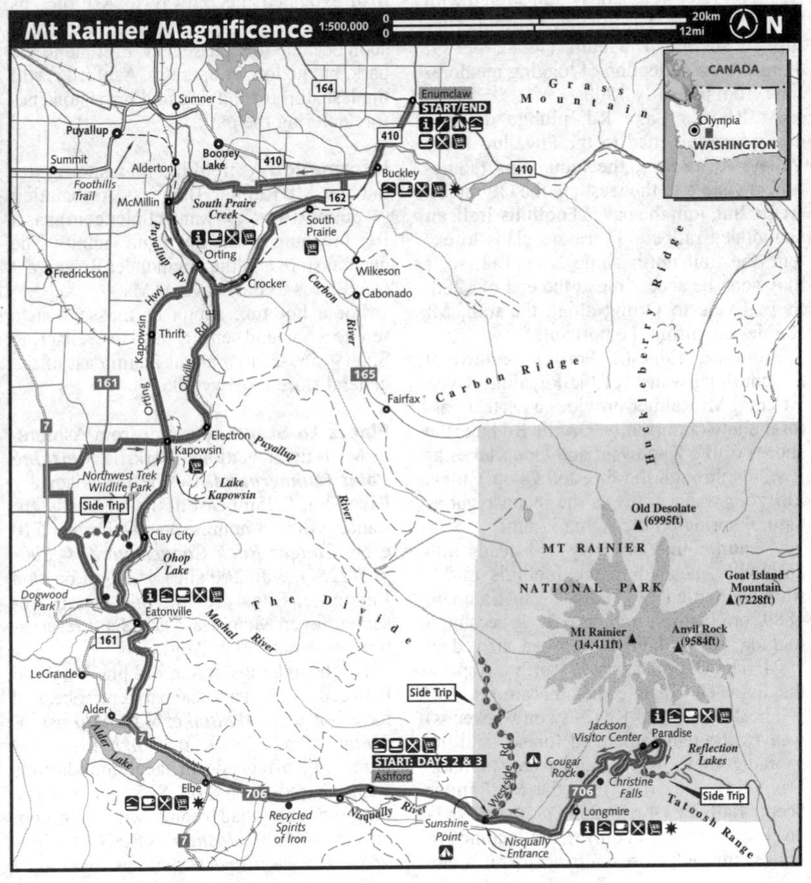

The ***Mint Alehouse*** *(☎825-8361, 1608 Cole St)* offers pizza, salads, burgers and sandwiches from $5, plus, of course, beer! At ***Seeder's Steak & Brew House*** *(☎ 802-6685, 1502 Initial St)* prices range from $11 to $32.

Day 1: Enumclaw to Ashford

6-10 hours, 60.1mi

Cycle through farmlands, dropping into the Puyallup River valley. The route undulates through forests and farms passing through Orting (19.2mi) and Eatonville (40.1mi), both blessed with the spectacular backdrop of Mt Rainier. The only real climbs are in and out of Eatonville.

Look over your left shoulder as Mt Rainier escorts you out of Enumclaw, and follows you several miles beyond Buckley. Begin on Hwy 410, a busy 3mi stretch with a wide shoulder. The **Buckley Foothills Historical Society Museum** (☎ 829-1289; 3.3mi) has a collection of logging memorabilia from the early 1900s.

At Rhodes Lake Rd, plunge down a curvy forested road to the **Puyallup River Valley**. At 12.9mi, the mountains (sometimes) visible to the west are the Olympics. At 16.2mi, join the paved **Foothills Trail**, an abandoned railbed. There are plans to extend the trail north along Hwy 162, so it may soon be accessible at the end of 128th St E. Cycle to Orting along the trail, Mt Rainier engulfing the horizon.

From the bridge (23.9mi), look down at the churning waters of the Puyallup River. At 26mi Mt Rainier provides a perfect pastoral photo opportunity. Orville Rd hugs the shores of the Kapowsin and Ohop lakes as it winds through the forested Ohop Valley. Fill your water bottle at the inconspicuous natural spring on the right (37.6mi).

A short climb on Hwy 161 leads into **Eatonville**, nestled in the foothills of Mt Rainier. Settled by Thomas van Eaton in 1889, originally a trading post, it became a logging town when the railroad arrived in 1904. The Ohop Bakery is worth a stop for the divine chocolate-coated macaroons.

The Alder Cutoff Rd (busy on weekends) weaves through farms and forests, and the sporadic views of Mt Rainier are stunning. From tiny Elbe (52.1mi), the **Mt Rainier Scenic Railway** (☎ 569-2588 *or* ☎ 888-783-2611, W www.mrsr.com) steam locomotive winds through forests to Mineral Lake (1½ hours; Jun–Sept). If you're into trains, stay in a caboose at the ***Hobo Inn*** *(☎ 569-2500)*. Peek at the **Evangelische Lutherische Kirche**, a tiny Lutheran church built in 1906 for German settlers. It measures a mere 18ft by 24ft and is topped with a 55ft steeple.

Allow time for a stop at the unique outdoor sculpture park, **Recycled Spirits of Iron** (☎ 569-2280; 55mi). Among Dan Klennert's amazing sculptures welded from antique scrap metal, the *pièce de résistance* for any cyclist is the 15ft-high penny farthing.

Ashford

☎ 360

The small town of Ashford is 6mi west of the Nisqually entrance to Mt Rainier National Park. In 1904, Tacoma Eastern Railroad extended the railway to Ashford, its last stop. Originally a logging railroad, it soon became the 'passenger' railroad to the park, but no longer operates. Ashford is still the last stop for lodging and provisions before entering the park.

Information Ashford has no visitor center but the Mt Rainier Business Association (☎ 569-0910, W www.mt-rainier.com) has a free brochure on the town and vicinity. The general store and the Highlander Restaurant (see Places to Eat) have ATMs.

For a hot tub, sauna or massage in a serene woodland setting, head to Wellspring Spa (☎ 569-2514), about 2.5mi east of the general store on Hwy 706.

Places to Stay About 6mi from Ashford, in Mt Rainier National Park, is ***Sunshine Point Campground***. Beside the Nisqually River, it is 0.25mi east of the Nisqually entrance, with 18 nonreservable sites for $10 each. ***Cougar Rock Campground*** *(☎ 800-365-2267)*, with 200 sites, is 2.3mi beyond Longmire. Sites are $12 and can be reserved (open Memorial Day–Sept; reservations essential Jul & Aug).

All the lodgings in Ashford line Hwy 706 between Ashford and the park entrance, and have hot tubs! ***Whittaker's Bunkhouse & Motel*** *(☎ 569-2439, e bunkhouse@mashell.com)* offers dorm accommodations with shared bath for $25 per person. Single/double/quad rooms with bathroom cost $65/65/90. ***Jasmer's B&B*** *(☎ 569-2682, W www.jasmers.com)* has two rooms from $60, plus they can book an array of cabins in the area. A little further down Hwy 706, the ***Nisqually Lodge*** *(☎ 569-8804 or ☎ 888-674-3554)* has doubles from $80. An elegant country inn, ***Alexander's Inn*** *(☎ 569-2300 or ☎ 800-654-7615, W www.alexanderscountryinn.com)* is 4mi beyond Ashford. Rooms with bathroom start at $110, including breakfast. ***Wellspring Spa*** (see Information) also has cabins from $79.

In the park, the ***National Park Inn*** (Longmire) and the ***Paradise Inn*** are both National Historic landmarks. Built in a spectacular 5400ft setting in 1917, Paradise Inn is the grander of the two. Rooms without/with bath start at $75/112 (open mid-May through Sept). In a rustic setting, the cozy National Park Inn is open all year. Rooms start at $74/104. Both inns serve all meals. Make your (essential) reservations through **Mt Rainier Guest Services** (☎ 569-2275, W www.guestservices.com/rainier).

Places to Eat Serving the community since 1905, ***Suver's Ashford General Store*** *(30402 Hwy 706)* has most necessities. For sweet snacks and espresso, head to the ***Whittaker's Bunkhouse & Motel Cafe*** (see Places to Stay). ***The Highlander Restaurant & Bar*** *(☎ 569-2953, 30319 Hwy 706)* has cheap breakfast, lunch and dinner, with home-made pies for dessert. Go upscale at ***Alexander's Inn*** (see Places to Stay), where dinners include duck, chicken, and trout from their own pond. Breakfast and lunch are also served.

Day 2: Ashford Circuit

4½–8 hours, 48.6mi

Make an early start for this stunningly scenic ride up to Paradise. The word is *up* right from the start, 24mi of up, but once you reach the aptly named Paradise, the return is an exhilarating downhill.

Warm up with the easy 6mi ride to the Nisqually park entrance. The $5 bike entry fee is valid for one week. It's a while until the foothills give way to Mt Rainier views, however, the lower reaches of the park are a fairyland of **old-growth forests**. Many trees stretch 150ft into the sky above.

The Nisqually River follows playfully alongside the road. Cross Kautz Creek (9.4mi), a glacier-fed stream, and marvel at the first views of the mountain, or hike one of the trails.

Longmire (12.4mi) is the site where James Longmire built a mineral hot springs lodge. Today, the buildings include the ***National Park Inn*** (see Places to Stay), Wilderness Information Center, **Longmire Museum**, plus National Park offices. The museum, in the original park headquarters, has displays of the park's early days and natural history. A self-guided hike, the 0.7mi **Trail of the Shadows** passes the site of the former Longmire Springs Hotel, plus the springs.

After Longmire the real climbing begins. Views of the mountain and the **Tatoosh Range** abound. The walk to the **Christine Falls** viewpoint (16.8mi) is a welcome break. The one-way road 'to Paradise via viewpoint' is awesome. From **Ricksecker Point**, the mountain seems as if it's at arm's length.

After **Narada Falls** (21.4mi), the road wiggles steeply to Paradise. The area is laced with **hiking trails**. Pick up the free *Paradise Area Trails* map from the **Henry M Jackson Visitor Center** (24.1mi). Visit the impressive lobby at the ***Paradise Inn*** (24.4mi; see Places to Stay).

The descent begins on the one-way road through alpine meadows. The side trip (26.7mi) to **Reflection Lakes** shows some of Mother Nature's best architecture; the lakes offer a striking mirror image of the mountain.

Whoosh! It's all downhill to Ashford.

Side Trip: Westside Rd

26mi return

The 13mi gravel Westside Rd is a popular mountain bike route, often used by cyclists

Warning

Lights on!

Even though you will be cycling to Paradise in daylight, there are two reasons to have your lights on. Once in the park, the shoulder becomes quite narrow, often only 12 to 18 inches wide. The old-growth forests in the park's lower elevations are at times so dense that the light is poor. Both front and rear lights will enhance visibility.

Cycling in the Park

In Mt Rainier National Park, cyclists may only ride on public roads and campground roadways, not on park trails. The only mountain-bike route is Westside Rd (see Side Trip).

to reach the trailheads. The first 3.2mi of the road is open to motor vehicles, and is easy cycling on a hybrid or mountain bike.

From Fish Creek (3.2mi) a mountain bike is essential. From the road there are views of Mt Wow to the southwest. At 7mi, reach Round Pass (elevation 3900ft); a 0.9mi trail to Lake George and a 2.4mi trail to Gobblers Knob Lookout begin here.

Descend to cross the Puyallup River (3500ft), climbing to cross St Andrews Creek at 11.3mi (3800ft), where a trail leads to Denman Falls. The road ends at Klapatche Point (4100ft).

Bikes are not allowed on any of the trails off the Westside Rd. Early in the season, check for road flooding.

Day 3: Ashford to Enumclaw

6–10 hours, 64.3mi

Retrace the route from Day 1 for the first 20mi to Eatonville, then it's a short side trip to a wildlife park. Undulating hills, forests and farmlands make up most of the day. Following a steep descent into Orting is an idyllic bikepath along the Carbon River.

Glide down into Eatonville, continuing the descent for another 1mi. The 3mi section on Hwy 161 can be busy but there is a wide shoulder. **Dogwood Park** (23.1mi) affords another great view of Mt Rainier, with an interesting historical marker.

The side trip (25.8mi) travels to **Northwest Trek** (☎ 832-6117 or ☎ 800-433-8735, w www.nwtrek.org), a 635-acre wildlife park with animals native to the Northwest. Ride for 2mi on hilly Jensen Rd to Hwy 161. Turn left, cycle 0.1mi, then turn right onto Trek Dr E for 1mi. Adults pay $9 (open Mar–Oct).

Except for a busy stretch on Hwy 7, it's farm roads most of the way to Kapowsin. Mt Rainier is larger than life as you leave Orting along the Carbon River on the peaceful **Foothills Trail**, undoubtedly one of the most gorgeous stretches of reclaimed rail-trail in the world. The paved path lasts about 4mi, and the route continues on the quiet South Prairie–Carbon River Rd. At time of publication there were plans to extend the trail to South Prairie and Buckley.

With Mt Rainier again demanding attention, you'll hardly notice the final climb. Return to Enumclaw on Hwy 410.

North Cascades Contrasts

Duration	5 days
Distance	247mi
Difficulty	hard
Start	Mt Vernon
End	Wenatchee
Cues & Elevation Profiles	pp358–9

A two-for-one spectacular, this ride contrasts wet, wild, western Washington with dry yet dramatic Eastern Washington. From start to finish the ride is breathtaking; striking scenery, giant vistas, mighty rivers and stunning peaks thrill at every turn.

Ease into the ride alongside the Skagit River, winding through its shady valley. Hit the North Cascades Hwy, the lifeline of North Cascades National Park, where mind-boggling mountains and teal-green lakes will blow you away. Drink in every bit of scenery, a feast for the eyes beyond belief, as the road climbs to a crescendo at Washington Pass, then drops down with a divine descent to the Methow Valley, where rolling hills replace rugged mountains.

Meander through the Methow, connecting with the mighty Columbia River. A delicious vein of flourishing apple orchards contrasts with the arid earth all the way to Wenatchee.

HISTORY

Farming has been the economic foundation of the lower Skagit Valley since the 1870s. Farming still occupies the land, with tulips the dominant crop. Further up the valley, logging and mining were the mainstays. Seattle City Light saw the Upper Skagit River's potential, and, in 1924, built the first of three dams, harnessing the waters for hydro-electricity, and company towns such as Diablo and Newhalem were built.

The gem of the northern mountain range is the North Cascades National Park and Recreation Area. Modern day exploration of the area began with Alexander Ross, who in 1814 crossed today's southern park boundary. In 1968, the 505,000-acre North Cascades National Park, and Ross Lake and Lake Chelan National Recreation Areas were established. In 1972, the paved North Cascades Hwy (Hwy 20), considered to be one of the most scenic roads in the country, officially opened, linking west and east. In 1988,

Congress designated approximately 92% of the three park areas as wilderness.

On the east side of the Cascades, Native Americans lived in the Methow Valley for some 9000 years. The first Europeans came to the area in 1811. With gold as the original lure, settlements began in 1883. It wasn't until 1972 and the highway opening that tourism arrived and the area boomed.

The word synonymous with the Columbia River and the Wenatchee River Valley, is 'apple'. In the 1890s the semi-arid lands were 'reclaimed' for orchards. Later, irrigation projects along the Columbia River created an even more fruitful area.

NATURAL HISTORY

The Skagit River cuts a narrow valley through the North Cascades, an area of rugged alpine peaks, glaciers, deep valleys and glacial lakes. The mountains were formed from the buckled seafloor of an ancient micro-continent. Ice-Age glaciers further crowded the range. In the southwestern corner of the park, carved by glaciers, is the spectacular 55mi-long Lake Chelan.

The North Cascades divide the state, the wet western slopes thick with Douglas fir and Western red cedar, the drier eastern slopes sparsely forested with ponderosa pine. Black bears and mountain lions frequent the backcountry, mountain goats scramble among rugged mountain slopes, and marmots laze on rocks in the sun. Bald eagles are in abundance, especially in winter around Rockport. In summer, birds to look for are black swifts, Clark's nutcrackers and mountain chickadees.

The Upper Methow River flows through a straight, steep-walled valley, cut by a glacier during the most recent Ice Age. The valley widens at Winthrop and Twisp, and the Methow flows into the Columbia.

Central Washington is dominated by the Columbia River and its dams. This massive river, the third-largest in the USA, begins in the mountains of British Columbia, cuts through the center of Washington, then slices through the Cascades to the Pacific.

PLANNING

When to Ride

The North Cascades Hwy can open from sometime in late April until October or early November. Opening and closing dates are decided by snow levels; call ☎ 800-695-7623 or the North Cascades visitor center (☎ 206-386-4495).

Several businesses depend on the highway to determine their annual opening and closing times. Don't plan to ride before Memorial Day or after early October.

> **Warning**
>
> 
>
> Campers can enjoy several campgrounds on Days 2 & 3. Others must be prepared to complete both days in one, as there are no lodging options between Marblemount and Mazama. Finish the day in Mazama, instead of Winthrop, to cut 13mi off the distance. It's a long day, so start by 7am.

Maps & Books

For basic overview maps, this ride is covered on two Square One maps, *Northwest Washington* and *Washington's Okanogan* (each $4.95; 6mi to an inch). If the DeLorme Atlas & Gazetteer is your supplement map, pages 67, 83–4, 95–100 and 109–13 cover the ride. If the Benchmark Atlas is your choice, then reference pages 42–5, 58–60 and 73–4. For an excellent hiking map, purchase Trails Illustrated's *North Cascades National Park* ($9.95).

For hikers, there is a plethora of books, including *100 Hikes in the North Cascades* by Ira Spring & Harvey Manning ($14.95) and *Hiking the North Cascades* by Erik Molvar ($15.95).

What to Bring

As with all mountain areas, the weather is changeable. Sun can turn to rain in minutes; pack warm clothes and rain gear. See the Warning box; you may want to bring camping gear.

GETTING TO/FROM THE RIDE

Mt Vernon

From Seattle, the most scenic and bike-friendly option is the train.

Bus The bus station is at 1101 S 2nd St. From Sea-Tac, Bellair Airporter Shuttle (☎ 800-235-5247, W www.airporter.com) has a service to Mt Vernon ($28, two hours, 10 a day). The service continues to Anacortes and the ferry terminal for rides in the San Juan Islands. Bikes cost $10 each way and must be in a box.

Greyhound runs from Seattle to Mt Vernon ($9, 1½ hours, five a day).

Train The train station is at 725 College Way. Amtrak's Cascades service departs twice daily for Mt Vernon ($18, 1½ hours). One daily train leaves Vancouver, BC for Mt Vernon ($21, 2½ hours). Bikes cost $5 and are carried in the bicycle section of the baggage car. No boxing is required but advance reservations must be made.

Wenatchee

Air Horizon Air (☎ 800-547-9308, 🅦 www.horizonair.com) flies seven times a day to Seattle ($100, one hour). Bikes must be boxed and cost $50 each way; there's no room for tandems.

Bus The bus station is at 300 S Columbia St. Northwestern Trailways (☎ 800-366-3830, 🅦 www.nwadv.com/northw/) departs Wenatchee for Seattle ($24, four hours, two a day) and Spokane ($24, 3½ hours, one a day). Bikes ($15) must be boxed or bagged.

Train Amtrak has one daily service to Seattle ($38, 4½ hours) but, at the time of publication, would not load bikes in Wenatchee. The station is at the end of Kittitas St.

THE RIDE

Mt Vernon

☎ 360

Named after George Washington's home in Virginia, Mt Vernon is on the banks of the Skagit River, and spills across both sides of the I-5.

Founded in 1870 to serve the logging trade, farming soon took over due to the rich soil of the river valley. Today, the area around Mt Vernon is one of the most productive agricultural areas in the Northwest. Its most famous crops are the spring-blooming daffodils, tulips and irises.

Mt Vernon's 'old town' (downtown) is west of the I-5 while the newer area sprawls north and east.

Information The Mt Vernon Chamber of Commerce (☎ 428-8547, 🅦 www.mvcofc.org) is at 117 N First St.

Downtown, a Bank of America is on the corner of Kincaid and Cleveland Sts. Several banks are at the intersection of Riverside St and College Way, a block from the Amtrak station.

Art's Bike Shop (☎ 336-5277) is downtown at 310 W Montgomery St. Rent bikes at Back Country Outfitters (☎ 336-3554, 🅦 www.bcogear.com), 100 E Montgomery St, in the Old Town Grainery.

Internet access is available at the Mt Vernon Library, 315 Snoqualmie St.

Things to See & Do From late March to early May, the fields around Mt Vernon are ablaze with color, when first **daffodils**, then **tulips** and finally **irises** cover the fields (see the boxed text 'Tulip Pedals').

Mt Vernon has a charming **old town**. Stop at the historic **Lincoln Theatre**, 712 First St, which has a still-operational, 1926 Wurlitzer organ, used in the silent film era.

In winter, watch for **trumpeter swans** and **snow geese**.

Places to Stay The *Skagit Valley Fairgrounds (☎ 336-9453, 1410 Virginia St)*

Tulip Pedals

If it's April and you're anywhere between Mt Vernon and La Conner, don't look up in the sky to see a rainbow, look down at ground level. From late March through early May, the tulip and daffodil fields reveal their rainbow hues. If it wasn't for the mountain backdrop, you could be in the Netherlands.

This rich, fertile area is known as the Skagit flats. Bucolic countryside, mountain views and flat terrain offer pleasant cycling year-round but in April it's time to hit the back roads. Don't expect to be alone; only 60mi from Seattle, the area swarms with day-trippers. April events are plentiful during the Skagit Valley Tulip Festival (🅦 www.tulipfestival.org), including the family-oriented Tulip Pedal Bike Ride (☎ 360-428-0404).

The best way to cycle the area is to obtain the free tulip field map (available from the Mt Vernon Chamber or the Tulip Festival Web site). Meander the back roads, south of Hwy 536, using the tulip and daffodil icons on the map as a guide. Avoid weekends, and for the quietest roads, make an early weekday start.

offers camping on the grass areas for $12 per tent. The office is open weekdays 8.30am to 4.30pm; after hours, check in with the caretaker. Camping is not available during Fair Week (mid-Aug).

Most Mt Vernon hotels are alongside the I-5 on Freeway Dr, about 1mi from the station. ***Best Western College Inn*** *(☎ 424-428 or ☎ 800-793-4024, cnr W College Way & Freeway Dr)* has singles/doubles from $71/76, with continental breakfast. Heading north, ***Comfort Inn*** *(☎ 428-7020, 1910 Freeway Dr)* charges $80 per room, including deluxe continental breakfast. ***Tulip Inn*** *(☎ 428-5969 or ☎ 800-599-5969, 2200 Freeway Dr)* charges $50/55.

Places to Eat For self-caterers, ***Robert's Red Apple*** *(820 Cleveland St)* is downtown. Close to the station is an ***Albertson's*** supermarket *(E College Way & Riverside Dr)*. For baked goods try ***City Bakery & Cafe*** *(514 S First St)*.

There are ***fast-food outlets*** one block west of the station. Downtown, the ***Thai House*** *(☎ 336-2966, 616 S First St)* is a local favorite. The ***Skagit River Brewing Company*** *(☎ 336-2884, 404 S 3rd St)* serves pizzas, sandwiches and pub food at lunch and dinner. The cozy ***Grainery Restaurant*** *(☎ 336-3046, 100 E Montgomery St)*, in the Old Town Grainery, offers pasta, meat and seafood dishes.

Day 1: Mt Vernon to Marblemount

4½–8 hours, 51.3mi

It's easy riding along the Skagit River. There are no major hills, just a couple of gradual climbs between Concrete and Rockport, the start of the Cascade foothills.

Leave Mt Vernon behind, and it's not long before you're cycling through fields of cows and admiring views of the **Cascade foothills**, the tip of Mt Baker to the northeast. Loop under Hwy 9 onto the S Skagit Hwy (7.5mi), and for the next 20mi have the gorgeous valley road almost all to yourself. For the most part, the S Skagit Hwy (hardly a highway at all) hugs the **Skagit River**. On the south side of the road, small waterfalls trickle. In shady spots, mossy trees wearing green, velvety jackets line the road. Watch for **Mt Baker**, especially the last couple of miles before Day Creek (17mi).

'Welcome to Concrete' announce the huge concrete silos as you pass the town (33.8mi), once the site of a huge cement plant, which closed in 1968. If you think the name Concrete is uninspiring, the town's original name was Cement City!

Rockport State Park (41.4mi) makes a great camping spot and offers numerous **hiking** trails through old-growth forest. Beyond Rockport, the **Skagit River Bald Eagle Natural Area** is the winter stopping point for hundreds of bald eagles.

On the way into Marblemount stop at the **Cascadian Farm** roadside stand (45.8mi) for delicious organic berry shakes or ice cream.

Marblemount

☎ 360

Marblemount is the last 'town' on Hwy 20 for 75mi, and a sign announces that it has the last tavern for 89mi. More importantly, for the 75mi between here and Mazama there are no services except a small shop in Newhalem.

For information try the North Cascades Chamber of Commerce (☎ 873-2210, W www.marblemount.com). Next door to the post office (Milepost 106), the general store has an ATM. Most businesses line Hwy 20 between Mileposts 103 and 106.

The Marblemount Ranger Station (☎ 873-4500) issues backcountry permits (open daily May–Sept).

Places to Stay & Eat The ***Clark's Skagit River Resort*** *(☎ 873-2250 or ☎ 800-273-2606, W www.northcascades.com, Milepost 104)* is one-stop lodging. Choices include tent sites for $15, a variety of cabins with or without kitchen from $59 to $129, and their ***Brookhaven B&B***, $89 per room with breakfast. There's also ***The Eatery***, serving home-cooked breakfasts, lunches and dinners.

Totem Trail Motel *(☎ 873-4535, W www.totemtrail.com, Milepost 102.8)* has eight comfortable singles/doubles from $45/50. A Victorian house on the Skagit River, the ***Salmonberry Way B&B*** *(☎ 873-4016, Milepost 108)* has rooms from $49.

For groceries, ***Marblemount Mercantile*** is at Milepost 106. For pizza, burgers, espressos and shakes, head to ***Marblemount Drive-In*** *(☎ 360-873-9309, Milepost 105.7)*. The ***Buffalo Run*** *(☎ 873-2461, Milepost 106)* features buffalo and venison burgers alongside traditional menu items.

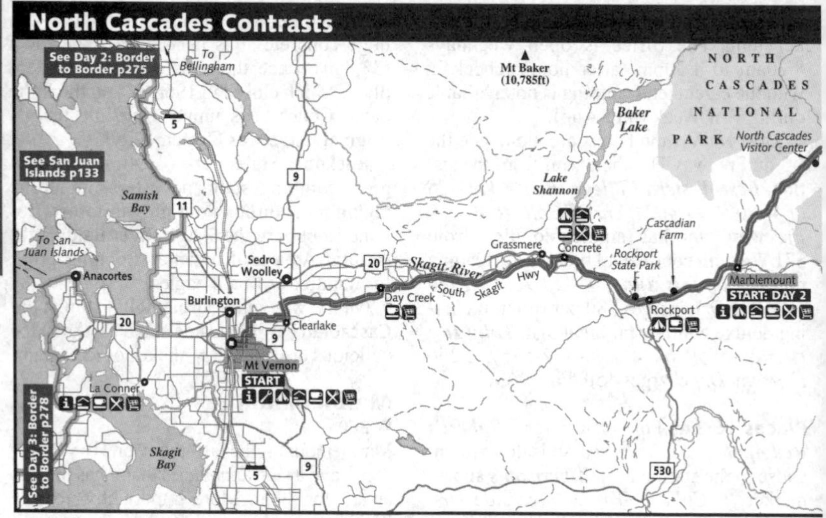

Day 2: Marblemount to Colonial Creek Campground

2½–4 hours, 24.6mi

Hwy 20 continues along the Skagit River. Now in the mountains, there are a couple of short climbs after Newhalem. Allow time for the short side trips. Organize a Skagit Dam tour ahead of time.

It's an easy gradient as the Skagit escorts you from Marblemount to Newhalem. The **North Cascades visitor center** (side trip, 13.6mi; ☎ 206-386-4495, W www.nps.gov/noca) has information on camping and trails, plus interesting flora, fauna and geology exhibits. Collect a park map, and the *North Cascades Challenger* for current events.

Tiny **Newhalem** (14.8mi) may not look like much but behind the company houses are some surprises. In the ***Skagit General Store***, your last chance for groceries, pick up the free pamphlet *Walking Tour of Historic Newhalem* and try their home-made fudge. The pamphlet directs you to two short, splendid trails, the **Ladder Creek Falls & Garden** (a side trip at 15.1mi) and **Trail of the Cedars**.

From Newhalem the road steepens, and the views become more magnificent by the minute. At 16.1mi, activate the 'Bikes in Tunnel' flashing light and illuminate your own lights. Walk the **Gorge Overlook Trail** (a side trip at 17.6mi) for fabulous views of the turquoise waters of **Gorge Lake**. Across from the side trip turnoff is the **Gorge Creek Falls Lookout**.

An exciting descent allows you to marvel at the changes in the Skagit River. At 20.1mi a side trip leads to Diablo, and **Skagit Dam Tours** (☎ 206-684-3030, W www.cityofseattle.net/light/tours/skagit.asp). Choose the four-hour deluxe tour, including a boat trip, a ride up the incline railway and lunch ($25); or the 90-minute Dam Tour ($5).

The 2mi climb alongside **Diablo Lake** will have you stopping to catch your breath, not from the climb, but from the breathtaking views. Glide down to Colonial Creek and bid the Skagit *adieu*.

Colonial Creek Campground

On Diablo Lake's Thunder Arm, ***Colonial Creek Campground***, popular with boaters and kayakers, has 162 nonreservable sites ($12).

Day 3: Colonial Creek Campground to Winthrop

6–10 hours, 63.9mi

It's mostly up to Washington Pass. Enjoy the views. Time permitting, hike from one of the many trailheads en route.

Begin with a steep climb to the **Diablo Lake Overlook** (1.6mi). The jade hues of glacier-fed Diablo Lake are striking, and **Colonial Peak, Davis Peak** and **Sourdough**

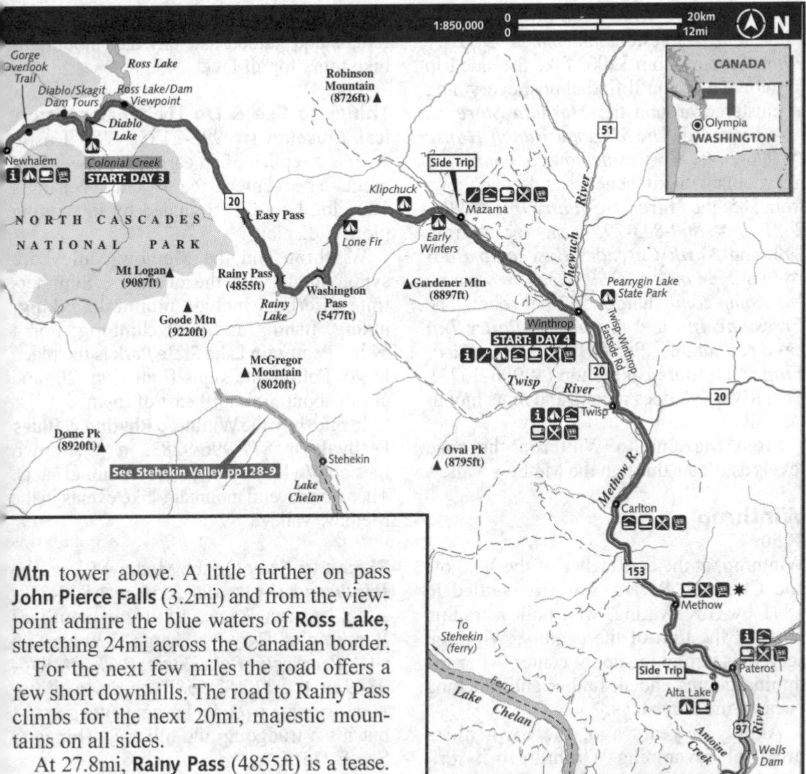

Mtn tower above. A little further on pass **John Pierce Falls** (3.2mi) and from the viewpoint admire the blue waters of **Ross Lake**, stretching 24mi across the Canadian border.

For the next few miles the road offers a few short downhills. The road to Rainy Pass climbs for the next 20mi, majestic mountains on all sides.

At 27.8mi, **Rainy Pass** (4855ft) is a tease. After reaching the top, the road drops steeply. It's demanding pedaling for the 2.7mi ascent to Washington Pass but stunning views reward as you cycle past **Liberty Bell**. At **Washington Pass** (32.7mi; 5477ft), take a breather and walk the **Washington Pass Overlook**, an easy 0.5mi path with incredible views of **Liberty Bell** and **Early Winter Spires**.

Plunge downhill. The first 7mi are steep, with gradients of up to 7%, then it's an exhilarating freewheel to Mazama. The dramatic contrast between west and east is evident, firs and cedars replaced by pines.

Maintained by the Forest Service (☎ 509-996-4000 or ☎ 877-444-6777), three camping grounds (with drinking water) are on the descent to Mazama: ***Lone Fir*** (39.1mi), ***Klipchuck*** (45.9mi) and ***Early Winters*** (48.4mi).

For noncampers, Mazama (50.4mi; area code ☎ 509) may be your preference for an overnight destination. Choices are limited. In order of appearance on the route: the luxury

Freestone Inn *(☎ 996-3906 or ☎ 800-639-3809, ⓦ www.freestoneinn.com, 17798 Hwy 20)* has rooms from $200. Take the side trip into town and you'll find almost everything is clustered around the ***Mazama Store*** on Lost River Rd. The ***Mazama Ranch House*** *(☎ 996-2040, ⓦ www.methow.com/mazama)* has rooms with kitchenettes and great views from $85; the ***Mazama Country Inn*** *(☎ 996-2681 or ☎ 800-843-7951)* has rooms from $90; and ***North Cascades Basecamp B&B*** *(☎ 996-2334 or ☎ 866-996-2334, ⓦ www.ncbasecamp.com)* charges $82 per room. The ***Freestone Inn*** and ***Mazama Country Inn*** have restaurants. For BBQ, try the ***Burnt Finger***. D-Tours Bike Shop (☎ 996-3673), Lost River Rd, does repairs and rents mountain bikes.

From Mazama to Winthrop the road levels as it cuts through the Methow Valley.

Winthrop

☎ 509

Winthrop, at the confluence of the Methow and Chewuch Rivers, was first settled in 1891 by Guy Waring, who built a trading post. At the turn of the century, Winthrop served as a mining supply center. After the mining booms ended, timber and ranching became the mainstays.

About 30 years ago, the town did a great job revamping Winthrop in its original Old West theme, with wooden boardwalks and Western storefronts. With its distinct frontier feel, Winthrop thrives on tourism, boasting fabulous mountain biking and cross-country skiing (see the boxed text 'Methow Valley: Mountain-Biking Mecca' opposite).

Information The Winthrop Chamber visitor center (☎ 996-2125 or ☎ 888-463-8469, ⓦ www.methow.com) is at the corner of Hwy 20 as it turns right in town. The Methow Valley Ranger Station (☎ 996-4000), on Hwy 20 0.2mi before Winthrop, has information on hiking, mountain biking, flora and fauna.

Farmer's State Bank, 159 Riverside Ave, has no ATM. Tenderfoot Grocery, 177 Riverside Ave, and Winthrop Red Apple supermarket, 1mi south of town on Hwy 20, both have ATMs.

For bicycle needs, go to Winthrop Mountain Sports (☎ 996-2886 or ☎ 800-719-3826, ⓦ www.winthropmountainsports.com), 257 Riverside Ave. They offer mountain bike rentals and guided half-day/day mountain-bike tours for all levels.

Things to See & Do The **Schafer Historical Museum** (☎ 996-2125), 285 Castle Ave, is a replica of an early Methow settlement. The centerpiece is Guy Waring's 1897 log house, surrounded by interesting pioneer displays.

Winthrop and the Methow Valley are synonymous with the outdoors. Summertime offerings include **mountain biking, hiking, fishing** and **rock climbing**. For a swim, **Pearrygin Lake State Park** is the place to go. Follow the signs from Hwy 20, and climb about 5mi northeast of town.

In mid-July the **Winthrop Rhythm & Blues Festival** (☎ 877-996-9283, ⓦ www.nwblues.com/winthrop/) draws national acts. There are several mountain-bike events in the Methow Valley.

Places to Stay On the Methow River, the ***Winthrop KOA*** *(☎ 996-2258 or ☎ 800-562-2158, ⓦ www.koa.com)*, 1.2mi south of Winthrop on Hwy 20, charges $20 per tent site. ***Pearrygin Lake State Park*** *(☎ 996-2370 or ☎ 800-452-5687 for reservations, ⓦ www.parks.wa.gov)* has tent sites for $13 but it's a trudge up the hill (see Things to See & Do).

The ***Duck Brand Hotel*** *(☎ 996-2192 or ☎ 800-996-2192, ⓦ www.methownet.com/duck, 248 Riverside Ave)* has only six rooms but lots of atmosphere. The rooms, from $55, are above the restaurant, which can be noisy until 9.30pm.

The ***Trails End Motel*** *(☎ 996-2303 or ☎ 877-996-2339, ⓔ trail-end@methow.com, 130 Riverside Ave)* has rooms from $63, including a continental breakfast.

Beside the Methow River, the ***Riverside Lodge*** *(☎/fax 996-394/3701, 281 Riverside Ave)* has a hot tub overlooking the river, plus in-room refrigerators, microwaves and coffeemakers. Rooms start at $75. Next door, ***Hotel Rio Vista*** *(☎ 996-3535 or ☎ 800-398-0911, ⓦ wwwmethow.com/~riovista/, 285 Riverside Ave)* also has a hot tub. The rooms, from $85, have refrigerators.

If you're having trouble finding lodging, contact **Methow Valley Central Reservations** *(☎ 509-996-2148 or ☎ 800-422-3048, ⓦ www.methow.com/lodging/)*.

Methow Valley: Mountain-Biking Mecca

When winter's snows melt, skiers bid adieu to the valley's 125mi of cross-country ski trails, which in summer become a mountain biker's playground. The area of the Methow Valley between Mazama and Twisp offer a variety of off-road opportunities, from easy circuits to tough single-track rides in valleys, forests and on mountainsides. In addition, there are plenty of forest service roads and trails to explore.

The season opens with the **Boneshaker** (☎ 455-7657, Ⓦ www.roundandround.com), a weekend of downhill and cross-country races for all skill levels. The **Tuesday Evening Race Series** is on the first and third Tuesday of June, July and August (contact Winthrop Mountain Sports; see Information, p126). The **Methow Valley Sports Trails Association** (☎ 996-3287, Ⓦ www.mvsta.com) maintains many of the trails and sponsors the annual **Methow Valley Mountain Bike Festival**, three days jam-packed with events in early October. They can provide information on the trails, as can the Ranger Station (see Information, p126), local bike shops and Sun Mountain Lodge. Maps are available at bike shops and the Ranger Station.

The luxurious **Sun Mountain Lodge** (☎ 996-2211 or ☎ 800-572-0493, Ⓦ www.sunmountainlodge.com), 9.2mi southwest of Winthrop by road, has more than 40mi of mountain-bike trails of varying levels, and is one of the most popular areas to mountain bike in the Methow. Mountain bikes can be rented from the Activities Shop. The trails are open to everyone, and a free trail map is available. The **Winthrop Trail** is an 8mi ride up to Sun Mountain from Winthrop.

Sold in bike shops for $2 is the **One Ride Guides** series, oversized single-sheet maps and route descriptions of Methow Valley mountain-bike rides. More rides can be found in Falcon Press' *Mountain Biking: Methow Valley* ($10.95).

Trails in the Methow include the **Big Valley Ranch Trail** (6mi; beginner), **Buck Mountain** (12mi; intermediate), **Lightning Creek** (13mi; intermediate/advanced) and **Starvation Mtn** (25mi; advanced). The **Methow Community Trail** is an 18mi beginner trail connecting Winthrop and Mazama.

Places to Eat The ***Tenderfoot Grocery*** *(177 Riverside Ave)* is downtown and ***Winthrop Red Apple*** supermarket is 1mi south of town on Hwy 20.

The enormously popular ***Duck Brand Cantina*** (see Places to Stay) serves breakfast, lunch and dinner. The menu is extensive and the outside seating area is worth the wait.

The ***Winthrop Brewing Company*** *(☎ 996-3183, 155 Riverside Ave)* has microbrews on tap, plus pub food. Across the road is ***The Riverside Grill*** *(☎ 509-996-2444, 162 Riverside Ave)*.

Day 4: Winthrop to Chelan

6–10 hours, 62.7mi

It's gentle cycling through the pastoral Methow Valley. Two-thirds of the way into the day's ride the Methow greets the Columbia, a mighty water source defining its way through arid landscape. About 10mi after the confluence, there's a huge climb with huge views.

Begin on a lovely stretch of the Eastside Rd overlooking the Methow Valley. If you detour to Twisp (9.6mi), a worthwhile stop is the ***Cinnamon Twisp Bakery*** *(116 N Glover St)*; try their oatmeal fudgies.

From Twisp the Methow River leads the way. Soon after Carlton, **fruit orchards** line the road to the historic town of **Methow** (31.5mi), with its old log schoolhouse. Here, the first orchards in the valley were established in 1888. **Alta Lake State Park** (a side trip at 41.1mi) is a favorite spot for boaters and anglers, with a swimming beach and camping.

The **Rest-A-While Fruit Stand** (42.3mi; open May–Oct) sells fresh fruit, from cherries to nectarines, and naturally, apples.

At 51.9mi turn off Hwy 97, and climb steeply. Catch your breath at the top; the views of the Columbia are fabulous. Aptly named Apple Acres Rd presses through apple orchards and stark canyon-like terrain. At 58.8mi the road emerges, and again the Columbia comes into view.

Chelan

☎ 509

The mighty glaciers that carved Lake Chelan created one of Washington's most

Stehekin Valley

How can anyone resist a mountain-bike ride through a pristine Cascade mountain valley that has hardly changed since the first settlement 150 years ago? What's more, the 'road' sees only one shuttle bus and the cars of the 70 year-round residents of this remote community. The gravel road is virtually all your own. Marvel at waterfalls, towering mountains, glacier-fed streams and rugged forests as you ride through one of the North Cascades greatest treasures.

Planning

Mountain weather is unpredictable so bring rain gear and warm clothes.

Mountain bikes can be rented from Discovery Bikes (☎ 509-884-4844, W www.stehekinvalley.com), PO Box 8, Stehekin, WA, 98852, located outside the Courtney Log Office. North Cascades Stehekin Lodge also rents mountain bikes.

It's certainly worth staying overnight, or a few days, to take in the valley and its activities – hiking, rafting, fishing and horseback riding.

Getting to/from the Ride

Chelan Airways (☎ 682-5555, W www.chelanairways.com) operates a daily floatplane service to Stehekin ($120 return, 30 minutes). They can't transport bikes.

The *Lady Cat* ($89 return) will give you seven hours at Stehekin. Other boat combinations are cheaper but allow less time; see Things to See & Do for Chelan (p129).

Stehekin

There are no phones in Stehekin. Phone numbers listed are answered in Chelan. There is one public credit-card phone for outgoing calls and a radio-telephone at the Golden West visitor center at the landing.

There are plenty of camping options in the valley (see the map). Free backcountry permits required for campgrounds are available at the visitor center.

At the landing, ***North Cascades Stehekin Lodge*** (☎ *682-4494*) has basic rooms from $75.

More than a place to stay, Courtney's ***Stehekin Valley Ranch*** (☎ *682-4677 or* ☎ *800-536-0745,* W *www.courtneycountry.com)*, 9mi up the valley, is an experience. Rustic cabins in an unmatched setting, great food and welcoming hosts make the $65 per person rate, including all meals, worth every cent. Advance reservations are essential.

The Stehekin Lodge has a small ***shop*** and an uninspiring ***restaurant*** with meals from $12. If camping, bring food from Chelan. The ***Stehekin Pastry Company*** (on the ride) has baked goods and snacks. The ***Stehekin Valley Ranch*** serves hearty, delicious dinners nightly for about $15; reservations essential.

The Ride

3–4 hours, 24.4mi

Vary the length of your ride according to the time available between boats.

From the visitor center/landing, go northwest along the lake. As the locals would say, you are heading 'up-valley', and up it is, with a gradual elevation gain of 650ft to Tumwater Bridge. Zip along for the 4mi of paved road, the rushing waters of the Stehekin River on your left. At 2mi, stop at the ***Stehekin Pastry Company*** for snacks and drinks.

Pass the one-room **schoolhouse**. At 3.5mi, it's a 1mi roundtrip to the mighty 312ft cascade of **Rainbow Falls**. At 3.7mi, another 1mi roundtrip leads to the historic 1912 **Buckner Orchard**, the apple trees still bearing fruit, and an 1889 homestead cabin.

After Harlequin Bridge the unpaved road begins. The road hugs the river's edge, the valley floor thickly forested, until at 9mi the views open at the ***Stehekin Valley Ranch***. Climb a further 2mi and look down at the milky waters as Agnes Creek meets the Stehekin River.

High Bridge (11mi) is a world unto itself. Stand on the bridge and look down the narrow gorge into a jumble of mossy trees, turbulent water, massive boulders and overhanging limbs.

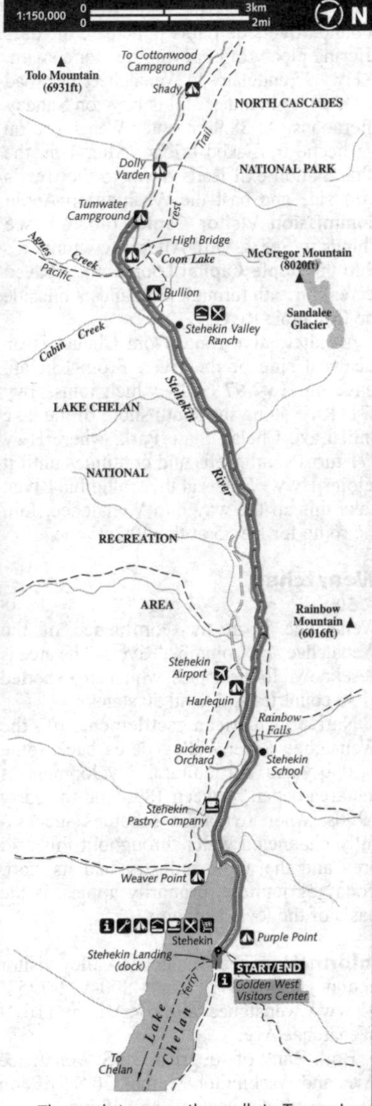

The road steepens, then rolls to Tumwater campground (12mi). Continue for another 0.2mi to Tumwater Bridge, with a marvelous vantage point over the river. (From here, the road continues on the east side of the river, and it is possible to ride another 10mi to Cottonwood Campground on double track.) Retrace the outward route back to Chelan.

spectacular lakes, and, at 1500ft, the third-deepest lake in the USA. The 55mi-long lake, never more that 2mi wide, occupies a stunning glacial valley stretching from the eastern edge of the North Cascades to the town of Chelan.

A watersports destination, Chelan is Central Washington's summer playground. It is a resort town, and the jumping off point for boat trips on the lake and hiking in North Cascades National Park.

Information The Lake Chelan visitor center (☎ 682-3503 or ☎ 800-424-3526, 🅦 www.lakechelan.com), 102 E Johnson Ave, is a great resource.

Both Bank of America, 101 E Johnson Ave, and Washington Mutual, 106 E Chelan Ave, have ATMs.

John Page runs Pedal Paddle Lake Chelan (☎ 682-9211) out of his garage at 228 W Nixon Ave. He repairs bikes and has parts on hand. He has a self-guided bike tour of the nearby Manson area ($0.50).

For Internet access, Electrik Dreams (☎ 682-8889) is in the Chelan Plaza, corner Manson Rd and Lake St.

Things to See & Do The **Chelan Museum** (☎ 682-5644), corner Woodin Ave and Emerson St, has exhibits of local history, Native American artifacts and an apple-box label collection. Pick up a mural map from the Visitor Center. The 15 **murals** painted on Chelan's buildings each contain an apple in some form, either obvious or hidden.

Rent **kayaks** and other **water toys** from Chelan Boat Rentals (☎ 682-4444), 1210 W Woodin Ave.

The **boat trip to Stehekin** is incredibly popular. Stehekin itself is a slice of paradise nestled in the Cascades. For a mountain-bike ride there, see the boxed text 'Stehekin Valley', however, the boat journey alone is worth the trip. The Lady of the Lake (☎ 682-4584, 🅦 www.ladyofthelake.com) ferries people 55mi up the lake several times daily (1¼–4 hours each way, $23–89 return, both depending on the type of boat, bikes $13 return). There are no roads to Stehekin, the only way in is by boat, plane or foot (over Cascade Pass from the Marblemount side). Stehekin has only one road, the few cars that use it are barged in. Choose a day trip or stay longer.

Places to Stay In town, ***Lakeshore RV Park*** *(☎ 682-8023; Manson Rd, Don Morse Park)* has tent sites for $24. ***Lake Chelan State Park*** *(☎ 682-5031 or ☎ 800-452-5687 for reservations, W www.parks.wa.gov)*, 9mi from town on the south shore of Lake Chelan, has campsites for $13.

Chelan has several motels. The ***Apple Inn*** *(☎ 682-4044, 1002 E Woodin Ave)* has rooms from $59. The ***Midtowner*** *(☎ 682-4051* or *☎ 800-572-0943, 721 E Woodin Ave)* has rooms from $75. Both motels have a pool and hot tub.

Hike up the hill to the 1902 Victorian ***Quail's Roost Inn B&B*** *(☎ 682-2892* or *☎ 800-681-2892, W www.aquailsroostinn.com, 121 E Highland Ave)* for the views and the wraparound porch. Rooms start at $89 (two-night minimum summer weekends).

For resort-style lodging, and a splurge, the definitive Lake Chelan resort is ***Campbell's*** *(☎ 682-2561 or ☎ 800-553-8225, W www.campbellsresort.com, 104 W Woodin Ave)*. With 170 waterfront rooms, restaurants, pools and more, expect rooms priced from $166 in summer.

Places to Eat Pick up groceries at ***Safeway*** *(cnr Manson Rd & Columbia St)*. Head to ***Flying Saucers Espresso*** *(116 S Emerson St)* for great coffee. Start your day at the ***Apple Cup Cafe*** *(☎ 682-2933, 804 E Woodin Ave)*, open breakfast, lunch and dinner.

Worth the 2mi ride out of town is dinner overlooking the lake at ***Deepwater Brewing & Public House*** *(☎ 682-2720, 225 Hwy 150)*. Excellent pastas, burgers, steaks and salads are on the menu, alongside their beers. In town, ***Peter B's Bar & Grill*** *(☎ 682-1031, 116 E Woodin Ave)* serves pastas, steaks and salad beside Riverwalk Park. For a Mexican lunch or dinner, try ***La Laguna*** *(☎ 682-5129, 114 N Emerson St)*.

Day 5: Chelan to Wenatchee

4–7 hours, 44.5mi

Follow the curves of the Columbia. 'Apple' is the word of the day; miles of orchards adorn the river's banks. As the season progresses, you can almost hear the trees laden with fruit groaning under their weight.

Leave Chelan, passing the fruit-packing plants of Trout and Blue Chelan. Plunge down an exciting descent to the river and across Beebe Bridge to the east bank. The road hugs the river, and **fruit stands** abound. **Riverside parks** punctuate the day, offering plenty of opportunities for a swim.

Hwy 97 undulates to Wenatchee. The road has a wide shoulder, and is busy on Sunday afternoons. At 38.9mi, enter Wenatchee on the hectic trafficked bridge. After 1mi, the Olds Station exit leads down to the river's west side and past the **Washington Apple Commission Visitor Center** (40.4mi; see Things to See & Do). After a few turns it's onto the **Apple Capital Loop Trail**, a paved recreation path through parklands alongside the Columbia River.

An alternative route from Chelan is on the west side of the river. From Chelan, leave on Hwy 97 (Alt), which joins Hwy 971. Ride along the south shore of the lake until Lake Chelan State Park, where Hwy 971 turns south (left) and continues until it rejoins Hwy 97 (Alt) at the Columbia River. Take this all the way into Wenatchee. Join the route for Day 5 at the 40.2mi cue.

Wenatchee

☎ 509

Wenatchee is at the confluence of the Wenatchee and Columbia Rivers. The area is best known for its apples, which are exported to 30 countries and to all 50 states.

Native American settlement of the Wenatchee River Valley dates back some 11,000 years. Agricultural development of the area began between 1890 and the early 1900s, when irrigation schemes successfully channeled water throughout this arid area and the apple industry had its start. Today agriculture, primarily apples, is the basis of the local economy.

Information The Wenatchee Valley visitor center (☎ 663-3723 or ☎ 800-572-7753, W www.wenatcheevalley.org) is at 116 N Wenatchee Ave.

Both Bank of America, 30 S Wenatchee Ave, and Washington Mutual, 30 S Mission St, have ATMs, as does the Safeway.

Full Circle Cycle Shop (☎ 663-8025) is at 318 S Chelan Ave. For Internet access, the Computer Park Cafe (☎ 667-9337) is at 518 N Wenatchee Ave.

Things to See & Do Don't leave Wenatchee without visiting the **Washington Apple Commission Visitor Center** (☎ 662-

3090 or ☎ 800-57APPLE, Ⓦ www.bestapples.com), 2900 Euclid Ave. There are displays of apple production, and juice samples.

Unload your panniers before visiting Ohme Gardens (☎ 662-5785, Ⓦ www.ohmegardens.com). Perched on a bluff, 4mi north of Wenatchee on Hwy 97 (Alt), this is a serene escape overlooking the valley. The final mile up is a killer but worth the effort.

About 8mi north of town, past the Ohme Gardens, is Rocky Reach Dam (☎ 663-8121, Ⓦ www.chelanpud.org). A Columbia River dam, the complex has fish-viewing windows, two museums and groomed grounds with picnic facilities.

Day 5 ends with a 3mi section of the **Apple Capital Loop Trail**. Cycle the entire 10mi loop, crossing the Columbia twice and hugging both the east and west shorelines.

One of the premier cycling events in the area is the **Apple Century Ride** (Jun, Ⓦ www.wenatcheesunrise.org/century). The ride attracts 800 to 1000 cyclists.

Places to Stay Convenient for campers, the route passes through ***Wenatchee Confluence State Park*** *(☎ 663-6373 or ☎ 800-452-5687 for reservations, Ⓦ www.parks.wa.gov)* at 41.1mi. Tent sites cost $13. There are also four campgrounds along the river on the Day 5 route: ***Beebe Bridge Park*** (4.6mi), ***Daroga State Park*** (20mi), ***Orondo River Park*** (24mi) and ***Lincoln Rock State Park*** (34mi).

Hotels, motels and restaurants line N Wenatchee Ave. The bike-friendly ***Economy Inn*** *(☎ 663-8133 or ☎ 800-587-6348, Ⓦ www.economyinn.4mg.com, 700 N Wenatchee Ave)* has comfortable singles/doubles from $45/50 with continental breakfast. ***Ramada Limited*** *(☎ 665-8585 or ☎ 877-203-8585, Ⓦ www.ramada.com, 1017 N Wenatchee Ave)* offers a substantial continental breakfast. Rooms start at $59. The ***WestCoast Wenatchee Center Hotel*** *(☎ 662-1234 or ☎ 800-426-0670, Ⓦ www.westcoasthotels.com, 201 N Wenatchee Ave)* has rooms from $99/109. All the hotels have pools. The ***Apple Country B&B*** *(☎ 664-0400, Ⓦ www.applecountryinn.com, 524 Okanogan St)* has rooms from $65, including a full breakfast.

Places to Eat A ***Safeway*** supermarket is at 501 N Miller St. For local produce, visit the ***Wenatchee Valley Farmers Market*** at the Riverfront Park at the end of Fifth St (8am–noon, Wed & Sat, May–Oct).

For Italian food, ***Visconti's*** *(☎ 662-5013, 1737 N Wenatchee Ave)* has pastas starting from $13. ***The Windmill*** *(☎ 665-9529, 1501 N Wenatchee Ave)* has been open since 1931. Steaks and prime rib, from $19, are the specialties; seafood is also on the menu. Atop the WestCoast Wenatchee Center Hotel, (see Places to Stay) with views of the river, the ***Wenatchee Roaster & Ale House*** serves breakfast, lunch and dinner. Known for smoked and roasted dinners from $14, it also does salads and burgers.

Don't forget to eat an apple! This area boasts the country's best.

San Juan Islands

☎ 360

Islands typically conjure up images of paradise, and the San Juans could indeed be described as a cycling paradise. Forested shorelines, secluded coves, fabulous seascapes, wildlife watching, bucolic vistas and quiet roads await cyclists.

The ferry weaves through the islands, lulling the visitor into 'island time', and the slow, peaceful character of these islands, each with its own distinctive charm. Cyclists can smile as they board the ferry with their trusty steed (or walk on, if renting a bike), avoiding the long summer lines of cars.

The islands are in western Washington's banana belt. Protected by the Olympic Mtns and Vancouver Island, they are sunny 247 days of the year, with summer temperatures averaging about 70°F. Add to that kayaking, hiking, historic sites, mountains, lakes, whale watching, galleries and gourmet food; all adventures to be had during rides on the three largest islands, Lopez, Orcas and San Juan.

HISTORY

Prior to British and Spanish explorers visiting in the 18th century, the islands were inhabited by Native Americans. In the mid-1800s, both British and American settlements sprang up. Both nations claimed the islands, and in 1859 they nearly came to blows on San Juan Island over the shooting of a marauding pig, resulting in the Pig War. Eventually, the USA's claim of ownership prevailed, the islands becoming part of the USA in 1871.

Traditionally islanders have been farmers and/or fishers, but during the last 20 years tourism has engaged a large percentage of locals. The islands have also become a haven for artists, writers, retirees and, more recently, tele-commuters.

NATURAL HISTORY

The San Juan archipelago lies between Washington's northernmost coast and Vancouver Island, Canada. Depending on the definition of island, rock or reef, and the tides, the total island count varies from 457 to more than 700; only about 200 are named.

The islands, created during the Ice Age, are actually the peaks of eroded mountains; the waterways between are the sunken valleys. The islands are hilly. The highest peak, Mt Constitution (2409ft), is on Orcas Island.

Madrona trees line the beaches and coves; Douglas firs cover rocky outcroppings and march up slopes straight from the water's edge; and salal and ferns make their presence known on forest floors.

The surrounding waters are a marine wonderland home to seals, otters, sea lions, porpoises, salmon, clams, crabs and orcas. On land, black-tailed deer, squirrels and rabbits (introduced in the 1800s) abound. The skies are a feast for birdwatchers, with eagles, hawks, herons, oystercatchers, woodpeckers, gulls, ospreys, belted kingfishers, Canada geese and hummingbirds.

PLANNING

Bring binoculars to the islands, for bird, seal and whale watching.

When to Ride

The mild climate lends itself to a long cycling season. Attractive to cyclists and hoards of vacationers are the warm, drier summer months. The shoulder months (April, May, Sept & early Oct) offer good weather and fewer crowds. Weekends are busy from April to early October.

Maps & Books

Great Pacific Recreation Maps' *Recreation Map & Guide: San Juan Islands* (1:70,000; $4.95) is clear and well documented. The reverse side is crammed with useful services information and maps of the main towns.

A comprehensive guide to the islands is Marge & Ted Mueller's *Essential San Juan Islands Guide* ($14.95). Nature lovers and birdwatchers should pick up Evelyn Adams' *San Juan Islands Wildlife: A Handbook for Exploring Nature* ($14.95) or *Birding in the San Juan Islands*, by Mark G Lewis & Fred Sharpe ($10.95).

Take Your Time

The three rides described for the San Juan Islands are set up as day rides. To take full advantage of the side trips, the plethora of island activities, and to allow for ferry travel time, indulge in 'island time' and plan on at least two days to fully explore each island.

Information Sources

San Juan Islands Visitor Information Service (☎ 468-3663 or ☎ 888-468-3701, W www.guidetosanjuans.com) is not open to the public. Call or visit the Web site for general information and the free *Your Guide to the San Juan Islands*, packed with practicalities.

Several tourist publications are distributed free. Three are published by local newspapers: The Anacortes American's *San Juanderer* (W www.gosanjuans.com); The Sounder's *San Juans Beckon*; and The San Juan Journal's *Springtide* (W www.sanjuanjournal.com). Pick them up on the ferry or around the islands.

GATEWAY CITIES

Anacortes

See Anacortes (pp274–7) for information about accommodations and other services.

GETTING TO/FROM THE RIDES

Anacortes is the nearest town to the public ferries to the islands, and Mt Vernon has the nearest train station, plus a bus service to Anacortes. See Getting to/from the Ride for the North Cascades Contrasts ride (pp121–2) for details of transport from Seattle to Mt Vernon. More expensive ferries go to the islands from Seattle and Bellingham.

Bus

From Mt Vernon, Skagit County Transit (SKAT; ☎ 757-4433, W www.skat.org) provides one of the best public transport deals in the world. To encourage transit use passengers and bikes are free. Every bus has a bikerack. Bus 513 leaves Mt Vernon to the ferry terminal via Anacortes (1½ hours, five a day). On some runs a connection is required at March Point Park & Ride with Bus 410.

Bellair Airporter Shuttle (☎ 800-235-5247, **W** www.airporter.com) operates bus services to Anacortes and the ferry terminal from Sea-Tac ($31, 3 hours, 10 a day). Bikes must be boxed and cost $10 each way.

Bicycle

From Mt Vernon train station, it's 21mi to the San Juan Islands ferry terminal. The ride begins through the farms of the Skagit Valley, famous for their tulips (see the boxed text 'Tulip Pedals', p122), then travels busy Hwy 20 for almost 3mi. Take back roads along the water, with Mt Baker views, to Anacortes.

From the station, go west on College Way, turning left onto Riverside Dr (0.2mi). Continue for 1mi, crossing the I-5 freeway before turning right onto Washington St, right again onto 1st St, then immediately left onto Division St/Hwy 536 W.

Pass the Lefeber Bulb Company and Museum (5.3mi) and, at 5.7mi, continue on Young Rd (don't take Hwy 536). At 8mi, turn right, then right again at the Farmhouse Inn (8.3mi) onto Hwy 20. A shoulder on Hwy 20 leads to a bridge with a bikepath over the Swinomish Channel. At the end of the bridge (11mi), turn right onto March's Point Rd, past the Indian Art Gift Shop.

At 13.4mi continue straight onto Hwy 20, veering right onto Fidalgo Bay Rd (14.2mi). To the right across the water, Mt Baker

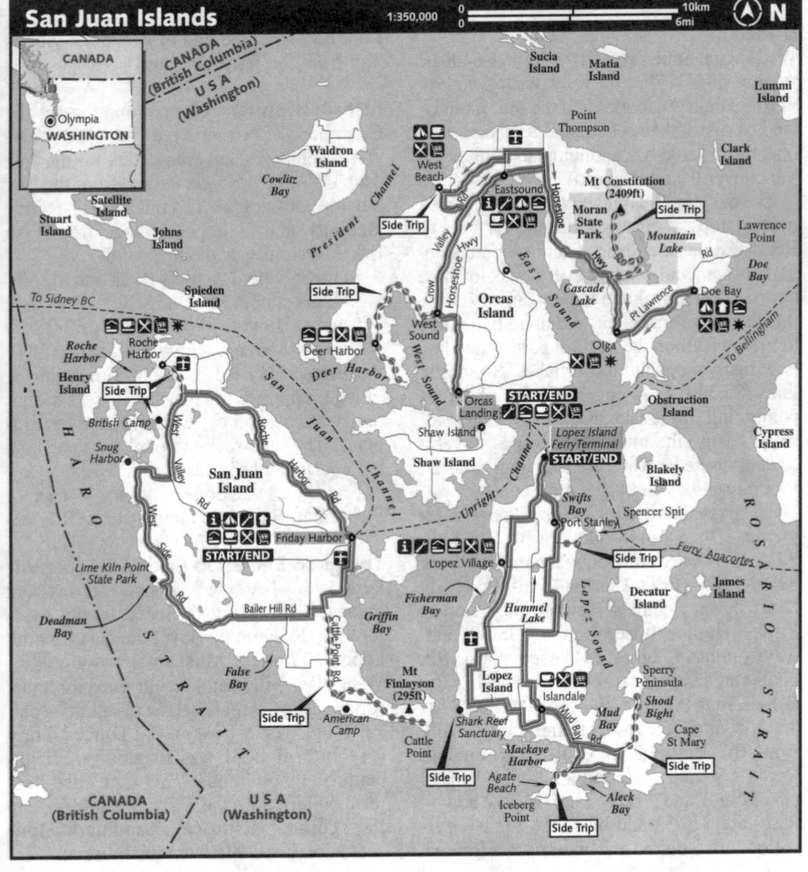

dominates. At 16.5mi turn right onto S Ave, then left onto 34th (16.6mi), right onto R Ave (16.7mi), left at 13th (17.9mi), with an immediate right onto Commercial. From Commercial turn left at the lights onto Hwy 20 (18.1mi). It's now 3mi to the ferry terminal!

Retrace the route to return to Mt Vernon, however, mind two tricky parts. The first is at 3.9mi where Fidalgo Bay Rd ends at Hwy 20. Cross Hwy 20 with extreme caution and continue on the other side for 0.8mi until the left turn onto March's Point Rd. The second complication is at the end of the bridge over the Swinomish Channel. At the end of the bridge (8.4mi), take an immediate hard left onto Josh Green Rd. After 0.2mi turn left onto an unsigned road, which leads under the bridge. Curve left with the road 'to Hwy 20 East' and again enter Hwy 20 (8.9mi).

Boat

Washington State Ferries (☎ 206-464-6400 or ☎ 800-843-3779, W www.wsdot.wa.gov/ferries) links Anacortes and the four main islands, Lopez, Shaw, Orcas and San Juan, with one ferry per day continuing to Sidney on Vancouver Island (Canada).

The daily international run to Sidney (three hours) stops at Friday Harbor (1¾ hours). Regular domestic ferries from Anacortes depart to some/all islands every two to three hours. It's a 45-minute trip to Lopez Island, the closest to Anacortes, and up to two hours to Friday Harbor, the furthest port, depending how many stops the ferry makes. Roundtrip fares ($5.30 for passengers, $3 for bikes) are paid going to the islands (both ways to Sidney). Lastly, the inter-island ferries travel a circular route between the four main islands; foot passengers and bikes are free.

The passenger-only *Victoria Clipper* catamarans (☎ 206-448-5000 or ☎ 800-888-2535, W www.victoriaclipper.com) run from Seattle to Victoria, Canada (mid-May–early Sept). From Seattle's Pier 69, they stop at Friday Harbor (three hours, $38/59 one-way/roundtrip, bikes $10 each way). Six bikes can travel per trip; reserve ahead.

San Juan Shuttle Express (☎ 888-373-8522, e info@orcawhales.com) travels daily from the Bellingham Cruise Terminal to Orcas Landing (1¼ hours), Lopez Village (1¾ hours) and Friday Harbor (2¼ hours). Fares are $20/33 and bikes are $3/5. Reservations are required and bike space is limited.

Lopez Island

Duration	4–6 hours
Distance	31.2mi
Difficulty	easy
Start/End	Lopez Island ferry landing
Cues & Elevation Profile	p359

Lopez is known as the 'Bicycle Isle'. Largely agricultural, Lopez lures the cyclist with gentle inclines, striking seascapes, sheep-studded fields and picturesque farmhouses. Stop to hike through an old-growth forest, stare at seals (bring binoculars) or enjoy a seaside picnic. There's no question that this friendly isle beckons 'Come Cycle'.

THE RIDE (See Map, p133)

Lopez Village

Lopez Village, the hub of island activity, is 4mi from the ferry landing.

Information For information, contact the Chamber of Commerce (☎ 468-4664, W www.lopezisland.com). Pick up the free *Map & Guide of Lopez Island* from the box outside Odlin Park (1.2mi from the ferry landing), and in Lopez Village from Fish Bay Mercantile or the museum.

In the village, Islanders Bank and the Village Market both have ATMs.

Lopez Bicycle Works (☎ 468-2847, W www.lopezbicycleworks.com), 2847 Fisherman Bay Rd, is about 1mi from the village, opposite the marina. It rents mountain or cross bikes, tandems and recumbents. The bike-racks throughout the island are courtesy of this shop.

Log on at the Lopez Library, corner of Fisherman Bay and Hummel Lake Rds.

Things to See & Do Laid-back **Lopez Village** is a cluster of shops, eateries and houses, with a tiny business district overlooking Fisherman Bay. The unassuming **Lopez Historical Museum** (☎ 468-2049), Weeks Rd, will keep you intrigued for hours (open May–Sept, Fri–Sun, noon–4pm; Jul–Aug, Wed & Thurs). The **Lopez Library** (see Information) was originally a 19th-century schoolhouse. This and other historic buildings on the island are described in the **Lopez Historical Landmark Tour** brochure, available from the museum.

Galleries are scattered around the island. Take a glimpse into the creative spaces of artists during the **Lopez Island Artists' Studio Tour** (Labor Day weekend). The rest of the year, visit **Chimera Gallery**, in Lopez Village, for a sampling of arts and crafts.

In the village, the **Farmers Market** sells local produce and crafts (Sat 10am–2pm, May–Sept).

Lopez Kayaks (☎ 468-2847, Ⓦ www.lopezkayaks.com), next door to Lopez Bicycle Works (see Information), has sea-kayak rentals and guided trips. MacKaye Harbor Inn (see Places to Stay) also rents kayaks.

Don't miss the side trips to **Spencer Spit** (at 3.7mi) and **Shark Reef** (21.8mi).

Places to Stay Beachfront ***Odlin County Park*** *(☎ 468-2496 or ☎ 378-1842 for reservations, Ferry Rd)* is 1.2mi from the ferry. Campsites cost $12 each. Stunning views, beaches and hiking trails make ***Spencer Spit State Park*** *(☎ 468-2251 or ☎ 800-452-5687 for reservations, Ⓦ www.parks.wa.gov, Baker View Rd)*, 5mi from the ferry, a popular spot. Sites cost $6 to $13. Neither campground has showers; head to the public restrooms in the Village or the Marina for coin-operated showers.

Lopez Farm Cottages & Tent Camping *(☎ 800-440-3556, Ⓦ www.lopezfarmcottages.com, 555 Fisherman Bay Rd)* blends camping and cottages. The 10 campsites, in a secluded setting ($28 per double) include morning coffee and showers. The cozy cottages (from $125) have a kitchen, hot-tub access and include a continental breakfast.

Next to the marina, ***Islander Lopez Resort*** *(☎ 468-2233 or ☎ 800-736-3434, Fisherman Bay Rd)* has motel-style rooms (some with kitchenettes), a pool and hot tub. Prices begin at $80 (two-night minimum, Jul & Aug).

Built to resemble a Victorian mansion, the ***Edenwild Inn*** *(☎ 468-3238 or ☎ 800-606-0662, Ⓦ www.edenwildinn.com)*, Lopez Village, bids you to sit on the porch and watch the world go by. Rooms, with breakfast, start from $110.

On the south end of the island, the ***MacKaye Harbor Inn*** *(☎ 468-2253 or ☎ 888-314-6140, Ⓦ www.san-juan.net/mackayeharbor)*, built in 1904, has an irresistible location. Rates for the four rooms begin at $99, with breakfast.

Places to Eat Look no further than Lopez Village for all your edibles.

The ***Lopez Village Market*** caters to your supermarket needs. Visit ***Vita's*** for the makings of a superb picnic. For luscious local ice cream, stop at the ***Lopez Island Creamery*** in the Village or grab a pint from the market.

Head to ***Café Verdi*** for lattes or ***Holly B's*** for baked goods. In the pharmacy, the ***Soda Fountain*** serves soups, sandwiches, malts and sundaes, with an old-fashioned soda fountain. The ***Vortex Juice Bar & Good Food*** has smoothies and healthy snacks (open 10am–6pm).

The place for burgers and great fish tacos is ***Bucky's Grille*** *(☎ 468-2595)*. For superb dining, great sunset and water views, the ***Bay Cafe*** *(☎ 468-3700)* has main courses from $16. Reservations are absolutely essential.

Day Ride: Lopez Island Circuit

After a climb from the ferry landing, the route offers gentle cycling with easy climbs. Cruise effortlessly down hills, alongside harbors and through rolling pastures.

Begin on forested roads, then glide down to the water's edge as Port Stanley Rd hugs the shoreline with expansive **views** across Swifts Bay. At 3.7mi is a side trip to **Spencer Spit**, stretching toward, but not quite reaching, Frost Island. Walk the trail to the spit and along this skinny finger dividing the lagoon, a favorite stop for migratory birds.

The **Port Stanley Schoolhouse** (4.2mi) was built in 1917. Squeeze your brakes for the descent on fir-lined Lopez Sound Rd. Pass the current Lopez School and follow Center Rd, with fields of sheep and houses dating to the early 1900s.

The side trip (13.8mi) rewards with stunning **Mt Baker views** across Rosario Strait. Sperry Peninsula, once a popular summer camp, is now the private property of Microsoft co-founder Paul Allen.

Bucolic vistas continue to picturesque MacKaye Harbor. Pass fishing fleets on the side trip (15.8mi) to **Agate Beach**, where picnic tables make a great lunch spot.

The **Shark Reef Sanctuary** side trip is a must. The 10-minute walk through dense **old-growth forest** ends with glorious **views** across San Juan Channel to Cattle Point on San Juan Island. Turn left and walk another five minutes to view offshore rocks, a favorite hangout for **harbor seals**.

The route winds towards the Village, with a spectacular descent along postcard-perfect **Fisherman Bay**. Turning into **Lopez Island Vineyards**, you'd be forgiven for thinking you'd arrived in France. Be sure to taste their Madeleine Angevine and Siegerrebe (open noon–5pm, Wed, Fri & Sat).

Orcas Island

Duration....5–8 hours
Distance....42.8mi
Difficulty....moderate-hard
Start/End....Orcas Landing
Cues & Elevation Profile....p359

Mountain meets maritime. Orcas, the largest of the islands, is also the most challenging. Prepare for lots of ups and downs, dramatic coastline and picturesque harbors. Mt Constitution soars up from sea level, and pushing the pedals to reach the top is worth it for the outstanding views. For a change of pace, hike the trails lacing Moran State Park.

THE RIDE (See Map, p133)

Eastsound & Orcas Landing

Saddlebag-shaped Orcas Island is almost bisected by East Sound. The ferry dock is on the south of the island's western half. The main town, Eastsound, is 9mi from the ferry dock, at the northern extreme of East Sound, where the two halves of the island meet.

Information Orcas Island Chamber of Commerce (☎ 376-2273, Ⓦ www.orcasisland.org) is at 254 N Beach Rd, Eastsound (closed weekends). Pick up the free *Orcas Island Map & Guide*. If closed, there are racks of information outside the office. In the same building, log on at OrcasOnline. Key Bank, 210 Main St, has an ATM.

Also on N Beach Rd, the friendly staff at Wildlife Cycles (☎ 376-4708, Ⓦ www.rockisland.com/~wildlifecycles) rent mountain bikes. At Orcas Landing, Dolphin Bay Bicycles (☎ 376-4157, Ⓦ www.rockisland.com/~dolphin) also rents bikes (open Memorial Day–Labor Day).

The Orcas Island Lodging Information Hotline is ☎ 376-8888.

Things to See & Do In Eastsound, stop at the **Orcas Island Historical Museum** (☎ 376-4849, N Beach Rd), a collection of log cabins with interesting exhibits (open Memorial Day–1 Oct, Tues–Sun, 1–4pm). In the museum grounds, the **Farmers Market** has a host of local produce and crafts (Sat 10am–3pm, May–Sept).

The highlight of Orcas Island is **Moran State Park** (☎ 376-2326), dominated by **Mt Constitution**. The 5252-acre state park, the fourth-largest in Washington, has more than 30mi of **hiking trails**, and is graced with lakes, waterfalls, mountain biking trails (check with bike shops for access times), lots of wildlife and spectacular views. Available free is *Your Guide to Moran State Park*, with a map and information on the 15 hiking trails.

The waters around Orcas Island are ideal for **sea kayaking**. Shearwater Adventures (☎ 376-4699, Ⓦ www.shearwaterkayaks.com), across from Wildlife Cycles, offers classes, tours and rentals. For **whale watching**, contact Eclipse Charters (☎ 376-6566 or ☎ 800-376-6566, Ⓦ www.sanjuanweb.com/OrcasIsEclipse); reservations required.

Two miles from Eastsound, opposite the golf course on Horseshoe Hwy W, **Crow Valley Pottery** (☎ 376-4260, Ⓦ www.CrowValley.com) is in an historic 1866 log cabin. It features work by about 70 Northwest artists. See more pottery at Westsound (on the ride).

Places to Stay Five miles southeast of Eastsound, ***Moran State Park*** *(☎ 376-2326 or ☎ 800-452-5687 for reservations, Ⓦ www.parks.wa.gov, Horseshoe Hwy)* has more than 150 campsites. Hiker/biker sites cost $6 (no reservations).

Orcas has two low-key, laid-back resorts. ***West Beach Resort*** *(☎ 376-2240 or ☎ 877-937-8224, Ⓦ www.westbeachresort.com, Enchanted Forest Rd)*, 3mi from Eastsound, is in a secluded corner on a west-facing beach. Campsites cost $25, cottages from $90 per night. The cafe serves snacks and espresso. Kayak, canoe and boat rentals are available.

Doe Bay Resort *(☎ 376-2291, Ⓦ www.doebay.com)*, off Point Lawrence Rd, is best described as 'funky alternative'. Nestled between a forest and a cove, this 45-acre property has campsites from $12, dorm rooms from $16, plus yurts, domes and cabins from $42. There's a clothing-optional hot tub. The restaurant serves breakfast and dinner (mid-Jun–mid-Sept).

The bike-friendly ***Kangaroo House B&B*** *(☎ 376-2175 or ☎ 888-371-3604, www.KangarooHouse.com, 1459 N Beach Rd)*, a 1907 Craftsman-style home, is 1mi north of Eastsound. Rooms, including sumptuous breakfast and use of hot tub, begin at $85.

The 1888 ***Outlook Inn*** *(☎ 376-2200 or ☎ 888-688-5665, www.outlook-inn.com, Main St)* has shared-bath rooms from $79. Rooms in the new wing cost from $125. The front rooms have East Sound water views.

At Orcas Landing, the gracious 1904 ***Orcas Hotel*** *(☎ 376-4300 or ☎ 888-672-2792, www.orcashotel.com)* has a dozen rooms ($79–189 for doubles).

Places to Eat The ***Orcas Market*** is at Orcas Landing. In Eastsound, ***Island Market*** faces Prune Alley. For artisan breads, sandwiches and cheeses find ***Rose's Breads & Specialties*** in Eastsound Square (closed Sun).

At Orcas Landing, the ***Orcas Hotel Bakery*** has baked goods, espresso and cafe meals. For fine dining ***Octavia's*** *(☎ 376-4300)*, in the Orcas Hotel, has pasta and seafood mains with a Northwest flair.

In Eastsound, ***Portofino*** *(☎ 376-2085, A St)* has pizza. For good-value Italian fare, try ***La Famiglia Ristorante*** *(☎376-2335, Prune Alley)*.

On a warm evening, dine in the outdoor courtyard at ***Bilbo's Festivo*** *(☎ 376-4728, N Beach Rd)*. Enjoy Mexican and Southwest meals from $10.

The restaurant at the ***Outlook Inn*** (see Places to Stay) serves all meals. The evening menu features Thai, vegetarian and Northwest specialties from $15.

Day Ride: Orcas Island Circuit

Orcas is hilly, and the hills start early and continue for the entire ride. By far the winner of the biggest 'hill' award is the side trip to the summit of Mt Constitution. The route is possible in one day but to enjoy the side trips, allow at least two full days.

At 2.5mi, resist the temptation to take the slightly shorter route on Horseshoe Hwy. This thoroughfare is very busy, especially from the ferry to Eastsound.

Follow the madrona-lined Deer Harbor Rd down to tiny West Sound and its harbor views. Take a peek in the **Crow Valley School Museum** (6.1mi), built in 1888 as a one-room school. On the downhill stretch to Eastsound, dazzling **hanging sculptures** from the Howe Gallery line the road (8.5mi).

Climb out of Eastsound to **Moran State Park**. Just before the archway entrance, a right turn (13.1mi) leads to Rosario Resort, originally the mansion of shipbuilding magnate and Seattle mayor Robert Moran, who donated most of the land to the park. Cycling there is difficult due to the narrow, steep, winding road.

Cruise through the thickly forested park to the sparkling waters of **Cascade Lake** (13.8mi), reminiscent of an alpine setting. The climb up Mt Constitution is only for the fittest (see Side Trip).

The one-lane bridge (15.1mi) is the park boundary. The reasons to stop at Olga (16.7mi) are ***Cafe Olga*** and **The Orcas Island Artworks**, both in a quaint 1938 building.

It's up and down to the turnaround point at **Doe Bay** (20.1mi; see Places to Stay), a great place to picnic or hang out. Use the **hot tub** or have a **massage** (both for a fee). Follow the outward route back towards Eastsound but continue on Terrill Beach Rd (30mi).

The side trip to **West Beach** leads to West Beach Resort (see Places to Stay), a good spot for a drink, with great sunsets. **Right Place Pottery** is at the end of West Beach Rd and **Orcas Island Pottery** (34.6mi) is on the route.

The side trip to **Deer Harbor**, overlooking West Sound, climbs through forest before the glide down to an exquisite harbor setting.

Side Trip: Mt Constitution

9.4mi return

Make sure your brakes are up to the descent, and take lots of water for the ascent. The road is windy, and is busiest on weekends. The first 3mi are the toughest, as you tackle switchbacks and gradients of up to 15%. Watch for bald eagles and deer. The gradient eases at Little Summit (3mi).

At the top, congratulate yourself, then climb the observation tower for a 360-degree view of the San Juan Islands, Vancouver Island, Mt Baker and the mainland. It's easy to see why this is reputed to be one of the best maritime views in the USA, if not the world. If the ride seems too daunting, there are several hiking options to the top (see Things to See & Do).

San Juan Island

Duration .... 3–5 hours
Distance 25.9mi
Difficulty .... easy–moderate
Start/End .... Friday Harbor visitor center
Cues & Elevation Profile p360

Don't be deceived by the short length of this route; history, wild coastline, seaside parks, marine wildlife and an intriguing mausoleum easily fill the day. Allow time to explore Friday Harbor, the 'big city' of the islands.

THE RIDE (See Map, p133)

Friday Harbor

Information The island visitor center (☎ 378-5240, Ⓦ www.sanjuanisland.org), upstairs at the corner of Spring and Front Sts, is 200yd from the ferry landing.

The National Park visitor center (☎ 378-2240, Ⓦ www.nps.gov/sajh), 125 Spring St, has brochures, information and an excellent map for both National Historic Parks, English and American Camps (site of the Pig War).

Key Bank is at 95 Second St. Interwest Bank is on the corner of Argyle and Spring Sts. Island Bicycles (☎ 378-4941, Ⓦ www.islandbicycles.com), 380 Argyle St, includes tandems in its rental bikes. The Menu Bar, 435B Argyle St, has Internet access (closed Sun).

Things to See & Do The **San Juan Historical Museum** (☎ 378-3949, Ⓦ www.sjmuseum.org), 405 Price St, is on the outskirts of Friday Harbor. Housed in an 1890s farmhouse, it commemorates the island's early pioneer life (open Thurs–Sat, May–Sept; Tues & Thurs other months).

The waters around here are the best place in the islands for spotting whales. Learn about these and other marine mammals at the **Whale Museum** (☎ 378-4710 or ☎ 800-946-7227, Ⓦ www.whalemuseum.com), 62 First St. Presentations are offered both at the museum and **Lime Kiln State Park** by museum-trained naturalists.

Several companies offer **whale-watching tours**; for a boat excursion, try Salish Sea Charters (☎ 378-8555, Ⓔ salishsea@interisland.net). **Guided kayak treks** from Roche Harbor are operated by San Juan Safaris (☎ 378-1323 or ☎ 800-450-6858, Ⓦ www.sanjuansafaris.com). The visitor center has brochures on most tours.

Get the **Friday Harbor Gallery Guide** (Ⓦ www.fridayharbor.net/gallery-guide) and explore the 12 or so galleries in town.

Friday Harbor hosts the biggest party on the islands, the **San Juan Jazz Festival** (☎ 378-5509 or ☎ 888-825-9390, Ⓔ jazz@sanjuanjazz.org; mid-Oct).

Places to Stay Five miles from Friday Harbor, ***Lakedale Campground*** *(☎ 378-2350 or ☎ 800-617-2267, Ⓦ www.lakedale.com, 4313 Roche Harbor Rd)* has sites (including 10 bicycle-only sites) from $16. On the western shore, ***San Juan County Park*** *(☎ 378-2992 or ☎ 378-1842, 380 Westside Rd)* has 20 sites; book ahead. ***Pedal Inn*** *(☎ 378-3049, 1300 False Bay Rd)* has primitive hiker/biker sites for $5 per person (Jun–Sept).

Wayfarer's Rest *(☎ 378-6428, Ⓦ www.rockisland.com/~wayfarersrest, 35 Malcolm St)* is the only hostel in the islands, with dorm beds for $20 and a four-person cabin for $50 (closed Jan & Feb).

There are more than two dozen B&Bs on the island. These bicycle-friendly options are in lovely old houses in Friday Harbor: ***Blair House B&B*** *(☎ 378-5907 or ☎ 800-899-3030, 345 Blair Ave)* has shared bathrooms from $85 and peaceful grounds; ***Argyle House B&B*** *(☎ 378-4084 or ☎ 800-624-3459, 685 Argyle St)* has rooms from $95.

Friday's Historical Inn *(☎ 378-5848 or ☎ 800-352-2632, Ⓦ www.friday-harbor.com, 35 First St)*, a renovated 1891 hotel in the town center, has rooms with shared/private bath from $90/135, including breakfast.

Places to Eat Self-caterers should head for ***King's Supermarket*** *(160 Spring St)*. ***Felicitations*** *(120 Nichols St)* has bakery items (closed Mon). Friday Harbor provides lots of eating options. Cafes line the waterfront

Watch for orcas around San Juan Island

and the area behind the ferry terminal. Get a casual breakfast, lunch or dinner at ***Fat Cat Cafe*** *(☎ 378-8646, 1 Nichols St Walk)*. For brews and pub food, head to the ***Front Street Ale House & San Juan Brewing Company*** *(☎ 378-2337, 1 Front St)*.

For Mexican, go to ***Amigos*** *(☎ 378-8226, 40 Spring St)*; Middle Eastern, to ***Maloula's*** *(☎ 378-8485, 1 Front St)*, upstairs from the Ale House; or Italian, ***Bella Luna*** *(☎ 378-4118, 175 First St)*. Try ***China Pearl*** *(☎ 378-5254, 51 Spring St)* if you're craving Chinese. For excellent dining with innovative Northwest cuisine visit the ***Springtree Cafe*** *(☎ 378-4848, 310 Spring St)* and the ***Place Next to the San Juan Ferry*** *(☎ 378-8707, 1 Spring St)*; reservations essential.

Day Ride: San Juan Circuit

It's a hilly day cycling the perimeter of the island. The hardest climb is at the mid-point of the ride.

Pastoral views are quickly revealed. Visit **San Juan Vineyards** (3.6mi), in an 1896 schoolhouse (open noon–6pm in summer). Forested Roche Harbor Rd, interspersed with farms, terminates at Roche Harbor, the side trip destination (8.2mi). Another side trip (9.5mi) goes down a short, steep road to **British Camp**. The remains of the 1860s British military facility are in a gorgeous setting on Garrison Bay. Pick up the *Historic Guided Walk* from the box in the parking lot. The area offers two short **hiking trails**.

At 9.9mi fields of alpacas greet you. Water views disappear until **San Juan County Park** (14.2mi; see Places to Stay). It's a grind up the hill but the rewards are a wonderful (narrow) road through a thick mossy forest, ending in an exciting descent to **Lime Kiln State Park**. Also known as Whale Watch Park, it was the first park in the world devoted to whale watching. Sightings of resident pods of **orcas (killer whales)**, and sometimes minke whales, offer spectacular sights in the waters of Haro Strait. A trail leads to the main viewing area (bring binoculars and patience), equipped with picnic tables and interpretive panels. The white Lime Kiln Lighthouse is used as a research station by the Whale Museum (see Things to See & Do).

Glide along, 100ft above the water, taking in marvelous marine vistas. The road gradually turns inland through rural landscape.

The side trip to **American Camp** (22.9mi) offers a completely different look at the island. The southeast corner offers huge panoramas on this windswept grassy peninsula, flanked by pounding surf beaches and mountain views. Two buildings remain at the camp, plus a visitor center and interpretive trail. Stroll along the miles of **beach** or **hike** to Jackle's Lagoon or the top of Mt Finlayson for views of the Cascades and the Olympics. South Beach, the longest public beach on the island, is home to **shore birds** and bald eagles – if you're lucky, you might catch a glimpse of a pod of whales. **Cattle Point** is at the tip of the peninsula. From here, Lopez Island lies one mile across the channel, and short walks lead to the beach and lighthouse.

Gently undulating hills make it an easy ride back to Friday Harbor.

Side Trip: Roche Harbor & Mausoleum

4.2mi return

The first stop is the impressive but hard-to-find McMillin family mausoleum, in a serene spot in the woods. About 1.3mi along the side trip, turn right at the arch and proceed uphill for 0.15mi to the cemetery. Just 0.05mi beyond the cemetery, a dirt path (Fire Lane) leads to the **Afterglow Vista Mausoleum**. Return to the arch and follow the road (right) 'to the Resort' as it descends past the old **lime quarries and kilns** to Roche Harbor Resort (W www.rocheharbor.com).

The grand, still-popular **Hotel de Haro**, built in 1886 by limestone king John McMillin, is the centerpiece of this seaside hamlet. The brochure, *A Walking Tour of Historic Roche Harbor* ($1) is worth picking up in the lobby. Ride past the hotel, with the harbor on your left, and pass the small **Our Lady of the Good Voyage Chapel**. Continue on the service road, then turn left through the arch back to the main route.

Southeastern Washington

☎ 509

Tucked away in the southeastern corner of the state is an area too often overlooked by travelers. Two distinctive types of terrain characterize the area, the perfect, undulating hills of the Palouse Range, and the massive canyon cut by the Snake River. Quiet roads, gentle farmlands, expansive views and deep canyons are some of the delights that await cyclists.

HISTORY

The original inhabitants of this area were Native Americans. The Palouse tribe lived along the Lower Snake River. Further east, the Nez Percé tribe inhabited the area along the Clearwater River, and are credited with the development of the Appaloosa horse.

Lewis and Clark were the first white explorers in the region in 1805, making their way through the Clearwater and Snake River valleys to the Columbia River.

In 1858, resistance from the Palouse tribe led to a battle with US Army troops. Under the command of Colonel Edward Steptoe, the US troops were defeated at Steptoe Butte.

Gold was discovered in Idaho and Montana in 1862 and miners swarmed to the area. In the 1870s, miners gave way to homesteaders, who began farming around Pullman and Moscow, Idaho. They transformed an area of open prairie into one of the USA's premier farming regions, and today agriculture remains the backbone of the economy.

NATURAL HISTORY

Sometime before the last Ice Age, prevailing southwesterly winds blew across the lava-covered Columbia Plateau. The dust created dunes that accumulated into steep-sided rolling hills with very fertile soil, called loess. Early French traders gave the Palouse its name, derived from the French word *pelouse* (lawn). The region stretches from south of Spokane to just north of the Snake River. Wheat and legumes dominate the crops.

The Palouse is home to two buttes, Steptoe and Kamiak. Buttes are outcroppings of pre-Cambrian rock, with lava flows covering the lower ground around the rock 10 to 30 million years ago. Geologists use the term steptoe to refer to this type of landform.

The Snake River originates in Yellowstone National Park and winds through Idaho, Oregon and Washington to join the Columbia River near Pasco, 1036mi from its source. The canyon walls are primarily basalt, resulting from lava flows as recently as six million years ago.

INFORMATION

When to Ride

The Palouse is like an artist's palette, changing colors with the seasons. In May and June, the hills of the Palouse don a velvety, green jacket. In summer, the fields of golden wheat ripple in the breeze, and in fall the harvested hills display their yellow hues. The weather is pleasant between May and early October, August being the hottest month.

Maps

There's a dearth of maps on the area. The best are in the DeLorme *Washington Atlas & Gazetteer* (pages 43 & 57) and Benchmark's *Washington Road & Recreation Atlas* (pp93 & 106–7).

GATEWAY CITIES

Spokane

Spokane is the largest city between Seattle and Minneapolis, and the second-largest city in Washington.

Washington's first trading post was located here in 1810, and in 1881 the Northern Pacific began building a transcontinental rail line through Spokane. Spokane flourished in the 1880s as a gold capital, after the discovery of gold and other precious metals in nearby Cœur d'Alene, Idaho.

Like so many towns in the West, fire destroyed the business area in 1889. It was rebuilt in brick rather than wood.

Spokane gained recognition in 1974, hosting an extremely successful world fair. The city spruced up a rundown area along the river, and today this site, Riverfront Park, remains the city's centerpiece.

Information Spokane visitor center (☎ 747-3230 or ☎ 800-248-3230, Ⓦ www.visitspokane.com) is at the corner of W Main Ave and Browne Sts.

On W Riverside Ave, a US Bank is at 428, and a Bank of America is at 601. Both have ATMs.

For bicycle repairs and rentals, Spoke'N Sport (☎ 838-8842), 212 N Division St, is a few blocks east of the visitor center.

Spokane Library (☎ 444-5300), corner Main Ave and Lincoln St, has Internet access.

Things to See & Do Undeniably, the heart of Spokane is **Riverfront Park**. Straddling the Spokane River the park is laced with walking and cycling **paths**, and has an **ice-skating rink**, small **amusement park**, **IMAX theater**, and a 1909 hand-carved **carousel**. **Spokane Falls** are at the west end of the park.

The **Spokane River Centennial Trail** runs northwest from Riverfront Park to Riverside State Park, and east to Cœur d'Alene, Idaho (see the boxed text below).

Spokane has its share of museums. Paying tribute to the city's native son, Bing Crosby, is the **Bing Crosby Memorabilia Room** (☎ 328-4220, ext 4297), 502 E Boone Ave, at Gonzaga University, the crooner's alma mater.

With more than 1000 participants, the annual two-day **Tour des Lacs Ride** (☎ 455-7657, W www.roundandround.com/tdl.htm) is on the last weekend in September. Four rides of varying length and difficulty go from Spokane to Cœur d'Alene, Idaho.

Places to Stay On the Spokane River, the huge ***Riverside State Park*** *(☎ 456-3964, W www.parks.wa.gov)* has first-come, first-served tent sites for $13. It is 6mi northwest of downtown Spokane and features 32mi of hiking trails, and can be reached on the Centennial Trail.

Most of the cheaper downtown hotels tend to be near the freeway or the railway line. South of the I-90 freeway, the ***Budget Inn*** *(☎ 838-6101 or ☎ 800-325-4000, 110E 4th Ave)* has singles/doubles from $49/53. Near the Amtrak station, the ***Ramada Limited*** *(☎ 838-8504 or ☎ 800-210-8465, W www.ramada.com, S 123 Post St)* costs $69/77, including a substantial continental breakfast. Close to Centennial Trail, the ***WestCoast River Inn*** *(☎ 326-5577 or ☎ 800-325-4000, W www.westcoasthotels.com, 700 N Division St)*, with pool, has rooms from $100.

Near the Centennial Trail and Gonzaga University, the elegant 1908 ***Marianna Stoltz House B&B*** *(☎ 483-4316 or ☎ 800-978-6587, W www.mariannastoltzhouse.com, 427 E Indiana Ave)* welcomes cyclists. Rooms start at $69/79, including breakfast.

Places to Eat A ***Safeway*** *(cnr 3rd Ave & Maple St)* is on the western edge of downtown. If you're riding the Centennial Trail east, detour for an espresso and bakery treat at the ***Rocket Bakery*** *(3315 N Argonne Rd)*.

Spokane offers a wide selection of restaurants. A good downtown bet is the ***Rock City Grill*** *(☎ 455-4400, 505 W Riverside Ave)* an Italian-American Grill.

Several eateries are in the old ***Flour Mill*** *(621 W Mallon Ave)*, on the north bank of the Spokane River. Among the choices are ***Clinkerdagger's Restaurant*** *(☎ 328-5965)*, serving Northwest cuisine, and the ***Riverview Thai Restaurant*** *(☎ 325-8370)*.

Getting There & Away Spokane is well serviced by air, bus and train services.

Spokane River Centennial Trail

While in Spokane, it would be a shame not to set aside time to cycle the Spokane River Centennial Trail. This glorious 37mi bikepath, mostly along the Spokane River, heads 14mi west from downtown to Nine Mile Dam, and east 23mi to the Washington-Idaho border. From the border, it continues a further 23mi as the North Idaho Centennial Trail to just east of Cœur d'Alene.

The idea of a bicycle/pedestrian path along the river was born in 1979. In 1986, the plan was to open a 10.5mi trail east of the city to coincide with Washington's 1989 Centennial. Today the trail extends 60mi, with plans to extend it 12mi beyond Nine Mile Dam.

One of the gems of the trail is the section through the city center from Gonzaga University through Riverfront Park to Spokane Falls. This segment is a superb example of an urban bikepath.

Heading east from downtown the trail offers gentle, mostly flat cycling as it hugs the river, utilizing portions of a disused rail line. The most spectacular section is the western segment from the TJ Meenach Bridge through Riverside State Park to Nine Mile Dam. The trail undulates high above the river through pine forests, offering great views, including the Bowl & Pitcher rock formation and a short side trip (1.5mi) to Deep Creek Canyon.

For trail information see W www.spokanecentennialtrail.org. Trail maps ($2) are available from the Web sites, where you can also find more basic maps. Generally the trail is well signposted, however, signs are often lacking for the first few miles out of downtown Spokane. It is tricky following the city streets, and a Spokane city map is a handy supplement to the trail map.

Air Alaska, Horizon, United Express, and Southwest fly between Spokane and Seattle. Horizon and Alaska have the greatest frequency with 20 flights daily; return fares are around $104 for the one-hour flight. Horizon also flies to Portland for $104 return.

Spokane Transit Authority (STA; ☎ 328-7433) runs airport–downtown buses every hour until 9.48pm ($0.75c, 30 minutes). Buses have bike racks and bikes are free. Spokane Cab (☎ 535-2535) charges about $15 for the 10-minute ride; request a minivan for your bike.

Bus Northwestern Trailways (☎ 800-366-3830, W www.nwadv.com/northw/) has one bus a day between Spokane and Seattle ($26, nine hours) and between Wenatchee and Spokane ($24, 3½ hours). Greyhound offers service between Seattle and Spokane ($26, seven hours, five a day).

Train Amtrak has one train a day between Spokane and Seattle ($81, eight hours).

Snake & Spiral Circuit

Duration	3 days
Distance	139.5mi
Difficulty	moderate
Start/End	Pullman
Cues	pp360–1

Drop down from the hills of the Palouse through the Wawawai Canyon to meet the Snake River. This haunting canyon leads to the twin towns of Clarkston and Lewiston, start points for Hells Canyon Tours.

What comes down must go back up to Pullman, and the serpentine Old Spiral Highway is that 'up'. Enjoy enormous views as you wind up this straggling strand of spaghetti clinging to the canyon wall.

Day 3 showcases classic Palouse landscape. Soft, sensuous hills and big, old barns present timeless rural images. Take the side trip and climb Kamiak Butte, cycle through pine forests and venture into Idaho. Finish the day along a paved rail trail.

GETTING TO/FROM THE RIDE

Pullman

Air Horizon Air (☎ 800-547-9308, W www.horizonair.com) flies to Pullman from Seattle ($140 return, one hour, four daily). Bikes must be boxed ($50 each way). The small planes cannot carry tandems.

Bus Northwestern Trailways (☎ 800-366-3830, W www.nwadv.com/northw/) operates buses between Spokane and Pullman ($15, 1½ hours, two a day). Bikes ($15) must be boxed or bagged.

Link Transportation (☎ 800-359-4541, W www.linktrans.com) runs minibuses between Pullman and Spokane/Spokane International Airport (1¾ hours, $45/65 one way/return, three to five a day). Bikes are $10 each way, subject to space availability. Boxed bikes are preferable.

Bicycle It's an 80mi ride from Spokane to Pullman. Take food and water as there aren't many services en route.

Leave Spokane east on the Centennial Trail. At Argonne Rd turn right, stopping at the Rocket Bakery (3315 N Argonne Rd). Continue over the I-90 freeway, where Argonne Rd becomes Dishman-Mica Rd, which in turn becomes Madison Rd. Turn left onto the Palouse Hwy, then right after about 1mi onto Hwy 27. Continue until Pullman. See Maps (p140) for help with this route.

THE RIDE

Pullman

Pullman's origins date back to 1877, when it was called 'Three Forks' due to its position at the confluence of the Missouri Flat Creek, Dry Fork Creek and south fork of the Palouse River. It is believed that it was renamed in 1881, after George Pullman (of Pullman railroad sleeping-car fame). Fire destroyed the wooden buildings of downtown Pullman in 1890. Rebuilt in brick, many of the buildings remain.

In 1892, the state opened the Washington Agricultural College here. With just 21 students, this was the forerunner of Washington State University (WSU), today Washington's major agricultural school, with more than 22,000 students and faculty.

Information The Pullman chamber of commerce (☎ 334-3565 or ☎ 800-365-6948, W www.pullman-wa.com), 415 N Grand Ave, is closed Sundays. The WSU visitor center (☎ 335-8633, W www.wsu.edu/visitor), one block south at 225 N Grand

Ave, is in the old Union Pacific railroad depot. It has a campus map walking tour, plus basic tourist information.

A Bank of America and US Bank are on E Main St. The town's bike shops are: B&L Bicycles (☎ 332-1703), 219 E Main St, and Follett's Mountain Sports (☎ 332-2259), 236 E Main St. Both are closed on Sunday. Internet access is available at the campus libraries.

Things to See & Do A culture buff could spend days on the WSU campus, well endowed with museums and collections. The **Museum of Art** (☎ 335-1910) specializes in Northwest art, contemporary and Old Master prints, and American paintings. With more than 2000 specimens of petrified wood, the **Jacklin Collection** (☎ 335-3009) is the largest display of its kind in the western USA. There is also a **Museum of Anthropology** (☎ 335-3936), an **Historic Films Collection** (☎ 335-5618), two **Herbariums**; the list goes on.

On campus, don't miss **Ferdinands** (☎ 335-2141) at the WSU Creamery, offering ice cream, milkshakes and the exceptionally tasty **Cougar Gold cheese**, all produce of WSU's dairy herd. Visit the observation room and watch cheese being made.

Pullman's **National Lentil Festival** (☎ 334-3565) is on the last weekend in August. Sample lentil salads, lentil enchiladas and even lentil ice cream. There's also a parade.

In late July, head to Moscow, Idaho on the Chipman Trail (see Day 3) for the annual **Whitepine Classic Bike Tour**, a century, metric century and family ride sponsored by the Moscow Central Lions Club (☎ 208-882-2814).

Places to Stay The ***Pullman RV Park*** *(☎ 334-4555, ext 228)* in the city park, less than 1mi from the city center, near South and Riverview Sts, has tent sites for $6. For camping away from the city, ***Kamiak Butte County Park*** *(☎ 397-6238)*, on Day 3, has $10 campsites. ***Wawawai County Park*** *(☎ 397-6238)*, Day 1, has campsites on the Snake River for $10. Both county parks have running water and flush toilets.

The ***Manor Lodge Motel*** *(☎/fax 334-2511, 455 SE Paradise St)* has singles/doubles for $39/49, with microwaves and refrigerators. The ***American Travel Inn Motel*** *(☎ 334-3500, W www.palouse.net/allamerican, 515 S Grand Ave)* has rooms for $47/52. Just off the Chipman Trail, the ***Quality Inn Paradise Creek*** *(☎ 332-0500 or ☎ 800-669-3212, 1050 SE Bishop Blvd)* has a jacuzzi. Rooms start at $65/75. All lodgings add a surcharge on graduation and football weekends.

Places to Eat For supermarket needs, stock up at ***Dissmore's*** *(1205 N Grand Ave)*. Students need coffee. For espresso, the ***Daily Grind*** *(230 E Main St)* also serves soup, sandwiches and baked goods. Across the road, ***Basilio's Italian Cafe*** *(☎ 334-7663, 337 E Main St)* has good-value pasta, plus sandwiches and salads. For Mexican, ***Rancho Viejo*** *(☎ 332-4301, 170 S Grand Ave)* has mains from $8. ***Pizza Pipeline*** *(☎ 332-1111, 630 E Main St)* is also popular.

A favorite hangout for both students and faculty is ***Rico's Tavern*** *(☎ 332-6566, 200 E Main St)*. It has a large beer selection, burgers and sandwiches. ***Swilly's*** *(☎ 334-3395, 200 Kamiaken St)* has an interesting and varied menu, serving lunch and dinner ($11–19).

Day 1: Pullman to Clarkston

4–7½ hours, 45.9mi

This is the easiest day of the ride. The route rolls over the Palouse and down to the Snake River. The only significant climb is up Main St, Pullman, the first half-mile of the day. There's very little traffic until the last few miles before Clarkston. Carry food and drinks as there are no shops en route.

Main St (0.2mi) confronts you with a steep hill first thing in the morning. Rounded hills usher you past farms to the top of the Wawawai Canyon. It's a 5mi freewheel through the canyon's tight walls. Take a moment to absorb the quietness, only the chirping of birds breaking the silence.

Wawawai derives its name from the Native American word *wa* meaning 'talk, talk, talk', or 'council ground'. In the late 1800s, settlers grew fruit on the Wawawai flats, now submerged by the Lower Granite Dam. At this time, Wawawai was a huge fruit-shipping port. The **Wawawai County Park** makes a great picnic spot. This 50-acre wildlife sanctuary has camping (see Places to Stay for Pullman), picnic facilities, an interpretive trail with great views, and a wetland area.

Along the river there are very basic recreation areas for boaters. **Rock formations** shape the canyon walls. The road turns east as you ride within sight of **Chief Timothy State Park**, the island only accessible from Hwy 12 on the other side of the river (see Places to Stay for Clarkston).

At the Port of Wilma (42.3mi), milled logs of all shapes and sizes await their departure. The **Red Wolf Crossing Bridge** over the Snake to Clarkston honors the chief of the Nez Percé tribe.

Clarkston

In 1805, the expedition of Meriwether Lewis and William Clark (see the boxed text, p15) followed the Clearwater River to the Snake River, setting up camp at the rivers' confluence. The hospitable Nez Percé tribe supplied them with food to continue their exploration. Today the twin towns bear the names of the explorers.

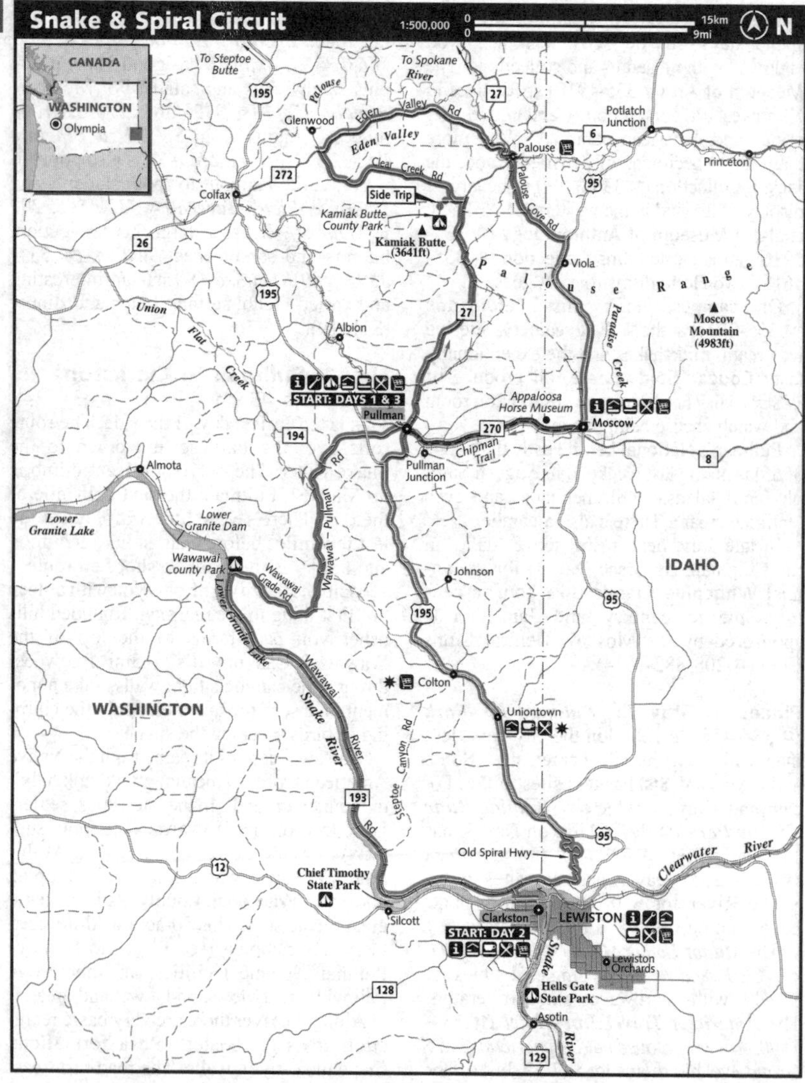

RICHARD CUMMINS

See Seattle's Space Needle...

RICHARD I'ANSON

...enjoy the vibrant arts scene...

RICHARD CUMMINS

...explore the harborside by night...

RICHARD CUMMINS

...be enticed off your bike by alluring aromas...

RICHARD CUMMINS

...and marvel at the architecture.

DONALD C & PRISCILLA ALEXANDER EASTMAN

JOHN ELK III

Washington's North Cascades: cycle to Diablo Lake (L), or spend sunrise at majestic Lake Chelan (R).

JOHN ELK III

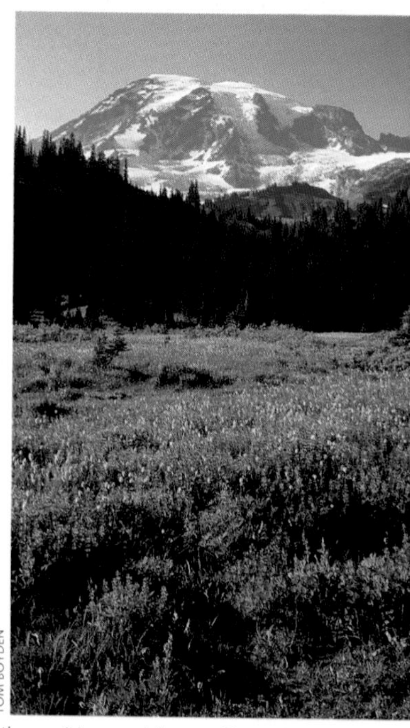

TOM BOYDEN

Watch whales near San Juan Island's Lime Kiln Lighthouse (L), or watch magnificent Mt Rainier (R).

JENNIFER SNARSKI

Oregon wilderness: views of the Wallowa Mountains.

RICHARD CUMMINS

JENNIFER SNARSKI

Columbia River Gorge National Scenic Area: enjoy fall colors at Shepperds Dell (L), dense forests (R)...

JENNIFER SNARSKI

...and the chance to give yourself a day off the bike while you stretch your legs on scenic hiking trails.

JOHN ELK III

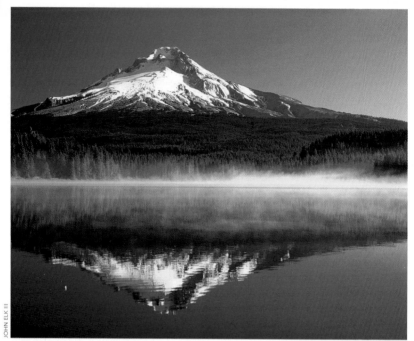

Extreme Oregon: take in views of its highest peak, the 11,240ft volcanic Mt Hood...

BRENT WINEBRENNER

...or take a well-earned rest on the shores of Crater Lake, the USA's deepest lake.

There was no settlement here until 1860, the beginning of the Idaho gold rush. The confluence of the Snake and Clearwater was the head of steamboat navigation from Portland, and the area boomed as a transport and trade center. Today Lewiston, with its grain loading docks, is the USA's most inland port, 470mi from the Pacific Ocean.

Clarkston, Washington, on the west side of the Snake River, is across the bridge from Lewiston, Idaho, and is the smaller and younger of the two towns.

Information The Clarkston chamber of commerce (☎ 758-7712 or ☎ 800-933-2128, Ⓦ www.clarkstonchamber.org) is at 502 Bridge St. The Lewiston chamber of commerce (☎ 208-743-3531 or ☎ 800-473-3543, Ⓦ www.lewistonchamber.org) is at 111 Main St, Suite 120. Both are closed weekends. Both have the *Clearwater & Snake River National Recreation Trail* bikepath map.

A US Bank is on the corner of 6th and Poplar Sts, and a Bank of America is on 6th and Elm Sts. For bicycle needs, you'll have to go to Lewiston. TNT Bicycles (☎ 208-798-8727) is at 620 Main St. Pedals-n-Spokes (☎ 208-743-6567), 829 D St, has mountain bike rentals. Both are closed Sunday. Log on at the Clarkston Library at 5th and Sycamore Sts.

Things to See & Do Set aside time to visit **Hells Canyon**. Just south of the Washington border, in Oregon, it's the deepest river gorge in North America, cutting a chasm more than 1mi deep. It begins 50mi south of the twin cities. Several companies offer **jet boat tours**. Beamers (☎ 758-4800 or ☎ 800-522-6966, Ⓦ www.hellscanyontours.com) leave from the dock in front of the Quality Inn in Clarkston. River Quest Excursions (☎ 208-746-8060 or ☎ 800-589-1129, Ⓦ www.riverquestexcursions.com) depart from the Hells Gate State Park Marina.

Hells Gate State Park (see Places to Stay) has a swimming beach, mountain-bike and hiking trails, plus an interpretive center. **Chief Timothy State Park** (see Places to Stay), on a landscaped island in the Snake River with more than 11,000ft of freshwater shoreline, has plenty of swimming options. Just before crossing the bridge to the island, the **Alpowai Interpretive Center** tells of the area's geologic and human history.

Both chambers of commerce provide a list of commemorative **Lewis and Clark sites**.

The **Greenbelt Trail**, a 6mi paved pedestrian and cycle path, runs south alongside the Snake River from Clarkston to the small town of Asotin, where you'll find the **Asotin County Museum** (☎ 243-4659), corner 3rd and Filmore Sts. Several buildings, including a pole barn with an huge collection of branding irons, and a 1927 one-room schoolhouse, make up the museum. The gem is the main building, with a 1900s pump organ, a collection of telephone switchboards, an 1897 music box (ask for a demonstration) and an 11,000-year-old mammoth's tusk (open Tues–Sat, 1–5pm).

Places to Stay The closest campground is ***Hells Gate State Park*** *(☎ 208-799-5015, Ⓦ www.idahoparks.org)*, 4.5mi south of Lewiston. Access the park by cycling the Lewiston Levee Parkway Trail, on the east side of the Snake River. Campsites cost $12. On an island in the Snake River, 8mi west of Clarkston on Hwy 12, is ***Chief Timothy State Park*** *(☎ 758-9580 or ☎ 800-452-5687 for reservations, Ⓦ www.parks.wa.gov)*. Tent sites cost $13. Both parks have showers.

Hacienda Lodge *(☎ 758-5583 or ☎ 888-567-2287, 812 Bridge St)* has single/double motel rooms for $32/42. The ***Best Western RiverTree Inn*** *(☎ 758-9551 or ☎ 800-597-3621, 127 Bridge St)* has a pool, hot tub and sauna. Rooms start at $59/69. On the river, the ***Quality Inn*** *(☎ 758-9500 or ☎ 800-228-5151, 700 Port Dr)* has rooms from $72/80.

Highland House *(☎/fax 758-3126, 707 Highland Ave)* has rooms from $55/70. The English owner transformed this Victorian house into a piece of England; she even serves a real English breakfast.

Places to Eat Shop at ***Albertson's*** supermarket *(400 Bridge St)*. The ***Sage Baking Company*** *(720 6th St)* has delicious bakery items (closed Sun & Mon).

Paraiso Vallarta *(☎ 751-9077, 518 Bridge St)* has Mexican meals from $6. For Chinese food, ***Bamboo Gardens*** *(☎ 758-8898, 907 6th St)* has mains from $6.50. ***Tomato Bros*** *(☎ 758-7902, 200 Bridge St)*, offers wood-fired pizza from $10, pastas from $6 and Italian specialties from $12.

For great food with a view of the Snake River try ***Rooster's Landing*** *(☎ 751-0155,*

1550 Port Dr). Head over to Lewiston for more culinary options.

Day 2: Clarkston to Pullman

3½–6 hours, 36.5mi

A short day with a big climb in Idaho, followed by gentle hills to Pullman with a stop in an historic town.

You'll need to be warmed up for the **Old Spiral Highway**. This road, engineered in 1914, known locally as the Lewiston Grade, snakes up the canyon wall, climbing 2000ft in 7mi. Today it is known as the 'old' highway, as off to the east the 'new' highway takes most of the traffic, leaving this quiet road for sightseers and intrepid cyclists. Stop periodically and soak up views of the rivers and Blue Mtns. At 11.7mi, an historic marker tells of Lewiston's development. At the top, bear with the traffic entering the busy stretch of highway, before Idaho's Hwy 95 and Washington's Hwy 195 split. Back in Washington, it's relaxing cycling as the Palouse uplands spread before you.

Tiny **Uniontown** (18.8mi) is a surprise. To see the splendid 1904 **St Boniface Catholic Church**, turn left on W Woodworth St, go up two blocks and turn left onto St Boniface St. The church has the original five altars, statues, and stained glass windows. Next door is the **Churchyard Inn**. Built in 1905 as a parish house, it was converted to a convent in 1913. Today it is a B&B. Leaving Uniontown, look left at the oft-photographed **wagon-wheel fence** (19.4mi). In Colton (22mi), turn right onto Steptoe St and follow the steeple to **St Gall's Church**, built in 1905. Picturesque farms and patterned fields will charm you all the way back to Pullman.

I Made the Grade!

For more than 20 years, on the third Saturday in June, cyclists have gathered for the great Lewiston-Clarkston hill climb cycling challenge, the annual 'I Made the Grade' ride up the Lewiston Grade. The 18mi ride begins at Chief Timothy State Park, then climbs the Old Spiral Highway. Rewards are a sense of achievement, panoramic views, participation in a fun event and, best of all, a T-shirt emblazoned with the words 'I Made the Grade'. For the event, cyclists carry as little as possible for the 2000ft climb, however, on Day 2 of the Snake & Spiral Circuit, you can feel exceptionally proud when you reach the top, on a *loaded* bike!

The ride is organized by the First Presbyterian Church of Clarkston (☎ 758-3381), 1122 Diagonal, Clarkston, WA 99403.

Day 3: Pullman–Palouse Circuit

5½-9 hours, 57.1mi

The Palouse Range treats you to a roller coaster ride, the heftiest climb of the day is about 8mi before Moscow, Idaho. End the day with easy cycling on a rail trail. Take provisions as there is only one small ***shop*** (in Palouse) until Moscow.

Hwy 27 cuts through the **wheat fields** of the hilly Palouse. Depending on the time of year, the colors vary from rich greens to golden yellows. The short side trip to **Kamiak Butte** (12.1mi) gives you the opportunity to hike the 3.5mi **Pine Ridge Trail** through a thick conifer forest to the top of 3641ft-high Kamiak Butte, its geology almost identical to Steptoe Butte. From the top exceptional **views** of the Palouse are your reward. This is a good spot for **bird-watching**. Warblers, nuthatches, and pygmy and great-horned owls inhabit the forests.

Pause at the crest of the hill (15.1mi) for an expansive view; an incredible Palouse tapestry stretches before you. Drop down and the stand of pine trees (19.8mi) is likely to make you forget you're in the Palouse. Eden Valley Rd offers views as far afield as Steptoe Butte. In fall, it's easy to imagine you're in the desert – from a distance, the hills covered in golden wheat stubble appear like sand dunes.

After the triple set of railway tracks (31.2mi), there is a short, steep climb through shady streets of historic houses into the town of **Palouse**. The road then drops in to the town center (32mi). Once the thriving 'wheat capital', today the town's buildings show damage from the floods of 1996, many businesses, sadly, still empty and boarded up.

Turn onto Hwy 95 (Idaho) for the climb up Steakhouse Hill. **Moscow** (46.8mi) is home to the University of Idaho, and like Pullman, is very much a university town. As the route leaves Moscow, the **Paradise Path** winds through the campus to connect with the **Bill Chipman Trail**, a 9mi paved recreation rail trail. At the state line (49mi), the **Appaloosa Horse Museum & Heritage Center** presents the history of the Appaloosa horse.

GON

Highlights

- waterfalls of the Columbia River Gorge
- volcanic peaks and ancient lava flows near Bend
- Klamath Basin, home to more than 200 bird species
- Crater Lake, deepest and bluest in the USA
- vast, spectacular Baker and Grande Ronde Valleys
- Elkhorn Range and the Wallowa Mountains

Special Events

- Oregon Shakespeare Festival (Feb–Nov) Ashland
- Rose Festival (Jun) Portland
- Waterfront Blues Festival (Jun) Portland
- Sternwheeler Days (Jun) Cascade Locks
- Oregon Brewers Festival (Jul) Portland
- Chief Joseph Days (Jul) Joseph

Cycling Events

- Cycle Oregon (Sept)
- Cascade Cycling Classic (Jul) Bend
- Bridge Pedal (Aug) Portland

Food & Drink Specialties

- microbrews – Mirror Pond Pale Ale at Deschutes Brewery (Bend), Terminator Stout at Fulton Pub (Portland) & India Pale Ale at Terminal Gravity Brewery (Enterprise)
- blackberries, wild and ripe for the picking in fall

CHRIS MELLOR

Oregon

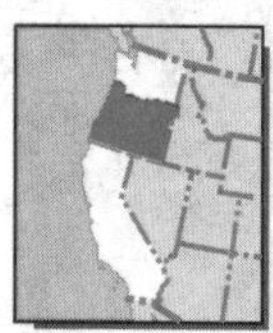

A vast state, the USA's ninth-largest at 98,386 sq mi (with only some three million people), Oregon offers an extraordinary range of possibilities for the cyclist. The Portland region includes the Columbia River Gorge National Scenic Area, with more than 70 waterfalls. Easy cycling amid vineyards and orchards is found in the Willamette River Valley, the 60mi wide basin between the Cascade Mtns and the coastal range. Central Oregon contains lava and obsidian (glass formed by the cooling of molten lava) flows and alpine lakes. Southern Oregon boasts the bird-filled Klamath Basin; Crater Lake, the USA's deepest; and the wild and scenic Rogue River. The northeastern region has a completely different flavor. It's the Wild West, complete with ranches and wheat fields, remote sagebrush-covered hills and the Wallowa Mtns, containing 19 of Oregon's 25 highest peaks.

HISTORY

The history of Oregon is inextricably linked to the story of some 53,000 immigrants who arrived via the Oregon Trail, the greatest human migration in US history. They forever changed the land and the lives of the Native Americans who called the region home.

Starting in the 1840s, farmers, traders and their families followed the 2000mi overland path. Oregon City in the Willamette Valley was their destination, but when this area became saturated, settlement spread to the valleys of eastern Oregon.

Oregon officially became a US territory in 1848. It entered the Union as a free state in 1859. Throughout the region, native tribes clashed with white settlers – fighting to protect the natural resources that sustained them. In the south, Rogue River tribes opposed settlement. Modocs fought US troops, and eastern Oregon's Nez Percé fled north. Most Native Americans were incarcerated on reservations, some as far away as Oklahoma.

From the 1880s, the grasslands of Eastern Oregon were taken over by ranchers and then by homesteaders. The high lava plains in the central part of the state were tilled and planted with wheat. Arguably, the long-term result of such settlement was the ever-increasing destruction of the natural world, including over-fishing, over-logging and the damming of rivers for hydroelectric power.

By the end of the 19th century, Portland was a boomtown, acting as the trade conduit for agricultural products from the inland valleys. Portland was the terminus of the Northern Pacific Railroad, which in 1883 linked the region to eastern USA. Shortly thereafter, a rail line linked Portland to San Francisco. By 1890, Portland was one of the world's largest wheat-shipment points.

By WWII, Oregon had become the nation's largest lumber producer; in the 1980s nearly all the state's ancient forests were slated for logging. In the years following, environmentalists have waged battles – in the courtroom, the streets and forests – to try to halt or slow deforestation.

NATURAL HISTORY

Oregon has an extremely diverse landscape. The rugged coast gives way to densely forested mountains of the Coast Range, and then to the wide and fertile Willamette River Valley. Further south the Umpqua River and Rogue River valleys drain a tightly contorted series of mountain canyons. East of the volcanic Cascade Mtns, green valleys shift to arid uplands. In central Oregon's Deschutes River Valley savannas drop away into immense canyons carved through lava flows. The Ochoco and Blue Mtns amble through central and eastern Oregon. In the northeastern part of the state, the peaks of the Wallowa Mtns are ragged and craggy, formed by glaciers during the last Ice Age.

The old growth is mostly gone but you'll see plenty of trees in Oregon. The Douglas fir (up to 250ft high) and western red cedar (about 200ft) are used for the building industry. Slightly smaller, the Ponderosa pine, with its distinctive orange, jigsawed bark is prevalent east of the Cascades, as well as elsewhere. Also common east of the Cascades are lodgepole pines. Back cottonwood, a hardwood used for paper, grows by rivers and streams. Although there are many evergreens, you'll see brilliant fall color and ripe blackberries.

In the understory of established forests grow ferns, rhododendrons and Oregon grape. Old-mans beard is a gray-green lichen that clings to trees and is eaten by deer. Mosses and mushrooms abound in the moister regions.

It won't be hard to find blue Steller's jays, crows and ravens. Keep your eyes open for woodpeckers. Near water are graceful blue herons and loons, as well as lots of ducks.

Among the larger animals are elk, deer and black bears. Little critters include deer mice, chipmunk squirrels, raccoons and beavers. Streams are home to their own distinct salmon populations.

CLIMATE

The Oregon Coast gets about 77 inches of rain a year; the Willamette Valley, 20 inches. Watered by about 37 inches a year, Portland isn't as rainy as its reputation. But the city is often cloaked in grayness due to Pacific marine clouds. Southwest Oregon experiences a warmer summer – temperatures in the nineties – than Portland, the Willamette Valley or the coast, and is much drier. The Cascade Mtns block wet Pacific air and, as a consequence, much of central and eastern Oregon is arid: Bend gets as little as 12 inches of precipitation annually, much of it in snowfall. Eastern stretches of the state are even drier and, in the summer, hotter.

INFORMATION

Local visitor centers and chambers of commerce, detailed in individual rides, are a good source of information.

Maps

A useful state overview is given by the *Oregon Bicycling Guide*. It shows all highways, indicating traffic volume, major road grade, whether there is a shoulder, wind patterns, climate and rules of the road. For a free copy, write to Oregon Department of Transportation, 355 Capitol St NE, Salem, OR 97301-3871 or call ☎ 503-986-3556.

Unwieldy but handy are the *Oregon Road & Recreation Atlas*, published by Benchmark Maps; and DeLorme's *Oregon Atlas & Gazetteer.* Benchmark distinguishes (not always accurately) between paved and unpaved roads.

Adventure Cycling's *TransAmerica Bicycle Trail* map sections one and two are helpful for heading inland to Eugene from the Border to Border ride and for cycling from Eugene to Baker City for the Wild West Roundup ride. For copies, contact Adventure Cycling (☎ 406-721-1776 or ☎ 800-721-8719, Ⓦ www.adv-cycling.org), PO Box 8308, Missoula, MT 59807.

Books

Cyclists with unlimited time to explore the endless variety of blissful byways may wish to own *Bicycling the Backroads of Northwest Oregon* or *Biking the Great Northwest: 20 Tours in Washington, Oregon, Idaho & Montana*, both published by the Mountaineers. If dirt is your thing, get a copy of *Oregon: A Guide to the Classic Trails*, part of Menasha Ridge Press' *America by Mountain Bike* series.

By David Alt and Donald Hyndman, *Roadside Geology of Oregon* erupts with explanations of why Oregon looks as it does. The *Well-Traveled Casket: A Collection of Oregon Folklife*, by Tom Nash and Twilo Scofield, presents quirky tales from Oregon's past. *Salmon Nation: People and Fish at the Edge* (Ecotrust, Portland) is a thought-provoking collection of essays about the relationship between this iconic fish and the human inhabitants of the Pacific Northwest.

Information Sources

Contact Oregon Tourist Commission (☎ 503-986-0000 or ☎ 800-547-7842, fax 986-0001, Ⓦ www.traveloregon.com) at 775 Summer St NE, Salem, OR 97301.

For information on hiking and camping in state parks, visit Ⓦ www.prd.state.or.us or call ☎ 800-551-6949. For campground reservations call ☎ 800-452-5687 or visit Ⓦ www.ReserveAmerica.com.

Bicycle Transportation Alliance (BTA; ☎ 503-226-0676, Ⓦ www.bta4bikes.org), 717 SW 12th Ave, Portland, is a nonprofit organization working to promote bicycle use and to improve bicycling conditions in Oregon. It has chapters throughout the state.

GATEWAY CITIES

Portland

☎ 503

Portland has been called the most bicycle-friendly city in the United States. Cyclists will find not only a well-developed system of bike routes – including bikepaths and striped

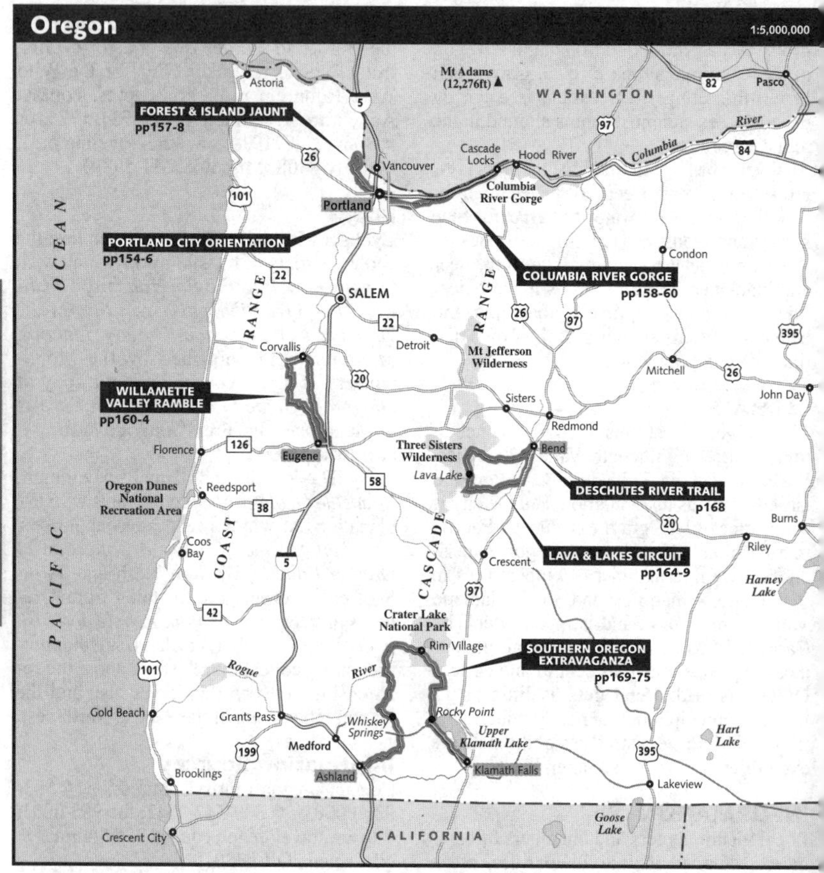

bike lanes – but considerate drivers and numerous side streets with little or no traffic. Sitting at the confluence of the Columbia and Willamette Rivers, with its major neighborhoods straddling the Willamette, bridges are major arteries in Portland. Many of these have recently been redesigned for cycling.

The city of Portland (with a population of around 650,000) has a busy but laid-back downtown and several vibrant neighborhoods, each with a distinct identity. Portlanders invariably locate themselves in one of the city's quadrants; likewise street addresses bear such a designation. The Willamette River is the east-west divider; Burnside St divides north from south. The unsung 'fifth quadrant' is North Portland, roughly bounded by the Willamette River and Hwy 99.

Today, Portland is known for its forward-thinking urban planning and is home to universities, nonprofit organizations and high-tech companies.

Information The Portland Oregon Visitors' Association (POVA; ☎ 503-275-8355 or ☎ 877-678-5263, W www.travelportland.com) is at 701 SW 6th Ave, in Pioneer Courthouse Square. It stocks oodles of information and sells tickets for local entertainment and events. Also on the square is a Tri-Met office, offering transit information and permits for taking bikes on buses and the MAX line.

Two free maps to the city are helpful: the *Portland Visitor's Map*, available at the visitor center and at museums and other

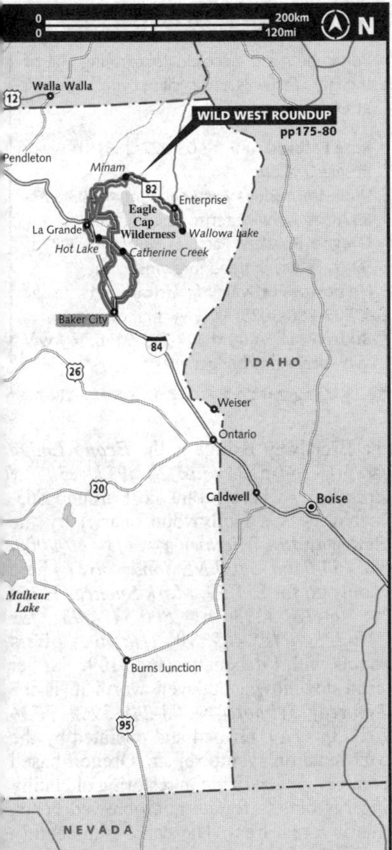

tourist sites; and Powell's Books *Walking Map of Downtown Portland*, found at all Powell's stores, including its Travel Store (☎ 503-228-1108), in Pioneer Courthouse Square (which also offers foreign currency exchange). For more complete coverage of the city and environs, try Rand McNally's *Portland, Oregon City Map*. The Metro Transportation Department (☎ 503-797-1742), 600 NE Grand Ave, Portland, produces the indispensable *Bike There*. Look for it in bike shops, too.

A handy post office is in the Pioneer Courthouse at the corner of SW 6th Ave and Yamhill St.

Check email at the Multnomah County Central Library (☎ 503-988-5123), 801 SW 10th Ave.

River City Bicycles (☎ 503-233-5973), 706 SE Martin Luther King Jr Blvd, is a large, friendly store. Make sure to eyeball the roof sculpture. Comrades at the Bicycle Repair Collective (☎ 503-233-0564), signed 'Bike Stuff', at 4438 SE Belmont, repair bikes and sell parts. The shop also rents workspace and offers supervised maintenance instruction. Conveniently located at 2025 SE Hawthorne Blvd is Coventry Cycle Works (☎ 503-230-7723). This is the place for information on the city's cycling events. To gawk at some beautiful classic bikes, visit the small, service-oriented Sellwood Cycle Repair (☎ 503-233-9392) at 7639 SE Milwaukie Ave. Mountain-biking enthusiasts will appreciate Fat Tire Farm (☎ 503-222-3276), 2714 NW Thurman St, which rents bikes.

Things to See & Do For more attractions, see the Portland City Orientation ride (p156).

The Bicycle Transportation Alliance (☎ 503-226-0676) offers **bicycle tours** of the city. Friends and employees of Sellwood Cycle Repair lead early morning rides; inquire at the shop for details.

Amble along Portland's **South Park Blocks**, between SW Park and SW 9th Aves, to spot Portland State University students philosophizing on the grass. Here, too, is the **Portland Art Museum** (☎ 503-266-2811), 1219 SW Park Ave. The museum's **Northwest Film Center** (☎ 503-221-1156) shows foreign, classic and experimental films year-round and hosts festivals.

A preserve of Victorian architecture, the district that surrounds the **Skidmore Fountain**, at SW 1st Ave and SW Ankeny St, bustles from March to December with the **Saturday Market** (should you need a tie-dyed shirt).

To satisfy literary longings, stop by **Powell's City of Books** (☎ 503-228-4651, Ⓦ www.powells.com), 1005 W Burnside St.

For a night out, go the **Crystal Ballroom** (☎ 503-225-0047), 1332 W Burnside St, which has live music – from jazz to rock to swing to tango – as well DJ dance nights.

The West Hills behind Portland's downtown are home to **Washington Park**. Here you'll find the **International Rose Test Gardens**, one of the USA's oldest such gardens, sprawling on 4.5 acres with fountains and hundreds of sweet-smelling varieties of rose. On a clear day there's also a stunning view of 11,240ft-high Mt Hood. For tree lovers, the **World Forestry Center** (☎ 503-228-1367) offers arboreal education. Visit the formal **Japanese Garden** (☎ 503-223-1321) with its teahouse and garden. Architecture buffs will want to visit the **Pittock Mansion** (☎ 503-823-3624), completed in 1914 for the then-editor of the *Oregonian*.

It is well worth cycling over the majestic **St Johns Bridge** in North Portland. Travel from the Eastside to the Westside for stunning views of Forest Park.

Places to Stay Portland has a good range of central accommodations.

Budget Portland's two HI-AYH hostels are hospitable and conveniently located, charging $15/18 members/nonmembers for dorm beds. ***Hostelling International-Portland, Northwest Neighborhood*** *(☎ 503-241-2783, W www.2oregonhostels.com, 1818 NW Glisan)* is in an upscale neighborhood, full of restaurants, vintage- and new- clothing stores, and bars. ***Hostelling International-Portland, Hawthorne District*** *(☎ 503-236-3380, W www.portlandhostel.com, 3031 SE Hawthorne Blvd)* has a large front porch for relaxing.

Mid Range The ***Downtown Value Inn*** *(☎ 503-226-4751, 415 SW Montgomery St)* has singles/doubles for $50/55. Just across the Broadway Bridge is the ***Econo Lodge*** *(☎ 503-284-5181, fax 287-9711, 305 N Broadway)* where rooms cost around $65. In Northeast's Hollywood district try the ***Rodeway Inn Midtown*** *(☎ 503-460-9000, fax 460-0460, 3800 NE Sandy Blvd)* where rooms go for $54/59. ***Mark Spencer Hotel*** *(☎ 503-224-3293 or ☎ 800-548-3934, fax 510-223-7848, 409 SW 11th Ave)* offers rooms with kitchenettes for $109. Further from downtown, but well worth it, is the ***Kennedy School*** *(☎ 503-249-3983, 5736 NE 33rd Ave)*. Owned and operated by the McMenamin's empire, an Oregon-based company specializing in restoring old buildings as outlets for its microbrewed beers, this is a real treat. The early-20th-century building's 35 guest rooms, around $109, are former school classrooms, now artfully decorated. The complex has a movie theater, restaurant, atmospheric bars serving microbrews, a heated soaking pool and more.

B&Bs A smaller B&B is the ***Terwilliger Vista*** *(☎ 503-244-0602 or ☎ 888-244-0602, 515 SW Westwood Dr)*. The 1941 Georgian Colonial in the West Hills has five rooms from $75 to $125. If you prefer a tranquil rural setting, stay at ***River's Edge B&B*** *(☎ 503-621-9856, fax 9784, 22502 NW Gillihan Rd)* on Sauvie Island (see Forest & Island Jaunt, p157–8), about 11mi out on a busy road from Portland. Rooms cost $75, including breakfast, use of a kitchenette, TV and books.

Top End Luxurious accommodations can be had at the ***Heathman Hotel*** *(☎ 503-241-*

Bikes on Portland Transit

Tri-Met is Portland's network of buses and MAX light-rail trains. All buses are equipped with a two-bike rack and MAX train cars have designated spaces for bikes (though neither tandems nor recumbents are allowed). At the time of writing you need a Bikes on Tri-Met permit ($5) – although the permit is under revision and may be scrapped. It is available from many bike shops as well as the Portland State University Information & Transportation Center (☎ 503-725-8759), in the Urban Center Plaza at 506 SW Mill St; and the Tri-Met office at Pioneer Courthouse Square. You'll need to view a short film explaining the rules of bikes on transit. For more information call the Bikes on Tri-Met hotline (☎ 503-962-7644).

Portland's Festivals

Portlanders are disposed to partying. All of the city's festivals and cycling events are well attended:

Rose Festival (Jun) ☎ 503-227-2681, W www.rosefestival.org
Waterfront Blues Festival (Jun) ☎ 503-973-3378, W www.waterfrontblues.com
Oregon Brewers Festival (Jul) ☎ 503-778-5917, W www.oregonbrewfest.com
Homowo Festival of African Arts (Aug) ☎ 503-288-3025, W www.homowo.org
Bridge Pedal (Aug) ☎ 503-281-9198, W www.providence.org/bridgepedal

4100 or ☎ 800-551-0011, 1001 SW Broadway) for $159 and up. The attractive bar and restaurant are at street level.

Places to Eat No cyclist will go hungry in Portland. There are a number of good choices for people with big appetites and small budgets, starting with the vendors who feed weekday workers from carts parked on the city's sidewalks and plazas. Several are found in Pioneer Courthouse Square, including ***Honkin' Huge Burritos***, where just that goes for $4.50. The ***Taste of India*** cart is at the corner of SW Alder St and 9th Ave.

Westside For groceries close to central downtown, head to ***Fred Meyer*** *(cnr 20th Ave & Burnside St)*. Planning a picnic? Grab a sandwich at the ***Great Harvest Bread Co*** *(810 SW 2nd Ave)*. ***World Cup Coffee & Tea Service*** *(1740 NW Glisan St)* is a tranquil place to start your day. ***Una Mas*** *(914 NW 23rd Ave)* puts fresh salsa on its burritos ($3–5). Delicious ***India House*** *(1038 SW Morrison St)* offers a $6.95 lunch buffet, and serves slightly pricier dinner. Fill up on pizza and beer at ***Old Town Pizza*** *(226 NW Davis St)*. The funky old building (supposedly a former brothel) is furnished with mismatched 'antiques' – including some very rickety chairs. Reasonably priced salads, pastas and good, crisp pizza are on the menu at ***Pizzicato*** *(cnr NW Glisan & 23rd Ave)*.

For spinach ravioli and fancier dishes, head to ***Tuscany Grill*** *(☎ 503-243-2757, 811 NW 21st Ave)* for dinner. For a celebration try ***Veritable Quandry*** *(☎ 503-227-7342, 1220 SW 1st Ave)*, serving creative meat, seafood and pasta ($15–20).

Eastside Shop for groceries at ***Safeway*** *(2800 Hawthorne Blvd)* or the smaller ***Daily Grind*** *(4026 Hawthorne Blvd)*. The ***Cup & Saucer*** *(3566 SE Hawthorne Blvd)* is a hub of the neighborhood for three meals a day. Cell phones are banned and basic grub is in the $6 to $8 range. The ***Bread & Ink Cafe*** *(3610 SE Hawthorne Blvd)* serves up cheese blintzes ($7) and duck, seafood and vegetable meals (to $17) on white tablecloths.

Vegetarians won't want to miss the ***Paradox Cafe*** *(3439 SE Belmont St)*. The menu offers vegetarian or vegan food, from the four-grain pancakes ($4) to the tempeh Reuben sandwich ($5). The restaurant's name may refer to the one lonely meat dish on offer (a hamburger).

For pub grub try the pizza and people-watching at the McMenamin's-owned ***Bagdad*** *(3702 SE Hawthorne Blvd)*. It also has a movie theater in which you can eat and drink. At the ***Horse Brass Pub*** *(4534 SE Belmont St)* the beer list is longer than your arm. On weekends you can watch English football in the wee hours, working up an appetite for a traditional English breakfast, served at 10am. The ***Laurelthirst*** *(☎ 503-232-1504, 2958 NE Glisan St)*, named for the Laurelhurst neighborhood, has more of a bar/club vibe and hosts live music.

For creative, flavorful Italian dishes and voluminous glasses of red wine, try ***Il Piatto*** *(☎ 503-236-4997, 2348 SE Ankeny St)*. The pumpkin ravioli approaches perfection in the $10 range; meat dishes are around $14.

Getting There & Away Portland is well connected to other West Coast cities.

Air Portland airport (☎ 503-460-4234 or ☎ 877-739-4636, W www.portofportlandor.com), 7000 NE Airport Way, is served by many airlines. Alaska Airlines (☎ 503-249-4075 or ☎ 800-252-7522) flies to San Francisco. Its Seattle-based sister airline, Horizon (☎ 800-547-9308), flies between Portland and Seattle and also serves Vancouver, BC, in Canada. Southwest Airlines (☎ 503-221-9792 or ☎ 800-435-9792) flies between Portland and Oakland, California. Fares vary depending on the season, day and time of travel.

The MAX train runs from the airport through the Eastside to the city center ($1.55). Tri-Met city bus number 12 runs from the airport to SW 6th Ave and SW Main St, downtown ($1.55, 45 minutes) and has two bike racks. The only problem with these options is that the Bikes on Tri-Met permit (see the boxed text 'Bikes on Portland Transit', p152) is not available at the airport. Negotiation with the driver is your best bet.

Bikes will have to travel as boxed luggage on the Grayline Express airport shuttle, which leaves the airport every 45 minutes, 5am to midnight, serving downtown hotels ($15/22 one way/return).

To cycle from the airport (around 7mi) exit the terminal following signs to 82nd

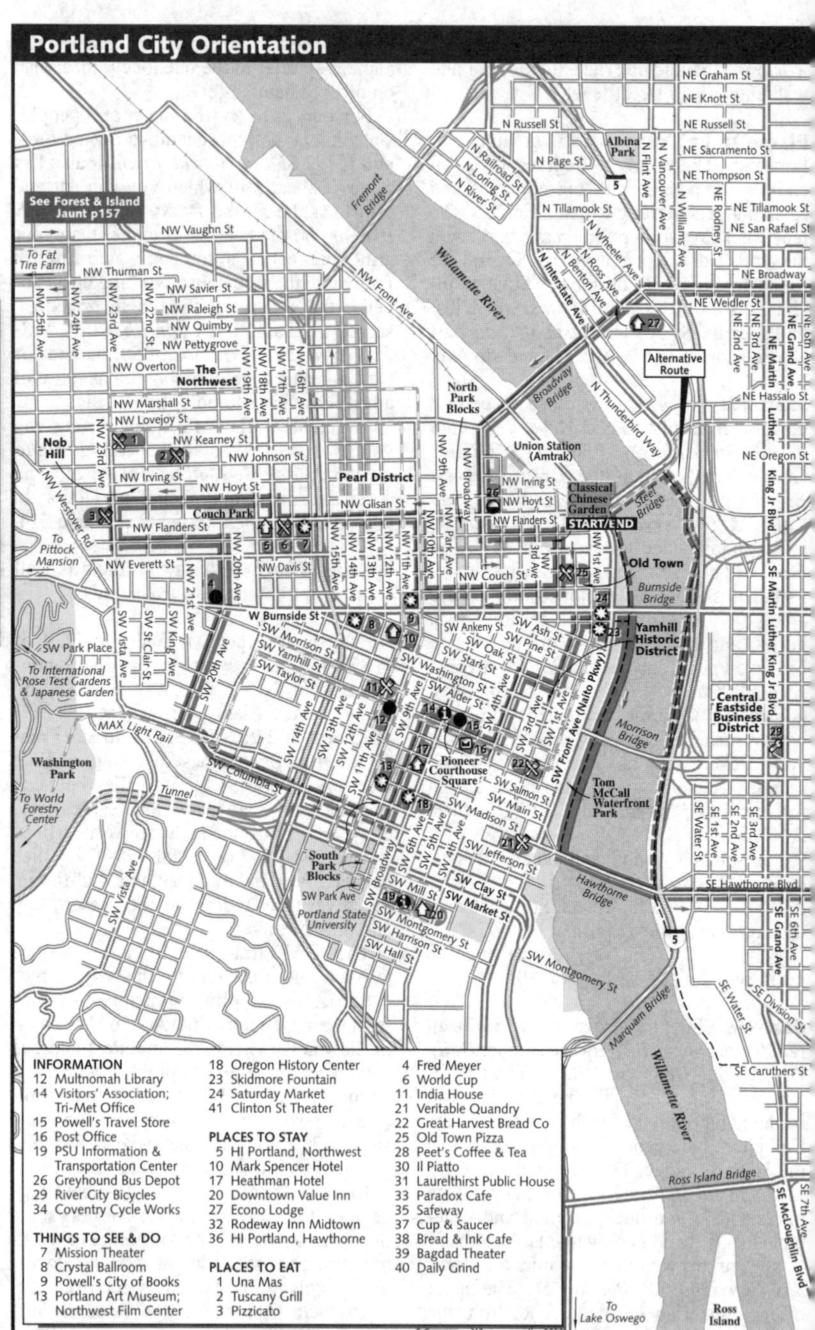
Portland City Orientation
See Forest & Island Jaunt p157
To Fat Tire Farm
To Pittock Mansion
To International Rose Test Gardens & Japanese Garden
Washington Park
To World Forestry Center
Nob Hill
The Northwest
Couch Park
Pearl District
North Park Blocks
Union Station (Amtrak)
Classical Chinese Garden
START/END
Old Town
Yamhill Historic District
Pioneer Courthouse Square
South Park Blocks
Portland State University
Tom McCall Waterfront Park
Central Eastside Business District
Albina Park
Alternative Route
Willamette River
Fremont Bridge
Broadway Bridge
Steel Bridge
Burnside Bridge
Morrison Bridge
Hawthorne Bridge
Marquam Bridge
Ross Island Bridge
Ross Island
To Lake Oswego
MAX Light Rail
Tunnel
INFORMATION
12 Multnomah Library
14 Visitors' Association; Tri-Met Office
15 Powell's Travel Store
16 Post Office
19 PSU Information & Transportation Center
26 Greyhound Bus Depot
29 River City Bicycles
34 Coventry Cycle Works
THINGS TO SEE & DO
7 Mission Theater
8 Crystal Ballroom
9 Powell's City of Books
13 Portland Art Museum; Northwest Film Center
18 Oregon History Center
23 Skidmore Fountain
24 Saturday Market
41 Clinton St Theater
PLACES TO STAY
5 HI Portland, Northwest
10 Mark Spencer Hotel
17 Heathman Hotel
20 Downtown Value Inn
27 Econo Lodge
32 Rodeway Inn Midtown
36 HI Portland, Hawthorne
PLACES TO EAT
1 Una Mas
2 Tuscany Grill
3 Pizzicato
4 Fred Meyer
6 World Cup
11 India House
21 Veritable Quandry
22 Great Harvest Bread Co
25 Old Town Pizza
28 Peet's Coffee & Tea
30 Il Piatto
31 Laurelthirst Public House
33 Paradox Cafe
35 Safeway
37 Cup & Saucer
38 Bread & Ink Cafe
39 Bagdad Theater
40 Daily Grind

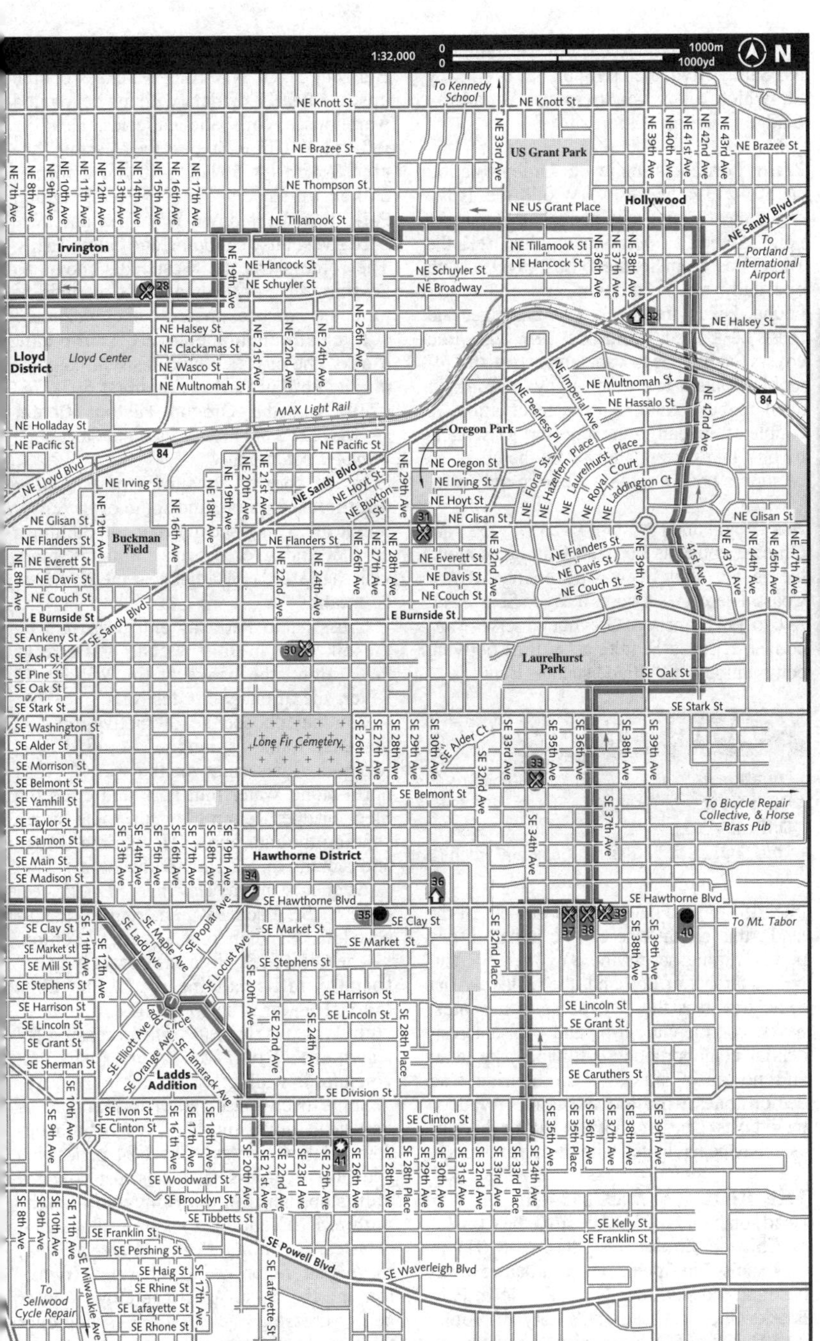
1:32,000
0
0
1000m
1000yd
N
To Kennedy School
NE Knott St
NE Knott St
NE Brazee St
NE Brazee St
US Grant Park
NE Thompson St
NE US Grant Place
Hollywood
NE Tillamook St
NE Tillamook St
NE Hancock St
NE Hancock St
NE Schuyler St
NE Schuyler St
NE Broadway
NE Sandy Blvd
To Portland International Airport
Irvington
NE 7th Ave
NE 8th Ave
NE 9th Ave
NE 10th Ave
NE 11th Ave
NE 12th Ave
NE 13th Ave
NE 14th Ave
NE 15th Ave
NE 16th Ave
NE 17th Ave
NE 19th Ave
NE 33rd Ave
NE 36th Ave
NE 37th Ave
NE 38th Ave
NE 39th Ave
NE 40th Ave
NE 41st Ave
NE 42nd Ave
NE 43rd Ave
28
32
NE Halsey St
NE Halsey St
Lloyd District
Lloyd Center
NE Clackamas St
NE Wasco St
NE Multnomah St
NE Multnomah St
NE Hassalo St
NE 21st Ave
NE 22nd Ave
NE 24th Ave
NE 26th Ave
NE 42nd Ave
84
MAX Light Rail
NE Holladay St
NE Pacific St
NE Pacific St
84
Oregon Park
NE Peerless Pl
NE Imperial Ave
NE Lloyd Blvd
NE Irving St
NE Irving St
NE Sandy Blvd
NE Hoyt St
NE Hoyt St
NE Buxton St
NE Oregon St
NE Floral St
NE Hazelfern Place
NE Laurelhurst Place
NE Royal Court
NE Laddington Ct
NE Glisan St
NE Glisan St
NE Glisan St
31
NE Flanders St
NE Flanders St
NE Flanders St
Buckman Field
NE Everett St
NE Everett St
NE Davis St
NE Davis St
NE Davis St
NE Couch St
NE Couch St
NE Couch St
NE 8th Ave
NE 12th Ave
NE 16th Ave
NE 18th Ave
NE 19th Ave
NE 20th Ave
NE 21st Ave
NE 22nd Ave
NE 24th Ave
NE 26th Ave
NE 27th Ave
NE 28th Ave
NE 29th Ave
NE 32nd Ave
NE 39th Ave
41st Ave
NE 43rd Ave
NE 44th Ave
NE 45th Ave
NE 47th Ave
E Burnside St
E Burnside St
SE Sandy Blvd
SE Ankeny St
SE Ash St
30
Laurelhurst Park
SE Pine St
SE Oak St
SE Oak St
SE Stark St
SE Stark St
SE Washington St
SE Alder St
Lone Fir Cemetery
SE Alder Ct
SE Morrison St
SE Belmont St
SE Belmont St
33
SE Yamhill St
SE Taylor St
SE Salmon St
SE Main St
SE Madison St
SE 26th Ave
SE 27th Ave
SE 28th Ave
SE 29th Ave
SE 30th Ave
SE 32nd Ave
SE 33rd Ave
SE 34th Ave
SE 35th Ave
SE 36th Ave
SE 37th Ave
SE 38th Ave
SE 39th Ave
To Bicycle Repair Collective, & Horse Brass Pub
SE 13th Ave
SE 14th Ave
SE 15th Ave
SE 16th Ave
SE 17th Ave
SE 18th Ave
SE 19th Ave
Hawthorne District
34
36
SE Hawthorne Blvd
SE Hawthorne Blvd
35
SE Clay St
SE Clay St
37
38
39
40
To Mt. Tabor
SE Poplar Ave
SE Maple Ave
SE Ladd Ave
SE Market St
SE Market St
SE Market st
SE Mill St
SE Stephens St
SE Stephens St
SE Locust Ave
SE 11th Ave
SE 12th Ave
SE 32nd Place
SE 38th Ave
SE 39th Ave
SE Harrison St
SE Harrison St
SE Lincoln St
SE Lincoln St
SE Lincoln St
Ladd Circle
SE Grant St
SE Grant St
SE Elliott Ave
SE Orange Ave
SE Tamarack Ave
SE 20th Ave
SE 22nd Ave
SE 24th Ave
SE 28th Place
SE Sherman St
SE Caruthers St
Ladds Addition
SE Division St
SE Ivon St
SE Clinton St
SE Clinton St
SE 10th Ave
SE 9th Ave
SE 16th Ave
SE 17th Ave
SE 18th Ave
41
SE 20th Ave
SE 21st Ave
SE 22nd Ave
SE 23rd Ave
SE 25th Ave
SE 26th Ave
SE 28th Ave
SE 28th Place
SE 29th Ave
SE 30th Ave
SE 31st Ave
SE 32nd Ave
SE 33rd Ave
SE 33rd Place
SE 34th Ave
SE 35th Ave
SE 35th Place
SE 36th Ave
SE 37th Ave
SE 38th Ave
SE 39th Ave
SE Woodward St
SE Brooklyn St
SE Tibbetts St
SE Kelly St
SE Franklin St
SE Franklin St
SE 8th Ave
SE 9th Ave
SE 10th Ave
SE 11th Ave
SE Pershing St
SE Powell Blvd
SE Waverleigh Blvd
SE Haig St
SE Rhine St
SE Lafayette St
SE Rhone St
SE 17th Ave
SE Milwaukie Ave
SE Lafayette St
To Sellwood Cycle Repair

Ave. Take NE 82nd Ave south. Turn right on NE Sandy Blvd, then right on NE Broadway St, which takes you over the Broadway Bridge to Union Station.

Train Portland's majestic Union Station (☎ 503-273-4865), 800 NW 6th Ave, is the city's most glamorous arrival or departure point. Amtrak's *Coast Starlight* line treks the West Coast from Seattle to Los Angeles, with one daily run northbound and one southbound. Bikes are checked as baggage, and must be boxed. Amtrak's *Cascades* line covers the Eugene to Vancouver (British Columbia) route a few times a day: bikes don't need to be boxed; make a reservation. A couple of the daily runs transport passengers by bus; bikes aren't allowed on the buses, so be sure to book a spot on the train-only runs.

Bus Greyhound (☎ 503-243-2357), 550 NW 6th Ave, connects Portland with cities along the I-5, the major freeway traversing the West Coast. There are six buses a day to Seattle and five to San Francisco. Greyhound serves Vancouver, BC, via Seattle, as well as outlying communities of Portland such as Bend.

Portland City Orientation

Duration....................................3–5 hours
Distance 15mi
Difficulty ....easy
Start/End.............Classical Chinese Garden

Intended to give new arrivals the 'lay of the land', this circuit ride can be joined at any point. Cutting across the SW, NW, SE and NE quadrants of Portland, the relatively flat route traverses the city, passing museums, parks, commercial strips and pleasant residential neighborhoods. Utilizing bike lanes and no-traffic side streets, the ride also demonstrates why Portland is much lauded by cyclists. Cues are not needed for this ride as it may be navigated with the map supplied.

THE RIDE (See Map, p154–5)

Head south on NW 3rd Ave from the **Classical Chinese Garden** (☎ 503-228-8131) in Portland's **Old Town**, where urban renewal has replaced skid row. Cross the **North Park Blocks**, then pass **Powell's City of Books** (☎ 503-228-4651). It occupies an entire block but the entrance and bike racks are on W Burnside St. On NW 10th Ave check out the upscale **Pearl District**, with its renovated warehouses, lofts and galleries. Heading left on NW Glisan St, pass the **Mission Theater & Pub** (☎ 503-223-4031), a former church turned cinema. Pass leafy **Couch Park**, then peer down NW 21st and NW 23rd Aves, busy shopping and eating strips. The route skirts the West Hills (home to **Washington Park**), then SW Columbia St turns the ride back toward the city center.

Cycle through the lovely **South Park Blocks**, the city's cultural district, containing the **Portland Art Museum** (☎ 503-276-4249) and the **Oregon History Center** (☎ 503-222-1741), with its eight-story-high *trompe l'oeil* mural.

In the core of downtown pass **Pioneer Courthouse Square**, and some of the city's **public art**. You'll see majestic old buildings on SW 2nd Ave. If your timing is good, visit the **Saturday Market** near the **Skidmore Fountain**.

Cross Naito Parkway and turn right on the bikepath in **Tom McCall Waterfront Park**, along the banks of the Willamette River, site of many city festivals.

You may choose the alternative route on the **East Bank Esplanade**. Some of this bikepath floats right on the water! (Turn north along Waterfront Park and cross the Steel Bridge. Rejoin the main route by ascending the ramp up to Hawthorne Bridge and picking up SE Hawthorne Blvd.)

After crossing the Hawthorne Bridge veer right on SE Ladd Ave, entering Portland's best designed neighborhood, **Ladds Addition**.

The Clinton St environs boasts bicycle-friendly traffic-calming roads. The **Clinton St Theater** is between SE 25th and SE 26th Aves. Gazing east when crossing SE Hawthorne Blvd, **Mt Tabor**, an extinct volcano, is visible.

Some tricky navigation is involved as you head north on 41st Ave, which becomes NE 42nd Ave. The I-84 pedestrian and bike overpass, which is also a MAX train stop, lands in the **Hollywood neighborhood**. It's home to many shops and eateries, including ***Peet's Coffee & Tea***, serving strong brew. Pass charming **Irvington** and the oh-so-American **Lloyd Center** before crossing back to the Westside over the Broadway Bridge.

Forest & Island Jaunt

Duration...3–6 hours
Distance...45.9mi
Difficulty...easy
Start/End...Union Station, Portland
Cues...p362

Get ready for variety! This ride starts amid urban sophistication and industrial grit; climbs past stately homes; takes you off-road through tall trees allowing occasional glimpses of volcanic peaks; rolls alongside a major river port; and loops through fertile farmland on an island in the Columbia River. The total elevation gain is about 1400ft.

HISTORY & NATURAL HISTORY

Forest Park was officially designated as a park in 1947. At almost 5000 acres, this is the USA's largest urban forested park, full of hiking and biking trails and virtually undeveloped.

In the early 19th century, explorers Lewis and Clark named the island Wappato after an indigenous plant. About 20 years later, dairy cattle belonging to the Hudson's Bay Company grazed on the island under the care of Laurent Sauvé, after whom it became known as Sauvie Island. Much of the island, the largest in the Columbia River, is for the birds: 20 sq mi of it make up a wildlife refuge, year-round home to great blue herons and temporary accommodation to flocks of migrating sandhill cranes.

PLANNING

Rand McNally's *Portland, Oregon City Map* covers the ride. July and August are the least rainy months, but a sunny day in September, with cool breezes and fallen leaves, is best.

GETTING TO/FROM THE RIDE

On the north end of downtown, Union Station is at the end of NW 6th Ave.

Bus

If you opt to return from Sauvie Island by bus, the No 17 runs Monday to Saturday. Catch it in the parking lot nestled next to the island side of the Sauvie Island Bridge. You need a bike permit: see the boxed text 'Bikes on Portland Transit'(p152).

THE RIDE

Leaving Union Station, the route weaves through Portland's **Pearl District**, with its antique shops and galleries, and then through the industrial flatlands. NW Thurman St climbs through the **West Hills**, perhaps the city's swankiest neighborhood. The residents of these huge homes have **Forest Park** as their backyard. There's a water fountain and information at the park entrance (3.4mi).

Leafy Leif Erickson Dr, a dirt and gravel hiker/biker trail, is 12mi of blissful cycling. Be mindful of pedestrians, as you wind in and out of trees, catching glimpses of **Mt St Helens**, **Mt Adams**, and the river port below. Hidden driveways line Germantown Rd and traffic may be heavy on the downhill, as it will be on Hwy 30, which has a bike lane.

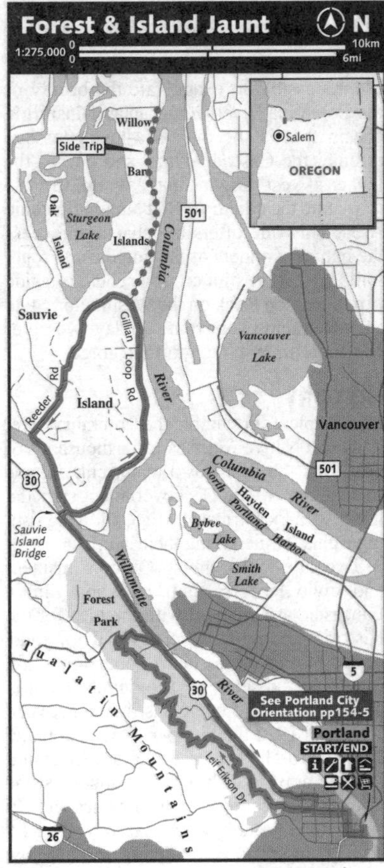

After crossing the Sauvie Island Bridge turn left and make an immediate U-turn through the parking lot (20.7mi). Pick your own fruit at the **Pumpkin Patch** or purchase their tasty apple cider. In the fall, this farm store also offers the chance to get lost in a **cornfield maze**. If you have time take the side trip to a charming **swimming beach** (27.2mi). Take the short walk to see the **dike** (28.4mi) that makes agriculture on the island possible. This is also a great **bird-watching** spot. Just before the bridge there's a ***grocery*** (33.6mi).

Columbia River Gorge

Duration..2 days
Distance..70.7mi
Difficulty............................easy–moderate
Start/End...Gresham City Hall MAX Station
Cues & Elevation Profile..................p362

It's impossible to exaggerate the beauty of the Columbia River Gorge, an awe-inspiring chasm that is the only sea-level passage through the Cascade Mtns, and one of the few east-west canyons in the world. In 1986 it became the country's first National Scenic Area. This ride offers the chance to access the natural wonders of the gorge using road, trail and a short stint on I-84. There is a side trip to Beacon Rock on the Washington State side. Retracing your route on day two gives you more time in the glorious gorge.

HISTORY

With its plentiful salmon, the Columbia River sustained Native Americans for thousands of years and the area was a major cultural and trading center. The US government signed a treaty with local tribes in 1855, allowing fishing rights (while taking their land).

Two late-19th-century Oregon business and civic leaders, Sam Hill and Simon Lancaster, are credited with the idea for the Historic Columbia River Hwy. They journeyed to Europe to learn about mountain roads and, subsequently, convinced Oregon to finance the project. Constructed between 1913 and 1922 the highway was to connect Portland to The Dalles. The graceful design and the craftsmanship of its tunnels, stone bridges and guardrails inspires respect. In subsequent years it was replaced by the I-84 but is being restored and parts of it are now hiker/biker trails. Experiencing this road by bicycle is sublime.

NATURAL HISTORY

During the most recent Ice Age, which lasted until 15,000 years ago, 2500ft-high glaciers filled the valleys that drained western Montana. An enormous lake covering 3000 sq mi formed behind the ice dam. When the water level grew high enough, it floated the ice, and the entire lake of melted water and icebergs rushed through, scouring out the Columbia watercourse and cutting away the canyon walls. The many waterfalls along the gorge were formed when the floods flushed away the stream paths that entered the Columbia River, causing the streams to tumble over towering cliffs.

PLANNING

When to Ride

The gorge is extraordinarily popular, the historic highway narrow, and most tourists come by car. The best cycling is on weekdays; late spring, early summer, or early fall are best. Avoid summer weekends. The waterfalls will be flowing most heavily in the spring, the trees lining the highway golden in autumn.

Maps

Bike There! (see Information, pp150–1) shows the ride start and how to get there by bike. The *Springwater Corridor* map is free from Portland Parks and Recreation (☎ 823-2223, Ⓦ www.parks.ci.portland.or.us). The free *East Multnomah County Bikeways Bicycling Guide* (☎ 248-5050) shows the ride start and how to connect to the historic highway. The *Historic Columbia River Highway* brochure, available from the Portland visitor center, shows which sections of the restored road are hiker/biker only.

GETTING TO/FROM THE RIDE

Train

Ride the MAX train east to Gresham City Hall Station.

Bicycle

To cycle to the ride start from Portland (about 10mi), take the Springwater Corridor bikepath from SE Johnson Creek Blvd and SE 45th Ave. Exit the bikepath and head north on Eastman Parkway (bike lane) to the Gresham City Hall MAX station.

THE RIDE
Portland

See Portland (pp149–56) for information about accommodations and other services.

Day 1: Portland to Cascade Locks

4–6½ hours, 35.2mi

The route climbs to stunning views of the Columbia River before descending into the lush, ferny gorge on a narrow but glorious road. Hiking trails to towering waterfalls beckon cyclists to hop out of the saddle. The tree-lined hiker/biker section of the route passes a fish hatchery before reaching tiny Cascade Locks.

Leave Gresham's 'strip mall' hell behind as Stark St becomes a wooded downhill with a bike lane. When crossing the Sandy River ride on the sidewalk instead of the narrow roadway (5.4mi).

Once on the Columbia River Hwy the scenery becomes more spectacular with each mile. The **Crown Point Vista House** (12.8mi) sits atop a craggy point of basalt. Built between 1916 and 1918, the unusual building, a stone octagon, has striking views of the Columbia River and Washington State.

A steep and winding descent leads to **Latourell Falls** (15.4mi), followed by **Shepperds Dell** (16.6mi). Now you're in the heart of the gorge: steep walls tower over the road on the right and there's a drop-off to the left. Trees shade the hand-crafted stone guardrails that line the more dangerous sections of the road. After **Wahkeena Falls** (21mi) comes the most famous sight in the gorge, **Multnomah Falls** (21.6mi). At 624ft, this is the second-highest nonseasonal waterfall in the nation. Take a short hike to **Benson Bridge**, built in 1914 by Italian stonemasons and overlooking the second drop of the falls. Worth the work is a longer hike to a viewpoint of the top of the falls. Afterwards, get a good meal at the ***restaurant*** in the 1925 **Multnomah Falls Lodge**.

Oneonta Gorge (23.9mi), a narrow chasm cut into a thick basalt flow by Oneonta Creek, is spectacular. Walls more than 100ft high arch over the stream. Intrepid, waterproof hikers can travel about half a mile between the sheer walls to the 75ft falls; all around are rare, cliff-dwelling plants that thrive only in this moist, shadowy environment.

There's camping at ***Ainsworth State Park*** *(25.3mi; ☎ 503-695-2301 or ☎ 800-551-6949)* with hiker/biker sites for $5 per night.

At 32.2mi there's a **viewpoint** of the **Bonneville Dam** and the landslide called **Bridge of the Gods**. Walk your bike down five flights of stairs (32.4mi), followed by **Eagle Creek fish hatchery** and ***Eagle Creek Campground*** *(☎ 541-386-2333, fax 541-386-1916)*

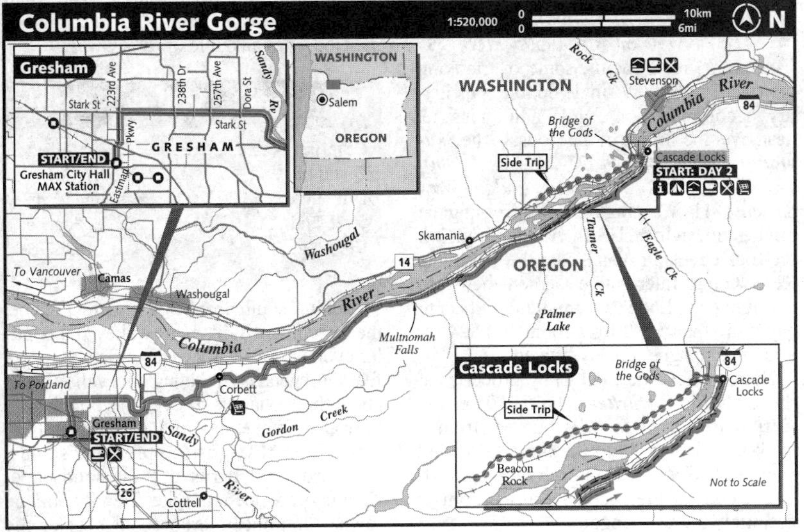

at 32.9mi. Sites cost $12 (no reservations). The 13mi Eagle Creek Trail starts at the campground and takes hikers to Wahtum Lake, intersecting with the Pacific Crest Trail (see the boxed text, p46) at 7.5mi.

Cascade Locks

☎ 541

Cascade Locks is most famous for the other Bridge of the Gods, a steel cantilever bridge spanning the Columbia.

The visitor center (☎ 374-8619), is in the Marine Park complex, on Wanapa St (also spelled Wa-Na-Pa). Also in the complex is the **Historical Museum** (☎ 374-8535), displaying Native American artifacts and the early transportation history of the Gorge.

In late August the town hosts the **Sternwheeler Days Festival** (☎ 374-8619), featuring riverboat rides, craft displays and lots of salmon. Book lodging in advance.

Places to Stay & Eat On the banks of the Columbia River is the ***Cascade Locks Marine Park*** *(☎ 374-8619, fax 374-8428, Wanapa St)*. Sites cost $15 (no reservations). From Wanapa St/Hwy 30, take Forest Lane 1mi east out of town to grassy sites at the ***KOA Cascade Locks*** *(☎ 374-8668, W www.koa.com, 9841 NW Forest Lane)*. This isn't the backcountry, either, there's a store, laundry, swimming pool and more. Sites cost around $20; cabins for two cost $30 to $40.

The ***Best Western Columbia River Inn*** (*☎ 541-374-8777 or ☎ 800-595-7108, 735 Wanapa St*) rents rooms, some overlooking the river, for $79/89 single/double. For luxury accommodations, golf and massage, head over the Bridge of the Gods, to the ***Skamania Lodge*** (*☎ 509-427-7700 or ☎ 800-221-7117; 1131 Skamania Lodge Way, Stevenson*) in Washington. After crossing the bridge, turn right on US 14. At 1.5mi turn left on Rock Creek Dr. You'll pass the Columbia River Gorge Interpretive Center, then turn uphill into the Lodge's compound. Expect to pay more than $100 for a room and $24 for a full champagne Sunday brunch.

Back in Cascade Locks buy groceries at the ***Columbia Market***. The 1950s-esque ***East Wind Drive In*** sells burgers from a walk-up window. Enjoy a pizza ($14) and beer at the ***Salmon Row Pub*** *(Wanapa St)*. The wood-paneled, cozy dining room is definitely a local hangout.

Day 2: Cascade Locks to Portland

3–6 hours, 35.5mi

This day starts with a relatively flat side trip and then retraces yesterday's route after a few minor deviations (4.9–7.9mi). Eventually the bikepath may be extended, eliminating the need to ride on I-84. To check on trail extensions, call the Oregon Department of Transportation (☎ 503-731-8200).

Side Trip: Beacon Rock State Park

16.2mi return

Bridge enthusiasts will love crossing the **Bridge of the Gods**, high above the Columbia. Acrophobes might not, and certainly should not look down; it's 135ft to the water.

Turn left on Washington's Hwy 14. At about 2mi is the **Bonneville Dam** (☎ 374-8820) – call ahead to see if it is open to visitors.

Continue west on Hwy 14 to **Beacon Rock**. Reckoned to be the second largest monolith in the world (after the Rock of Gibraltar), Beacon Rock was almost blown up early in the century by the Army, who needed rock pieces to support a jetty. It's a very steep 0.75mi climb to the top of the 848ft rock, but the views are spectacular. There are opportunities for **rock climbing** and **hiking**. The state park (☎ 509-427-8265 or ☎ 800-233-0321), across Hwy 14 from Beacon Rock, has ***camping*** for $10 per night. The small town of Stevenson, 2.3mi east of Bridge of the Gods, has a couple of ***restaurants***.

Willamette Valley Ramble

Duration	2 days
Distance	104.6mi
Difficulty	easy–moderate
Start/End	Eugene
Cues	pp362–3

Stretching south from Portland to Eugene, the agricultural Willamette Valley is a popular cycling destination. This circuit is a perfect short getaway. Although the valley holds about three-quarters of Oregon's population, the route offers empty rural roads, plus riverside bikepaths. Farms, produce stands, vineyards and barns dot the landscape. Evenings are spent in bike-friendly college towns sampling microbrewed beer or the nectar of the local grapes. Mild temperatures and easy access by train make the ride accessible.

HISTORY

The Willamette Valley was home to a large number of Native Americans before the arrival of settlers. The Chinook and Calapooian tribes were the most numerous until their numbers were decimated by diseases introduced by whites, who also forced these tribes onto the Grande Ronde Reservation. Vying for control of the area were Brits and Americans; the latter won. More than 50,000 people had arrived in Oregon by 1855; of these, many New Englanders settled the rich agricultural valley, founding churches and schools. Catholics and Methodists, along with Quakers, German Utopian Communists and Mennonites, made the valley their home.

Grapes play a part in the region's history dating back to the Oregon Trail days, when vines were introduced. However it wasn't until the 1960s that vintners began establishing it as a premium wine-growing region.

NATURAL HISTORY

The Willamette Valley, which once had extensive wetlands, has been altered by human contact since Native Americans burned forested areas to create grasslands. Oregon Trail settlers began the transition to the farmlands that, along with many small towns and growing cities, now dominate the area. An amazing variety of crops flourish here, including fruit, vegetables, flowers, holly, Christmas trees, hazelnuts, herbs, grass and grass seed, and grapes. Three national wildlife refuges, William L Finley, Ankeny and Baskett Slough, were created in the 1960s.

PLANNING

When to Ride

All these crops just wouldn't grow without a little rain, now would they? But the upside for cyclists is that they need summer and early-fall sunshine, too. In July and August wineries are likely to have longer opening hours, though in the fall you might catch a glimpse of a grape harvest. In late September the college campuses in Eugene and Corvallis will be abuzz, and the countryside ablaze with color. The Eugene Celebration (☎ 541-682-5215) is late that month.

Maps

As it covers most of the ride, the *Albany & Mid-Willamette Valley Bicycle Map* is well worth the $4 it costs to buy. Get your copy from the City of Albany Graphic Services (☎ 541-917-7768), 333 Broadalbin SW, Albany, OR 97321. *Get in Motion: the Eugene Springfield Bicycle Map* shows how to get into, around and out of town. It's free from the City of Eugene (☎ 541-682-5218); leave your address on the answering machine and the map will be mailed to you. *Corvallis Area Bikeways* is free from the Department of Public Works (☎ 541-757-6916), PO Box 1083, Corvallis, OR 97339. The *Oregon Bicycling Guide* (see Maps, p149) has an inset of the region.

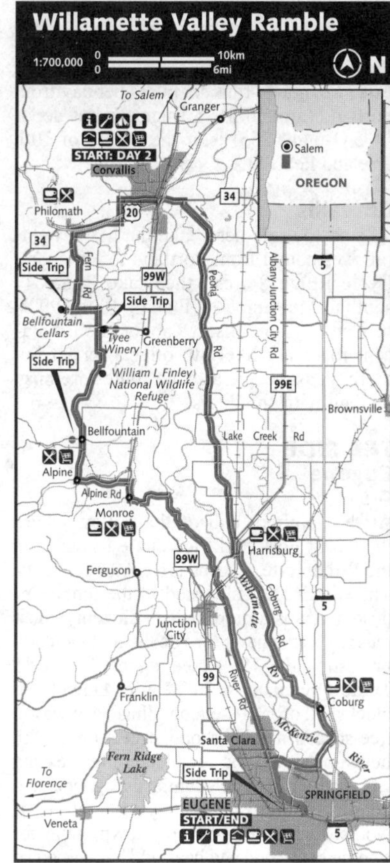

What to Bring

The Willamette Valley appellation is known for its excellent pinot noir wines; bring a corkscrew.

GETTING TO/FROM THE RIDE

Eugene

There are two good ways to reach the north-south Willamette Valley trek.

Train Amtrak's *Cascades* line is your best bet, with a service from Portland to Eugene five times daily. However, three of those runs are by bus, with no space for bicycles. So, cyclists have two trains to choose from; make a reservation for your bicycle and arrive early. A sample Portland–Eugene (2½ hours) fare is $14; bikes cost an extra $5. Northbound, there are two bike-accepting departures from Eugene's station (☎ 541-687-1383), 433 Willamette St.

Bus Greyhound runs six buses per day from Portland (around $13). Eugene's bus depot (☎ 541-344-6265) is at the corner of 10th Ave and Pearl St.

Corvallis

To start the ride here, take the MAX light-rail westbound from Portland to Hillsboro. Cycle Route 8 west, then take Route 47 south to McMinnville. Pick up Route 99 W headed for Corvallis. It's about 76mi. Adjacent roads are likely to offer a longer but more pleasant ride as state routes are busy – albeit with shoulders.

THE RIDE

Eugene

☎ 541

At the southern end of the valley, where the Coast Fork and McKenzie Rivers join the Willamette, Eugene is a city of contrasts. The working class, rooted in the timber industry, versus a more radical citizenry, most recently in the news for vocally and violently protesting the 1999 meeting of the World Trade Organization in Seattle. Downtown blocks full of 1960s-era buildings give way to tree-shaded neighborhood streets lined with bungalows, and the architecturally pleasing University of Oregon campus. Loggers, academics, anarchists, oh my! Somehow, it works. Eugene is a friendly town, great for finding tasty food and beer, and has earned its reputation as a cycling haven: bike lanes and paths abound. It's also home to several frame builders, including Bike Friday folding bikes.

Information The Lane County visitor center (☎ 800-547-5445), PO Box 10286, Eugene, OR 97440, is on Olive St one block west of Willamette St.

The new library, corner 10th Ave and Olive St, was under construction at the time of research. Hutch's (☎ 345-7521) 960 Charnelton St, is a full-service bike shop. The shop with the best name is Paul's Bicycle Way of Life (☎ 342-6155), in a brick building called the 'Farmer's Union' on W 5th Ave.

Things to See & Do Visit the Lane County **Farmers Market**, corner E 8th And Oak Sts (open Sat Apr–Nov, 9am–5pm).

The **Hult Center for Performing Arts**, corner 6th Ave and Willamette St, is the venue to hear the opera and symphony or see the ballet. Call the concert line at ☎ 682-5746. Old movies, and foreign and art films are best viewed in the **Bijou**, a distinctly non-cinema-like building at 492 E 13th Ave.

Check out **local and touring bands** at divey but cool John Henry's, 136 E 11th Ave. **Live entertainment** – from African drumming to punk rock – is on the bill at the historic Woodmen of the World or **WOW Hall**, 291 W 8th Ave.

The **Eugene Celebration** (☎ 682-5215; late Sept) brings a colorful parade to the city, along with arts, crafts and food.

Places to Stay A great bet for camaraderie and safe bike parking is the ***Eugene International Hostel*** *(☎ 349-0589, 2352 Willamette St)*. Dorm beds cost $15/18 members/nonmembers. There's a private room for $30/38 single/double.

The ***Timbers Motel*** *(☎ 343-3345 or ☎ 800-643-4267, 1015 Pearl St)* charges $43. Ask about the cheaper basement rooms. The ***Downtown Motel*** *(☎ 345-8739, 361 W 7th Ave)* charges $39/50.

The Campbell House *(☎ 343-1119 or ☎ 800-264-2519, 252 Pearl St)* is one of Eugene's luxury B&Bs, in a refurbished home near Skinner Butte. Rates range from $80 to $350.

Places to Eat The ***Kiva*** *(125 W 11th Ave)* sells groceries, wine and beer. Strong coffee and baked goods are served in a bright, clean storefront at ***Full City Coffee Roasters*** *(cnr W 13th Ave & High St)*. For breakfast, try ***Morning Glory*** *(Willamette St)*, right next to the train station (closed Mon). On the same block, ***Cafe Navarro*** *(454 Willamette St)* serves vegetarian and meat dishes in the $12 range. Across the street in a funky old building is ***Oregon Electric Station*** *(cnr 5th Ave & Willamette St)*, serving lunch and dinner. Crab cakes cost $18.

There are some excellent pubs and bars in Eugene. There are too many TVs but the beer is good at ***Steelhead Brewing Co*** *(199 E 5th Ave)*, where you can also fill up on burgers ($7) or fish and chips ($10). ***Max's*** *(550 13th Ave)* is a bar with live music. The ***High Street Brewery & Cafe*** *(1243 High St)*, in an old house, serves McMenamins microbrews and sandwiches, salads and pasta (all about $7). Sit on the front porch or in the back garden and you're likely to meet other cyclists.

Day 1: Eugene to Corvallis

4½–7 hours, 56.8mi

Begin today at the Lane County Courthouse, corner E 8th Ave and Oak St. Flat for several miles, the route leaves Eugene behind for farm country, rolling hills and mountain views. The total elevation gain is about 1200ft.

Early on, the route joins a multi-use path along the Willamette River (keep the river on your right), and for about 5mi it's smooth sailing on the path and sleepy streets of a signed 'bike route.' As suburban congestion starts to drop away, look for the **Thistledown Farm** (8.8mi) produce shop and its fields of pick-your-own flowers. Follow signs 'To Monroe' on quiet, rolling roads that head away from the Willamette. The landscape alternates between agriculture and forest. Mountains of the **Coast Range** are in the distance.

Monroe (26.1mi) has a small ***store*** and the ***Chat 'n' Chew*** cafe, serving burgers and grilled cheese. Smaller Alpine (30.8mi) has a ***tavern*** and a ***store***. If you're carrying a picnic lunch take a left on Dawson Rd at 33.5mi for the side trip to Bellfountain Park. Dine at the **85ft-long picnic table**, possibly the longest in the world, cut from one 422-year-old Douglas fir tree. If you're a lumbermill buff visit the Hull-Oakes Lumber Company 2mi further, where you can see one of the largest remaining **wigwam burners**. Call (☎ 424-3112) for an appointment.

A moderate climb takes you into the trees and past the **William L Finley National Wildlife Refuge**, a sanctuary for elk, falcons, egrets and indigenous plant species; you'll see the gravel access road. At 41.3mi turn right on Greenberry Rd for the side trip to **Tyee Winery** (☎ 753-8754; open 12–5pm weekends Apr–Dec; plus Fri & Mon Jul–Aug; or by appointment). The farm's two-mile nature trail passes a beaver pond and offers views of 4097ft Mary's Peak. For the side trip to **Bellfountain Cellars**, stay on Llewellyn Rd at 44mi and turn right on the gravel driveway after about 1mi.

Turning on Applegate St at 49.1mi, follow a somewhat confusing bike route through the small town of Philomath; watch for 'bike route' signs. Ride through the famous **Irish Covered Bridge** at 54.3mi.

OREGON

Corvallis

☎ 541

Corvallis is a welcoming town at the base of the Coast Range. Striped with bike lanes and surrounded by miles of farms, orchards and vineyards, it doesn't have the funky edge that Eugene has. However, the downtown vintage storefronts are full of shops and cafes, and the neighborhood streets lined with Victorian homes. About 30 parks and the Willamette riverfront make it a charming place to visit.

Information The Corvallis visitor center (☎ 757-1544) is at 420 NW 2nd St. Bike 'n' Hike (☎ 753-2912) is on the corner of 2nd St and Adams Ave and Corvallis Cyclery (☎ 752-5952) is at 344 SW 2nd St.

Things to See & Do Perhaps to bolster its somewhat slow pace of life, Corvallis likes to hold festivals, including July's **da Vinci Days** (☎ 757-6363), celebrating art, science and technology; and the **Fall Festival**, with handicrafts and food.

Don't miss the architecturally striking **Benton County Courthouse** at 110 NW 3rd St. Built from 1888–9, it's Oregon's oldest courthouse still used for its original purpose (open Tues–Sat). Check out the downstairs public bathrooms and vault.

Learn to **swing dance** and then practice your moves (or hear **live rock-n-roll**) at Squirrels, 100 SW 2nd St. It's across the street from the **Majestic Theater**, built in 1913 as a vaudeville house. Today it features community theater.

Places to Stay & Eat There's camping at the river in ***Willamette City Park*** ($9; open Mar–Oct) on Goodnight Ave. You can't reserve sites. Contact the Corvallis Department of Parks and Recreation (☎ 766-6918) for information.

Basic rooms at the ***Super 8 Motel*** *(☎ 758-8088 or ☎ 800-800-8000, fax 758-8267, 407 NW 2nd St)* cost $56/66 single/double. The nearby ***Econo Lodge*** *(☎ 752-9601 or ☎ 800-553-2666, 345 NW 2nd St)* has rooms for $44/50. Rooms are slightly cheaper at the ***Towne House Motor Inn*** *(☎ 753-4496, 350 SW 4th St)*. A little farther from downtown, the ***Harrison House B&B*** *(☎ 752-6248, 2310 NW Harrison Blvd)* has four rooms in the $100 range.

Buy groceries at ***Safeway*** *(cnr 3rd St & Adams Ave)*. ***New Morning Bakery*** *(219 SW 2nd St)* serves coffee, baked treats and lunch items cafeteria-style.

Downtown, ***Evergreen Indian Cuisine*** *(136 3rd St)* serves lunch and dinner. For deviled Guinness beef ($14) or warm spinach salad ($7) washed down with Irish whiskey, ease into a wooden booth at ***Kells*** *(137 SW 2nd St)*.

Near the university there are several inexpensive, casual restaurants. Brush elbows with students and professors over coffee at the ***Beanery*** *(2541 NW Monroe Way)*. ***Interzone*** *(1561 Monroe Way)* is a hip hangout; the coffee shop offers live music. ***Tarntip Thai*** *(2535 NW Monroe Way)* is open for lunch and dinner. Nearby are ***Bombs Away Cafe***, a ***taquería*** *(2527 Monroe Way)* and ***American Dream Pizza*** *(2525 Monroe Way)*. Fancier dishes are prepared at ***Magenta*** *(1425 Magenta)*. One vegan dish graces the menu.

Day 2: Corvallis to Eugene

3–5½ hours, 47.8mi

This day provides easy cycling (450ft is the total elevation gain) without many turns or interruptions. Enjoy the low traffic volume, flat terrain and views.

In the fall, stop for **U-Pick Blueberries** (4.7mi). Enjoy views of 649ft **Saddle Butte** and, in the distance, high, snow-capped peaks. A tidy Mennonite farming community (look for school children playing baseball in traditional dress) enjoys a beautiful spot near Harrisburg (23.9mi), where there are a few shops and ***restaurants***. The Willamette Valley grows 98% of the world's hazelnuts, or **filberts**, as they're called. If you've never seen a filbert orchard, now is your chance. Coburg (36.4mi), a former mill town on the McKenzie River has a multitude of **antique shops** and a ***cafe***. Stop on the pedestrian bridge over the Willamette to watch the white water, and then keep the river on your left as you retrace the Day 1 route.

Side Trip: Skinner Butte

1.8mi return

Since the day has been seriously flat, head uphill on this side trip. Turn right on Cheshire Ave (no sign) where the bikepath ends at a parking lot, and left on Skinner Butte Loop. The winding climb gains 270ft in elevation over 1.2mi, passing a columnar basalt rock formation under constant assault from rock climbers. At the top there's a great view. On the way down take the first left (E 3rd Ave) and a right on Pearl St, rejoining the main route.

Lava & Lakes Circuit

Duration	2 days
Distance	85.2mi
Difficulty	moderate–hard
Start/End	Bend
Cues & Elevation Profiles	p363

About all Central Oregon has to offer are volcanoes, obsidian flows, crystal-clear lakes and rushing rivers...making it a haven for outdoors enthusiasts of all stripes. Cyclists could easily spend longer than two days on this ride. The High Desert Museum near Bend warrants several hours, and a few more could be spent just down the road at Lava Lands visitor center, part of the Newberry National Volcanic Monument. The side trip to Newberry Crater to see the massive obsidian flow adds a grueling climb but is well worth it.

HISTORY

Once the domain of the Wasco tribe, Oregon Trail travelers and gold seekers also settled here. In 1855 native tribes were moved to the Warm Springs Indian Reservation and years of drought defeated would-be farmers. In the 1940s the government built irrigation dams along the Deschutes River and agriculture flourished.

NATURAL HISTORY

Much of the area south of Bend has been influenced by the Newberry Volcano, a shield volcano built by countless eruptions of fluid lava that began about 600,000 years ago. At its summit is a caldera (large crater) containing two lakes. Its flanks have more than 400 cinder cones (conical hills composed of volcanic debris with a central vent) and fissure vents. Immense lava flows traveled along the Deschutes River drainage – changing the river's course (for great views of this – do the Deschutes River Trail mountain-bike ride; see the boxed text, p168). The many lakes along the Cascade Lakes Scenic Hwy were also created by these lava flows damming streams, or by smaller craters filling with water. The most recent volcanic activity, about 1300 years ago, produced the amazing Big Obsidian Flow, covering 700 acres.

PLANNING

When to Ride

Ride June through October; during other months part of the route will be closed by snow. During summer the ski lift on Mt Bachelor is open to sightseers. In fall many of the trees change color.

Maps

As Bend is the fastest growing city in Oregon, the street grid surrounding the old downtown is undergoing many changes. Cyclists will want the *Deschutes County Bicycling Guide*, available free from Deschutes County Department of Public Works (☎ 541-388-6581), at 61150 SE 27th St, Bend, OR 97702. The *Indexed Street Map of Bend* by MapWorks and *Pittmon's Map of Bend and Redmond* (both $3) are available from Bend Mapping and Blueprint Inc (☎ 541-389-7440) at 922 NW Bond St.

GETTING TO/FROM THE RIDE

Bend

This region is not easy to access by public transport. You may wish to rent a car and drive to Bend. It's also possible to cycle here.

OREGON

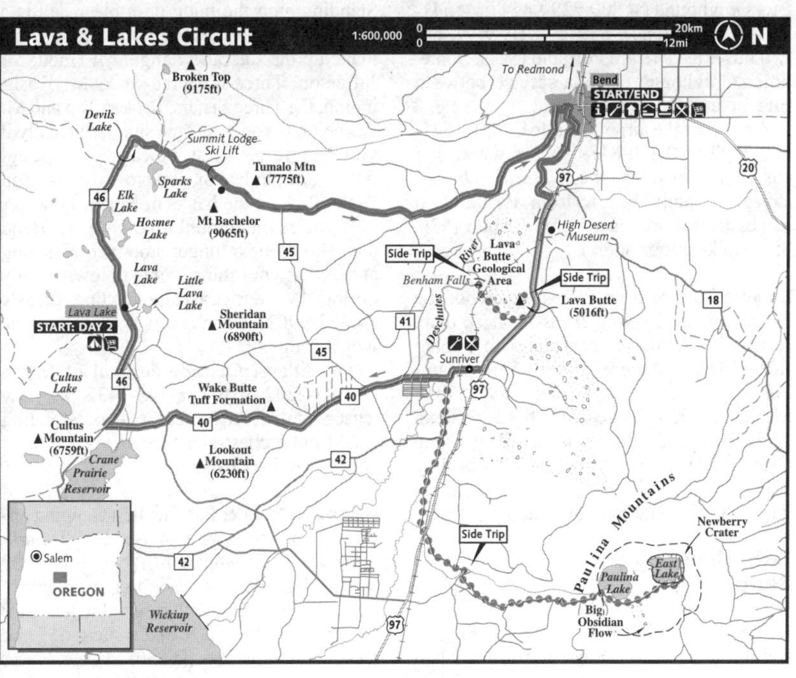

Air The Redmond/Bend airport is southeast of Redmond on US 97, 18mi north of Bend. United Express and Horizon Air fly here from Portland ($75 one way), Eugene, Seattle and San Francisco. The CAC Airport Shuttle (☎ 541-389-7469 or ☎ 800-847-0157; Ⓦ www.cactrans.com) goes to Bend for $19. If you call ahead, the shuttle can take boxed bikes. To cycle from the airport take Old Bend–Redmond Hwy, then OB Riley Rd into Bend.

Train The closest Amtrak station is Chemult, about 65mi south of Bend. The southbound train leaves Portland daily at 2.00pm, arriving in Chemult at about 8pm. If you need to overnight here try the ***Chemult Motel*** *(☎ 541-365-2228, Hwy 97)*.

To cycle from Chemult to Bend head north on busy Hwy 97. This is not a bike-friendly road, but you can pick up parallel Huntington Rd in La Pine. A longer option is to take Hwy 97 north from Chemult to the Crescent Cutoff, and then take the Cascade Lakes Hwy (Hwy 46) into Bend, in effect joining the ride midway.

Bus Greyhound (☎ 800-229-9424 or ☎ 541-382-2151 in Bend), 63076 N Hwy 97, has two buses a day from Portland ($21). Sometimes Greyhound offers a service between Eugene and Bend. Call ahead.

As well as the airport shuttle CAC (☎ 541-389-7469 or ☎ 800-847-0157; Ⓦ www.cactrans.com) operates the *Central Oregon Breeze*, a daily bus to/from Portland. It leaves from Portland's Union Station ($36, $5 for bikes; four hours).

Bicycle To ride from Eugene to Bend, use the Adventure Cycling *Trans-America* map, section 2. The route intersects with Coburg Rd (see Day 2 of the Willamette Valley Ramble, p164) at the McKenzie River. Take McKenzie View Rd west to Hill Rd; go south on Hill Rd and Old Mohawk Rd to Camp Creek Rd. Head east to Walterville; join Hwy 126 E eastbound and cycle over Santiam Pass (4817ft). The journey is about 130mi.

THE RIDE

Bend

☎ 541

Historically, Bend was a base for loggers and a trading center. Since the 1960s when nearby Mt Bachelor began to be developed as a ski destination, the town and surroundings have grown into a major resort community. Cycling visitors would do well to steer clear of the sprawling, busy US 97 and hang out in the charming downtown area.

Information The Central Oregon visitor center (☎ 389-8799 or ☎ 800-800-8334), 63085 N US 97, is a bit out of the way. Instead of making the trek cyclists may prefer to call for information or just collect brochures from local shops describing the area's attractions.

Century Cycles (☎ 389-4224), 1135 NW Galveston Ave, rents mountain bikes. The friendly mechanics here will also help you out with a touring set-up and negotiate the rental rate.

The Bend Public Library is downtown, corner Wall St and Kansas Ave, and offers free Internet access.

Things to See & Do Cycle up **Pilot Butte**, on the east side of town less than 1mi out on the Greenwood Ave/US 20 bike lane. The road circles up steeply for just over 1mi. Standing atop the butte on a clear day is a great way to see several of the peaks that make up the **Cascade Range**: Mt Hood, Mt Jefferson, Three-Fingered Jack, Mt Washington, the Three Sisters, Broken Top and Mt Bachelor. It's an awesome sight, especially if you picture all these volcanoes erupting! Afterwards, relax in downtown's beautiful **Drake Park** on the banks of Mirror Pond.

If you're into **mountain biking**, the Bend area should be a longer stopover. If gazing at racers is your thing, come to town in July during the **Bend Cascade Cycling Classic** (☎ 382-5962), when racers from around the world compete.

The August **Cascade Festival of Music** (☎ 383-2202 or ☎ 888-545-7435, Ⓦ www.cascademusic.org) features outstanding acts, from orchestral arrangements to choral concerts to jazz bands.

Places to Stay & Eat The best camping option is 5mi northwest of Bend at ***Tumalo State Park Campground*** *(☎ 382-3586 or ☎ 800-452-5687, Ⓦ www.oregonstateparks.org, OB Riley Rd)*, with reservable tent sites for around $15; hiker/biker sites, $5; and tepees and yurts, around $30.

The least expensive lodging option, the ***Bend Cascade Hostel*** *(☎ 389-3813, 19 SW Century Dr)*, is basic but clean. Dorm beds cost $14; private rooms cost more. It's $2 per day to store baggage – if you want to do the ride traveling light.

Dozens of motels line 3rd St/US 97 and Greenwood Ave/US 20. Rooms at the ***Palms*** *(☎ 382-1197, 645 NE Greenwood Ave)* have microwaves and/or complete kitchens, and cost $30 to $45. The ***Dunes Motel*** *(☎ 382-6811, 1515 NE 3rd St)* has singles/doubles for $45/59 weekdays and $89/99 weekends. Rooms at the ***Best Western Inn & Suites*** *(☎ 382-1515, 721 NE 3rd St)* cost $55 to $89.

For a treat, stay across from Drake Park at ***Lara House B&B*** *(☎ 388-4064, 640 NW Congress Street)* for $65 to $95.

Devore's Natural Foods and the ***Newport Ave Market*** are across from each other less than 1mi from the center of Bend. Head west on Newport Ave to 12th St.

Wake up at ***Cup of Magic*** *(1304 NW Galveston Ave)*, a funky cafe whose treats include exceptional home-made bagels.

Wall and Bond Sts in the downtown area are home to plenty of reasonably priced eateries. Eggs and French toast for under $10 are fresh and tasty at ***Alpenglow*** *(1040 NW Bond St)* in the center of town. Nearby ***Yoko's Japanese Restaurant*** *(1028 NW Bond St)* serves lunch and dinner. At ***Pizza Mondo*** *(811 NW Wall St)* a medium broccoli bianco costs $14.50; slices are also available.

Serving food ($10–20) and great micro-brewed beer late into the evening is the ***Deschutes Brewery & Public House*** *(1044 NW Bond St)*. If you prefer dining in a less rowdy atmosphere, head to the ***Pine Tavern Inn*** *(☎ 382-5581, 967 NW Brooks St)*. Steak, pasta and seafood meals cost $12 to $20.

For a beer and a game of pool head to locals' haunt ***Westside Tavern***, easy to find on NW Galveston Ave, just west of the river.

Day 1: Bend to Lava Lake

5–7½ hours, 45.4mi

There's a bit of stop and start as the route beckons you off your bike at the High Desert Museum and Lava Lands visitor center, along with negotiating four-wheel travelers on busy but shouldered US 97. Soon it heads into the thick walls of Oregon's evergreens, and gently climbs to the Cascades Lakes Hwy.

Avoiding the most built up part of US 97, ride through Bend's Old Mill district, where the oversized red buildings and defunct smoke stacks are complemented nicely by Cascade peaks. (For a simpler route, continue on Bond St at 1.2mi, instead of turning left on Wilson Ave. Bond St becomes Blakely Rd, rejoining the route a little over 2mi into it.)

At ***Riverwoods Country Store*** (7.2mi) the route joins busier, faster Hwy 97. At 9.2mi, give the must-see **High Desert Museum** (☎ 382-4754, W www.highdesert.org) several hours. Indoor galleries chronicle the history of the Columbia Plateau Native Americans and the overland migration of the American West. Outside, see the 'critters' that typify the high desert. There's also a ***cafe***.

After the climb on Hwy 97 you'll be ready to stop again at 13.9mi at **Lava Lands visitor center** (☎ 593-2421). Turn right here for an 8mi return side trip to Benham Falls (see the 'Deschutes River Trail' boxed text, p168). You can cycle amid traffic up steep Lava Butte for close-up views of the massive lava flow, which you'll see from a distance on Day 2. **Lava River Cave** is at 15.2mi.

For an alternative to Hwy 97 turn right on Cottonwood Dr (15.6mi) and cycle 2.4mi to Sunriver, a part residential/part vacation rental community that seems overly groomed and eerily sterile. If you follow signs and posted maps to Sunriver Village, you'll hook up with the primary route again by turning right on S Century Dr. There are ***restaurants*** and a **bike shop**.

The turnoff for the Newberry Crater side trip is at 19.2mi. The rest of the day alternates between the forest and more open vistas of distant buttes. At 28.5mi, look for **Wake Butte Tuff formation**. At 38.6mi, join the Cascade Lakes Hwy. ***Cultus Lake Resort*** *(☎ 541-408-1560)* rents cabins (by the week only) and has a ***restaurant***. Instead, camp at lovely Lava Lake or Little Lava Lake, which offer great views of Mt Bachelor and cold, clear water for swimming – or for chilling cans of beer bought at the Lava Lake store.

Side Trip: Newberry Crater

52.2mi return

At the juncture of three major fault zones in Central Oregon (and not part of the Cascade Range), Newberry Crater covers more than 500 sq mi and is the largest shield-shaped volcano in the contiguous USA. Native

OREGON

Deschutes River Trail

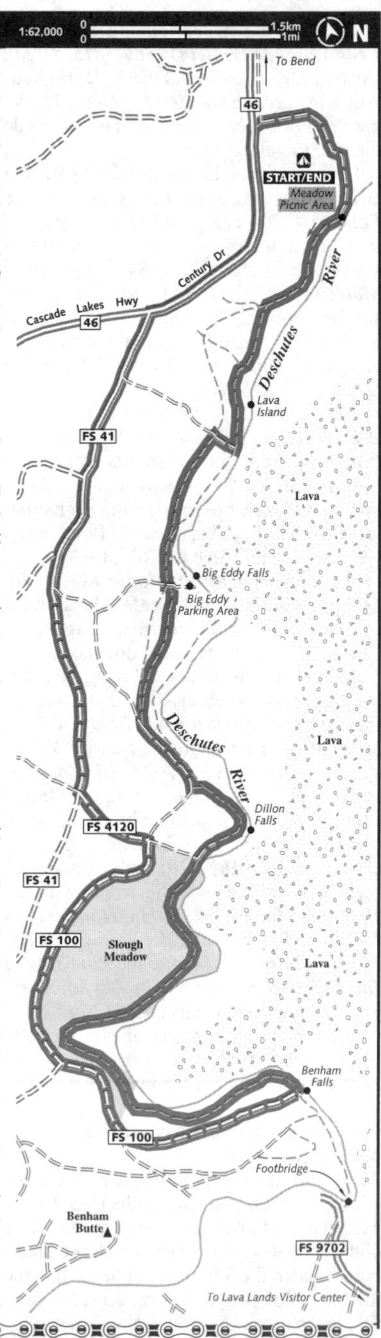

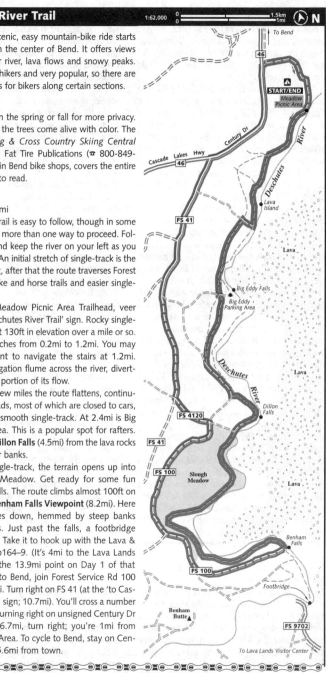

This incredibly scenic, easy mountain-bike ride starts around 6mi from the center of Bend. It offers views of a white-water river, lava flows and snowy peaks. It's also open to hikers and very popular, so there are alternative routes for bikers along certain sections.

Planning

Ride weekdays in the spring or fall for more privacy. In early October the trees come alive with color. The *Mountain Biking & Cross Country Skiing Central Oregon* map by Fat Tire Publications (☎ 800-849-6589), available in Bend bike shops, covers the entire area but is hard to read.

The Ride

2–4 hours, 17.6mi

This well-worn trail is easy to follow, though in some stretches there is more than one way to proceed. Follow bike signs and keep the river on your left as you head upstream. An initial stretch of single-track is the most challenging, after that the route traverses Forest Service roads, bike and horse trails and easier single-track.

Starting at Meadow Picnic Area Trailhead, veer right at the 'Deschutes River Trail' sign. Rocky single-track gains about 130ft in elevation over a mile or so. Lava Island stretches from 0.2mi to 1.2mi. You may need to dismount to navigate the stairs at 1.2mi. You'll see an irrigation flume across the river, diverting a substantial portion of its flow.

For the next few miles the route flattens, continuing on gravel roads, most of which are closed to cars, alternating with smooth single-track. At 2.4mi is Big Eddy parking area. This is a popular spot for rafters. View beautiful **Dillon Falls** (4.5mi) from the lava rocks flanking the river banks.

Following single-track, the terrain opens up into marshy Slough Meadow. Get ready for some fun whoop-de-do hills. The route climbs almost 100ft on the way up to **Benham Falls Viewpoint** (8.2mi). Here the river tumbles down, hemmed by steep banks with evergreens. Just past the falls, a footbridge crosses the river. Take it to hook up with the Lava & Lakes Circuit, pp164–9. (It's 4mi to the Lava Lands visitor center – the 13.9mi point on Day 1 of that ride). To return to Bend, join Forest Service Rd 100 (FS 100) at 8.4mi. Turn right on FS 41 (at the 'to Cascade Lakes Hwy' sign; 10.7mi). You'll cross a number of roads before turning right on unsigned Century Dr at 14.9mi. At 16.7mi, turn right; you're 1mi from Meadow Picnic Area. To cycle to Bend, stay on Century Dr; you're 5.6mi from town.

American arrowheads made of obsidian collected here have been found throughout western America.

At 19.2mi turn left on S Century Dr. Turn left on Paulina-Eastlake Rd/Hwy 21 and cross Hwy 97. Along this road, ***Prairie Campground*** *(☎ 388-5664)*, about 11mi into the side trip, is a good place to stop if you want a night's sleep before the grueling climb up the crater.

The **visitor center** (☎ 536-8802), with knowledgeable staff, is at 21.3mi. This climb is from about 4500ft to 6350ft. ***Paulina Lake***, near the center, and ***East Lake***, about 5mi farther on the main road, are resorts with camping, cabins and restaurants. A must-see is the **Big Obsidian Flow**, which formed when silica-rich lava cooled quickly and hardened into rock before its atoms managed to organize themselves into crystalline structure. Walking amidst the shiny, black, jagged natural volcanic glass is otherworldly.

Lava Lake & Little Lava Lake

☎ 541

There are many campgrounds along the Cascade Lakes Hwy. Two of the nicest are ***Little Lava Lake*** and neighboring ***Lava Lake*** *(☎ 382-9443 for both)*. They are about 1mi off the Cascade Lake Hwy where Day 1 ends (turn right on the access road). Take a left at the intersection for Lava Lake and a right for its little brother, where sites cost $5. Lava Lake has a ***lodge*** that sells groceries and rents boats. RVs fill this one's pricier camping area ($22 per site).

Day 2: Lava Lake to Bend

3½–5 hours, 39.8mi

Tree-lined, rural roads wind past lakes and pristine marshlands and under high mountain peaks, before cresting the pass at Mt Bachelor, and descending back into Bend.

Elk Lake Resort (5.7mi; 0.3mi off the main road) has a restaurant with a deck overlooking the river. It can be windy cycling down to the lovely spot. There's a hill climb and then a short descent to **Devils Lake** (10.6mi). Past a huge lava flow is **Sparks Lake** (12.9mi) in a grassy meadow. Look for birds. With the Sisters at your back, climb steeply toward the almost perfectly conical 9065ft Mt Bachelor. Before Labor Day a **ski lift** operates from Summit Lodge (17.6mi), taking visitors to the top of the mountain. Descend into Bend, stopping for a dramatic view of Lava Butte, the Newberry lava flow and Paulina Peak (30.2mi).

Southern Oregon Extravaganza

Duration	4 days
Distance	193.7mi
Difficulty	hard
Start	Klamath Falls
End	Ashland
Cues & Elevation Profiles	pp364–5

This is the perfect ride for wildlife watchers, geology buffs, tree-huggers, campers and Shakespeare lovers – provided they are strong cyclists. Valley vistas and views of snowy Mt Thielson and Mt Scott alternate with tree-lined stretches of road. A steady but gentle climb makes its way to the rim of Crater Lake, and a side trip circles the caldera of the ancient volcano. Joining the wild and scenic Rogue River, the route rushes downhill before heading deeper into the trees for challenging climbing and, finally, the best descent in Oregon: into Ashland, where creature comforts and highbrow culture abound.

HISTORY

Tribes of Native Americans, including the Klamath and Modoc, populated the Klamath Basin before the arrival, in 1825, of white trappers from Hudson's Bay Company. Eventually the Native Americans were forced onto a reservation which subsequently shrank from 1560 sq mi to nothing. Logging, ranching and agriculture took over.

The communities of Southern Oregon, settled in large part by displaced Southerners and Confederate soldiers, differ from those of the Willamette Valley, settled mostly by more well-off New Englanders. To this day, Southern Oregon is a more politically conservative region, although some younger and more left-leaning folks arrived in the 1960s to set up farms or communes. Thespians prevent Ashland from becoming too stodgy.

NATURAL HISTORY

The 185,000 acres of shallow lakes and marshes of Klamath Basin were irrevocably changed in 1905 when the US Bureau of Reclamation began a campaign to convert wetlands to farmlands. Less than a quarter of historic wetlands remain intact. The Upper Klamath Lake is the largest body of fresh water west of the Rocky Mtns and home to more than 400 species of wildlife, including the largest concentration of bald eagles in the USA.

Mt Mazama, a 12,000ft-high volcano, violently erupted about 7,000 years ago, scattering pumice and ash for hundreds of miles. The summit collapsed; snowfall and rain filled Crater Lake, the USA's deepest lake, which formed in the caldera. The legacy of this volcanic eruption is also apparent in the magnificent Annie River Gorge and the lava flows through which the turbulent Rogue River rushes.

Near Ashland, the Siskiyou Mtns are rich in vivid yellowish-green peridotite and mottled green serpentinite rock that originally formed as ocean bedrock. The terrain is strikingly different from other parts of the state.

PLANNING

When to Ride

On one particularly hilly, isolated stretch of this route you'll be wishing you would see someone – anyone – even someone in a car. But many roads have the potential to be quite crowded. More than half a million people a year come to Crater Lake. Try to time this part of the route for a weekday. Early fall is quite scenic but don't push it past mid-September or you could freeze. Rim Dr closes from the first snow until April, when things thaw out a bit.

Ashland's Shakespeare Festival runs from February through November; buy tickets in advance and book lodging ahead of time.

Maps

The *Klamath County Bicycling Guide and Klamath Falls Area Bikeways* is handy for navigating your way out of Klamath Falls and beyond. Get a free copy from the Klamath County Department of Public Works (☎ 541-883-4697), 305 Main St, Klamath Falls. The *Oregon Bicycling Guide* (see Maps, p149) shows all of the route's roads.

What to Bring

Hill climbs are an incentive to travel light but bring lots of snack food, and refill water bottles whenever you can, especially in Prospect – there's *nothing* between there and Ashland.

GETTING TO/FROM THE RIDE

To turn this ride into a circuit, cycle 64mi over incredibly hilly but scenic terrain on US 66 from Ashland back to Klamath Falls. Stop for home-baked pie in Pinehurst. See the Optional Return Route on the map.

Klamath Falls

Amtrak offers service to Klamath Falls. The southbound *Coast Starlight* line passes through Portland daily at 2pm, arriving in Klamath Falls at 10pm. Northbound from California, the train arrives at around 8am.

Ashland

The only transport from Ashland is Greyhound bus (☎ 541-482-8803 in Ashland). Buses to Portland leaves three times a day from the Mr C Market at 2073 Hwy 99, about 2mi north of town. A bus leaves downtown Ashland every half hour and stops at Mr C Market; ask at the visitor center for details.

THE RIDE (See Map, pp172–3)

Klamath Falls

☎ 541

A fairly sleepy town, Klamath Falls had its heyday in the early 20th century, when the railroad arrived. Hotels, theaters and saloons flourished, frequented not only by local loggers and ranch hands but visiting Californians, too. Today, K Falls, as it is often called, still has the railroad but is otherwise economically challenged. It's also one of the most conservative communities in Oregon. The town is the gateway to fabulous cycling in the Klamath Basin, Crater Lake and Rogue River areas.

Information Tiny Klamath Falls is easy to navigate. The chamber of commerce (☎ 884-5193), 701 Plum Ave, shares premises with a bank.

Numerous brochures are also available at the **Klamath County Museum** (☎ 883-4208), 1451 Main St, where you can see natural history displays and historical interpretations of the Modoc War (1869–73). Learn more about Native American history at the impressive **Favell Museum of Western Art & Indian Artifacts** (☎ 882-9996), 125 W Main St.

Bicycle Jones (☎ 850-2453), 719 Main St, is well equipped and the owner can recommend local **mountain-bike trails** (closed Sun & Mon).

Places to Stay & Eat The ***Maverick Motel*** *(☎ 882-6688, fax 885-4095, 1220 Main St)* is a no-frills operation at $42 for single or double. In a more corporate spirit, the ***Quality Inn*** *(☎ 882-4666, fax 883-8795, 100 Main St)* charges about $70.

There's a ***Safeway*** *(Klamath Ave)* a block off Main St. Enjoy coffee and the namesake dish at the ***Daily Bagel*** *(cnr Main & 7th Sts)* in an attractive building. Ask for the mandarin cuisine spicy at ***Dynasty Restaurant*** *(106 Main St)* – if pressed, staff will admit to knowing what tofu is. Good for pizza, beer, video games and pool is the ***Old Town Pizza Company*** *(722 Main St)*. For dinner and dancing head to ***Mac Z's*** *(1111 Main St)*, where the salmon goes for $16.

Day 1: Klamath Falls to Rocky Point Resort

3–5 hours, 30.2mi

The beginning of the day offers a vista of the southern tip of Upper Klamath Lake, before climbing away from the lake's edge, alongside coniferous trees. The route flattens out, passing grazing cows with views of white-capped peaks, before dropping back to the lake and its bird-filled marshy edges.

The route heads out of town on residential streets past well groomed lawns and crosses the Link River, at the southern tip of **Upper Klamath Lake**, almost 30mi long and up to 8mi wide. Lakeshore Dr affords views of the water and **wildlife** – look for pelicans – before joining Hwy 140, which gains 600ft over 3.3mi to the 4760ft summit of wooded Doak Mt. From 8.2mi Hwy 140 has no shoulder for 19mi. The road curves and descends, offering views of 9495ft **Mt McLoughlin** to the west and the **Upper Klamath National Wildlife Refuge** to the east. At 24.2mi, the ***Odessa Creek Campground*** is 1mi off the road; at 26mi is the ***Odessa Market*** and ***Julie's Java Joint***. Across the road are tall aspen trees that turn golden in September.

Rocky Point Resort

☎ 541

On the northwest shore of Upper Klamath Lake in the Winema National Forest, ***Rocky Point Resort*** *(☎ 356-2287, fax 356-2222, 28121 Rocky Point Rd)* is attractive and popular with boaters, fishers, wildlife watchers and photographers. Cabins cost $80; the smaller guest rooms, $55. ***Camping*** costs $14. There's a ***shop*** selling fishing tackle, bait and snacks and a pricey but good ***restaurant*** in a small lodge. While you wait for a table, sit by the fire under huge deer antlers, then dine with a view of Pelican Bay. Entrees cost $12 to $20; reservations recommended.

Cycle the 30mi to Rocky Point by early afternoon, rent a **canoe** or **kayak** and paddle the **Klamath Canoe Trail**, to visit the beautiful wetlands of Upper Klamath Lake.

Day 2: Rocky Point Resort to Rim Village

4–8 hours, 45.9mi

Heading through the woods and into broad pastureland, the route eventually climbs steadily to Crater Lake, with a total elevation gain of 3400ft.

Watch for snakes on uphill Westside Rd. Reclaimed pastureland is dotted with cows and boasts views of 8036ft **Pelican Butte** to the west. Cycling east on Sevenmile Rd through a wide basin the views are sweeping; you can see down the arrow-straight road to Fort Klamath, and all around are peaks. **Mt Scott**, the highest in Crater Lake National Park at 8929ft high, is easily recognizable; look west of it to discern the outline of the Crater Lake rim.

Fort Klamath (21.7mi) is barely a town but accommodations and food are available. ***Crater Lake Resort*** at Fort Creek Campground *(☎ 381-2349, Hwy 62)*, just south of Fort Klamath, rents cabins for $50/60 single/double and tent sites for $5. For 'groceries, liquor, guns and ammunition', shop at ***Fort Klamath General Store***. It also serves food.

Mt Thielson (9182ft) looms in the distance before the route heads uphill. On the long climb see huge trees teetering on the edges of deep **Annie Creek Canyon**, carved into ash spewed by the eruption of Mt Mazama.

About 7mi from the rim of Crater Lake is a **ranger kiosk** (38.6mi) followed by Mazama Village (38.9mi). ***Mazama Village Campground*** *(☎ 830-8700)* charges $13; the camp ***store*** has limited food options. The ***Mazama Village Motor Inn*** *(☎ 830-8700, fax 830-8514)* rents somewhat gloomy rooms from $100. Stay here if you're too tired for the climb to Rim Village or if you can't afford the upscale Crater Lake Lodge.

An initially gradual climb steepens after the **Steel Visitor Center**. This is one of the

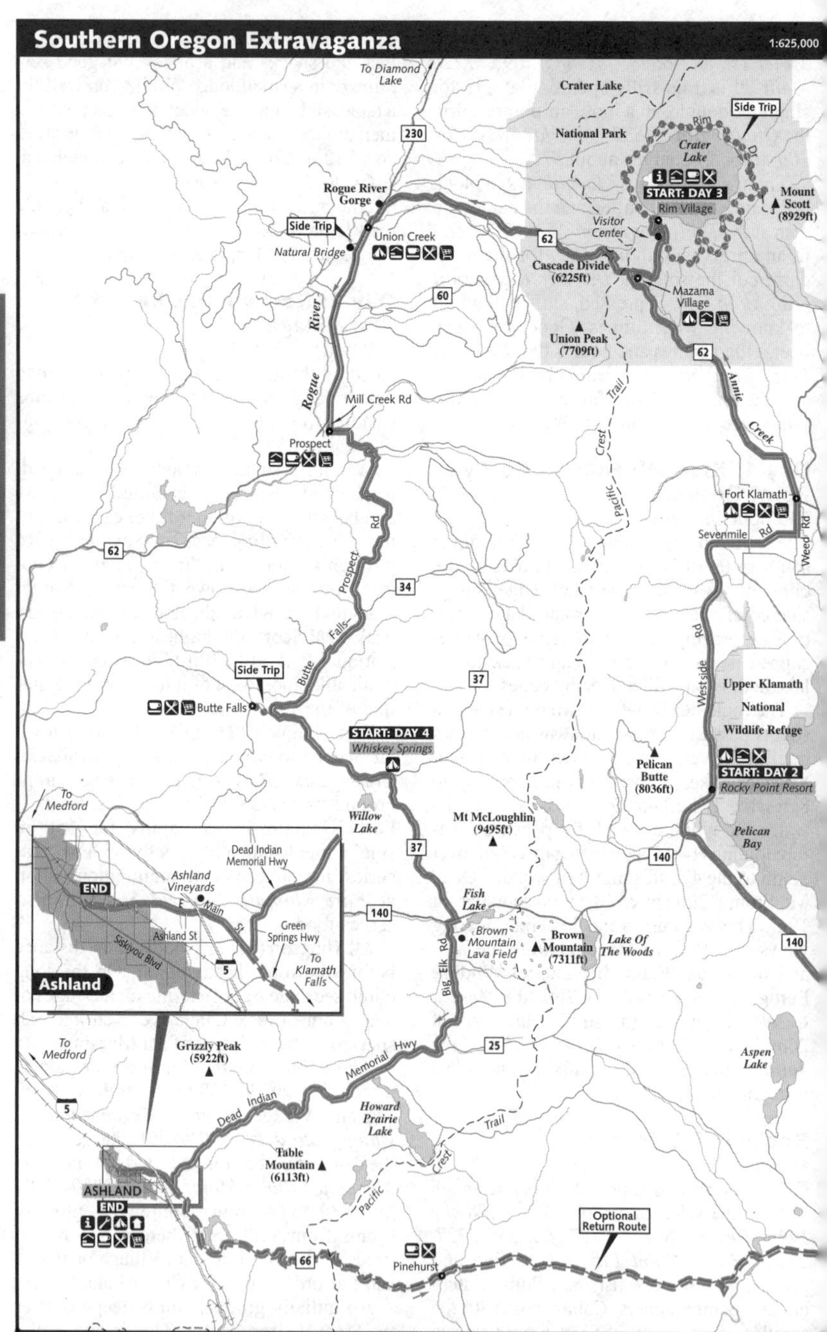

Southern Oregon Extravaganza
1:625,000
To Diamond Lake
Crater Lake National Park
Side Trip
Rim Dr
Crater Lake
START: DAY 3
Rim Village
Mount Scott (8929ft)
Visitor Center
Rogue River Gorge
Side Trip
Natural Bridge
Union Creek
Cascade Divide (6225ft)
Mazama Village
Union Peak (7709ft)
Rogue River
Mill Creek Rd
Prospect
Annie Creek
Pacific Crest Trail
Fort Klamath
Sevenmile Rd
Weed Rd
Prospect Rd
Butte Falls
Side Trip
Butte Falls
START: DAY 4
Whiskey Springs
Westside Rd
Upper Klamath National Wildlife Refuge
START: DAY 2
Rocky Point Resort
Pelican Butte (8036ft)
Mt McLoughlin (9495ft)
Pelican Bay
To Medford
Willow Lake
Fish Lake
Brown Mountain Lava Field
Brown Mountain (7311ft)
Lake Of The Woods
Big Elk Rd
Dead Indian Memorial Hwy
Ashland Vineyards
END
E Main St
Ashland St
Siskiyou Blvd
Green Springs Hwy
To Klamath Falls
Ashland
To Medford
Grizzly Peak (5922ft)
Aspen Lake
Howard Prairie Lake
Table Mountain (6113ft)
ASHLAND
END
Optional Return Route
Pinehurst
230
62
60
34
37
140
25
5
66

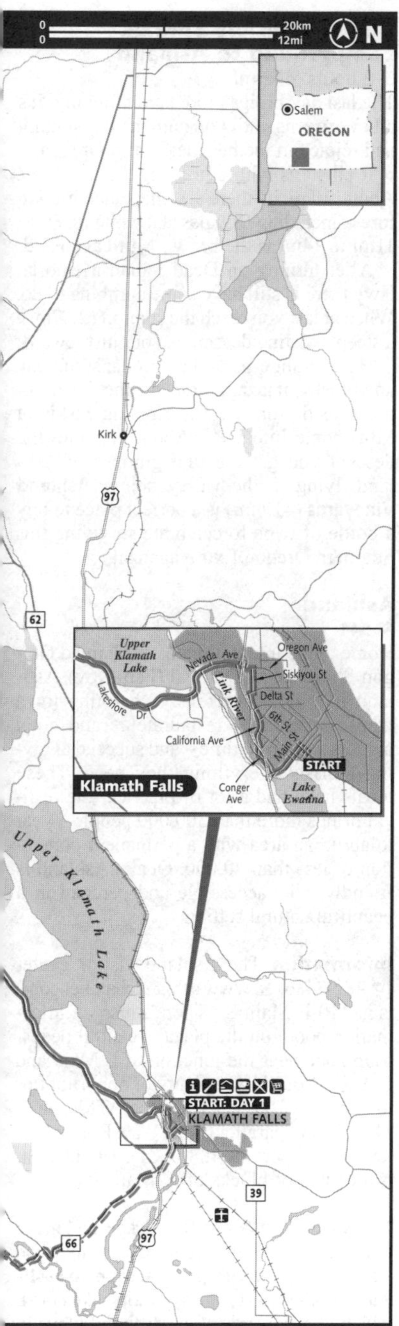

best ascents in Oregon. The first sight of the startlingly blue **Crater Lake** is breathtaking.

Side Trip: Crater Lake Rim Drive

32.6mi return

Need a challenge? This side trip is your ticket: the total elevation gain is 3800ft. Start in Rim Village and head west. Take Rim Dr past Hillman Peak, the highest point on the rim. At about 4mi is the **Wizard Island** overlook and trailhead to the **Watchman** (see Things to See & Do, below). At 10.7mi is the steep path down to **Cleetwood Cove** from where boat tours depart. From the trailhead at 17mi, it's a 2.5mi hike to the highest point in the park, the 8929ft summit of Mt Scott. Just past here is a short side road to **Cloudcap Overlook**, the highest point on Rim Dr (8070ft).

Rim Village

☎ 541

Rim Village is bustling with tourists who take more photographs than hikes or rides. The Rim Village Visitor Center, in a cabin, is closed in winter. The gift shop has an ATM. At the time of writing, management of the national park was changing. As a result, some services in Rim Village may change.

Things to See & Do Cyclists should ride the **Rim Drive** side trip. If you want to get closer to that amazingly blue water, take a **boat tour** from Cleetwood Cove. Tours stop at **Wizard Island** from late June to early September, weather permitting. Numerous **hikes** grant views of the lake. Try the **Watchman**: a short hike ascends to a hut, perched at 8013ft, used as a fire lookout. It offers a great view of **Phantom Ship**, a lava dike rising 160ft above the lake.

Places to Stay & Eat The ***Crater Lake Lodge*** *(☎ 830-8700, fax 830-8514)*, dating from 1909, has luxurious rooms from $145. Make reservations six months in advance or cross your fingers and call the morning of the day you want to stay. Make dinner reservations at the lodge's ***restaurant*** *(☎ 594-1184)*, where entrees cost about $20.

If you blew the bank on a lodge room, burgers and pizza are served on paper plates at the ***Llao Rock Cafe*** (under $10). The ***Watchman Restaurant*** serves dinner. Both are in the same complex as the gift shop.

Day 3: Rim Village to Whiskey Springs Campground

6–10 hours, 73.1mi

Most of this day is spent in the trees, starting with a fast descent from Crater Lake, gliding through the Rogue River Valley and ending up in hilly, timber-covered logging areas that feel eerily devoid of life.

The descent is almost as good as the climb as you retrace yesterday's route. Back at Mazama Village you join Hwy 62 and the road becomes an exercise in linear perspective, shaded on either side by tall trees. At 8.4mi the route crosses the **Pacific Crest Trail** (see the boxed text, p46). Joining Hwy 230, the route also joins the **Rogue River**. Often described as 'wild and scenic' this rushing, turbulent river deserves the moniker, as it forces its way through the forests of the Cascades. Stop and walk the 0.25mi trail (25.6mi) to a viewpoint of the **Rogue River Gorge**. Stay at nearby tiny Union Creek (25.7mi) if you want more time to explore the Rogue wilderness. ***Union Creek Campground*** *(☎ 770-5146 or ☎ 560-3400, fax 865-2795)* is right in town on Hwy 62, with 75 sites for $10 per night (no reservations; open mid-May–mid-Oct.) ***Union Creek Resort*** *(☎ 560-3565; 56484 Hwy 62)* is on the National Register of Historic Places. Whether you stay or not, stop at ***Beckie's Cafe***, across the street, for home-baked pie.

The side trip to **Natural Bridge** (26.9mi) is well worth it. Take the short hike to a viewpoint where the Rogue flows through a lava tube for 200ft, creating the so-called bridge.

Prospect (38.9mi) has a less-than-delicious ***pizza parlor*** and the ***Prospect Historical Hotel*** *(☎560-3664, fax 560-3825)*, decorated in frilly, Victorian decor.

The rest of the day is hilly and tiring. Beware gravel trucks on Butte Falls-Prospect Rd until 44.3mi, where they turn off. At 64.2mi take the side trip to Butte Falls. It's 1.2mi to the tiny town, with a ***store*** and a couple of ***cafes***. About 2mi off the route at 71.3mi, ***Willow Lake Resort*** *(☎ 774-8183)* has campsites and four cabins.

Whiskey Springs Campground

☎ 541

This ***campground*** *(☎ 770-5146 or ☎ 560-3400, fax 865-2795)* has 33 tent sites for around $10 (May–Sept; no reservations). Bring your own food; firewood is available.

Day 4: Whiskey Springs Campground to Ashland

6–8 hours, 44.5mi

The last day brings more hard climbing. It's all evergreens until you gain the last summit and rejoice in the best descent in Oregon.

It all starts with a grueling, 7.2mi climb. About 10mi in there's some older growth forest, including Douglas and white fir. From 11mi to 14mi is the **Brown Mtn Lava Field**.

After turning on Dead Indian Memorial Hwy there is still have some climbing to do. When at last you reach the summit (27.7mi), a steep, twisting descent is your just reward.

Here, orange-barked madrona, scrub oak and brushy manzanita replace the thick, oppressive fir forests. The rippling Siskiyou Mtns come into view. About 5mi into the descent you get the first glimpse of Ashland, lying in the valley below. **Ashland Vineyards** (41.6mi) is a perfect place to buy a bottle of wine to celebrate surviving this Southern Oregon Extravaganza!

Ashland

☎ 541

Home to the internationally acclaimed Oregon Shakespeare Festival (Feb–Nov), Ashland is a self-consciously charming town whose merchants, restaurateurs and hotel owners work overtime – and succeed at giving tourists everything they need. These locals have had a lot of practice: the festival brings more than 300,000 people a year to an urban area with a permanent population of less than 20,000. Quaint Ashland is friendly, bike-accessible and perched in a beautiful natural setting.

Information The Ashland visitor center (☎ 482-3486, Ⓦ www.ashlandchamber.com) is at 110 E Main St. There's also an information booth on the plaza, a central pedestrian zone near the junction of E Main and Oak Sts. You'll have plenty of opportunities to withdraw money from the ATMs on E Main St and parallel Lithia Way. Rogue Valley Cycle Sport (☎ 488-0581), 191 Oak St, is a couple of blocks off E Main St.

Things to See & Do Buy tickets and make lodging reservations well in advance to attend a play during the **Oregon Shakespeare Festival** (☎ 482-4331, Ⓦ www.orshakes.org), which runs upwards of ten different plays in three theaters each year. The festival began in 1935 when a local college professor, Angus Bowmer, convinced Ashland residents to sponsor two of the Bard's plays in a dilapidated building that reminded him of the Globe Theater. The festival stages a variety of plays; past bills have featured works from Euripides to Tennessee Williams to contemporary plays. The Shakespeare plays are all staged at the fantastic Elizabethan Theater (early Jun–early Oct only). The ticket office is at 15 S Pioneer St. If you didn't purchase in advance, queue at the ticket office at 6pm on show nights to score unclaimed tickets.

Places to Stay & Eat Fight over the video games in the rec room at ***Glenyan Campground*** *(☎ 488-1785, 5310 Hwy 66)*, about 2.5mi south from the intersection of Dead Indian Memorial Hwy and Hwy 66 (see Day 4). Tent sites cost $17. Less than 0.5mi farther south is ***Emigrant Lake Campground*** *(☎ 774-8183, fax 826-8360, Hwy 66)*. The road climbs a bit but the pleasant sites ($14) dot a hillside next to oak trees and you can cool down on the waterslide.

Ashland Hostel *(☎ 482-9217, 150 N Main St)* is just three blocks north of the town plaza. Beds cost $14/15 members/nonmembers.

There are tons of motels in and around town. Your best bet for a clean, friendly well-situated place is the ***Timbers Motel*** *(☎ 482-4242, fax 482-8723, 1450 Ashland St)*, where a queen bed costs $67/72 single/double.

In an historic building, the ***Columbia Hotel*** *(☎ 482-3726 or ☎ 800-718-2530, 262 1/2 E Main St)* has a boarding house vibe. Bathrooms are shared and rates range from $49 to $105.

To check on availability at one of the numerous B&Bs, call the ***Ashland B&B Clearinghouse*** *(☎ 488-0338 or ☎ 800-588-0338)*.

Get caffeinated at locally owned ***Rogue Valley Roasting Co*** *(917 E Main St)*. Baked goods and other cafe fare are available for under $5. For salads, soup and sandwiches (around $5), try ***Grizzly Peak Roasting Co*** *(First St)*, just off E Main St. Sit-down breakfast costs $9 at the ***Ashland Bakery & Cafe*** *(38 E Main St)*, where if you're lucky you'll overhear festival gossip; dinners get fancier and pricier ($12–14). Pizza at ***Macaroni's*** *(58 E Main St)* costs from $10.

Waiters with Italian accents serve the pasta at ***Il Giardino*** *(5 Granite St)*. Dinner for two with wine costs around $40. The ***Firefly Restaurant & Bar*** *(23 N Main St)* on the plaza offers live jazz on Monday, along with haute-cuisine entrees for $18 to $25.

Wild West Roundup

Duration	6 days
Distance	289mi
Difficulty	hard
Start/End	Baker City
Cues & Elevation Profiles	pp365–6

The American West has been mythologized in books, films and ballads. But you'd hardly call Oregon the Wild West, right? This ride proves otherwise: windy roads connect classic Western towns and ranching valleys; cloud shadows paint mountainsides; and blue skies meet golden sagebrush. The cycling is challenging and the landscape different from other rides in this chapter.

Perhaps the most difficult part of the state for cyclists to access, Northeastern Oregon is also the most rewarding. Pioneers on the Oregon Trail passed through here, no doubt discouraged by the sometimes rough terrain and harsh weather, but dazzled by the region's extraordinary beauty, including the Wallowa and Blue Mtn Ranges. Modern adventurers, however, have the advantage of towns settled long ago.

To keep the mileage down, the best lodging option is to camp. However, you can put in longer days and stay in motels. If you plan to stay in tiny Elgin or Union, book ahead.

HISTORY

In 1804–6, Lewis and Clark's Corps of Discovery (see the boxed text, p15) engaged in trading with the region's many Native American tribes, most notably the Nez Percé. However, when white gold seekers arrived, eventually encroaching on the Wallowa Mtns, the ancestral home of the Nez Percé, relations quickly deteriorated. A series of tit-for-tat murders began the Nez Percé War in 1877. Fleeing for Canada, Chief Joseph and 800 Nez Percé were defeated in Montana and sent to reservations in Oklahoma. When the Union Pacific railroad came through La Grande and Baker city in the 1880s, the area quickly filled with farmers and ranchers.

PLANNING

When to Ride

Make sure you know there's no snow when you're planning to do this ride. Your best bet is July to early September – but always prepare for sun, rain, wind and chilly temperatures, especially if you're camping.

Maps

The *Oregon Bicycling Guide* provides an overview of the route. For more detail use either the DeLorme or Benchmark Atlas (see Maps, p149). Helpful, too, are some locally published *Road Bike Route* brochures. Contact the La Grande/Union visitor center (☎ 800-848-9969), Suite 200, 1912 Fourth St, La Grande, OR 97850, to request the following free brochures: *Valley Loop*; *Union, North Powder, Catherine Creek*; *Imbler, Summerville*; and *Foothill Road.*

What to Bring

On Days 2, 4 and 5, this ride overnights at campgrounds with no other services. Bring food supplies for the entire journey or be sure to load up in towns with services, although the choice will be somewhat limited.

GETTING TO/FROM THE RIDE

Baker City

This is not an easy region to get to with a bike.

Bus The Greyhound Bus depot (☎ 523-5011), 515 Campbell St, is served by three buses a day eastbound, and three westbound, along its Portland–Boise (Idaho) route. From Portland it's a 6½-hour, $47 journey.

Bicycle It's only 240mi from Bend (p166–7), the start/end town of the Lava & Lakes Circuit ride – so what are you waiting for? Take the Old Redmond Hwy north from Bend to Redmond. Pick up Canal Boulevard to O'Neill Hwy. Take State Route 126/US 26/SR 7 to Baker City.

THE RIDE (See Map, pp178–9)

Baker City

☎ 541

Located where the Powder River leaves the Blue Mtns and enters its wide agricultural valley, Baker City is one of the region's oldest commercial centers. A hopping town in the 1880s, full of miners, cowboys, shepherds, shopkeepers and loggers, it is less bustling now but retains an old-fashioned charm. Wide streets are flanked by Victorian Italianate buildings housing shops, restaurants and hotels. Although many of these are listed with the National Register of Historic Places, current-day proprietors don't put on airs and everyone is friendly. Noteworthy 1929 **Hotel Baker** (now apartments) is one of the tallest buildings in Oregon east of the Cascades.

Information The Baker County visitor center (☎ 523-3356 or ☎ 800-523-1235) is at 490 Campbell St. Everything you need can be found on 1st, Main and Resort Sts between Place Ave and Campbell St. The public library, with Internet access, is at the corner of Resort and Madison Sts. Flagstaff Sports (☎ 523-3477), 2101 Main St, Suite 17, is the local bike shop.

Things to See & Do The **Oregon Trail Regional Museum** (☎ 523-9308), corner Grove and Campbell Sts, has an extensive mineral collection. The 23,000-sq-ft **National Historic Oregon Trail Interpretive Center** (☎ 523-1843) is about 4mi east of town on Hwy 86. If you can spare the time, it's worth it. Pre-book a room if you're coming to town during the July **Miners' Jubilee** (☎ 800-523-1235), featuring a carnival and bull riding.

Places to Stay & Eat The ***Oregon Trail Motel & Restaurant*** *(☎ 523-5844 or ☎ 800-628-3982, 211 Bridge St)* has rooms for $46 with continental breakfast. Comparably priced is the ***Friendship Inn*** *(☎ 523-6571, 134 Bridge St)*. The ***Best Western Sunridge Inn*** *(☎ 523-6444 or ☎ 800-233-2368, 1 Sunridge Lane)*, by the visitor center, charges $60 to $80 for comfortable rooms. ***Geiser Grand Hotel*** *(☎ 523-1889 or ☎ 888-434-7374, fax 523-1800, 1996 Main St)* is in a gorgeous, historic landmark building with a restaurant and saloon. Rooms start at $79.

Albertsons *(cnr Resort & Madison Sts)*, by the library, sells groceries. Get breakfast at the ***Front Street Cafe & Coffee Co*** *(1840 Main St)*. ***Barley Brown's Brew Pub*** *(2190 Main St)* serves up seafood, pasta and fish and chips from $7 to $10. The best place in town for hungry cyclists is ***Pizza a' Fetta*** *(☎ 523-6099, 1915 Washington St)*. The friendly owner-chefs make great pizzas (from $15) topped with more fresh vegetables than you'll see anywhere else in eastern Oregon.

Day 1: Baker City to Hot Lake

4–7 hours, 43.9mi

This relatively flat route traverses broad Baker Valley, at the foot of the Blue Mtns, passing ranches and podunk towns.

US Hwy 30 from Baker City to Haines offers views of the Elkhorn Range of the Blue Mtns to the west, and the high Wallowa peaks to the northeast. On the smooth road, prepare to be passed by rumbling pick-ups driven by ranchers. The wide valley may also be windy.

At 11.5mi is rinky-dink Haines – don't blink – with its **1880s Park**, home to a few 'historic' buildings and information about the history of cattle ranching. There's a ***general store*** and the friendly ***Frontier Tavern***, serving food as well as libations. Here the road narrows but there's very little traffic. At 18.4mi you'll cross the **45th parallel**, midway between the Equator and the North Pole. Stop and rest under the water tower in **North Powder** (20.5mi), where there's also a ***cafe***.

From 25mi to 28mi the road is up and down, with some 500ft of climbing (possibly into the wind); look behind for striking views of the Elkhorn Range. As you head downhill along Pyles Creek, listen for a lonesome whistle and look for an endless freight train rumbling in the shadow of Craig Mtn, to the west.

Get a snack or espresso at ***Hometown Hardware*** in Union (37mi). There's also the grand ***Union Hotel*** *(☎ 562-6135, 326 N Main St)*. A good gravel road (43.4mi) affords views of steaming **Hot Lake** and the abandoned hotel (see the boxed text 'The Haunted Sanatorium', above).

The Haunted Sanatorium

As early as 1864, white settlers recognized Hot Lake's economic viability and built a series of lakeside resorts at the edge of the eight-acre lake. The grandest of all was built in 1906, a huge sanatorium/hotel with hundreds of rooms. In the 1930s a fire destroyed the grand ballroom and library.

The Hot Lake resort closed in the 1980s and is widely considered to be haunted. It certainly is creepy, standing abandoned by the side of the road near the site where 2½ gallons per minute of nearly-boiling water reach the surface of a pond, steaming. Hear any screams?

Hot Lake

☎ 541

There's nothing here but the ***Hot Lake RV Resort*** *(☎ 963-5253 or ☎ 800-994-5253, 65182 Hot Lake Lane)* and the ghosts of vacationers past. However, it's a great place to stay, at the edge of the Grande Ronde Valley and in the shadow of **Elk Mtn** (5463ft) and **Mt Emily** (6110ft). According to the resort's brochure, this spot was known to Native Americans as 'Peace Valley'. Pitch a tent for $13 and use the showers and laundry facilities. There's also a small ***store***.

Day 2: Hot Lake to Minam State Park

4½–8 hours, 52.4mi

The route becomes more rigorous on Day 2, heading through the Grande Ronde Valley and joining up with the Wallowa River.

Decent gravel leads to lovely Foothill Rd, at the base of the **Blue Mtns**. On the outskirts of **La Grande** is **Birnie Park** (9.5mi). This spot was an encampment for Oregon Trail emigrants getting ready to climb the Blue Mtns. Closer into town you'll pass the **La Grande Visitor Center** (10.8mi), corner Adams Ave and Fourth St. If you're hungry go to ***Foley Station*** at 1011 Adams Ave. La Grande also has a bike shop, several ***restaurants***, a ***Safeway***, banks and a few motels, including the ***Royal Motor Inn*** *(☎ 963-4154, 1510 Adams Ave)*.

Mt Glen Rd climbs past the **Pioneer Monument** (15.2mi), a wind-swept late-19th-century graveyard, as you cycle under the shadow of **Mt Emily** to the west. Summerville (27mi) has a ***store*** and ***bar***. Descend past what appears to be millions of dead trees at the **Boise Cascade Mill** (35.8mi) and into Elgin. Here you'll find an ATM, ***store***, the ***Elgin City Center Motel*** *(☎ 437-2441)* and a few ***restaurants***.

Golden wheat fields line Hwy 82 as it climbs **Minam Hill**. Trees take over again as a 5mi steep, winding descent drops from **Minam Summit** (46.9mi) into a canyon along the Wallowa River.

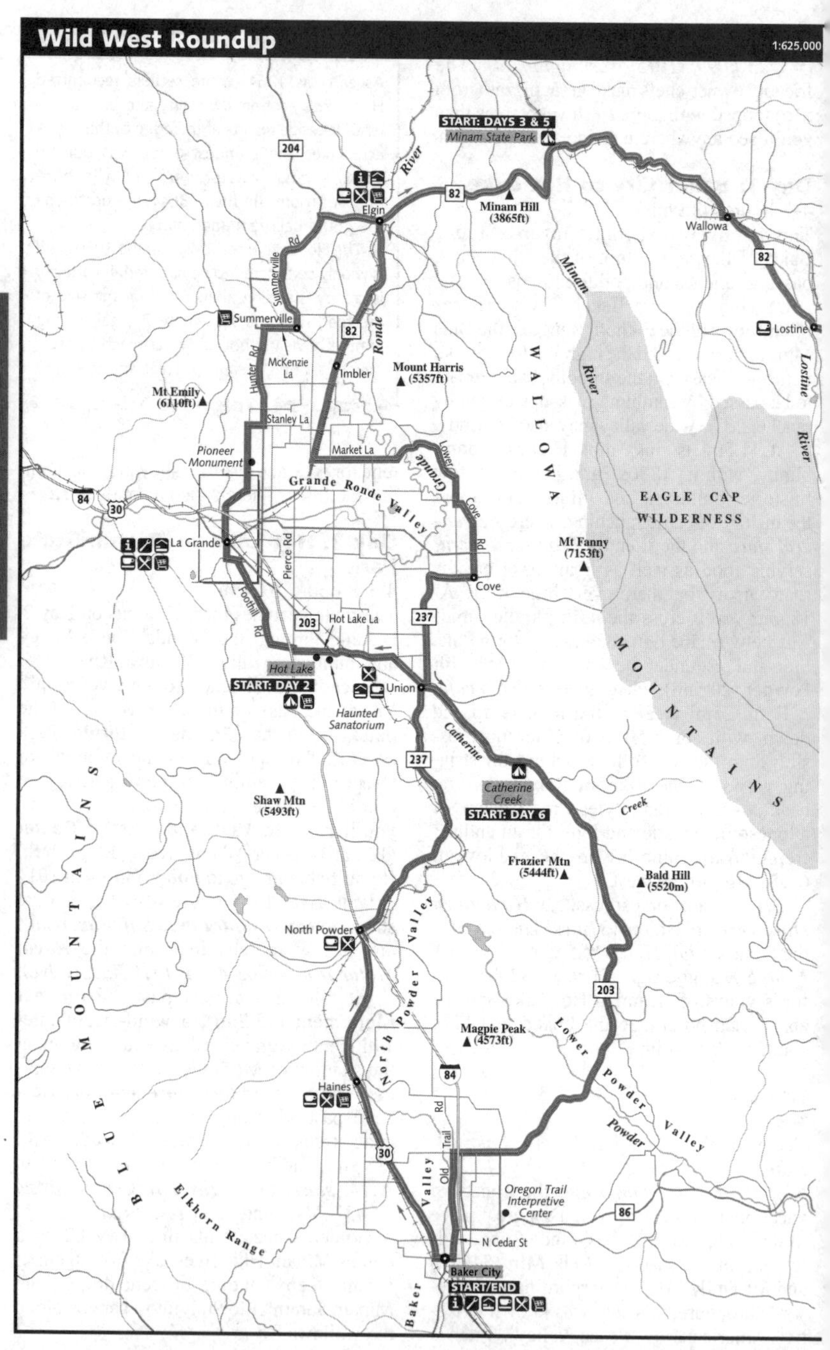

Wild West Roundup
1:625,000
START: DAYS 3 & 5
Minam State Park
Minam Hill (3865ft)
Wallowa
Lostine
Lostine River
Minam River
WALLOWA MOUNTAINS
EAGLE CAP WILDERNESS
Mt Fanny (7153ft)
Elgin
Summerville Rd
Summerville
Hunter Rd
McKenzie La
Imbler
Ronde
Mount Harris (5357ft)
Mt Emily (6110ft)
Stanley La
Market La
Lower Grande
Pioneer Monument
Grande Ronde Valley
Cove Rd
Cove
La Grande
Pierce Rd
Foothill Rd
Hot Lake La
Hot Lake
START: DAY 2
Haunted Sanatorium
Union
Catherine Creek
START: DAY 6
Shaw Mtn (5493ft)
Frazier Mtn (5444ft)
Bald Hill (5520m)
North Powder
North Powder Valley
Magpie Peak (4573ft)
Lower Powder Valley
Powder
Haines
Old Trail Rd
Oregon Trail Interpretive Center
N Cedar St
Baker City
START/END
Baker Valley
Elkhorn Range
BLUE MOUNTAINS

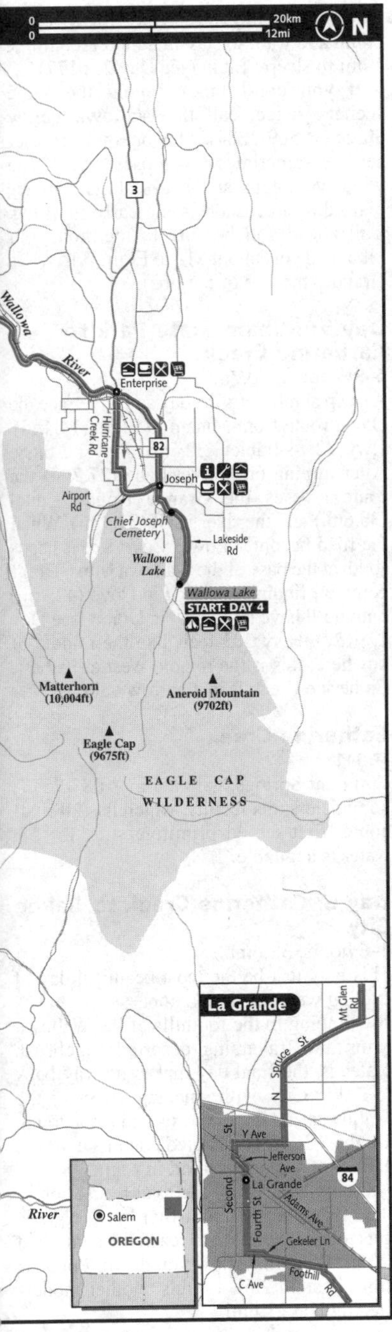

Minam State Park

☎ 541

Fall asleep listening to the Wallowa River, which runs through this scenic campground in a steep valley filled with evergreens. Your neighbors may be deer, elk, bears, cougars and the odd mountain sheep. Sites cost $7 to $10. You can't make reservations but call ***Minam State Park*** *(☎ 432-8855 or ☎ 800-551-6949)* for information.

Day 3: Minam State Park to Wallowa Lake

4–8 hours, 47.7mi

Gradually climbing past the farms of the **Wallowa Valley**, you start to see the high peaks that give the Wallowa Mtns the nickname the **Switzerland of America**.

A slow, steady climb through **Wallowa River Gorge Canyon** lasts for about 9mi before breaking out to a beautiful agricultural valley. Tiny Lostine (22.6mi) has a ***tavern***. Continue to climb, with the looming **Matterhorn** in the distance to the southwest. You'll come to the ***Wilderness Inn*** *(☎ 426-4535, 301 W North St)* before reaching Enterprise's 1890s town center (32.9mi), which has a few ***restaurants***. Not to be missed is funky, one-of-a-kind ***Terminal Gravity Brewery*** *(803 School St)* just off Hwy 82 toward Joseph. This oasis of counter culture is reason enough to stay in Enterprise. Enjoy a beer on the front porch.

There's more climbing to Joseph (41.5mi) where there's a bike shop, ***hotels*** and restaurants, including the delicious ***Wildflour Bakery*** *(Hwy 82/N Main St)*.

Out of town the route passes farms on a tiny back road with vistas of the (often snow-capped) 9000ft peaks of the Wallowas. Stop to pay respects at **Chief Joseph Cemetery** (43mi). Observe some of the best-preserved examples of glacial moraines in North America.

Wallowa Lake

☎ 541

Under the shadow of the glacier-carved jagged peaks of the Wallowas, this state park is breathtaking. From 4450ft in the park, take the 15-minute **Wallowa Lake Tramway** to 8150ft, atop Mt Howard. This is the steepest vertical lift in North America. Views of four states, the **Eagle Cap Wilderness** and the **Seven Devils of Idaho** are spectacular from the 2.5mi of hiking trails.

If there's a warm spell in late September, don't miss the **Alpenfest**, featuring crafts, food, yodelers and dancing in a rustic hall.

Places to Stay & Eat Camp at the ***State Park*** *(☎ 432-4185 or ☎ 800-551-6949)* for $17 or $4 per person at the hiker/biker sites; keep your food out of reach of black bears and cougars. (For information on safe camping in bear country, see Touring Dangers & Annoyances, pp63–6.)

Treat yourself to the ***Wallowa Lodge*** *(☎ 4342-9821, fax 432-4885)*, where rooms range from $70 to $135. Cabins with kitchens cost $85 to $175. Warm up by the fireplace before dining in the pricey but elegant ***restaurant***. There is a ***general store*** across from the lodge.

Day 4: Wallowa Lake to Minam State Park

5–7 hours, 45.7mi

Quicker than retracing yesterday's exact route, follow Hwy 82 all the way back – enjoy the descent on a wide shoulder. This saves 2mi. Today you'll only climb 100ft in elevation so if you're ready for a bigger climb and want to stay in a motel, continue 14mi to sleepy Elgin (see Day 2, p177).

If you don't fancy seeing the same scenery twice, call the **Wallowa Valley Stage** (☎ 569-2284). This one-man courier service sometimes takes passengers. The white van stops at the gas station on the main drag in Joseph in the early morning. Call ahead and be sure to mention your bike. It'll cost about $11 to Elgin, $14 to La Grande (the end of the line).

Survival Tactics for Vegetarians in the Wild West

'Honey, there's not a vegetarian for 300mi.' This is not what I wanted to hear from the cafe owner that cold day in the small town of Elgin. But I wasn't surprised. Northeastern Oregon is cattle country, and proud of it. Non-carnivores will do OK in larger towns catering to tourists but in some of the tinier hamlets may have to overdose on cheese sandwiches or starve – not to mention face ridicule.

Come prepared, as the challenging, rugged terrain will stimulate your appetite. Bring plenty of snacks and shop for groceries in the larger towns. Even if you're not carrying a camp stove, bring dehydrated soup; you'll be able to get boiling water in small groceries.

Luckily, the cafe owner was wrong: just 50mi down the road in Enterprise, I sat down to a steaming bowl of vegetarian chili and a microbrewed beer at Terminal Gravity. The next day I had a delectable burrito at the Wildflour in Joseph. There are a few civilized culinary outposts, even in the Wild West.

Day 5: Minam State Park to Catherine Creek

5–8½ hours, 60.7mi

A steep climb starts the day as you retrace the Day 2 route from Minam to Elgin (14.4mi). Hwy 82 to Imbler (22.5mi) may be busy. After turning on Market Lane (27.7mi) the route crosses the Grande Ronde Canal (30.6mi) and the river itself (32.9mi). When the road becomes Lower Cove Rd, it heads south at the base of the Wallowa Mtns. Don't count on finding anything in Cove (42.7mi) but you'll have more luck in Union (see Day 1, p177). Hwy 203 feels like the middle of nowhere; this is the remote West at its best. Catherine Creek is in a narrow valley.

Catherine Creek

☎ 541

Emigrant Springs State Park (☎ 983-2277) administers this facility, which has 20 first-come, first-served primitive sites for $8; water is available.

Day 6: Catherine Creek to Baker City

4–6 hours, 38.6mi

This may just be the most beautiful day of cycling we cover in Oregon.

Climbing in the foothills of the Wallowa Mtns and traversing deserted sagebrush plateaus, the final day makes its way back to Baker City, with amazing views of the Wallowas and the Elkhorns and some tough climbs. It's fairly deserted country until the end – buy water and food in Elgin.

From about 1.9mi the road heads uphill. It's moderately steep at first but the grade gets tougher at 3.9mi to reach the summit at 6.3mi. Wind may slow you down. Pondosa **store** is at 14.2mi. There's another moderate climb at 21.6mi.

CALIFORNIA

Highlights

- Big Sur coastline
- sightseeing by bicycle in San Francisco
- 'clothing optional' hot springs in Northern California's Wine Country
- dense redwood forests along the Avenue of the Giants
- Anza-Borrego Desert
- wild Catalina Island

Special Events

- Tournament of the Roses Parade (Jan) Pasadena/LA
- Italian Street Painting Festival – San Luis Obispo (Apr) & Santa Barbara (May)
- Castroville Artichoke Festival (May) near Monterey
- Gay & Lesbian Pride Celebration (Jun) Los Angeles
- Gilroy Garlic Festival (Jul) near San Juan Bautista
- Apple Festival (Oct) Julian

Cycling Events

- Tour of Borrego (Feb) Borrego Springs
- Gourmet Century (Apr) Santa Ynez Valley
- Tour of the Unknown Coast (May) Ferndale
- Strawberry Fields Forever Century (May) Santa Cruz
- Healdsburg Harvest Century Bicycle Tour (mid-Jul)
- Solvang Century (Mar) Santa Ynez Valley

Food & Drink Specialties

- artichokes (deep-fried, steamed, you name it) Santa Cruz & Monterey
- sourdough bread, authentic ethnic food and monster burritos in San Francisco
- Fine dining and exceptional, hard-to-find wines in the Wine Country
- Apples in the Russian River Valley & Julian
- Jodi Maroni's sausages on Venice Beach

GREGOR CLARK

Northern California

This chapter features rides around the San Francisco Bay area, plus a few to the north and two in Yosemite National Park to the east. The region is vast and large areas of interest have been left out due to their inaccessibility by public transport or lack of cyclist-friendly infrastructure. All the coastal rides can be linked to the Border to Border ride (pp269–353) and all rides except those in Yosemite lie along US 101, which parallels the Coast Range east of the Pacific Ocean and west of Sacramento Valley.

Spectacular coastal scenery, wine-tasting opportunities, giant redwoods and fun urban exploration are the chapter's highlights. The thrill of seeing Yosemite National Park by bike or mountain biking above the rim of Lake Tahoe are exciting but only possible from June to October.

NORTHERN CALIFORNIA

HISTORY

Though it lies at the geographic midline of the state, San Francisco Bay has always been the social and economic hub of 'Northern' California. It was missed by the British pirate/explorer Sir Francis Drake, who landed his boat just north at Point Reyes in 1579, but not by Gaspar de Portolá, who came looking for Monterey Bay while establishing Spanish missions two hundred years later. By this time (1776) there were already Russian hunting forts established north of San Francisco and British trading posts in the Sacramento Valley.

The next party on the scene was the newly formed United States. In 1845 American settlers – fed up with Mexican rule and disillusioned with their own government's promise to purchase California – staged a revolt in Sonoma. They laid siege to the town square, raised a bear-emblazoned flag and proclaimed the territory the Bear Flag Republic. (California's flag still bears the bear and the words 'California Republic'.)

It was a short-lived venture, however, as the USA proclaimed war on Mexico the following year and received California (plus Arizona and New Mexico) in the Treaty of Guadalupe Hidalgo in 1848. Gold was discovered in the Sierra Nevada foothills a few months later.

Over the next 15 years, more than 380,000 people came to try their luck in California's gold rush. The completion of the Transcontinental Railroad (1869) further promoted the state, bringing people and goods from the east coast to Sacramento and San Francisco.

As Southern California developed, Northern California's natural resources, especially water, fueled its growth. This is still a divisive point in political and economic battles between 'north' and 'south': 75% of California's water comes from Northern California, and 75% of that goes to Southern California.

Slower growth, less congestion and affordability have long attracted people to Northern California. But with San Francisco and the Silicon Valley in pole position of the dot-com revolution, the Bay Area is increasingly congested and affordable housing is scarce. Since 1995, much of the dairy and orchard land north of the Napa Valley has been replanted with vines. Still, the roads north of San Francisco remain much less traveled than those to the south.

NATURAL HISTORY

The 'Coast Range' runs along most of the coast, with gentle foothills in the east and rocky cliffs plunging into the Pacific on the west. San Francisco Bay divides the range roughly in half. The North Coast is famous for its redwoods, giant beauties with spongy red bark, flat needles and olive-size cones.

South of Humboldt County, where annual precipitation is considerably less, plant life is less specialized. Inland, from the east side of the Coastal Range to the western foothills of the Sierra Nevada, you'll find California black oak, with broad leaves (bristly at the ends) and gray-black bark. The smooth, shiny acorns from these trees were a staple for California Native Americans.

The coast offers many chances to see California's aquatic mammals, including northern elephant and harbor seals, California sea lions and sea otters. California gray whales are often visible off the coast from December to March when they head to warm waters in Mexico. Once in a while you'll see them breaching but usually you

Oaks of California

While California's conifers get all the press, the tree most emblematic of the California landscape is the oak. From Oregon to Baja, the Pacific to the Sierra, California's 20 oak species occupy an impressive diversity of habitat.

Largest is the valley oak. These giants favor fertile river valleys and can live up to 600 years, soar to more than 100ft, and spread – as did the famous Hooker Oak of Butte County – wide enough to shade thousands of people from the summer sun. The 11 species of shrub oaks, a ground-hugging 3 to 16ft, can survive everything from toxic serpentine soils to frequent all-consuming fires to semi-desert conditions, and are important members of California's chaparral ecosystems. While most of California's oaks are evergreen, a few drop their leaves in response to drought or cold.

Naturalists consider the oak to be a 'hub' or 'keystone' species. Roughly 5000 insect species, 80 species of amphibians and reptiles, 100 species of birds and 60 mammals are associated with California's oaks. They provide food – acorns, leaves, twigs, sap, roots, pollen – and shelter on more than 30 million acres, benefiting everything from fungi, toads and wasps to wood rats, black bears, great horned owls and feral pigs.

Gaen Murphree

can just spot the spray from their blowholes and part of their back or tail.

Coastal birds include gulls and grebes, terns, cormorants, sandpipers, and sanderlings that like to chase waves from the shore.

CLIMATE

A typical weather forecast for San Francisco and the north coast, at any time of year, is 'fog at night and morning, burning off by midday'. Fog is especially noticeable in summer when hot inland temperatures cause a mist to rise from the cooler ocean waters offshore.

East of the Coast Range, the climate is less affected by the Pacific Ocean. Summer days can exceed 100°F. Winter temperatures are slightly cooler than in San Francisco, though they rarely drop below freezing. It rains for an average of three days per week from January to April.

The Sierra Nevada has a typical mountain climate that varies with altitude. Snow usually dumps in earnest by December and lasts until early May, though the foothills can remain clear of snow in mild years.

INFORMATION

Maps & Books

Krebs Cycle Products (W members.cruzio.com/~krebsmap/), PO Box 7337, Santa Cruz, CA 95061, publishes hand-drawn, wonderfully detailed maps, including *California North Coast*; *North San Francisco Bay & Wine Country Bike Touring Map*; and *Lake Tahoe & Gold Country*. These are not always available in bike shops; mail order is recommended (about $10 per map).

Available at most bookstores, DeLorme's *Northern California* atlas ($15) is best used as a planning resource because of its size.

Lonely Planet's *California* and *San Francisco* guides are excellent complements to this book. For long stays, *Out to Eat – San Francisco* and *San Francisco City Map* may also be useful. CitySync *San Francisco* is Lonely Planet's digital city guide for Palm OS hand-held devices. Purchase or demo CitySync *San Francisco* at W www.citysync.com. Mountain bikers should pick up a copy of Linda Gong Austin's *Mountain Bike!: Northern California* (Menasha Ridge; $13), or *Mountain Biking Northern California's 100 Best Trails* (Fine Edge Productions; $16).

GATEWAY CITIES

San Francisco

☎ 415

It was less than 250 years ago that San Francisco Bay was 'discovered' by Gaspar de Portolá, when his party mistook it for Monterey Bay. Since then, San Francisco has been a sleepy Mexican mission town, earned the sobriquet 'Barbary Coast', been leveled by earthquake and rebuilt in Victorian fashion, hosted the birth of the 1950s Beat movement, kicked off the Summer of Love in Golden Gate Park and welcomed Gay Pride. Most recently, its upwardly mobile Internet generation has catapulted living costs past those of New York City's. What consistently tops the polls as America's favorite city is now also America's most expensive place to live.

San Francisco (*never* called 'Frisco' or 'SF' by locals) is an amalgam of distinct

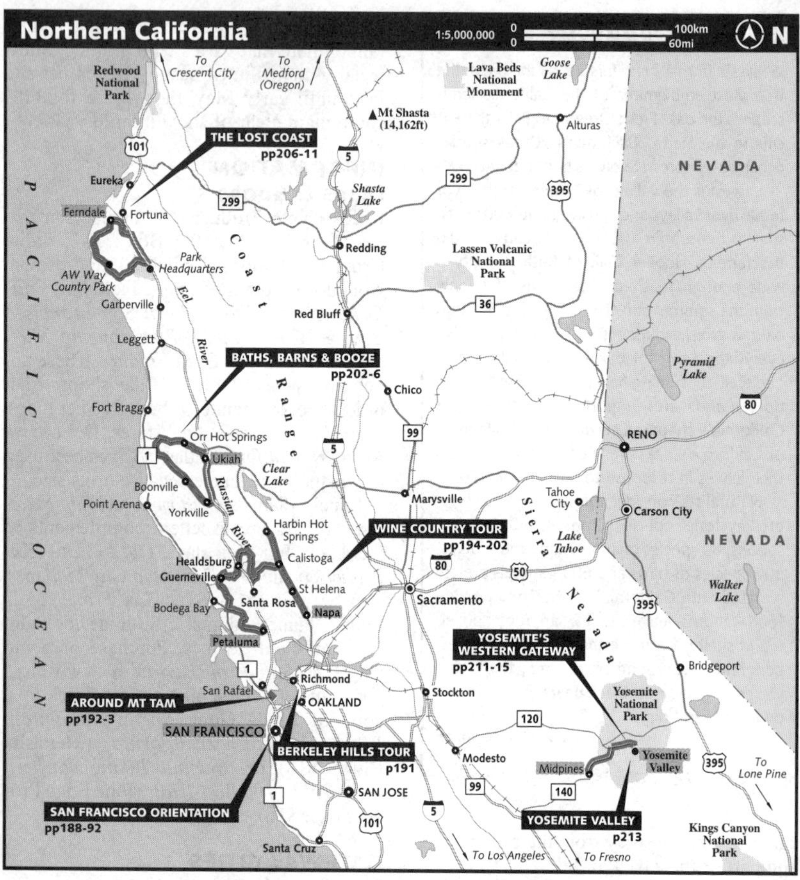

neighborhoods – all compressed into a 7-by-7-mile thumbnail of a peninsula.

While the topography can be intimidating to cyclists, San Francisco is a bike-friendly city that welcomes and respects people on two wheels. A fun city ride (see San Francisco Orientation ride, pp188–92) knocks quite a few 'must-sees' off the list, and there is great riding in Marin Co and the East Bay, both accessible by bike or public transport.

Information The San Francisco visitor center (☎ 391-2000), on the lower level of Hallidie Plaza, corner Market and Powell Sts, is in the heart of the city. Find statewide information and discount coupons at the California Welcome Center (☎ 956-3493), second level, Pier 39, Fisherman's Wharf.

The *San Francisco Street Map & Visitor Guide* is available free at many hotels. The Rand McNally Map Store (☎ 777-3131), corner Market and 2nd Sts, is a good place to pick up maps and guidebooks.

The main post office is the Civic Center Post Office (☎ 800-725-2161), 101 Hyde St.

Most public libraries have Web access; the main branch (☎ 557-4400), corner Larkin and Grove Sts, near the Civic Center BART/Muni station, has 160 terminals. Convenient Internet cafes include Yakety Yak (☎ 885-6908), 679 Sutter St, and Muddy Waters Coffeehouse (☎ 621-2233), 260 Church St.

San Francisco has terrific bike shops, including the Bike Hut (☎ 543-4335) at

Townsend and Embarcadero (Pier 40), a non-profit organization that teaches at-risk youth how to repair bikes and run a small business.

Valencia Cyclery (☎ 550-6601), 1065 Valencia St, Mission District, has a selection of tools available for public use, as does Missing Link Bicycle Cooperative (☎ 510-843-4763), 1988 Shattuck Ave, Berkeley. The Start to Finish shops have a good selection of parts, books and clothing; they're in Upper Haight (☎ 750-4760), 672 Stanyan St; Marina District (☎ 202-9830), 2530 Lombard St; and SoMa (South of Market; ☎ 243-8812), corner 2nd and Brannan Sts.

For rentals, try Avenue Cyclery (☎ 387-3155), corner Stanyan and Waller Sts, near Golden Gate Park in the Upper Haight; or American Bicycle Rental (☎ 931-0234), 2715 Hyde St, Fisherman's Wharf.

Bay Area Roaming Tandems (☎ 759-9413, **W** www.cruzers.com/~glennandpat) is a fun-seeking club that fills its niche well.

Things to See & Do San Francisco's downtown tourist center is **Union Square**, surrounded on all sides by landmark hotels, classy shops and the city's main department stores. Don't miss Maiden Lane, on the east side of the square, and the city's only Frank Lloyd Wright building at No 140. San Francisco's dense **theater district** lies immediately southwest of the square, crumbling from there into dismal Tenderloin.

In a building by Swiss architect Mario Botta, the **San Francisco Museum of Modern Art** (SFMOMA; ☎ 357-4000), 151 3rd St, has particularly strong American abstract expressionist and photography collections. Across 3rd St are the **Yerba Buena Gardens**, including galleries, short-term exhibits and a theater at the Yerba Buena Center for the Arts (☎ 978-2787). Adjacent, **Sony Metreon Entertainment Complex** (☎ 369-6000) is a 350,000-sq-foot high-tech mall with stores, restaurants, 15 movie screens, an IMAX theater and three theme-park attractions.

Nob Hill is a classy district atop one of the city's famous hills. Besides hotels and their top-floor bars, Nob Hill has **Grace Cathedral**, 1100 California St, with bronze doors cast from Ghiberti's Gates of Paradise in Florence, Italy, and a Keith Haring altarpiece.

Chinatown is a great place for casual wandering, soaking up the hectic atmosphere and stumbling across interesting little corners and alleys. A good starting point is the dragon-studded **Chinatown Gate** at the Bush St entrance to Grant Ave.

North Beach started as the city's Italian quarter. The Beats took over in the 1950s, adding jazz clubs, City Lights Bookstore (founded and still owned by poet Lawrence Ferlinghetti) and Vesuvio Cafe (Dylan Thomas and Jack Kerouac's favorite hang-out). It remains one of the liveliest parts of the city, a great place for watching people over a cheap meal, a cold beer or a strong coffee.

Adjacent to North Beach is Telegraph Hill, crowned with one of San Francisco's prime landmarks: the 210ft **Coit Tower** (☎ 362-0808), built in 1934. Inside is a superb series of Diego Rivera–style murals, painted by 25 local artists as part of a 1930s Works Project Administration project. The tower elevator offers no better views than those from below.

For a Japanese-style communal bath, try **Kabuki Hot Springs** (☎ 922-6000), 1750 Geary Blvd, in the heart of Japantown.

Places to Stay No matter where you stay, reservations are a good idea on summer weekends and over holiday periods.

Camping & Budget San Francisco doesn't have any campgrounds convenient to its center. The closest camping is on Angel Island (reached by a Golden Gate Ferry), at ***Pantoll Station*** *(☎ 415-388-2070)* in Mt Tamalpais State Park (see the Around Mt Tam ride, pp192-4); and at ***Battery Alexander*** *(☎ 415-331-1540)* in the Marin Headlands. Within 30mi are the campgrounds at Olema and Montara (see Days 24 and 25 of the Border to Border ride, pp323–8).

The hostel scene, on the other hand, is quite good. Large and well-equipped ***HI San Francisco Downtown*** *(☎ 788-5604, 312 Mason St)* is a stone's throw from Union Square. A bed in a dorm or double rooms costs $16, and bikes can be kept in either.

Near Chinatown, the friendly ***Pacific Tradewinds Guest House*** *(☎ 433-7970, 680 Sacramento St)* is a well-maintained 4th-floor hostel (no elevator) with dorm beds ($16) and a fully equipped kitchen. Bikes are kept in a small but secure hallway. In SoMa, the ***San Francisco International Student Center*** *(☎ 487-1463, 1188 Folsom St)* is an aging hostel with a kitchen, small dorms ($15) and bike storage in the lobby.

The ***Green Tortoise Hostel*** *(☎ 834-1000, 494 Broadway)* has beds in dorms for two to six people ($17), and a few private rooms ($39). They offer free breakfast, kitchen and laundry facilities, and an indoor bike rack.

There's a purpose-built bike room at ***HI Fishermans Wharf*** *(☎ 771-7277)*, in Building 240 at Fort Mason. Beds are $15, and there's a 1am curfew.

Mid-Range Space is at a premium in San Francisco hotels, so you'll have to bring your bike inside your room wherever you go. The following were chosen for their proximity to the Bay Area Rapid Transit system (BART) and relatively flat surroundings. The snug 42-room ***Dakota Hotel*** *(☎ 931-7475, cnr Post & Taylor Sts)*, near Union Square, has small rooms for $79 to $120.

On the edge of the Tenderloin, near Civic Center BART, the ***Phoenix Motel*** *(☎ 776-1380 or ☎ 800-248-9466, 601 Eddy St)* has boxy rooms ($109 to $119, including breakfast) surrounding a swimming pool.

Of three Best Western hotels on 7th St, between Mission and Howard Sts in SoMa, ***Hotel Britton*** *(☎ 621-7001 or ☎ 800-444-5817, 112 7th St)* is cheapest (from $85).

Top End For the quintessential San Francisco experience, spend $389 to $3000 for a room at the opulent ***Westin St Francis*** *(☎ 866-411-4766, 335 Powell St)*, right on Union Square. More fun, intimate and economical are ***Hotel Boheme*** *(☎ 433-9111, 444 Columbus Ave)*, in the heart of North Beach, and ***Hotel Triton*** *(☎ 800-433-6611, 342 Grant Ave)* at the foot of Chinatown's gate. Both have rooms from around $160. For a change of scenery, stay on your own yacht near Fisherman's Wharf. ***Dockside Boat & Bed*** *(☎ 392-5526)* charges $125 to $340 per couple, including a light breakfast. Bikes can stay locked on shore.

Places to Eat It's a crime not to eat well and exotically in this culinary quilt that has more restaurants per capita than any other city in the USA. Among the many Italian eateries in North Beach, ***Molinari*** *(373 Columbus Ave)* remains the best traditional delicatessen (no tables). ***Mario's Bohemian Cigar Store*** *(566 Columbus Ave)* no longer sells cigars but turns out tasty focaccia sandwiches, strong espresso and rich tiramisu. For dinner, ***L'Osteria del Forno*** *(☎ 982-1124, 519 Columbus Ave)* is a real gem – it's romantic, small and run by two pleasant Italian women who craft tasty thin-crust pizzas and sophisticated antipasti (closed Tues).

Chinatown has many haunts for authentic fare but the best for soups and thick Shanghai noodles is ***DPD*** *(cnr Kearny & Jackson Sts)*. On the other end of the spectrum is the elegant ***Empress of China*** *(☎ 434-1345, 838 Grant Ave)*, with its Han Dynasty art, superb

Free & Outdoors in SF

Free outdoor entertainment abounds in San Francisco, especially in summer, when many of the city's big performance companies – and some of its smaller ones – sponsor events in the open air.

On summer Sundays the **Stern Grove Festival** (☎ 252-6252) presents free performances in the Stern Grove Amphitheater, corner Sloat Blvd and 19th Ave, Inner Sunset. The open-air amphitheater is a beautiful spot to enjoy a picnic while listening to the San Francisco Symphony or big-name jazz artists.

One of the city's most popular outdoor events is **Shakespeare in the Park** (☎ 422-2222). Each year one play is performed in parks throughout the Bay Area, and in September it comes to Golden Gate Park.

The second Sunday in September is **Opera in the Park**, also in Golden Gate Park, a noncostumed concert celebrating the opening of the opera season.

The **San Francisco Mime Troupe** (☎ 285-1717 or ☎ 415-285-1720 for schedule information) performs at parks throughout San Francisco and the East Bay all summer. Don't expect any silent, white-faced mimes – this is political musical theater in the *commedia dell'arte* tradition.

For music downtown, the **Noontime Concert Series** (☎ 255-9410) puts on a varied repertoire of free classical music performances in Old St Mary's Church, corner Grant Ave and California St, every Tuesday (donations appreciated). On Fridays during summer there are **lunchtime jazz concerts** in Justin Herman Plaza and, if you prefer the shade, in Redwood Plaza next to the Transamerica building.

Scott McNeely

food and view (full meals cost $15–25). ***Yank Sing*** *(427 Battery St)* is said to have the best dim sum this side of Hong Kong.

If you're here during crab season (mid-Nov–Jun), enjoy Dungeness crab and sourdough bread from a sidewalk stand at ***Fisherman's Wharf***. For a restaurant on the Wharf, you can't beat ***Alioto's*** *(☎ 673-0183, 8 Fisherman's Wharf)*, with great views and entrees from $13 to $20.

The bricolage of cheap eats around Haight St include Cajun/Creole brunch items at ***Crescent City Cafe*** *(1418 Haight St)*; East African, Eritrean and Ethiopian food at ***Massawa*** *(1538 Haight St)*; reasonably priced and *really* good sushi at ***Hama-Ko*** *(108-B Carl St)*, near Cole St; and outstanding Thai at ***Thep Phanom*** *(☎ 431-2526, 400 Waller St)*, near the lower part of Haight St.

In the Mission District, ***Taquería Can-Cun*** *(cnr Mission & 19th Sts)* is one of the most popular purveyors of burritos while the ***Slanted Door*** *(☎ 861-8032, 584 Valencia St)*, near 17th St, is everybody's favorite swank Vietnamese restaurant (entrees $6–14).

A high-end splurge with a view of the Bay Bridge is ***Boulevard*** *(☎ 543-6084, 1 Mission St)*, designed to look like a belle époque Parisian salon. Over at Fort Mason, ***Greens*** *(☎ 771-6222)*, in Building A, is one of the city's best-known vegetarian restaurants with a tremendous view of the Golden Gate Bridge (main meals $9–18).

Getting There & Away BART (☎ 650-992-2278, W www.bart.gov) is a subway system linking San Francisco with the East Bay. In the city, the route runs beneath Market St; the Powell St station is the most convenient to Union Square. Bikes are allowed in any car but the first car of the train and are prohibited from Embarcadero to 16th St/Mission during peak hours (7–9am, 5–6.30pm).

Air The Bay Area's major airports are San Francisco International Airport (SFO), on the west side of the bay, and Oakland airport, a few miles across the bay on the east side. The majority of international flights use SFO; at Oakland 'international' means Mexico and Canada. Both airports are important domestic gateways but travelers from other US (particularly West Coast) cities may find cheaper flights into Oakland, a hub for discount airlines such as Southwest.

A Burrito Primer

California is famous for its spa cuisine, the kind that looks pretty on the plate but leaves both the stomach and pocketbook empty. Cyclists should ignore the advice of California 'foodies', eschew the advertisements in airline magazines and turn their ravenous attention to *real* California Cuisine: the burrito.

The flour tortilla may have originated in Sonora, Mexico (where maize was scarce), but its purpose evolved as it spread north. When it reached California in the 19th century, Mexican agricultural laborers were utilizing its glutinous flexibility to create self-contained, easily transported rice-and-bean lunches.

Today's burritos are much more complex. San Francisco's Mission District is famous for its bulging burritos of rice, beans, grilled meat, salsa, guacamole and sour cream in a flour tortilla wrapped in aluminum foil. When eating a Mission-style burrito, remember the old adage: never eat anything bigger than your head.

Burritos in Los Angeles, and southwards, tend to be more true to the original form: beans, cheese and meat wrapped in a tortilla, often served 'wet' with a rich red sauce and copious amounts of cheese melted over the top. In San Diego, burritos may be stuffed with grilled shrimp or fish and shredded cabbage.

Creative taquerías offer tofu and sautéed vegies, and black or whole pinto beans along with the usual refried variety. In most places, one $3 to $5 burrito is often more food than a single person can chow down in a sitting.

Don't attempt riding from either airport – it's not particularly attractive and involves busy roads. Instead, keep your bike in its box and take a door-to-door shuttle.

American Airporter Shuttle (☎ 546-6689) and Lorrie's (☎ 334-9000) charge $5 extra for a bike and Quake City (☎ 255-4899) charges $10 extra; they all charge a base fare of around $13 between SFO and downtown. Super Shuttle (☎ 558-8500) charges $50 one way ($13 without a bike).

Economizers can take SamTrans (☎ 800-660-4287) express bus No 3X ($1) from SFO to reach the Colma BART station. From here BART trains go to downtown San Francisco. The bus holds two bikes on a front rack and two inside.

From Oakland, Bayporter Express (☎ 467-1800 or ☎ 877-467-1800) charges $25 to downtown San Francisco, $18 to Berkeley, plus $5 for a boxed bike.

Bus All bus services arrive at and depart from the Transbay Terminal (☎ 495-1575), corner Mission and 1st Sts, two blocks south of Market St. Locally, AC Transit (☎ 510-839-2882) operates buses to the East Bay while Golden Gate Transit (☎ 932-2000) buses go north to Marin and Sonoma counties.

Greyhound Lines (☎ 800-231-2222, W www.greyhound.com) has multiple buses daily to Los Angeles (LA; $35), Portland ($55), Seattle ($55) and other destinations.

Train Amtrak (☎ 800-872-7245) trains stop at Emeryville station, on the east side of the Bay between Berkeley and Oakland. From here service continues to San Francisco (the Ferry Building, Transbay Terminal or SFO) by bus. The bus fare is incorporated into the Amtrak ticket. Daily connections operate between San Francisco and Seattle ($130), Portland ($104) and LA (via Bakersfield; $63), with connecting trains to points all over the USA.

San Francisco Bay Area

The Bay Area offers great riding, most of it north of the Golden Gate Bridge in Marin and east of the Bay Bridge in the East Bay (Berkeley/Oakland) hills. Part of the fun is getting to the rides, on BART or by ferry. After finishing the rides listed here, check with local bike shops or pick up Ray Hosler's *Bay Area Bike Rides* for more.

San Francisco Orientation

Duration	4–6 hours
Distance	29.8mi
Difficulty	easy–moderate
Start/End	SF Ferry Building
Cues	p367

In a city as compact as San Francisco, 30mi covers just about every corner of the city. Except for the *really* hilly 'hoods of Russian Hill and Nob Hill, and the exceptionally

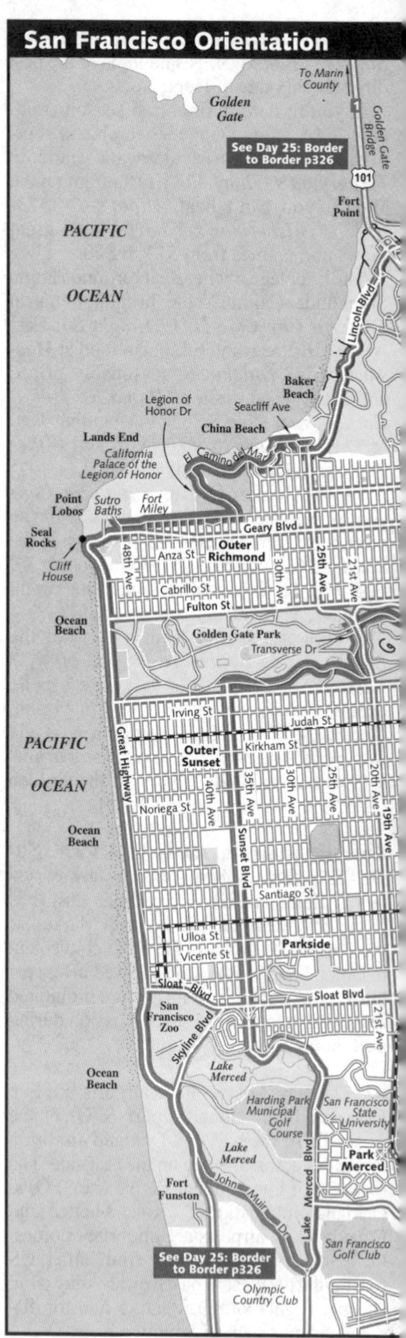

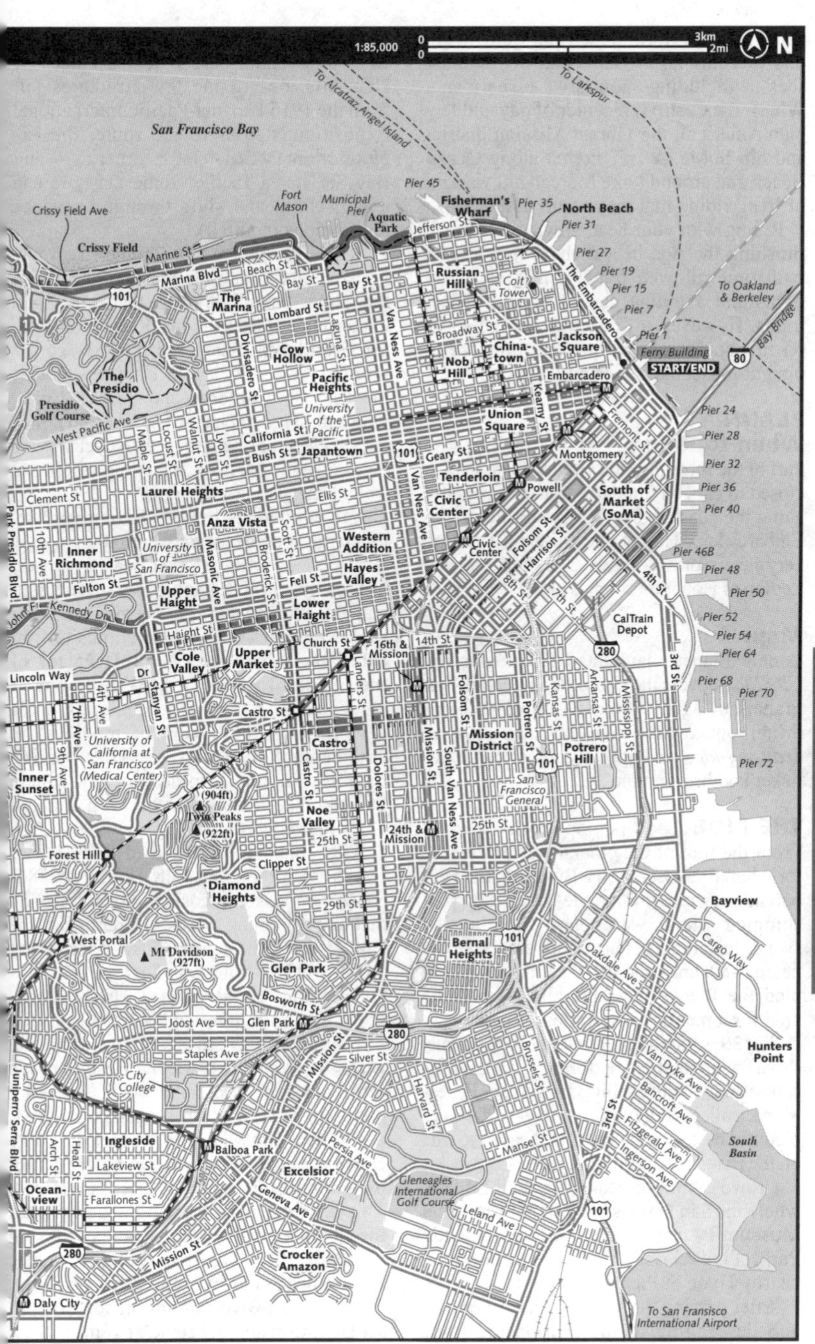

NORTHERN CALIFORNIA

dense areas of North Beach and Chinatown, this ride hits all of San Francisco's 'must sees', including touristy Fisherman's Wharf, the Castro (epicenter of gay and lesbian America), the vibrant Mission district and hip SoMa. A 7mi stretch along Ocean Beach and around Lake Merced allows a bit of 'real' riding that may result in a sweat.

Riding with your head down could mean finishing the ride in less than three hours, with time allowed for stopping at traffic lights and avoiding car doors and pedestrians. However, a full day could be spent on this socio-cultural *tour de force*, stopping at museums, shops and pubs.

PLANNING

When to Ride

Part of the route through Golden Gate Park is closed to cars on Sundays, though car traffic along the coast and pedestrian traffic on the Embarcadero, Haight and Castro Sts can be very heavy on weekends. The Palace of the Legion of Honor museum is closed Mondays.

Maps

Lonely Planet's laminated *San Francisco City Map* covers the entire ride in detail. San Francisco Muni (W www.transitinfo.org/Muni) puts out the excellent *Muni Street & Transit Map*, available at stores, cable car ticket booths or online.

THE RIDE (See Map, pp188–9)

From the foot of the clocktower of the historic San Francisco Ferry Building, the Embarcadero wraps around the waterfront, past shipping piers, warehouses and a few swank restaurants. This entire area was beneath I-80 until the 1989 earthquake toppled the freeway and literally opened the area for a massive restoration project.

Pier 39 is the focus of touristy Fisherman's Wharf, with its street performers, boats to Alcatraz and vendors selling fresh crab. Pedestrians, roller skaters and skateboarders are plentiful here so you may find it easier to ride on the road; be careful of the streetcar tracks.

Crowds thin out near Ghiradelli Square, where the **San Francisco National Maritime Museum** (☎ 556-8177) overlooks Aquatic Park. Five classic ships are moored at nearby Hyde St Pier.

After passing through part of Fort Mason and descending to the Marina the route heads straight towards the Golden Gate. A worthy deviation here is to the **Palace of Fine Arts**, one of the few structures left from the 1915 Panama-Pacific International Exposition. Closer to the route, the **Exploratorium** (☎ 561-0360), corner Lyon and Bay Sts, has a Tactile Dome that you can crawl, climb and slide through (advance reservations required).

Before the foot of the bridge, the route turns uphill through the **Presidio**, a Spanish then American military base that is now part of the Golden Gate National Recreation Area. The **Presidio Museum** (☎ 561-4331), corner Funston Ave and Lincoln Blvd, documents the history of California and the West Coast, with a military emphasis. The Presidio police are sticklers for giving tickets to cyclists who don't obey traffic laws, including coming to a complete stop at stop signs.

A tight bit along Lincoln Blvd gives way to a large shoulder from which to enjoy the cliff-top views above **Baker Beach**, prettiest of the city's beaches and popular with sunbathers. After a jaunt past the million-dollar homes of Seacliff, the route climbs to Lincoln Park, where the **California Palace of the Legion of Honor** (☎ 863-3330), one of San Francisco's premier art museums, holds a world-class collection of medieval to 20th-century European art. After visiting the museum, the steep descent of Clement St looks like it's straight out of a Richard Diebenkorn painting.

After rounding the bend of Point Lobos you'll reach the 1863 **Cliff House** (☎ 386-3330), famous for its cocktail-hour views and memorabilia-hung walls. Underneath the Cliff House is the superb **Musée Mécanique** (☎ 386-1170), with a collection of early-20th-century arcade games, risqué Mutoscope motion pictures and player pianos.

There's a bikepath along the wind and wave swept shores of Ocean Beach but it's often covered with sand; cyclists usually prefer the road, which has a generous shoulder. Where Great Hwy turns east the route encounters a few busy roads before wrapping around the south end of Lake Merced. This reservoir is neither an integral part of the city or a terribly scenic spot but the 7mi bikepath offers carefree riding. (Cut the extra mileage out by turning left off Great Hwy on Sloat Blvd and turning left on Sunset Blvd to rejoin the route at 18mi.)

The route follows a (bumpy) bikepath along Sunset Blvd to **Golden Gate Park**, which stretches almost halfway across San Francisco's 7mi-wide peninsula. Riding through this mega-park is extremely enjoyable, and the attractions within (gardens, lakes, sporting facilities and a host of outstanding museums) are worth a day in themselves. Park information, including a detailed map ($2.25), is available from McLaren Lodge (☎ 831-2700) at the park entrance at Fell and Stanyan Sts.

The route re-enters the urban landscape with gusto, cruising through the **Haight-Ashbury** area, known locally as 'the Haight'. During the heady years around (and including) the Summer of Love, the neighborhood was populated with musicians such as the Grateful Dead, Jefferson Airplane and Janis Joplin. Heavy (but slow) traffic, and a wild variety of shops and people, could be distracting enough that you may want to walk.

A short ride on Divisadero takes you to **The Castro**, a similarly dense scene with an entirely different cast of characters. 'Cruising the Castro' has nothing to do with bicycles and everything to do with human eye candy.

On 18th St, the route passes Mission Dolores Park and enters what is known as the **Mission District**, one of the city's oldest. Until recently it was a primarily Spanish-speaking enclave. Gentrification is evident but it remains a colorful neighborhood of thrift stores, taquerías, funky bars and murals.

Berkeley Hills Tour

This easy tour provides a great way to incorporate a ride, and stunning views of the Bay Area, into a day exploring Telegraph Ave, where the Free Speech movement of the 1960s was born. The ride starts at the North Berkeley BART station, heads up into Tilden Regional Park and descends past the Lawrence Hall of Science to UC Berkeley campus and its botanic gardens. The best map for this ride is *A Rambler's Guide to the Trails of the East Bay Hills* (Olmstead Bros Map Co; ☎ 415-658-4869). The ride is possible year-round, though rain could make the descent pretty hairy.

The Ride

1–1½ hours, 9mi

Emerge from the North Berkeley BART station on its east (uphill) side and turn right to go to Hearst Ave. Take Hearst Ave east (towards the hills) for 0.5mi to Shattuck Ave and turn left. Berkeley's 'gourmet ghetto', on Shattuck Ave between Cedar and Rose Sts, is home to a wonderful array of artisan shops and restaurants – from Alice Waters' ***Chez Panisse*** *(1517 Shattuck Ave)*, birthplace of 'California Cuisine', to the collectively owned ***Cheeseboard*** *(1504 Shattuck Ave)*, which sells a variety of cheeses and bakes delicious breads and pastries.

Turn right on Rose St and left on Spruce St to begin a 2mi ascent. At the top of Spruce St, continue straight, on redwood-lined Wildcat Canyon Rd, into Tilden Regional Park.

In 1.7mi, a restroom and water fountain precede the Brazil Building, originally built for the 1939 World's Fair. Turn right here onto Shasta Rd for a short but very steep climb up to Golf Course Rd. Turn left to pass the golf course and climb 0.8mi, out of the park, to Grizzly Peak Blvd.

Continue straight onto Centennial Dr, which quickly begins a steep descent to the **Lawrence Hall of Science** (☎ 510-642-5132), an interactive children's science museum with a wonderful view of San Francisco and Mt Tamalpais. After a vertigo-inducing dive of 1.2mi, you'll reach the **University Botanic Garden** (☎ 510-642-3343). The ride levels off through the remainder of Strawberry Canyon to where it meets Stadium Rim Way at Memorial Stadium, UC Berkeley's elegant football stadium.

Turn left, then right and left again on Warring St to wind past sororities and fraternities for 0.3mi. At Dwight Way, turn right and descend to Telegraph Ave. Get off your bike to explore the pedestrian-heavy zone lined with bookstores, cafes, music shops and streetside craft vendors. ***Raleigh's*** *(2438 Telegraph Ave)* is an excellent place for a beer, game of pool or pub meal.

Take Telegraph Ave north 0.4mi to where it runs into the UC Berkeley campus at Bancroft Ave. To reach the Downtown Berkeley BART station, turn left on Bancroft Ave and descend to Shattuck Ave, where you'll see the station's entrance. The more scenic route is through the lovely UC Berkeley campus whose 328ft **Campanile** (officially named Sather Tower) is modeled on St Mark's Basilica in Venice.

In the home stretch, the route turns off Mission St and heads through the **South of Market** (SoMa) district along Folsom St. This hotbed of Internet industry is a little bleak for passers through, though new cafes and restaurants are sprouting like wild weeds. A final turn towards **Pac Bell Park** leads back to the Embarcadero to finish the loop after passing under the Bay Bridge.

Around Mt Tam

Duration	4–6 hours
Distance	35.1mi
Difficulty	moderate–hard
Start/End	Ferry terminal, Larkspur
Cues	p367

This circuit of Mt Tamalpais (lovingly referred to as Mt Tam) is the Bay Area's ultimate escape from the city. The mountain's broad shoulders and noble cap dominate most views of the Bay Area but from the fringes of her skirt Mt Tam is ever elusive. Instead, the focus is on Marin County's quaint towns, stands of redwoods that shade moisture-loving ferns and moss, and a ridgeline that seems to float between the Pacific Ocean and San Francisco Bay.

One-third of the ride is relatively flat while the rest is a succession of real climbs and smaller hills. There's ample opportunity to feed and hydrate at the early and late stages of the ride, with an undeveloped stretch of land in the middle, tended by Marin Municipal Water District and Mt Tamalpais State Park.

PLANNING

Maps

AAA's *Marin County* or *San Francisco Bay Region* maps cover the route well. For maximum topographic detail, buy *A Rambler's Guide to the Trails of Mt Tamalpais & the Marin Headlands* ($4; Olmstead & Bros Map Co; ☎ 510-658-6534).

GETTING TO/FROM THE RIDE

The Golden Gate Ferry (☎ 923-2000 from SF or ☎ 455-2000 from Marin) leaves from behind the San Francisco Ferry Building, corner The Embarcadero and Market St (one hour, $3 weekdays, $5 weekends).

Bus riders will have to join the ride in Mill Valley, which still makes for a pleasant route. Golden Gate Transit bus No 10 goes from downtown San Francisco – the Civic Center, corner Polk & McAllister Sts, and Transbay Terminal, corner Mission & 1st Sts – to downtown Mill Valley from 7am to 7pm daily (1½ hours, $2.35).

THE RIDE

The introduction to this route is a study in contrasts: the bikepath follows a finger of the Corte Madera Ecological Reserve, crossed by freeway overpasses and flanked by planned waterfront communities of South Marin. Contemplate Mt Tam as you approach Magnolia Ave and get a taste of Marin County living at ***Woodlands Market*** (2.6mi), in the small community of **Kentfield**. The Village Peddler (2.4mi; ☎ 461-3091), 1161 Magnolia Ave, has a small repair and retail shop that sells maps.

Heading counterclockwise around the mountain, the route changes names many times as it follows small streets parallel to Sir Francis Drake Blvd, the primary traffic artery. Most of the little towns here were once railway stops on a line that ran from Mill Valley to the coast. The bigger ones, such as **Ross** and **San Anselmo**, have stately old homes and a wealth of antique stores, fine ***restaurants*** and ***cafes*** in their one-block centers.

Reaching Fairfax (6.5mi) is a highlight for most, since ***Fairfax Coffee Roasters*** *(☎ 451-1825)* has outstanding coffee and pastries. This popular pre-ride gathering spot also signifies where the route turns southwest and starts to climb up Fairfax-Bolinas Rd.

Traffic can be busy between Fairfax and the **Meadow Club** golf course, but cars are generally used to cyclists around here. In the distance, to the right, are White Hill and (just out of sight) Repack Hill – the grassy ridge and knob where some of the country's first mountain-bike rides took place (see the boxed text 'Mountain Biking in the USA', p42).

The route passes a trailhead for the **Pine Mtn Loop** (10.2mi), another legendary Mt Tam mountain-bike ride; across the route is a short walking trail to a scenic viewpoint.

The watery fingers of **Alpine Lake** become visible as the route begins a rolling downhill towards the lake's northern edge.

A few hairpin turns and dappled sunlight necessitate caution, but otherwise there's nothing but pleasure until reaching the Alpine Dam. Hikers park at the far side of the bridge for the **Cataract Trail** – a 3mi footpath flanked by waterfalls.

A steep, serpentine climbs takes you from lake level to the intersection with West Ridgecrest Blvd. At the intersection, which is *not* the end of the climb but is a popular rest point, trailheads lead to Bolinas and Stinson Beach. From here the route follows an exposed ridgeline. Below, at sea level, is the town of **Bolinas** – a funky artists community known for continually removing all road signs pointing to it.

Just off Pan Toll Rd (20.6mi), where the route begins its descent towards Mill Valley, is the **Mountain Theater**, an outdoor amphitheater used for summer concerts and Shakespearean fests. If you've not had your fill of climbing, follow East Ridgecrest Blvd (left) for a 1.2mi, 262ft ascent to a parking lot at Mt Tam's east peak.

Pan Toll Rd swings left (northeast) at the **Pan Toll Ranger Station**, with maps and information, water and bathrooms. About 3mi further, the ***Mountain Home Inn*** offers hot meals, lodging and a cozy atmosphere.

Turning off Panoramic Hwy (26.6mi) leads to the steep streets above **Mill Valley**, where the route changes names several times but follows an obvious downhill flow. At Miller Ave the route goes right to pass ***Whole Foods Market***, which has a fabulous deli, coffee and salad bar; going left on Miller Ave will take you (0.25mi) to downtown Mill Valley, an old logging town that's worth a visit. You'll find the ***Depot Bookstore & Cafe*** *(☎ 383-2665, 87 Throckmorton Ave)* at the hub of Mill Valley activity.

The route from Mill Valley involves one short climb and some zig-zagging through Corte Madera before a bikepath leads back to **Larkspur**. Larkspur's two-block downtown includes the Parisian bistro atmosphere of the ***Left Bank*** *(☎ 927-3331, 507 Magnolia Ave)* and the famed ***Red Boy Pizza*** *(☎ 453-3138)*, in the shopping center, corner Magnolia Ave and Doherty Dr. From here it's an easy ramble back to Bon Air and the bikepath that returns to the ferry landing.

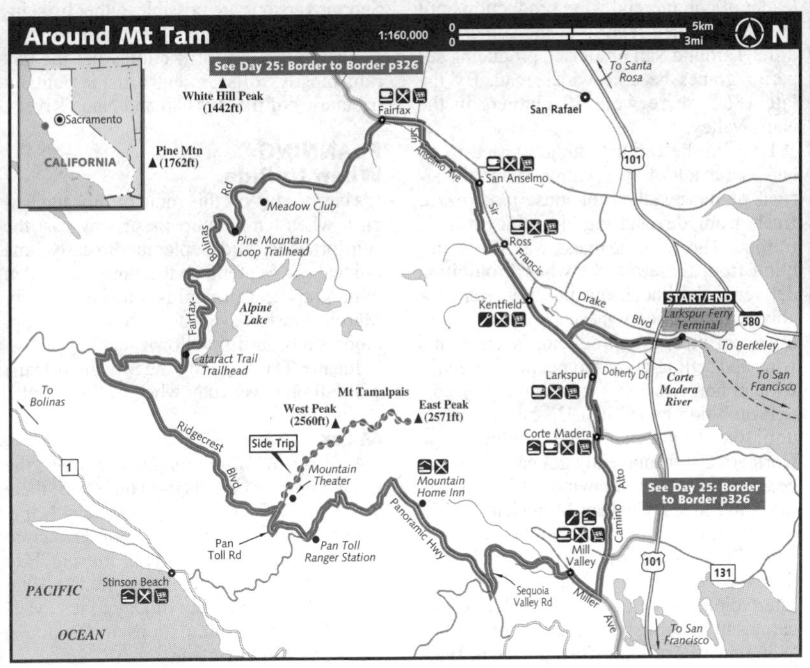

Wine Country

Most of California's wine comes from the heavily agricultural Central Valley. But the wines that have put California on the connoisseur's map, even caused the French and Italians to give hearty, if envious, approval, are those produced in the parallel Napa and Sonoma Valleys. This is where, back in the 1970s, California's independent wineries began creating award-winning vintages that quickly garnered worldwide acclaim.

Besides the rustic beauty of vineyards, wildflowers and green and golden hills, the Wine Country offers Spanish and Mexican history, mud baths and spas at Calistoga, and literary connections with Robert Louis Stevenson and Jack London.

HISTORY

Early Spanish and Mexican settlers began producing wine in the Napa and Sonoma Valleys. But it was Hungarian Count Agoston Haraszthy who started the modern wine business in 1857, when he began cultivating grapes in Sonoma Valley. LA remained the leader of commercial wine production until the 1860s, when reports of the cooler conditions around San Francisco producing superior grapes became widespread. By the late 1860s there were 50 vintners in the Napa Valley.

Later in the century things started to go bad as a result of cheap imports and the arrival of the deadly root louse *phylloxera*, fresh from devastating the vineyards of Europe. The wine business was still stumbling from these attacks when Prohibition delivered the knock-out in 1919. Remarkably, a handful of wineries somehow continued in business, producing sacramental wine and selling grapes to people who made wine at home, which Prohibition allowed.

Prohibition ended in 1933 but it was not until the 1960s that wine production in Northern California really got back into high gear. In 1976 at a blind wine-tasting competition in France, Chateau Montelena's 1973 chardonnay and a 1973 cabernet sauvignon from Stag's Leap outscored French Bordeaux wines – putting Napa Valley on the international wine map. In 1981 'Napa' became an established appellation, while 'Sonoma' was officially recognized in 1983.

INFORMATION

Books

Frommer's *Portable California Wine Country* is a compact edition with useful information about wine tasting and individual wineries, plus lengthy coverage of restaurants.

Wine Country Tour

Duration	6 days
Distance	209.9mi
Difficulty	easy–moderate
Start	Petaluma
End	Napa
Cues	pp367–8

This near-circuitous route rolls through green dairylands, traverses the redwood-heavy Russian River resort area, spends a day among lesser-known vineyards of the Alexander Valley and overnights at a 'clothing optional' hot springs before descending to (and through) the fabled Napa Valley. Mileage is short on most days, allowing time to tipple and saunter through historic towns. Shorter versions are possible, either by skipping sections or using public transport.

There are a few stiff climbs but the terrain mostly rolls among hillsides cut by tributaries of the Russian and Napa Rivers.

PLANNING

When to Ride

It's best to stay off this route in July and August, when temperatures soar way past the comfort zone. Mid-September to early June is ideal. In September the vines are laden with grapes; from mid-January to early March mustard, used as a cover crop, blooms a beautiful yellow.

Ideally, Day 6 (along the Silverado Trail) will fall on a weekday when traffic is light.

Maps

AAA's *Bay & Mountain Section* covers the route, minus two roads used on Day 5; there are AAA offices in Petaluma and Napa. Krebs Cycle Products' *North San Francisco Bay & Wine Country Bicycle Touring Map* details all of the route except the last 10mi of Day 4 and first 23mi of Day 5; it's available ($10.95) at bike shops in Petaluma, Calistoga and St Helena.

GETTING TO/FROM THE RIDE

Greyhound buses stop in Calistoga and St Helena for those who wish to alter or shorten the route.

Petaluma

Golden Gate Transit bus No 80 runs daily between downtown San Francisco and Petaluma's central bus depot, corner 4th and C Sts ($5); bus No 74 runs northbound in the evening and southbound in the morning (Mon–Fri).

Taking Greyhound from San Francisco will mean a late start – buses arrive in Petaluma at 2pm and 11.30pm ($10). Amtrak runs five buses per day from the Martinez station to Petaluma ($9), with the earliest arriving at 11am. The stop for Amtrak and Greyhound buses is Petaluma's City Library, 0.8mi east of downtown Petaluma via Washington St To reach Walnut Park, turn left out of the library parking lot and left on Petaluma Blvd.

Napa

Napa's Transit Center is at the corner of Pearl and Main Sts, next to Mervyn's in the Napa Town Center outdoor shopping mall; there is a ticket booth but no indoor waiting area. From the Transit Center, VINE (☎ 707-255-7631) buses run through the Napa Valley (stopping at Calistoga, St Helena and other towns along Hwy 29), and to the Vallejo Ferry terminal ($1.50) from where Baylink ferries (☎ 877-643-3779) connect to the San Francisco Ferry Building ($8).

Amtrak buses run daily from Napa's Wine Train Station, 1275 McKinstry St, two blocks east of Main St via First St, to Amtrak's Martinez station ($8), with connections to downtown San Francisco.

THE RIDE (See Map, p196)

Petaluma

☎ 707

On US 101, 38mi north of San Francisco, Petaluma is a funky old town surrounded by rich dairylands that have been its economic mainstay since the late 1800s. The small downtown of brick buildings, from around 1900, is flush with cafes and restaurants. It's a convenient launch pad for cyclists but not a town that people go out of their way to visit.

Information The Historical Library & Museum (☎ 778-4398), corner 4th and B Sts, is the best source of information. Banks, restaurants and shops are concentrated within a few blocks along Kentucky St and Petaluma Blvd (north-south), Washington St and Western Ave (east-west).

The Bicycle Factory (☎ 763-7515), 110 Kentucky St, is a good repair shop.

Places to Stay & Eat Campers can ride 3.8mi north from downtown along Stony Point Rd to the ***KOA Camping Resort*** *(☎ 763-1492, 20 Rainsville Rd)*, where tent sites cost $31.

The best cheap motel in town is ***Casa Grande Motel*** *(☎ 762-8881, 307 Petaluma Blvd S)*, with $65 rooms. Other options are not as good when arriving by bike because they're near the highway, north of downtown on the east side of US 101. In a pinch, try ***Motel 6*** *(☎ 765-0333, 1368 N Mcdowell Blvd)*, with rooms from $57, and ***Quality Inn*** *(☎ 664-1155, 5100 Montero Way)*, with rooms from $88.

Petaluma Market *(210 Western Ave)* has a full selection. For a deli sandwich ($5) or pasta dinner ($8), try the cozy ***La Famiglia Deli Cafe*** *(220 Western Ave)*. ***Aram's*** *(131 Kentucky St)* serves breakfast for under $5, plus big Mediterranean-influenced lunches for around $7. ***Cotija's*** *(330 Western Ave)* is said to have the most authentic Mexican food ($5) but you'll have to go to ***Velasco's*** *(190 Kentucky Ave)* for a margarita with your meal ($10).

Day 1: Petaluma to Guerneville

6–7 hours, 45.9mi

This day starts in the broad, grass-blanketed dairylands outside Petaluma and ends on the thickly forested banks of the Russian River. Start early enough on this longish route for a dip in the river when you arrive in Guerneville.

Ascending out of Petaluma, the route quickly leaves suburbia behind. The Pacific Ocean is around 10mi west, but you'd never know because farm smells are much stronger than any ocean breeze.

A 2mi stretch along the Tomales-Petaluma Rd can be busy but has a good shoulder and smooth pavement. The first sign of life you see may be in **Valley Ford** (27.5mi), founded as a dairy and cattle center in 1893. Here the ***Valley Ford Market*** acts as 'town central' and has an adequate

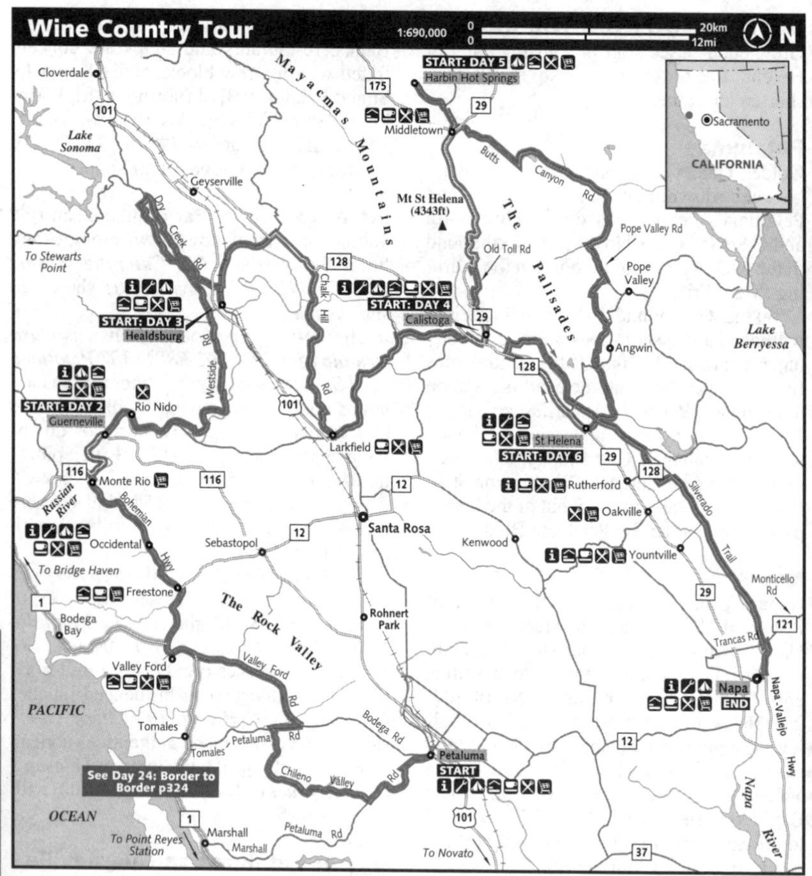

deli section, plus burritos and fresh produce. The ***Valley Ford Hotel*** (☎ *876-3600*) offers lodging ($55–98) and full meals, while the ***Route 1 Diner*** serves $6 burgers.

After a stint on busy Hwy 1 (Valley Ford Rd), the route takes smaller, narrower roads. Berry bushes and willow are thick along the Valley Ford-Freestone Rd, which parallels Ebabias Creek before climbing to meet Bodega Hwy; pavement is uneven here, and there's no shoulder.

The hamlet of **Freestone** (32.1mi) has an unlikely but wonderful reason to stop: ***Wildflour Bread*** (closed Tues–Thurs). This bakery uses all organic ingredients and wood-burning brick ovens for its whimsical breads. Tasting is encouraged and there's a picnic table out back.

North of Freestone, the Bohemian Hwy climbs a narrow and twisting path through redwood trees to **Occidental** (35.7mi). Founded as a logging town in the 1850s, this is a good place to stay if Guerneville seems too far. Besides a market and several small restaurants, ***Negri's*** (☎ *823-5301*) and the ***Union Hotel*** (☎ *874-3555*) both serve Italian dinners and offer historic rooms for around $65.

Take caution on the last 10mi, along the busy and narrow Bohemian Hwy through thick forests of redwood, pine and fir. Numerous church-affiliated summer camps line the road, and just before **Monte Rio** (41.8mi) is a turn-off to the Bohemian Grove, annual pow-wow grounds for political and industrial big-wigs. The ride ends at the main intersection in Guerneville, corner Hwy 116 and Armstrong Woods Rd.

Guerneville

☎ 707

The Russian River begins in the mountains north of Ukiah and flows south, making a sharp turn west towards the ocean just south of Healdsburg. It's this area of the lower river that is known as the Russian River resort area. Laid-back and very open, Guerneville (population 7300) is the area's hub. The Russian River chamber of commerce (☎ 869-9000) is at 16209 1st St (open Mon–Fri 10am–5pm, Sat 11am–4pm). Use the Internet at Coffee Bazaar (see Places to Eat).

Locals come to shop or partake in the many live performances (music, theater etc) held throughout the summer. Visitors come to explore the only grove of virgin redwoods in this area at **Armstrong Redwoods State Reserve**, 2.5mi north of town on Armstrong Woods Rd. There's a $5 fee to drive into the park but cyclists enter free – the grove of giant trees is right near the entrance.

Playing in the **river** is popular too. Rent a canoe, paddle boat or inner tube at Johnson's Beach (☎ 869-2022) at the river end of Church St downtown.

Places to Stay Camping at ***Austin Creek State Recreation Area*** (part of Armstrong Redwoods State Reserve) costs $5 for cyclists but the campground is 3.5mi and 1000ft up from the reserve entrance, 2.5mi north of town. A better option near the Reserve is ***Faerie Ring Campground*** *(☎ 869-2746, 16747 Armstrong Woods Rd)*, 1.5mi from town. On the Day 2 route are the well-shaded ***Schoolhouse Canyon Campground*** *(☎ 869-2311, 12600 River Rd)*, 3.5mi east of town; and, next to one another, ***Riverbend Campground*** *(☎ 887-7662, 11820 River Rd)* and ***Hilton Park Campground*** *(☎ 887-9206)*, both on the river 4.3mi from town. Sites at all four campgrounds cost $15 to $18.

Fife's *(☎ 869-0656, 16467 River Rd)* is an attractive 'mostly gay' resort right on the river, with $75/89 singles/doubles. ***Johnson's Beach Resort*** *(☎ 869-2022, 16241 1st St)* has beach access and a variety of lodging options, from $50 motel rooms to $175 cabins that sleep six. ***Riverlane Resort*** *(☎ 869-2323, 16320 1st St)* has family-style cabins on the river for $63 to $120.

Ridenhour Ranch House Inn *(☎ 887-1033 or ☎ 888-877-4466, 12850 River Rd)* is beside Korbel winery 2.8mi along the Day 2 route. It has lovely rooms with private bath and breakfast for $95/105.

Places to Eat A ***Safeway*** supermarket is at the corner of Hwy 116 (River Rd) and Mill St. ***Coffee Bazaar*** *(14045 Armstrong Woods Rd)* is a popular spot for coffee, baked goods and Internet service.

Hub Cap Cafe & Deli *(16337 Main St)* serves home-cooked meals until late for under $10. ***Main Street Station*** *(16280 Main St)*, has pizza, sandwiches and salads, and live jazz several nights a week.

For fine dining, make reservations at the ***Applewood Restaurant*** *(☎ 869-9093, 13555 Hwy 116)*, across the Guerneville Bridge at the Applewood Inn.

Day 2: Guerneville to Healdsburg

3–6 hours, 34.6mi

This easy day follows the Russian River north (upstream) from Guerneville through the newly chic wine region west of Healdsburg. There are no services en route, so leave Guerneville with the day's food supply (you can get water and snacks from wineries). The small farm roads are rarely flat.

You've barely left Guerneville when the wine tasting begins. **Korbel Champagne Cellars** (2.8mi) offers free tours of its grandiose facility, which produces some of America's most well-known, if not highly lauded, sparkling wine. After joining Westside Dr (5.2mi), a very steep 0.1mi section takes you out of the redwoods and into a landscape of oak, madrona and bay trees.

Davis Bynum Winery (9.8mi) makes highly touted zinfandel and chardonnay. **Rochioli Vineyards & Winery** (11.6mi) is said to have the most sought after pinot noir vines in the USA, likened to the best of Burgundy. Neighboring **Hop Kiln Winery** (11.8mi), housed in a hops-drying barn built in 1905, is worth a visit even if tasting isn't on the agenda. **Rabbit Ridge** (14.8mi) has a picnic area and produces unusual (for California) wines such as marsanne, sangiovese, dolcetto, barbera and grenache.

After Rabbit Ridge, the road widens and drops to the valley floor as it approaches the main turnoff for Healdsburg at 16.9mi. West Dry Creek Rd is primarily a farm road used by vintners. Alongside the vineyards are beautiful old homes and apple and pear orchards. Vines on the west side of this valley are said to produce wines rich with blackberry and raspberry flavors; those on the east side have more prominent plum and currant flavors. **Quivira Vineyards** (22.3mi) is among the best of Dry Creek Valley wineries, especially known for zinfandel.

The route along the valley's west side is more heavily traveled but there is a good shoulder and fine pavement all the way.

Healdsburg

☎ 707

This friendly town continues to grow, and become more sophisticated, as its surrounding wineries attract more visitors each year. The heart of town is Spanish-style Healdsburg Plaza; a fun place for browsing, having a coffee or catching free entertainment on weekends. In mid-July, cyclists converge here to begin the Healdsburg Harvest Century Bicycle Tour and its preceding bike expo.

Healdsburg's visitor center (☎ 433-6935) is a block south of the plaza at 217 Healdsburg Ave. Healdsburg Spoke Folk Cyclery (☎ 433-7171), 249 Center St, has knowledgeable staff and a good selection.

Visit the **Healdsburg Museum** (☎ 431-3325), 221 Matheson St, for a walking-tour map of historic homes or to see exhibits on northern Sonoma County history, including Pomo and Wappo Native American tribes (open Tues–Sun 11am–4pm).

Places to Stay At 2.4mi on the Day 3 route, the ***Alexander Valley Campground*** *(☎ 433-7247 or ☎ 800-640-1386, 2411 Alexander Valley Rd)*, operated by WC 'Bob' Trowbridge Canoe Trips, has 75 campsites on the bank of the Russian River, for $8 per person.

An extra 15mi north, there are tent sites for $27 at the ***Cloverdale Wine Country KOA*** *(☎ 894-3337 or ☎ 800-368-4558, 26460 River Rd)*.

Older motels a few blocks south of the plaza include the ***Fairview Motel*** *(☎ 433-5548, 74 Healdsburg Ave)* with rooms for $50 to $85; and the ***L&M Motel*** *(☎ 433-6528, 70 Healdsburg Ave)* with rooms from $63. On the north edge of town, the ***Healdsburg Travelodge*** *(☎ 433-0101 or ☎ 800-499-0103, 178 Dry Creek Rd)* charges $89/109 weekday/weekend.

A nice B&B in town is the ***Healdsburg Inn on the Plaza*** *(☎ 433-6991 or ☎ 800-431-8663, 110 Matheson St)* with rooms from $155.

Places to Eat Construct a picnic at the ***Oakville Grocery*** *(124 Matheson St)* on the southeast corner of Healdsburg Plaza. Its pastries and coffee are a big hit in the morning. More utilitarian is the ***Safeway*** *(1115 Vine St)*.

South of the plaza, the ***Singletree Inn*** *(165 Healdsburg Ave)* serves pancakes, eggs, burgers and other breakfast and lunch items for under $10. ***Bistro Ralph*** *(109 Plaza St)* is a casual but elegant little place on the plaza, serving lunch ($8) on weekdays and dinner ($10–15) every night. A block north of the plaza, ***Ravenous*** *(117 North St)*, beside the Raven Theater, is very popular for its eclectic, mostly organic lunches ($6–10) and dinners (around $12). Join locals for a steak at the ***Western Boot Steakhouse*** *(9 Mitchell Lane)*, north of the Plaza; entrees start at $9.

Day 3: Healdsburg to Calistoga

4–5 hours, 37mi

Arguably the least scenic day of the tour, this route connects the Alexander and Napa Valleys.

The roads between Healdsburg and the **Alexander Valley Vineyards** (6.6mi) and **Field Stone Winery** (7mi) are thoroughly trafficked with good pavement and shoulders.

Turning into the Chalk Hill Valley along one of the area's most beloved cycling routes, you'll cross the **Macama Historical Bridge** (8.5mi), which looks like two half-bridges joined at the middle. Its post-WWII construction was complicated by the sharp angle at which the road meets the creek bed.

Chalk Hill gets its name from the texture of its soil, which is laden with ash from volcanic Mt St Helena (a feature of Day 4). According to the folks at **Chalk Hill Winery** (13mi) this soil is what makes their land so good for growing chardonnay and sauvignon blanc grapes; stop by to taste-test the theory.

A constant serpentine undulation past ranches, vineyards and oak trees takes you out of the valley and past **Shilo Regional Park**, which has restrooms and a picnic spot with a good view of the vineyards.

After this lovely section it's a shame to come to the suburban sprawl of Larkfield

NOW THIS IS A RATHER CHEEKY LITTLE NUMBER! ..WHAT A PITY YOU HAVE TO KEEP STEERING!
DON HATCHER

(18.1mi). Make the most of it by having an ice cream at one of the ***fast-food joints*** on Old Redwood Hwy. The climb up Mark West Springs Rd may have you sucking exhaust but once on Franz Valley Rd (25.9mi) the scene turns rural once again. Mounting and descending several north-south running ridges, the route makes its way to Napa Valley. The day ends at the corner of Lincoln and Washington Aves.

Calistoga

☎ 707

Somehow, despite its famous mud baths, mineral water and wineries, Calistoga has managed to stay unpretentious and folksy. Could it be the covered sidewalks? Or the buildings dating back to the 1840s? Maybe it's because the numerous spas in town are a little dilapidated?

Guiseppe Musante began bottling Calistoga mineral water here in 1924, but the town's name came from Sam Brannan, who founded it in 1859. He believed that it would emulate the New York spa town of Saratoga, perhaps as the Cali-stoga of Sara-fornia.

Along Lincoln Ave, which stretches from Hwy 128 across to the Silverado Trail, the visitor center is behind the Old Railroad Depot, 1458 Lincoln Ave. Palisades Mountain Sport (☎ 942-9687), at 1330 Gerard St just off Lincoln Ave, serves cyclists well.

Things to See & Do The **Sharpsteen Museum**, 1311 Washington St, has a collection of dioramas showing scenes from the town's colorful history, and a restored cottage from Sam Brannan's original resort.

Basking up to your neck in a tubful of mud is the thing to do in Calistoga. **Mud-bath packages** take 60 to 90 minutes and cost from around $45. You start off semi-submerged in hot mud, followed by a shower, then a soak in hot mineral water. An optional steam bath and a cooling towel-wrap follows. The treatment can be extended to include a massage. Discount coupons are sometimes available from the visitors center, which also has listings of spa centers. It's wise to book ahead.

More unusual would be a **flight** with Calistoga Gliders (☎ 942-5000, 1546 Lincoln Ave; $80–$135). Getaway Adventures (☎ 942-0332), 1117 Lincoln Ave, offers **mountain-biking trips**.

Places to Stay A few blocks north of the town center, the ***Napa County Fairgrounds*** *(☎ 942-5111, 1435 Oak St)* charges $10. The scenery is much better at ***Bothe-Napa Valley State Park*** *(☎ 942-4575)*, 3.3mi south of town on Hwy 29; it's a 0.2mi climb to the campground from the park entrance. Tent sites ($12) can be reserved through Reserve America *(☎ 800-444-7275, W www.reserveamerica.com)* for April through October and are first-come, first-served the rest of the year.

A great deal in the center of town is the ***Calistoga Inn & Brewery*** *(☎ 942-4101, 1250 Lincoln Ave)*, with 18 simple rooms (shared bath) for $65/$90 weekday/weekend.

Rooms at ***Nance's Hot Springs*** *(☎ 942-6211, 1614 Lincoln Ave)* all have kitchenettes and cost $67 midwinter, $100 and up in summer. Spa treatments are extra. The ***Roman Spa Motel*** *(☎ 942-4441, 1300 Washington St)* includes free use of its three mineral pools (mud baths and massage packages are extra) in the $76/106 weekday/weekend price.

Places to Eat Lincoln Ave has plenty of dining possibilities, with the gourmet deli at ***Palisades Market*** *(1506 Lincoln Ave)* among the best. Across the street is ***Cal Mart*** grocery store.

Locals say that the ***Calistoga Inn & Brewery*** (see Places to Stay) has one of the best kitchens in town, serving microbrews and burgers ($6) in the bar, refined California food in the dining room (entrees start at $11). ***Checkers*** *(1414 Lincoln Ave)* is a popular gourmet pizza place that also serves large salads and sandwiches ($6–12). Across the street, ***Sarafornia Cafe*** serves big breakfasts for around $8.

Day 4: Calistoga to Harbin Hot Springs

3–4 hours, 19.9mi

This short day allows a morning of wandering around Calistoga, an afternoon of lounging and hiking at Harbin Hot Springs and an hour (or more) of climbing in between.

Just outside Calistoga the climb up volcanic Mt St Helena (4343ft), crowning feature of the Mayacmas Mtns, begins. The first climb begins along the narrow and twisting Old Toll Rd, past fruit orchards and magnificent rock outcroppings of the Palisades (a sub-range of the Mayacmas). The road can be rough and is very steep in a few sections but rarely sees cars and gets year-round shade.

After turning onto Hwy 29 (4.3mi) there is further climbing along this very busy road. **Robert Louis Stevenson State Park** (6.8mi; LHS) is at the summit, near where the author and his wife honeymooned in an abandoned cabin while he collected notes for *Silverado Squatters*. There's a 5mi hiking trail to the summit of Mt St Helena (4343ft), known as 'Spyglass Hill' in Stevenson's *Treasure Island*.

It's a thrilling descent with a small shoulder and good pavement to the Collayomi Valley, where the climate is much drier than on the west of the Mayacmas. Following Helena Creek, the route cruises into Middletown (15.5mi) – you may opt to stay here if Harbin's 'clothing optional' scene isn't your thing.

The final 4mi follow the creek that drains Harbin's hot pools. The grade of Harbin Springs Rd is such that you may feel frustrated for going so slowly without realizing you're actually ascending: about 500ft over 1.5mi.

Harbin Hot Springs & Middletown

☎ 707

A resort on 1160 acres, ***Harbin Hot Springs*** *(☎ 987-2477 or ☎ 800-622-2477, W www.harbin.org)* is tucked into a crook of the earth atop a natural hot spring that feeds four pools: cold, warm, hot and REALLY hot. It's a peaceful place that attracts a good mix of New Agers and weekend getawayers. There are numerous hiking trails into the surrounding hills, nightly entertainment, movies and daily yoga classes, all included in the $10 'membership' fee payable upon arrival.

Weekday/weekend rates are: $25/30 per person to camp; $35/50 for a dorm bed; $55/75 for a single; and $80/110 for a double. Reservations are recommended in summer and for weekends year-round. The ***restaurant*** serves excellent organic meals for around $15 and the natural food store has everything you'd need (at good prices) to make a meal in the communal vegetarian kitchen.

Resembling a service town in the middle of the USA, Middletown has a good choice of eating options along its main street (Hwy 175). For lodging, there's only one choice: the ***Middletown Motel*** *(☎ 987-7330)*, on the west end of town, which has $55 rooms. ***Hardesters Market & Hardware*** has a full selection and good deli. ***CJ's Cafe*** does a good job with breakfast and lunch ($5–7) while the ***Mt St Helena Brewing Co*** serves salads, burgers and hearty appetizers (around $10) with their homemade beers. ***Perri's Deli*** is said to make good sandwiches and ice creams.

Day 5: Harbin Hot Springs to St Helena

4–5 hours, 35.1mi

Today's route explores the rural 'backside' of the Mayacmas range and descends back to the Napa Valley.

Mt St Helena dominates the western view while cruising down from Harbin Hot Springs. From Middletown, Butts Canyon Rd is quiet, flat and straight until it makes a sharp jog left (east) to circle the northern shore of Detert Reservoir and enter the Guenoc Valley. In the 19th century, actress Lilly Langtry had a ranch house here, where she entertained Hollywood's elite in notoriously garish fashion. Now her acreage is part of **Guenoc Winery** (10.3mi) and her restored house is part of the view from their tasting room.

After climbing up a volcanic ridge along Butts Creek, the route descends into the broad and pastoral Pope Valley. **Litto's Hubcap Ranch** (21.1mi), with its 2000 or so displaced metal disks, is a genuine piece of oddball Americana that's impossible to miss.

Pope Valley Winery (21.3mi) is the last non-Napa winery on this ride. 100-year-old buildings and fine chenin blanc are worth a stop (weekends only).

Climbing out of the valley is a rather pleasant experience via the Ink Grade (21.6mi; no shoulder, good pavement), which snakes through redwood trees and private fruit orchards. A short descent and 3.5mi roll on White Cottage Rd puts you at the edge of the Napa Valley. A descent from 29.7mi accelerates on Howell Mtn Rd (32.8mi); traffic is fast and caution is required. The last 1mi crosses the Napa Valley to meet Hwy 29.

St Helena

☎ 707

High-end boutiques and swank cafes occupy St Helena's historic buildings along a four-block stretch of Hwy 29 (called Main St in town). It's a bustling pedestrian scene that can be charming at best, annoyingly crowded at worst (generally summer weekends). Its old movie theater shows two films nightly, and the free **Silverado Museum** (☎ 963-3757), 1490 Library Lane, has a fascinating collection of Robert Louis Stevenson memorabilia (open Tues–Sun).

The chamber of commerce (☎ 963-4456) is in Suite A, 1010 Main St. Saint Helena Cyclery (☎ 963-7736), 1156 Main St, can take care of all cycling needs.

On the north edge of town is the regal 1883 Rhine House, home to **Beringer** (☎ 963-4812), the oldest continuously operating winery in Napa. A free tour includes a tasting and a visit to the extensive tunnels that burrow into the hill behind the winery. About 2mi further north, **Bale Grist Mill State Historic Park** (☎ 963-2236) features a 36ft wheel, dating from 1846, that ground the local farmers' grain to flour. A hiking trail connects the park to adjacent Bothe-Napa Valley State Park.

Places to Stay See Places to Stay for Calistoga (p199) for information on camping at ***Bothe-Napa Valley State Park***, midway between St Helena and Calistoga.

El Bonita Motel *(☎ 963-3216, 195 Main St)* has rooms from $95 to $150. In the center of town ***Hotel St Helena*** *(☎ 963-4388, 1309 Main St)* dates from 1881 and has 18 rooms (some with private bath) from $165 to $195. The ***Harvest Inn*** *(☎ 963-9463 or ☎ 800-950-8466, 1 Main St)* offers 54 rooms in a Tudor-style building for $120 and up.

Places to Eat A ***Safeway*** supermarket *(cnr Hunt & Railroad Aves)* is one block east of Main St. The ***Model Bakery*** *(1357 Main St)* serves great scones, muffins and coffee (closed Mon). ***Gillwoods Cafe*** *(1313 Main St)* is a straightforward diner with meals for $5 to $10. ***Armadillo's*** *(1304 Main St)* serves decent Mexican food ($6–12) in a festive setting.

St Helena has interesting places for a classy meal but reservations are imperative. ***Tra Vigne*** *(☎ 963-4444, 1050 Charter Oak Ave)*, on the south edge of town, has a long-standing reputation for some of the best food in the valley (entrees $18–25). The ***Cantinetta*** in Tra Vigne's walled garden patio is a deli and wine shop that serves quicker, cheaper meals than the main restaurant. In a dramatic setting next to Beringer, the ***Wine Spectator at Greystone*** *(☎ 967-1010)* is run by the renowned Culinary Institute of America; entrees cost around $20.

Day 6: St Helena to Napa

4–6 hours, 37.4mi

If wine tasting is not your thing, think about catching the bus back to Napa. Otherwise, start early and plan on stopping frequently on this connect-the-wineries ride.

The Silverado Trail runs parallel to Hwy 29 on the east side of the Napa Valley. It's much less traveled than Hwy 29 but is still heavily trafficked, especially on weekends. There are no serious climbs, nor any flat sections.

Passing **Beringer Vineyards** (1mi) and **Bale Grist Mill State Historic Park** (13.1mi; for both attractions, see St Helena town information above), the route takes busy Hwy 29 north for 7.1mi before crossing the valley on Dunaweal Lane. The purpose of what may seem like a detour are two great wineries: **Clos Pegase** (7.7mi), designed by postmodernist architect Michael Graves; and **Sterling Vineyards** (7.8mi), with a hilltop tasting room accessed by gondola. A ride on the Silverado Trail lasts for 12mi before the route cuts through the heart of the vines along picture-perfect Conn Creek Rd, recalling the valley's humble agricultural beginnings. **Caymus** (21.2mi) makes an outstanding white (blend) called Conundrum and award-winning cabernets that you can taste by appointment; real wine lovers should make the effort and call ahead.

Rejoining the Silverado Trail, the route climbs gradually to gain expansive views of the vines. A gentle descent lands in the valley's southern end, where the two favorites among many wineries are Disney-owned **Silverado Vineyards** (27.3mi) and **Stag's Leap** (28.3). The latter's Cabernet Sauvignon outscored a French Bordeaux in 1976 to put Napa Valley on the world's wine map.

The last 3mi of the route are exceptionally busy with traffic.

Napa
☎ 707

The town that lends its name to such a highfalutin' region is surprisingly pedestrian. Its history as a port town (the Napa River flows south to San Pablo Bay, which joins San Francisco Bay) is superseded by its place as service center for the smaller towns in the valley. Besides the unpretentious shops downtown, the only thing to see is the tiny **Napa County Historical Society Museum** (☎ 224-1739), 1219 1st St, with displays on wine making and local history.

Next to the transit center, the Napa Valley visitor center (☎ 226-7459), 1310 Napa Town Center, has maps, a list of local accommodations, and train and bus schedules. Bicycle Trax (☎ 258-8729), corner Soscal Ave and 3rd St, has a repair shop and good supply of gear.

Places to Stay & Eat There's camping at ***Skyline Wilderness Park*** *(☎ 252-0481, 2201 Imola Ave)*, 0.6mi south of town on Soscal Ave, then 1.2mi east on Imola Ave. It's not terribly pretty but there are hot showers and $10 sites.

The ***Travelodge*** *(☎ 226-1871, 800 Coombs St)* is central and has a pool; rooms are $82/88 weekday/weekend. Marilyn Monroe and Elvis Presley are said to have slept (not together) at the ***Napa Valley Wine Lodge*** *(☎ 224-7911 or ☎ 800-696-7911, 200 South Coombs St)*, close to town, with rooms for $60 to $74. The ***John Muir Inn*** *(☎ 257-7220 or ☎ 800-522-8999, 1998 Trower Ave)* is in the sprawl of the city, with rooms for $95 to $135.

Ralphs Grocery Store is in the Bel Air Plaza. ***Downtown Joe's*** *(902 Main St)* incorporates microbrewery and restaurant and operates from breakfast ($5) to dinner ($6–11). Nearby ***PJ's Cafe*** *(1001 2nd St)* serves straightforward burgers, sandwiches, pastas and pizzas for under $10. ***Taquería Tres Hermanos*** *(1122 1st St)* is a good spot for burritos. For pizzas and Italian dishes in a stylish setting, make a reservation at ***Bistro Don Giovanni*** *(☎ 224-3300, 4110 St Helena Hwy)*; entrees are $13 to $17.

Baths, Barns & Booze

Duration	3 days
Distance	104.3mi
Difficulty	moderate
Start/End	Ukiah
Cues	p368

This short tour explores one of California's most highly touted but still up-and-coming wine regions, plus two of the state's finest breweries. Along the way are once-prosperous sheep ranches and still-prosperous fruit orchards, and hot springs at the end of Day 2.

The Navarro River and its tributaries have carved a hilly route through this section of the Coast Range, making flat stretches of pavement the rare exception.

PLANNING
When to Ride

In late September and early October the vines and trees of this region are laden with fruit. Rain comes in November and by February parts of Hwy 128 risk being covered by the Navarro River.

Hwy 128 gets busy on weekends with holiday-makers heading for Mendocino. If riding on a weekend is unavoidable, start on Sunday so you'll be riding against traffic.

Maps

AAA's *Mendocino and Sonoma Coast Region* does a good job of covering the entire route. It's available from any AAA office, including the one in Ukiah (☎ 707-462-3862), 601 King's Court Rd.

What to Bring

If you secure reservations at Orr Hot Springs you can choose not to camp on this ride.

GETTING TO/FROM THE RIDE

To link this ride with the Border to Border ride, it's 14.7mi from Comptche (Day 2) to

Mendocino (see Day 22, pp319–21, of the Border to Border ride).

Ukiah

The transport hub in Ukiah is a covered bus stop with a pay phone at the entrance to the Mendocino County Airport (private planes only) on S State St.

Greyhound operates two buses daily to/from San Francisco ($32, $15 per boxed bike). MTA (☎ 707-462-1422 or ☎ 800-696-4682) buses connect Ukiah to Santa Rosa ($13) and Mendocino ($4) daily; each bus can transport two bikes (no charge) on a front rack.

Amtrak buses depart from Burger King. Daily bus services from San Francisco go via the Emeryville and Martinez stations (around $30). Bikes are allowed at no extra charge if there's room. Call ahead to find out how much space is available.

As there is no official station here, buy a roundtrip or onward ticket at your point of departure. MTA bus tickets can be purchased on board with exact fare.

THE RIDE

Ukiah (See Map, p204)

☎ 707

North of San Francisco by 104mi and 60mi east of the Pacific Ocean, Ukiah is the Mendocino County seat. It is home to administrative offices, places to stay and eat, and not much else. Attractions lie in the surrounding Yokayo Valley, a fertile producer of pears and winery grapes. Consider Ukiah a launch pad and fueling point, then hop on the saddle to see where the region's beauty lies.

Information The chamber of commerce (☎ 462-4705), 200 S School St, one block west of State St, has maps and information for the entire county.

Ukiah's motels, banks, restaurants and shops lie along a 3mi stretch of State St, divided into North State St and South State St by Perkins St.

Both Dave's Bike Shop (☎ 462-3230), 846 S State St, and Denny Bicycles (☎ 462-8426), 246 N State St, have maps and make repairs.

Places to Stay & Eat Budget motels along State St are your best bet. ***Motel 6*** *(☎ 468-5404 or ☎ 800-466-8356, 1208 State St)* has rooms for $38/44 single/double. ***Rodeway Inn*** *(☎ 462-2906, 1050 State St)* has a swimming pool, picnic/barbecue area, free continental breakfast and rooms for $49/55. The ***Sunrise Inn*** *(☎ 462-6601, ⓔ rooms@sunriseinn.net, 650 S State St)* offers free local phone calls from its $38/41 rooms. In a quiet neighborhood close to downtown, the ***Sanford House B&B Inn*** *(☎ 462-1653, 306 S Pine St)* has five rooms for $75 to $100.

The large ***Safeway*** *(653 S State St)* is open 24 hours. Ukiah's best coffee house is ***The Coffee Critic*** *(476 N State St)*, with live music most weekends. ***Ellie's Mutt Hut & Vegetarian Cafe*** *(732 S State St)* serves a varied menu of tasty vegetarian and meat dishes. For pasta, try ***Angelo's Italian Restaurant*** *(☎ 707-462-0448, 920 N State St)*, which has reasonable prices and plenty of vegetarian dishes.

Day 1: Ukiah to Boonville

5–7 hours, 46mi

This ride climbs from the wide, flat Yokayo Valley to the hilly Anderson Valley, both flush with vineyards and fruit orchards. Between them is quiet, oak-covered ranch land.

The traffic of Ukiah quickly disappears upon reaching East Side Rd, an easy 13mi stretch through vineyards. Most of these grapes become wine under supervision of **Fetzer Vineyards** whose tasting room (16.1mi) is open daily.

The main reason to detour into central Hopland (17mi) is to visit the **Mendocino Brewing Company**, one of California's first brewpubs. There is also a ***grocery store*** and ***B&B***. Barely 1mi south of Hopland, on Hwy 101, the **Real Goods' Solar Living Center** offers tours of its 12-acre site dedicated to sustainable living practices.

From here it's an undulating climb along a curvy but lightly used road to Hwy 128. The route rhythmically dips and crests, down to tributaries of the Navarro River and up the sides of their V-shaped valleys. The shoulder is narrow to non-existent along most of Hwy 128 but traffic is generally light (weekends excepted).

Yorkville (33.6mi) has a ***market*** with a good deli and marks the start of the southern Anderson Valley's wine region. Places to taste include the 100% organic **Yorkville Vineyards & Cellars** (34.5mi) and award-winning **Martz Vineyards** (38.7mi).

As the route descends to Boonville, hub of the Anderson Valley, the surrounding hills appear lower but more dramatically sculpted – the result of forceful erosion from water that has picked up speed as it gets closer to its destination on the coast.

Boonville

☎ 707

Locals developed Boonville's dialect, called 'Boontling', at the end of the 19th century to distinguish themselves from outsiders. The older population is still a bit closed but nearly half of the 800 folks who live here now are Mexican-American field laborers.

The two-block town is easy to navigate but assistance is available from a rack of brochures outside Otto's Ice Cream, on the north side of Hwy 128, or from the chamber of commerce (☎ 895-2379, W www.andersonvalleychamber.com).

The award-winning **Anderson Valley Brewing Co** (☎ 207-2337), on Hwy 253, offers two tours daily.

Places to Stay & Eat There is no camping in Boonville but ***Indian Creek Campground*** *(☎ 895-2465)*, just before Philo on Day 2, has $10 sites but no showers. ***Hendy Woods State Park*** *(☎ 800-444-7275)*, 2.9mi past Philo, then 0.5mi south (left) on the Greenwood-Philo Rd, has $1 hiker/biker sites and hot showers.

Other accommodations here cater to city dwellers looking for a weekend away. Whether dining or staying, reservations are

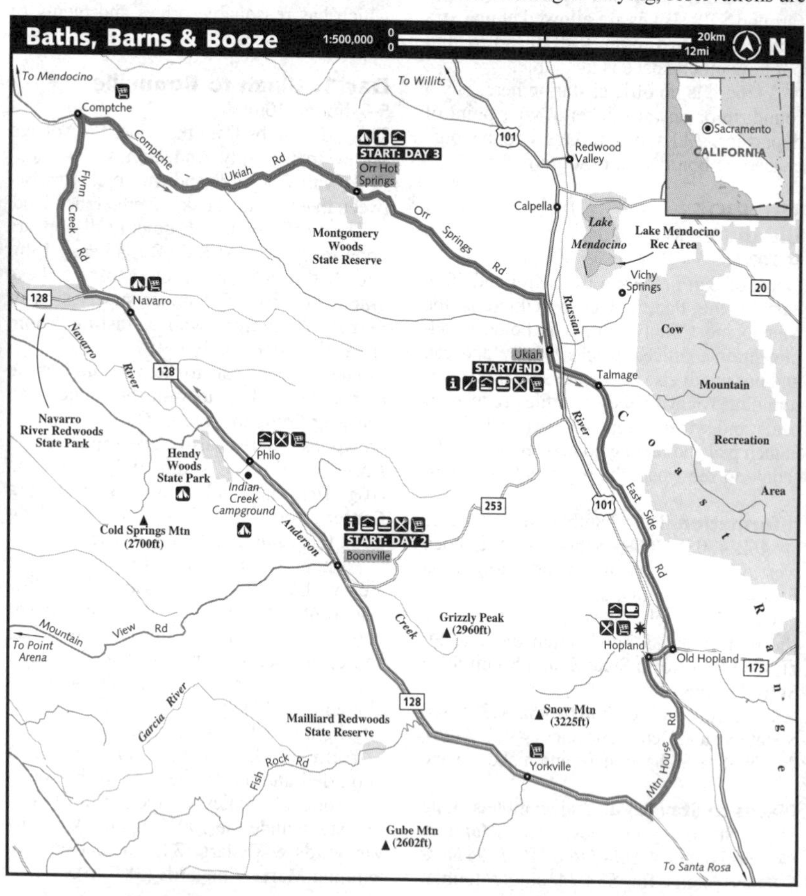

recommended at the excellent ***Boonville Hotel*** *(☎ 895-2210, 14050 Hwy 128)*. It has 10 rooms from $75 to $200 (including breakfast) and an outstanding dining room for lunch and dinner. The ***Anderson Creek Inn*** *(☎ 895-3091, 12050 Anderson Valley Way)* has five rooms for $110 to $170, including breakfast.

There's a filtered water machine and good selection of food at ***Anderson Valley Market & Deli*** *(Hwy 128)*. The valley's most popular food and libation destination is the ***Buckhorn Saloon*** *(14081 Hwy 128)*, which pours Anderson Valley Brewing Co beer and serves a variety of food ($6–11). Also recommended are the fresh, mostly organic takeaway items at ***Boont Berry Farm*** *(Hwy 128)*, across from the Boonville Hotel.

Day 2: Boonville to Orr Hot Springs

3½–5 hours, 42.9mi

Beginning among wineries and ending beneath the redwoods, this day completes a U-turn from Hwy 128 to the Comptche-Ukiah Rd, to end at a clothing optional resort.

North of Boonville the shoulder widens and pavement improves, making the 6mi to **Philo** relatively easy. Groceries and deli items are available at ***Lemon's Market***. The ***Wellspring Renewal Center*** *(☎ 895-3893)*, 1.1mi south (right) from Hwy 128 at the end of Ray's Rd, is highly recommended. The produce and freshly squeezed juice at ***Gowan's Oak Tree*** (8.3mi) is unbeatable.

From here the route passes a winery every half-mile or so. Tasting rooms are generally open daily. **Husch Vineyards** (10.6mi) welcomes picnickers to its lovely grounds and pours highly regarded wines. Across Hwy 128, atop a potentially daunting perch, **Roederer Estates** produces Anderson Valley Brut, a nice sparkling wine.

Most vines here yield chardonnay and pinot noir grapes. Without the intense heat experienced inland, these grapes hold less residual sugar and thus make light chardonnays and earthy pinot noirs.

After passing the ***grocery store*** and post office at Navarro (13.1mi), the route joins the Navarro River through a veritable tunnel of trees designated as **Navarro River Redwoods State Park** (16.3mi). There are 23 first-come, first-served ***campsites*** ($1 per hiker/biker) 6mi further west on Hwy 128.

Flynn Creek Rd is used by lumber trucks going from Mendocino to Boonville but traffic is light in the middle of the day. At Comptche (26.1mi), the ***Comptche Store*** offers a small selection but a big dose of backwoods California soul. This is the last place to buy food for the night.

The 2.2mi climb up Bowman Ridge is rewarded by a gentle stretch through pine forest and a 1.5mi downhill where pine is replaced by manzanita trees, which like the drier inland climate.

Final strokes take you along the South Fork of Big River through **Montgomery Woods State Reserve**. There is a primeval feel to the old growth redwoods and ferns here, worth exploring on a walk along the 2mi Montgomery Woods trail.

Orr Hot Springs

☎ 707

This clothing-optional ***resort*** *(☎ 462-6277)* was built in the 1820s to soothe the bones of weary sheep ranchers and give the residents of Mendocino a social destination. After many years of inactivity, the place was revitalized and rebuilt by 'Berkeley hippies' in the 1970s. It now enjoys an elegant, manicured appearance with a slightly 'New Age' vibe. The spring that feeds the various hot and cold pools (all untreated) originates 400ft below ground and bubbles to the surface at around 100°F.

Campsites or a bed in the 12-room dormitory cost $36 per person, including use of the pools, large kitchen and cozy lodge. Rooms and cabins with private baths cost $95 to $200. Day-use is $20 ($10 on Mondays).

Reservations are recommended but are only done by return phone call, so plan ahead. A very limited selection of ***vending machine*** food is available.

Day 3: Orr Hot Springs to Ukiah

2–3 hours, 15.4mi

A steep and steady climb, rolling ridge ride and kick-ass downhill comprise this final day.

Your soaked, mellowed muscles get no warm-up for the hill that climbs up from Orr Hot Springs to the backbone of the Coast Range. A false summit comes after 3mi, from where you have the last views west. It's common to see a layer of fog hanging over the coast in the form of a blurry gray line just above what looks like the horizon.

At the true crest of the ridge (4.3mi) is an oak-covered knoll that, when ascended on foot, offers splendid views.

There is little shoulder on the hand-cramping downhill to Ukiah. The ride's end, through central Ukiah, is less than scenic.

The North Coast

From the Russian River area up to the Oregon border, California's rugged north coast holds some of the state's finest natural attractions, including forests of 1000-year-old coast redwoods and a rocky, brooding coastline still being carved by crashing waves. Wet weather keeps the population of the small towns here relatively stable.

Coast redwoods, found in a narrow 450mi strip along the Pacific Coast from Central California to southern Oregon, grow nowhere else on the continent. These towering beauties are named for the color of their wood and bark, and can live up to 2200 years, grow to 368ft (the tallest tree ever recorded) and achieve a diameter of 22ft at the base. The trees' structure, likened to a nail standing on its head, is unique in how shallow their root system is in relation to their height – only 10 to 13ft deep but spreading out 60 to 80ft around the base of the trees. Standing on the needle-padded floor of a redwood forest, surrounded by the silence and fresh scent, is akin to a religious experience.

HISTORY

Before members of the Russian-American Fur Company arrived in 1806, the coast was plied by the Wiyot tribe. In the 1850s, Humboldt Bay became an important whaling station and disembarkation point for miners seeking gold on the Trinity and Klamath Rivers. As populations in the mining camps increased, Eureka became a supply town – first of mining equipment and then of lumber. By 1854 schooners made regular supply trips between San Francisco and Humboldt Bay which, by then, had upwards of 70 lumber mills in its environs.

Railroad systems were laid down and, by 1914, Humboldt County was connected to San Francisco by rail. The Louisiana Pacific pulp mill, near Eureka, and Pacific Lumber Company (PALCO) in Scotia are still operating but they are all that has withstood the over-cutting of forests and the subsequent move towards more sustainable economies.

In 1997, Julia 'Butterfly' Hill climbed a 200ft, 1000-year-old redwood named Luna to prevent PALCO from cutting it down. She descended two years later, having secured the tree's preservation and her own place in the annals of environmental history.

GATEWAY CITIES

Eureka

See Eureka (pp313–15) for information about accommodations and other services.

The Lost Coast

Duration	3 days
Distance	106.3mi
Difficulty	hard
Start/End	Ferndale
Cues	p369

This is an intensely beautiful ride through remote, pristine and majestic country. Where US 101 jogs east (south of Eureka) the coast juts west, stretching to reach its westernmost point in the Lower 48 states at Cape Mendocino. The transition from redwood forest to windswept coast is not easy: you must climb over the rugged ridge-and-valley topography of the King Range, cut by tributaries to the Mattole and Eel Rivers, rising to more than 4000ft within 3mi of the coast. Only strong-legged hill-lovers need embark.

PLANNING

When to Ride

This part of the state can be cold and wet year-round, though the driest months are generally from May through October. Gray whales migrate past in late April and early May.

In summer, the coast may be shrouded in fog while temperatures inland (at Humboldt Redwoods State Park, for example) reach towards 100°F. In winter, the King Range (between Humboldt Redwoods State Park Headquarters and Honeydew) can, but rarely does, get snow.

Around 5000 cyclists converge to ride all or part of this route during the Tour of the

Unknown Coast Ride (W www.tuccycle.org) in the second weekend of May.

Maps

AAA's *Northern California Section* map does a good job of covering the entire route. It's available from any AAA office, including the one in Eureka (☎ 707-443-5087), 707 L St. Krebs' *California North Coast* map has more detail and topography but may only be available in San Francisco or by mail.

What to Bring

Camping is the best mode of lodging on this ride. There are stores en route but not at the overnight stops on Days 1 and 2.

GETTING TO/FROM THE RIDE

The first day of this ride overlaps Day 19 (p315) of the Border to Border ride.

The nearest transportation hub is Fortuna, 6.7mi northeast of Ferndale. Greyhound buses stop here (on request) en route between San Francisco ($31) and Seattle ($108). Amtrak buses connect Fortuna to the train station in Martinez ($32), from where trains and buses make the one-hour journey to San Francisco.

To get from Fortuna to Ferndale, load your bike on the front rack of a Redwood Transit System bus (☎ 443-0826; weekdays only; $1). To ride, exit Fortuna on Main St (going west), enter US 101 (yes, it's a bike route!) for 1.1mi. Exit on Fernbridge Dr and turn left on Hwy 211, which goes south 4.7mi to Ferndale.

THE RIDE (See Map, p208)

Ferndale

☎ 707

This idyllic little dairy farming community, founded in 1852, feels as if time has passed it by. Century-old Victorian buildings and homes are still in use, well-preserved and lovingly tended. The town **cemetery** could be straight from a Stephen King novel.

It's got traces of tourist trap, but most of the time the five-block Main St remains quiet, offering ample space to browse the antique stores, eat ice cream and poke around the **Kinetic Sculpture Museum**, 580 Main St, which pays tribute to what might be California's quirkiest race (see the boxed text 'Kinetic Sculpture Race', p209).

The visitor center (☎ 786-4477, W www.victorianferndale.org/chamber) sends out information by request.

Places to Stay Charging $5, the ***Humboldt County Fairgrounds*** *(☎ 786-9511, cnr Van Ness & 5th Sts)* offers camping on the lawn.

Francis Creek Inn *(☎ 786-9611, 577 Main St)* has four cozy rooms for $62, including morning pastries. ***Ferndale Laundromat & Motel*** *(☎ 786-9471, 632 Main St)* has two units at $55, each with two bedrooms, kitchen and private bath. ***Fern Motel*** *(☎ 786-5000, 332 Ocean Ave)* has rooms and suites for $65 to $125.

Ferndale's elegant Victorians are naturals for B&Bs. The ***Gingerbread Mansion Inn*** *(☎ 786-4000 or ☎ 800-952-4136, cnr Brown & Berding Sts)*, one block east of Main St, is a fancy 1899 Victorian mansion, now a four-star B&B. It offers the utmost in service and elegance, with 11 large rooms from $140 to $350 and a back porch for bike storage.

Shaw House *(☎ 786-9958, 703 Main St)* was the first permanent structure to be built in Ferndale. The house, called 'Fern Dale' for the 6ft ferns that grew here, is now a B&B with seven rooms from $85 to $145 and a garage for bikes.

A Ferndale landmark and headquarters of the annual Tour of the Unknown Coast Ride, the ***Victorian Inn*** *(☎ 786-4949 or ☎ 888-589-1808, 400 Ocean Ave)*, has 12 rooms for $85 to $125 (full breakfast on weekends; cereal, pastries and coffee on weekdays) and a conference room to store bikes.

Places to Eat Along Main St you'll find ***Valley Grocery***, the ***Ferndale Meat Co*** for big deli sandwiches and ***Sweetness & Light*** for old-fashioned candy treats.

The ***Ferndale Pizza Co*** *(607 Main St)* turns out a great variety of pizzas with fresh toppings for around $10 (closed Mon). For a nice dinner ($8–15), locals favor the northern Italian food at the ***Hotel Ivanhoe*** *(315 Main St)* and the steaks and seafood at ***Curley's Grill*** *(460 Main St)*.

Day 1: Ferndale to Humboldt Redwoods State Park

4–5 hours, 34.8mi

There are a few short, steep climbs as the route goes east to join the course of the Eel

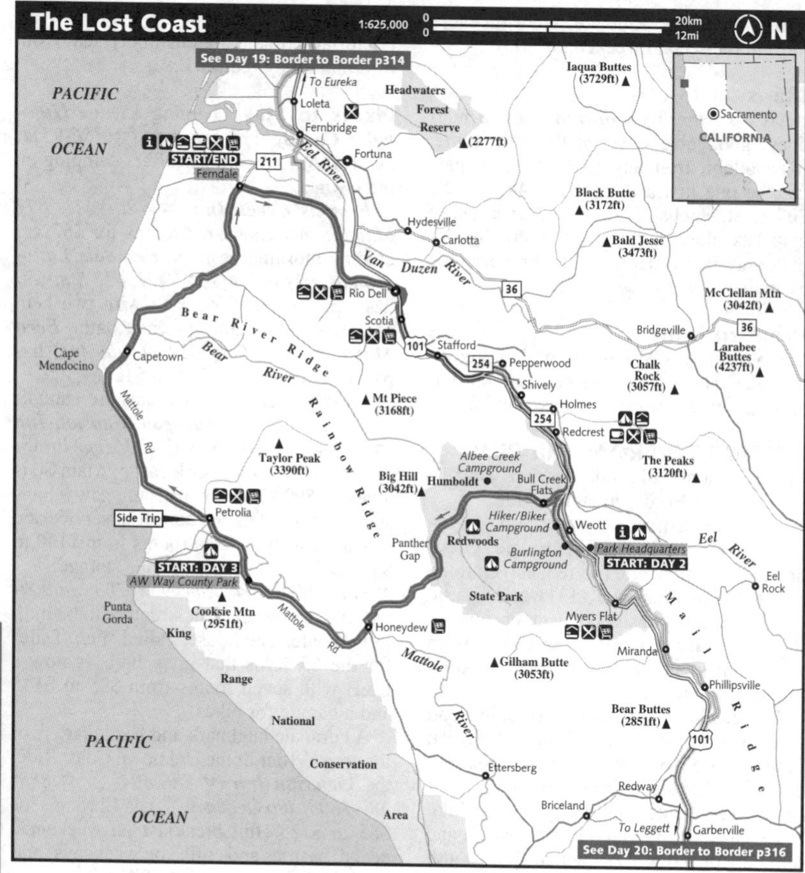

River. Small ***resorts*** pepper the route, offering food stores and occasional lodging.

South of **Scotia** (14.3mi) the route necessarily takes the freeway (it's well signed as a bike route and has a big shoulder) before exiting on to the **Avenue of the Giants** (19.8mi). This 33mi redwood corridor is a highlight of any trip to California. Pick up a free *Avenue of the Giants Auto Tour* map/brochure from a box at the north end of the avenue or at the park visitors center. **Redcrest** (26.3mi) is the last place to buy food and best place to find a motel room if you don't intend to camp.

Weott (33.1mi) marks the northern boundary of Humboldt Redwoods State Park. In summer there's a good deal of activity in Weott, but from October to May it's basically vacant. Here, you'll pass the overnight camping options.

Humboldt Redwoods State Park

☎ 707

This 80-sq-mi state park holds some of the world's most magnificent old-growth forest. The park headquarters (☎ 946-2263) on the Avenue of the Giants, 1.7mi south of Weott, has museum displays and useful books and maps (open daily 9am–7/8pm in summer, 10am–4pm in winter).

Sites at the hiker/biker ***campground*** (33.3mi on Day 1) cost $5. For a hot shower you'll have to go to ***Burlington Campground***, beside the visitors center and open year-round, or ***Albee Creek Campground*** (9.3mi on Day 2; open late May–mid-Oct).

NORTHERN CALIFORNIA

The nearest motels and food are in Redcrest; see p315 for information on accommodations and other services.

Day 2: Humboldt Redwoods State Park to AW Way County Park

5–6 hours, 35.5mi

A fairly short but hilly day, this leg takes you from the redwood forests over the rugged King Range on the legendary Mattole Rd. Used by loggers and fishermen in days gone by, it's now primarily a tourist route that gets infrequent use past the first 10mi.

After retracing Day 1's final miles along the Avenue of the Giants, the route turns west to follow Bull Creek through enormous stands of redwoods. The **Rockefeller Forest** (8.7mi) is one of the most spectacular groves in the redwoods, home to the world champion Giant Tree, Tall Tree and others that you can see up close on a 1.5mi loop foot trail.

Most visitors turn back here or at ***Albee Creek Campground*** (9.3mi). From here to Panther Gap (20.9mi) it's a steady, twisting climb that hits 10% grades in several sections. The road is narrow, has no shoulder and gets quite bumpy but you may have it to yourself. A just reward is the panoramic view and thrilling descent to the Mattole River and the outpost of Honeydew (25.7mi). The one business here is the ***Honeydew Country Store*** *(☎ 629-3310)*, well-stocked with backpacking food, produce and microwaveable items (and microwave).

Kinetic Sculpture Race

The Kinetic Sculpture Race was born in 1969 when Ferndale artist Hobart Brown decided to spruce up his son's tricycle. After creating a wobbly, five-wheeled red 'pentacycle', he raced it, against four other odd contraptions, down Main St on Mother's Day (which was also the conclusion of the Ferndale Arts Festival). The race was expanded in the early 1970s to two days, coming from Fields Landing, on Humboldt Bay south of Eureka; now it has grown to a three-day, 38mi amphibious event, coming all the way from Arcata and attracting thousands of spectators and usually around 40 to 60 entrants. The race is held annually on Memorial Day weekend.

Nancy Keller

The last 10mi along the Mattole River are relatively flat, with a few short hills to end the day.

AW Way County Park

☎ 707

An idyllic expanse of grass on the river bank, ***AW Way County Park*** *(☎ 445-7651)* has campsites for $12, cold showers and a campground attendant on duty year-round. Swimming in the river is terrific, though it can get shallow in late summer and fall.

The nearest motels are in Petrolia, 6.4mi away (see Day 3).

Day 3: AW Way County Park to Ferndale

5½–7 hours, 36mi

This day is similar to Day 2 in that it's short but challenging. The scenery, however, is remarkably different.

Continuing along the Mattole River, you'll pass manicured sheep and cattle ranches before Lighthouse Rd (5.5mi) turns towards the coast at the edge of Petrolia, site of California's first oil well (1865). For a short side trip at the 6.4mi mark, continue on Lighthouse Rd for 3mi to where hiking trails continue to the sea and up to the rocky cliffs at Punta Gorda.

In town, the ***Petrolia General Store*** (☎ 629-3455) is a hub of activity and has a good general selection. ***Lost Coast Lodge*** *(☎ 629-3355, 42 Main St)* and ***Ziganti's Motel*** *(☎ 629-3593, 29615 Mattole Rd)* offer accommodations. The ***Hideaway*** (5.6mi) and ***Yellow Rose*** (6.9mi) both serve sandwiches, burgers and steaks.

It's a rolling 5mi out of the Mattole River valley to where the route meets the sea. An incredibly scenic stretch takes you towards Cape Mendocino along an isolated beach where big chunks of rock, haven for birds and threat to ships, perch offshore.

Even the strongest cyclists may walk some of the hills between the cape and Capetown (21.6mi), where sheep and cows graze right up to the sand. There are no services. Leaving this pastoral setting is the hardest work of the day, as you climb switchbacks that end at a false summit. The real summit affords great views of Humboldt Bay to the north, with Ferndale immediately below. Take care on the final descent that ends abruptly in town.

The Sierra Nevada

The Sierra Nevada is the longest continuous mountain range with the highest peak (Mt Whitney, 14,496ft), the largest and deepest alpine lake (Lake Tahoe), the tallest waterfall (Yosemite Falls), and what many call the finest mountain scenery. Extending 430mi through eastern California from the southern end of the Cascade Range near Lassen Peak to the Mojave Desert, it is 40mi to 80mi wide, an area roughly equivalent to that of the French, Swiss, and Italian Alps combined.

HISTORY

At least 7000 years ago, Native Americans living in the western foothills and eastern Sierra crossed the mountain passes in summer to trade, notably seashell beads and pinyon pine nuts.

Spanish missionaries and 18th-century explorers ventured infrequently into the mountains. European trappers and surveyors explored the area in the early 19th century, but it was the 1848 discovery of gold in the western foothills near Coloma that brought a flood of gold seekers known as the 'forty-niners' across the range.

John Muir's activities in the latter part of the 19th century brought recognition to the Sierra, with two national parks established in 1890, and the Sierra Club formed in 1892. By the end of the 1930s, the entire Sierra had been explored and mapped, and the major peaks had all been climbed.

NATURAL HISTORY

The Sierra Nevada comprises a single, continuous yet diverse ecosystem. Between 3500ft and 6000ft in the lower montane zone, mixed conifers predominate and active

Mountain Biking in the Sierra Nevada

California's most prominent mountain range offers arguably its best mountain biking. When the trails are clear of snow (late Jun–early Oct), mountain bikers share the dirt with hikers and equestrians throughout most of the range. National parks have more restrictive rules than national forests or areas managed by the BLM but there is plenty of riding in or near any Sierra destination.

Books & Maps

Carol Bonser & RW Miskimins have published several good guides, including *Mountain Biking South Lake Tahoe's Best Trails* and *Mountain Biking the High Sierra*.

Check with the local ranger station for trail maps, permits and access guidelines. Krebs' *Lake Tahoe & Gold Country Bicycle Map* is invaluable for its detail and topography but may only be available at bike stores in the Lake Tahoe region (or by mail order; see Information, p183).

Trails

One of the hands-down favorite trails in the Sierra is the 14mi **Marlette Flume Trail**, which runs along the eastern edge of Lake Tahoe, from Spooner Lake to Nevada's Hwy 28. Spooner Lake Outdoor Co (☎ 888-858-8844, W www.theflumetrail.com) rents bikes, sells maps and runs a biker's shuttle ($10) from a little cabin at the trail's start.

Primarily a ski resort, **Mammoth Mtn**, in the Eastern Sierra off Hwy 395, becomes a mountain-bike park in summer. A one-day bike rental costs $25, and $35 gives you access to as much lift-served downhill riding as you can handle. The Kamikaze Downhill on the last weekend in June is one of the fastest races on the professional circuit.

In the western foothills of the Sierra, along Hwy 49, the old mining camp of Downieville is known for the **Downieville Downhill**, a course that descends 5000ft in 12.4mi and is rated the 'best downhill route in the USA' by a popular bicycle magazine. Downieville Outfitters (☎ 530-289-0155), in the heart of Downieville, spends all summer shuttling people to the top of the course ($10) and fixing their bikes at the bottom. Bike rental costs $25 to $45.

Also in the western foothills, about 4mi south of Auburn, the North and Middle Forks of the American River converge where mountain bikers from Sacramento and the Bay Area converge: in the **Auburn State Recreation Area**. The California Department of Parks and Recreation office (☎ 530-885-5648), on Hwy 49 about 2mi south of Auburn, is a good source of trail maps and information.

bushy-tailed Douglas squirrels are readily seen. Coyote, black bear, mule deer and black-crested Steller's jay reside here, and between 6000ft and 8500ft in the upper montane zone. In this higher section, the two-needled lodgepole pine and California red fir thrive. Lodgepole chipmunk and golden mantled ground squirrel are common.

In the subalpine zone, between 8500ft and 10,500ft, trees are shorter, more widely spaced and often twisted by wind. Five-needled whitebark pine prevails, with mountain hemlock on moist north-facing slopes and gnarled foxtail pine on dry, rocky slopes. Yellow-bellied marmots thrive in rocky areas, as does the loud-voiced, gray Clark's nutcracker. Meadows here host a multitude of wildflowers.

Above tree line at more than 10,500ft in the alpine zone, the meadows are lush with grasses and wildflowers, and Belding's ground squirrel and rosy finch are characteristic. On the rocky slopes live small, round-eared American pika.

CLIMATE

The Sierra Nevada has the mildest, sunniest climate of any major US mountain range. Prevailing westerly winds bring moist Pacific air over the mountains between October and April, when 80% of annual precipitation falls as snow. Snow can fall during any month and weather generally changes rapidly.

The warmest time in the mountains is from mid-July to mid-August when day high temperatures range from 70° to 90°F. Night temperatures at the highest elevations drop to freezing even in midsummer.

From August to early September, days are warm and the weather is stable. From September to mid-October, skies are generally clear and nights cold, often below freezing.

PLANNING

Information Sources

The USFS (W www.fs.fed.us) provides information for national forests and wilderness areas and issues wilderness permits.

Books

In John Muir's *Gentle Wilderness: The Sierra Nevada*, his writings are accompanied by modern photographs. *Yosemite & the High Sierra*, by Ansel Adams, the most renowned photographer of the Sierra, offers a compilation of his finest images and most exuberant writings. For cyclists who also love to hike, Lonely Planet's *Hiking in the Sierra Nevada* is a great buy.

Yosemite's Western Gateway

Duration	4–5 hours
Distance	34.3mi
Difficulty	moderate–hard
Start	Bug Hostel, Midpines
End	Yosemite Lodge
Cues & Elevation Profile	p369

This route follows the wild, scenic Merced River for 30mi, treating the cyclist to gorgeous scenery and culminating with a dramatic entrance into Yosemite, crown jewel of California's national parks. This ride will have special appeal for newcomers – experience the valley's magic for the first time by bike rather than through a car window.

HISTORY

The Southern Sierra Miwoks lived in Yosemite Valley for millennia, fishing, hunting and gathering acorns from the area's abundant black oaks. They named the valley Ahwahnee – 'place of the gaping mouth' – and called themselves Ahwahneechee. Their word for grizzly bear – *uzumati* – evolved into the name Yosemite.

In 1851, conflict between gold miners and local Miwoks culminated in non-native discovery of Yosemite Valley and the forcible removal of the Ahwahneechee from their homeland. The area's remarkable beauty was captured in drawings and photographs, and Yosemite soon became an emblem of the American wilderness. Its rapidly spreading fame led Abraham Lincoln to establish Yosemite Valley as the world's first state park (under Californian jurisdiction) in 1864. Thanks to the efforts of John Muir and others passionate about Yosemite, thousands of acres surrounding the valley achieved national park status in 1890, and the valley was transferred to federal protection in 1906.

NATURAL HISTORY

Rivers and glaciers both played a role in the formation of Yosemite Valley. The Merced River, which still dominates the valley floor, began its erosive work more than 50 million years ago; however, the dramatic contours of the U-shaped valley you see today are primarily the result of glacial action over the past million years. The valley's awe-inspiring granite walls include El Capitan, the largest single slab of exposed granite in the world, and Half Dome, which towers over the valley's eastern end at 8842ft. Yosemite is said to have the world's greatest concentration of significant waterfalls; the most notable is Yosemite Falls, the tallest waterfall in North America at 2425ft. The valley's many trees include maple, black oak, dogwood and ponderosa pine. Commonly sighted animals include black bear, mule deer and western gray squirrels. Giant sequoia trees grow at three locations within the park, all outside the valley.

PLANNING

When to Ride

This ride is best from mid-April to late May, and from early September to late October, when weather conditions permit cycling but roads are less crowded than in summer. Wildflowers along the Merced River are especially beautiful in April; Yosemite waterfalls are most dramatic in May; and fall foliage in Yosemite Valley peaks in late October. Summer brings oppressive heat to the Merced River valley and heavy tourist traffic the entire length of Hwy 140.

Maps & Books

AAA's *Yosemite & Central Sierra* map covers the route in detail, although the ride is quite straightforward and requires minimal navigation.

GETTING TO/FROM THE RIDE

Midpines

Train Amtrak's San Joaquin train runs twice daily from the San Francisco Bay Area (Oakland/Emeryville) to Merced ($29, three hours). A connecting Amtrak bus continues to the Bug Hostel in Midpines ($8, one hour). Bikes travel free on convenient racks aboard the train and can be transferred unboxed to the luggage compartment under the bus. The early morning run from Oakland/Emeryville reaches Midpines before noon, allowing cyclists to continue to Yosemite the same day.

Bus Greyhound (☎ 209-722-2121), 710 W 16th St, operates several buses daily to Merced from LA ($28, 6½ hours) and San Francisco ($24, four hours).

Yosemite Area Regional Transportation System (YARTS; ☎ 877-989-2787, **W** www.yarts.com) runs four daily buses to Midpines ($4; two on weekends) from the Merced Transportation Center, corner 16th and O Sts. Some buses are equipped with bike racks, others have luggage space for bikes underneath.

Yosemite Lodge

Bus Two daily Amtrak buses run from Yosemite Lodge to the Merced train station. A third bus operated by YARTS runs on weekdays to the Merced Transportation Center. Note that on Amtrak buses the driver will accept a YARTS ticket if the bus is not already full with Amtrak passengers – this will save you money. Fare is $8 one way if traveling on a YARTS ticket (these can be purchased at Yosemite Lodge) or $17 if traveling on an Amtrak ticket. Travel time to Merced is 2¼ hours.

Bicycle This route can be ridden in reverse, from Yosemite to Midpines, offering cyclists an exhilarating long downhill run along the Merced River to Briceburg, followed by a hellish 3mi climb back to the Bug Hostel.

THE RIDE (See Map, p214)

Midpines

☎ 209

Midpines sits in the Sierra foothills about halfway between the Central Valley and Yosemite National Park. The town has a store, a couple of places offering cabins and camping, and an excellent hostel, which is the starting point for this ride.

Information The best local source of information is the Yosemite Bug Hostel. The friendly and well-informed staff can recommend hikes, mountain-bike rides, rafting and other outdoor activities in the area.

Midpines doesn't have a bike shop but the Bug Hostel rents bikes and publishes a free mountain-bike map for the region.

The closest ATMs are in Mariposa (7mi west) and at the Yosemite View Lodge (20mi east).

Yosemite Valley

This family-friendly, flat and easy ride on bikepaths and traffic-free roads offers an enjoyable introduction to the wonders of Yosemite Valley. You can join the ride at any point along the valley floor, but we start at the Yosemite Lodge bike rental stand.

Maps & Books

Yosemite Lodge and Curry Village bike stands carry the *Yosemite Valley Bikeways* map (free), which shows this route in its entirety, as does the *Yosemite Official Map & Guide* (supplied when you pay your entry fee).

The Ride

1–1½ hours, 8mi

Heading south from the Yosemite Lodge bike rental stand, the bikepath soon enters a beautiful meadow with sweeping views to both sides of the valley. At Swinging Bridge (0.5mi) the route crosses the Merced River, providing photo opportunities of **Yosemite Falls** (2425ft), the park's highest waterfall and one of the world's most dramatic. The path next parallels the roadway for 2mi, skirting another giant meadow before crossing Southside Dr and entering the forest. At 2mi the **LeConte Memorial** is a striking granite building. Built in 1903 as the first park headquarters, it now houses a publicly accessible Sierra Club library.

At 2.8mi the bikepath feeds into a wide road closed to motorized traffic. Passing through fragrant pine forest adjacent to Curry Village and Upper Pines Campground, the route soon reaches Happy Isles Bridge. Here the Merced River rages turbulently below, still fired up from its wild ride down nearby Vernal and Nevada Falls. It's well worth parking your bike just beyond the bridge and hiking the 2mi **Mist Trail** to get a closer look at these falls.

About 1mi further on, the route's only hill climbs briefly but steeply to **Mirror Lake**, which is slowly evolving into a meadow. Up top a short loop trail affords magnificent views of **Half Dome**'s sheer rocky face.

After zooming back downhill, the route leaves the main road behind, following an idyllic 1mi course through the trees, and crossing two bridges over the Merced River. This stretch is ideal for picnicking or contemplating the forest's serene beauty.

At 6.8mi the route re-enters the more heavily touristed part of the valley near Yosemite Village. Here you'll find the park **visitor center** plus a full array of other services. A short meander through another meadow leads back to Yosemite Lodge.

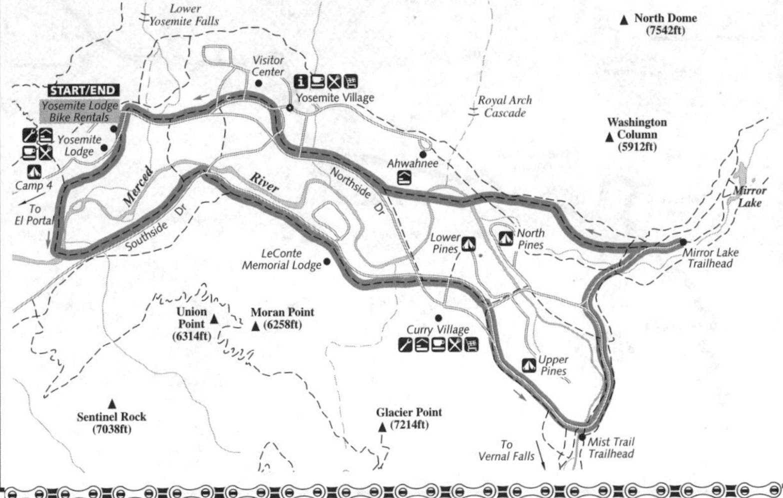

Things to See & Do The **Merced Wild and Scenic River corridor**, with easy access at the Briceburg Information Center just north of Midpines, provides fantastic opportunities for outdoor recreation. The beautiful Merced River Trail hugs the river's northern edge for several miles and is open to mountain bikers and hikers. Swimming, rafting and camping are also possible along the river.

Places to Stay & Eat The obvious choice, ***Yosemite Bug Hostel*** *(☎ 966-6666, W www.yosemitebug.com)* offers numerous services and a variety of lodging options. Hostel rooms cost $16, campsites $17, tent cabins $40, and private rooms $40 to $125. The common area features couches, guitars, Internet access, kitchen, laundry and a reasonably priced ***restaurant***. There's also a swimming hole just five minutes away. The only drawback to staying at the Bug is the long, steep, unpaved driveway!

Other lodging options in Midpines include ***Yosemite/Mariposa KOA*** *(☎ 966-2201 or ☎ 800-562-9391)* with tent sites for $26 and cabins for $47, and ***Muir Lodge*** *(☎ 966-2468)* with motel rooms priced from $43 to $65.

Day Ride: Midpines to Yosemite Lodge

4–5 hours, 34.3mi

This ride commences with a precipitous 1000ft drop from the base of the Bug Hostel driveway to the historic Briceburg Information Center on the Merced River. The route continues upstream all the way to Yosemite Valley, always in sight of the raging waters and rugged banks that earned this stretch of the Merced federal designation as a Wild and Scenic River. Across the river an unpaved hiking and mountain-biking trail is visible most of the way, following the old railway bed used by the Yosemite Valley Railroad from 1907 to 1945. Unfortunately this trail doesn't go all the way to Yosemite, so you're stuck with the busy traffic along Hwy 140. Still, the views from the highway are fantastic, and the road surface is good.

At 17mi the route detours across the river onto Foresta Rd, providing a momentary respite from traffic. You rejoin Hwy 140 at El Portal (19.4mi), where the main attraction is

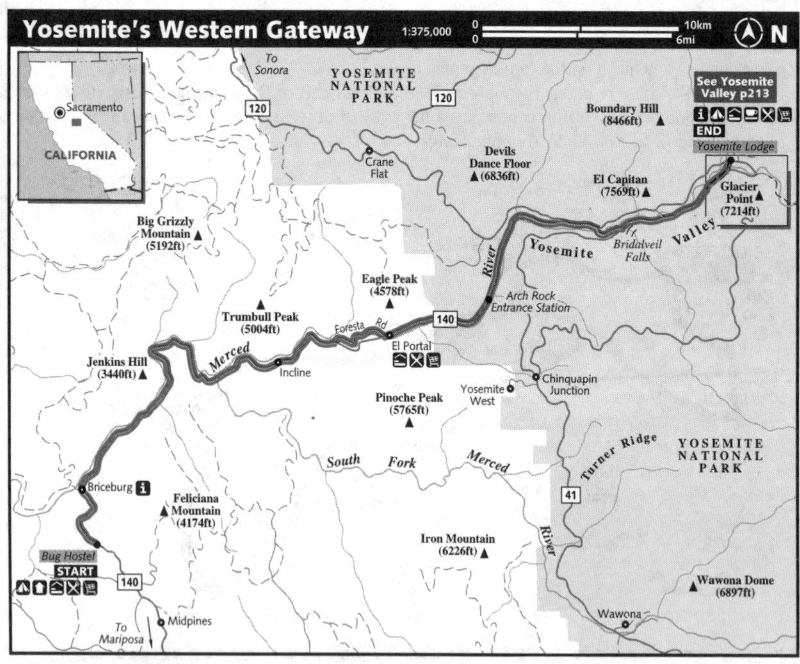

a ***general store*** offering provisions for the long ascent into the national park.

The steepest, narrowest part of the climb begins at 21mi and continues until you reach the park entrance 2mi later. Here you must pay the $10 reduced entrance fee (non-cyclists pay $20). Your climbing efforts are rewarded by dramatic views of rapids, falls, and enormous boulders. This section is not for the squeamish – the road here is barely wide enough for two motor vehicles, and a massive stone wall along the road's right edge gives you nowhere to go if a car passes too close.

The highlight of the ride is the entrance into Yosemite Valley near the 29mi mark. Here, after several steady miles of climbing, the route levels out, revealing the dramatic granite cliffs, waterfalls and vast meadows for which the park is famous.

Yosemite Valley

☎ 209

Yosemite Valley is one of the most spectacular spots on earth, a lush patchwork of meadows and forests bordered by enormous granite cliff faces. It forms the geographical, scenic and touristic heart of Yosemite National Park. Although occupying only seven sq mi (out of a total park area of 1200 sq mi), the valley receives nearly four million visitors annually. The resulting congestion can turn main roads into parking lots during the summer months.

For cyclists, the 8mi Yosemite Valley bikepath (see the boxed text, p213) provides an alternative way of enjoying the park. The circuit is suitable for riders of all ages and affords wonderful vistas of most of the valley's most famous attractions, including Half Dome and Yosemite Falls. There is currently talk of expanding the park's network of bikeways by creating a bike- and pedestrian-only zone along Northside Dr, presently one of the valley's main motor vehicle thoroughfares. Our map of this circuit also shows the locations of valley services.

Information Yosemite Valley visitor center is on the north side of the valley, in the complex of buildings known as Yosemite Village.

There are ATMs in the valley's three main tourist complexes – Curry Village, Yosemite Village and Yosemite Lodge.

Bikes can be rented at the Yosemite Lodge and Curry Village bike stands. Trailers for children are also available.

Things to See & Do Yosemite Valley provides virtually limitless opportunities for **outdoor recreation**. Aside from cycling, the most popular pursuits are hiking, rock climbing, photography and just plain gawking at the valley's grandeur.

Places to Stay & Eat Staying in Yosemite Valley requires serious planning, as rooms and campgrounds usually fill up months in advance. Reservations for all indoor accommodations listed here must be made through ***Yosemite Concession Services Corporation*** *(☎ 252-4848, 🆆 www.yosemitepark.com)*.

The cheapest campground is ***Camp 4***, 1mi west of Yosemite Village. Its walk-in sites are popular with climbers and cost $5 per person, first-come, first-served. People line up for sites as early as 4am on summer weekends. As each site accommodates six people, you may have to share. Sites in the valley's three other campgrounds – ***Lower Pines***, ***Upper Pines*** and ***North Pines*** – cost $18 and can be reserved up to five months in advance *(☎ 800-436-7275, 🆆 reservations.nps.gov)*. Hot showers cost $2 at the nearby Camp Curry Shower House.

Curry Village offers no-frills canvas tent cabins for $48, plus heated wooden cabins for around $57/75 without/with bath. Hotel rooms are available here for $87 to $103 and at ***Yosemite Lodge*** for $87 to $130.

Yosemite's classiest lodging is the ***Ahwahnee Hotel***, dating back to 1927. The attractive wood-and-stone building is tucked away at the edge of a meadow overhung by sheer granite walls. Rooms cost $319 and can be booked one year and one day in advance.

Food in the valley ranges from fast food and deli items to formal dinners at the Ahwahnee. Numerous casual eateries are available in Curry Village, Yosemite Village and Yosemite Lodge. The first two also have grocery stores.

Ahwahnee Hotel Dining Room and Bar *(☎ 372-1489)* has more character than anywhere else in the valley. The grand old Dining Room serves three meals a day plus an elaborate $20 Sunday brunch. Dinner reservations are advised.

Central California

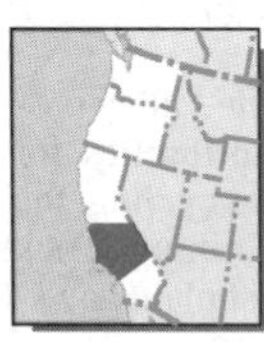

This section covers the long coastal strip between San Francisco and Los Angeles, from San Mateo County in the north to Ventura County in the south. The rides visit classic California places such as Santa Barbara, Big Sur, Monterey Bay, the Salinas Valley and the San Andreas Fault, while also exploring one-lane back roads, sleepy historical towns, 18th-century Spanish missions and secluded redwood groves unknown to the average Californian.

HISTORY

Central California's human history goes back more than 10,000 years. The main indigenous groups were the Esselen near Monterey Bay and Big Sur, the Salinan between the Salinas Valley and the coast, and the Chumash from San Luis Obispo (SLO) south. These peoples established hundreds of villages, basing their diet on the area's abundant marine life, wild game and acorns.

HAYDEN FOELL

Graceful 18th-century missions show California's rich Spanish heritage

From the mid-16th century, Spanish boats plied the waters offshore seeking mythical riches and a northern passage to the Atlantic. Disappointed in what they found, they did not establish permanent settlements until the late 18th century. Gaspar de Portolá's 1769 overland expedition from San Diego to San Francisco Bay, intended to fend off Russian designs on Alta California, paved the way for the building of forts and missions which ultimately secured the region for Spain. The Spanish chain of 21 missions was heavily concentrated on the Central Coast, with 11 such churches established between Santa Cruz and Ventura from 1770 to 1804. Contact with Europeans proved disastrous for California's native peoples, who were forced into servitude, infected with unfamiliar diseases and ultimately dispossessed of both their land and their traditional way of life.

Along with the missions, the Spanish established military strongholds at Santa Barbara and Monterey. Monterey quickly rose to prominence as the capital of Alta California, and after 1821 became a thriving trade center under Mexican rule. Yankee encroachment on the region culminated with Commodore John Sloat's raising of the US flag over Monterey's Custom House in 1846.

NATURAL HISTORY

Central California boasts a dazzling array of natural features. Vast redwood forests cloak the Santa Cruz Mtns, while smaller groves reach deep green fingers into Big Sur's precipitous coastal canyons. Monterey Bay, with its remarkable abundance of sea life, is the centerpiece of the world's largest marine sanctuary. Whales migrate offshore between December and April, and otters continue their comeback from the brink of extinction in the California Sea Otter Refuge between Carmel and Cambria. Critical coastal wetlands are preserved at Elkhorn Slough, while the Ventana Wilderness shelters the endangered California condor.

The Salinas River flows 150mi from its headwaters east of SLO to its mouth at Monterey Bay, draining Southern California's largest coastal basin and watering the state's second most productive agricultural

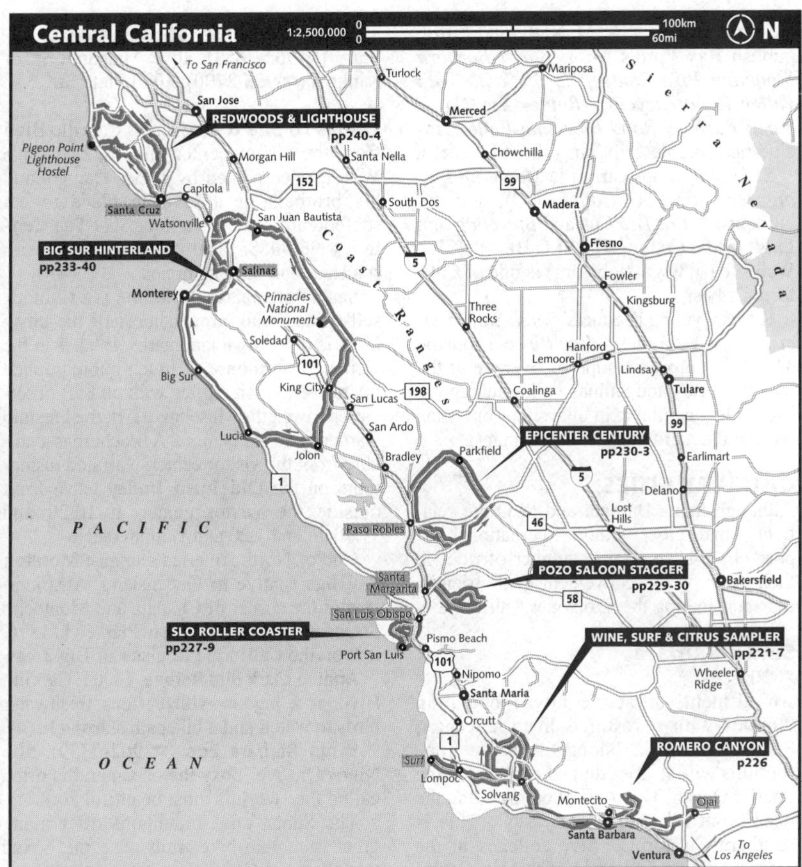

valley. The San Andreas Fault runs the entire length of Central California; graphic proof of the earth's slow creep can be seen in the dramatically offset stream channels south of Parkfield, and the displaced ancient volcanic rock formations of Pinnacles National Monument.

The variety of native oak species and habitats is exceptional, while cultivated orchards and vineyards add dashes of color and symmetry.

CLIMATE

Central California, while less rainy than the north, shares many of the same climate features. Winter (Nov–Mar) is the wettest season. Snow falls occasionally in the higher mountains but at sea level even frost is rare.

Spring and fall are pleasantly clear and warm, both inland and on the coast. Summer temperatures climb beyond 90°F in the interior valleys while coastal temperatures are often 20°F cooler.

INFORMATION

Maps & Books

An unbeatable resource is AAA's *Coast & Valley Section* map, covering everything from San Francisco to Ventura (☎ 805-682-5811, W www.aaa-calif.com). Caltrans (☎ 805-549-3111) publishes the free *District 5 Bicycle Map*, charting state highway elevations from Santa Cruz to Santa Barbara.

AAA's Santa Barbara and SLO County maps are excellent, as is the *Official Santa Barbara County Cycling Map*, free from most area bike shops. McNally and Loftin publish Ray Ford's *No 4: Santa Barbara Mountain Bike Routes*, *No 6: Santa Ynez Valley Road Bicycling Routes* and *No 7: Santa Barbara Road Bicycling Routes*, including route descriptions (about $3 each).

SLO bike shops carry the *Mountain Biking Map for SLO County* ($9), and the guidebooks *Fat Tire Fun* and *Bicycling San Luis Obispo County*. The SLO Bicycle Club Web site (W www.slobc.org) is one of California's best.

Krebs Cycling Products' *South San Francisco Bay & Monterey Bay Bicycle Touring Map* ($10) provides superb coverage of the Monterey Bay and Salinas Valley subregion. It is widely available in bike shops or online (W members.cruzio.com/~krebsmap/).

GATEWAY CITIES

Although Santa Barbara and SLO are relatively small cities without international airports, both have a large number of rides in their vicinity and convenient cycle-friendly transport linking them to wider California.

Santa Barbara

☎ 805

An affluent, attractive city (population 90,000) with a restored historic center, Santa Barbara lies along the Santa Ynez foothills with its toes dipped casually in the Pacific Ocean. The rows of palms along the oceanfront bikepath clearly say: 'This is southern California.' Five colleges in the area, including a campus of the University of California (UCSB), give the town a youthful population. Its rugged backdrop offers great mountain-biking opportunities.

Information The Tourist Information Center (☎ 965-3021, W www.santabarbaraca.com), corner Cabrillo Blvd and Garden St, is tiny and very busy.

Montecito Bank & Trust on the corner of State and Carrillo Sts has an ATM, as does Von's supermarket, corner Victoria and Chapala Sts.

Open Air Bicycles (☎ 962-7000), 224 Chapala St, adjacent to the Amtrak station, and Velo Pro Cyclery (☎ 963-7775), 629 State St, open every day. Wheel Fun Rentals (☎ 966-6733), 22 State St, near the railway, rents 21-speed, front-suspension mountain bikes.

Log on at the City of Santa Barbara Library (☎ 962-7653), 40 E Anapamu St; or Kinko's (☎ 966-2700), 1030 State St.

Things to See & Do Across Cabrillo Blvd from the visitor center, the 1872 Stearn's Wharf, once owned by James Cagney and his brothers, is a favorite place to eat seafood and watch sea lions. The **Sea Center** (☎ 962-0885) features touch tanks with sea stars and sea anemones.

Santa Barbara's **Red Tile Tour** is a 12-block self-guided walk around most of the city's historic downtown landmarks. It takes in the County Courthouse, a much-photographed Spanish-Moorish edifice with an 85ft observation tower, the Museum of Art, the Presidio Gardens and many more. A brochure is available from the visitor center. Narrated history tours on the **Old Town Trolley** leave from outside the visitor center at 10.20 and 11.50am and 1.20 and 2.50pm daily.

One of North America's largest **Moreton Bay figs** (native to Queensland, Australia) shades the corner of Chapala and Montecito Sts, near the Amtrak station. Planted in 1876, it is on the California Register of Big Trees.

Andrée Clark Bird Refuge, 1400 E Cabrillo Blvd, is a lagoon with various freshwater birds to watch and a bikepath skirting it.

Santa Barbara Zoo (☎ 962-5339), 500 Niños Dr, overlooks the ocean and is often called the 'world's most beautiful zoo'.

The Santa Ynez mountains offer many great mountain-bike trails. See the boxed text 'Romero Canyon' (p226).

Places to Stay & Eat Hiker/biker ***camping*** is available at El Capitan and Refugio State Beaches (the latter has hot showers) on the Day 3 route (and Day 32 of the Border to Border ride), but is best at Carpinteria State Beach, on Day 33 of the Border to Border ride. Cost is $3 per person with coin showers and a one-night limit.

Blue Sands Motel *(☎ 965-1624, 421 S Milpas St)* has large quiet doubles from $55 with a continental breakfast. ***Adobe Motel*** *(☎ 966-7505, 26 E Haley St)* has doubles with king beds for $75/125 weekday/weekend. ***Motel 6*** *(☎ 564-1392 or ☎ 800-466-8356, 443 Corona del Mar)*, 0.9mi east of the visitor center, charges $88 a double. The ***Motel 6*** *(☎ 800-466-8356)* 11mi away at Carpinteria charges only $49 a double. Motels clustered on Castillo St such as ***Colonial Beach Inn*** *(☎ 963-4317 or ☎ 800-649-2669, 206 Castillo St)*, ***Tropicana Inn*** *(☎ 966-2219 or ☎ 800-468-1988, 223 Castillo St)*, and adjacent ***Santa Barbara Beach Travelodge*** *(☎ 965-8527 or ☎ 800-578-7878)* charge around $120/140 weekday/weekend.

Von's supermarket *(cnr Victoria & Chapala Sts)* is open from 6am to midnight. A ***farmers market*** is held on the 500 and 600 blocks of State St (Tues 4–7.30pm; 3.30–6.30pm in winter). Fresh food is also available from ***Tri-County Produce Wholesale*** next to the railway line on Milpas St.

Restaurants to suit every taste exist in town. For many more options, ask the visitor center for a copy of 'The Map', a restaurant, shopping and entertainment guide. ***Be Bop Burgers*** *(☎ 966-1956, 111 State St)* is an old-style diner and family fun restaurant. Burgers range from $3 to $5, there are sandwiches, soups and salads, and breakfast pancakes from $2. Beach bums and surfers head for ***The Endless Summer*** *(☎ 564-4666, 113 Harbor Way)* a bar/cafe with delicious views and fresh seafood by the boats. ***Left at Albuquerque*** *(☎ 564-5040, 803 State St)* can fill even a cyclist with Mexican/Southwestern food – nachos, tamales, tacos, enchiladas – for around $9. ***Santa Barbara Fishouse*** *(☎ 966-2112, 101 E Cabrillo Blvd)* offers classy dining opposite the water with fresh local fish dishes from $12 to $19. ***Blue Shark Bistro*** *(☎ 564-1700, 21 W Victoria St)* serves upmarket burgers, risotto, chicken and beef (to $30).

Getting There & Away Although not an international gateway, Santa Barbara is convenient for domestic air, bus and train travel.

Air Santa Barbara's airport, served by numerous domestic airlines, is 10mi northwest of town in Goleta. Daily flights go to Los Angeles (LA), San Francisco, Phoenix and Denver. Cycling from the airport to downtown is straightforward, via the Coast and Crosstown bike routes. Turn right out of the parking lot, following signs to Santa Barbara, then join the Coast Route bikepath immediately after crossing under Hwy 217 (0.6mi).

Bus Greyhound (☎ 965-7551) is at 34 W Carrillo St downtown. Nine buses daily go to LA ($14/24 one way/return, three hours), seven to San Diego ($23/44, six hours), six to SLO ($19/34, three hours), and five each to Salinas ($34/67, six hours) and San Francisco ($32/60, nine hours).

Train The train station is at 209 State St, two blocks from the waterfront. Service to/from LA and San Diego is especially good, with five trains traveling the route daily. Two trains run daily to/from SLO, and one to/from Oakland-San Francisco. Fares from Santa Barbara include LA $22/44, SLO $26/52, San Diego $43/86, Salinas $48/96 and San Francisco $67/134.

San Luis Obispo (SLO)

☎ 805

SLO is a relaxed, friendly town with a large student population, dramatically situated 10mi inland in a valley of extinct volcanoes leading to the sea. Spanish padres chose this as their fifth California mission site in 1772. Modern day SLO-town, as locals tend to call it, is still centered on the old mission plaza. A beautiful creek runs through downtown, a pedestrian walkway taking full advantage of its leafy greenness.

Information The visitor center (☎ 781-2777, W www.slochamber.org) is at 1039 Chorro St, near Mission Plaza.

Numerous ATMs can be found downtown on Marsh, Higuera and Santa Rosa Sts.

An excellent bike shop just east of downtown is Art's Cyclery, (☎ 543-4416), 2140 Santa Barbara St.

Free Internet access is available at the public library (☎ 781-5991), corner Osos and Palm Sts (closed Sun).

Things to See & Do The mountain biking is excellent all around SLO. Some of the best trails are in the hills behind campus at Cal Poly State University, and along the coast in **Montaña de Oro State Park**.

The **farmers market**, on Higuera St between Nipomo and Osos Sts, is a fun place to eat, hear live music and mingle (Thurs 6–9pm).

Bubblegum Alley, a local curiosity between 733 and 737 Higuera St, runs between walls plastered with discarded chewing gum.

Historic **Mission San Luis Obispo**, in the heart of downtown, has a museum with exhibits on Chumash and mission life.

Places to Stay Eight miles west of town, ***El Chorro Regional Park*** *(☎ 781-5930, Ⓦ www.slocountyparks.com)* has campsites from $18. Further west, beautiful ***Montaña de Oro State Park*** *(☎ 528-0513 or ☎ 800-444-7275, Ⓦ www.cal-parks.ca.gov)* offers beachside sites for $7. The $20 sites at ***Avila Hot Springs*** *(☎ 595-2359, Ⓦ www.avilahotsprings.com)*, 8mi south of town, are noisy and near the road but close to Sycamore Mineral Springs' 24-hour hot tubs.

Hostel Obispo *(☎ 544-4678, Ⓦ www.hostelobispo.com, 1617 Santa Rosa St)* is a delightful hostel two blocks from the train station. Cyclists Elaine Simer and Tom Parks offer a 'self-propelled' discount rate of $15. They have four private rooms for $40/45 members/non-members. Rates include a sourdough-pancake breakfast.

Motels are clustered in two locations near downtown: on the north end of Monterey St, and on Olive St (near the junction of Hwy 101 and Santa Rosa St). Decent budget options include the ***Los Padres Motel*** *(☎ 543-5017 or ☎ 800-543-5090, 1575 Monterey St)*, charging from $39; and ***Coachman Inn*** *(☎ 544-0400, 1001 Olive St)*, as low as $28/35 per single/double midweek. Slightly more upscale is the ***Adobe Inn*** *(☎ 549-0321 or ☎ 800-676-1588, 1473 Monterey St)*, where the price ($55–110) includes full breakfast. The ***Garden Street Inn*** *(☎ 545-9802 or ☎ 800-488-2045, Ⓔ innkeeper@gardenstreetinn.com, 1212 Garden St)* offers B&B in an 1887 Victorian ($110–190), with bike storage on its back deck.

A wonderfully tacky extravaganza of pink decor and massive stonework, the ***Madonna Inn*** *(☎ 543-3000 or ☎ 800-543-9666, Ⓦ www.madonnainn.com)* offers unique rooms ($117–310). If the price is too steep, it's worth visiting their cafe and restrooms – the circular red booths are a hoot, and the clam shell sinks and waterfall grotto urinals are big enough to bathe in.

Sycamore Mineral Springs *(☎ 595-7302 or ☎ 800-234-5831, Ⓦ www.sycamoresprings.com, 1215 Avila Beach Dr)* is a refurbished historic spa 9mi south of town, offering rooms with private hot tubs ($127–308), breakfast included. Hot-tub rentals are available for non-guests 24 hours a day.

Places to Eat Just north of downtown is ***Scolari's*** *(cnr Johnson Ave & Marsh St)* supermarket. ***New Frontiers*** *(896 Foothill Blvd)* is a good natural-food market. ***Trader Joe's*** *(237 Higuera St)* sells delicious, ready-to-cook frozen food and specialty groceries. ***House of Bread*** *(☎ 542-0255, 858 Higuera St)* bakes great bread and pastries.

For quality Mexican fast food, try ***Taco Roco*** *(281 Santa Rosa St)* near motel row, open till 3am weekends.

Mo's Smokehouse BBQ *(☎ 544-6193, 970 Higuera St)*, winner of numerous annual awards, serves fantastic barbecue. Its recipes were gleaned from all over the USA on a cross-country road trip (see the wall map). ***Linnaea's*** *(1110 Garden St)* is a pleasant downtown cafe with delicious baked goods, a nice back patio and live music nightly in summer. ***Thai Palace*** *(☎ 594-1744, 1015 Court St)* has tasty Thai food, including many vegetarian options. ***Big Sky Cafe*** *(☎ 545-5401, 1121 Broad St)*, one of SLO's most popular eateries, serves American and international meals in a big room under a starry ceiling. Gotta try their beignets! ***Fishdaddy's*** *(☎ 545-8226, 1040 Broad St)* features nouvelle Mexican cuisine overlooking the creek.

Getting There & Away There are several convenient options for cyclists leaving or entering SLO.

Air The airport is served by United and American Airlines, with several non-stop flights daily to/from LA and San Francisco. From downtown, take Broad St east 3mi, then turn right on Aero Dr.

Bus Greyhound (☎ 543-2121) is at 150 South St. Six buses leave daily for LA ($30/58 one way/return, five hours), Santa Barbara ($19/34, two hours), San Diego ($49/92, eight hours), Salinas ($24/48, three hours) and San Francisco ($40/76, six hours).

Train The train station is at 1011 Railroad Ave (east end of Santa Rosa St). Amtrak's Coast Starlight comes through once daily in each direction, northbound to Salinas and Oakland, southbound to LA. Bikes cost $5 and must be boxed.

Amtrak's *Pacific Surfliner* has its northern terminus at SLO. A southbound *Surfliner* leaves SLO daily for Santa Barbara, LA and San Diego; the return train is also daily. Bikes travel free on convenient racks.

Fares from SLO include Santa Barbara $26/52, LA $36/72, San Diego $46/92, Salinas $28/56, and Oakland-San Francisco $46/92.

Central Coast

The Central Coast epitomizes all the advantages usually associated with Southern California (healthy lifestyle, beaches, good weather, relaxed attitude) without having fully succumbed to many of its vices (hideous traffic, smog, wall-to-wall mall culture). The road and mountain biking are both so good in this region, it's worthy of an entire book! With unparalleled natural beauty, bike-friendly cities and an excellent public transit system, this is a destination that will make any cyclist smile.

Wine, Surf & Citrus Sampler

Duration	4 days
Distance	158.1mi
Difficulty	moderate–hard
Start	Surf
End	Ojai
Cues & Elevation Profiles	pp370–1

This ride offers a smorgasbord of Central Coast experiences, from wine tasting to breathtaking coastal panoramas to Danish kitsch to vast seas of citrus and avocado groves to a rugged climb on a remote dirt road through the Santa Ynez Mtns. Southbound cyclists on the Border to Border ride can use this as an alternate route from Lompoc to Santa Barbara or Ventura.

NATURAL HISTORY

The Santa Ynez Valley occupies a triangle of land at the junction between two of California's principal mountain chains. To the south lie the Santa Ynez Mtns, the westernmost extension of the Transverse Ranges, while to the northeast lie the San Rafael Mtns, the southernmost extension of the Coast Ranges. Among California mountains, the Santa Ynez range is unique in that it runs east-west. As a result, its seaward slopes get full southern exposure, and despite heavier rainfall its microclimate is drier than on the inland side.

PLANNING

When to Ride

This ride is beautiful year-round. March and April are particularly enjoyable, with fields full of wildflowers and the Santa Ynez Valley's two biggest cycling events, the Solvang and Gourmet Centuries. Immediately after heavy winter rains, the dirt section and stream crossings on Day 3 may become treacherous; inquire locally if in doubt.

What to Bring

You'll want good tread on your tires, if not an actual mountain bike, for the dirt section on Day 3. A pair of sturdy sandals is also very useful for the stream crossings that morning.

GETTING TO/FROM THE RIDE

Surf

Reach Amtrak's Surf-Lompoc station from SLO or Santa Barbara. The daily morning train from SLO ($10, one hour) permits a full day of cycling with breakfast in Lompoc. The daily train from Santa Barbara ($12, 1½ hours) requires cyclists to split Day 1 into two, due to its 7pm arrival and the total lack of accommodations in Surf; the best option is to overnight in Lompoc (8.5mi inland).

Ojai

Bicycle This ride can enjoyably be extended 15mi beyond Ojai to Ventura via the Ojai Valley and Ventura River bikepaths. From Ojai, retrace the Day 4 route on the Ojai Bikepath to Hwy 150, then continue straight on the bikepath to Ventura, where you can join Day 33 (pp341–4) of the Border to Border ride or catch public transit.

Bus South Coast Area Transit (☎ 643-3158, **W** www.scat.org) runs bus No 16 hourly from the corner of Fox St and E Ojai Ave in Ojai to Main and Figueroa Sts in Ventura ($1, 50 minutes). From here it's only a few blocks to Greyhound and Amtrak.

Five buses leave daily from Ventura's Greyhound station (☎ 653-0164), corner E Thompson Blvd and S Palm St. They head to LA ($12/24 one way/return, 2½ hours), Santa Barbara ($7/13, 40 minutes), SLO ($19/34, 3½ hours) and San Francisco ($32/60, 11 hours).

Train Amtrak's Ventura station is on the corner of Harbor Blvd at Figueroa St. Several trains leave daily for Santa Barbara ($8/16, 45 minutes) and LA ($13/26, two hours). One train goes to SLO ($21/42, four hours).

THE RIDE

Surf

☎ 805

Surf is nothing more than a lonely railway stop hidden in the coastal dunes of Vandenberg Air Force Base at the western terminus of a lightly traveled dead-end road. There's a magical feeling of seclusion disembarking in a place so remote. Surf is also a more convenient place to bring a bike (thanks to the easy-to-use bike rack system) than Lompoc, Buellton or Solvang, all three of which are accessible only by bus and therefore require you to box your bike en route to the ride.

The only services at Surf are a pay phone and a restroom.

Day 1: Surf to Solvang

3–5 hours, 33.7mi

Start at the beach and follow the Santa Ynez River inland to the Danish-style tourist town of Solvang. Most of the ride is through farm country on quiet roads, with only moderate changes in elevation.

From the windswept railroad siding at Surf (where surfers indeed throng in the early morning hours) it's an easy ride east on class 2 bike lane through cultivated flower fields to Lompoc (8.5mi). At 10.1mi is the detour to La Purísima Mission (see Side Trip). The ride briefly joins the Border to Border route, then turns east and drops into the beautiful Santa Ynez River Valley on Santa Rosa Rd (13.1mi). The next 17mi wind languidly through attractive old walnut orchards and new vineyards, with vistas of the river flanked by graceful hills on either side. Two small **wineries** offer tasting as you approach the intersection with busy US Hwy 101.

Buellton (30.7mi) is a nondescript freeway town a stone's throw from Solvang. It has ***fast-food outlets*** and a ***Motel 6*** *(☎ 688-7797)* charging $40/45 for singles/doubles. It is also home to the nearest ***campground*** to Solvang and a great ***barbecue restaurant*** (for both, see Places to Stay & Eat for Solvang, p224).

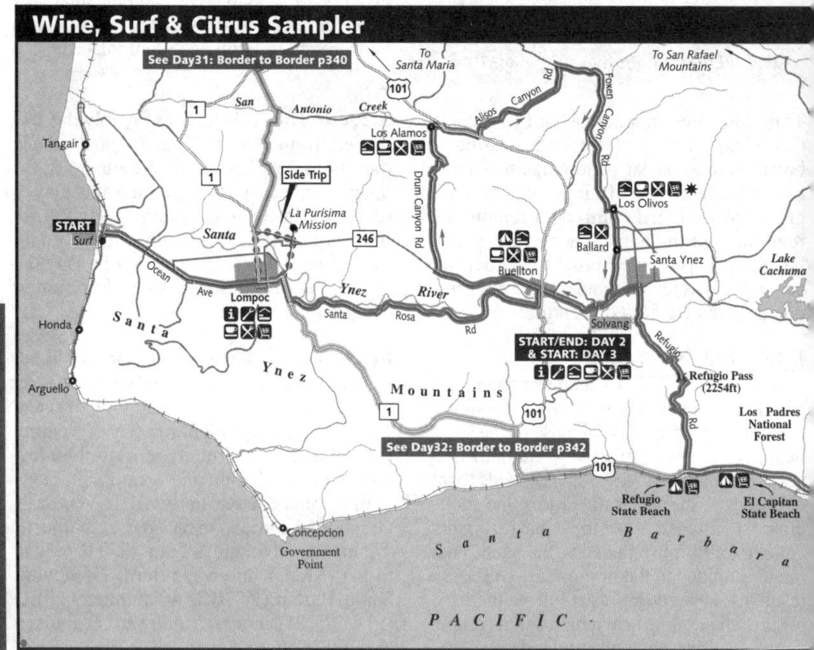

Side Trip: La Purísima Mission State Historic Park

7mi return

La Purísima, founded in 1787, was California's eleventh mission and today is preserved as a state historic park (☎ 733-3713), with buildings, gardens and even livestock painstakingly reassembled to simulate 19th-century conditions. Periodically throughout the year costumed docents give demonstrations on Chumash traditions and mission life. Turn off the route at 10.1mi, taking H St north for 2.7mi, then Purísima Rd east 2.1mi to the park entrance (entry costs $2). To rejoin the main route, take Mission Gate Rd south 0.4mi and Hwy 246 west 1.8mi, then turn left (south) at the Hwy 1/Hwy 246 junction (11.6mi mark on the cue sheet).

Solvang

☎ 805

Arriving in Solvang is like stumbling upon a Disneyfied Denmark. Despite the town's kitsch exterior, it actually does have a proud Danish heritage going back to 1911, when Midwesterners of Danish extraction came here to found a traditional folk school. Solvang's current 'theme park' look, replete with faux half-timbered buildings and windmills, was the brainchild of a local resident who came back from WWII inspired to give the town a European makeover. Below the surface, however, some authentic Danish touches remain. Solvang's cuisine features *aebleskiver* (pronounced able-skeever; tasty pancake-like balls with jam), *frikadeller* (Danish meatballs) and *medisterpolse* (Danish sausage). **Solvang's oldest windmill**, a ramshackle but picturesque affair dating back to 1922 and now designated a county historical landmark, sits in a field 2mi north of town on Fredensborg Canyon Rd. Alas, the folk school which constituted the town's original *raison d'être* was lost to termites in the 1970s!

Information The visitor center (☎ 688-6144 or ☎ 800-468-6765, W www.solvangusa.com) has an office at the corner of Mission Dr and Fifth St, where the ride cues start and stop; and another at 1639 Copenhagen Dr.

The most central ATM is at Mid-State Bank, 1660 Copenhagen Dr.

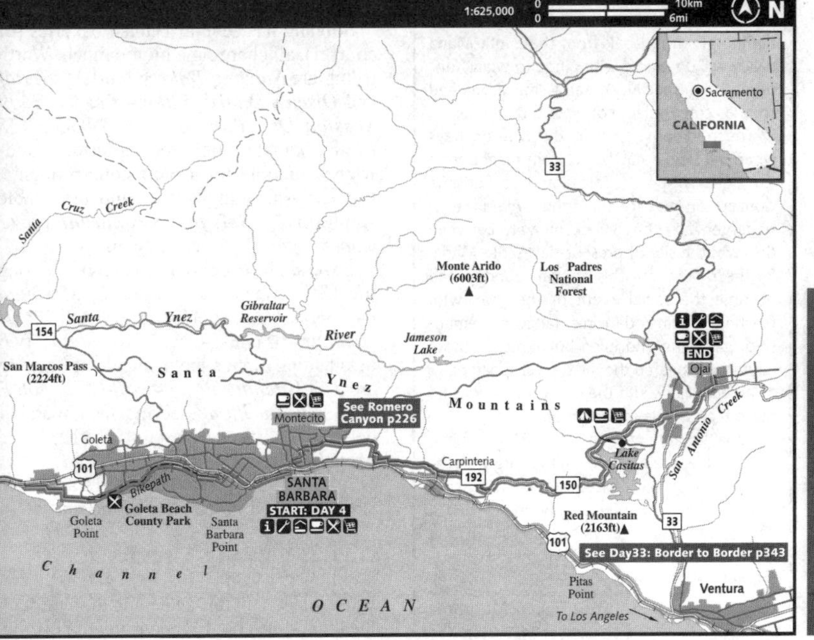

Dr J's Bicychiatry (☎ 688-6263), 1661 Fir Ave, is a small but very helpful bike shop just north of Mission Dr.

Things to See & Do The **Mission Santa Ynez**, founded in 1804 as California's 19th mission, is an unexpectedly peaceful oasis only a few hundred yards from the center of town, its beautiful gardens filled with palm and pepper trees.

Nojogui Falls State Park is a charmed spot 7mi southwest of town, accessible by a lightly traveled paved road. From downtown, cycle south on Alisal Rd, which climbs 500ft before dropping into idyllic oak and sycamore grassland. The graceful ribbon-like falls are a 10-minute walk from the parking lot.

Solvang's two free, small **museums** (Hans Christian Anderson Museum, 1680 Mission Dr, and Elverhoj Museum, 1624 Elverhoy Way) offer glimpses into Danish culture, the former cataloging the life of the famous author, the latter showcasing traditional Danish rooms alongside historical displays.

Places to Stay & Eat The ***Flying Flags RV Park*** *(☎ 688-3716; 180 Ave of the Flags, Buellton)* charges $18 for lackluster but grassy campsites.

Solvang Gardens Lodge *(☎ 688-4404, 293 Alisal Rd)* and ***Hamlet Motel*** *(☎ 688-4413, 1532 Mission Dr)* are two of Solvang's better budget motels, each offering rooms from $39/69 midweek/weekend. Several other motels on Mission Dr compete for the Cutest Scandinavian Name award, their prices varying greatly with the season. Solvang's biggest and fanciest place is the ***Royal Scandinavian Inn*** *(☎ 688-8000 or ☎ 800-624-5572, W www.solvangrsi.com/main.shtml, 400 Alisal Rd)*, where rooms cost $55 to $159.

The area's biggest supermarkets are ***Nielsen's*** *(608 Alamo Pintado Rd)* and ***El Rancho Market*** *(2886 Mission Dr)*, both east of town on the Day 3 route. The latter has an excellent deli. ***Solvang Market & Deli*** *(475 Fifth St)* is a smaller in-town alternative. On Wednesday afternoons there's a ***farmers market*** on First St.

Solvang has several Danish bakeries (of course!), all charging a bit too much. Worth trying are ***Solvang Bakery*** *(460 Alisal Rd)* and ***Olsen's Danish Village Bakery*** *(1529 Mission Dr)*. ***Panino*** *(☎ 688-0608, 475 First St)* makes delicious gourmet sandwiches suitable for a wine country picnic. For early-morning coffee and affordable Aebleskiver, ***Solvang Restaurant*** *(1672 Copenhagen Dr)* opens at 6am.

Several places serve Danish food. Among the better ones are ***The Little Mermaid*** *(☎ 688-6141, 1546 Mission Dr)* and ***Bit O' Denmark*** *(☎ 688-5426, 473 Alisal Rd)*. Two outstanding dinner spots outside of Solvang are ***The Hitching Post*** *(☎ 688-0676; 406 E Hwy 246, Buellton)*, serving incomparably delicious oak-fired barbecue since 1952, and ***Mattei's Tavern*** *(☎ 688-4820; Hwy 154, Los Olivos)*, a 19th-century hotel and stagecoach stop converted into a cozy restaurant.

Santa Maria–Style Barbecue

For some of the tastiest seared cow this side of the Sierra Nevada, Santa Maria–style barbecue is a must-eat. Take prime top sirloin, cut to four-inch-thick hunks, roll in salt, garlic salt and pepper, spear onto 8ft-long metal rods, and lower onto glowing coals. Only slightly green red oak from the Santa Maria Valley will do. Serve with pinquito beans (another local specialty), salsa, macaroni and cheese, green salad, coffee and ice cream.

The tradition began in the Mission days when *vaqueros* (cowboys) from neighboring San Luis Obispo de Tolosa and La Purísima Concepción met for the annual *matanza*, or slaughter, at a huge rock midway between the two: the site of present-day Santa Maria. By the rancho era this annual roundup had become the social event of the year, with feasting, singing, dancing, fancy horsemanship, gambling and even bullfights. In those days, they speared the meat on stripped poles of green willow, and the barbecue pit was no more than a hole in the ground.

Today's Santa Marians are still barbecuing. But don't let them catch you messing with the recipe. To protect the tradition, the Santa Maria Valley Chamber of Commerce had it copyrighted – right down to the salsa. To taste it for yourself, try Buellton's Hitching Post restaurant (see Places to Stay & Eat for Solvang).

Gaen Murphree

Day 2: Solvang Circuit

4–6 hours, 44.8mi

Ride unladen on this sweeping loop through the local wine country, returning to Solvang.

JOHN ELK III

JOHN ELK III

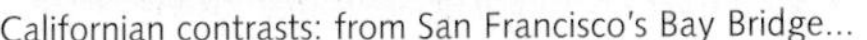

Californian contrasts: from San Francisco's Bay Bridge...

...to Yosemite's Half Dome.

ANTHONY PIDGEON

Pack a picnic and cycle from vineyard to vineyard through California's Wine Country.

RICHARD CUMMINS

JOHN ELK III

At day's end in San Francisco relax on Baker Beach (L), or take a moonlit ride through the streets (R).

LOUISE PRESTON

JOHN ELK III

Cycle in Central California's golden glow, or buckle up for a ride of a different kind in Salinas.

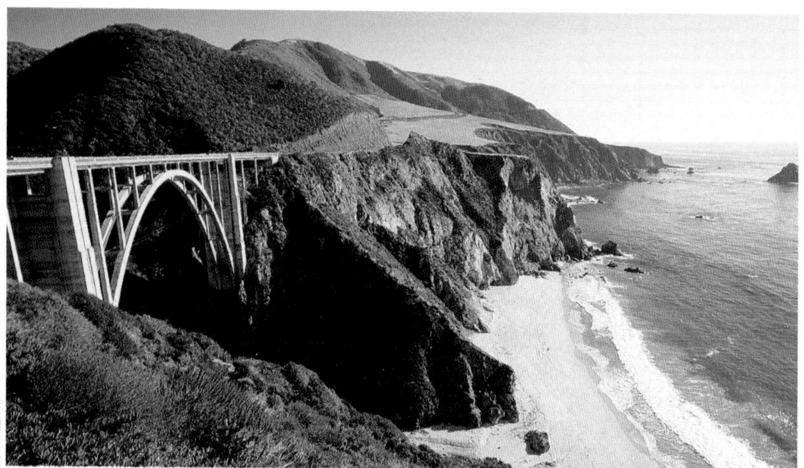
JOHN ELK III

California's Big Sur coast offers miles of stunning Pacific Ocean views.

RICHARD CUMMINS

RICHARD CUMMINS

Santa Cruz: enjoy the breathtaking natural beauty or hang up your hat in ranch country.

Except for two short stretches of busy highway, traffic is extremely light. Gorgeous views of vineyards and mountains compensate for occasionally challenging terrain.

From Solvang, retrace the Day 1 route to Buellton (3mi), then continue west on busy four-lane Hwy 246. The pleasant traffic-free riding begins in earnest at Drum Canyon Rd (9.2mi), which eventually narrows to one lane as it snakes steeply up to a summit offering commanding views of the countryside. An equally sinuous downhill (watch for broken pavement!) leads to sleepy historical Los Alamos (18.5mi), a nice spot for lunch, with ***market***, **parks** and ***restaurants***.

From here, briefly follow the wide shoulder of busy Hwy 101 before reentering tranquil vineyard country. The remaining stages are delightful, with wineries offering tasting every 2mi to 5mi. The **Bedford Thompson Winery** is at 23mi. **Zaca Mesa Winery** (29.1mi) and **Firestone Vineyard** (a short side trip down Zaca Station Rd at 33.8mi) are among the region's oldest, both dating from 1972, and **Fess Parker Winery** (32.3mi) is quickly becoming a local institution with its ritzy Spa Hotel in nearby Los Olivos. Cheese and crackers are sold at several of the wineries' stores. Beware of drinking too much, as there are a couple of tough climbs in this stretch. The long downhill into Los Olivos beginning at 35mi is pure bliss, with dramatic views of the wine country and the San Rafael Mtns to the east.

Los Olivos (38.8mi) has several tasting rooms, plus the option of an early dinner at historic ***Mattei's Tavern*** (see Places to Stay & Eat for Solvang). From here it's an easy ride on a bike lane back to Solvang.

Day 3: Solvang to Santa Barbara

5–7 hours, 43.8mi

This is the hardest day of the tour, with limited services and several early challenges, including nine stream crossings and a steep, rutted climb up the flank of the Santa Ynez Mtns on unpaved Refugio Rd (former home of Ronald Reagan). From the summit (2254ft), a long paved descent plummets through lemon and avocado groves towards **Refugio State Beach** (18.1mi), offering spectacular coastal views. The remaining miles are mostly flat and within sight of the Pacific, combining long stretches of bikepath with a grind along Hwy 101.

While the steep, 3.5mi dirt section is easiest on a mountain bike, it can be managed on a touring bike with good tires, or walked. The advantage to this route is that there are virtually no cars. For cyclists unfazed by fast-moving traffic, an alternative (paved) route is scenic Hwy 154 past Lake Cachuma. From Solvang, take Hwy 246 east, then Hwy 154 south towards San Marcos Pass (2224ft). At Paradise Rd (13mi), exit the busy highway and hook up with a series of steep but more lightly traveled roads through the mountains to Santa Barbara (Stagecoach Rd, Camino Cielo, and either Gibraltar Rd or Painted Cave Rd/Old San Marcos Pass Rd).

The main route sees no towns for the first 30mi, so consider stocking up at the excellent ***El Rancho Market deli*** (2.7mi). In summer, small ***stores*** at Refugio and **El Capitan** (20.5mi) Beaches are also open. Also recommended is the ***Beachside Bar/Cafe*** at **Goleta Beach County Park** (33.8mi).

The final leg is on a bikepath extending 7mi from Goleta to the edge of downtown Santa Barbara. It's just one of many well-signed bikeways, indicating what a fantastic cycling city this is.

Santa Barbara

See Santa Barbara (pp218–21) for information about accommodations and other services.

Day 4: Santa Barbara to Ojai

4–5 hours, 35.8mi

After yesterday's demanding climb, Day 4 is almost a relief. There are still a few good ascents, all of them on paved road, as you cross the Santa Ynez Mtns one last time. The early stages pass through the wealthy and beautifully landscaped town of Montecito (3.9mi) in the hills above Santa Barbara. Further south, Hwy 192 emerges into agricultural country, with citrus and avocado groves and flower nurseries everywhere. The stretch along Gobernador Canyon Rd (15mi) is especially picturesque and less busy than the state highways. From the junction with Hwy 150, it's a steep climb to West Casitas Pass (20.5mi), then a quick descent and another rise to East Casitas Pass (23,2mi), which affords beautiful views over Lake Casitas and into the Ventura River Valley. It's mostly downhill from here to the Ojai Valley Bikepath, which continues into central Ojai.

Romero Canyon

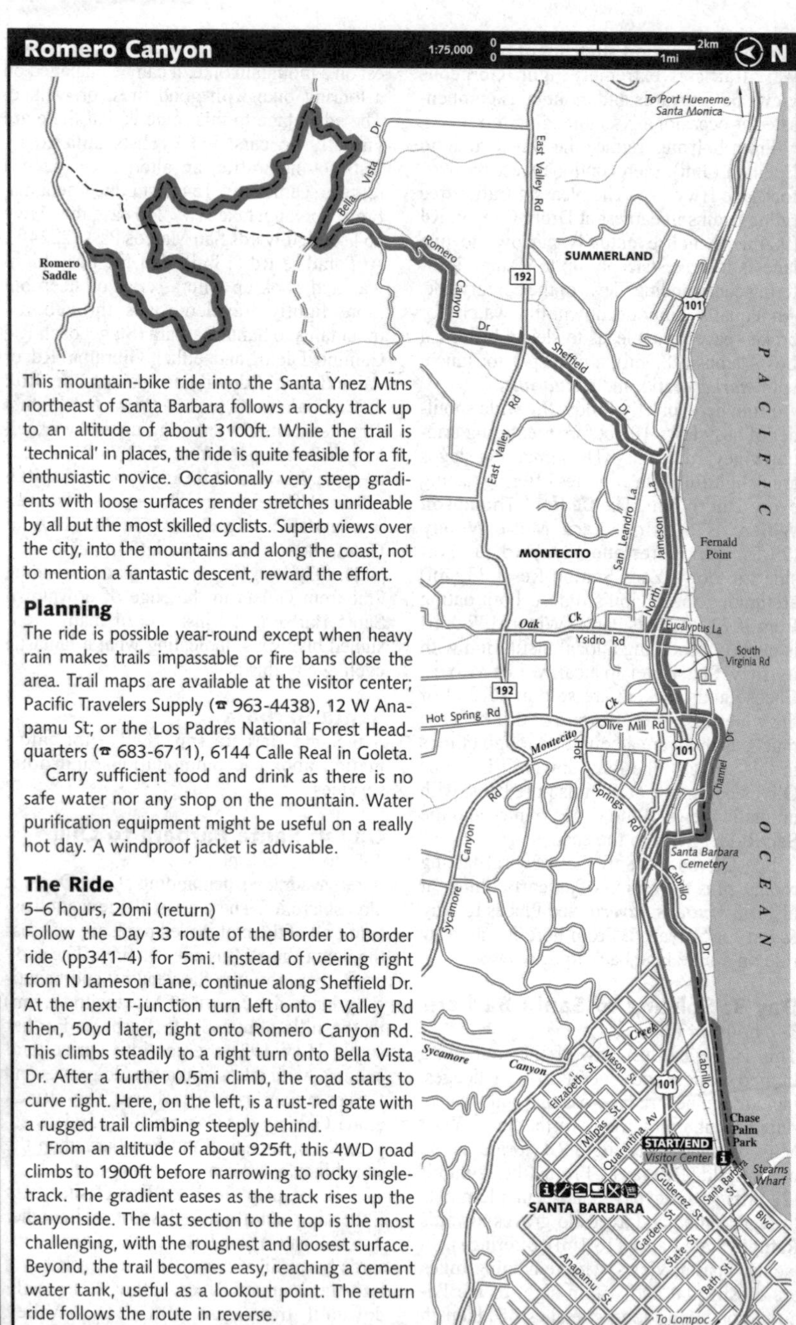

This mountain-bike ride into the Santa Ynez Mtns northeast of Santa Barbara follows a rocky track up to an altitude of about 3100ft. While the trail is 'technical' in places, the ride is quite feasible for a fit, enthusiastic novice. Occasionally very steep gradients with loose surfaces render stretches unrideable by all but the most skilled cyclists. Superb views over the city, into the mountains and along the coast, not to mention a fantastic descent, reward the effort.

Planning

The ride is possible year-round except when heavy rain makes trails impassable or fire bans close the area. Trail maps are available at the visitor center; Pacific Travelers Supply (☎ 963-4438), 12 W Anapamu St; or the Los Padres National Forest Headquarters (☎ 683-6711), 6144 Calle Real in Goleta.

Carry sufficient food and drink as there is no safe water nor any shop on the mountain. Water purification equipment might be useful on a really hot day. A windproof jacket is advisable.

The Ride

5–6 hours, 20mi (return)

Follow the Day 33 route of the Border to Border ride (pp341–4) for 5mi. Instead of veering right from N Jameson Lane, continue along Sheffield Dr. At the next T-junction turn left onto E Valley Rd then, 50yd later, right onto Romero Canyon Rd. This climbs steadily to a right turn onto Bella Vista Dr. After a further 0.5mi climb, the road starts to curve right. Here, on the left, is a rust-red gate with a rugged trail climbing steeply behind.

From an altitude of about 925ft, this 4WD road climbs to 1900ft before narrowing to rocky singletrack. The gradient eases as the track rises up the canyonside. The last section to the top is the most challenging, with the roughest and loosest surface. Beyond, the trail becomes easy, reaching a cement water tank, useful as a lookout point. The return ride follows the route in reverse.

Ojai

☎ 805

The Ojai Valley is a fertile mosaic of fields, palm trees and citrus groves cradled by tall and occasionally snowcapped mountains. It has long been a center for healing, spirituality and the arts. The town's most prominent landmark is the stucco post office tower at the corner of Signal St and E Ojai Ave. Most local businesses are concentrated within a few blocks of here, spreading east-west along Ojai Ave.

Information The visitor center (☎ 646-8126, fax 646-9762, w www.the-ojai.org) is at 150 W Ojai Ave. Bank of America, 205 W Ojai Ave, and Wells Fargo Bank, 202 E Matilija St, have ATMs. Ojai Bicycles (☎ 646-7736), 108 Canada St, is a full-service shop with rentals.

Things to See & Do Ojai makes a great base for **mountain biking** and **hiking** trips into the surrounding **Los Padres National Forest**. For local trail information, visit the Forest Service Ranger Station (☎ 646-4348) at 1190 E Ojai Ave. Good 'there and back' **road biking** is possible north of town on Hwy 33 towards Pine Mtn Summit and east of town on Hwy 150, which runs flat through orange groves for 2mi before climbing steeply for beautiful panoramas of the valley. The **Ojai Valley Museum**, in an historic converted church at 130 W Ojai Ave, has exhibits on local history plus a native plant garden. Various places around town offer **spa treatments**; inquire at the visitor center.

Places to Stay & Eat The ***Lake Casitas Recreation Area*** *(☎ 649-2233)*, 6mi west of town on Hwy 150, has campsites from $15, with snack bar, store and showers but no swimming. Primitive campsites are available throughout Los Padres National Forest – among the most accessible is beautiful ***Wheeler Gorge*** *(☎ 800-280-2267)*, 8mi north of town on Hwy 33, with sites from $12.

Rose Garden Inn *(☎ 646-1434 or ☎ 800-799-1881, w www.rosegardeninnofojai.com, 615 W Ojai Ave)*, with sauna, jacuzzi and swimming pool, has singles/doubles for from $69/79. ***Hummingbird Inn*** *(☎ 800-228-3744, w www.hummingbirdinnofojai.com, 1208 E Ojai Ave)* charges $87/97. The hilltop ***Ojai Retreat*** *(☎ 646-2536, w www.ojairetreat.com, 160 Besant Rd)* is a meditative spot west of town, with rooms/cottages from $50/120. ***Blue Iguana Inn*** *(☎ 646-5277, w www.blueiguanainn.com, 11794 N Ventura Ave)* features Southwestern-style adobe rooms with cooking facilities from $95/135 midweek/weekend.

Starr Market *(131 W Ojai Ave)* is the most central supermarket. ***Rainbow Bridge/Rainbow Kitchen*** *(211 E Matilija St)* is a good natural foods market and deli. Delicious fresh-baked bread is available from ***Bill Baker's German Bakery*** *(457 E Ojai Ave)*. ***Ojai Coffee Roasting Company*** *(337 E Ojai Ave)* is a lively cafe popular with locals. Friendly ***Bonnie Lu's*** *(328 E Ojai Ave)* serves delicious breakfasts featuring huge glasses of local orange juice. ***Boccali's*** *(☎ 646-6116, 3277 Ojai-Santa Paula Rd)* is an Ojai institution, serving pasta and pizza in a country setting 2mi east of town. On the pricier side, ***The Ranch House*** *(☎ 646-2360, S Lomita Ave)*, west of town, features fresh herbs, award-winning gourmet food and streamside seating in a lovely garden while ***Suzanne's Cuisine*** *(☎ 640-1961, 502 W Ojai Ave)* has received rave reviews from *Gourmet Magazine* and the *LA Times*. Numerous other restaurants are scattered along Ojai Ave.

San Luis Obispo County

The SLO Roller Coaster, Pozo Saloon Stagger and Epicenter Century rides all fall within this county, and are covered on one map (p228).

SLO Roller Coaster

Duration	3–4 hours
Distance	31.1mi
Difficulty	moderate–hard
Start/End	San Luis Obispo
Cues & Elevation Profile	p371

This circuit begins with an easy meander to a picturesque port, then climbs steeply into the surrounding hills for dramatic views of nine extinct volcanoes.

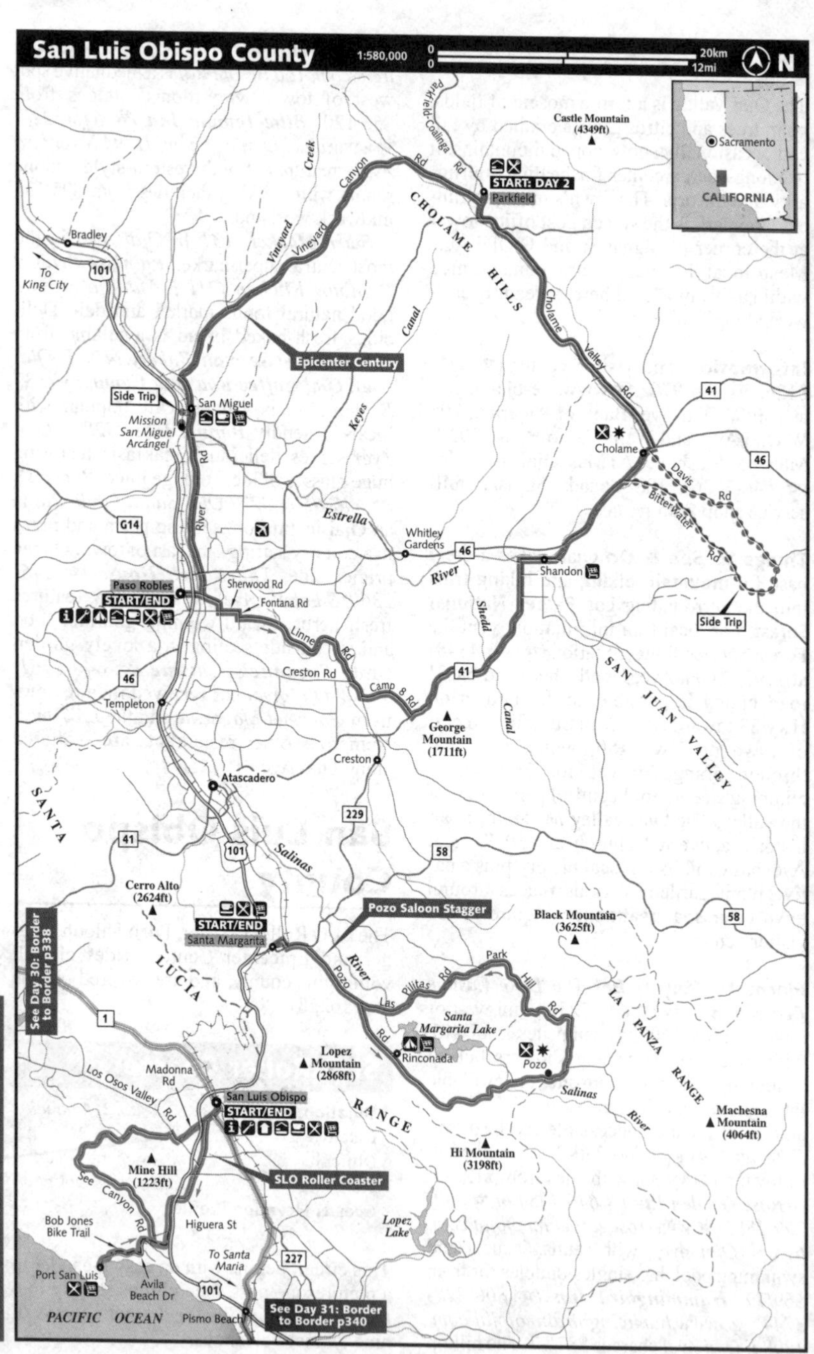
San Luis Obispo County
1:580,000
0
20km
0
12mi
N
Sacramento
CALIFORNIA
Castle Mountain (4349ft)
START: DAY 2
Parkfield
Parkfield-Coalinga Rd
Vineyard Canyon Rd
Vineyard Creek
CHOLAME HILLS
Cholame Valley Rd
Bradley
To King City
101
Canal
Epicenter Century
Side Trip
San Miguel
Mission San Miguel Arcángel
Keyes
River Rd
Cholame
41
46
Davis Rd
Bitterwater Rd
G14
Estrella
Whitley Gardens
River
Shandon
Paso Robles
START/END
Sherwood Rd
Fontana Rd
Linne Rd
Shedd
Side Trip
Creston Rd
Camp 8 Rd
SAN JUAN VALLEY
Templeton
George Mountain (1711ft)
Canal
Creston
Atascadero
SANTA
229
Salinas
58
Cerro Alto (2624ft)
START/END
Santa Margarita
Pozo Saloon Stagger
See Day 30: Border to Border p338
Black Mountain (3625ft)
LUCIA
River
Pozo Rd
Las Pilitas Rd
Park Hill Rd
LA PANZA RANGE
Santa Margarita Lake
Rinconada
Pozo
Lopez Mountain (2868ft)
Salinas
River
Los Osos Valley Rd
Madonna Rd
San Luis Obispo
START/END
RANGE
Machesna Mountain (4064ft)
Hi Mountain (3198ft)
Mine Hill (1223ft)
See Canyon Rd
SLO Roller Coaster
Bob Jones Bike Trail
Higuera St
Lopez Lake
To Santa Maria
227
Port San Luis
Avila Beach Dr
101
PACIFIC OCEAN
Pismo Beach
See Day 31: Border to Border p340

NATURAL HISTORY

One of SLO's most striking features is the series of oddly shaped hills with dramatic rocky outcroppings surrounding the town. Known as the Nine Sisters or Morros, these are extinct volcanoes whose cooled magma core has eroded differently from the surrounding rock. From the summit of the ride you get a fantastic bird's eye view of all nine peaks. Particularly noticeable are Morro Rock (576ft), which rises dramatically from the Pacific Ocean at Morro Bay; Hollister Peak (1404ft), which has a natural spring at its base and was sacred to the local Chumash tribe; and Bishop Peak (the tallest at 1559ft), whose rock was used in the construction of many local buildings.

PLANNING

When to Ride

This ride can be done year-round. During the rainy season, it's worth inquiring about the condition of the dirt stretches near the summit.

Maps & Books

AAA's *San Luis Obispo County* map covers the entire route.

What to Bring

If you're riding a touring bike, make sure your tires have good tread for the dirt road descent at the end of the ride.

THE RIDE

The first few miles are congested and noisy as the route parallels Hwy 101 south, but there's a bike lane the whole way. At 7.3mi things improve, with the Bob Jones Bike Trail following the old Pacific Coast Railway bed through a leafy corridor to Avila Beach. From here a paved road leads to the railway's historical terminus at Port San Luis (11.3mi).

In its heyday a century ago Port San Luis was known as Port Harford and served as a major transport hub. Steamship passengers to/from San Francisco connected with the Pacific Coast Railway line here. From 1887 to 1933 the railway continued south all the way to Los Olivos in Santa Barbara County.

Nowadays Port San Luis is a relaxed place, with great coastal views, a long pier, the ***Portside Marina store*** and the 24-hour ***Fat Cats Cafe***. The 1890 lighthouse on the point to the west is currently under restoration as a maritime museum. Just east of town is the entrance to Diablo Canyon Nuclear Power Plant; its construction in a cove adjacent to an earthquake fault during the early 1980s prompted serious controversy.

The route backtracks 3mi before joining lightly traveled See Canyon Rd, which winds and climbs gently through apple orchards, then turns dramatically steeper at 18.8mi. Three dirt sections make the going bumpier near the summit but the steepest segments are paved. Views of the Nine Sisters volcanoes and the coast beyond are phenomenal.

The rest of the ride is a long swooping downhill – enjoy, but exercise caution on the dirt sections. Busy traffic and bike lanes resume as you re-enter SLO.

Pozo Saloon Stagger

Duration	4–5 hours
Distance	41.5mi
Difficulty	moderate
Start/End	Santa Margarita
Cues & Elevation Profile	p371

This circuit leads to a 19th-century saloon in a secluded valley, combining beautiful riding with living history.

HISTORY

The Pozo valley was first settled in the mid-1800s. By the 1860s the saloon here was serving as a Wells Fargo stagecoach station and Pony Express mail stop on the busiest route between SLO and the Central Valley. A late 1870s gold strike east of here enhanced the town's importance, and by 1882 the local population of 850 was served by two hotels, three saloons and various other frontier enterprises. The early 1900s saw a decline in Pozo's fortunes as the gold boom ended and Hwy 466 (now State Hwy 46) bypassed the town to the north. In 1920 Prohibition closed down the saloon but the building remained, reopening in 1967 under the ownership of a former SLO county sheriff.

PLANNING

When to Ride

This ride is best on a Saturday, when the saloon is open and good public transport is available between SLO and Santa Margarita.

The route is beautiful year-round, though more challenging on hot summer days (late May–early Oct).

Maps & Books

AAA's *San Luis Obispo County* map covers the entire route.

What to Bring

Bring enough provisions for the hot and dry return leg, where you will encounter neither stores nor water sources.

GETTING TO/FROM THE RIDE

Santa Margarita

Bus Central Coast Area Transit (☎ 541-2228) bus No 9 leaves SLO (corner of Osos and Monterey Sts) every Saturday at 9.10am, arriving at Santa Margarita (cnr Encina Ave & El Camino Real) 25 minutes later. One-way fare is $1, with rack space for two bicycles. The return bus is at 4.46pm.

Weekday buses are more frequent but the saloon is closed. The saloon is open on Sunday but no buses run, so you'll need to ride all the way from SLO (see Bicycle).

Bicycle Cycling from SLO to Santa Margarita is a possible but challenging 11mi trip. From Mission Plaza, take Monterey St north for 1.2mi, then follow busy Hwy 101 north 3.8mi before crossing to the west side, where a steep, winding dirt road leads to the summit of Cuesta Grade (a 1300ft total elevation gain from SLO). From the summit it's another 4mi downhill to Santa Margarita, first paralleling Hwy 101 on a frontage road, then continuing on the freeway itself to the Santa Margarita exit. To return to SLO, retrace your steps.

THE RIDE (See Map, p228)

The first 10mi are gently undulating, traversing pretty farmland at the base of the Santa Lucia Mtns. Just beyond the small Rinconada store (8.3mi; the last chance for food and water before Pozo) the road begins its steepest climb of the morning, crossing briefly into Los Padres National Forest near the summit. A long downhill leads to your first crossing of the upper Salinas River, which flows languidly beneath rocky outcroppings. About 2mi later you enter the wide and peaceful Pozo valley.

Pozo (17.9mi) itself is nothing more than a small cluster of buildings and a forest service office nowadays. The **saloon** (☎ 438-4225) menu is straightforward Western fare (burgers, chili, nachos and beer) while the decor features old photos, dollar bills plastered to the ceiling and a mahogany bar carried around Cape Horn a century and a half ago (open Fri 5–8pm, Sat 11am–6pm & Sun 9am–5pm). Out front is an old hitching post and a cottonwood tree planted in the 1850s. A leafy backyard and deck with picnic tables provide the venue for occasional performances by big name musicians. In April Pozo hosts the annual **Whisky Highland Games**, where men in kilts hurl stones and logs competing for bottles of single-malt scotch.

The return trip to Santa Margarita leads through increasingly arid ranch country, with no cars in sight most of the way. A series of short climbs and descents culminates in the final summit at 28.5mi. At 36.2mi, shortly after crossing the Salinas River headwaters on an old metal bridge, rejoin the outbound route and head back to Santa Margarita.

Epicenter Century

Duration	2 days
Distance	84.8mi
Difficulty	moderate–hard
Start/End	Paso Robles
Cues & Elevation Profiles	p272

This ride heads inland from the Salinas Valley and into vast, sparsely settled country along the San Andreas Fault. En route are two off-beat California tourist attractions, the James Dean Death Spot and the tiny town of Parkfield, locally dubbed the earthquake capital of California. Services are few and far between, but the quiet roads are a cyclist's dream. The side trip on Day 1 adds the mileage to justify the ride's title.

NATURAL HISTORY

This section of the San Andreas Fault Zone has made its presence felt repeatedly during the past century and a half, with six earthquakes of 6.0 Richter magnitude or greater centered under Middle Mtn north of Parkfield and another centered in nearby Coalinga. At the time of writing, seismologists were still waiting for the next big one to hit.

PLANNING

When to Ride

This ride is especially pleasant in spring, when hills are green and wildflowers at their peak. For an extra treat, ride in early May during one of Parkfield's two annual festivals – you'll need to camp or book well in advance.

Maps & Books

AAA's *San Luis Obispo County* map covers the entire route.

GETTING TO/FROM THE RIDE

Paso Robles

Train The Paso Robles train station, corner Eighth and Pine Sts, is just south of the central plaza. Amtrak's *Coast Starlight* passes through once daily in each direction but will not load or unload bicycles, since Paso Robles is an unstaffed station. The best bet is to take the train to SLO, then catch a local CCAT bus from there (see Bus).

Bus Paso Robles is easily reached by local bus from SLO. Central Coast Area Transit (☎ 541-2228) runs 14 buses every weekday and three on Saturday from SLO (corner Palm and Osos Sts) to the Paso Robles train station. The fare is $1.75, with rack space for two bikes.

Greyhound also stops in front of the train station. Six northbound and four southbound buses run daily: San Francisco ($35/70 one way/return, six hours), LA ($38/76, six hours), Salinas ($21/42, two hours) and Santa Barbara ($24/48, 3½ hours).

Bicycle Cyclists heading south on the Border to Border route can cut across from Cambria (Day 30) to Paso Robles via grueling but gorgeous Santa Rosa Creek Rd, Hwy 46, Vineyard Dr and Peachy Canyon Rd.

THE RIDE (See Map, p228)

Paso Robles

☎ 805

Paso Robles is a small city set amid vineyard, horse and almond orchard country halfway between San Francisco and LA. Downtown is centered on the attractive plaza bordered by 12th, Spring, 11th and Pine Sts. Spring St is the main north-south thoroughfare. Bus and train stations are just southeast of the plaza.

Information The visitor center (☎ 238-0506, fax 238-0527, 🅦 www.pasoroblesch amber.com) is at 1225 Park St. There's also a welcome center inside the train station. Be sure to ask for the brochure *Bicycle Routes In & Around Paso Robles*.

There are many ATMs on Spring St. The best local bike shop is Bikemasters (☎ 237-2453), 1030 Railroad St, near the plaza.

Things to See & Do There is great **road biking** all around Paso Robles. Four recommended routes west of town are Peachy Canyon Rd, Adelaida Rd, Chimney Rock Rd and Vineyard Dr, all of which meander through hilly vineyard and almond orchard country with light traffic.

Wine tasting is increasingly popular in the region; inquire at the visitor center.

About 30mi north of town, Lake San Antonio County Park runs **Eagle Watch Tours** (☎ 888-588-2267; open Jan–Mar).

Places to Stay & Eat Camping at ***California Mid-State Fairgrounds*** *(☎ 239-0655, 2198 Riverside Ave)* costs $20, including hot showers (closed late Jun–mid-Aug & for big events).

Two centrally located budget motels are ***Melody Ranch Motel*** *(☎ 238-3911 or ☎ 800-909-3911, cnr Spring & Ninth Sts)* with rooms from $38; and ***Relax Inn*** *(☎ 238-3013 or ☎ 800-210-9897, 730 Spring St)* with midweek rates from $30. ***Adelaide Inn*** *(☎ 238-2770 or ☎ 800-549-PASO, 🅦 www.adelaideinn.com, 1215 Ysabel Ave)* is slightly fancier, with rooms from $45 to $78. The spiffiest place in town is the historic but heavily remodeled ***Paso Robles Inn*** *(☎ 238-2660 or ☎ 800-676-1713, 🅦 www.pasoroblesinn.com, 1103 Spring St)*, offering basic rooms from $95 and rooms with private hot tub from $150.

Ralph's *(2121 Spring St)* is the biggest downtown supermarket. There's a ***farmers market*** *(cnr 14th & Park Sts)* every Tuesday from 3 to 6pm. ***House of Bread*** *(807 12th St)* offers delicious baked goods, with free samples. ***Joe's Place*** *(☎ 238-5637, 608 12th St)* is a popular local breakfast/lunch spot just off the central plaza. ***Alloro*** *(☎ 238-9091, 1215 Spring St)* is an award-winning new Italian restaurant serving lunch and dinner. Several other eateries line the streets around the central plaza.

Day 1: Paso Robles to Parkfield

5–7 hours, 51.6mi

After escaping Paso Robles' eastern sprawl, the route emerges into open ranch country, where occasional suburban homes alternate with vineyards and horse farms. At 15.3mi the route joins Hwy 41, which despite its 'main highway' status is not particularly busy as it winds through bald hills. Shandon (27.6mi) offers the first chance to refill water bottles and rest in the shade, with its well-stocked ***market*** and pleasant park. Beyond Shandon the route merges onto busy Hwy 46 for 6.4mi, where speeding rigs provide a jolting wakeup call.

Cholame (34.5mi) is the **site of James Dean's infamous 1956 auto crash** and now a pilgrimage site for Dean buffs from around the world. (If you arrive here towards sunset, with the eastern hills turning brilliant shades of pink and gold, you'll understand how easily a driver could get distracted.) The ***Jack Ranch Cafe*** is an entertaining spot to observe James Dean wannabees in action over pie and coffee. Outside is a bizarre modern art memorial to Dean, funded by a Japanese businessman three decades after Dean's death.

The mostly flat home stretch follows the fault line north for 15mi into Parkfield.

Side Trip: San Andreas Fault Circuit

20.5mi return

This side trip makes a large loop with the San Andreas Fault at the center, offering a glimpse of the interior's vast, lonely beauty. Turn right off the main route onto Bitterwater Rd at 33.3mi, then climb steadily for 7mi to 2000ft Palo Prieto Pass. After leveling off for a couple of miles, the route climbs steeply again for 1mi as it continues straight onto Annette Rd, just past the picturesque old Greensberg store (abandoned). From the summit (2385ft) there are fabulous views of open hills and the valley, with occasional coyotes roaming about. About 1mi further on, a left onto Davis Rd sends you coasting 9mi back to Cholame, past streambeds offset by the fault's north-south shiftings.

Parkfield

☎ 805

Parkfield (population 37) is a peaceful and friendly backcountry oasis with a quirky claim to fame as the most dependably earthquake-prone town in California. Set in a grand ranching valley, the town center consists of an inn, a cafe, a schoolhouse, an abandoned Santa Fe rail car turned gift shop, an old water tower, a pleasant park, an artistic fountain and a few residences. It's the kind of place where you can spend half an hour in the middle of the road stargazing without hearing or seeing a car. Parkfield sits directly astride the San Andreas Fault – in 1985 its history of regular seismic activity enticed US Geological Survey scientists to install dozens of high-tech measuring devices here. Ironically, since the USGS arrived no major earthquakes have shaken Parkfield.

Things to See & Do The **V6 Ranch**, 5mi north of Parkfield, is a working horse and cattle ranch offering a lake for swimming, fishing and boating, miles of hiking and cycling trails, and cattle drives in spring and fall. The ranch is open to all inn guests; you must simply sign a legal disclaimer before entering ranch property.

Parkfield's annual **rodeo** and **bluegrass festival** are on the first and second weekends in May respectively.

The Cal Poly Wheelmen (W www.calpoly.edu/~wmenclub), one of SLO's main bike clubs, hold the **Parkfield Classic Mountain Bike Race** every fall.

Places to Stay & Eat Frequented by locals as well as Parkfield's intermittent tourist population, cozy ***Parkfield Cafe*** *(☎ 463-2421)* serves classic cowboy fare on check tablecloths in front of an enormous stone fireplace. The decor features historic photos, and earthquake maps and memorabilia (closed Sun except for breakfast & Wed).

Parkfield Inn *(☎ 463-2421, just across from the cafe)* may be the only show in town but it's a wonderful place. The six spacious motel rooms, hand-hewn by the owners using local lumber and stones, cost $45/65 midweek/weekend, including continental breakfast (advance booking advised). Rooms have coffee makers, fridges and taxidermy displays in place of phones and TVs. There's a large front porch with giant chairs and rockers perfect for reading and anticipating the next big quake.

Free camping on the inn grounds can sometimes be arranged if you're eating your meals at the cafe. Ask at the counter.

In case you fall in love with the area, secluded cabins can be rented at the nearby ***V6 Ranch*** *(☎ 463-2354)*.

Day 2: Parkfield to Paso Robles

3–4 hours, 33.2mi

This short leg, coupled with the Parkfield Inn's noon checkout time, allows you to sleep in or explore the valley while waiting for the cafe to open for lunch. The entire route has very light auto traffic. There's one big hill to climb, after which it's a long downhill coast to the Salinas River. At 23.4mi a short side trip crosses the river to historic Mission San Miguel Arcángel, founded in 1797 as the 16th California mission. The remaining 10mi into Paso Robles gently undulate along the river's east bank.

Monterey Bay & Salinas Valley

This is a region rich in scenic beauty, from the turquoise waters and imposing coastal hillsides of Big Sur to the quintessentially Californian oak grasslands of the interior. Early Spanish padres favored this land as the setting for two of their first three missions, and John Steinbeck's passionate connection to the region inspired many of his best novels. The Salinas Valley and the eastern edges of Monterey Bay remain the agricultural heartland of Central California, where many of the state's vegetables – and most of America's strawberries and artichokes – are grown.

Big Sur Hinterland

Duration	5 days
Distance	250.3mi
Difficulty	moderate–hard
Start/End	Salinas
Cues & Elevation Profiles	pp272–4

Combine history and scenic beauty by following sleepy back roads through some of Central California's prettiest landscapes. Visit two mission churches that still retain the ambience of early Spanish days and conclude with a spectacular swing up the Pacific coast. Highlights include the estuarine wildlife refuge at Elkhorn Slough, the dramatic rock formations of Pinnacles National Monument, the stunning coastline of Big Sur, the small mission town of San Juan Bautista, and the bucolic isolation of Mission San Antonio. You'll also cross the broad Salinas Valley and pass several locales immortalized by author John Steinbeck.

PLANNING

When to Ride

This ride is best from mid-March to mid-May, after the worst of the winter rains. The entire route is beautiful at this time, with brilliant green hills and wildflowers. Summer is the least appealing time, due to intense heat inland, periodic military maneuvers at Fort Hunter-Liggett, plus busy tourist traffic, headwinds and chilly fog on Hwy 1. Major slides occasionally close Hwy 1 in winter between Lucia and Big Sur; call Cal Trans (☎ 800-427-7623 or ☎ 916-445-7623) for information.

Maps & Books

AAA's *Monterey Bay Region* map covers most of this ride.

What to Bring

Because there are no motels or restaurants at Pinnacles National Monument, you'll need a tent, sleeping bag and basic cooking gear, unless you prefer to rent these at the campground or add 31mi to Day 2 by pushing on to King City. Carry extra food and water, as there are several long stretches without services.

GETTING TO/FROM THE RIDE

Salinas

Bus Greyhound (☎ 424-4418) is at 19 W Gabilan St. Buses leave daily for LA ($38/72 one way/return, nine hours), Santa Barbara ($34/67, 5½ hours), SLO ($24/48, three hours), San Diego ($48/90, 10–12 hours) and San Francisco ($18/32, three hours).

Monterey-Salinas Transit (☎ 424-7695) run buses Nos 20 & 21 several times daily from Central Ave and Salinas St to Monterey's Transit Center (55 minutes, $3).

Train The train station (☎ 422-7458), 11 Station Place, is just north of downtown on the east side of W Market St/Hwy 183. Amtrak's *Coast Starlight* passes through town once daily in each direction, southbound to

LA ($50/94, 9 hours) and northbound to Oakland ($16/32, 3 hours), Portland ($91/173, 22 hours), and Seattle ($104/198, 26 hours). Bikes must be boxed. Monterey is connected by train to Oakland-San Francisco ($23/46, 2½ hours), SLO ($28/56, 3½ hours), Santa Barbara ($48/96, six hours), LA ($66/132, nine hours) and San Diego ($79/158, 12½ hours).

Bicycle Cyclists on the Border to Border route can reach Salinas from Moss Landing (Day 27; pp330–2) by following Day 1 of this ride in reverse.

THE RIDE (See Map, p236)

Salinas

☎ 831

In contrast to its ritzier neighbors on the Monterey Peninsula, Salinas is a down-to-earth working town whose economy is still based on the region's agricultural wealth. The city has recently made efforts to spruce up its attractive historic downtown district, but large-scale tourism remains refreshingly absent.

Information The visitor center (☎ 424-7611, fax 424-8639, e salinas@salinaschamber.com) is at 119 E Alisal St.

Community Bank of Central California is one of several Main St banks with ATMs.

Bobcat Bicycles (☎ 831-753-7433), 141 Monterey St, is a friendly full-service bike shop two blocks from the Steinbeck Center.

Things to See & Do Completed in 1998, the **National Steinbeck Center** (☎ 796-3833, w www.steinbeck.org) is a spacious and appealing museum celebrating the life and work of Salinas' native son, author John Steinbeck. Displays on individual novels alternate with others tracing Steinbeck's personal life. A map at the entrance indicates the Central California locales that served as inspirations and/or settings for his novels. The Center hosts a Steinbeck Festival every August. Buffs may also want to visit the author's birthplace and childhood home at 132 Central Ave, and grave site at the Garden of Memories Cemetery, both in Salinas.

The **California Rodeo** (w www.carodeo.com), an annual event since 1911, brings hundreds of professional cowboys and cowgirls to Salinas every July for four days of riding, roping, chili cookoffs and cowboy poetry.

River Rd is a sleepy two-laner paralleling the Salinas River for 30mi, passing old farmhouses and vineyards, and offering pleasant cycling.

Wine tasting and **agro-tourism** are increasingly popular in the area; inquire at the Chamber of Commerce.

Places to Stay & Eat Reasonable motels near the downtown area include: ***Country Inn*** *(☎ 757-8383, 126 John St)*, with rooms from $38, and the ***Best Inn Salinas Motor Lodge*** *(☎ 424-4801, w www.bestinn.com,*

California's Spanish Place Names

From Terra Incognita to subdivided suburbia, California's Hispanic heritage is embedded in its place names.

Hip LA began life as El Pueblo de Nuestra Señora la Reina de los Ángeles de Porciúncula, named for the Catholic feast day on which Gaspar de Portolá's landmark expedition camped nearby. Explorers as far back as Cabrillo had described California's mountains as snowy. But not until missionary-explorer Pedro Font's 1776 glimpse of the Range of Light did the name Sierra Nevada stick. Even many non-Spanish names turn out to be Spanish in origin. Today's Russian River was originally dubbed the Río Ruso by scouts sent up from Mission San Rafael to spy on foreign fur trappers. And the venerable redwood was first named by the Portolá expedition's intrepid Father Crespi. At a loss for words to identify these towering giants of the forest, he called them simply *palos colorados*, red sticks.

Then there are the contrived names such as Hacienda Heights, Rio Dell, Tierra Blanco, Solromar and Mesa Dump Rd – all invented in the past 100 or so years by land sharks and city boosters cashing in on the nostalgia for all things Spanish.

And 'California' itself? The name derives from a popular Spanish novel circa 1510 that depicts a fabled island 'near to the Terrestrial Paradise', inhabited by gorgeous Amazon-like women who wear gold armor and ride wild beasts. Hollywood – here we come!

Gaen Murphree

109 John St), starting from $49. More upmarket is the ***Holiday Inn Express*** *(☎ 757-1020, 131 John St)*, charging from $79, including continental breakfast.

Three of the town's biggest ***supermarkets*** are clustered near the corner of S Main St and Blanco Ave, west of town.

Several good restaurants are within walking distance of the Steinbeck Center and motel row. ***Villa Cafe*** *(8 Midtown Lane)*, just off Main St, serves authentic and inexpensive Mexican food, including homemade corn tortillas. ***First Awakenings*** *(171 Main St)* is a popular breakfast spot in an historical building. The British-owned ***Penny Farthing Tavern*** *(9 E San Luis St)* has pub food and 16 British beers on tap. ***Spado's*** *(☎ 424-4139, 66 W Alisal St)*, voted best restaurant in Salinas five years in a row, is a great Italian lunch and dinner spot.

Day 1: Salinas to San Juan Bautista

4–6 hours, 42mi

Within minutes you leave the urban center of Salinas and enter flat coastal farming country. The rest of the ride remains rural and becomes increasingly hilly, meandering through strawberry and artichoke fields, horse pastures and a marine bird sanctuary en route to historic San Juan Bautista.

At 13.1mi, the small coastal town of Moss Landing makes a great spot for a late breakfast or early lunch. The ***Lighthouse Harbor Grille*** on Hwy 1 serves delicious fried artichokes, seafood and apple pie. **Elkhorn Slough National Estuarine Research Reserve** (19.7mi; closed Mon & Tues) has an excellent network of trails allowing you to observe the 267 species of birds that flock to these coastal wetlands. When the reserve is closed you can birdwatch at **Kirby Park Public Access**, 2.6mi further up the estuary.

Elkhorn and Aromas both have stores. Just beyond Aromas you climb the day's only significant hill. Your efforts are rewarded when a long, coasting descent through a beautiful eucalyptus grove drops into flat farm country on the outskirts of San Juan Bautista.

San Juan Bautista

☎ 831

Considering its jam-packed history and proximity to San Francisco and Silicon Valley, San Juan Bautista is a remarkably tranquil place. Its historic main street, beautiful mission and gardens, and crowing roosters can make you feel as though you've stepped back in time to a more rural and Spanish-influenced California. In its 1860s heyday, San Juan was a bustling place, with hotels, saloons, and as many as seven different stagecoach lines passing through. In the 1870s the town almost became the seat of newly formed San Benito County but nearby Hollister won instead, and San Juan has kept a lower profile ever since. The town does plenty to cater to tourists but doesn't suffer from the trend towards commercial development, which has engulfed so much of the greater Bay Area.

Information The visitor center (☎ 623-2454, fax 623-0674, Ⓦ www.san-juan-bautista.ca.us) is at 1 Polk St.

ATMs are at South Valley National Bank, corner Third and Mariposa Sts, and San Benito Bank, in Windmill Plaza just east of downtown.

The closest bike shop is Muenzer's Cyclery (☎ 637-2121), at 221 Fifth St in Hollister, 12mi east and just a short detour off the Day 2 route.

Things to See & Do The **Mission San Juan Bautista** sits on California's only surviving original Spanish plaza and is the largest of the state's 21 mission churches, with spacious gardens and a museum adjoining. Of particular interest are the church's interior tile floors, which bear the footprints of animals from two centuries ago. In 1957, Alfred Hitchcock chose this mission as the setting for *Vertigo*, although the belltower seen in the film is a Hollywood reconstruction of an earlier tower destroyed by dry rot and termites.

Lining the sides of the plaza opposite the mission are the buildings of **San Juan Bautista State Historic Park**. Most notable are the Castro-Breen Adobe (1838), once a Mexican government building; the old Plaza Hotel (1858), famous in its heyday for fine French and Italian cuisine; the Plaza Stable (1861); and Plaza Hall (1868). The park's beautiful garden features roses, hollyhocks, prickly pear cactus, and pepper trees introduced by the mission fathers. There are chickens descended from birds from the island of Minorca. A Spanish orchard is filled

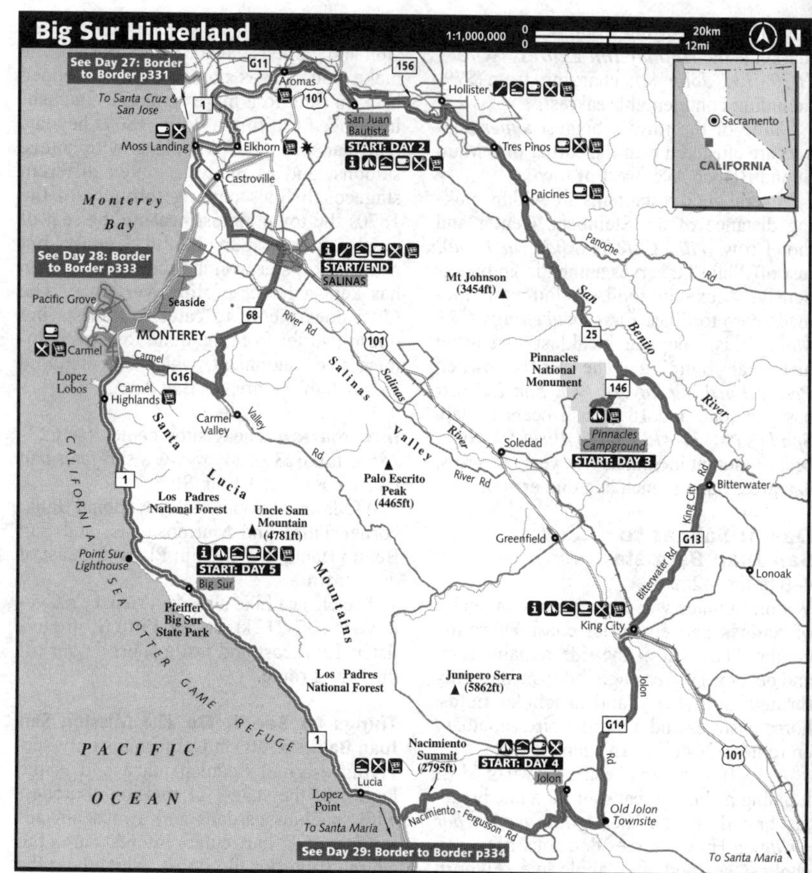

with olive, pomegranate, guava, fig and other fruit trees.

In December the Mission is the setting for **traditional Mexican Christmas plays** performed by El Teatro Campesino (☎ 623-2444), 705 Fourth St, a San Juan-based theater group that has achieved international recognition.

Places to Stay & Eat Just southeast of town, ***Mission Farm RV Park*** *(☎ 623-4456, 400 San Juan-Hollister Rd)* has tent sites with hot showers, charging $12/20 for one/two people. ***McAlpine Lake & Park*** *(☎ 623-4263, 900 Anzar Rd)*, 3mi northwest of town on the Day 1 route, charges $29 for a tent site or $44 each for two very basic cabins (bring a sleeping bag and reserve in advance).

The town's only motel, ***San Juan Inn*** *(☎ 623-4380, cnr The Alameda & Hwy 156)*, charges from $79 for basic rooms. Central ***Posada de San Juan*** *(☎ 623-4030, 310 Fourth St)* is a modern place masquerading as an historic inn, with an attractive Spanish-style lobby but fairly ordinary rooms starting at $98.

Additional ***motels*** can be found in Hollister, 12mi east on the Day 2 route.

Windmill Market *(301 The Alameda)*, just east of town, has the town's largest grocery selection plus a deli. ***San Juan Bakery*** *(cnr Third & Polk Sts)* sells fresh-baked bread, pastries, sandwiches and drinks. ***Mission Cafe*** *(cnr Third & Mariposa Sts)* is a great local hangout for breakfast and lunch. ***Jardines de San Juan*** *(☎ 623-4466,*

115 Third St) serves Mexican food and margaritas on a festive outdoor patio.

Day 2: San Juan Bautista to Pinnacles

4–6 hours, 43.7mi

Meander through flat farmland for the first 10mi, then skirt the edges of rapidly growing Hollister before leaving urban California for good. Climb slowly along the San Andreas Fault line into the beautiful oak valleys of the interior. The only busy stretch of road is Hwy 25 just south of Hollister but the good shoulder compensates for the traffic. Beyond Tres Pinos cars are few and far between.

There are no restaurants or motels at the end of today's ride, unless you choose to push on 31mi to King City. On weekdays the store at Pinnacles (see Places to Say & Eat) has very limited hours, so plan accordingly. After Hollister (12.3mi), the small towns of Tres Pinos (18.2mi) and Paicines (23.5mi) are the only two possible lunch spots, with a couple of ***restaurants*** in the former and a ***general store with deli*** in the latter.

Between Tres Pinos and Paicines are the San Benito County Fairgrounds, home to a **saddle horse show** and **rodeo** (Jun). At Paicines, an historical marker commemorates the **New Idria quicksilver mine**, which did a booming business in Gold Rush days but is now a ghost town down a 54mi dead-end road. The Paicines area also gained historical prominence when notorious outlaw Tiburcio Vasquez botched a robbery here in 1873, murdering three people and prompting a statewide pursuit that resulted in his hanging two years later.

The 20mi after Paicines are idyllic but totally without services. Pinnacles Campground, the only place to spend the night in this area, lies just outside the national monument's boundaries.

Pinnacles National Monument

☎ 831

Pinnacles National Monument, established in 1908, protects an improbable landscape of rocky volcanic spires jutting out of the surrounding oak-covered hills. The Pinnacles are the remnant of an ancient Southern California volcano split by the San Andreas Fault. The volcano's western half sheared off millennia ago and has been moving steadily northward along the fault line, protected initially from erosion by tilting and subsidence, then exposed as the surrounding rock has eroded.

Things to See & Do Pinnacles is a **rock-climbing** mecca and there are beautiful **hiking trails** and **caves** to explore. Thanks to its isolation and nearly a century of protected status, the park offers superb opportunities for **wildlife viewing** and **star gazing**. Commonly seen animals are deer, bobcats and wild pigs. **Park headquarters** (☎ 831-389-4485) is 3mi west of the campground via a paved road. Please note that bicycles are strictly prohibited from all hiking trails.

Places to Stay & Eat The ***Pinnacles Campground & Store*** *(☎ 389-4462, W www.pinncamp.com)* has tent sites set among meadows and trees, with hiking trails leading into the park. Rates are $7 per person, with a $28 maximum for up to six people. There is a swimming pool (Apr–Oct) and hot showers. Reservations (online or by phone) are advisable. They also rent tents, sleeping bags and stoves. The adjacent camp store has limited and variable hours; call ahead for details.

Day 3: Pinnacles National Monument to Jolon

5–7 hours, 56.7mi

Day 3 is more challenging than the previous two in terms of both distance and hills. For the first 15mi the route follows the San Andreas Fault south through remote country. Rugged, tortured-looking hills are visible on the North American Plate to the east, with pastoral oak grasslands on the Pacific Plate to the west.

At 16.4mi the route climbs steeply west from the settlement of Bitterwater (no services) into the Gabilan Mtns, fictional home of the Hamilton family in Steinbeck's *East of Eden*. From the summit (17.6mi), sweeping views unfold towards the Salinas Valley, and you get one last glimpse of the Pinnacles peeking above oak foothills on the northern horizon.

A gradual 13mi descent drops into King City (31mi), where the ***Safeway supermarket*** (530 Canal St) is the only big grocery store until Day 5. There are plenty of lunch spots in town, with an emphasis on Mexican food and freeway restaurants.

Monterey County Agricultural & Rural Life Museum (☎ 385-8020), in San Lorenzo Park, is a side trip at 32.2mi; continue to the west end of Broadway. It has photos and displays highlighting the valley's two centuries as an agricultural center. On weekends (1–3pm), tour the adjacent historical farmhouse, one-room schoolhouse and train depot.

Exiting King City, cross the Salinas River to Jolon Rd and reenter sleepier territory. At the time of writing, a bike bridge was under construction from San Lorenzo Park to Jolon Rd, eliminating the need to cross the nerve-wracking Hwy 101 bridge (32.5mi). The route from here is straightforward, although the last climb is a killer. From the summit (43.7mi), it's an easy coast to Fort Hunter-Liggett, modern-day home of historic Mission San Antonio. Just before entering the army base, look for the **old Jolon town site** (51.3mi) to your left. The 1876 stagecoach stop and general store is still standing, with a plaque telling its story.

Jolon/Mission San Antonio

☎ 831

Jolon is no longer a town except in name. In the 1860s it was founded as a supply station for miners heading towards the coast. The town thrived and nearly became the county seat but went into decline after the railroad bypassed it in favor of King City. William Randolph Hearst bought the town and all the surrounding land in the 1920s, then sold it 20 years later to the army. The young John Steinbeck spent summers near here on his grandfather's ranch. His second novel, *To A God Unknown*, was set in the Jolon Valley.

The only modern settlement in the Jolon Valley is Fort Hunter-Liggett, a military reservation improbably juxtaposed against the peaceful solitude of the surrounding hills. The fort has several services, including the Hacienda Guest Lodge, a snack bar and bowling alley, a movie theater and an ATM.

Things to See & Do The only tourist draw out here is beautifully restored **Mission San Antonio**, half a mile northwest of the Hacienda. San Antonio was founded in 1771 as the third California mission. Despite the proximity of the military base, this place retains its serenity, with birdsong filling the air. In front of the church stands an olive tree planted in 1836 while nearby the remains of aqueducts and old mission buildings poke through the grass. Inside is a wonderfully eclectic museum and a colonnaded garden with European cypresses surrounding a fountain.

Just south of the mission, Del Venturi Rd strikes out northwest towards the rocky outcroppings known as the Indians in **Los Padres National Forest**. About 20mi down this road is a primitive campground where intrepid souls will find excellent **hiking** and **mountain biking** opportunities.

On Friday and Saturday night, **movies** are screened at the army base. The nearby Hacienda Bowl (☎ 831-386-2194) features **Night Owl bowling** with glow-in-the-dark pins.

Places to Stay & Eat The ***Fort Hunter-Liggett Campground*** *(☎ 386-2550)*, just inside the entrance gate (51.7mi on Day 3), charges $20 for a trailer (two-night minimum, reservations essential) or $5 for a campsite – you'll more likely be surrounded by hunters than by other cyclists. An alternative is the no-frills ***Ponderosa Campground***, 12.7mi west of the Hacienda in Los Padres National Forest (12.7mi on Day 4). The water supply is intermittent, and the fee is $10 per night.

The obvious choice is ***The Hacienda Restaurant, Lounge & Guest Lodge*** *(☎ 386-2900, W www.usawines.com/hacienda)*, a striking Spanish Colonial Revival building designed by architect Julia Morgan for William Randolph Hearst in 1929. Originally a hunting lodge where Hearst entertained the likes of Clark Gable and Teddy Roosevelt, the Hacienda is now open to the public. Prices range from $28/33 for singles/doubles with shared bath to $125 for an extravagant suite sleeping four. All rooms have fridges and microwaves, some have VCRs.

The adjoining ***restaurant*** serves lunch daily and dinner every day except Sunday. Next door, the ***Hacienda Lounge*** has a full bar (closed Sun). Down the hill is a ***snack bar*** serving breakfast.

Day 4: Jolon to Big Sur

5–7 hours, 54.8mi

This is one of the best routes in California, with beautiful scenery the whole way and virtually no traffic for the first 26mi. There is no guaranteed water source until you hit highway 1 (26mi). At 1.9mi, the route crosses a one-lane bridge over the San Antonio River, then climbs briefly before leveling out into a vast oak savanna landscape. As you enter Los Padres National Forest at 10.3mi, the Santa Lucia Mtns close in and the route ascends steadily along the Nacimiento River. A river crossing at 16.3mi signals the beginning of the 3mi steep ascent to Nacimiento Summit (2795ft). From here it's a screaming 7mi plunge down to the ocean, with dramatic views of the mountainsides and the Pacific glinting far below. Once you hit the coast, a series of less abrupt hills leads along cliffs and bluffs to Big Sur.

The only services en route are at ***Lucia Lodge*** *(☎ 667-2391)*, where a small store and restaurant provide limited fare and rental cabins are available. There are also campgrounds south of Lucia at Kirk Creek (26.5mi) and Limekiln State Park (28.5mi).

McWay Falls are in Julia Pfeiffer Burns State Park at 43.7mi. Take the short, signed walk under the highway to this spectacular waterfall cascading 80ft to a sandy beach. Two little-known ***campsites*** (☎ 800-444-7275, 🅦 www.reserveamerica.com/usa/ca/juli) are available at the top of the falls for $12 per night; bookings essential.

Big Sur

☎ 831

El pais grande del sur (the big country to the south) was the name 19th-century Spanish settlers gave the then-unexplored wilderness south of Carmel. More a region, or an experience, than a discrete place, Big Sur's coast stretches from Carmel to San Simeon. Its remoteness and raw beauty are awe inspiring and it is eminently cyclable. Big Sur village is strung out nearly 4mi with Pfeiffer Big Sur State Park in the middle.

Information Big Sur Station (☎ 667-2315) is the ranger station and park visitor center. Big Sur Chamber of Commerce (☎ 667-2100, 🅦 www.bigsurcalifornia.org) publishes a free annual tourist paper, *El Sur Grande*, available everywhere in the area, listing all Big Sur's campgrounds, parks, businesses and events.

Big Sur River Inn General Store has an ATM. There is no bike shop or public Internet access.

California Condor

On 5 April 2001, five condors soared out of their training pen and into Central California's Ventana Wilderness, bringing to 53 the total number of these endangered birds living in the wild.

Before the arrival of the Europeans, California's vast wilderness provided North America's largest raptor room to roam and plenty of carcasses to scavenge. Driven to the brink of extinction by poisoning, shooting and habitat loss, by the mid-1980s only nine wild condors remained.

In a controversial move to save the species, US Fish and Wildlife officials rounded up the survivors for a captive breeding program in the San Diego and Los Angeles zoos. By the early 1990s, the first young condors were released. Raised by zookeepers using condor puppets, most proved unfit for life in the wild. Condors are social animals who preen one another, fly and forage in groups, and click their beaks in greeting. To survive in the 'real world', the zoo-bred condors had to learn a thing or two. Today's young chicks are more typically raised by their parents and then mentored by wild-caught condors before being released.

The program appears to be working. In March 2001, biologists for the Grand Canyon flock spotted their first egg. And the Ventana flock has begun foraging its own food, rather than relying on calf carcasses trotted out by researchers in dead of night.

Gaen Murphree

Things to See & Do One of the favorite pastimes at Big Sur is to 'do nothing', according to tourist brochures. Nothing, that is, except relax, replenish the spirit and take in the area's beauty – on a quiet beach, atop a sea cliff or on a ridge.

Pfeiffer Beach, Big Sur's most popular, is about 2mi along unsigned Sycamore Canyon Rd, the only paved, ungated road west of Hwy 1 between Pfeiffer Big Sur State Park and the post office. A short path leads from the parking area to where cliffs tower above the sand and a large arched rock offshore gleams in the sunset.

Molera Horseback Tours (☎ 625-5486) runs beach **horse rides** in Andrew Molera State Park (Apr–Dec).

Watch for **California condors**, North America's largest and most endangered land bird, soaring in the sky. From near extinction, condors are making a comeback through captive breeding and reintroduction. To report sightings or get more information contact Ventana Wilderness Society (☎ 455-9514, **W** www.ventanaws.org).

Big Sur Blues Festival (☎ 667-2422) is held in late October and a three-day **Jazz-Fest** (☎ 667-1530, **W** www.bigsurjazz.org) is in May.

Big Sur International Marathon (☎ 625-6226, **W** www.bsim.org), late April, and the 10-kilometer **Big Sur River Run** (☎ 624-4112, **W** www.bigsurriverrun.org) in October, are the area's major sweatfests.

Places to Stay & Eat The ***Pfeiffer Big Sur State Park*** has hiker/biker camping ($3 per person with coin showers) while ***Big Sur Campground & Cabins*** *(☎ 667-2322)* has tent sites for $15/24 single/double ($26 a double on weekends), canvas-sided cabins from $42/50 weekday/weekend, motel-style cabins for $87/97 and two-bedroom riverfront cabins with kitchen for $155/165.

Big Sur River Inn *(☎ 667-2700 or ☎ 800-548-3610, **W** www.bigsurriverinn.com)*, on the right entering Big Sur village's outskirts, has rustic rooms overlooking the Big Sur River for $80 weekdays, $90 weekends. It has a store and the ***River Inn Country Restaurant***.

Glen Oaks Motel *(☎ 667-2105)*, on Hwy 1 in adobe buildings with a garden setting, has doubles for $85 year-round. Next door, ***Ripplewood Resort*** *(☎ 667-2242)* has cabins with kitchens and private bathrooms for around $100. Ask for a quiet room near the river, farther from the highway. The resort ***coffee shop*** serves good breakfast and lunch, and the adjacent ***grocery store*** stocks fresh produce.

Ventana Inn *(☎ 667-2331 or ☎ 800-628-6500)* is stylish, low-key and high-priced, a combination that attracts Hollywood highfliers such as Robert Redford, Tom Cruise and Mel Gibson. Mortals who can't afford the $300 to $800 rooms in the complex, which has a Japanese bathhouse, sauna, sun deck and pools, can sample the ambience over dinner in its romantically rustic restaurant. Impeccable service, artistic and tasty dishes and, of course, high prices, are the hallmarks.

Big Sur River Inn General Store sells groceries. Uphill, 1.1mi south of Big Sur Station, is the post office in a strip of shops called Big Sur Center. Here ***Big Sur Bazaar*** *(☎ 667-2197)*, a combination store, deli and all-purpose shop, has the cheapest supplies in town.

The ***Village Pub*** *(☎ 667-2355)*, adjacent to the River Inn store, serves meals. The soups, fish and chips and vegie burgers are cheap. ***Bonito Road House*** *(☎ 667-2264)* serves fish, steak, chicken and pasta with some class.

Day 5: Big Sur to Salinas

5–7 hours, 53.1mi

The first half of Day 5 follows the most famous 25mi of the Big Sur coastline. At Carmel (26mi) the route turns inland and climbs one last mountain pass before dropping back to the welcome flatness of the Salinas Valley. An alternative for people who have had enough climbing is to continue north along the coast to Monterey and end the ride there.

The entire coastal stretch is breathtakingly beautiful. **Andrew Molera State Park** (4.4mi), **Point Sur Lighthouse** (7.1mi) and **Point Lobos State Reserve** (23.9mi) provide convenient excuses for getting out of the saddle and taking a closer look.

Redwoods & Lighthouse

Duration	2 days
Distance	105.8mi
Difficulty	hard
Start/End	Santa Cruz
Cues & Elevation Profiles	p382

This challenging ride connects the coastal towns of Santa Cruz and Pescadero via a lightly traveled inland passage through the redwoods. En route you'll pass through California's oldest state park; negotiate tough climbs and a hair-raising unpaved descent; visit 19th-century coastal towns; have the chance to stay at an historic lighthouse; and follow the ridgeline of the Santa Cruz Mtns before rejoining the sea at Santa Cruz.

This route can be shortened by taking city bus No 35 to Boulder Creek on Day 1 and back from Felton on Day 2.

PLANNING

When to Ride

March, April and May are beautiful months for a ride in this area, with wildflowers blooming everywhere and creeks running full. September and October are among the warmest and least foggy months, with picturesque pumpkin fields adding appeal. Be cautious after winter rainstorms, as the dirt sections can become waterlogged.

Maps & Books

Krebs Cycle Products publishes the very useful *South San Francisco Bay & Monterey Bay Bicycle Touring Map* and the *SF Peninsula/Santa Cruz Mountains Mountain Biking Map*, available in many local bike shops for $9.95.

What to Bring

A mountain bike is advisable for the rugged dirt sections on Day 1, although experienced road bikers with good tires (and perhaps a devil-may-care attitude would also help) can get by. Make sure to bring plenty of food and water, especially for the 42mi section without services on Day 2.

GETTING TO/FROM THE RIDE

Santa Cruz

Bus Greyhound runs several buses daily to/from its downtown depot (☎ 423-1800), 425 Front St. Routes include San Francisco ($12/22 one way/return, three hours), SLO ($23/46, five hours), Santa Barbara ($32/60, eight hours) and LA ($39/75, 10 hours).

Train There's no train station in Santa Cruz but Amtrak passengers arriving in San Jose can transfer onto Amtrak Thruway bus number 22 (timed to meet all incoming trains). It continues to the Santa Cruz Metro Center, corner Pacific Ave and Elm St. The fare is $10/20 from Oakland, $63/118 from LA.

On weekdays Caltrain (☎ 650-508-6455 or ☎ 800-660-4287, Ⓦ www.caltrain.com) runs frequently from San Francisco to San Jose ($5.25, 1¾ hours), where you can catch also SCMTDs (☎ 831-425-8600) Hwy 17 Express bus to Scotts Valley or Santa Cruz (one hour, $2.25).

THE RIDE (See Map, p242)

Santa Cruz

☎ 831

A laid-back beach and college town, Santa Cruz has a young population of 55,000 and streets on which bicycles (and even bike lanes) are common. It's a popular weekend escape from San Francisco; songwriter Neil Young lives in the nearby mountains. Downtown has a pedestrian-friendly, traffic-calmed core. The University of California (UCSC) campus is 2.5mi northwest of the center.

Information Downtown Information Center is at 1126 Pacific Avenue (☎ 459-9486, fax 429-1512 Ⓦ www.downtownsantacruz.com). For the free Santa Cruz County Regional Transportation Commission bike-route map, phone ☎ 460-3200.

Bank of America, at 1128 Pacific Ave; Coast Commercial Bank, at 720 Front St; Santa Cruz Commercial Credit Union, on Front St's 500-block; and the Safeway supermarket all have ATMs.

The Bicycle Trip (☎ 427-2580), 1127 Soquel Ave, is an excellent bike shop. Ask for its *5 Great Bike Trips in Santa Cruz County* maps.

Internet access is available at the library (☎ 420-5600), corner Church and Center Sts, or the 24-hour Kinko's (☎ 425-1177), 105 Laurel St.

Things to See & Do It's worth wandering along pedestrianized Pacific Ave to appreciate attractive **stone buildings** such as the 1895 former Santa Cruz County Bank building.

Santa Cruz boardwalk is a 1906 beachfront amusement park on Beach St. Its famous rides include the half-mile-long Giant Dipper roller coaster and the 1911 carousel, both National Historic Landmarks.

Santa Cruz City Museum of Natural History (☎ 420-6115), 1305 E Cliff Dr, is on the east side of the San Lorenzo River and fronted by a gray whale figure. Its highlight is the fossil skeleton of a 12-million-year-old sea cow, local relative of the dugong of Australasia. Behind the museum, migratory monarch butterflies perch in the trees from October to March.

Beach activities and **surfing** are popular. Boards and gear can be rented; try Shoreline Surf (☎ 458-1380) at 125 Beach St.

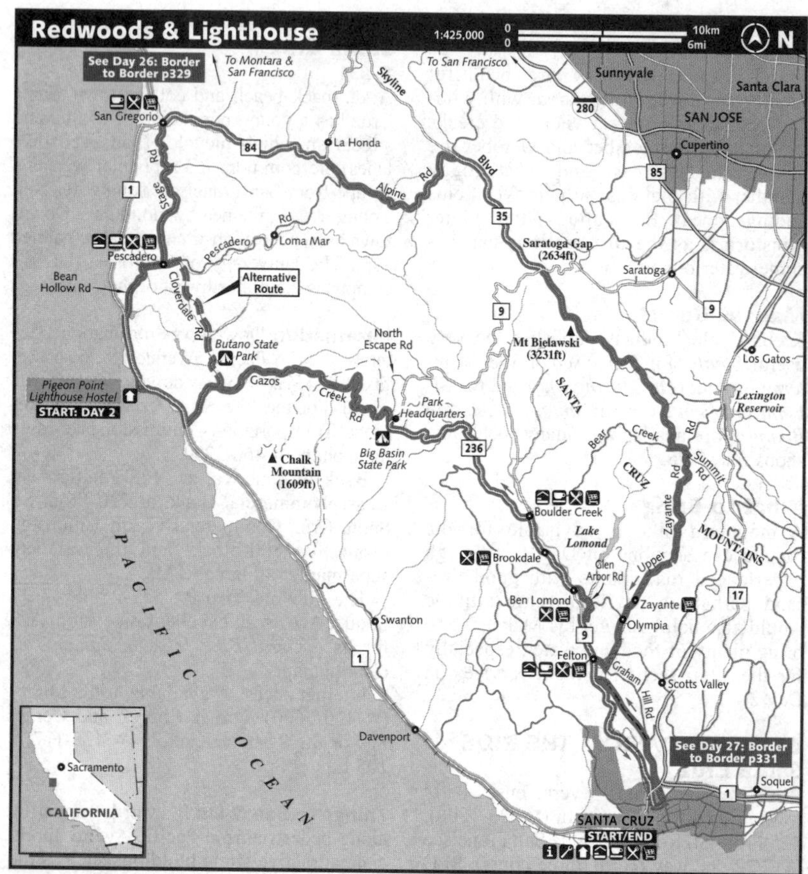

Richard Schmidt (☎ 423-0928) or Club-Ed (☎ 459-9283) offer surfing lessons from $50 per hour.

Three-hour long **whale-watching** trips (Nov–Apr) and **harbor cruises** leave the municipal wharf. Fares start at $17/6 respectively. Timetables are available from Stagnaro's (☎ 427-2334) kiosk on the wharf.

Places to Stay & Eat Hiker/biker camping (with a two-night maximum) is available at stunning, cliff-top ***New Brighton Beach State Park*** *(1500 Park Ave, Capitola)* for $3 per person with coin-operated showers. Turn south off Soquel Ave 7mi east of the visitor center. Beware: gangs of raccoons attack nightly at 3am.

Excellent ***Santa Cruz Hostel*** *(☎ 423-8304, e info@hi-santacruz.org, 321 Main St)* has beds in restored 1870s cottages on Beach Hill, two blocks from the beach, for $15/18 members/nonmembers. Private rooms are available for two or more people for a minimum $35. Reservations advised.

Many motels but not many cheap rooms is a summer reality in Santa Cruz. Motels further from the beach offer more room for less money – check along Mission Rd (Hwy 1) and in the streets running back from Beach St. Most motels within easy walk of the beach charge from $100. An exception is ***Super 8 Motel*** *(☎ 426-3707, 338 Riverside Ave)*, which has doubles from $65. ***Econo Lodge*** *(☎ 426-3626 or ☎ 800-553-2666, 550 2nd St)*, near the boardwalk, has doubles for $135/175 weekday/weekend. ***Days Inn*** *(☎ 423-8564 or ☎ 800-325-2525, 325 Pacific Ave)* charges $155 a double despite an ordinary location and indifferent welcome, while luxury ***West Coast Santa Cruz Hotel*** *(☎ 426-4330 or ☎ 800-325-4000, 175 W Cliff Dr)* has rooms with ocean views for $209/239 weekday/weekend, plus a pool, sauna, restaurant and bar.

A ***Safeway*** supermarket *(cnr Morrissey Blvd & Water St)* is 1.1mi from the visitor center. A ***farmers market*** *(Cedar St)* is held between Walnut and Lincoln Sts (Wed 2.30–6.30pm; call the Visitors Council for locations on other days). ***Zoccoli's Italian Deli*** *(☎ 423-1717, 431 Front St)* serves good takeaway coffee and sandwiches, and has outdoor tables.

Lulu Carpenter's *(☎ 429-9804, 1545 Pacific Ave)* is a popular downtown cafe serving inexpensive focaccias, sandwiches, desserts and coffee. ***The Bagelry*** *(☎ 429-8049, 320A Cedar St)* is a good place for breakfast.

Pontiac Grill *(☎ 427-2290, 429 Front St)* is an authentic recreation of a 1950s diner with burgers from $5.

Little Shanghai *(☎ 458-2460, 1010 Cedar St)* is a cheap, simple and well-patronized Chinese restaurant. ***Benten*** *(☎ 425-7079, 1541 Pacific Ave)* offers good-value sushi.

Day 1: Santa Cruz to Pigeon Point

5–6 hours, 40.1mi

Despite the moderate distance, Day 1 is challenging, with several steep ascents and an 8mi dirt stretch through the mountains. The route dives and climbs through gorgeous, secluded redwood groves while traversing two state parks. Long stretches are closed to motorized traffic, making even the difficult sections seem less taxing.

An initial congested stretch followed by a steep climb up busy Graham Hill Rd gives way to the tranquility of the paved Pipeline Trail through **Henry Cowell Redwoods State Park**. The trail's early stages encourage despair, with a brake-melting descent and grueling uphill. Soon, however, the park's serene beauty eclipses all concern for physical discomfort, with deep sylvan canyons, sweeping views of the San Lorenzo River valley, and a final passage through a large open meadow.

The stretches along crowded state Hwy 9 are a rude awakening but the route calms down for good as you head towards Big Basin, California's oldest state park (1902). Boulder Creek (14.7mi) is the last dependable chance to buy food before Pescadero, although the park headquarters (24mi) has water, restrooms, an information desk, and a ***small store*** (opens weekend Mar–Dec).

Just past park headquarters, unpaved Gazos Creek Rd threads through some of the park's most pristine stands of old growth. Pay careful attention at 30.3mi, where the road veers right along a rusted metal fence, then plunges headlong down a steep gorge. The views and sense of solitude are well worth the effort, and the road soon levels out, rolling slowly towards the ocean after rejoining pavement at 32.3mi.

An important junction is at 35.6mi – continuing straight here will take you to Pigeon Point Lighthouse Hostel while the alternative route onto Cloverdale Rd leads to ***Butano State Park campground*** (1.2mi; see Places to Stay & Eat) and the town of Pescadero (6.2mi).

Pigeon Point & Pescadero

☎ 650

While the ride stopover is at Pigeon Point, most services are at Pescadero. Founded in 1856, this relaxed small community is tucked into a farming valley just inland from the ocean. The few services are clustered near the intersection of Stage Rd and Pescadero Rd. An ATM is at First National Bank of California, 239 Stage Rd.

Things to See & Do The **Pescadero State Beach & Preserve**, 6mi north of Pigeon Point and 2mi west of Pescadero at the junction of Pescadero Rd and state Hwy 1, is a beautiful mix of sand and coastal marshland with abundant birdlife. For weekend tours, call ☎ 879-2170.

Butano State Park, 5mi south of Pescadero on Cloverdale Rd, has hiking trails, fire roads for mountain biking and a campground (see Places to Stay & Eat).

Places to Stay & Eat Tucked into a redwood grove, ***Butano State Park*** *(☎ 879-2040 or ☎ 800-444-PARK, Cloverdale Rd)* is 1.2mi north of the Day 1 route. It has 39 campsites with cold water only for $12 per night.

The destination for this ride, and a great place to stay, is picturesque ***Pigeon Point***

Lighthouse Hostel *(☎ 879-0633, Pigeon Point Rd)*, 6mi southwest of Pescadero just off Hwy 1. Dorm beds cost $15/18 for HI members/nonmembers. Private rooms cost $45/51.The hostel is extremely popular and reservations are strongly advised. Kitchen facilities and simple food items such as soup and cocoa are available. If you prefer to eat in town, the 6mi ride is very pretty – simply follow directions from the Day 2 cue sheet.

The only place to stay in town is the rustic and charming ***Pescadero Creekside Barn*** *(☎ 879-0868, W www.pescaderolodging.com, 248 Stage Rd)*, offering a single unit for the romantically inclined, with a clawfoot bathtub, stereo, VCR, microwave and fridge for $95 per night midweek, $235 for Friday and Saturday nights combined (two-night minimum on weekends).

For delicious cinnamon rolls, bread and deli sandwiches, check out ***Norm's Market*** *(287 Stage Rd)*. The cheapest eats in town are at ***Mercado y Taquería Los Amigos*** *(1999 Pescadero Rd)*, serving tacos and other Mexican food, with a ***grocery*** next door.

Duarte's Tavern *(☎ 879-0464, W www.duartestavern.com, 202 Stage Rd)* is one of coastal California's hidden gems, a wonderfully atmospheric family-run place that is famous for its artichoke soup, olallieberry pie and seafood. Reservations are essential on weekends. Breakfast is served daily from 7am.

Day 2: Pigeon Point to Santa Cruz

6–8 hours, 65.7mi

Get ready for a series of extreme climbs with an exhilarating 20mi downhill to end the day. The route begins by winding along an old stagecoach route through century-old eucalyptus groves and fields of pumpkins and wildflowers. It links two of northern California's most appealing small coastal towns, Pescadero (6mi) and San Gregorio (13.3).

From San Gregorio – where a visit to the ***general store*** is highly recommended – climb a broad river valley, enter the redwood forest, and begin the long ascent to the crest of the Santa Cruz Mtns. Once you're on top (38.7mi), the route undulates along the ridgeline, narrowing to one lane at points and zigzagging gracefully beneath a canopy of trees. One last plunge lands you in a deep redwood-filled canyon, within 7mi of Santa Cruz. Parallel the San Lorenzo River the rest of the way.

Southern California

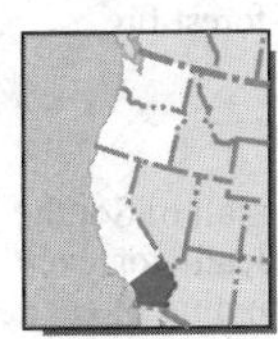

This section covers the state's sunny southern extremity, from Los Angeles (LA) to the Mexican border, and from Catalina Island to the Anza-Borrego Desert. The rides range from urban excursions in LA and San Diego to remote rambles through awe-inspiring island and desert landscapes.

HISTORY

Numerous indigenous peoples inhabited Southern California before European arrival, in settlements ranging from large coastal Chumash villages to tiny Cahuilla settlements in the less hospitable desert. Trade between neighboring peoples was widespread, with mountain Kumeyaay acting as intermediaries between coastal and desert tribes, and Channel Islands people shuttling goods to the mainland on large plank canoes. Particularly prized were high-quality soapstone bowls, tools, and other implements made on Catalina Island, which found their way as far as the American Southwest.

The earliest European exploration of California began here in the south. In 1542 Juan Rodríguez Cabrillo put the Southern California coast on Spanish maps for the first time; 60 years later Sebastián Vizcaino gave many places their present-day names (San Diego, Catalina, Santa Barbara). In 1769 the Spanish founded their first Alta California presidio and mission in San Diego, and within five years overland expeditions led by Pedro Fages and Juan Bautista de Anza had ventured across the southern mountains and deserts. By 1798 five missions had been established between present-day LA and San Diego.

Despite these early settlements, Southern California remained less populated than the north until the late 1800s, when rail access and the discovery of oil prompted a massive influx of new residents. Rapid growth continued in the 20th century, spurred in part by the exodus from the Dust Bowl, the dream

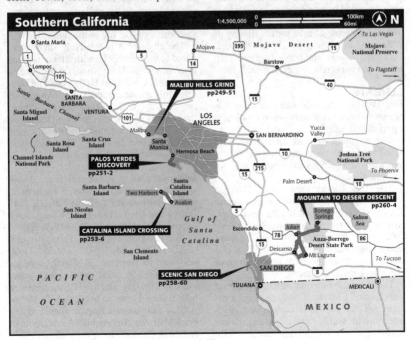

Southern California
1:4,500,000
0 100km
0 60mi
N
Santa Maria
Lompoc
Santa Barbara Channel
SANTA BARBARA
VENTURA
Santa Miguel Island
Santa Rosa Island
Santa Cruz Island
Channel Islands National Park
Mojave
Mojave Desert
Barstow
To Las Vegas
Mojave National Preserve
To Flagstaff
MALIBU HILLS GRIND
pp249-51
LOS ANGELES
Malibu
Santa Monica
Hermosa Beach
SAN BERNARDINO
Yucca Valley
Joshua Tree National Park
To Phoenix
Palm Desert
PALOS VERDES DISCOVERY
pp251-2
Santa Barbara Island
Two Harbors
Santa Catalina Island
Avalon
San Nicolas Island
CATALINA ISLAND CROSSING
pp253-6
Gulf of Santa Catalina
San Clemente Island
MOUNTAIN TO DESERT DESCENT
pp260-4
Borrego Springs
Salton Sea
Julian
Escondido
Anza-Borrego Desert State Park
Descanso
Mt Laguna
SAN DIEGO
To Tucson
SCENIC SAN DIEGO
pp258-60
TIJUANA
MEXICALI
PACIFIC OCEAN
MEXICO

of an earthly paradise, and the rise of the movie industry in Hollywood.

NATURAL HISTORY

The area from LA south to the Mexican border is much drier and more developed than the Central Coast. Loss of native animal and plant habitat is especially acute in the LA basin. However, outlying areas such as Catalina Island and the Anza-Borrego Desert teem with life. Particularly fascinating is Anza-Borrego, which provides native habitat for bighorn sheep, California fan palm trees and a plethora of flowering desert plants. East of San Diego, the forests of Rancho Cuyamaca State Park contain the richest mix of oak and conifer species anywhere in Southern California, including incense cedar, which are usually associated with more northerly climes.

Catalina Island's isolated geography has led to the evolution of eight endemic plant species, and helped protect other species whose mainland habitat has been lost to urbanization. Native mammals include the Catalina Island fox, a small, inquisitive member of the fox family whose numbers have dwindled in recent years. The island is home to a non-native herd of bison descended from the 14 brought over for the filming of a Zane Grey movie in 1924. Offshore, Catalina's waters are home to giant kelp forests and the bright orange Garibaldi fish.

CLIMATE

This is where the rain stops and the sun begins. Winter is the only season with any significant rainfall.

The southern coastal climate is mild year-round, with warm days (average daily temperature 57–75°F), cool nights and occasional fog.

The low desert areas near Borrego Springs can have pleasantly warm, sunny days anytime from October through April, with daytime temperatures reaching above 70°F even in winter. Summer months (May–Sept) bring blistering 100°F heat and cause many tourist services to shut down or scale back their operations.

The mountains around Julian, Cuyamaca Rancho and Cleveland National Forest receive several snowfalls each winter, with intermittent warm spells melting snow. Spring, summer and fall days are generally pleasant, although snowfalls are sometimes recorded as late as May, and Santa Ana winds in the fall increase the risk of forest fire.

INFORMATION

Maps & Books

No single regional map covers all of Southern California in sufficient detail for cyclists. See Planning at the beginning of each ride for the best local resources. Lonely Planet publishes several useful guides to the region, including *California*, *Los Angeles*, *CitySync Los Angeles*, *Los Angeles City Map* and *San Diego & Tijuana*.

Los Angeles Region

GATEWAY CITIES

Los Angeles

☎ 213 downtown ☎ 323 Hollywood
☎ 310 West LA, Malibu & the beaches

LA is a place that no traveler should omit from a must-see list. The big houses, fast cars, fancy clothes, elegant restaurants and designer drugs – of which LA has more than its share – are not only the aggrandizement of the 'American dream' but also statements of LA mentality: what you see may be gone tomorrow, so live life to the fullest today.

The city of LA is relatively small compared to the metropolis with which its name is synonymous. Hollywood, for instance, is a part of LA, but West Hollywood and Beverly Hills are independent cities. Angelenos rely heavily on the automobile to navigate the network of freeways that bind this urban sprawl but bikes can make their way around LA's side streets just fine. That said, there are few established bike routes.

Information LA visitor centers are downtown (☎ 213-689-8822) at 685 S Figueroa St, and in Hollywood (☎ 323-689-8822), 6541 Hollywood Blvd. There is a 24-hour multilingual events hotline (☎ 213-689-8822).

The LA Department of Transportation (LADOT; ☎ 213-485-9957 or ☎ 580-1199) will send its free (though slightly cumbersome) 'bikeway guide' maps, which cover most of the city and highlight suggested bike routes. Easier to use is AAA's *Metropolitan Los Angeles* map, available at any branch of the Automobile Association of Southern California.

The main post office (☎ 213-617-4543 or ☎ 800-275-8777 for regional branches) is at 900 N Alameda St; postal code 90017.

Internet terminals are available at most libraries. For coffee with your connection, try the Interactive Cafe (☎ 310-395-5009), 215 Broadway, near Santa Monica's Third St Promenade; or Cyber Java (☎ 310-581-1300), 1029 Abbot Kinney Blvd in Venice, with a 24-hour branch (☎ 323-466-5600), 7080 Hollywood Blvd, Hollywood.

Helen's Cycles is a local chain that has reliable service and good prices. There's one near UCLA at 1071 Gayley Ave (☎ 310-208-8988), and in Manhattan Beach (☎ 310-643-914) at 1570 E Rosecrans Ave. In Santa Monica is H&M Bike Shop (☎ 323-221-4425), 3424 N Broadway, near Third St Promenade.

You'll also find a number of bike rental stands, which usually have a minimal set of tools, along the South Bay Bike Trail, the 22mi stretch of sidewalk that skirts the sand from Malibu in the north to Palos Verdes in the south. Perry's Rentals (☎ 310-452-7609) has four outlets.

The LA Wheelmen (W www.lawheelmen.org) welcome all (helmeted) cyclists on their 9am Sunday rides that start at the corner of Olympic and La Cienega Blvds.

Things to See & Do Few areas of LA have as much to offer per square mile as downtown. Reach the top of historic Bunker Hill via **Angels Flight** – built in 1901 as 'the shortest railway in the world'. Near the base is the acclaimed **Museum of Contemporary Art** (MOCA; ☎ 213-626-6222; closed Mon), 250 S Grand Ave, with works from the 1940s to the present.

Between 3rd and 4th Sts is the **Grand Central Market**, a bustling food bazaar in business since 1917. Across the street at 304 Broadway is the elegant Bradbury Building (1893).

The Civic Center contains the most important of LA's city, county, state and federal office buildings, the most distinctive of which is the **City Hall** (1928), which served as the 'Daily Planet' building in the *Superman* movie and the police station in *Dragnet*.

The heart of El Pueblo de Los Angeles, founding site of LA (1781) is **Olvera St**, a narrow, block-long passageway that's been an open-air Mexican marketplace since 1930.

Getting into a Studio

If you've always dreamed of seeing your favorite TV show in the flesh, your best bet is to watch a taping. Doing so is easy – and tickets are free – but plan well ahead because the most coveted shows such as *Friends* are usually booked up for months. Production season runs from August through March. All shows have minimum age requirements (usually 16 or 18). On the day of the taping, come to the studio early to guarantee getting a seat, as tickets are distributed in excess of capacity.

The 'central clearing house' for studio tickets is Audiences Unlimited (☎ 818-753-3483 for recorded information or ☎ 818-753-3470 for tickets, W www.tvtickets.com), Bldg 153, 100 Universal City Plaza, Universal City, CA 91608. It handles distribution for almost 30 shows, including *Friends* and *The Drew Carey Show*.

You can contact some of the major studios directly: CBS Television Center (☎ 323-852-2458), 7800 Beverly Blvd, Los Angeles, CA 90036; Paramount Guest Relations (☎ 323-956-5575 for recorded information or ☎ 323-956-1777 for tickets), 860 N Gower St, Hollywood; NBC Tickets (☎ 818-840-3537 for recorded information or ☎ 818-840-3538 for tickets), 3000 W Alameda Ave, Burbank, CA 91523.

You can also see live filming taking place by obtaining a 'shoot sheet', a list detailing the locations where movies, TV programs, videos and commercials are being shot that day; it's available online (W www.seeing-stars.com/ShootSheet) or for a small fee in person from the LA Film & Video Permit Office (☎ 323-957-1000), 7083 Hollywood Blvd. The list does not reveal which actors are involved in the shoot or whether it's indoors or outdoors.

Andrea Schulte-Peevers

It's home to LA's oldest building, the refurbished Avila Adobe (1808). **Union Station**, built in 1939, is the last of the great railroad stations in the USA. Its impressive marble-floored waiting room decked with massive original chandeliers and elegant leather armchairs has starred in a fistful of movies.

The seaside city of Santa Monica is one of the most agreeable in LA, with its early 20th-century pier and colorful **Third St Promenade**, a pedestrian mall extending for three long blocks from Wilshire Blvd south to Broadway. **Main St**, flanked with boutiques and hip eateries, runs south for 2mi to Venice. Here the chief attraction is **Ocean Front Walk**, where you can buy spicy sausages, get your fortune told or your body pierced, or pump it up with body builders at Muscle Beach.

More than 2000 marble-and-bronze stars are embedded in the sidewalk along the **Hollywood Walk of Fame**, stretching east from La Brea Ave to Gower St and south along Vine St between Yucca St and Sunset Blvd. **Mann's Chinese Theater**, 6925 Hollywood Blvd, is the most famous of Hollywood movie palaces. Leaving a foot or handprint in wet cement has been a special honor since Douglas Fairbanks, Mary Pickford and Norma Talmage started the tradition.

Stylish and sophisticated, Beverly Hills centers its wealth on **Rodeo Dr**, lined with designer boutiques.

The **Getty Center** (☎ 310-440-7300), atop a Brentwood hillside at 1200 Getty Center Dr, unites the art collections that were assembled by oil magnate J Paul Getty.

Beaches are LA's major natural asset. Surfing, sailing, swimming, in-line skating (rollerblading) or volleyball are all enjoyed by locals and visitors year-round. Arguably the nicest beaches are those of Santa Monica, Manhattan and Hermosa Beach.

Places to Stay The favorite saying of real estate hawkers and movie producers applies to travelers looking for accommodations in this vastly dispersed city: 'location is everything'.

Camping & Budget LA's campgrounds cater to RVs, are on the beach and open year-round. ***Malibu Beach RV Park*** *(☎ 310-456-6052 or ☎ 800-622-6052, 25801 Pacific Coast Hwy)* is the only one with tent spaces ($17–20). ***Dockweiler Beach RV Park*** *(☎ 310-322-4951 or ☎ 800-950-7275, 12001 Vista Del Mar)*, in Playa del Rey, is under the flight path of LAX. Sites cost $15 to $25.

The ***Hollywood International Hostel*** *(☎ 323-463-0797 or ☎ 800-750-6561, 6820 Hollywood Blvd)* is big and lively, with small dorm rooms ($14 per bunk) and a few private rooms ($32). It offers free breakfast, a communal kitchen, Internet access, gym and laundry. Bikes stay in the reception area.

A block from shopping and the beach in Santa Monica, the ***HI Los Angeles*** *(☎ 310-393-9913 or ☎ 800-909-4776, ext 05; 1436 2nd St)* has dorm beds ($18–20), a large kitchen, library, theater, laundry and bike storage room. There is a 2am curfew.

Best of the bunch is ***Los Angeles Surf City Hostel*** *(☎ 310-798-2323 or ☎ 800-305-2901, 26 Pier Ave)*, surrounded by the shops, restaurants and bars of Hermosa Beach (14mi south of Santa Monica on the South Bay Bike Trail). It offers free airport pick-up (keep your bike in its box), ocean-view dorms ($15) and doubles ($35), plus a kitchen and free breakfast. Bikes stay in the hallway, or in your room.

Mid-Range A good hotel near downtown is the family-run Best Western ***Dragon Gate Inn*** *(☎ 213-617-3077 or ☎ 800-282-9999, 818 N Hill St)*, with large rooms ($70–110) where bikes are welcome.

On a quiet street near Mann's Chinese Theater, the ***Liberty Hotel*** *(☎ 323-962-1788, 1770 Orchid Ave)* is a friendly place with large rooms ($44/45 single/double), a guest laundry and patio where bikes are kept. A step up in service, the ***Hollywood Celebrity Hotel*** *(☎ 323-850-6464 or ☎ 800-222-7017, 1775 N Orchid Ave)* offers spacious $85 rooms (good for bike storage) and delivers continental breakfast to your room. At the nearby ***Highland Gardens Hotel*** *(☎ 323-850-0535 or ☎ 800-404-5472, 7047 Franklin Ave)* rooms ($60/65) wrap around a leafy, quiet courtyard where bikes can stay. Janis Joplin overdosed in room 105 on 3 October, 1970.

Cheap but charming in Santa Monica is the ***Sea Shore Motel*** *(☎ 310-392-2787, 2637 Main St)*, where bikes stay in your room ($68). The ***Hotel Shangri-La*** *(☎ 310-394-2791 or ☎ 800-345-7829, 1301 Ocean Ave)* has long been a sentimental favorite. Rooms start at $130, including continental breakfast and afternoon tea; bikes can stay in a room off the lobby.

One of LA's best bargains remains the ***Cadillac Hotel*** *(☎ 310-399-8876, 8 Dudley Ave)*, right on Venice's Ocean Front Walk. It offers spacious rooms ($78–120) with ocean views, a gym, rooftop deck and coin laundry.

Top End If you've got $200 to $750 to spend on a room, put yourself in the lap of luxury and ocean waves at ***Shutters on the***

Beach *(☎ 800-334-9000; 1 Pico Blvd, Santa Monica)*, or surround yourself with Beverly Hills' boutiques and beautiful people at the opulent ***Regent Beverly Wilshire*** *(☎ 310-275-5200, 9500 Wilshire Blvd)*.

Places to Eat Downtown's ***Grand Central Market*** *(cnr Broadway & 4th St)* is a fun place to gaze and graze. Pick up fresh produce, cheeses and baked goods for a picnic, or sidle up to one of the counters for a tamale, grilled sausage or noodle soup.

One of LA's oldest Mexican restaurants (since 1924), and the best on Olvera St, is ***La Golondrina*** *(W-17 Olvera St)*, where meals start at $10. Another LA institution, in business since 1908, ***Philippe's The Original*** *(1001 N Alameda St)* serves juicy roast beef sandwiches ($4) and coffee for $0.90.

Hamburger Hamlet *(6914 Hollywood Blvd)* is perfect for grabbing a quick burger, sandwich, salad or pasta ($6–$10). Celebrities are often spotted curing their hangovers with all-beef dogs at ***Pink's Hot Dogs*** *(711 La Brea Ave)*.

Main St in Santa Monica offers a range of upscale dining options, including the lofty ***Röckenwagner*** *(☎ 310-399-6504, 2435 Main St)*, where mains cost around $18.

Venice is more casual, with places such as the ***Sidewalk Cafe*** *(1401 Ocean Front Walk)* serving big plates of old-fashioned American fare for under $10.

In Hermosa Beach, eat Hawaiian-style breakfast or lunch ($5) at ***Beach Hut No 2*** *(1342 Hermosa Ave)*; grilled fish, salads, sandwiches and tasty beers at ***Brewski's*** *(49 Pier Ave)*; or nicer Italian fare (around $10) at ***Buona Vita*** *(439 Pier Ave)*.

Getting There & Away Along with New York, LA is the major international gateway to the USA.

Air Los Angeles international airport (LAX; ☎ 310-646-5252) is one of the world's busiest hubs, served by all major airlines.

Super Shuttle (☎ 310-450-2377 or ☎ 800-258-3826) charges $13 to $20 for door-to-door service, no extra charge for boxed bikes. Prime Time (☎ 800-262-7433) has similar fares and charges $5 extra for each bike.

The free 24-hour Shuttle C bus stops outside each terminal every 10 to 20 minutes and goes to the LAX Transit Center, from where public buses will take you anywhere in greater LA. Metropolitan Transportation Authority (MTA; ☎ 800-266-6883, **W** www.mta.net) has the largest fleet of buses, each equipped to take two bikes on a front rack. Santa Monica's Big Blue Bus (☎ 310-451-5444) serves much of the Westside, as well as Santa Monica and Venice Beach, but does not accommodate bikes.

It is possible, but not scenic and a little scary, to ride from LAX to the South Bay Bike Trail: exit the airport on Lincoln Blvd (going north), go left (west) on Westchester Parkway and ride 2.5mi to where Pershing Dr parallels the beach; turn right (north) to access a ramp that leads down to the bikepath; Hermosa Beach is 3mi south, Santa Monica is 11mi north.

Bus Greyhound connects LA with cities all across North America. The 24-hour main terminal (☎ 213-629-8421), corner E 7th and Alameda Sts, is in a rough area but the station is safe enough inside. Other Greyhound stations are at 1409 N Vine St, Hollywood (☎ 323-466-6384) and on 4th St between Colorado Blvd and Broadway in Santa Monica. Buses depart almost hourly to San Diego ($15), Santa Barbara ($13) and San Francisco ($36).

Train Amtrak (☎ 800-872-7245, **W** www.amtrak.com) arrives and departs from historic Union Station, 800 N Alameda St. Interstate trains stopping in LA are the *Coast Starlight* to Seattle ($106); the *Southwest Chief* with daily departures to Chicago ($199); and the *Sunset Limited* with three services a week to Orlando, Florida ($273). The *San Diegan* connects LA with Santa Barbara ($14) and San Diego ($22).

Malibu Hills Grind

Duration	5 hours
Distance	31.1mi
Difficulty	hard
Start/End	Santa Monica Pier
Cues	p375

A kick-ass ride for hill lovers, this route is a favorite workout of local cyclists. Topanga Canyon cuts east-west from the Pacific to the San Fernando Valley, through the Santa

Monica Mtns and some of LA's woodiest enclaves. Climbing out of the canyon is challenging but the views from atop Fernwood Ridge are some of the finest in Southern California. Food and water are available at Fernwood (9.9mi) and in Malibu.

PLANNING

When to Ride

Start in the early morning, when most traffic is going down-canyon, or mid-morning when commuter traffic has subsided. All but the last 2.5mi of climbing is in the shade. Afternoon winds can sweep down the canyon, making left turns on the already-hairy descent quite tricky.

Maps

AAA's *Metropolitan Los Angeles – Western Area* is good, though any decent map of Malibu and/or Santa Monica should do.

GETTING TO/FROM THE RIDE

MTA bus Nos 20 (to/from Beverly Hills), 22 (to/from Century City), 33 and 333 (both to/from downtown) stop at the Santa Monica Visitor Center, on Ocean Ave above the Pier's entrance.

THE RIDE

Follow the South Bay Bike Trail north from the Santa Monica Pier to Will Rogers State Beach. When roller skaters and pedestrians crowd this route, you may prefer to ride along the Pacific Coast Hwy (PCH).

Once the route leaves the beach it follows the PCH for a short stint before turning north. The glitz and glamour of LA quickly disappear as Topanga Canyon's only road takes you through its steep, rocky flanks covered with California laurel, anise and wild mustard. There is little shoulder for most of the way and the road can be strewn with rocks that tumble from above.

After gentle climbing, the route takes a hard uphill turn on Fernwood Pacific Dr. The ***cafe*** and ***natural foods store*** at this turn are cyclist-friendly, with outstanding coffee and pastries and healthy deli fare.

The next 3mi, known as the 'Fernwood climb', twist through one of LA's most alternative communities. Pick-up trucks and VW vans are more prevalent than BMWs for a change. About 2mi into the climb, the houses are sparser and glimpses of the awesome rock heap you've been climbing are more frequent. Another 1mi of steep climbing puts you almost on top of the ridge, at a scenic spot from where the road levels a bit. Million-dollar homes, large cacti, sage and rock formations cohabit on this chunk of land that feels surprisingly remote.

The route then traverses the ridge separating Topanga Canyon from Las Flores

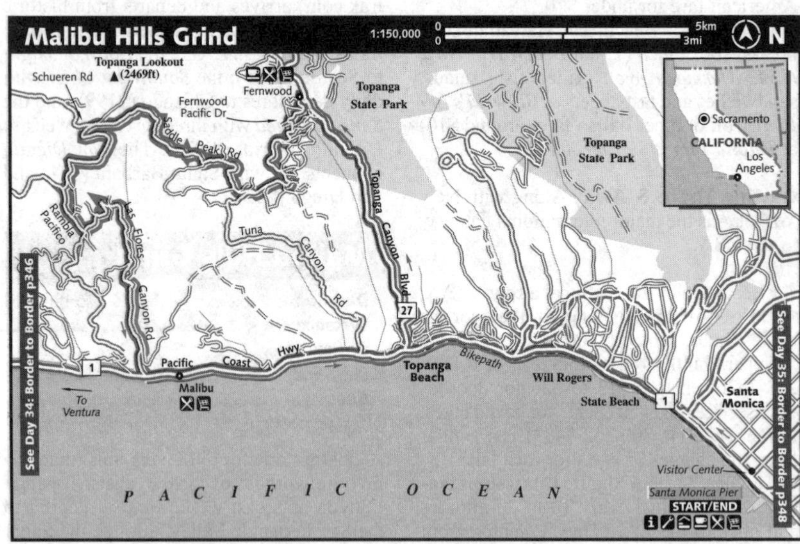

Canyon, immediately north. Upon reaching the ridge's northern end, Schueren Rd descends briefly to Rambla Pacifico, which may eventually be connected to the PCH. For now, follow Las Flores Canyon Rd, one of the most exciting downhills in the USA, with 2mi of tight turns and 10% grades that appear to float above the Pacific Ocean. Shoulders are narrow to non-existent and the road can be strewn with rocks, so use extreme caution.

The downhill ends at the PCH from where it's a straight shot back to the bikepath; to reach it cross the parking lot where Temescal Canyon Rd hits the highway (27.7mi).

Palos Verdes Discovery

Duration .... 4 hours
Distance 28.5mi
Difficulty .... easy–moderate
Start/End .... Hermosa Beach Pier
Cues & Elevation Profile p375

Palos Verdes (PV), the rocky precipice separating Santa Monica Bay from San Pedro Bay, is Mediterranean in every way: from its Spanish-style villas (a tile roof is required by the neighborhood planning department) to its bougainvilleas and the rocky cliffs that plunge into the cobalt sea. The circuit of PV is a regular weekend ritual for many LA cyclists. It offers stunning views of Catalina Island, a chance to see whales from December to April and an excuse to leave the saddle and explore tidepools. PV is also a horse-loving community with a plethora of bridle trails.

You may see some of PV's most graceful (but very noisy) denizens on this ride: peacocks, introduced in the 1920s by a real estate developer.

PLANNING

Maps

AAA's *Southern Area Metropolitan Los Angeles* map is useful for this ride.

GETTING TO/FROM THE RIDE

MTA bus No 439 goes from downtown to the Hermosa Beach Pier, via LAX. On the South Bay Bike Trail, it's a 14.6mi ride from the Santa Monica Pier to the Hermosa Beach Pier.

HUGH D'ANDRADE

Gray whales may be spotted as they migrate along the Pacific Coast.

THE RIDE (See Map, p252)

Leaving the sand at Hermosa, passing **King Harbor** and the Redondo Beach pleasure pier, the route heads south towards Palos Verdes, the southern end of Santa Monica Bay (Malibu is at the north end).

Turning away from the coast, the route climbs through the Hollywood Riviera to Palos Verdes Blvd. The bikepath here is bumpy and often covered with eucalyptus berries, so most cyclists stay on the road's generous shoulder. After rounding the bend and heading west past **Malaga Cove Plaza**, where there's a small ***store*** and ***cafe***, Palos Verdes Blvd becomes Palos Verdes Dr W.

Weaving around the wave-cut terraces towards Palos Verdes Point, the road eventually turns north towards Lunada Bay (7.6mi). This affluent neighborhood is serviced by a good ***market*** and great Italian restaurant, ***Viva La Pasta***. A wide, smooth shoulder makes the going great for the next several miles.

At Point Vicente, Palos Verdes Dr W turns to Palos Verdes Dr S. The **Point Vicente Interpretive Center** (10mi) has a small exhibit about the gray whales that pass en route from the Arctic Sea to Baja California. Access the rocky beach from the **parking lot**, 0.5mi further.

A better trail to the beach is at **Abalone Cove Shoreline Park** (11.8mi), where a grassy expanse above the cliffs is popular for picnicking (no restrooms). The ecological reserve of Abalone Cove has large tidepools that are great for exploring at low tide.

On the opposite side of the road and 0.2mi south from the park is **Wayfarer's Chapel**, designed by Lloyd Wright, son of Frank Lloyd Wright, in 1949. The glass structure is enveloped by a thick grove of trees that make the fairy-tale space look and feel like a greenhouse.

From here the road gets exceptionally bumpy as a result of the continually shifting land below. There is little shoulder and frequent road construction for the next 2mi. Known locally as 'Portuguese Bend', this area had a big Portuguese population in the

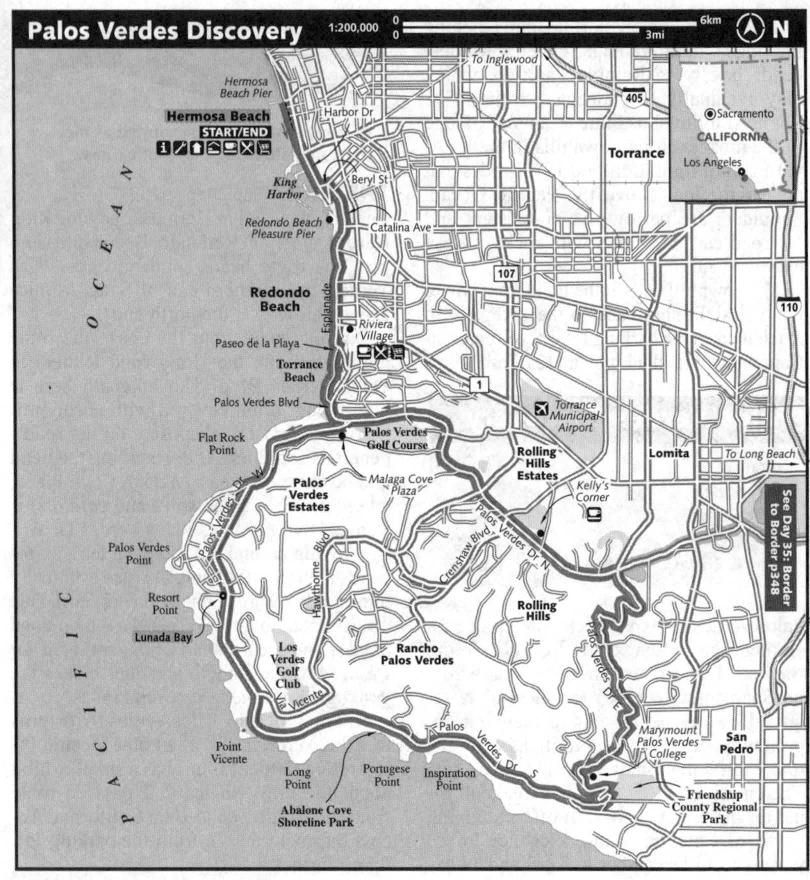

mid-1800s when Palos Verdes was an important whaling station.

From 14.8mi the route turns off Palos Verdes Dr S to climb steadily up Palos Verdes Dr E to the top of Palos Verdes. **Marymount Palos Verdes College** (16.7mi) marks the beginning of a fabulous 4.5mi descent affording views of San Pedro and LA's main shipping harbor.

Once you've turned west on Palos Verdes Dr N it's a fairly straightforward 4.8mi back to the coast. A bridle path and bumpy bikepath parallel the road most of the way. Be sure to stop at ***Kelly's Korner*** (22.3mi) for a sandwich, ice cream or just to see the beautiful saddles, blankets and tack they carry.

Back on the coast you can rejoin the South Bay Bike Trail or stay high along the Esplanade for quicker pedaling. Two blocks inland, Riviera Village has a good ***brewery***, several ***cafes***, ***restaurants*** and plenty of clothing boutiques. The Hermosa Beach Pier is 4mi north.

Catalina Island

Only one hour by boat from the traffic-choked LA basin, Santa Catalina Island (known as Catalina Island) is a world apart. This is what coastal Southern California might have been without the internal combustion engine and the mania for wall-to-wall development. With just two small settlements, a strict limit on automobile traffic and a wide array of scenic roads and trails, Catalina Island is a cyclist's dream. See Natural History (p246) for information on the island's plants and animals.

HISTORY

Human presence on Catalina dates back over 7000 years. The island's original inhabitants used Catalina's abundant high-quality soapstone for bowls, tools and other implements that were prized and traded throughout the American Southwest. In the 1800s Spanish and Mexican ownership gave way to a succession of American miners, ranchers, and land speculators hoping to make their fortunes.

The island's development as a tourist destination started in the late 19th century and hit its stride in the 1920s, when chewing-gum magnate William Wrigley built many of the town's landmark buildings and successfully courted large crowds of visitors from nearby LA. Catalina also experienced a brief period of fame as a manufacturer of ceramics in the 1930s, as evidenced by the beautiful tilework adorning Avalon's streets.

Catalina Island Crossing

MOUNTAIN-BIKE RIDE

Duration	3–4 hours
Distance	23mi
Difficulty	moderate–hard
Start	Two Harbors
End	Avalon
Cues & Elevation Profile	p376

This mountain-bike ride traverses the rugged and largely uninhabited interior of Catalina Island, offering spectacular ocean and mountain vistas, plus a chance to see buffalo and other wildlife. Although short in miles, the ride is challenging because of the steep climbs involved. It can be done in either direction but is described here from north to south, allowing you to experience a sheer 1500ft drop from the mountains into Avalon rather than an excruciating morning climb. Ferry transport is available at either end.

PLANNING

When to Ride

Cycling on Catalina is pleasant year-round. April is a particularly nice month, when days are warm but not too hot, winter rains have subsided, hotels are still charging low-season prices, and bike permits are at their cheapest. Summer is the priciest and most crowded season but the best for ocean sports and evening entertainment. Special events can enhance your trip – check out the calendars at w www.visitcatalina.org and w www.sci co.com/twoharbors/mainevent.html; see the boxed text 'Desert Island Diversions', p254.

Maps & Books

The Catalina Island Conservancy provides a free map of all the island's cyclable roads and trails when you purchase your bike permit.

Franko's Map of Catalina Island, widely available at stores in Avalon and Two Harbors, is also a good resource.

What to Bring

You'll need a bike permit from the Catalina Island Conservancy in Avalon (☎ 310-510-2595, w www.catalinaconservancy.org) or the Two Harbors visitor center (☎ 310-510-0303). Buying a permit makes you a part of their cycling association and provides insurance in case of an accident. As the insurance policy is renewed annually on 1 May, all permits are valid from the date of purchase through 30 April. Permits cost $13 (Feb–Apr), $25 (Nov–Jan), $38 (Aug–Oct), $50 (May–Jul). The Conservancy requires that you use a mountain bike with good tires and wear an approved bike helmet (both available for rent in Avalon). Rangers are on duty to enforce these rules. Carry plenty of water and some food, as services are limited along the route. Camping gear will allow you to overnight at one of the island's remote beachside campgrounds.

GETTING TO/FROM THE RIDE

Two Harbors/Avalon

Catalina is just a short boat ride from Southern California's mainland. Three companies provide transportation to/from the island.

Boat Catalina Express (☎ 310-519-1212 or ☎ 800-481-3470, w www.CatalinaExpress .com) offers year-round daily boat service to Avalon from San Pedro (1¼ hours), Long Beach (one hour) and Dana Point (1½ hours). Boats also run from San Pedro to Two Harbors year-round (1½ hours; daily in summer). Fares are $21/41 one way/return, higher from Dana Point; bikes cost $3 extra each way. Less frequent service is available between Two Harbors and Avalon ($14 one way, bikes $3).

The Catalina Explorer (☎ 877-432-6276, Ⓦ www.catalinaferry.com) runs boats from Dana Point to Avalon ($21/42, bikes $5, 1½ hours) daily in summer, weekends only from late March to mid-May. Daily services also run in summer between Avalon and Two Harbors daily ($15/25, bikes $5, one hour).

Catalina Flyer (☎ 949-673-5245 or ☎ 800-830-7744, Ⓦ www.catalinainfo.com) runs boats from Newport Beach to Avalon ($38 return, bikes $7) daily from March through November, less frequently in winter.

Train The most convenient way of combining train and boat travel to Catalina is to take Amtrak's daily shuttle bus between LA's Union Station and San Pedro's Catalina Terminal. To use this service you must have a connecting Amtrak train ticket between LA and some other destination.

Bicycle The Border to Border ride passes through Newport Beach (pp347–9), allowing easy connections to the Catalina Flyer boat.

Desert Island Diversions

Maybe it's the margaritas, or perhaps the folks in Two Harbors have spent a few too many hours in the Southern California sun. Whatever the case, the annual calendar of events for this Catalina Island community displays a unique breed of creative inspiration. If you've ever wanted to test your skill at hurling dried buffalo dung or carving pumpkins underwater you shouldn't miss the **Catalina Buffalo Chip Toss** (Sept) and the **Halloween Jacques-o-Lantern Contest** (Oct). Then there's the annual **Easter Egg Hunt**, where participants are invited to dig eggs out of the sand 'before the ravens get 'um'. Nautically inclined canines take center stage at the summer **Yacht Dog Show** ('strut your mutt'). And aspiring brigands will love **Buccaneer Days**, where adults and kids alike hunt for buried treasure and prizes are awarded for the best pirate costume. See these Web sites for a complete list of events in both Two Harbors (Ⓦ www.scico.com/twoharbors/mainevent.html) and Avalon (Ⓦ www.visitcatalina.org).

THE RIDE
Two Harbors
☎ 310

This tiny company town straddles Catalina's narrow northern isthmus. With dirt streets and a slow pace of life in the off season, its spectacular setting has also made it a regular film location for dramatic sea battles.

Information The visitor center (☎ 510-0303, Ⓦ www.catalina.com/twoharbors) is on Isthmus Pier, where the ferries dock, and sells bike permits. There's an ATM outside the Harbor Reef Restaurant.

Things to See & Do Two Harbors is a great place for **outdoor activities** of all kinds, including snorkeling, diving, kayaking, swimming and cycling. Rentals for all sports are available through Two Harbors Dive and Recreation Center (☎ 510-4272, Ⓔ dive@scico.com). The best local **bike ride** takes you 8mi north of town, dipping in and out of coves and offering beautiful coastal views en route to Parsons Landing, a secluded beach with a small campground.

One of the most colorful annual events is the **Buffalo Chip Toss** in September.

Places to Stay & Eat On a bluff overlooking the ocean, ***Two Harbors Campground*** *(☎ 510-8368, Ⓦ www.catalina.com/camping)* charges $6/12 per person in winter/summer. It also rents equipment. ***Two Harbors Camping Cabins*** *(☎ 510-2800)* has spartan rooms for $25/$40 midweek/weekend (Oct–Apr).

Banning House Lodge *(☎ 510-4228* or *☎ 800-851-0217, Ⓦ www.catalina.com/twoharbors/mainlodging.html)* is an historic B&B with dramatic views of the isthmus. Rooms cost $79 to $149 depending on season.

Two Harbors' three eating options are clustered near the ferry landing. The ***general store*** sells groceries and camping supplies. ***West End Galley*** is an order-at-the-counter breakfast and lunch place. ***Harbor Reef Restaurant*** is pricier but equally informal, with a pool table, jukebox, dart boards and a full bar. Both have outdoor decks.

Mountain-Bike Ride: Two Harbors to Avalon

From the ferry landing in Two Harbors, the route climbs steeply into the surrounding hills, affording spectacular views of the

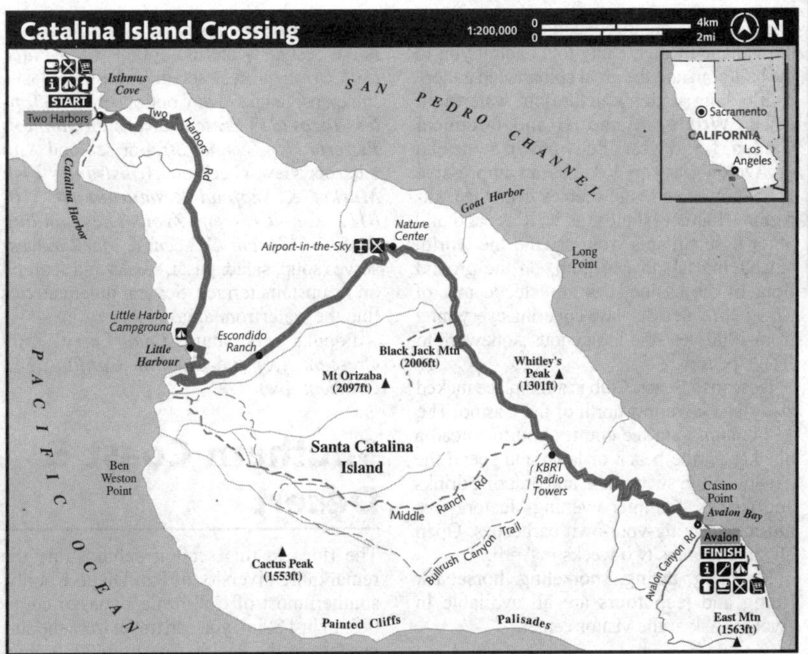

isthmus and the ocean on either side. Past the summit, the downhill to secluded Little Harbor beach is more gradual, with buffalo sightings possible. Phones and water are available at ***Little Harbor campground***. The day's longest climb (1500ft over 6mi) is broken briefly at **El Rancho Escondido** (9.5mi), where eucalyptus trees provide shade and horse corrals line the roadside. From here it's straight up to Catalina's **Airport-in-the-Sky** (13mi), where you'll find excellent displays on local and natural history, plus a good ***restaurant*** with a scenic outdoor deck. Pavement begins here, and the next 7mi undulate along the ridgeline, with unbelievably steep drop-offs to the island's eastern coves. The route's last 3mi plunge headlong down a narrow eucalyptus-lined road to the Mediterranean-style port of Avalon.

Avalon

☎ 310

Avalon is an appealing and compact town draped across steep hillsides surrounding a crescent-shaped cove. The business district is concentrated on waterfront Crescent St and a few smaller streets fanning out towards the hills. The south end of downtown is marked by the ferry landing, the north end by the eye-catching circular Avalon Casino. There's a delightful three-block pedestrian zone (walk bikes) on Crescent St between Metropole and Claressa Sts, with palm trees, fountains, tilework and benches.

Information Avalon's visitor center (☎ 510-1520, fax 510-7606, W www.visitcatalina.org) is on Green Pier, in the heart of the waterfront district. US Bank, corner Crescent and Metropole Sts, has a 24-hour ATM.

The Catalina Island Conservancy (☎ 510-2595, W www.catalinaconservancy.org), 125 Claressa St, issues cycling permits and maps.

Brown's Bikes (☎ 510-0986), on Crescent St near the ferry landing, is a full-service bike shop that rents mountain bikes.

Things to See & Do The stylish **Avalon Casino**, at the north end of the cove, is Catalina's most prominent landmark and well worth a visit. Opened in 1929, it boasts the world's largest circular dance floor. Downstairs are wonderful murals depicting underwater scenes, with nightly movie screenings and weekend organ concerts year-round in the vintage theater. Daily tours admit you to the ballroom and the great colonnaded gallery overlooking Avalon's picturesque waterfront.

The **Wrigley Memorial and Botanical Garden**, 1.5mi west of downtown at the end of Avalon Canyon Rd, has an impressive collection of endemic species from the California Channel Islands, as well as cacti and other desert plants from around the world.

Catalina Island Museum, on the ground floor of the casino, has an eclectic mix of Catalina-related displays covering everything from 7000-year-old indigenous stonework to 1930s pottery.

Descanso Beach Club is a fun place tucked away in a cove just north of the Casino. The $1.50 admission fee entitles you to spread a blanket on the beach or lawn and spend the day lounging, swimming, and ordering drinks and snacks. Summer evenings feature live music and bring-your-own barbecues. Open all summer plus two weeks in April.

Kayaking, **diving**, **snorkeling**, **horseback riding** and **jeep tours** are all available in Avalon. Ask at the visitor center.

Places to Stay & Eat With equipment, tent cabins and teepees for hire, ***Hermit Gulch Campground*** *(☎ 510-8368, Ⓦ www.catalina.com/camping)*, is near the Botanical Garden on Avalon Canyon Rd. Sites cost from $12 per person in (less Nov–Mar).

Hermosa Hotel *(☎ 877-241-1313, Ⓦ www.catalina.com/hermosa, 131 Metropole St)* is the most dependable budget option in town, with unheated rooms/cottages from $35/60 (less Nov–Apr). ***Catalina Beach House Hotel*** *(☎ 510-1078, 200 Marilla Ave)* has pleasant rooms starting at $35/65 winter/summer. Tucked away on a lane off Beacon St, ***La Paloma*** *(☎ 510-1505, Ⓦ www.catalina.com/lapaloma.html, Sunny Lane)* has cottages from $59/69 (Nov–March/Apr–Oct). The 1926 ***Zane Grey Pueblo Hotel*** *(☎ 510-0966 or ☎ 800-378-3256, Ⓔ michaelre2000@yahoo.com, 199 Chimes Tower Rd)* is the author's former home, perched on a hill north of town with swimming pool and spectacular views. Rates start at $59/139 (mid-Oct–May/Jun–mid-Oct). Waterfront ***Hotel Villa Portofino*** *(☎ 510-0555 or ☎ 888-510-0555, Ⓦ www.hotelvillaportofino.com, 111 Crescent Ave)* charges from $75/95 (Nov–Apr/May–Oct).

Von's Supermarket *(123 Metropole Ave)* is the best self-catering option. ***Joe's Place*** *(501 Crescent Ave)* serves good breakfasts. Inexpensive take-away options include ***Topless Tacos*** *(313 Crescent Ave)* and ***Antonio's Pizzeria*** *(114 Sumner St)*. For seafood with a harbor view, check out ***Armstrong's Fish Market & Seafood Restaurant*** *(☎ 510-0113, 306 Crescent Ave)*. ***The Landing*** *(☎ 510-1474, cnr Crescent & Marilla Aves)* serves soup, salad, pasta, steaks and seafood on its upstairs terrace. Several other eateries line the waterfront area.

Popular bars include ***Luau Larry's*** *(509 Crescent Ave)* and ***Catalina Cantina*** *(313 Crescent Ave)*.

Southern Coast & Desert

The rides in this section demonstrate the remarkable diversity of San Diego County, southernmost of California's coastal counties. In just 80mi, you can travel from the surf beaches of the Pacific Coast to 6000ft pine-filled summits to desert palm oases frequented by bighorn sheep. This was the first part of the state to be seen by Spanish explorers, and it is still strongly influenced by Mexico, which lies only a few miles to the south. It is an area rich in history, crisscrossed by the paths of early Native Americans, 18th-century Spanish explorers, 19th-century gold miners, and the United States' first transcontinental postal route.

INFORMATION

Maps & Books

The free *San Diego Region Bike Map* is a useful resource published by RideLink (☎ 800-266-6883). Lonely Planet's *San Diego & Tijuana* gives detailed information beyond the scope of this book. *Cycling San Diego*, by Jerry Schad & Nelson Copp, provides thorough coverage of road and mountain-bike rides throughout the county.

GATEWAY CITIES

San Diego

☎ 619

Encircling one of California's finest natural harbors and sprawling over the neighboring hills, San Diego is a city with many faces.

DAVID McCRAY

Undersea wonders await at Catalina Island...

GREGOR CLARK

Take the kids along; they love to cycle too!

RICHARD CUMMINS

...while LA offers urban grandeur (Pasadena).

RICHARD CUMMINS

Take a break from the saddle and go kayaking on Catalina Island.

JOHN ELK III

For true coast lovers...see California's Big Sur coast on the 37-day Border to Border ride.

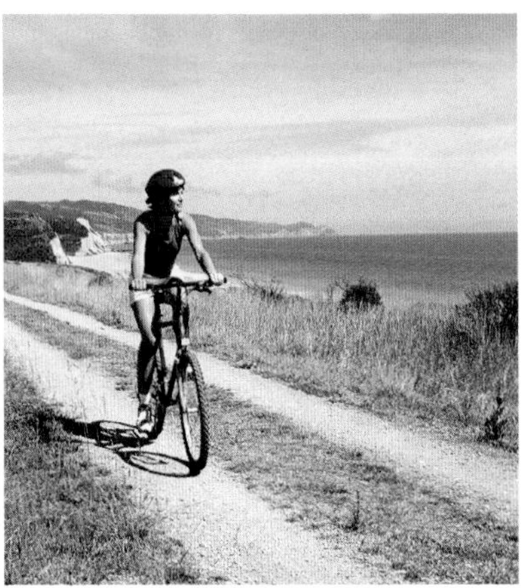
LEE FOSTER

Sea views near California's Point Reyes Station.

RICK GERHARTER

Quintessential California: surfers at Santa Cruz.

BRENT WINEBRENNER

For stunning Pacific Northwest coastal scenery, cycle in Oregon's Samuel H Boardman State Park.

Part historic Spanish settlement, part 21st-century city of skyscrapers, museums and parks, part Navy base, part freeway megalopolis, and part classic Southern California beach town, San Diego has a little something for everyone, including better cycling than you'd expect from a city its size.

Information San Diego's visitor center (☎ 236-1212, W www.sandiego.org), corner First Ave and F St, is directly adjacent to Horton Plaza in the heart of downtown. Pick up the *San Diego Region Bike Map* here.

Bike Tours San Diego (☎ 238-2444), 509 Fifth Ave, is a good multi-purpose bike shop in the Gaslamp Quarter, with local touring and mountain-biking information, plus rentals. Bernie's Bike Shop (☎ 224-7084), 1911 Cable St, is a helpful shop in Ocean Beach. Bike USA is a cycling superstore with several locations around San Diego.

Free Internet access is available at the San Diego library (☎ 238-6621), 820 E St.

Things to See & Do San Diego has plenty to keep you busy day and night. The city's liveliest food and entertainment district is the historic **Gaslamp Quarter** south of Broadway between 4th and 6th Aves. **Balboa Park**, just east of downtown, is a delightful mix of museums, gardens and open space, and houses the world-famous **San Diego Zoo**. Beach communities such as **Ocean Beach** offer a relaxed atmosphere, good bikepaths, and additional opportunities for outdoor recreation. **Old Town Historical Park** occupies the original town site established by early Spanish expeditions, and its reconstructed historical buildings are worth a visit.

All these attractions are visited on the Scenic San Diego ride (pp258–60).

Places to Stay With bike storage is on the third floor, ***HI-San Diego Downtown Hostel*** *(☎ 525-1531, e hisddwntwn@aol.com, 521 Market St)* has dorm beds from $21, double rooms for $50. A beachside alternative for people with proof of international travel is the ***Ocean Beach Hostel*** *(☎ 223-7873, W members.aol.com/OBIhostel/hostel, 4961 Newport Ave)*.

La Pensione Hotel *(☎ 236-8000* or *☎ 800-232-4683, cnr West Date & India Sts)* is a great deal in a pleasant Little Italy location. It charges from $50, with guest laundry. Moderately priced downtown chains include ***Motel 6*** *(☎ 236-9292 or ☎ 800-466-8356, 1546 Second Ave)*, charging from $46/52 for singles/doubles, and ***Super 8 Motel*** *(☎ 544-0164 or ☎ 800-537-9902, 1835 Columbia St)*, charging $65/69. Right next to Ocean Beach pier, the ***Ocean Beach Motel*** *(☎ 223-7191, 5080 Newport Ave)* offers doubles from $59 and rooms for four from $79. Nearby, the ***Ocean Villa Motel*** *(☎ 224-3481, 5142 W Point Loma Blvd)* has spacious rooms from $60, with easy access to the Ocean Beach bikepath.

A glitzier downtown option is the historic ***US Grant Hotel*** *(☎ 232-3121 or ☎ 800-237-5029, 326 Broadway)*, which has hosted 12 US presidents since 1910, and can host you too for $215 and up.

Places to Eat Open 24 hours is ***Ralph's Supermarket*** *(101 G St)*. An excellent health food market is the ***People's Organic Foods Co-op*** *(4765 Voltaire St, Ocean Beach)*, near Sunset Cliffs Blvd. The food court on the upper level of ***Horton Plaza*** offers international fast food at reasonable prices. ***Sun Cafe*** *(421 Market St)* serves inexpensive breakfast in an atmospheric former shooting gallery. The award-winning ***Cheese Shop*** *(627 Fourth Ave)* is a popular breakfast and lunch spot.

An enticing variety of pricier restaurants can be found in the Gaslamp Quarter down Fourth and Fifth Aves south of Broadway. Good options include ***Cafe Lulu*** *(419 F St)* for coffee and light meals in a cozy-chic environment; ***Bandar*** *(☎ 238-0101, 825 Fourth Ave)* for award-winning Persian food; ***Royal Thai Cuisine*** *(☎ 230-8424, 467 Fifth Ave)*; ***Star of India*** *(☎ 619-234-8000, 423 F St)*; and ***Sevilla Restaurant and Tapas Bar*** *(☎ 233-5979, 555 Fourth Ave)*.

Anthony's Fish Grotto *(☎ 232-5103, 1360 N Harbor Dr)* serves award-winning seafood overlooking the bay. Little Italy offers a dense cluster of Italian places on India St north of Date St. ***Caffe Italia*** *(1704 India St)* is an animated local hangout for coffee and sandwiches. ***Filippi's Pizza Grotto*** *(☎ 232-5095, 1747 India St)* has been a neighborhood institution since 1950, featuring an old-fashioned Italian deli and pizzeria.

In Ocean Beach, bustling Newport Ave offers something for every taste. Popular spots include ***OB Juice Bar*** *(5001 Newport*

Ave) for juice and vegetarian fare; ***Sapporo*** *(5049 Newport Ave)* for sushi; and ***Ortega's Cocina*** *(4888 Newport Ave)* for Mexican food.

Getting There & Away San Diego is well connected with the rest of California by plane, train and bus.

Air If you're flying internationally, you're more likely to enter LA, from where a bus/train/car to San Diego will be as quick and cheaper than a connecting flight. From other US cities, it's almost as cheap to fly to San Diego as it is to LA.

San Diego's airport is alarmingly close to downtown, requiring landing planes to come screeching in just a few hundred feet above residential rooftops. The good news is, the bike ride into town is easy. From Terminal 1, follow signs to Airport Exit/Harbor Island. In less than 0.5mi you'll cross N Harbor Dr and turn immediately left onto a waterfront bikepath that leads straight to the city center (3mi). From Terminal 2, follow signs for Airport Exit and look for the bikepath directly after crossing N Harbor Dr into Spanish Landing Park. Alternatively, take city bus 992 (The Flyer) from either terminal into downtown ($2, 10 min, departs every 10–15 min); its bike rack accommodates two bikes and boxed bikes are taken as luggage if space is available.

Bus Greyhound (☎ 239-3266) is at 120 W Broadway. It's a pretty seedy place, and train and local bus services are excellent, so you may prefer to let the 'Hound run without you. Thirty buses run daily to LA ($13/22, three hours), eight to Santa Barbara ($23/44, six hours), seven to San Francisco ($54/99, 11–15 hours), and six each to San Luis Obispo ($49/92, eight hours) and Salinas ($48/90, 11 hours).

Train The central Santa Fe Rail Depot (☎ 239-9021), corner Kettner Blvd and Broadway, is a magnificent old railway station with ornamental tiled walls and a fountain out front.

Amtrak train service from San Diego to LA and Santa Barbara is very frequent by American standards, and bikes travel free on convenient racks. Travel north of Santa Barbara is less frequent, and bikes must be boxed ($5 handling charge) for any destination north of San Luis Obispo. Non-discounted fares include LA ($29, three hours, 11 daily), Santa Barbara ($43, 5½ hours, four daily), San Luis Obispo ($46, 8½ hours, two daily) and Oakland-San Francisco ($96, daily).

Bicycle By far the most scenic way to bike into San Diego is via the coastal route (see pp351–3). The final day of the 37-day Border to Border ride passes through San Diego. Eastern approaches to the city are considerably less appealing due to suburban sprawl.

Scenic San Diego

Duration..................2–3 hours
Distance..................24.6mi
Difficulty..................easy–moderate
Start/End....Gaslamp Quarter trolley station

This circuit connects several of San Diego's most interesting neighborhoods and best-known tourist attractions. Much of the ride is flat, but a few steep hills along the way nudge it towards a 'moderate' rating. There are no cues for this ride, which can be navigated using the map supplied.

GETTING TO/FROM THE RIDE

The Gaslamp Quarter station is on the Trolley's Orange Line, just south of downtown near the corner of Fifth Ave and Harbor Dr.

THE RIDE

Begin by cruising north down Fifth Ave, heart of San Diego's historic **Gaslamp Quarter**. This neighborhood, inaugurated as 'New Town' in 1867, replaced Old Town as the city's center when the latter burned in 1872. The entire area is now a National Historic District, with many old buildings recently refurbished. The route passes the showy, modern **Horton Plaza** shopping complex, then heads north through **Little Italy** (1.5mi; still Italian, but much littler than it used to be thanks to 1960s freeway construction).

A circuitous maze through residential neighborhoods runs next to two picturesque **pedestrian bridges** across palm- and eucalyptus-filled canyons (carry your bike up and down stairs at either end). Turn left onto 6th Ave at 3.9mi. As Upas St dead ends for automobile traffic, continue straight on a footpath into verdant Balboa Park and zigzag down to a third pedestrian bridge, then climb your first steep hill of the day towards the **San Diego Zoo** (5.4mi; ☎ 231-1515 or ☎ 234-3153). The zoo boasts an outstanding collection of animals from every continent, with a botanical garden setting featuring coral trees, palms, orchids and exotic shrubs.

Where Zoo Dr feeds into a parking lot just left of the zoo entrance, continue straight (south) onto an unnamed fire lane (5.4mi), which soon joins Village Place, passing between the **Museum of Natural History** (☎ 232-3821) and the **Old Globe Theater** (☎ 239-2255). For 400yd a colonnade of beautiful neo-Spanish architecture along El Prado leads to the lovely fountain in the **Plaza de Panama**. Most of the surrounding buildings were originally constructed for the 1915–16 Panama-California Exposition. Balboa Park's best museums and gardens are all in this section; for a full list, see Ⓦ www.balboapark.org/museums.html. Passport to Balboa Park (☎ 239-0512), a multi-museum ticket good for seven days, is available for $30.

After leaving the park on Fifth Ave (6.4mi), head through residential neighborhoods to **Presidio Park** (10.1mi), chosen by the Spanish as the site for their first Alta California stronghold in 1769. Just below the Presidio lies **Old Town State Historical Park** (10.6mi; ☎ 220-5422), a collection of original and reconstructed historical buildings spread over what remains of San Diego's earliest town center. Guided tours are available daily (☎ 220-5422).

Just beyond Old Town a bikepath (11.1mi) takes you west along the San Diego river estuary, where you may see egrets, pelicans and other shore birds. After passing under a couple of bridges (the SeaWorld Side Trip, p260, begins at the second one), you enter Ocean Beach and soon emerge at **Dog Beach**, where San Diegans take their furry friends to play. A parking lot at 14.1mi leads to Brighton Ave, from where right turns on Abbot and Bacon Sts take you to Sunset Cliffs Blvd (15.4mi), where you'll see surfers, joggers and beautiful, rugged coastline. A very steep climb on Hill St (17.5mi) leads 300ft straight up to the crest of the peninsula, from where you can take a side trip

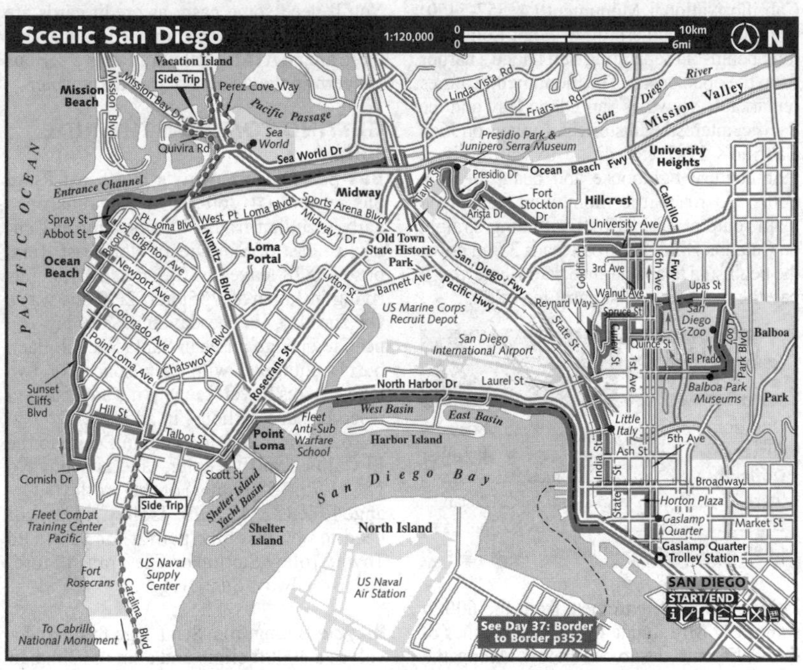

south to **Cabrillo National Monument** or continue back towards downtown.

The last 5mi of the ride are primarily on a bike/pedestrian path that sometimes looks more like a sidewalk and sometimes takes you through parking lots. It's easy cycling with views of the waterfront, the skyline and the planes coming in for a landing at San Diego International Airport.

Side Trip: SeaWorld

3.6mi return

If performing marine mammals and adventure rides are your thing, you'll enjoy SeaWorld (☎ 226-3901, W www.seaworld.com; admission $42), one of San Diego's best-known tourist attractions. Turn off the main route at 13.1mi and follow the bikepath north across a bridge towards Pacific Beach. Turn right on Quivira Rd and cross Mission Bay Dr onto Dana Landing Rd. Finally cross Ingraham St onto Perez Cove Way, which leads to the entrance. Bikes park free.

Side Trip: Cabrillo National Monument

7.5mi return

Cabrillo National Monument (☎ 557-5450) occupies the southern tip of Point Loma, the long peninsula separating San Diego's harbor from the open ocean. The monument features remarkable views of San Diego Bay and the Pacific, interesting historical displays on Juan Cabrillo's 1542 expedition to California, a 19th-century lighthouse and beautiful tidepools. To reach the monument, leave the main route at 18.1mi by continuing straight on Catalina Blvd. This road leads 3.5mi down the peninsula to an entrance gate where you'll pay the reduced cyclist entry fee of $2.

Mountain to Desert Descent

Duration	2 days
Distance	89.7mi
Difficulty	moderate–hard
Start	Julian
End	Borrego Springs
Cues & Elevation Profiles	p376

This is a ride of extremes, from the 6000ft summit of Mt Laguna to the vast reaches of the California desert far below. Along the way, the mixed oak and conifer forests around Julian and Cuyamaca Rancho State Park are noteworthy for their extraordinary species diversity. The ride also passes a number of important historical sites.

PLANNING

When to Ride

The best months to ride this route are October, November and mid-March through early May due to the radically different climates in the low desert and the alpine zone. October is Apple Festival season in Julian, a colorful but crowded time to visit. Mt Laguna, Julian and Anza-Borrego are popular getaway spots for San Diegans, so advance booking is essential on weekends; many places require a two-night minimum stay.

Maps & Books

AAA's *San Diego County* map covers the entire region. For in-depth coverage of desert roads and trails, the book/map *Anza-Borrego Desert Region* by Lowell & Diana Lindsay is recommended.

What to Bring

You'll need some cash, as credit cards are not accepted anywhere in Mt Laguna, and there are no ATMs. Dehydration is a serious concern in the desert – carry extra water.

GETTING TO/FROM THE RIDE

Julian

Bus San Diego County's Northeast Rural bus system (☎ 760-767-4287) runs once daily to Julian from El Cajon Transit Center just east of San Diego. Northeast Rural bus No 878 leaves El Cajon at 3.09pm, arriving in Julian at 4.35pm ($2.50 one way). On Tuesday, Wednesday and Saturday you need to change buses in Santa Ysabel. Each bus is equipped with rack space for two bikes. Bikes travel free, but it's advisable to reserve space 24 hours in advance.

To get from downtown San Diego to the El Cajon Transit Center, take city bus No 15 ($1.75, 75–90 min) or the Trolley's Orange Line ($2, 45 min). Trolley riders will need to obtain a bike permit for $3 at Old Town Trolley Station or The Transit Store, 102 Broadway, San Diego.

Bicycle Biking from San Diego to Julian involves a 4000ft climb and a lot of suburban sprawl in the early stages. If you're still interested, *Cycling San Diego* (see Maps & Books, p256) offers detailed descriptions of the best routes.

Borrego Springs

Bus Northeast Rural bus Nos 878/879 run from Borrego Springs (Christmas Circle) to El Cajon Transit Center daily ($3.25, 2½ hours). Transfer in Santa Ysabel is required on Tuesday and Thursday.

THE RIDE

Julian

☎ 760

Perched at the summit between ocean and desert, Julian is an old gold-rush town turned tourist boom town. Despite the cutesy shops, the obsession with apple pie and the hordes of people thronging the sidewalks every weekend, this remains an appealing place with an interesting history, and the surrounding countryside provides endless opportunities for recreation.

Information Julian's visitor center (☎ 765-1857, fax 765-2544, W www.julianca.com), 2129 Main St, is right in the center of town.

There's a 24-hour ATM at Valley Independent Bank, 2033 Main St.

R&B Bicycle Club (☎ 765-2200, W www.julianactive.com) organizes several annual bike rides in the Julian/Borrego Springs area.

Things to See & Do Julian's small downtown is an interesting place to stroll, with more than a dozen plaques indicating points of historical interest. The **Julian Pioneer Museum**, 2811 Washington St, has a collection of pioneer and Native American artifacts. A few blocks east of Main St, the **Eagle and High Peak Mines** (☎ 765-0036) offer guided tours of the gold mines that put Julian on the map. About 4mi south of town, the **California Wolf Center** (☎ 765-0030, W www.californiawolfcenter.org) gives Saturday afternoon presentations about the endangered gray wolf (reservations required).

Places to Stay & Eat About 5mi southwest of Julian, beautiful ***William Heise Regional Park*** *(☎ 619-565-3600)* has hiker/biker campsites with showers for $2.50 (one-night maximum), plus four rustic cabins for $35 (reserve well in advance).

The cozy cottages at ***Julian Farms Lodging*** *(☎ 765-0250, 2818 Washington St)* are among downtown's better deals at $74. Motel-style ***Julian Lodge*** *(☎ 765-1420 or ☎ 800-542-1420, cnr C & Fourth Sts)* charges $75 to $115, including continental breakfast. The historic and central ***Julian Hotel*** *(☎ 765-0201, W www.julianhotel.com, 2032 Main St)* has rooms from $82 to $185, including full breakfast.

Julian's many ***B&Bs*** are generally upscale affairs with amenities ranging from whirlpool tubs to afternoon teas to endless slices of Julian apple pie. The ***Julian Bed and Breakfast Guild*** *(☎ 765-1555, W www.julianbnbguild.com)* offers information on two-dozen establishments within the $85 to $175 range, many of them private homes. A cyclist-friendly, in-town option is ***Historical House*** *(☎ 765-1931, W www.historicalhouse.com, 2603 C St)*, charging $85.

Groceries and deli items are available at ***Jack's Grocery*** *(2117 Main St)* and ***Julian Market*** *(2202 Main St)*. ***Julian Coffee and Tea House*** *(1921 Main St)* opens at 5.30am daily for coffee and pastries. The town's most famous producer of apple pies is ***Julian Pie Company*** *(2225 Main St)*. ***The Bailey Barbecue*** *(cnr Main & A Sts)* has tasty barbecue. ***Romano's Dodge House Restaurant*** *(☎ 765-1003, 2718 B St)* serves pasta, pizza and calzone in a cozy historic setting. ***Rong Branch Restaurant*** *(☎ 765-2265, 2722 Washington St)* features Wild West fare, including steaks, buffalo burgers, soups and salads.

Day 1: Julian to Mt Laguna

4–6 hours, 36.9mi

Day 1 involves a lot of climbing, which tomorrow will be rewarded with extraordinary views and endless downhill bliss. The route begins by gradually ascending several hundred feet through the mixed oak and conifer forest south of Julian, then makes a switchbacking descent through Rancho Cuyamaca State Park, continuing downhill past big meadows and into increasingly dry and rocky country as it nears Descanso (20.5mi). Here the route heads east, with a long climb and equally long descent to Pine Valley. The last leg involves nearly 10mi of unbroken uphill along scenic and lightly traveled Sunrise Hwy from Pine Valley to Mt Laguna summit.

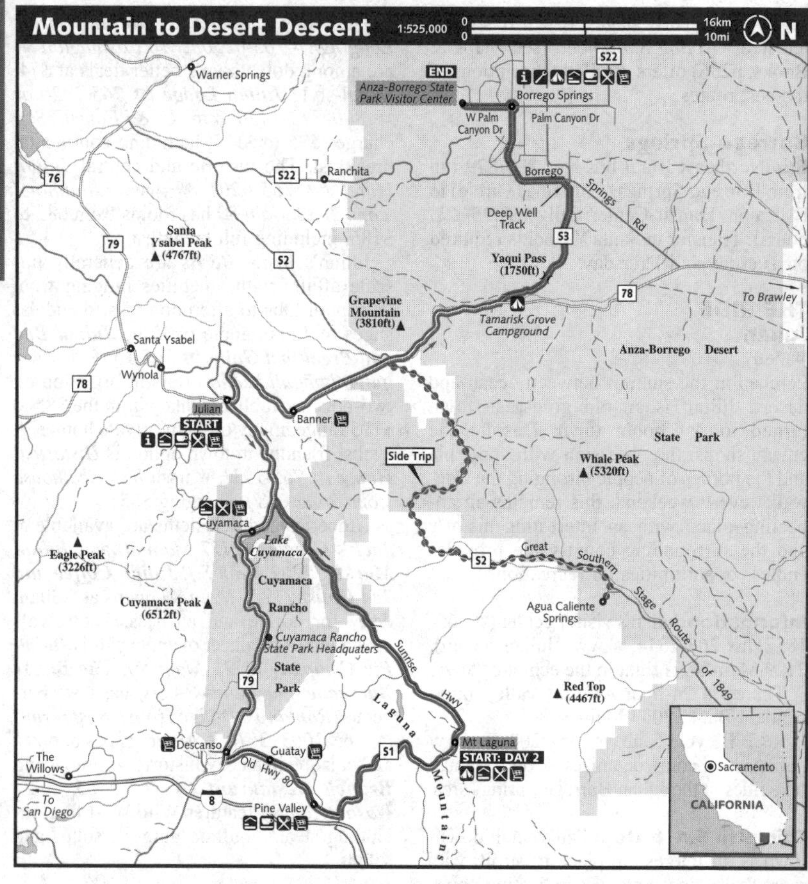

As it climbs, the road enters the alpine zone, with meadows, conifer forests and views south into Mexico.

At the 9mi mark, artificial **Lake Cuyamaca** is a popular fishing spot with a store and a couple of restaurants. Further on, **Cuyamaca Rancho State Park Headquarters** (14.3mi) has an informative visitor center in a beautiful, old, stone ranch house. The park also offers camping, hiking, horseback trails and excellent mountain biking. For details, pick up the flyer *Mountain Bike Trails in Cuyamaca Rancho State Park*.

The small towns of Descanso and Guatay (23mi) both have basic ***stores***. The slightly larger settlement of Pine Valley (25.7mi) makes a good lunch stop, with a few ***restaurants*** and a ***supermarket*** strung out along old Hwy 80. ***Major's Diner*** is one of the more popular eateries, serving breakfast, lunch and dinner. If you're too tired to continue to Mt Laguna, consider ***Pine Valley Sportsman's Lodge*** *(☎ 619-473-7666)*, charging $50/65 midweek/weekend.

Mt Laguna

☎ 619

Mt Laguna is not a town so much as a cluster of buildings providing services to Cleveland National Forest visitors.

The Laguna Mtn visitor center (☎ 473-8547) is open weekends, north of Laguna Mountain Lodge. There are no ATMs in town.

Numerous **hiking trails** start near Mt Laguna summit, including the Pacific Crest

Trail, which runs from Mexico to Canada (see the boxed text, p46). For a spectacular short hike, the Desert View Nature Trail is highly recommended.

Places to Stay & Eat Reserve as early as possible at ***Laguna Mountain Lodge*** (*☎ 445-2342 or ☎ 473-8533*). Motel units and cabins accommodating two to four people, some with fireplace and kitchen facilities, cost $45 to $110.

Near the summit, ***Burnt Rancheria & Laguna campgrounds*** (*☎ 877-444-6777 or ☎ 518-885-3639, W www.reserveusa.com*) has reserved and walk-in sites for $14.

Laguna Mountain Trading Post, adjacent to the lodge, sells groceries, drinks and provisions, and is the only place to buy food on the mountain Monday through Thursday.

The Blue Jay Lodge (*☎ 473-8844*) serves breakfast, lunch and dinner from 4pm Friday through 4pm Sunday. The saloon has a full bar, pool table, jukebox and piano. They also rent two cabins with fireplaces (but no kitchens) for $98.

Day 2: Mt Laguna to Borrego Springs

4–5 hours, 52.8mi

Day 2 plunges 5500ft from the mountains to the Anza-Borrego Desert. The first 10mi offer spectacular views down sheer drop-offs to the east, with the vast Salton Sea visible in the distance on clear days. From 14.2mi, the ride briefly retraces the Day 1 route back to Julian (20mi), a good lunch spot. Hwy 78 descends steeply down a beautiful canyon to the old Banner town site, beyond which the desert vistas open up dramatically. At 31.5mi the route reaches Scissors Crossing, where an historic stagecoach route leads south (see the Side Trip). Here the main route narrows again and snakes through rugged hills before beginning the day's only serious climb, to Yaqui Pass (1750ft). The summit affords spectacular views back to the desert floor, followed by an exhilarating 5mi descent into the Borrego Valley.

Aside from Julian, the only place to buy food is at the solitary Banner Store (26.7mi). The rangers at Tamarisk Grove Campground (39mi) sell bottled water and can point you towards tap water as well.

Side Trip: Butterfield Historic Stagecoach Route

44.4mi return

This overnight side trip heads through the desert to Agua Caliente County Park, following a famous stagecoach route known as the Southern Emigrant Trail or the Butterfield Overland Stage Route. This southern passage into California received heavy use between the late 18th century and the mid-19th century from explorers, settlers, miners, soldiers in the Mexican-American War, and the nation's first transcontinental mail service, the San Diego and San Antonio Line.

From Scissors Crossing (31.5mi), head south on county highway S2, a modern paved road following the original stage route. Plaques along the way provide interesting historical detail. Traffic is light and the scenery is dramatic, with the Laguna Mtns rising abruptly from the desert floor and ocotillo plants bursting with red flowers in spring. After 22.2mi, the ***Agua Caliente Campground*** (*☎ 858-565-3600*) has a small store and a hot spring-fed pool but no other services. Campsites cost $10.

Northeast Rural bus No 878 runs from Agua Caliente to Scissors Crossing on Saturday morning (bike rack reservation essential; ☎ 760-767-4287).

Borrego Springs

☎ 760

Borrego Springs sits in the middle of Anza-Borrego Desert State Park and is home to park headquarters. It's a sprawling community fond of portraying itself as 'Palm Springs without all the people'. A few golf resorts and pricey retirement communities dot the edges of the valley floor but otherwise Borrego Springs remains a sleepy place. Most of its businesses are spread along the mile-long main drag, Palm Canyon Dr. The business district's eastern edge is defined by Christmas Circle, a grassy, palm-fringed traffic circle, which is also the main bus stop in town. The town's two small shopping centers, The Mall and The Center, face each other across Palm Canyon Dr just west of Christmas Circle.

Information The ride ends at Anza-Borrego State Park visitor center (☎ 767-4205), 220 Palm Canyon Dr (weekends only Jun–Sept). It's at the western edge of town, where Palm

Canyon Dr dead ends in a parking lot at the base of the mountains. Numerous displays cover the park's flora and fauna, and the center hosts regular slide shows and activities. The Borrego Springs Chamber of Commerce (☎ 767-5555 or ☎ 800-559-5524, W www.borregosprings.org) is at 786 Palm Canyon Dr, just east of Christmas Circle.

ATMs are available at Borrego Springs Bank, 547 Palm Canyon Dr (in The Mall), and Wells Fargo Bank at 730 Christmas Circle.

Carrizo Bikes (☎ 767-3872), 648 Palm Canyon Dr, rents mountain bikes. Owner Dan Cain, a mountain-bike enthusiast and long-time resident, can recommend great rides in the area.

Things to See & Do Without question, the biggest draw in Borrego Springs is **Anza-Borrego Desert State Park**, the largest state park in California and one of the most spectacular. Go to the visitor center for information and tours etc.

Not to be missed is the **Palm Canyon Nature Trail**, which leads 1.5mi from Borrego Palm Canyon Campground to a beautiful oasis where nearly 1000 native California fan palm trees grow alongside a spring-fed stream bed. This is one of the largest palm oases in the USA. You'll also see waterfalls, and if you're lucky, some of the bighorn sheep from which the park derives half its name (*borrego* means 'sheep' in Spanish).

With a mountain bike, you can explore even more remote sections of the park. The free brochure *Bicycle Routes: A guide to bicycle riding at Anza-Borrego*, available at the visitor center, provides information on the park's 500-plus miles of mountain-bike trails and roads. For additional information on biking in the park, visit Carrizo Bikes (see Information).

Places to Stay & Eat Downhill from park headquarters, ***Borrego Palm Canyon Campground*** *(☎ 800-444-7275, W www.anzaborrego.statepark.org)* has sites with

HUGH D'ANDRADE

Watch for bighorn sheep in the Anza-Borrego Desert State Park

sweeping desert views, showers and sun shelters for $10.

Motel options include the 1950s-style ***Hacienda del Sol*** *(☎ 767-5442, e tblyon@ilaz.com, 610 Palm Canyon Dr)*, charging $55 and up, and the ***Oasis Motel*** *(☎ 767-5409, e Oasismotel@aol.com, 366 Palm Canyon Dr)*, with rates from $69. Both have pools.

Borrego Valley Inn *(☎ 767-0311, W www.borregovalleyinn.com, 405 Palm Canyon Dr)* offers Southwestern-inspired adobe rooms from $100, some with patios, kitchenettes and fireplaces.

Borrego's two supermarkets are the ***Center Market*** *(590 Palm Canyon Dr)* and ***Borrego Valley Foods*** *(cnr Palm Canyon Dr & Christmas Circle)*.

Jilberto's Taco Shop *(655 Palm Canyon Dr)* is popular with locals for cheap Mexican fast food. ***Borrego Bread Company*** *(551 Palm Canyon Dr)*, in The Mall, has espresso drinks, baked goods, sandwiches and pizza. ***Kendall's Cafe*** *(528 Palm Canyon Dr)*, in The Mall, is the best choice for breakfast and also serves lunch and dinner. ***Carlee's Place*** *(660 Palm Canyon Dr)* is a lively spot serving steaks, burgers, salads and pasta, with classic red vinyl booths and a full bar.

THE WEST COAST

Highlights

- crossing the whole country on two human-powered wheels
- spotting whales, seals and sea otters
- majestic mountains such as Rainier and St Helens
- Seattle's Experience Music Project
- camping in California's redwoods
- smelling (and riding) Fort Bragg's 'Skunk Train'
- architectural wonders along Monterey's 17-Mile Drive
- historic Spanish missions in California

Special Events

- Armed Forces Festival (May) Bremerton, WA
- Historic Homes Tours (early May & late Sept) and Wooden Boat Festival (Sept), Port Townsend, WA
- Glass Float (Oct) and Kite Festivals (early May & late Sept) Lincoln City, OR
- Cranberry Festival (mid-Oct) Bandon, OR
- Big Sur Marathon (Apr), Blues Festival (Oct) and Jazzfest (May) Big Sur, CA
- Clam Festival (mid-Oct) Pismo Beach, CA
- Jazz Festival (mid-Sept) and Blues Festival (late Jun) Monterey, CA

Cycling Events

- Lewis & Clark Discovery Ride (Oct) Fort Clatsop, OR
- Kinetic Sculpture Race (last weekend in May) Ferndale, CA
- LA Marathon & Bike Tour (Mar)
- Race Across America (RAAM; Jun) Portland, OR
- Lighthouse Century (Sept) San Luis Obispo, CA

Food & Drink Specialties

- seafood, especially razor clams, fresh chowder and Dungeness crabs
- shrimp and fish such as red snapper
- Tillamook cheddar cheese (OR)
- Bandon cranberries (OR)
- fish tacos and the multicultural cuisine of California

COREY RICH

The West Coast

The US West Coast lends itself to exploration by bicycle for many and varied reasons, not least being the natural wonders on show. The popularity of cycling in the region has spawned more facilities for touring cyclists and greater recognition of two-wheeled transport on the roads. The region includes some of the USA's most pristine environments and a very conservation-aware population. In the Northwest, sophisticated cities such as Vancouver and Seattle contrast with sparsely populated areas where near-wilderness prevails. Further south, wild ocean vistas and primeval forests give way to the laid-back cities and the casual, outdoor lifestyle of Southern California.

This section is unlike other chapters in the book, as it has a detailed map for each day of riding and the cue sheet and elevation charts are located with the maps, rather than at the back of the book.

CLIMATE

Prevailing northwesterly winds favor north to south travel in spring, summer and fall (May–Oct). Bad weather at any time, however, is often accompanied by southerly winds and it is advisable to have spare days in the itinerary to wait this out. The chance of bad weather decreases with each mile pedaled south. While the average wind speed is between four and 15mi/h, summer wind gusts of up to 60mi/h (80mi/h in winter) are not uncommon in Oregon, necessitating caution in exposed locations such as elevated bridges. For more information on regional climates see the other rides chapters.

INFORMATION

Books

Lonely Planet's *Vancouver*, *Pacific Northwest* and *California & Nevada* are excellent supplements to *Cycling USA – West Coast* with detailed sections on wildlife, activities and accommodations beyond the scope of this book.

The Lewis & Clark Trail, by Thomas Schmidt, is a guide to the expedition sites of note, including Fort Clatsop near Astoria, and gives detail of the entire journey.

Scenic Highway One, by Toby Rowland-Jones, is a comprehensively illustrated, full-color booklet showing the beauty of the California coastal highway, along with notes on some of the interesting towns and sights.

See also Maps (p270) under Planning for the ride.

Information Sources

Washington State Ferry schedules (☎ 800-843-3779) are available at visitor centers in towns and cities served by ferries.

State parks information is available at Ⓦ www.parks.wa.gov (Washington), Ⓦ www.prd.state.or.us (Oregon) and Ⓦ www.calparks.ca.gov (California).

GATEWAY CITIES

Vancouver

☎ 604

Vancouver's proximity to mountains, forests and ocean is impressive and makes it one of the world's most beautiful cities. Founded in 1867 around a sawmill on the south shore of Burrard Inlet, it is now a truly international center of almost 600,000 people straddling the Fraser River lowlands. People from about 100 different countries call it home.

Information The Travel InfoCentre (☎ 683-2000 or ☎ 800-663-6000), 200 Burrard St, is on the Plaza Level in the Waterfront Center. Ask for a free copy of *The Vancouver Book*, a visitor guide with information on shopping, accommodations and entertainment.

Major banks line Dunsmuir and Georgia Sts downtown and Denman St in the West End.

A very helpful bike shop is the touring-oriented Bike Doctor (☎ 873-2453), 163 W Broadway. The proprietor advises cyclists in Vancouver to 'be paranoid, be *very* paranoid' about bicycle theft and always lock up.

Other bike shops include: The Cyclepath (☎ 737-2344), 1421 W Broadway; Bike Way (☎ 254-5408), 831 Commercial Dr; and Bicycle Sports Pacific (☎ 682-4537), corner Pacific and Burrard Sts, and ☎ 988-1800 at 3026 Mountain Hwy, North Vancouver.

A number of camping stores are clustered on W Broadway. Try Altus Mountain Gear (☎ 876-5255), No 137; or The Backpackers Shop (☎ 879-4711), No 183.

Cycling information, mainly related to racing and events, is available from Cycling BC (☎ 737-3034, Ⓦ www.cycling.bc.ca) at Suite 332, 1367 W Broadway. The Vancouver Bicycle Club (☎ 733-3964, Ⓦ www.vbc.bc.ca) runs social rides. A Critical Mass ride starts at 5pm on the last Friday of each month at the Vancouver Art Gallery (Georgia St side).

Note that even though many cyclists don't bother to wear them, bicycle helmets are compulsory by law in British Columbia.

Things to See & Do The 405-hectare (1000-acre) jewel in the city's crown, **Stanley Park** features the one-way, 9km (5.5mi) seawall bikepath, accessed near the northwest end of Alberni St. The path passes under the noisy Lions Gate Bridge, and beneath and between interesting seaside rock formations with fabulous water views. An attractive walking trail with interpretive panels surrounds **Lost Lagoon**, a freshwater lake and bird refuge at the southern end of the park. **Beaver Lake,** in the park's interior, is seemingly isolated and remote from civilization.

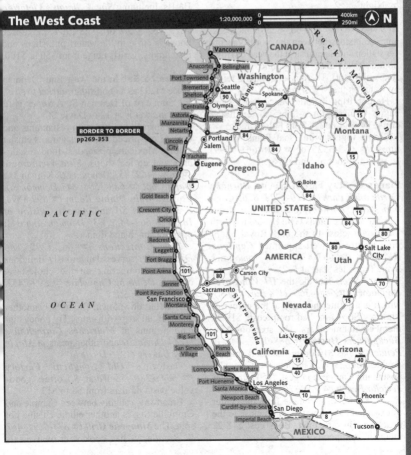

Tax

Most prices in Canada are quoted exclusive of tax. Allow an additional 7% Goods and Services Tax, plus another 7% provincial tax (in British Columbia) and, on Vancouver accommodations, a 3% city tax.

The West Coast

1:20,000,000 0 400km 0 250mi N

BORDER TO BORDER pp269-353

Vancouver, Anacortes, Bellingham, Port Townsend, Bremerton, Seattle, Shelton, Olympia, Centralia, Astoria, Kelso, Manzanita, Netarts, Portland, Salem, Lincoln City, Yachats, Eugene, Reedsport, Bandon, Gold Beach, Crescent City, Orick, Eureka, Redcrest, Leggett, Fort Bragg, Point Arena, Jenner, Point Reyes Station, San Francisco, Montara, Santa Cruz, Monterey, Big Sur, San Simeon Village, Pismo Beach, Lompoc, Santa Barbara, Port Hueneme, Santa Monica, Los Angeles, Newport Beach, Cardiff-by-the-Sea, San Diego, Imperial Beach, Spokane, Boise, Sacramento, Carson City, Las Vegas, Salt Lake City, Phoenix, Tucson

CANADA, Washington, Oregon, Idaho, Montana, UNITED STATES OF AMERICA, Utah, Nevada, California, Arizona, MEXICO, PACIFIC OCEAN, Rocky Mountains, Cascade Range, Sierra Nevada

Capilano Suspension Bridge (☎ 985-7474), 3735 Capilano Rd, North Vancouver, is a swaying wooden bridge, 140m long and 70m above the Capilano River, leading to meandering trails through old-growth forest and a 60m waterfall. It is accessible via the SeaBus ($2.50, bikes free) across Burrard Inlet then a ride of about 3km.

About 3mi along Capilano Rd, Grouse Mtn (☎ 984-0661) is famous for its 125-passenger **Skyride**, North America's largest aerial tramway. It operates every 15 minutes from 9am to 10pm daily, whisking passengers in about eight minutes to an altitude of 1100m – if it's clear, the views are fabulous.

Gray Line (☎ 879-3363 or ☎ 800-667-0882) offers **coach tours** from May to October, including the two-hour 'Vancouver by Night'.

BC Rail's *Royal Hudson* **steam train** (☎ 984-5246 or ☎ 800-663-8238) makes six-hour excursions between the North Vancouver station and Squamish at the head of Howe Sound (Wed–Sun & public holidays, June–mid-Sept). There is an option to return by water on the MV *Britannia*.

Harbor trips include Vancouver Champagne Cruises' three-hour sunset dinner cruise (☎ 688-6625) from False Creek.

Scenic flights with Float Plane Adventures (☎ 683-6525 or ☎ 800-661-5599) leave at the foot of Burrard St.

Places to Stay East of the city, ***Burnaby Cariboo RV Park*** *(☎ 420-1722; 8765 Cariboo Place, Burnaby)* has tent sites from $21. Across the Lions Gate Bridge in North Vancouver, close to the Park Royal Shopping Centre, is well-appointed ***Capilano RV Park*** *(☎ 987-4722, 295 Tomahawk Ave)*. Tent sites start at $22.

City hostels include the ***HI Vancouver Downtown*** *(☎ 684-4565, 1114 Burnaby St)*, which is a former nunnery at the corner of Thurlow St. A four-bed room costs $19/23 members/nonmembers. The spacious ***New Backpackers Hostel*** *(☎ 688-0112, 347 W Pender St)* has $10 dorm beds and singles/doubles for $25/35. Vancouver's original HI hostel and Canada's largest, ***HI Vancouver Jericho Beach*** *(☎ 224-3208; 1515 Discovery St, Kitsilano)* is remote from the center of town but has a great location close to the beach on Burrard Inlet. Beds cost $18/22 members/nonmembers.

Buchan Hotel *(☎ 685-5354 or ☎ 800-668-6654, 1906 Haro St)*, near Stanley Park 2km northwest of the tourist office, is a pleasant, older hotel with doubles from $80/99 with shared/private bath.

Nearby, the historic, ivy-covered ***Sylvia Hotel*** *(☎ 681-9321, 1154 Gilford St)* is in sight of English Bay. Rooms range from $65 to $125; kitchen suites start at $135.

Shato Inn Hotel *(☎ 681-8920, 1825 Comox St)*, off Denman St a couple of blocks from Stanley Park, has rooms with private bath/shower for $100.

Robsonstrasse City Motor Inn *(☎ 687-1674 or ☎ 888-667-8877, 1394 Robson St)*, has kitchenettes and a guest laundry, and charges $169 for a double.

North Vancouver has numerous attractive B&Bs, including ***Sue & Simon's Victorian Guest House*** *(☎ 985-1523 or ☎ 800-776-1811, 152 E 3rd St)*. The 1904 smoke-free house is close to the waterfront, shops and restaurants. Tariffs range from $50 to $100.

Places to Eat In the West End, Denman Place Mall has a good ***supermarket*** *(Nelson St)*, 50m east of Denman St. A ***Super Valu supermarket*** is at 1249 Davie St.

Denman St is lined with restaurants and cafes. Low-priced Asian restaurants cluster among Mexican, pizza, fast-food restaurants and coffee shops. ***Vina Vietnamese*** *(☎ 689-8462, 851 Denman St)*, Korean ***Ma Dang Cool*** *(☎ 688-3585, 847 Denman St)*, Chinese ***Main Dining Room*** *(☎ 899-8894, 833 Denman St)* and ***Assam Cuisine of India*** *(☎ 662-4432, 835 Denman St)* are all open for lunch and dinner.

True Confections *(☎ 682-1292, 866 Denman St)* serves dangerously delicious desserts. Competing on the cholesterol count is ***Death by Chocolate*** *(☎ 899-2462, 1001 Denman St)*.

Heading downtown, Davie St is another commercial strip with cafes. Try gooey cinnamon buns at ***Melriches Coffeehouse*** *(1244 Davie St)* and other treats at ***Maple Leaf Bakery*** *(1216 Davie St)*.

Gastown's ***Old Spaghetti Factory*** *(☎ 684-1288, 53 Water St)* offers good-value pasta dinners from $8 to $13.

Broadway, roughly between Cambie and Granville Sts, is another ethnic cuisine hot spot. The ***Mongolie Grill*** *(☎ 874-6121, 467 W Broadway)* has cook-your-own meals charged by weight (about $2.50 per 100g). The Russian ***Rasputin Restaurant*** *(☎ 879-6675, 457 W Broadway)* has live entertainment while the ***Afghan Horseman*** *(☎ 873-5923, 445 W Broadway)* advertises vegetarian dishes.

In Stanley Park, the refined ***Teahouse Restaurant*** *(☎ 669-3281)* at Ferguson Point has a garden setting and outdoor patio with fine views. Lunch main courses range from $11 to $17, dinners from $17 to $25. Get cheaper meals and takeaways at ***Prospect Point Cafe*** near the Lions Gate Bridge overlook.

Getting There & Away Arrive in Vancouver via international or domestic air services, or catch the bus or train.

Air Vancouver airport (Ⓦ www.yvr.ca) is 13km south of the city center on Sea Island at the mouth of the Fraser River. It is served by both major Canadian airlines, Air Canada and Canadian Airlines International, plus many US and Asian airlines.

To cycle downtown, head along Grant McConachie Way to Arthur Laing Bridge over the river's North Arm, veering left to Marine Dr. This becomes wide Granville St heading north to Granville Bridge into the city. Parallel minor streets to the west may be more pleasant to cycle but they are occasionally discontinuous, necessitating jogs (doglegs).

The Vancouver Airporter (☎ 946-8866 or ☎ 800-668-3141) runs a service between the airport and downtown hotels every half-hour ($10/17 one way/return), carrying boxed bikes free. Taxi fare between the airport and downtown is about $25.

Train Services run to Vancouver (and back) from across the country, the Rockies, provincial towns and the USA. Pacific Central Station is off Main St at 1150 Station St. For 24-hour information on fares and reservations, call ☎ 800-561-8630. Three trains a week travel each way on the route through Edmonton, Jasper and Kamloops. The three-day Vancouver–Toronto service costs $615 (less with advance purchase), plus $16 for a box and bike.

Amtrak Cascades (☎ 585-4848 or ☎ 800-872-7245) links Vancouver and Seattle via Bellingham (four hours, $21–33), carrying unboxed bikes free.

Bus Greyhound buses arrive at the train station from Calgary (four a day, about 16 hours, $117); Edmonton (two a day, 17 hours, $133); and Toronto (three days, $313). Bikes, which must be boxed, are charged by weight and distance as freight. For example, 20kg to Calgary costs $45. Bikes are not guaranteed to travel on the same bus. Greyhound also runs services across the border.

Border to Border

Duration	37 days
Distance	1838.3mi
Difficulty	moderate–hard
Start	Vancouver, British Columbia
End	Imperial Beach, California

A classic ride north to south across the USA from Canada to the border of Mexico. The full trek could be that once-in-a-lifetime journey that will yield enough experiences to entertain grandchildren, dinner guests or anyone you can corner for hours. It could also be a trip taken in stages, a state at a time over a few years. Scenery, history, wildlife and, when required, the services of civilization are all in abundance.

The ride uses quiet minor roads and bikepaths wherever possible but occasionally there is no such option and riders must brave major roads. On highways like 'the 1', as Hwy 1 is dubbed, and Hwy 101, road authorities have usually constructed adequate road shoulders and other cyclist amenities.

HISTORY

The popularity of cycling the West Coast led to official recognition of a route by Oregon and California road authorities for the American Bicentennial in 1976. Green signs with a bicycle symbol may still be seen in many places, despite theft and vandalism. The California Department of Transportation (Caltrans) published a map to its section of the route until 1982. Oregon's DoT still produces a free map/guide to the Coast Bike Route, which can be picked up at the Welcome Center in Astoria.

PLANNING

When to Ride

This ride is strongly recommended to be timed after the main tourist season (which officially ends with Labor Day on the first weekend of September). Traffic will be much lighter and accommodations in less demand, therefore cheaper. Riders who don't intend to add a lot of extra days for rest and/or side-tripping could safely start as late as the first week in October – the only major drawbacks are the rapidly shortening days and the increasing likelihood of rain, particularly in Washington and Oregon. A bonus is the fall displays of color. Locals recommend October as northern California's best month weather-wise, having the least fog and the rain yet to set in.

Maps

Unlike the other rides in this book, this special section is intended to be useable without having to buy a separate map. However, some cyclists may prefer to carry other maps that cover areas beyond the ride.

Benchmark Maps publishes a *Road & Recreation Atlas*, each about $20, for Washington (1:200,000), Oregon (1:250,000), and California (1:300,000), although the detail of smaller roads is poor. Each volume is too heavy and unwieldy for a bike but relevant pages could be extracted.

For general planning, Bartholomew World Travel Map series, *Western USA* (1:2,500,000, about $10) covers the West Coast and inland states of Montana, Wyoming, Colorado and New Mexico.

The *Commuter Cycling Map of Metro Vancouver* ($2.95), published by Davenport Maps Ltd, shows recommended routes and hills from North Vancouver to the US border. It is available at the Alternative Transportation Centre's Main Station Bikes Store (☎ 669-2453), 195 Main St; bike shops; and map retailers.

Long-distance Touring

If you plan to spend two months (or longer) cycling the West Coast you will have plenty of time to go all the way – riding from Canada to Mexico on the Border to Border ride! Or you could be creative and use the Border to Border ride to link several regions. Start with rides in Washington, catch a train to Portland for the rides in Oregon, then cycle to San Francisco on the Border to Border ride. Get the train to the Sierra Nevada and back, ride down to Santa Barbara, then train to San Diego.

If you have less time, see Suggested Itineraries (p28) for smaller-scale ideas.

What to Bring

A padlock for gear lockers is useful, especially if you're staying in hostels. A set of lightweight binoculars will make wildlife viewing easier.

Something campers planning to use hiker/biker sites in state parks will *not need* is a booking. Reservations aren't accepted. It's first-come, first-served but cyclists will not be turned away even during peak times – there's always room for one more small tent.

GETTING TO/FROM THE RIDE

Vancouver

See Getting There & Away for Vancouver (p269).

Imperial Beach

Retrace the outward route to San Diego. See Getting There & Away for San Diego (p258).

THE RIDE

Vancouver

See Vancouver (pp266–9) for information about accommodations and other services.

Day 1: Vancouver to Bellingham

6–11 hours, 68.2mi

Most of the day's ride is on easy terrain but follows a convoluted route in an urban jungle. There are only a couple of significant hills but, because of the distance and complicated navigation, it's advisable to start early. If time runs out, Blaine (41.1mi), immediately over the Washington border, has accommodations and supply options.

The ride begins with a jaunt through Vancouver's Gastown and Chinatown, then meanders through suburbs and satellite cities to cross the US border into Washington at sleepy Blaine.

Traffic conditions vary but wherever possible the route uses quiet suburban streets or semi-rural roads often signposted as bicycle routes and, after Blaine, flat-to-rolling rural roads with shoulders ranging from a wide 2yd to virtually zero.

The Ontario St bike route (from 1.8mi) uses a long straight suburban street with neat bike-accessible traffic barriers and bike traffic lights. There is one moderate climb lasting about 600yd, rising to a mere 60ft. At Commercial St leave the bike route. At Beresford St (9.7mi) the route joins the 'BC Parkway', a cycleway beneath, and parallel to, the SkyTrain route.

At 10.4mi, the bikeway is often busy with pedestrians. Parallel Beresford St is a reasonable alternative, becoming Prenter St at 11.3mi. After crossing busy King George Hwy via a pedestrian bridge (18.3mi), use the sidewalk then the shoulder. After about 0.3mi, veer right onto the bikeway under the SkyTrain viaduct.

At 29.6mi, 168th St marks the beginning of a more rural environment – small farms and agricultural land predominate until the US border at 38.7mi, after which bird-filled wetlands feature between Blaine and Bellingham. Blaine has motels – try ***Anchor Inn*** *(☎ 360-332-5539, 250 Cedar St)*, with doubles from $41 – and at nearby Birch Bay there's a ***hostel*** *(☎ 360-371-2180, 4639 Alderson Rd)*; to get there, stay on Bell Rd, signed to Birch Bay, instead of veering left at Loomis Trail Rd (44.5mi).

Bellingham

☎ 360

A sprawling conurbation of 61,000 people, Bellingham lies at the head of Bellingham Bay. It has a large pleasure port and a forested mountain backdrop which includes glacier-crowned Mt Baker. Its handsome old town perches on hills above the busy harbor while the suburbs (formerly separate communities) of Fairhaven, Sehome and Whatcom, spread east to Lake Whatcom and south to Chuckanut Bay.

Information Bellingham visitor center (☎ 671-3990 or ☎ 800-487-2032, w www.bellingham.org) is on the corner of Potter and Lincoln Sts.

Among the many banks, Frontier Bank (with a drive-/cycle-thru ATM) is on the inbound route at 3110 Northwest Ave. Bank of America is at 112 E Holly St. The supermarkets also have ATMs.

Kulshan Cycles (☎ 733-6440), downtown at 100 E Chestnut St, is excellent.

Free Internet access is available at Bellingham public library (☎ 676-6860), 210 Central Ave in the heart of downtown. Western Washington University (WWU) library also has computers open to the public. They are easier to access during the summer student holidays.

Things to See & Do **Whatcom Museum of History and Art** (☎ 676-6981) is in an imposing 1892 red-brick building, once Whatcom City Hall, at 121 Prospect St. Among its historical artifacts are displays of contemporary art.

At 2.1mi on Day 2, turn right to **Sehome Hill Arboretum**. The steep 0.9mi climb from the campus of WWU reaches a 165-acre park with interpretive walking trails and a lookout tower offering a panorama over the bay, harbor and downtown. The arboretum preserves species of the Pacific Northwest.

Ride around **WWU campus** checking out the older buildings' architecture and the sculptures – get a 'sculpture walk' brochure from the visitor center.

The **Interurban Trail**, off Old Fairhaven Parkway, 0.4mi east of 12th St, follows parts of a 1920s electric trolley line through cool forest.

San Juan Islands Shuttle Express (☎ 888-373-8522 or ☎ 671-1137, e info@orcawhales.com) operates **wildlife tours** from Bellingham harbor to view minke and killer whales, porpoises, seals and birds.

Places to Stay & Eat In the hilly hinterland near Lake Whatcom, ***Sudden Valley Camping Ground*** *(☎ 734-6430, ext 335)* charges $11 for pleasant sites but tired facilities. It's 5.3mi from the visitor center – go south on Potter St to a left on Lakeway Dr, then via N Terrace, Cable and Austin Sts and Lake Louise Rd, turning right at the bottom of a hill. About 8.6mi from town, ***Larrabee State Park*** also has camping (see Day 2, p274).

Bellingham Hostel *(☎ 671-1750; 107 Chuckanut Dr, Fairhaven Park)* has dorm beds for $15.

Many of the cheaper motels are along Samish Way, not far from WWU. ***Bay City Motor Inn*** *(☎ 676-9191 or ☎ 800-538-8204, 116 N Samish Way)*, with a work-out room and pool table, charges $45 a double. ***Bellingham Travelers Express*** *(☎ 734-1900, 202 E Holly St)*, signposted as Bellingham Inn, has a central location. Doubles start at $45. ***Val-U Inn Motel*** *(☎ 671-9600, 805 Lakeway Dr)* is a block south of the visitor center. Doubles cost $62.

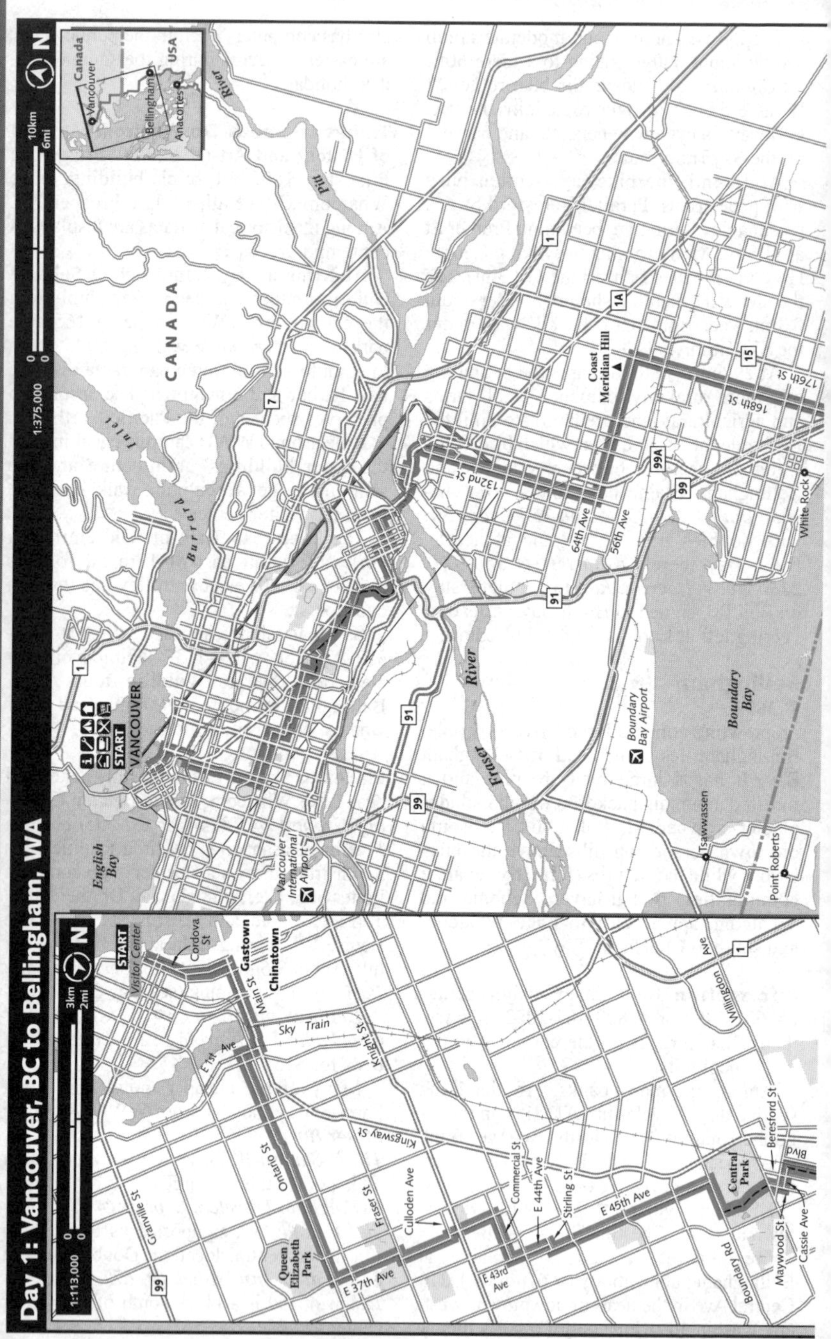
Day 1: Vancouver, BC to Bellingham, WA
1:113,000
3km
2mi
N
START
Visitor Center
Cordova St
Gastown
Chinatown
Main St
Sky Train
E 1st Ave
Knight St
Kingsway St
Granville St
Ontario St
Fraser St
Culloden Ave
Commercial St
E 44th Ave
Stirling St
E 45th Ave
Queen Elizabeth Park
E 37th Ave
E 43rd Ave
Central Park
Beresford St
Blvd
Maywood St
Cassie Ave
Boundary Rd
Willingdon Ave
1:375,000
10km
6mi
Canada
USA
Vancouver
Bellingham
Anacortes
CANADA
Pitt River
Burrard Inlet
English Bay
VANCOUVER
START
Vancouver International Airport
Fraser River
Boundary Bay Airport
Boundary Bay
Tsawwassen
Point Roberts
White Rock
Coast Meridian Hill
132nd St
64th Ave
56th Ave
168th St
176th St
1
1A
7
15
91
99
99A

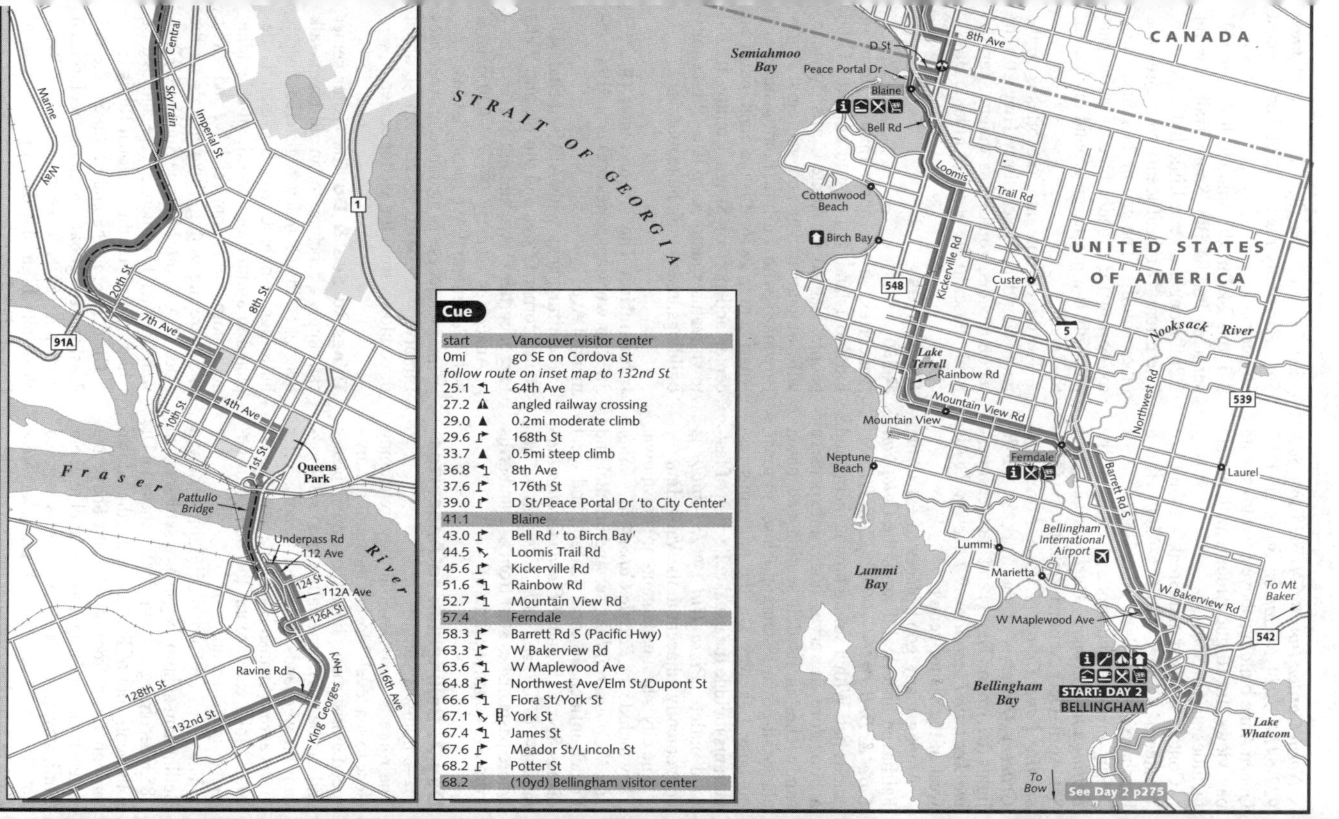
CANADA
UNITED STATES OF AMERICA
STRAIT OF GEORGIA
Semiahmoo Bay
Lummi Bay
Bellingham Bay
Lake Terrell
Lake Whatcom
Nooksack River
Fraser River
Queens Park
Pattullo Bridge
Blaine
Birch Bay
Custer
Ferndale
Laurel
Lummi
Marietta
Neptune Beach
Cottonwood Beach
Mountain View
Bellingham International Airport
START: DAY 2
BELLINGHAM
See Day 2 p275
To Mt Baker
To Bow
8th Ave
D St
Peace Portal Dr
Bell Rd
Loomis
Trail Rd
Kickerville Rd
Rainbow Rd
Mountain View Rd
Northwest Rd
Barrett Rd S
W Bakerview Rd
W Maplewood Ave
Central
SkyTrain
Imperial St
Marine Way
20th St
7th Ave
8th St
10th St
4th Ave
1st St
Underpass Rd
112 Ave
124 St
112A Ave
126A St
116th Ave
King Georges Hwy
Ravine Rd
128th St
132nd St
1
5
91A
539
542
548
Cue
start Vancouver visitor center
0mi go SE on Cordova St
follow route on inset map to 132nd St
25.1 64th Ave
27.2 angled railway crossing
29.0 0.2mi moderate climb
29.6 168th St
33.7 0.5mi steep climb
36.8 8th Ave
37.6 176th St
39.0 D St/Peace Portal Dr 'to City Center'
41.1 Blaine
43.0 Bell Rd ' to Birch Bay'
44.5 Loomis Trail Rd
45.6 Kickerville Rd
51.6 Rainbow Rd
52.7 Mountain View Rd
57.4 Ferndale
58.3 Barrett Rd S (Pacific Hwy)
63.3 W Bakerview Rd
63.6 W Maplewood Ave
64.8 Northwest Ave/Elm St/Dupont St
66.6 Flora St/York St
67.1 York St
67.4 James St
67.6 Meador St/Lincoln St
68.2 Potter St
68.2 (10yd) Bellingham visitor center

North Garden Inn *(☎ 671-7828 or ☎ 800-922-6414, 1014 N Garden St)* is an 1897 Queen Anne building above downtown with bay views. Its 10 guest rooms with private facilities start at $80.

Contact the Bed and Breakfast Guild of Whatcom County (☎ 676-4560) for a brochure and details of other B&Bs.

Buy produce and arts and crafts at the ***Bellingham Farmers' Market*** (10am–3pm Sat, April–Oct). At other times try the ***Community Food Co-op*** *(1220 N Forest St)*. ***Grocery Outlet*** is at the York St traffic lights (67.1mi on Day 1) and another ***supermarket*** *(cnr Lincoln St & Lakeway Dr)* is west of the visitor center.

Among many good places to eat in the Fairhaven historical district, the ***Colophon Cafe & Deli*** *(☎ 647-0092, 1208 11th St)* stands out. With a strong bovine theme and a bookstore, it serves huge, inexpensive sandwiches in its deli section and has a classy sit-down restaurant. Closer to town, on busy Lakeway Dr, the numerous restaurants include the usual collection of fast-food outlets. ***Pizza Hut*** *(☎ 733-5660)* is conveniently adjacent to the Val-U Inn.

The city's best restaurants are downtown. They include the ***Pacific Cafe*** *(☎ 647-0800, 100 N Commercial St)*, serving oriental and French-influenced local seafood and meat dishes from $15, and ***Il Fiasco Cucina Italiana*** *(☎ 676-9136, 1309 Commercial St)*, where pasta dishes start from $12 and grills from $15 (open weekdays).

Day 2: Bellingham to Anacortes

3¼–6 hours, 37.6mi

The route is fairly level all day, remaining close to sea level. Most of the roads are low-speed tourist routes but are narrow in places and can be busy, especially close to Bellingham on weekends. Frequent turnouts offer views across Samish Bay to the San Juan Islands. Take care around the 8mi point because sight lines are poor.

The town of Fairhaven (3.3mi), now a Bellingham suburb, began as a settlement in 1853, becoming a city in 1890. Chuckanut Dr rolls gently out of Fairhaven, trending down through forest from about 100ft above the water. It descends right to sea level at about 14mi, staying low and level across exposed flats to tiny Bow (16.4mi). ***Larrabee State Park*** (8.6mi) has camping for $8 a double.

At 24mi on the right is the ***Bay View State Park*** entry road. Hiker/biker sites cost $6 per person.

From 24.7mi the smooth, level, gravel-surfaced Padilla Bay Shore Trail runs for 2.2mi along a dike at Little Indian Slough. The estuary wetland teems with birds and other wildlife. The gap in the entry gate is too narrow for a loaded bike. If taking panniers off is a hassle, go around one end of the fence.

The direct route into Anacortes is on the wide shoulders of very busy Hwy 20. The recommended route uses quieter parallel roads closer to the water of Fidalgo Bay.

Anacortes

☎ 360

Anacortes, at the northernmost point of Fidalgo Island, is home to around 14,000 people. Named for Annie Curtis Bowman, wife of map maker and geologist Amos Bowman, who built a home, store and wharf here in 1876, it is the main industrial center and port of Skagit County. Its old town features many solid late-19th-century buildings, many with huge murals.

Information The visitor center (☎ 293-3832, W www.anacortes.org) is at 819 Commercial Ave.

Plentiful banks with ATMs include US Bank, corner O Ave and 9th St; and Wells Fargo, corner O Ave and 8th St.

Anacortes Cyclery (☎ 293-6205) is at 2012 Commercial Ave (near 21st St).

Internet access is available at Anacortes Library (☎ 293-1910), 1209 9th St, about three blocks from the visitor center.

Things to See & Do The visitor center can supply a brochure for an **old-town walk** that takes in the many registered historic buildings. Annie Curtis Bowman is depicted in a **mural** on the side of a building at the corner of Commercial Ave and 8th St, and there are **vintage bike murals** on the sides of Anacortes Marine Supply & Hardware, corner Commercial Ave and 2nd St, which is itself on the National Register.

On R Ave, at the end of 9th St, the **WT Preston 'snagboat'**, a sternwheeler used from the 1880s to keep the Skagit River clear, sits high and dry (open Memorial Day–Labor Day).

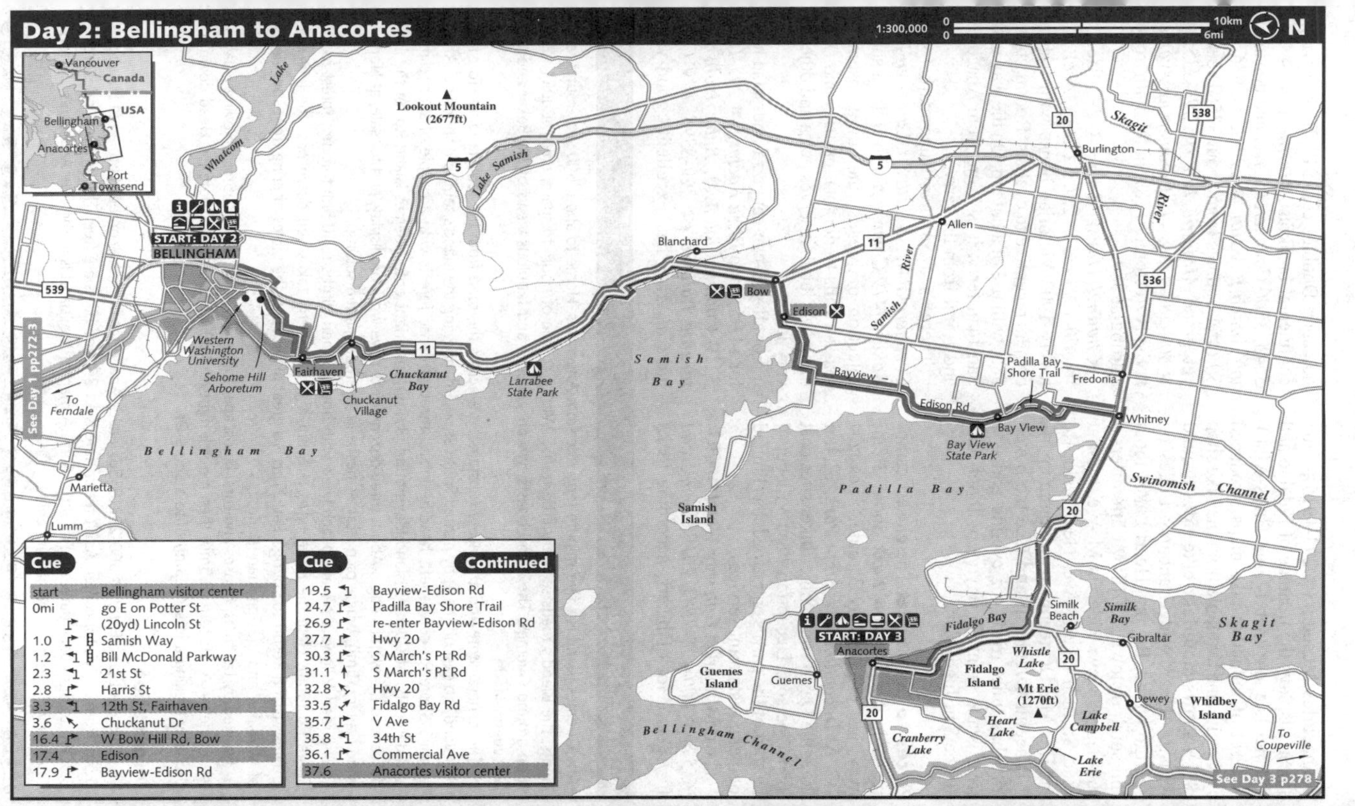

Cue	
start	Bellingham visitor center
0mi	go E on Potter St
	(20yd) Lincoln St
1.0	Samish Way
1.2	Bill McDonald Parkway
2.3	21st St
2.8	Harris St
3.3	12th St, Fairhaven
3.6	Chuckanut Dr
16.4	W Bow Hill Rd, Bow
17.4	Edison
17.9	Bayview-Edison Rd

Cue Continued	
19.5	Bayview-Edison Rd
24.7	Padilla Bay Shore Trail
26.9	re-enter Bayview-Edison Rd
27.7	Hwy 20
30.3	S March's Pt Rd
31.1	S March's Pt Rd
32.8	Hwy 20
33.5	Fidalgo Bay Rd
35.7	V Ave
35.8	34th St
36.1	Commercial Ave
37.6	Anacortes visitor center

Anacortes Museum (☎ 293-1915), 1305 8th St, displays the heritage of Fidalgo and Guemes Islands (open 1–5pm Thurs–Mon).

A set of mountain-bike maps, produced by the city and available from the bike shop ($11), shows **mountain-bike rides** around Whistle, Heart and Cranberry Lakes on Fidalgo Island. Beyond Heart Lake, about 8mi south of town, 1270ft **Mt Erie** offers a 360-degree view. Ride via M Ave, right at 32nd St, then take H Ave, Heart Lake Rd and Erie Mtn Dr steeply to the summit park.

Peaceful **Guemes Island** (see the boxed text) has quiet roads for cycling and is a great island jaunt for anyone without time for the San Juan Islands.

Places to Stay & Eat The closest camping is in ***Washington Park*** about 3.5mi away, just off the Day 3 route. Sites cost $12. At ***Deception Pass State Park***, 12.4mi along the Day 3 route, hiker/biker sites cost $6 per person. Deception Pass Village, at the start of the park's entry road, has limited food and restaurant services.

The downmarket ***Gateway Motel*** *(☎ 293-2655 or ☎ 800-428-7583, 2019 Commercial Ave)* gets a lot of bikers, according to its manager. Doubles cost $49. Both serving a continental breakfast, ***Marina Inn*** *(☎ 293-3545, 3300 Commercial Ave)* and nonsmoking ***Anaco Bay Inn*** *(☎ 299-3320, 916 33rd St)* offer doubles from about $75. The small yet grand ***Majestic Inn*** *(☎ 293-3355 or ☎ 800-588-4780, 419 Commercial Ave)* is a lavishly restored 1889 hotel with rooms starting at $89.

Channel House B&B *(☎ 293-9382 or ☎ 800-238-4353, 2902 Oakes Ave)* is a lovely 1902 Victorian house with friendly owners receptive to cyclists. Rooms start at $85, with use of a hot tub. On the way to the San Juan ferry, it is 1.3mi from Anacortes, and 1.5mi from the ferry.

There is a ***Safeway*** supermarket *(cnr Commercial Ave & 12th St)*. ***La Vie en Rose Bakery*** *(419 Commercial Ave)* has a superb selection of breads (including rosemary/sea-salt rolls to die for), pastries and sweet things. At lunch it serves pizza and other savory items.

For all-you-can-eat pizza-and-salad lunch for $4.95, go to ***Pizza Factory*** *(☎ 293-1000, 3219 Commercial Ave)*. ***Bella Isola Ristorante Italiano*** *(☎ 299-8398, 619 Commercial Ave)* has excellent, good-value

Guemes Island

Tiny Guemes Island is a five-minute ferry ride from Anacortes. Home to about 500 year-round residents, the island's roads see very little traffic. With a couple of hours to spare, enjoy a quiet 12mi loop around Guemes. The island boasts two art galleries and fabulous views of Mt Baker and the San Juan Islands.

The general store and art gallery (upstairs), are across the road from the ferry landing. To circle the island, go east on the aptly named South Shore Rd, hugging the island's southern shoreline. After 1.6mi S Shore Rd curves left, heading inland through dense forests with a couple of short climbs and descents. At Guemes Island Playground (3.6mi), turn right onto Guemes Island Rd for the 1mi descent to the water's edge. About three dozen artists have work on display, and for sale, at Northwind Gallery (5mi), where picnic tables nestle in a serene garden setting.

The road follows a private beach lined with houses, then climbs for 0.5mi through forest to W Shore Rd (6mi). Here the route turns left, but a 1mi side trip takes you down past the low-key Guemes Island Resort to Young's Park. This is a great picnic spot, the tables offering front-row views of Mt Baker and the San Juan Islands.

Flanked by tall trees, houses and rural landscape, follow W Shore Rd for 2.5mi, enjoying Fidalgo Island views. A left turn (8.5mi), then a quick right (8.8mi) leads onto W Shore Dr. Head down to the ferry making a left (10.3mi) onto S Shore Dr.

Information

The Guemes Island Ferry (☎ 360-293-6356) leaves Anacortes from the corner of 6th and I Sts about 0.5mi from the visitor center. Adult return fare is $1.25, and bikes are free. The ferry operates from 6.30am to 6pm daily (later on Fri, Sat & Sun). A map of the island is in the free *Anacortes Visitors Guide*, available from the visitor center.

Italian food. Moderately priced, homemade meals are served at the olde-worlde ***Calico Cupboard*** *(☎ 293-7315, 901 Commercial Ave)*. ***Gere-a-Deli*** *(☎ 293-7383, 502 Commercial Ave)* is locally recommended for its sandwiches and Friday pasta dinners. For fine dining on Wednesday to Saturday evenings, try ***Nantucket Inn*** *(☎ 293-6007, 3402 Commercial Ave)*. ***New Olympia*** *(☎ 293-6911, 2001 Commercial Ave)* serves Greek fare.

Day 3: Anacortes to Port Townsend

3½–6 hours, 39mi

An easy ride follows mostly gently undulating roads reaching only about 400ft altitude. But there are three short, steepish pinches in the first 25mi. At 11.1mi take care at Hwy 20's two narrow bridges over Deception Pass onto Whidbey Island. The narrow sidewalk is an alternative if traffic is heavy – give way to pedestrians. A ferry (38.1mi) returns bicycles, cars and pedestrians to the mainland's Quimper Peninsula across Admiralty Inlet.

Outside the fire station on the left (3.3mi), see the **Elkhart Chemical Engine**, an example of 1920s fire-fighting technology. A one-way 2.3mi loop road in **Washington Park** through cool forest beside the water could be ridden as a side trip from here. (Continue ahead on Sunset Ave into the park, watching for wheel-munching speed bumps. There are lovely views of Rosario Strait islands as well as some good ups and downs.)

At Deception Pass, named by navigator George Vancouver in 1792, water flows through narrow gaps at five to eight knots and is between four and 37 fathoms (24ft to 222ft) deep.

The route rolls easily for 8mi on busy, mostly wide-shouldered Hwy 20 before turning off to the right and continuing past a ***store*** (20.3mi) and Whidbey Island Naval Air Station (20.5mi). The noise of traffic is replaced by that from aircraft taxiing and 'touch-and-go' landing practice.

The coastline facing the Strait of Juan de Fuca is often fogbound. Beyond a seemingly deserted village built right on the beach between the ocean and marsh flats, high coastal bluffs rise and the sea smell is strong. After a climb, the route cruises past small farms, descending again to meander at the water's edge.

A vehicular ferry departs Keystone Dock (38.1mi; ☎ 800-843-3779) about 16 times a day from 7.45am to 9.30pm for the 30-minute trip to Port Townsend ($1.85 per person, $0.35 per bicycle).

Port Townsend

☎ 360

Oldest town on the Olympic Peninsula, Port Townsend (population 8700) features a streetscape of restored 19th-century buildings along a waterfront with views of the oft-snowy Cascade and Olympic Mtns. Victorian mansions, many operating as B&Bs, perch above the bay. Port Townsend and Seattle, each established in 1851, competed for supremacy in Puget Sound trade until the 1890 cancellation of a rail link with Portland spelled doom for Port Townsend. The economy now depends on tourists attracted by stores selling antiques, rare books, expensive clothing and art.

Information Port Townsend visitor center (☎ 385-2722, W www.ptguide.com) is in a booth at 2437 E Sims Way (Hwy 20).

US Bank occupies a corner position at the junction of Hwy 20 and the exit road from the ferry; Interwest Bank is on the corner of Hwy 20 and Washington St.

PT Cyclery (☎ 385-6470) is at 100 Tyler St. There's an Internet cafe (☎ 385-9773) at 2021 E Sims Way.

Things to See & Do The visitor center has a free **guide map** to the historic downtown district; it will also help navigation around the rest of town. More than 70 points of interest are listed.

Jefferson County Historical Museum (☎ 385-1003), 210 Madison, in the old city hall building, documents the port's maritime and Native American history.

The **Marine Science Center** (☎ 385-5582), on Fort Worden park's pier, has an aquarium and touch tank.

Kayak Port Townsend (☎ 385-6240), at the corner of Monroe and Water Sts on the harbor, leads trips for all experience levels every day.

The **Wooden Boat Foundation** (☎ 385-3628, W www.woodenboat.org), 380 Jefferson St, a center for maritime education on Point Hudson northeast of downtown, rents rowboats. In early September, the **Wooden**

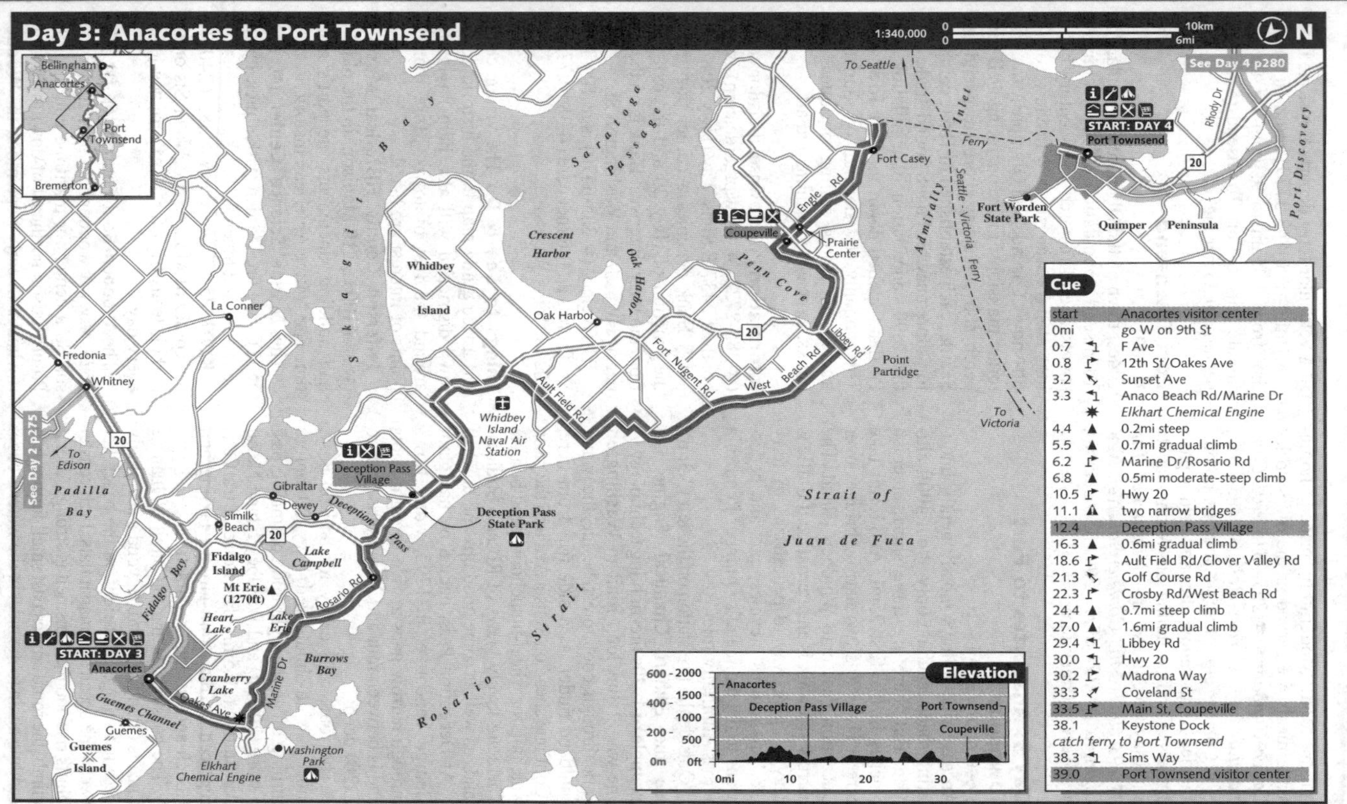

Day 3: Anacortes to Port Townsend
1:340,000
0 10km
0 6mi
N
See Day 2 p275
See Day 4 p280
START: DAY 3
Anacortes
START: DAY 4
Port Townsend
Cue
start Anacortes visitor center
0mi go W on 9th St
0.7 F Ave
0.8 12th St/Oakes Ave
3.2 Sunset Ave
3.3 Anaco Beach Rd/Marine Dr
Elkhart Chemical Engine
4.4 0.2mi steep
5.5 0.7mi gradual climb
6.2 Marine Dr/Rosario Rd
6.8 0.5mi moderate-steep climb
10.5 Hwy 20
11.1 two narrow bridges
12.4 Deception Pass Village
16.3 0.6mi gradual climb
18.6 Ault Field Rd/Clover Valley Rd
21.3 Golf Course Rd
22.3 Crosby Rd/West Beach Rd
24.4 0.7mi steep climb
27.0 1.6mi gradual climb
29.4 Libbey Rd
30.0 Hwy 20
30.2 Madrona Way
33.3 Coveland St
33.5 Main St, Coupeville
38.1 Keystone Dock
catch ferry to Port Townsend
38.3 Sims Way
39.0 Port Townsend visitor center
Elevation
Anacortes
Deception Pass Village
Port Townsend
Coupeville
600 - 2000
400 - 1500
1000
200 - 500
0m 0ft
0mi 10 20 30
Bellingham
Anacortes
Port Townsend
Bremerton
Fredonia
Whitney
La Conner
To Edison
Padilla Bay
Fidalgo Bay
Guemes Channel
Guemes
Guemes Island
Fidalgo Island
Mt Erie (1270ft)
Heart Lake
Cranberry Lake
Oakes Ave
Elkhart Chemical Engine
Washington Park
Marine Dr
Lake Erie
Burrows Bay
Rosario Rd
Lake Campbell
Similk Beach
Gibraltar
Dewey
Deception Pass Village
Deception
Pass
Deception Pass State Park
Skagit Bay
Whidbey Island
Whidbey Island Naval Air Station
Crescent Harbor
Oak Harbor
Ault Field Rd
Saratoga Passage
Fort Nugent Rd
West Beach Rd
Penn Cove
Coupeville
Libbey Rd
Prairie Center
Engle Rd
Fort Casey
Point Partridge
To Seattle
Admiralty Inlet
Seattle - Victoria Ferry
Ferry
To Victoria
Rosario Strait
Strait of Juan de Fuca
Fort Worden State Park
Quimper Peninsula
Rhody Dr
Port Discovery
20

Boat Festival celebrates the lore of wooden boat building. Yachts are displayed at Point Hudson Marina.

In late July, Fort Worden State Park hosts **Jazz Port Townsend** (☎ 385-3102 or ☎ 800-733-3608), attracting national acts.

Places to Stay & Eat Hiker/biker camping at ***Fort Worden State Park*** *(☎ 385-4730)*, over the hill north of town, costs $6 per person. Also in the park, the ***Olympic Hostel*** *(☎ 385-0655)* has dorm beds from $12.

Viewless rooms at ***Tides Inn*** *(☎385-0595 or ☎ 800-822-8696, 1807 Water St)* start at $65. Those with a view and jacuzzi on the deck cost $110. ***Harborside Inn*** *(☎ 385-7909 or ☎ 800-942-5960, 330 Benedict St)*, behind the visitor center, has doubles from $75. ***Port Townsend Inn*** *(☎ 385-2211 or ☎ 800-216-4985, 2020 Washington St)* has doubles from $78 to $98 ($175 with jacuzzi), including continental breakfast.

Ann Starrett Mansion *(☎ 385-3205* or *☎ 800-321-0644, 744 Clay St)*, is a smoke-free B&B where tariffs start at $99 a double.

From May to October, ***farmers' markets*** *(☎ 379-6959 ext 119)* are held near the city hall (Sat 8.30am–1pm) and in the ***Food Co-op*** on Lawrence St (Wed 3.30–6pm).

A 24-hour ***Safeway*** supermarket is at the next traffic lights, 0.3mi east of the visitor center.

Good light meals, excellent coffee, over-loud music and offhand service are available at ***Tyler Street Coffee House*** *(☎ 379-4185, 215 Tyler St)*. ***Silverwater Cafe*** *(☎ 385-6448, 237 Taylor St)* specializes in fresh northwest seafood, pasta and home-made desserts. ***The Public House Grills & Ales*** *(☎ 385-9708, 1038 Water St)* is more expensive, with $10 to $18 mains. For upmarket dining, try ***Belmont Inn*** *(☎ 385-3007, 925 Water St)*, Port Townsend's only remaining 1880s waterfront restaurant and saloon.

Day 4: Port Townsend to Bremerton

4½–8½ hours, 52.1mi

The route follows quiet roads for the day's first half. A number of niggling hills slow progress, although seldom rising above 200ft before the Hood Canal Bridge (26.3mi). Beyond, in Kitsap County, Hwy 3 is busy. Temporary relief arrives with the turn onto Lofall Rd (30.4mi) but, from Silverdale (42.7mi) onwards, suburbia generates traffic the rest of the hilly way to Bremerton. At 10.8mi, Port Hadlock has the last ***food store*** before the outskirts of Silverdale.

Early on, Discovery Rd rolls quietly with great views over Port Discovery and the often cloud-rimmed Olympia Range.

Don't be tempted by the sign to Shine Tidelands State Park, steeply downhill on the left at 25.7mi – there are no facilities. On the right at 30.2mi, **Kitsap Memorial State Park** is conveniently placed for a lunch break. Picnic tables, with beautiful views to the snowtipped Olympics, are 650yd inside the park, which also has a ***campground***.

Between the parks, Floating Hood Canal Bridge has a narrow, debris-strewn shoulder, busy traffic and a slippery metal rail angled across cyclists' path near its center. Signs advise walking this section but there is nowhere safer to walk. It would be more sensible to continue riding, carefully crossing the rail, and get off the bridge as soon as possible.

The approach to Bremerton is on busy suburban roads. Silverdale Cyclery (☎ 692-5508), off route at 42.7mi, is at 9242 Silverdale Way. From 47.1mi, Hwy 303 is a four-lane road with wide shoulders until the bridge into the city proper.

Bremerton

☎ 360

The largest town on the Kitsap Peninsula (40,000 people), Bremerton, with its excellent ferry connections, is basically a dormitory suburb of Seattle. It seems strangely deserted after 6pm and on Sunday when all downtown businesses shut up tight. The city is home to Puget Sound Naval Shipyard, the only west-coast yard capable of handling both nuclear and conventional ships. Bremerton is also home-port for the US Pacific Fleet. The frequent passenger ferry (about 40 minutes, bikes free) links the city to downtown Seattle. Timetables are available from most accommodations as well as the visitor center and ferry terminal.

Information The visitor center (☎ 479-3579, ⓔ visitorinfo@bremertonchamber.org) is on the corner of Pacific Ave and Burwell St (open weekdays).

Banks line Pacific Ave. Washington Mutual Bank is on the corner of 5th St; US

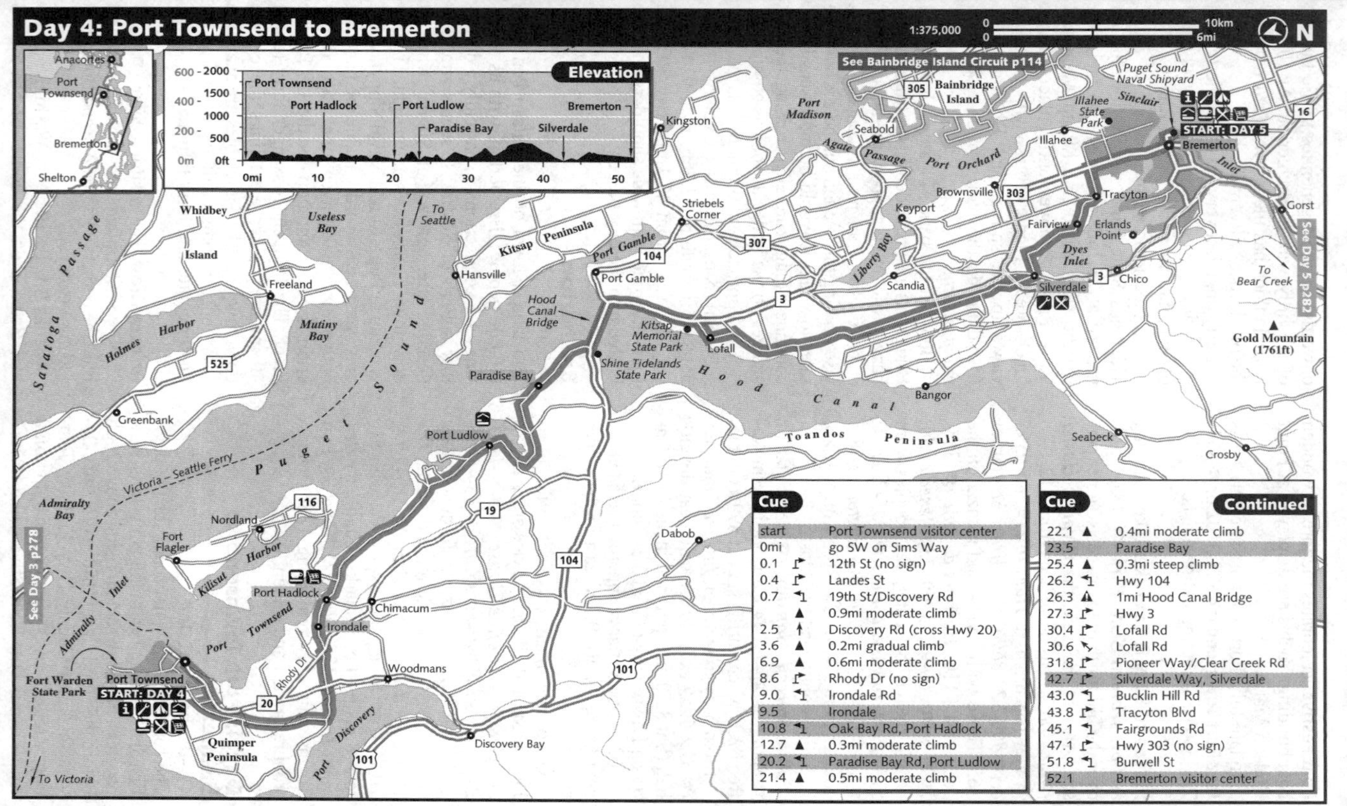

Cue	
start	Port Townsend visitor center
0mi	go SW on Sims Way
0.1 ↱	12th St (no sign)
0.4 ↱	Landes St
0.7 ↰	19th St/Discovery Rd
▲	0.9mi moderate climb
2.5 ↑	Discovery Rd (cross Hwy 20)
3.6 ▲	0.2mi gradual climb
6.9 ▲	0.6mi moderate climb
8.6 ↱	Rhody Dr (no sign)
9.0 ↰	Irondale Rd
9.5	Irondale
10.8 ↰	Oak Bay Rd, Port Hadlock
12.7 ▲	0.3mi moderate climb
20.2 ↰	Paradise Bay Rd, Port Ludlow
21.4 ▲	0.5mi moderate climb

Cue	Continued
22.1 ▲	0.4mi moderate climb
23.5	Paradise Bay
25.4 ▲	0.3mi steep climb
26.2 ↰	Hwy 104
26.3 ▲	1mi Hood Canal Bridge
27.3 ↱	Hwy 3
30.4 ↱	Lofall Rd
30.6 ↖	Lofall Rd
31.8 ↱	Pioneer Way/Clear Creek Rd
42.7 ↱	Silverdale Way, Silverdale
43.0 ↰	Bucklin Hill Rd
43.8 ↱	Tracyton Blvd
45.1 ↰	Fairgrounds Rd
47.1 ↱	Hwy 303 (no sign)
51.8 ↰	Burwell St
52.1	Bremerton visitor center

Bank is a block farther north; and West Sound Bank is on the corner of 2nd St.

Northwest Bike & Lock (☎ 479-3909) is at 820 Pacific Ave. An Internet cafe is at 206 Burwell St.

Things to See & Do Attractively refurbished 4th St contains the **Kitsap County Historical Museum** (☎ 479-62260), at 280 4th, showcasing the area's 100-year European history. Near where 4th St crosses Pacific Ave is the town's **art district**. The Amy Burnett Gallery at 408 Pacific Ave specializes in contemporary art on historical and local themes. The post office, corner 6th St and Pacific Ave, contains a fine 1930s **mural**, part of a depression-era public-art project.

There is a **Naval Museum** (☎ 479-7447) at 130 Washington Ave, and self-guided tours of the historic destroyer **USS *Turner Joy*** (☎ 792-2457), moored next to the ferry terminal at 300 Washington Beach Ave. **Harbor tours** of the navy's 'mothball fleet' leave from the Bremerton Boardwalk.

Summer pop concerts are on Friday evenings on the boardwalk near the ferry terminal. An armed forces festival, featuring one of the biggest parades in the USA, has taken place for more than 50 years on the third weekend in May.

Places to Stay & Eat Camping at ***Illahee State Park***, about 2mi along NE Sylvan Way east of Wheaton Way, costs $6 per person. The park has forest, sandy beaches and picnic facilities.

Super 8 Motel *(☎ 377-8881 or ☎ 800-800-8000, 5068 Kitsap Way)*, west of downtown, has doubles from $53 while ***Midway Inn*** *(☎ 479-2909* or *☎ 800-231-0575, 2909 Wheaton Way)* charges $59. ***Best Western Bremerton Inn*** *(☎405-1111 or ☎ 800-776-2291, 4303 Kitsap Way)* charges $79.

Highland Cottage B&B *(☎ 373-2235, 622 Highland Ave, e aoverson@hurricane.net)*, three blocks from the ferry terminal, charges $55 to $95.

There are 24-hour supermarkets along Kitsap Way – ***QFC*** is in the 4300 block and ***Safeway*** is near the corner of 11th St. All the usual fast-food chains are also represented on Kitsap Way, which is the busiest part of town after office hours. All-you-can-eat specials are advertised at the ***Family Pancake House*** *(☎ 479-2422, 3900 Kitsap Way)*.

Downtown, but open only until 5pm, are the ***Emperor's Palace*** Chinese restaurant *(☎ 377-8822, 3509 Kitsap Way)*, near the ferry dock, and ***Just Your Cup O'Tea*** *(☎ 377-9457, 305 Pacific Ave)*.

The nearest locally recommended after-hours, sit-down restaurant is north along Washington Ave and across the Manette Bridge to East Bremerton. ***The Boatshed*** *(☎ 377-2600, 101 Shore Dr)* serves seafood and pasta specialties.

Day 5: Bremerton to Shelton

3¾–6¾ hours, 42.1mi

The day begins with hills, first through the suburban area and continuing into the countryside. The high point is only 350ft in the hills near Bremerton. The hardest climb is a steep pinch from the turn onto Trails Rd (21.4mi), after which the road rolls along before plunging down into Shelton. Food is available from several stores along the route.

After the steep climb on Union Ave, starting at 3.4mi, be alert for the veer right onto W 3rd St – the sign is obscured and the only visible street sign identifies Poindexter St. From about 5mi, the route enters forested rolling terrain with water views before descending to parallel noisy Hwy 3. At 8mi, the route becomes quiet, forest-lined Old Belfair Hwy.

Unsigned Trails Rd (21.4mi) is distinguished by the purple rocks, buffalo and tepee at its junction with Hwy 106. About 4mi straight ahead on Hwy 106, ***Twanoh State Park*** has hiker/biker camping for $6 per person.

At 25.3mi, left off Mason Lake Dr, a **county park** makes a convenient picnic stop. At 35.3mi, the ***Lake Limerick store*** is on the left.

From the Shelton city limit (39.5mi) a bikepath brings relief from the busy, narrow-shouldered road.

Shelton

☎ 360

A town of 7700 people, Shelton is county seat of Mason County, proudly claiming to be one of the USA's fastest-growing counties. The town's historic center has undergone restoration, with wrought-iron lamp stanchions and hanging flower baskets accentuating its olde-worlde feel. Murals on downtown buildings also add interest.

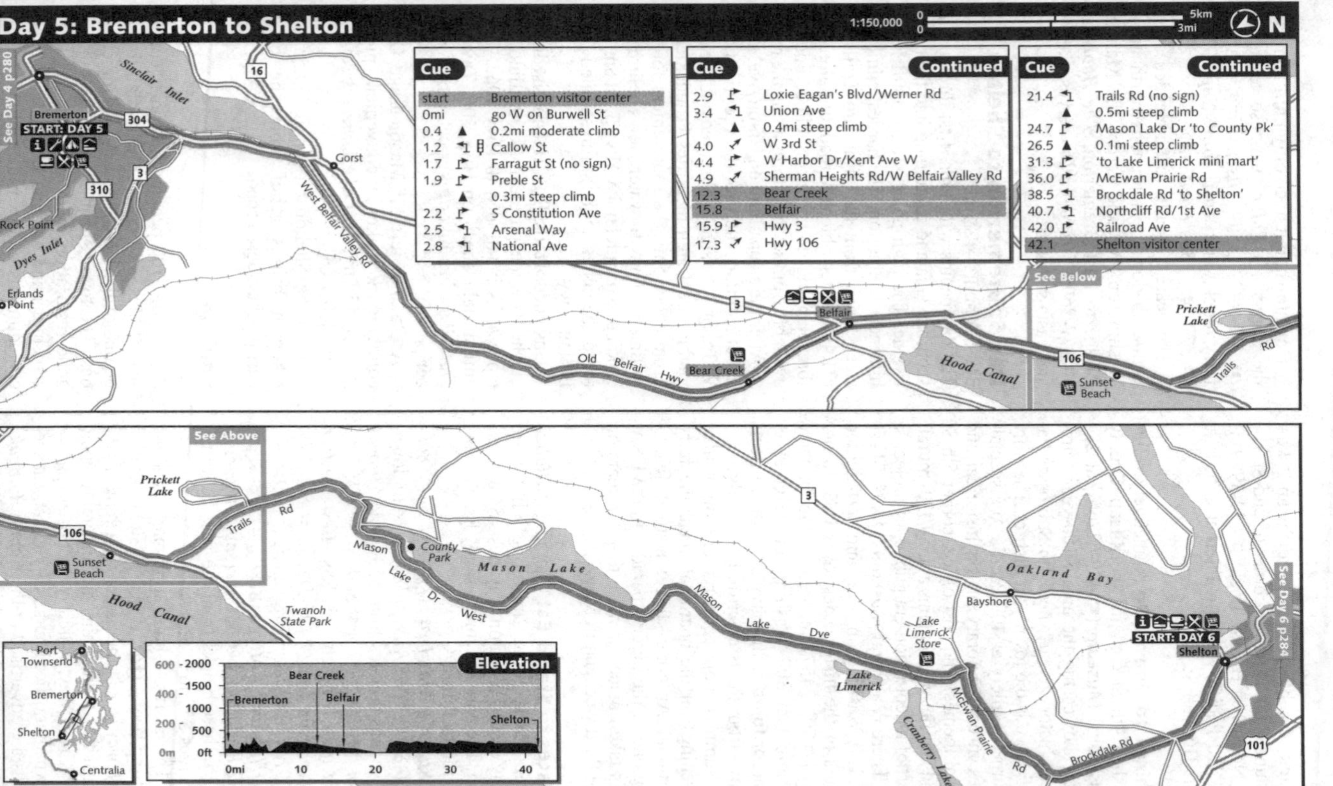
Day 5: Bremerton to Shelton
1:150,000
0 5km
0 3mi
N
Cue
start Bremerton visitor center
0mi go W on Burwell St
0.4 0.2mi moderate climb
1.2 Callow St
1.7 Farragut St (no sign)
1.9 Preble St
0.3mi steep climb
2.2 S Constitution Ave
2.5 Arsenal Way
2.8 National Ave
Cue Continued
2.9 Loxie Eagan's Blvd/Werner Rd
3.4 Union Ave
0.4mi steep climb
4.0 W 3rd St
4.4 W Harbor Dr/Kent Ave W
4.9 Sherman Heights Rd/W Belfair Valley Rd
12.3 Bear Creek
15.8 Belfair
15.9 Hwy 3
17.3 Hwy 106
Cue Continued
21.4 Trails Rd (no sign)
0.5mi steep climb
24.7 Mason Lake Dr 'to County Pk'
26.5 0.1mi steep climb
31.3 'to Lake Limerick mini mart'
36.0 McEwan Prairie Rd
38.5 Brockdale Rd 'to Shelton'
40.7 Northcliff Rd/1st Ave
42.0 Railroad Ave
42.1 Shelton visitor center
See Day 4 p280
Bremerton
START: DAY 5
Sinclair Inlet
16
304
3
310
Rock Point
Dyes Inlet
Erlands Point
Gorst
West Belfair Valley Rd
Old Belfair Hwy
Bear Creek
Belfair
Hood Canal
106
Sunset Beach
See Below
Prickett Lake
Trails Rd
See Above
Mason Lake Dr West
County Park
Mason Lake
Twanoh State Park
Mason Lake Dve
Lake Limerick Store
Lake Limerick
Cranberry Lake
McEwan Prairie Rd
Brockdale Rd
Bayshore
Oakland Bay
START: DAY 6
Shelton
See Day 6 p284
101
Port Townsend
Centralia
Elevation
600 - 2000
1500
400 - 1000
200 - 500
0m 0ft
0mi 10 20 30 40

Forestry has been important to the town since even before the Simpson Timber Company was founded here in 1890. Oysters are another important local product.

Information The visitor center (☎ 427-8168) is in the red caboose of the steam train parked at 230 W Railroad Ave. The nearby Chamber of Commerce (☎ 426-2021, 221 W Railroad Ave) also has information.

A West Coast Bank ATM kiosk is 100yd west of the visitor center on Railroad Ave.

Limited bike items such as puncture kits are available at Safeway.

Things to See & Do The **Mason County Historical Museum**, corner 5th St and Railroad Ave, is open afternoons (Tues–Sat). Wander the streets to see **murals** in the downtown area depicting the heritage of Shelton and Mason County. Note also the bronze and iron **statues** around town plus local **Native American art** in the town's galleries.

Shelton has **cinemas** (☎ 426-1000) at 517 W Franklin Ave.

Shelton's Mason County Fairground hosts the **County Fair** on the last weekend in July. The October **Oysterfest** (☎ 426-2021) is also at the fairground with vendors and exhibitors of seafood, wine and microbrews.

Places to Stay & Eat The nearest camping is a long way from town at ***Twanoh State Park*** – see the Day 5 route, p281. Stock up on supplies at Belfair if camping here.

Probably the cheapest in town, ***City Center Motel*** *(☎426-3397 or ☎ 888-771-2378, cnr 1st & Alder Sts)* has tired but clean rooms from $45. Two blocks from downtown, ***Shelton Inn*** *(☎426-4468 or ☎ 800-451-4560, 628 W Railroad Ave)* has good rooms from $53. On the outskirts, ***Super 8 Motel*** *(☎ 426-1654, 2943 Northview Circle)* charges $56.

On 7th Ave, between Franklin and Cedar Sts, is a 24-hour ***Safeway*** supermarket. A ***farmers' market*** is on 2nd St (10am–3pm Sat).

Vegetarians may have a lean time in town but could try ***Nature's Best Natural Foods*** *(☎ 426-7474, 131 W Railroad Ave)*; ***Dominos Pizza*** *(☎ 427-8700, 134 N 1st St)*; or the Mexican ***El Sarape*** *(☎ 426-4294, 318 W Railroad Ave)*.

Meat eaters can choose from ***Hungry Bear Steakhouse*** *(☎ 426-1101, 102 W Railroad Ave)*, ***Kobe Teriyaki Restaurant*** *(☎ 432-0533, 118 W Alder St)* or the more upmarket ***Steven's*** *(☎ 426-4407, 203 W Railroad Ave)*. ***Timbers Restaurant*** *(☎ 426-8757)* is attached to Shelton Inn. ***Xinh's Clam & Oyster House*** *(☎ 427-8709, cnr 3rd St & W Railroad Ave)* serves good but pricey seafood dinners.

Day 6: Shelton to Centralia

5½–10 hours, 62.6mi

Two or three moderate climbs punctuate this longish route, which is mostly on low-traffic roads. The high point is about 500ft, at 8.3mi along Cloquallum Rd, before the route descends in stages to the Satsop and Chehalis River valleys. Several small towns en route have food stores.

At 0.4mi, the route veers right at the KFC store onto Pioneer Way, staying parallel to Hwy 3 and climbing above it. Pretty Lake Isabella is visible on the left at 1.8mi. After 6.8mi the relatively quiet road, without a shoulder, takes easy grades through forest.

After crossing Hwy 8 onto Wakefield Rd (27.1mi), the route enters an open agricultural area. There are views to cooling towers of the inactive Satsop power plant. The route becomes S Bank Rd after the unsigned Chehalis River bridge (28.7mi) and mostly trends downwards or stays flat the rest of the way.

Centralia

☎ 360

Lying exactly halfway along the I-5 freeway between Seattle and Portland, Oregon (84mi each way), Centralia (population 13,500 people) and its conjoined twin, Chehalis, each boast historic red-brick centers oriented to the railroad tracks. Both also have new business districts alongside the interstate highway. Centralia is something of a shopping destination by virtue of its dozens of factory outlets, shops and discount malls near I-5 and the antique stores that dot the downtown area. Centralia is the only community in the Northwest founded by an African American. Former slave George Washington moved west from Missouri with the family that first owned him, then freed and adopted him. He established a land claim in 1852 near what is now downtown Centralia.

Information An information office (☎ 736-8730) is in the Amtrak station at 210 Railroad Ave. The main office for Centralia/

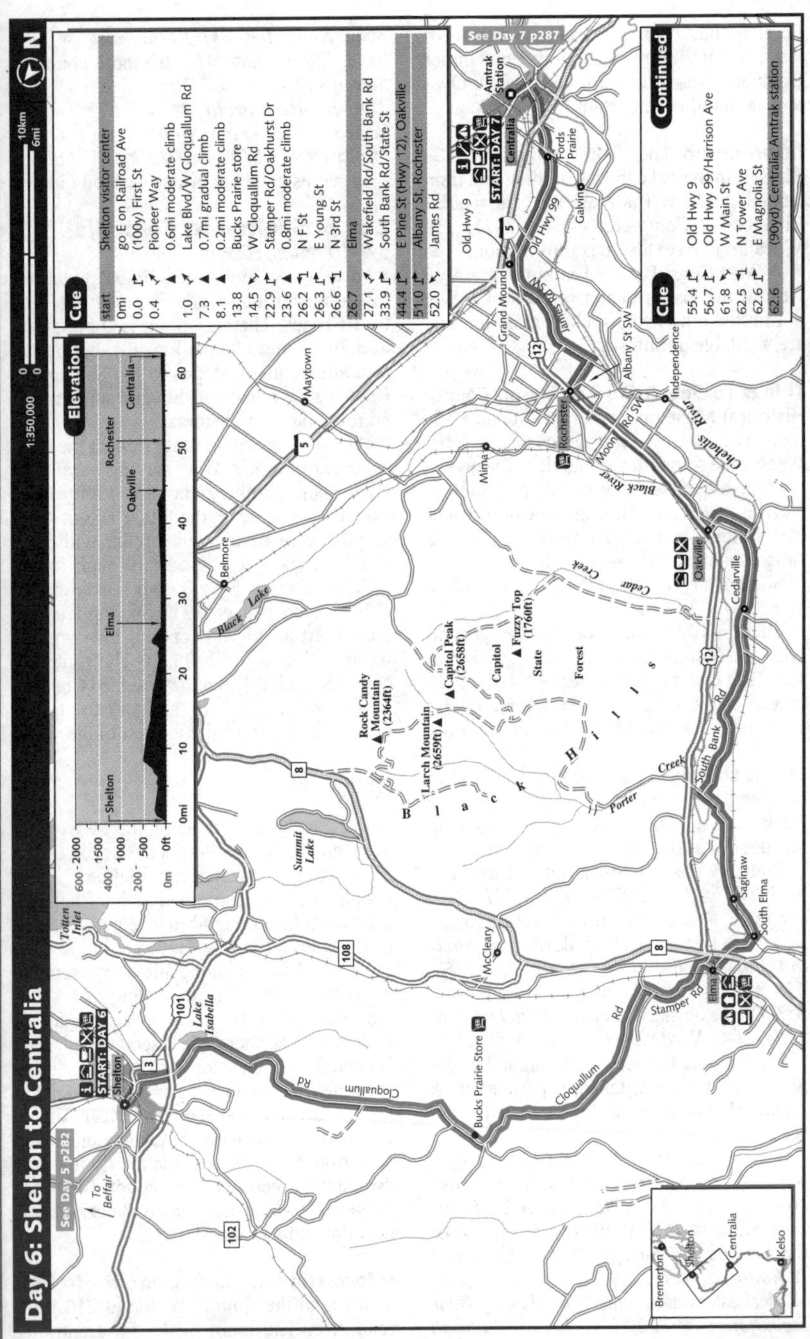
Day 6: Shelton to Centralia
See Day 5 p282
See Day 7 p287
1:350,000
0 10km
0 6mi
N
Cue
start Shelton visitor center
0mi go E on Railroad Ave
0.0 (100y) First St
0.4 Pioneer Way
0.6mi moderate climb
1.0 Lake Blvd/W Cloquallum Rd
7.3 0.7mi gradual climb
8.1 0.2mi moderate climb
13.8 Bucks Prairie store
14.5 W Cloquallum Rd
22.9 Stamper Rd/Oakhurst Dr
23.6 0.8mi moderate climb
26.2 N F St
26.3 E Young St
26.6 N 3rd St
26.7 Elma
27.1 Wakefield Rd/South Bank Rd
33.9 South Bank Rd/State St
44.4 E Pine St (Hwy 12), Oakville
51.0 Albany St, Rochester
52.0 James Rd
Cue Continued
55.4 Old Hwy 9
56.7 Old Hwy 99/Harrison Ave
61.8 W Main St
62.5 N Tower Ave
62.6 E Magnolia St
62.6 (90yd) Centralia Amtrak station
Elevation
2000
1500
1000
500
0ft
600
400
200
0m
0mi
10
20
30
40
50
60
Shelton
Elma
Oakville
Rochester
Centralia
START: DAY 6
Shelton
START: DAY 7
Centralia
Amtrak Station
To Belfair
Totten Inlet
Lake Isabella
Cloquallum Rd
Bucks Prairie Store
McCleary
Summit Lake
Black Lake
Belmore
Maytown
Rock Candy Mountain (2364ft)
Larch Mountain (2659ft)
Capitol Peak (2658ft)
Fuzzy Top (1760ft)
Capitol State Forest
Black Hills
Porter Creek
Cedar Creek
Mima
Rochester
Independence
Grand Mound
Old Hwy 9
Old Hwy 99
Galvin
Fords Prairie
James Rd
Albany St SW
Moon Rd SW
Black River
Chehalis River
Oakville
Cedarville
South Bank Rd
Saginaw
South Elma
Elma
Stamper Rd
Bremerton
Shelton
Centralia
Kelso
101
102
108
3
8
12
5

Chehalis is Tourism Lewis County (☎ 748-8885 or ☎ 800-525-3323, W www.chamberway.com) at 500 NW Chamber of Commerce Way, Chehalis.

The Bank of America is at the corner of Main and Pearl Sts.

Bike shops include Willie's Sport Shop (☎ 736-9994) at 113 W Main St and The Spokesman (☎ 748-6563) 1667 N National Ave, Chehalis.

There's an Internet cafe at 811 W Main St.

Things to See & Do Downtown has many interesting examples of early-20th-century architecture, notably the old **Fox Cinema** in Tower Ave. The **American Antique Furniture Market**, opposite, is worth a browse. More antique stores lie north, along Tower Ave. Note the bizarre expressionist metal creations visible from the road at the **Art Far**, corner Harrison Ave and N St, as well as the historical murals around town, especially near the station.

The **Veterans Memorial Museum** (☎ 330-7913), at 712 W Main St, exhibits service memorabilia. It was to move to Chehalis at the time of research. Also in Chehalis, the **Lewis County Historical Museum** (☎ 748-0831), 599 NW Front Way, in the old railway depot, depicts the sometimes violent history of the area.

Centralia holds an **Oktoberfest** at the fairgrounds on the south side of town.

Places to Stay & Eat Camp at city-operated ***Rotary Riverside Park*** *(☎ 736-7687, cnr Lowe & Harrison Aves)*, at the northern end of town. Self-registration hiker/biker sites cost $8 per person.

Riverside Motel *(☎ 736-4632, 614 Harrison Ave)* has doubles from $38; ***Park Motel*** *(☎ 736-9333, 1011 Belmont Ave)* charges $45; while ***Ferryman's Inn*** *(☎ 330-2094, 1003 Eckerson Rd)*, close to I-5, charges $48.

Grocery stores include ***Safeway*** *(1129 Harrison Ave)* and ***B&D Market*** *(601 N Tower)*. The usual fast-food restaurants spread along Harrison Ave around the I-5 underpass. Try ***Shari's*** *(☎ 736-0161, 933 Harrison Ave)*, open 24 hours.

Closer to downtown, ***Papa Ray's Family Cafe*** *(☎ 736-1188, 719 W Main St)* opens early and closes late.

A Centralia institution well worth a visit, the ***Olympic Club*** *(☎ 736-5164, 112 N Tower Ave)* is an atmospheric old bar and cafe dating from the 1910s.

Day 7: Centralia to Kelso

5–9 hours, 55.7mi

The route traverses mostly agricultural land, gradually gaining about 350ft to peak slightly above 450ft at 4.4mi. It then undulates, gradually losing the height after about 20mi. ***Stores*** near the Jackson House (19.2mi), at Toledo (27.2mi) and around Castle Rock (43.5mi) sell food. Take care at 11.6mi, when the road plummets down a short, steep grade signposted at 16%.

Matilda Jackson State Park, on the right at 18.8mi, has picnic tables. At 19.2mi, 0.1mi past a ***store*** at the US Hwy 12 crossing, is **Jackson House Historic Site**, which also has picnic facilities. The restored house was built in 1845 by John R Jackson, one of the first white settlers north of the Columbia River. The Jackson Hwy, which the ride uses, follows parts of the Cowlitz Trail. This led north from the Oregon Trail used by 19th-century pioneers traveling from Missouri to the west.

At 20.2mi, interpretive panels beside the road explain the complexities of **old-growth forest** environments and the interrelationship of its inhabitants.

Lewis and Clark State Park, on the right at 20.8mi, has camping but is closed between October and March. Views to the east at 23.6mi reveal volcanic Mt St Helens.

At 24.7mi, on the corner of Spencer Rd, a plaque commemorates the **Cowlitz Mission Site**, the first mission to bring Christianity to the natives, which was founded here in 1838. On the left at 28mi, the ***South Cowlitz County Regional Park*** has camping. At 31.5mi, Mandy Rd closely follows the Cowlitz River.

Near I-5 and on the left of Old Pacific Hwy, ***Paradise Cove RV Park*** (39.3mi; ☎ 274-6785) has tent sites for $14, RVs for hire at $18 and a small ***store***.

Side Trip: Mt St Helens Visitor Center

10.5mi return

Near Castle Rock, a hilly side trip northeast on Hwy 504 goes to Mt St Helens visitor center (☎ 274-2103) on Silver Lake. **Walking trails** with interpretive panels follow the lake shore with views to the still-distant 8363ft volcano that last blew its top in 1980. Inside the visitor center ($3 entry fee), displays tell the story of the eruption that changed the course of history, and of a river or two in the area (see the boxed text below). Across the road, ***Seaquest State Park*** has hiker/biker camping for $6 per person. Buy any required supplies at Castle Rock before heading here.

Kelso/Longview

☎ 360

Kelso (population 12,000) is across the Cowlitz River from its larger twin, Longview (33,000). The ride ends in Kelso but most services are at Longview. A planned industrial community established for Long-Bell Lumber Company employees in 1924, Longview was laid out in a series of concentric rings. An artificial lake and park meander through its center. The majority of logs cut from the southwest Washington forests come here to be milled or shipped from the deep-water port, mostly to Japan.

Information The Kelso Volcano & Visitor Center (☎ 577-8058) is at 105 Minor Rd, off Allen St after the Cowlitz River Bridge and the I-5 underpass. River Cities Chamber of Commerce (☎ 423-8400) is at 1563 Olympia Way, Longview.

Go to Longview for these services. Riverview County Bank is at 1011 Washington Way. Columbia Bank is on the corner of Commerce Ave and Broadway. Bob's Bicycle Shop (☎ 425-3870) is at 1111 Hudson St. Nearby Byman's Bikes (☎ 577-4481) is at 1165 Commerce Ave. The Internet Coffee House (☎ 423-3568) is at 550 27th Ave. Longview library (☎ 577-3380) is at 1600 Louisiana St.

Things to See & Do More industrial than tourist oriented, Longview/Kelso's attractions are limited. Ride along **Broadway** and through **Sacajawea Park** to get a sense of

When Mt St Helens Blew Her Stack

The most recent Mt St Helens eruption was one of steam, not lava. The molten rock that rose to the surface of the volcano during early 1980 was heavily infused with water, which at temperatures of 750°F is capable of enormous explosive power. As this piston of lava pushed closer and closer to the surface, it created a bulge on the north side of the peak that grew larger and more unstable with each passing day.

HAYDEN FOELL

On 18 May 1980, the rock finally gave way; the entire north face of Mt St Helens slid down the mountain in what geologists believe was the largest landslide in recorded history. The landslide carried mud, snow, ice and rock at speeds of 200mi/h, dumping them into Spirit Lake and 17mi down the North Fork Toutle River valley. At over 800°F, the mud-flows turned Spirit Lake into a boiling cauldron that instantly killed all fish and animal life.

Without the rock cover to hold them back, super-heated steam and gases finally broke through to the surface of the volcano, blasting a 15mi-high cloud of ash and rock into the air at speeds of 500mph. The blast hurtled through the forests north of the crater at speeds of 200mi/h, leveling 150 sq mi of forest in an instant.

The amount of mud and ash that was eventually carried downriver was enormous. Even navigation on the Columbia River was affected, as huge deposits of mud and ash closed the shipping channels between Portland and the Pacific for many weeks.

In the end, 59 people were killed in the blast while another 190 who were within the affected zone lived through the eruption. Almost 1000 people who lived mainly along the Toutle River were left homeless. Downwind from the eruption, several inches of ash settled between Yakima and Spokane, disrupting everyday life for months. While Mt St Helens has remained calm since 1980, geologists concur that another explosion is only a matter of time.

Bill McRae

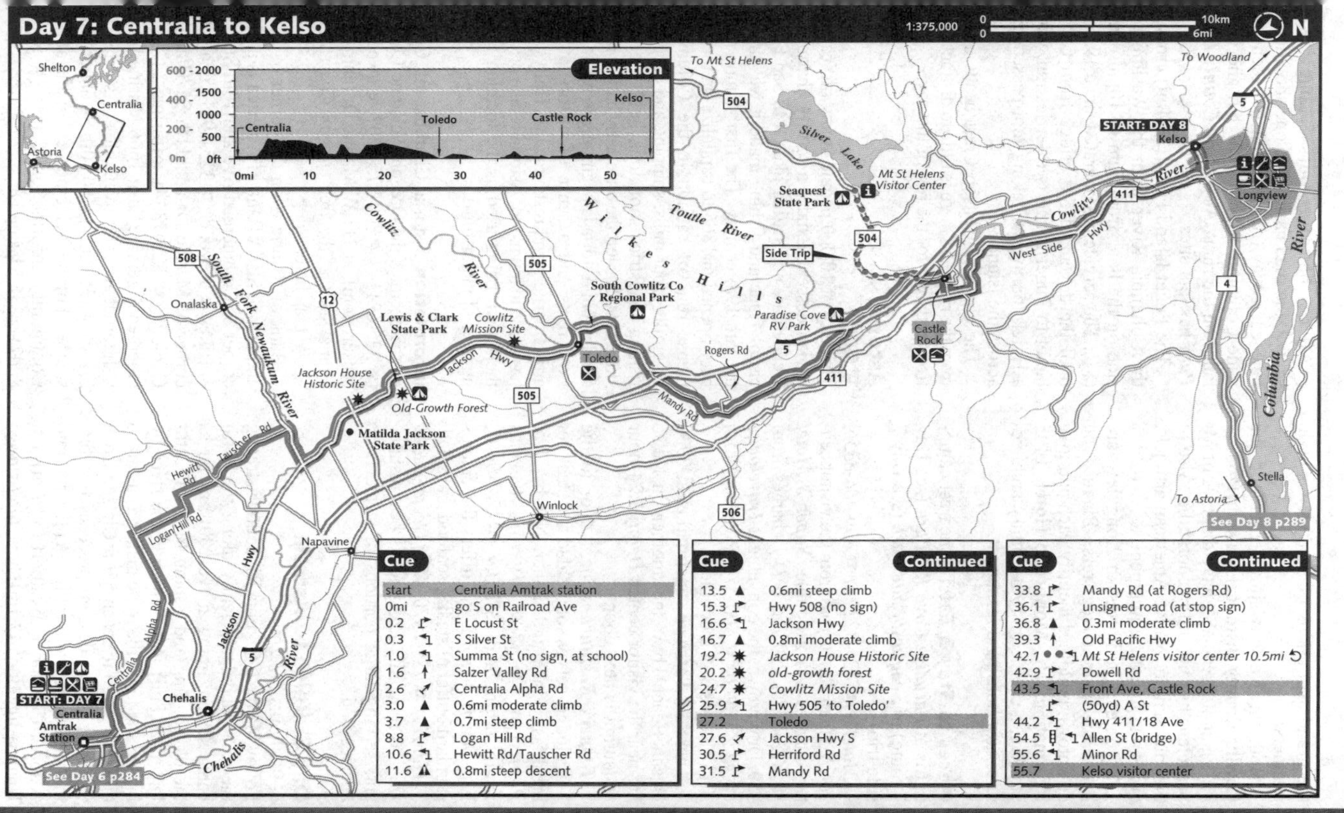
Day 7: Centralia to Kelso
1:375,000
0 10km
0 6mi
N
Shelton
Centralia
Astoria
Kelso
Elevation
600 - 2000
1500
400 - 1000
200 - 500
0m 0ft
Centralia
Toledo
Castle Rock
Kelso
0mi 10 20 30 40 50
To Mt St Helens
504
Silver Lake
Seaquest State Park
Mt St Helens Visitor Center
Side Trip
To Woodland
5
START: DAY 8
Kelso
Longview
411
Cowlitz River
West Side Hwy
4
Columbia River
Stella
To Astoria
See Day 8 p289
Wilkes Hills
Toutle River
Cowlitz River
508
South Fork Newaukum River
Onalaska
12
505
South Cowlitz Co Regional Park
Lewis & Clark State Park
Cowlitz Mission Site
Jackson Hwy
Toledo
Paradise Cove RV Park
Castle Rock
Rogers Rd
Mandy Rd
Jackson House Historic Site
Old-Growth Forest
Matilda Jackson State Park
Tauscher Rd
Hewitt Rd
Logan Hill Rd
Winlock
506
Napavine
Alpha Rd
Centralia
Chehalis
Chehalis
START: DAY 7
Centralia Amtrak Station
See Day 6 p284
Cue
start Centralia Amtrak station
0mi go S on Railroad Ave
0.2 E Locust St
0.3 S Silver St
1.0 Summa St (no sign, at school)
1.6 Salzer Valley Rd
2.6 Centralia Alpha Rd
3.0 0.6mi moderate climb
3.7 0.7mi steep climb
8.8 Logan Hill Rd
10.6 Hewitt Rd/Tauscher Rd
11.6 0.8mi steep descent
Cue Continued
13.5 0.6mi steep climb
15.3 Hwy 508 (no sign)
16.6 Jackson Hwy
16.7 0.8mi moderate climb
19.2 Jackson House Historic Site
20.2 old-growth forest
24.7 Cowlitz Mission Site
25.9 Hwy 505 'to Toledo'
27.2 Toledo
27.6 Jackson Hwy S
30.5 Herriford Rd
31.5 Mandy Rd
Cue Continued
33.8 Mandy Rd (at Rogers Rd)
36.1 unsigned road (at stop sign)
36.8 0.3mi moderate climb
39.3 Old Pacific Hwy
42.1 Mt St Helens visitor center 10.5mi
42.9 Powell Rd
43.5 Front Ave, Castle Rock
(50yd) A St
44.2 Hwy 411/18 Ave
54.5 Allen St (bridge)
55.6 Minor Rd
55.7 Kelso visitor center

the grand aspirations of Longview's civic planners.

Both the Kelso visitor center and the **Cowlitz County Historical Museum** (☎ 577-3119), at 405 Allen St, have displays of Mt St Helens history and memorabilia. Also in the museum are Native American artifacts, quilts and logging equipment.

Seventeen buildings in Longview are listed on historic registers. Plaques on downtown buildings identify each and give information. The **Monticello Hotel**, 1405 7th Ave, a classic of 19th-century architecture, now housing a restaurant.

Places to Stay & Eat The nearest camping is at ***Paradise Cove RV Park*** (see Day 7 route) or ***Seaquest State Park*** (see Day 7 side trip).

Motel 6 *(☎ 425-3229 or ☎ 800-466-8356, 106 N Minor Rd)*, across from the visitor center, charges $44 a double. ***Super 8 Motel*** *(☎ 423-8880, 250 Kelso Dr)* charges from $59. Downtown, the convenient ***Travelodge*** *(☎ 423-6460 or ☎ 800-578-7878, 838 15th Ave)* charges $45 a double.

There's a ***Safeway*** supermarket at 2930 Ocean Beach Hwy and another on Kelso Dr, near the visitor center. ***Denny's*** 24-hour restaurant is next door.

Toppers Restaurant, next door to the Travelodge, serves soup, salad and steak for breakfast, lunch and dinner. Nearby, ***The Pantry*** *(☎ 425-8880, 919 15th Ave)* has family dining and a ***Sizzler*** *(☎ 577-0607, 936 Ocean Beach Hwy)* offers the chain's standard buffet of steaks, seafood and salad.

Henri's *(☎ 425-7970, 4545 Ocean Beach Hwy)* is reputedly Longview's best restaurant, serving large portions of steak, lamb and seafood.

Day 8: Kelso to Astoria

5–9¼ hours, 57.2mi

Following the Columbia River downstream, the route undulates gently along the north bank, seldom going above 200ft, as far as the old logging and fishing town of Cathlamet (26.8mi). After crossing the river by bridge and ferry, the route makes a sustained climb of 2.3mi to reach 656ft Clatsop Crest (35.2mi). A fast descent precedes two further climbs before the final gentler run into Astoria. Cathlamet, Westport (30.9mi) and Knappa Junction (42.1mi) have ***food stores***.

After a 6mi drag out of Longview's sprawl, the road narrows to one shouldered lane each way, running flat between the wide Columbia River on the left and wetlands on the right. At 16.7mi, ***County Line Park*** has tent sites.

The Puget Island Ferry (30.4mi) crosses the Columbia River from the Washington side on the hour from 5am to 10pm daily ($1). The service has operated since 1925 – until the advent of the bridge from Cathlamet to Puget Island two ferries ran, with a Buick touring car taking foot passengers across the island.

The climb to Clatsop Crest heads away from the river and there is little to distract you from pedaling for the rest of the day.

Astoria

☎ 503

This city of 10,000 people, many of Scandinavian descent, exudes a scruffy charm. Its architecture and setting liken it to San Francisco. Trade and fishing made it wealthy in the late 19th century. The first salmon cannery opened in 1866 to capitalize on the immense runs of salmon in the Columbia. Sawmills, flour mills, shipping and deep-sea fishing industries soon took hold. Decline since 1900 has left the once-busy harbor near-derelict but Astoria is beginning to revitalize. Low rents and a sense of history attract artists, writers and restaurateurs. Hollywood has come to town, too; Astorians take pride in their town being used as the location for a number of major films.

Information Astoria Chamber of Commerce operates the Oregon Welcome Center (☎ 325-6311 or ☎ 800-875-6807, e awacc@seasurf.com), at 111 W Marine Dr (entry off Hume St). Get the free *Oregon Coast Bike Route* map here.

Bank of Astoria is on the corner of 11th and Duane Sts. A Bank of America is at the corner of Commercial Ave and 10th St.

Bikes & Beyond (☎ 325-2961) is at the corner of Marine Dr and 11th St. Hauer's Cyclery (☎ 325-7334), offering 24-hour emergency service, is at 1606 Marine Dr.

Internet access is available at Astoria Library (☎ 325-7323), 450 10th St, about 1mi southeast of the Welcome Center; and at the Community Information Center (☎ 325-8502), 1335 Marine Dr.

Day 8: Kelso to Astoria

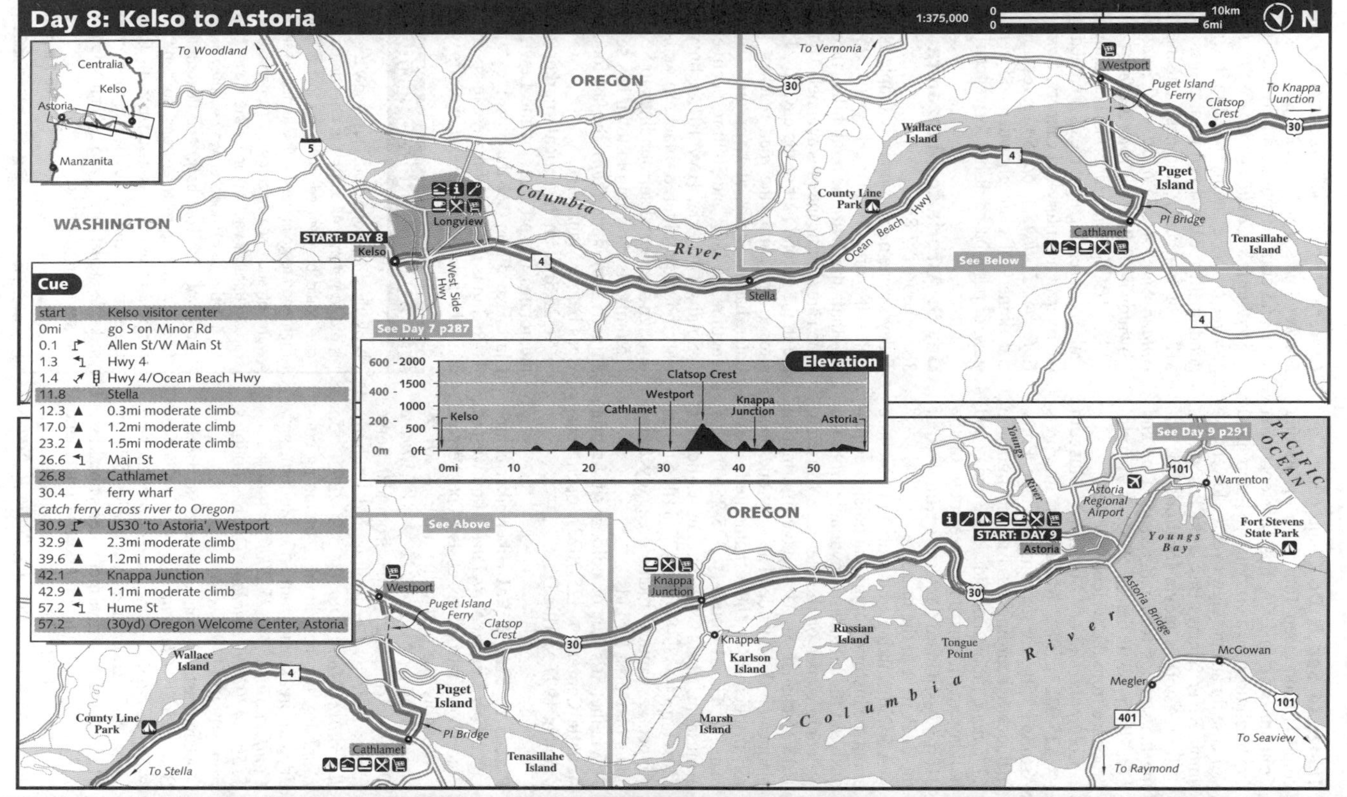

Cue

start		Kelso visitor center
0mi		go S on Minor Rd
0.1	↱	Allen St/W Main St
1.3	↰	Hwy 4
1.4	↗	Hwy 4/Ocean Beach Hwy
11.8		Stella
12.3	▲	0.3mi moderate climb
17.0	▲	1.2mi moderate climb
23.2	▲	1.5mi moderate climb
26.6	↰	Main St
26.8		Cathlamet
30.4		ferry wharf
catch ferry across river to Oregon		
30.9	↱	US30 'to Astoria', Westport
32.9	▲	2.3mi moderate climb
39.6	▲	1.2mi moderate climb
42.1		Knappa Junction
42.9	▲	1.1mi moderate climb
57.2	↰	Hume St
57.2		(30yd) Oregon Welcome Center, Astoria

Things to See & Do Climb 600ft Coxcomb Hill on steep 16th St to the **Astoria Column**. Built in 1926, this 125-foot tower can be climbed on a dizzying 164-step spiral staircase for an epic view over the lower Columbia River, Youngs Bay and Clatsop Spit.

Tour Astoria's **movie locations**, including the settings for *Kindergarten Cop* and *Free Willy*, with the $1 'Shot in Astoria' brochure from the welcome center.

Columbia River Maritime Museum (☎ 325-2323), 1792 Marine Dr, interprets Astoria's 150-year seafaring heritage. Entry includes a boarding pass to the lightship *Columbia*, moored outside. On Sunday and holiday afternoons, take free tours of the 210ft Coast Guard Cutter *Alert*, moored at the dock next to the museum.

A $3.50 walking-tour map and brochure about the **historic homes** that poise precipitously on the hillsides is available from the welcome center or the Heritage Museum, 1618 Exchange St. Most have information plaques on the outside. The only one open for inspection is the ornamented 1880s mansion, **Flavel House** (☎ 325-2563), now a museum, at 441 8th St. The **Children's Museum** (☎ 325-8669), 475 11th St, has puppets, a nautical theme area, toy trains and a play area for kids.

Whether it's hot or cold, visit **Astoria Aquatic Center** (☎ 325-7027), open yearround at 1997 Marine Dr.

Places to Stay & Eat Hiker/biker camping at ***Fort Stevens State Park***, 10mi west of Astoria on Clatsop Spit, costs $4 per person.

Probably the best-value motel is ***Rivershore Motel*** *(☎ 325-2921, 59 W Marine Dr)*, which has big doubles from $50. Some rooms have two bedrooms and kitchens. ***Bayshore Motor Inn*** *(☎ 325-2205, 555 Hamburg Ave)* has doubles, including continental breakfast, from $57. Modern, new ***Comfort Suites*** *(☎ 325-2000 or ☎ 800-228-5150, 3420 Leif Erickson Dr)* has doubles from $69 to $149.

Many historic homes operate as B&Bs. Bike-friendly ***Clementine's*** *(☎ 325-2005 or ☎ 800-521-6801, ⓔ jtaylor@clementines-bb.com, 847 Exchange St)* charges $70 to $135, including a gourmet biker's breakfast.

The ***Safeway*** supermarket is on Duane St, near 11th St. For organic produce, deli items and sandwiches, try ***Natural Foods Grocery*** *(1389 Duane St)*. ***Astoria Public Market*** *(cnr 9th St & Marine Dr)* sells produce and crafts (9am–2pm Sat, May–Oct).

Stephanie's Cabin *(☎ 325-7181, 12 W Marine Dr)* is a family restaurant serving good-quality seafood and meat dishes from $12. For northern Cantonese cuisine, try ***Golden Star*** *(☎ 325-6260, 599 Bond St)*. Downtown, ***T Paul's Urban Cafe*** *(☎ 338-5133, 1119 Commercial St)* is a casually upscale place serving light meals. Perched over the river in a century-old cannery, ***Cannery Cafe*** *(☎ 325-8642, 1 6th St)* serves lunches and dinners of clam chowder and venison stew, or pasta-based dishes for vegetarians.

Day 9: Astoria to Manzanita

3¼–6 hours, 37.8mi

Today's route navigation is as simple as possible – it's virtually all on Hwy 101. Balancing that, there are several hills, three of which are significant, plus a tunnel. All these are in the second half of the day. At 21.6mi, after a 3mi climb, the road reaches 400ft. Later, harder climbs of 1.7mi and 2.3mi in length reach 480ft and 500ft respectively.

South of Astoria, Hwy 101, a busy but flat, wide-shouldered blacktop, charges through semi-rural surroundings to Seaside (15.6mi). Its pleasant old town has several attractive ***cafes*** and ***shops***, the last food services before Manzanita.

At 22.3mi an **historical marker** commemorates the progress of the Lewis and Clark Expedition (see the boxed text, p15). At 26.2mi is the first of many viewpoints to coastal sea stacks, beaches and bluffs while,

This Ocean is Not So Pacific

Look, I'm not paranoid but I just know the sea is out to get me. All along the Oregon coast, one could be excused for being just a little frightened to go in the water. Numerous signs warn of such sea hazards as tsunami (ride rapidly uphill if you see one – the wave, that is, not the sign), sneaker waves (they'll get you if you turn your back) and floating logs (these weigh up to three tons, so don't be tempted to use one as a surf board). Then there's the rip current, cold water, submerged rocks, territorial surfers and…damn, I forgot my swimming costume!

Neil Irvine

2.6mi later, a marker explains the derivation of Cannon Beach's name. Nearby is the one of many, many little blue signs along the coast identifying tsunami evacuation routes. (It is remarkable, considering the inevitability of tsunamis, how many houses are built right on the beaches.)

The coast route's first tunnel (30.1mi) is well lit. The deafening noise traffic makes inside is alarming. Outside, a cyclist-operated button activates flashing lights to warn motorists.

Around 34mi, the road traverses Oswald West State Park, a forest of tall straight trees, which on a dull day can create an atmosphere of gloomy foreboding. West, Governor of Oregon from 1911 to 1915, was instrumental in the preservation of public access to 400mi of the state's coast from the Columbia River to California.

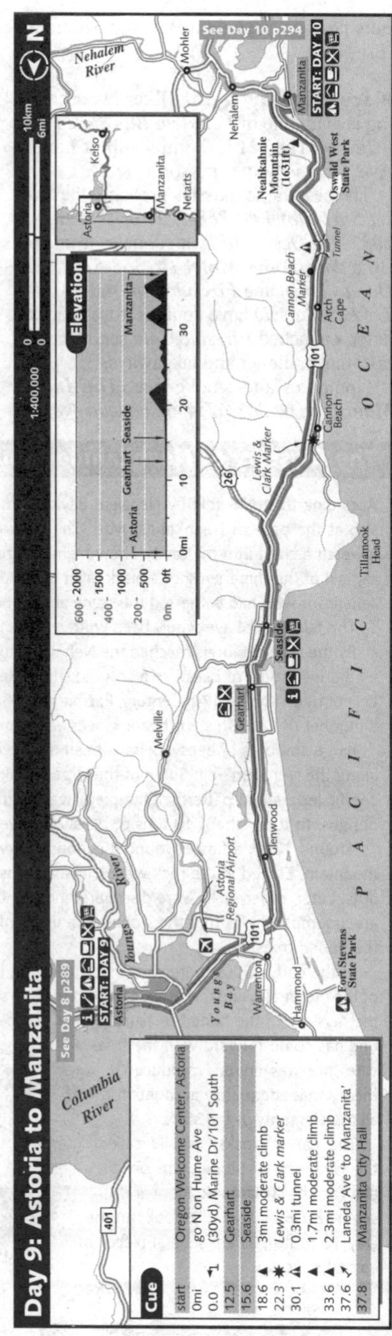

Manzanita

☎ 503

Tiny Manzanita (the name means 'little apple', from a dwarf plant common along the coast), with about 500 citizens, lies on the ocean side of the sand spit protecting Nehalem Bay. Jagged peaks of the nearby Coast Range reach 3000ft while, visible to the north of town, **Neahkahnie Mtn** (see the boxed text, p292) stands in 700ft cliffs in the Pacific waters. White-sand beaches stretch from the mountain to the end of Nehalem Spit.

Information Limited tourist information and brochures are available from Manzanita motels. There's a US Bank on the corner of Laneda and 5th Aves, but no bike shop. Internet access is available at the Oregon Coast Cyber Cafe (☎ 368-4411) at 183 Laneda Ave, behind the grocery store.

Things to See & Do Nehalem Bay State Park features **hiking** and **biking trails**. (It even has an airport for fly-in campers.)

Kayaks are available for hire by experienced users from Nehalem Bay Kayak Co (☎ 368-6055 or ☎ 877-529-2526) at 395 Hwy 101, Wheeler, or the company offers guided paddling tours.

Wine tastings are held daily at **Nehalem Bay Winery** (☎ 368-9463) about 1mi off Hwy 101 at 34965 Hwy 53, Nehalem.

The **Oregon Coast Tourist Train** (☎ 800-685-1719), a restored vintage diesel railcar, runs between Nehalem Bay and Tillamook (Fri–Sun).

Places to Stay & Eat Hiker/biker camping is available in ***Nehalem Bay State Park***, 0.2mi off Hwy 101, 0.8mi south of Laneda Ave. Cost is $4 per person.

The best-value motel is probably the ***Sunset Surf Motel*** *(☎ 368-5224 or ☎ 800-243-8035, 248 Ocean Rd)*, with doubles from $60. Both ***San Dune Motel*** *(☎ 368-5163, 428 Dorcas Lane)* and ***Fireside Inn*** *(☎ 368-1001, 114 Laneda Ave)* have doubles from $65. The latter's attached ***Fireside Cafe*** serves breakfast, lunch, dinner and takeaways.

Upmarket and smoke-free, ***The Inn at Manzanita*** *(☎ 368-6754, 67 Laneda Ave)* has rooms with spa and view deck from $105 to $150. ***The Arbors B&B*** *(☎ 368-7566 or ☎ 888-664-9587, e arbors@nehalemtel.net, 78 Idaho Ave)* charges $105 to $115 a double.

Manzanita Grocery & Deli *(193 Laneda Ave)* is open to 9pm. ***Manzanita News & Espresso*** *(500 Laneda Ave)* sells sandwiches, bakery items and environmentally sound shade-grown coffee.

Cassandra's Pizza *(☎ 368-5593, 60 Laneda Ave)* sells vegetarian and healthy pizzas. Locally recommended restaurants include ***Blue Sky Cafe*** *(☎ 368-5712, 154 Laneda Ave)*, which uses quality organic ingredients in a varied menu, and ***Left Coast Siesta*** *(☎ 368-7997, 288 Laneda Ave)*, serving fast, healthy, fresh Mexican-American

The Mystery of Neahkahnie Mountain

According to stories told by Nehalem Bay's Tillamook and Clatsop tribes, a Spanish ship landed long ago at the base of Neahkahnie Mtn. The crew dug a deep hole in the side of the mountain and lowered a chest into the cavity. Crew members placed heavy bags inside the chest and sealed it. The captain of the ship then shot a black sailor and laid his body on the chest before burying it. The Native Americans who had witnessed the scene abandoned the site, fearing the spirits of the murdered man.

This tale might have simply been written off as folklore, if it wasn't for a series of uncanny incidents.

By the time explorers reached the Nehalem Bay area, the tribes along northern Oregon had gathered a great deal of beeswax along the shore. Beeswax, used in candle making, was a common article of trade aboard 17th-century, Pacific-going Spanish vessels. Old shipping records document that a number of Spanish ships bearing beeswax were lost in the northern Pacific.

Large amounts of beeswax have been discovered along the northern coast of Oregon, especially along the Nehalem Spit. Some of the large chunks of beeswax found on the coast were carved with cryptic letters and patterns. One piece was engraved with the date 1679, others with crosses and designs. In total, about 10 tons of beeswax have been uncovered along the Oregon coast.

Around 1890, a farmer found a curiously carved rock in a meadow on the southern face of the mountain. Etched in the rock were Christian crosses, the letters D, E and W, arrows and a series of dots. Later, other rocks were discovered nearby that repeated the letters and designs. The immediate assumption was that the stones contained information that would, if properly decoded, lead to the buried treasure.

In the early 1900s there was a lot of digging in the side of the mountain, and many people claim to have solved the mystery of the buried treasure. However, noone has come forward with the treasure, nor has anyone produced a theory that adequately accounts for all the elements of the story.

The carved rocks, usually called the Neahkahnie Stones, are on display at the **Tillamook Pioneer Museum** (2106 2nd St, Tillamook, on the Day 10 route), as are several pieces of etched beeswax.

Bill McRae

HUGH D'ANDRADE

food. ***Sea Shack*** *(☎ 368-7897; 380 Marine Dr, Wheeler)* serves steak and seafood lunches and dinner.

Day 10: Manzanita to Netarts

3½–6½ hours, 40.1mi

The ride is mostly flat and often forested, with the only significant climbing on the Cape Meares loop after Tillamook (26.4mi), the last source of food before Netarts. A 1.2mi steep climb from sea level at 33.5mi reaches 530ft and two other easier hills follow after descents.

An **historical marker** at 15.8mi commemorates Captain Robert Gray's landing in August 1788. He was the first American in recorded history to set foot on Oregon's shore. Garibaldi's ***bakery*** (16.7mi) is worth a stop for morning tea.

Around Tillamook, rural scenery prevails. Ride within sight of beaches and bays until, nearer the town, grazing paddocks are backed by forested hills often wreathed in fog and low cloud. At 24.5mi, **Tillamook Cheese Factory** (☎ 815-1300) offers free self-guided tours, plus tastings, with cheese at low prices from its outlet store. The farmer-owned co-op was established in 1909. Opposite, across the factory parking lot, is the town's Chamber of Commerce/visitor center (☎ 842-7525, ⓔ tillchamber@wcn.net).

At 28.1mi, the route joins the delightful, well-signposted **Three Capes Scenic Route** – Capes Meares, Lookout and Kiwanda. The first section is flat with light traffic outside the high season, but rough and narrow without a shoulder.

Side Trip: Tillamook Naval Air Station Museum

8.4mi return

At Tillamook, stay on Hwy 101 for about 2mi, turning left onto rough, narrow Long Prairie Rd (where an ex-Navy jet is poised on a pedestal). After 650yd or so, turn right onto Blimp Blvd, following signs to the hangar. Flight fans will be in seventh heaven at **Tillamook Naval Air Station Museum** (☎ 503-842-1130; $8 per adult). The largest wooden building (1000ft by 296ft by 173ft) in the world, a hangar built for WWII airships, houses a great collection of military aircraft. WWI propeller-driven biplanes rub wings with WWII medium bombers and fighters (including the legendary P51 Mustang) as well as present-day, high-tech jet strike aircraft. Scenic flights (☎ 842-1942) take off from the adjacent airstrip.

Side Trip: Cape Meares Lighthouse

1.2mi return

At 35.4mi, on the right at the top of a hill, a dead-end road leads west and nearly 200ft down to **Cape Meares lighthouse**, about 0.6mi away. Additional attractions are dramatic views and wildlife spotting. From the same point, a Cape Meares walking track accesses a **'Big Spruce'**, roughly 200ft high. It's about a 10-minute return walk.

Netarts

☎ 503

Pronounced 'nee-tarts', this tiny coastal community nestles near the mouth of Netarts Bay and is happily untouristed.

Information The Terimore Motel (see Places to Stay & Eat) has limited tourist information. There is no bank, bike shop or public Internet access.

Things to See & Do Activities focus on the sea and the area is known for its excellent clamming and salmon fishing. Crabbing and beachcombing are also popular.

Rent a **boat** at Bayshore RV Park (see Places to Stay & Eat). Across the narrow bay, **sea lions** can be viewed.

Whiskey Creek Fish Hatchery (☎ 815-2555), signposted left off the Day 11 route 3.3mi south of town, can be inspected.

Places to Stay & Eat The ***Bayshore RV Park*** *(☎ 842-4012)*, on the left 1mi along the Day 11 route, charges $19 for tent sites. At 5.7mi on the right is the entry road for ***Cape Lookout State Park*** where hiker/biker camping costs $4 per person.

Sea Lion Motel *(☎ 842-5477, 4951 Hwy 6)* has large doubles with kitchens for $59. ***The Terimore*** *(☎ 842-4623 or ☎ 800-635-1821, 5105 Crab Ave)* has doubles from $45. Rooms with views cost $59 to $65. ***Edgewater Motel*** *(☎ 842-1300 or ☎ 888-425-1050, 1020 1st St W)* has luxury cabin units with ocean views and kitchens for $92.

Bayside Market *(Crab Ave)* has a reasonable selection of foods and is open until at least 8pm. Another ***grocery*** is a few yards south of Crab Ave on Hwy 6.

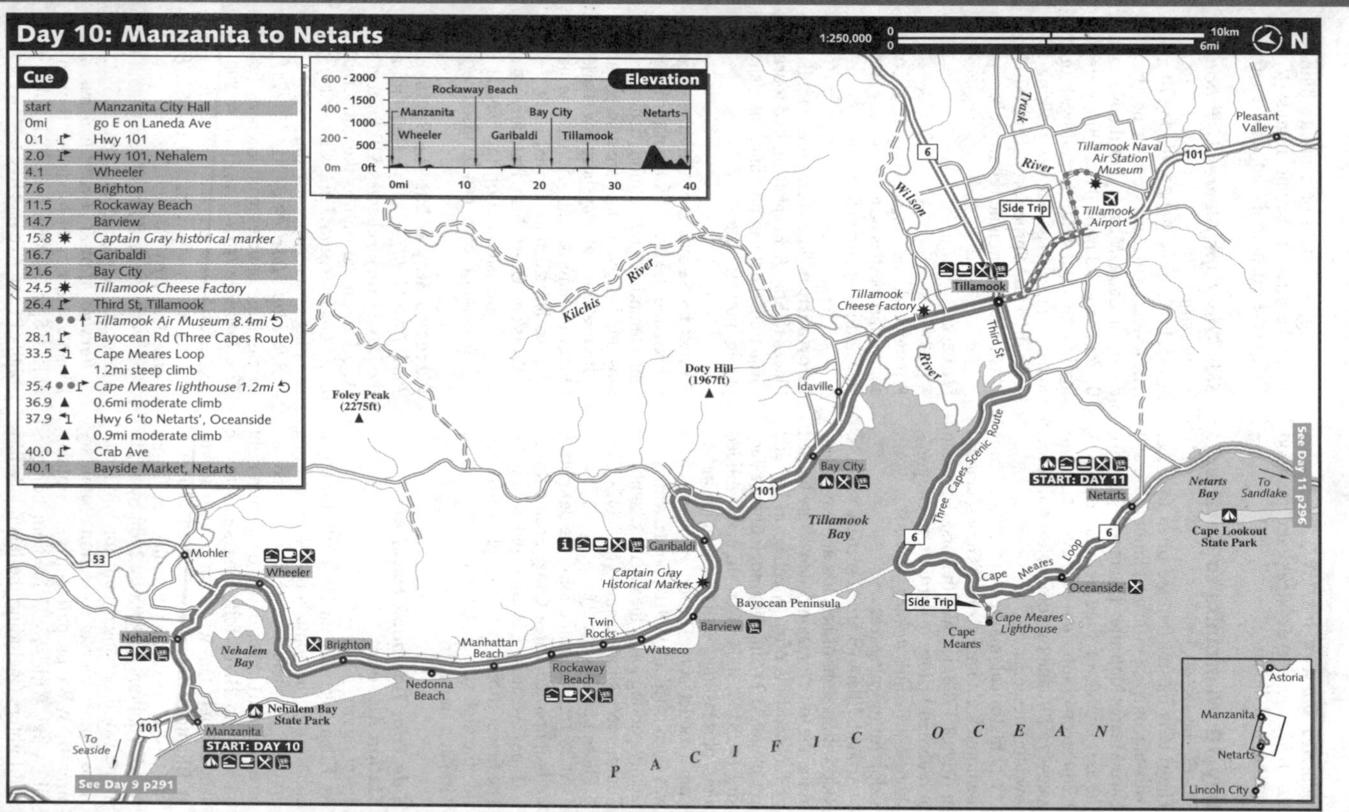
Day 10: Manzanita to Netarts
1:250,000
0
10km
0
6mi
N
Cue
start Manzanita City Hall
0mi go E on Laneda Ave
0.1 Hwy 101
2.0 Hwy 101, Nehalem
4.1 Wheeler
7.6 Brighton
11.5 Rockaway Beach
14.7 Barview
15.8 Captain Gray historical marker
16.7 Garibaldi
21.6 Bay City
24.5 Tillamook Cheese Factory
26.4 Third St, Tillamook
Tillamook Air Museum 8.4mi
28.1 Bayocean Rd (Three Capes Route)
33.5 Cape Meares Loop
1.2mi steep climb
35.4 Cape Meares lighthouse 1.2mi
36.9 0.6mi moderate climb
37.9 Hwy 6 'to Netarts', Oceanside
0.9mi moderate climb
40.0 Crab Ave
40.1 Bayside Market, Netarts
Elevation
600 - 2000
1500
400 -
1000
200 -
500
0m 0ft
0mi 10 20 30 40
Rockaway Beach
Manzanita
Wheeler
Bay City
Garibaldi
Tillamook
Netarts
Trask
River
Wilson
River
Pleasant Valley
Tillamook Naval Air Station Museum
Tillamook Airport
Side Trip
Tillamook
Tillamook Cheese Factory
Third St
Kilchis River
Doty Hill (1967ft)
Foley Peak (2275ft)
Idaville
Three Capes Scenic Route
START: DAY 11
Netarts
Netarts Bay
To Sandlake
See Day 11 p296
Cape Lookout State Park
Bay City
Tillamook Bay
Garibaldi
Captain Gray Historical Marker
Mohler
Wheeler
Cape Meares Loop
Oceanside
Side Trip
Cape Meares Lighthouse
Cape Meares
Bayocean Peninsula
Barview
Twin Rocks
Watseco
Manhattan Beach
Rockaway Beach
Nehalem
Nehalem Bay
Brighton
Nedonna Beach
Nehalem Bay State Park
Manzanita
START: DAY 10
To Seaside
See Day 9 p291
PACIFIC OCEAN
Astoria
Manzanita
Netarts
Lincoln City
6
101
53

The Schooner Lounge *(☎ 842-4988)*, at Netarts Boat Basin, offers grills, steak and fish from $13. About 2mi north of town at Oceanside, the pricey, slow ***Roseanna's Cafe*** *(☎ 842-7351)* offers seafood, pasta and chicken mains for around $16.

Day 11: Netarts to Lincoln City

4¼–7¾ hours, 48mi

The day is mostly on quiet roads but is marked by a solid climb of nearly 3mi from the 5.7mi point. The route reaches a maximum altitude of 875ft after 8mi before descending. Undulations continue all day with shorter, lower climbs from sea level through forest. Another high point of nearly 700ft comes after Neskowin (30mi). Grades ease after Otis (41.1mi), finishing with a gentle rise into Lincoln City. ***Food*** is available in several towns en route.

Cape Lookout Trail (8.3mi) is an easy/moderate 4.8mi return walk to a viewpoint. About 650yd down the trail is a memorial plaque where a 1943 plane crash killed 10 servicemen.

Sandlake Recreation Area (11.6mi) is a vast area of bare sand used by off-road vehicles. ***Cape Kiwanda RV Park*** (☎ 503-965-6230; 19.6mi) has tent sites for cyclists at $4 per person. There is a ***store***, ***takeaway food*** and ***indoor accommodations*** in the immediate vicinity.

Soon after Pacific City, the route returns to busy Hwy 101 (23.4mi), winding gently up to a **viewpoint** (27mi) to the south over wetlands. From 31.2mi, quiet Slab Creek Rd, the old scenic Hwy 101, meanders inland away from the constant roar of traffic on the newer section of main road. Back on the 101 beyond Otis at (coincidentally) around 45mi, the route crosses the 45th parallel of latitude.

Lincoln City

☎ 541

Lincoln City is an urban sprawl created by the merging of five previously separate towns, Oceanlake, Delake, Taft, Cutler City, and Nelscott. Population is around 6100. It lies only 3mi south of the 45th parallel, putting it nearly exactly halfway between the equator and the north pole. It's a popular family holiday destination because of its 7mi stretch of beaches, while its outlet stores on East Devils Lake Rd at Hwy 101 attract bargain hunters.

Information The visitor center (☎ 994-8378 or ☎ 800-452-2151, Ⓦ www.lcchamber.com) is in the City Hall complex at 801 SW Hwy 101.

Bank of America is at 1931 NW Hwy 101. Wells Fargo Bank is at 2300 NE Hwy 101.

The nearest bike shop, Bike Shop (☎ 265-7824), is about 25mi away at 223 NW Nye St, Newport (a short detour off the Day 12 route).

Internet access is available at Driftwood Library (☎ 996-2277), 801 SW Hwy 101.

Things to See & Do The **North Lincoln County Historical Museum** (☎ 996-6614), 4907 SW Hwy 101, features logging exhibits.

Browse numerous **galleries** such as American Shadows (☎ 996-6887) at 825 NW Hwy 101 and, nearby, Earthworks Gallery (☎ 557-4148), 620 NE Hwy 101, offering Native American arts and crafts, glass and clay objects, watercolors and artistic jewelry.

As home to two **kite festivals** (early May & late Sept), it's not surprising the city has a kite outlet. **Catch the Wind Kites** at 266 SE Hwy 101 has a vast array of colorful models. Fly them at the beach; the main access is at D River State Wayside in the center of town where the river, officially the world's shortest at 440ft, meets the ocean.

Glass blowing is big here and the annual **Float Festival** (Oct) sees hundreds of numbered colored glass balls hidden along the beaches. It's finders keepers but notify the visitor center when you find one.

Places to Stay & Eat Close to downtown is ***Devils Lake State Recreation Area*** *(☎ 994-2002 or ☎ 800-452-5687, NE 6th Dr)*, off Hwy 101. Hiker/biker sites cost $4 per person and yurts are available.

With a huge number of motel rooms available, cheap rates can be found all over town, especially out of season and along noisy Hwy 101. ***Budget Inn*** *(☎ 994-5281, 1713 NW 21st St)*, on the corner of Hwy 101, has doubles from $47/60 weekday/weekend (Fri & Sat). More pleasant lodgings are in the motels on the quieter streets as you ride into town. Try dated but quiet ***Whistling Wind Motel*** *(☎ 994-6155 or ☎ 800-667-5993, 3264 Jetty Ave)*. Doubles, some with kitchens and jacuzzis, start at $50/55. ***The Seahorse Oceanfront Lodging*** *(☎ 994-2101 or ☎ 800-662-2101, 2039 NW Harbor Dr)* is

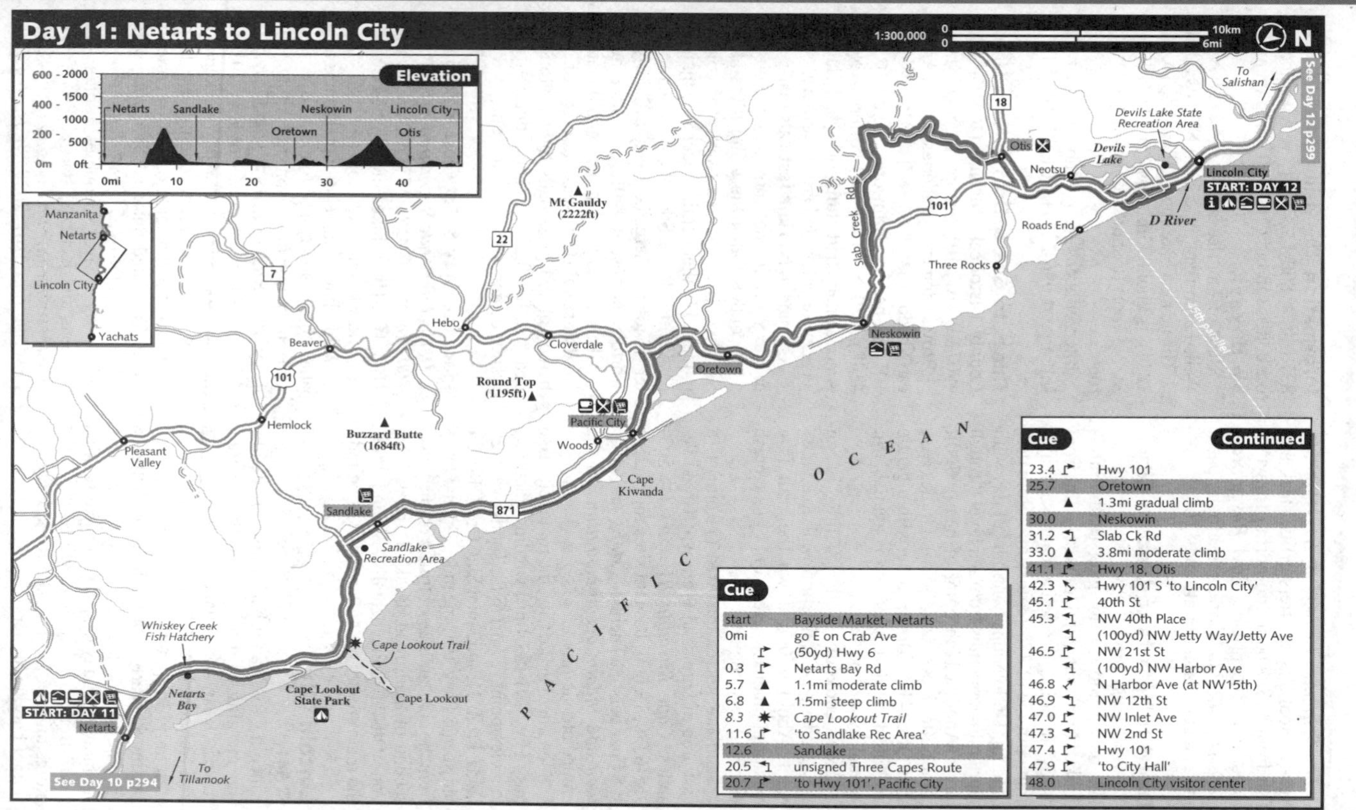
Day 11: Netarts to Lincoln City
1:300,000
10km
6mi
N
Elevation
Netarts
Sandlake
Oretown
Neskowin
Otis
Lincoln City
Manzanita
Netarts
Lincoln City
Yachats
See Day 12 p299
See Day 10 p294
START: DAY 11
START: DAY 12
Cue
start Bayside Market, Netarts
0mi go E on Crab Ave
(50yd) Hwy 6
0.3 Netarts Bay Rd
5.7 1.1mi moderate climb
6.8 1.5mi steep climb
8.3 Cape Lookout Trail
11.6 'to Sandlake Rec Area'
12.6 Sandlake
20.5 unsigned Three Capes Route
20.7 'to Hwy 101', Pacific City
Cue Continued
23.4 Hwy 101
25.7 Oretown
1.3mi gradual climb
30.0 Neskowin
31.2 Slab Ck Rd
33.0 3.8mi moderate climb
41.1 Hwy 18, Otis
42.3 Hwy 101 S 'to Lincoln City'
45.1 40th St
45.3 NW 40th Place
(100yd) NW Jetty Way/Jetty Ave
46.5 NW 21st St
(100yd) NW Harbor Ave
46.8 N Harbor Ave (at NW15th)
46.9 NW 12th St
47.0 NW Inlet Ave
47.3 NW 2nd St
47.4 Hwy 101
47.9 'to City Hall'
48.0 Lincoln City visitor center
PACIFIC OCEAN
Cape Lookout State Park
Cape Lookout Trail
Cape Lookout
Netarts Bay
Whiskey Creek Fish Hatchery
To Tillamook
Sandlake Recreation Area
Buzzard Butte (1684ft)
Round Top (1195ft)
Mt Gauldy (2222ft)
Pleasant Valley
Hemlock
Beaver
Hebo
Cloverdale
Woods
Pacific City
Cape Kiwanda
Oretown
Slab Creek Rd
Three Rocks
Roads End
Neotsu
Devils Lake
Devils Lake State Recreation Area
D River
45th parallel
To Salishan

excellent value; huge rooms with king-size beds and kitchenettes start at $68. ***Beachwood Oceanfront Motel*** *(☎ 994-8901 or ☎ 800-889-2037, 2853 NW Inlet Ave)*, entered off Jetty Ave, has ocean views; doubles start at $70. At ***Nordic Oceanfront Motel*** *(☎ 994-8145 or ☎ 800-452-3555, 2133 NW Inlet Ave)*, all rooms have sea views. Doubles cost $79.

For B&B, try the ***Brey House*** *(☎ 994-7123, 3725 NW Keel Ave)* with four rooms from around $80.

A ***Safeway*** supermarket is on the left of Logan Rd in the Lincoln City Plaza. ***Coast Health Foods*** *(2140 NW Hwy 101)* sells organic food (open Tues–Sat).

Along Hwy 101 is a wide variety of cafes and restaurants plus chains such as ***KFC***, ***Subway*** and ***Dairy Queen***. Casual ***Sungarden Cafe*** *(1826 NE Hwy 101)* caters for vegetarians, serves breakfast all day for $6, and dinner on Friday and Saturday. ***Williams Colonial Bakery*** *(1734 NE 1010)* also serves espresso coffee. ***Chameleon Cafe*** *(2185 NW Hwy 101)* serves healthy lunches and dinners. Stylish sit-down ***Galluci's Pizzeria*** *(☎ 994-3411, 2845 NW Hwy 101)* is open daily for lunch and dinner. Classy ***Blackfish Cafe*** *(☎ 996-1007,* 2733 NW Hwy 101*)*, serves seafood and grills for lunch and dinner (closed Tues).

Day 12: Lincoln City to Yachats

4½–8 hours, 49.9mi

The route is easy and flat on this leg, except for one notable climb that reaches 450ft at Otter Crest (16.1mi). Apart from Otter Crest Loop and a detour through Newport the ride is entirely on noisy Hwy 101, which has a shoulder. There are ***food stores*** roughly every 10mi and three short side trips to add interest.

Follow Hwy 101 south through Lincoln City's sprawl. The cliff at Spanish Head (1.8mi) offers fine views over Siletz Bay and Salishan Spit.

At 5.5mi, take a side trip onto Immonen Rd. Oregon's oldest glass-blowing studio, **Alder House** (☎ 541-996-2483), about 0.8mi along on the left, gives demonstrations on request. Samples and souvenirs are on sale.

Fogarty Creek State Recreation Area (9.4mi) is for day use only. **Boiler Bay** (10.7mi) has picnic tables and a viewpoint to where a coastal freight schooner exploded in 1910. Its boiler is still visible at low tide.

Depoe Bay (11.8mi) is the west coast's self-styled **'whale-watching capital'**. California Gray Whales, which measure up to 45ft and weigh 45 tons, pass here on their annual roundtrip migration between Alaska and Mexico.

At 13.8mi on the right are sea caves. Otter Crest Loop (14.2mi) is hilly but carries near-zero traffic and offers dramatic views south to the 1873 Yaquina Head lighthouse. **Otter Crest viewpoint** has a tourist information office and gift shop. Trees balance precariously on sea cliffs above caves and coastline vanishes into infinity. Adjacent **Cape Foulweather**, named by James Cook in 1778, was his first, inauspicious sight of 'New Albion', the Pacific Northwest of the American continent. Winds of up to 100mph are not unusual here and, when it's not windy, sea fogs are common.

A short side trip to **Devils Punchbowl State Natural Area** (17.4mi) reveals a collapsed sea cave and natural rock bridges. **Yaquina Head Lighthouse** is a side trip from 22.4mi. Its spectacular promontory location justifies the designation 'Outstanding Natural Area'. Prolific wildlife includes birds and sea mammals.

At 36mi on the left, **Brian McEnemy's woodcarving gallery** displays state-of-the-art chainsaw sculpture beside the road – among the large animal sculptures is Brian's depiction of himself, wielding his tool of trade.

Seal Rock (36.2mi), established in 1887, was the terminus of the first road to the coast from the Willamette Valley. Offshore, a remnant coastline of jagged volcanic rocks juts from the sea swells.

Waldport (41.4mi), first settled in 1879 on hopes of gold on the beach, now has ***food shops*** and a bike shop (see Information for Yachats, p298).

Yachats

☎ 541

This coastal town of 630 people (pronounced ya-**hots**; from the Chinook word Yahuts, meaning 'dark water at the foot of the mountain') is aptly named. It lies at the base of massive, volcanic Cape Perpetua.

The 20mi south of town are some of Oregon's most spectacular, and most windswept. Erosion-resistant basalt headlands push into the sea creating sheltered coves with little sand beaches between them.

Information Yachats Area Chamber of Commerce (☎ 547-3530 or ☎ 800-929-0477, W www.yachats.org) is at 241 Hwy 101.

Bank of the West, corner Hwy 101 and 5th St, has an ATM.

The nearest bike shop is Q's Bicycle Shop (☎ 563-5030) on Hwy 101 in Waldport (Day 12).

Log on at Shirley's (☎ 547-3292), opposite the visitor center; or at the library (☎ 547-3741; open 1–4pm Mon & Thurs–Sat).

Things to See & Do In the shape of a cross, the **Little Log Church Museum** (☎ 547-3976), 328 W 3rd St, has local historical artifacts. It was built in 1930 from local timber.

Ride the **804 Trail** at Smelt Sands State Recreation Site, 1mi north of town. The gravel coastal trail goes 3 to 4mi north along the reservation of old county road 804. Local pressure preserved it from takeover by adjoining landholders.

Visit a 1938 **covered bridge**, 8.5mi east of town. About 0.1mi south of the visitor center, turn left onto Yachats River Rd for 7mi, then turn left after crossing a concrete bridge. After another 1.4mi, the covered bridge spans the north fork of Yachats River. Built with a Queenpost-truss, it is one of the shortest in Oregon at 42ft. The visitor center has a brochure showing the locations of the 50 or so remaining covered bridges in the state.

Whale Watching

Each year, the longest migration known for any mammal takes place in the Pacific Ocean, when around 20,000 California Gray Whales make their annual 10,000mi roundtrip journey from the Arctic Sea and the warm lagoons of Baja California. Along the Oregon Coast, migration peaks in late December, when southbound whales can be spotted at the rate of about 30 an hour. Whales can also be spotted from March to May as they gradually meander back north. Most pass within 5mi of the shore and can be viewed from any coastal headland or ocean viewpoint.

Whales are air-breathing mammals and must frequently come to the surface for oxygen. They exhale with great force through a blowhole on the top of their heads, creating a warm vaporous cloud of mist (not water) 6 to 12ft high called a blow or spout. To see a blow, cast your gaze about halfway between the shore and the horizon and wait to see a burst of white mist. Blows can be seen with the naked eye but a pair of binoculars will make it much easier. Mornings and cloudy skies present the best conditions for whale watching.

Once a blow is sighted, watch for glimpses of the whale's head, knuckled back and flukes (tail). A whale's rhythmic breathing and diving usually follows a pattern of three to five short shallow dives spread one or two minutes apart, followed by one deep dive (sounding) lasting five minutes or more. A tail that breaks the surface usually indicates a sounding – watch for the whale to reappear about 300 to 400yd from where it was last sighted.

The uninitiated might find the sight of a blow unimpressive, even with a pair of binoculars. Vigilant whale watching pays off the first time a 30- to 40-ton whale is spotted breaching, propelling about half of its body out of the water, turning and splashing onto its side or back.

For a closer view, take a whale-watching trip; most ports have at least one charter operator. Roadside signs 'Whale Watching Spoken Here' indicate viewpoints staffed with volunteers who can help identify and interpret behavior. Viewpoints are typically staffed on weekends and extended holiday periods (such as Christmas and spring breaks) during the migration seasons. Visit W www.whalespoken.org for up-to-date locations and sightings.

Jennifer Snarski

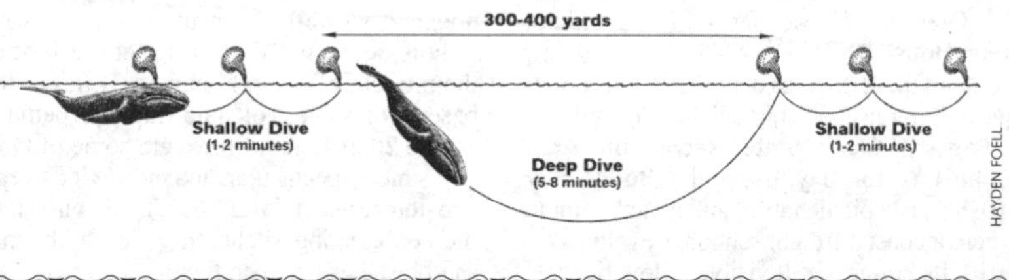

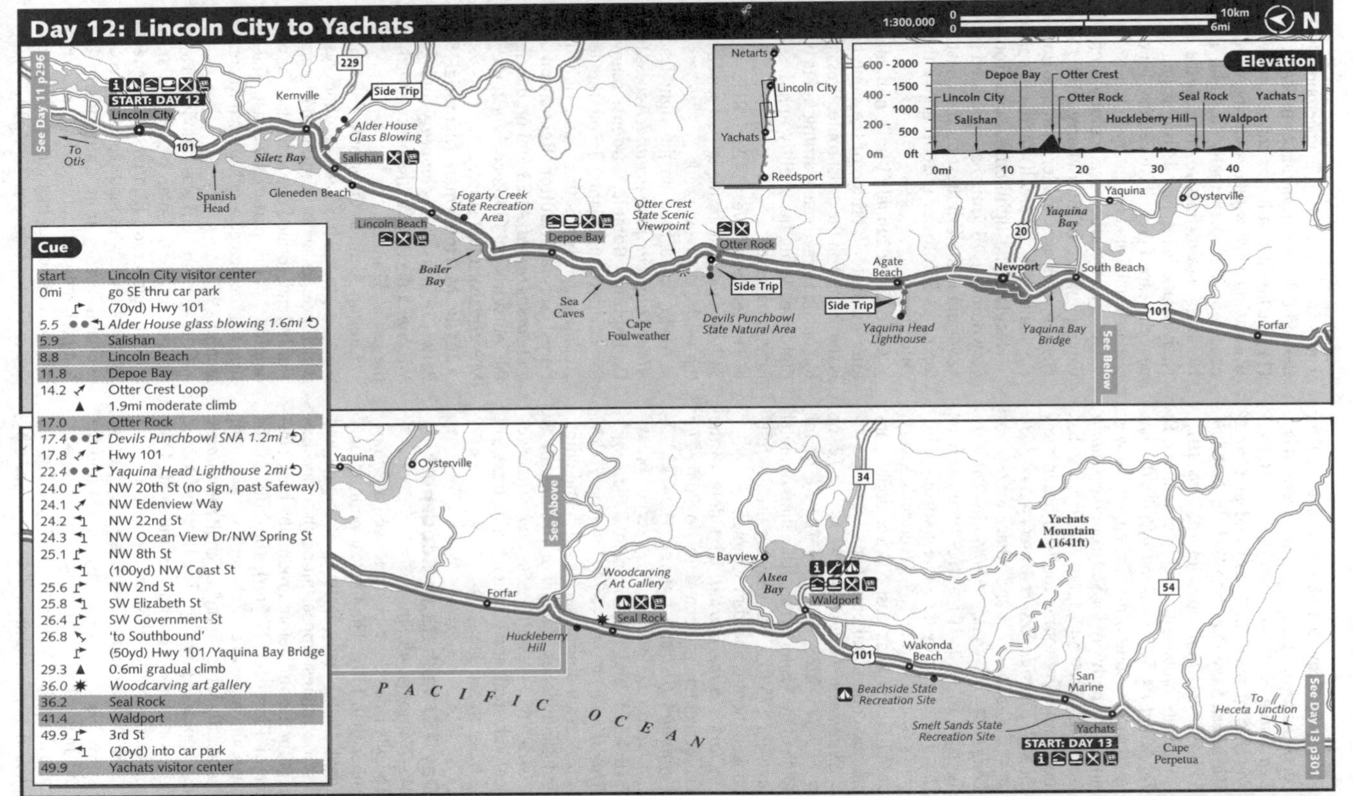
Day 12: Lincoln City to Yachats
1:300,000
0 10km
0 6mi
N
See Day 11 p296
START: DAY 12
Lincoln City
To Otis
101
Spanish Head
Kernville
229
Side Trip
Alder House Glass Blowing
Siletz Bay
Salishan
Gleneden Beach
Lincoln Beach
Fogarty Creek State Recreation Area
Boiler Bay
Depoe Bay
Sea Caves
Cape Foulweather
Otter Crest State Scenic Viewpoint
Otter Rock
Side Trip
Devils Punchbowl State Natural Area
Agate Beach
Side Trip
Yaquina Head Lighthouse
Newport
20
Yaquina Bay
Yaquina
Oysterville
South Beach
Yaquina Bay Bridge
101
Forfar
See Below
Netarts
Lincoln City
Yachats
Reedsport
Elevation
600 - 2000
400 - 1500
1000
200 - 500
0m 0ft
0mi 10 20 30 40
Lincoln City
Salishan
Depoe Bay
Otter Crest
Otter Rock
Huckleberry Hill
Seal Rock
Waldport
Yachats
Cue
start Lincoln City visitor center
0mi go SE thru car park
(70yd) Hwy 101
5.5 Alder House glass blowing 1.6mi
5.9 Salishan
8.8 Lincoln Beach
11.8 Depoe Bay
14.2 Otter Crest Loop
1.9mi moderate climb
17.0 Otter Rock
17.4 Devils Punchbowl SNA 1.2mi
17.8 Hwy 101
22.4 Yaquina Head Lighthouse 2mi
24.0 NW 20th St (no sign, past Safeway)
24.1 NW Edenview Way
24.2 NW 22nd St
24.3 NW Ocean View Dr/NW Spring St
25.1 NW 8th St
(100yd) NW Coast St
25.6 NW 2nd St
25.8 SW Elizabeth St
26.4 SW Government St
26.8 'to Southbound'
(50yd) Hwy 101/Yaquina Bay Bridge
29.3 0.6mi gradual climb
36.0 Woodcarving art gallery
36.2 Seal Rock
41.4 Waldport
49.9 3rd St
(20yd) into car park
49.9 Yachats visitor center
Yaquina
Oysterville
See Above
Forfar
Huckleberry Hill
Woodcarving Art Gallery
Seal Rock
PACIFIC OCEAN
Bayview
Alsea Bay
Waldport
34
101
Wakonda Beach
Beachside State Recreation Site
Yachats Mountain
▲(1641ft)
54
San Marine
Smelt Sands State Recreation Site
Yachats
START: DAY 13
Cape Perpetua
To Heceta Junction
See Day 13 p301

Places to Stay & Eat Hiker/biker ($4 per person) and yurt camping ($27, sleeps 6) is at ***Beachside State Recreation Site*** *(☎ 997-3641)*, 5mi north of town; and at ***Carl G Washburn State Park*** *(☎ 547-3416 or ☎ 800-551-6949)*, 11.6mi south, left off Hwy 101.

Yachats' motels fill quickly in summer. ***Ya Tel Motel*** *(☎ 547-3225, 640 Hwy 101)* has large rooms, some with kitchen, on the west side of the highway for $60 a double. ***Dublin House Motel*** *(☎ 547-3200, 251 W 7th St)* has mountain view rooms for $79, ocean view for $89. ***Fireside Resort Motel*** *(☎ 547-3636 or ☎ 800-336-3573)* and adjacent ***Overleaf Lodge*** *(☎ 547-4880, ☎ 800-338-0507)*, to the right of Hwy 101 at the 49mi mark on Day 12, are run by the same company. Fireside's rooms start at $69. Overleaf's luxury, ocean-view rooms cost $125 a double, including continental breakfast.

Shamrock Lodgettes *(☎ 547-3312* or *☎ 800-845-5028, 105 Hwy 101 S)*, 0.5mi south of the visitor center, has cabins or motel units for $75 to $118. They are usually fully booked months ahead in summer.

Clark's Supermarket, next door to the visitor center, is open daily to 9pm. ***The Landmark Bistro & Lounge*** *(☎ 547-3215, cnr Ocean Dr & Hwy 101)* serves breakfast, lunch and dinner from $7. ***Leroy's Blue Whale*** *(☎ 547-4794, 580 Hwy 101 N)* is for casual dining, serving fish and chips, and sandwiches. ***La Serre Restaurant & Bistro*** *(☎ 547-3420, 160 2nd St)* serves seafood, steak and chicken mains from $14 to $24 (closed Tues).

Day 13: Yachats to Reedsport

4½–7¾ hours, 48.8mi

Today's ride is best characterized as lumpy, rather than hilly. The highest point is only about 460ft. Many features of natural and historic interest appear along the way. Except for a 2.5mi detour around the busy center of Florence (27.7mi), the only major town, the route is entirely on Hwy 101 with a generally wide shoulder. Small ***food stores*** also appear at intervals. The latter half of the ride skirts the eastern edge of the sandy Oregon Dunes National Recreation Area.

The **Devils Churn** (2.6mi) is a deep narrow fissure, like a wedge, cut by the sea into the land. In rough weather the sea appears to boil. **Cape Perpetua Scenic Area**, 0.3mi farther, takes it name from another cape seen by James Cook in 1778. It is uncertain whether the name derives from that of the saint's day (11 Mar) on which it was charted or if Cook was having a bad wind day, during which the cape remained perpetually in sight. Black basalt gives a distinctive color to the cape. Native Americans found fishing and game near the cape before 19th-century European settlers established a military outpost.

Observe a **harbor seal colony** from the vantage point of **Strawberry Hill** (5mi). Harbor seals are smaller than sea lions or elephant seals and are distinctively spotted.

Heceta Head lighthouse, seen from the viewpoint at 13.7mi, has operated since 1894 and is the brightest on the coast. The top of its 56ft tower is 205ft above the Pacific Ocean.

Cape Creek tunnel (14mi), immediately after the historic bridge of the same name, is the second on the coast route. Press a button outside to activate warning lights before rapidly pedaling the slightly uphill, subterranean passage.

The **Sea Lion Caves** (14.8mi, RHS; ☎ 541-547-3111), said to be the largest sea caves in the world, can be viewed.

At 19.1mi a road on the right leads to ***Alder Dune camping ground***. Access to the **Darlingtonia Botanic Gardens**, renowned for carnivorous plants, is on the left at 20.8mi and, 0.1mi farther on the right, is the Forest Service's **Sutton Recreation Area** and ***campground***. At 23.5mi on the right at the outskirts of Florence is a huge Fred Meyer department store.

Jessie M Honeyman Memorial State Park (30.7mi) has ***camping*** and ***yurts***. Woahink Lake, part of the park, is visible on the left at 32.6mi.

Oregon Dunes Overlook (37.9mi) is worth a stop. The massive dune system, which extends about 45mi from Florence to North Bend, formed due to the lack of rocky outcrops on this part of the coast. The sand strip was dedicated as a National Recreation area in 1972.

Gardiner (46.6mi) was founded as a lumber port in 1850. South of town is an historical marker to frontiersman **Jedediah Smith** (48mi), who made the first recorded overland journey from California in 1828. A superb redwood forest near Crescent City is dedicated to his memory (see Things to See & Do for Crescent City, p307–9).

Day 13: Yachats to Reedsport

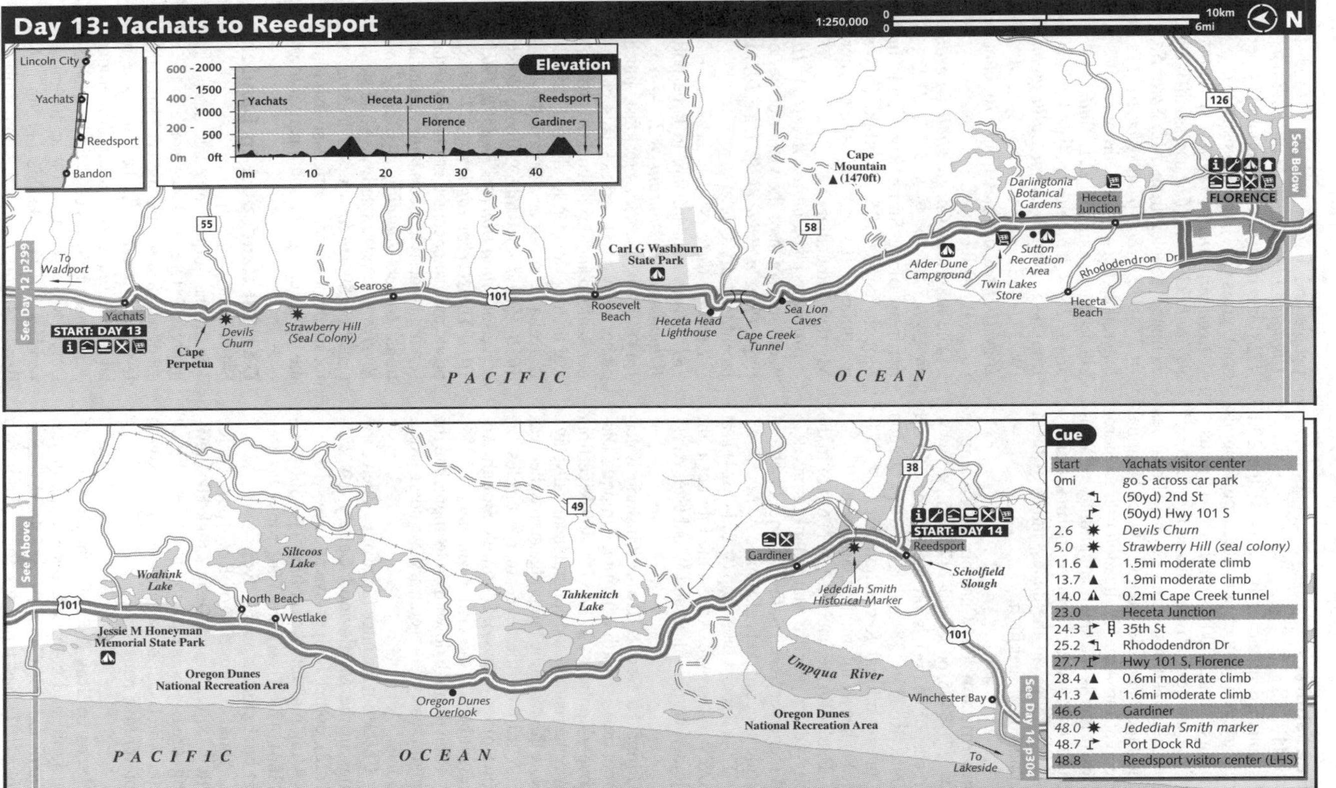

Cue

start		Yachats visitor center
0mi		go S across car park
	↰	(50yd) 2nd St
	↱	(50yd) Hwy 101 S
2.6	✸	*Devils Churn*
5.0	✸	*Strawberry Hill (seal colony)*
11.6	▲	1.5mi moderate climb
13.7	▲	1.9mi moderate climb
14.0	⚠	0.2mi Cape Creek tunnel
23.0		Heceta Junction
24.3	↱ 🚦	35th St
25.2	↰	Rhododendron Dr
27.7	↱	Hwy 101 S, Florence
28.4	▲	0.6mi moderate climb
41.3	▲	1.6mi moderate climb
46.6		Gardiner
48.0	✸	*Jedediah Smith marker*
48.7	↱	Port Dock Rd
48.8		Reedsport visitor center (LHS)

Reedsport

☎ 541

Established in the early years of the 20th century as a lumber port, Reedsport (population around 5000) is on the broad estuary of the Umpqua River. This is the center of the Oregon Dunes, with its miles of beaches and lakes, and the Oregon Dunes National Recreation Area is headquartered here. Downriver is the small community of Winchester Bay with its huge marina. Nearby are the tallest of the dunes, many of them hundreds of feet high.

Information The Chamber of Commerce (☎ 271-3495 or ☎ 800-247-2155, W www.reedsportcc.org) is on the corner of Port Dock Rd/Hwy 38 and Hwy 101. Oregon Dunes National Recreation Area (☎ 271-3611) has an information desk here.

Bank of America is at 178 N 6th St in the city center. Pacific State Bank is at 1975 Winchester Ave. Safeway and Price 'n' Pride supermarkets also have ATMs.

Bike Repairs bike shop (☎ 271-4624) is at 678 W Alder Ave. Access the Internet at the library, corner 4th St and Winchester Ave.

Things to See & Do The historic waterfront area is worth exploring. **Umpqua Discovery Center** (☎ 271-4816), 409 Riverfront Way, has natural and cultural history displays. Note the swinging rail bridge across the river.

A trail on the levee that encircles the town offers views of **Scholfield Slough**. Access it behind the visitor center.

Ride through downtown to appreciate the quaint early-20th-century wooden storefronts.

Check out the huge range of wooden carvings in the **Myrtlewood Gallery**, (☎ 274-4222), corner Juniper Ave and Hwy 101.

Umpqua Jet Adventure (☎ 800-353-8386), 423 Riverfront Way, runs two-hour **jet boat cruises** on the river.

About 3.5mi east of Reedsport beside Hwy 38, the grassy **Dean Creek Elk Viewing Area** is home to about 100 Roosevelt elk, which can be seen from turnouts with interpretive panels.

Places to Stay & Eat On the Day 14 route at 3.4mi and 6.4mi are two campgrounds. ***Surfwood RV Camp*** *(☎ 271-4020, 75381 Hwy 101)* has tent sites for $12 for two people and a ***store*** with basic food items. ***Umpqua Lighthouse State Park*** *(☎ 271-4118)* has hiker/biker camping ($4 per person), yurts ($27) and cabins ($35).

Economy Inn *(☎ 271-3671 or ☎ 800-799-9970, 1593 Hwy 101)* has small but well-equipped doubles from $42. ***Salty Seagull*** *(☎ 271-3729, 1806 Winchester Ave)* has large but rather noisy two-bedroom suites with kitchenettes from $55. ***Best Budget*** *(☎ 271-3686, 1894 Winchester Ave)* has doubles from $45. ***Best Western Salbasgeon Inn*** *(☎ 271-4831 or ☎ 800-528-1234, 1400 Hwy 101)* has doubles from $76, continental breakfast included.

The luxurious ***Cozy Cattail Guesthouse*** *(☎ 271-5444 or ☎ 877-271-4222)*, 5mi northeast along Smith River and Hudson Slough, costs $125 per night (two-night minimum). It's run by the owners of Myrtlewood Gallery.

Safeway *(Winchester Ave/Hwy 101)* is two lights south of the visitor center on the right. ***Price'n'Pride*** *(1300 Hwy 101)* is adjacent to Dairy Queen.

Leona's Cafe *(☎ 271-5297, 1501 Hwy 101)* serves standard fare in large portions. ***Windjammer Restaurant*** *(☎ 271-5415, 1281 Hwy 101)* is open for breakfast, lunch and dinner every day. It serves salads, clam chowder, seafood and shrimp cocktails with a nautical theme. Mexican food amid kitsch decor is available at ***Sol de Mexico*** *(☎ 271-0339, 1050 Hwy 101)* while Chinese cuisine is served at ***China Doll*** *(☎ 271-3590, 1903 Hwy 101)*. The ***Harbor Light*** *(☎ 271-3848)*, opposite the visitor center, is a family restaurant serving homestyle meals with vegetarian options. ***Ungers Landing*** *(☎ 271-3328, 345 Riverfront Way)* has daily fish and steak specials from $9. ***Du Bray's*** *(☎ 271-2502)*, noted for its flambé dishes, offers stylish dining at the golf course in the south part of town.

Day 14: Reedsport to Bandon

5–8¾ hours, 54.8mi

The first half of the day continues beside the impressive Oregon dunes, some of the highest of which are on the right at 21mi. Hills are few and low early on, then the route undulates from sea level to about 80ft around the 30mi mark before steep climbing on Seven Devils Rd, reaching 600ft at 40.4mi. ***Food services*** are at Lakeside (11.9mi), North Bend (24.9mi) and Charleston (34mi).

A short steep climb reaches the 65ft tower of **Umpqua River Lighthouse** (6mi; ☎ 271-4631 for tours). The existing lighthouse, built in 1891, replaced the first lighthouse in the Oregon Territory, built in 1857 at the river mouth. Across the road is a **whale-watching station** with interpretive panels and coin-operated binoculars.

Winchester Bay Wayfinding Point (a lookout at 7.4mi) has interpretive panels. **Umpqua Dunes trailhead** (12.7mi) is the start of a fascinating mile-long interpretive walk through a variety of dune ecosystems.

North Bend is home to Moe's Bike Shop (☎ 756-7536). In the back streets of North Bend, be sure to navigate carefully around the traffic island to stay on Florida Ave. Resupply at a huge ***Safeway*** (26.1mi; Virginia Ave) or fill up on candy (free tastings!) at **Cranberry Sweets Candy Factory Shop** (☎ 888-9824; 28.8mi; Newmark St).

Charleston has a ***store*** and a ***cafe***. You can rent bikes and **kayaks** at High Tide Rental (☎ 888-366).

Hilly **Seven Devils Rd** is narrow, winding, roughly surfaced but very attractive, being largely forested. Ridge-top sections offer distant views. Keep an ear out for fast-approaching traffic. The final section includes a thrilling downhill.

On the approach to Bandon, Hwy 101 crosses a busy bridge (52.3mi) without shoulders.

Side Trip: Cape Arago

11mi return

Head to rocky coast, a lighthouse and views to off-shore islands swarming with seals and sea lions on gently undulating Cape Arago Hwy. About 2mi along the return from the cape, take time to turn left (west) into **Shore Acres State Park** to see the formal gardens established in the 1920s by early Oregon entrepreneur Louis J Simpson. **Sunset Bay**, 4mi from the cape, has good hiker/biker ***camping***; ***yurts*** are also available by prior reservation (☎ 888-4902). Beautiful walking trails (part of the Oregon Coast Trail) are accessible at Sunset Bay.

Bandon

☎ 541

Bandon (population 2700) is one of the Oregon coast's real gems. Its Old Town houses many cafes, gift shops, art galleries and taverns. Noteworthy industries include cranberry farming and cheese-making.

Information Bandon visitor center (☎ 347-9616, Ⓦ www.bandon.com) is at the corner of 2nd St and Chicago Ave.

There are ATMs at: Western Bank, corner 11th St and Hwy 101; Security Bank, 1125 Hwy 101; and Bank of America, 1110 Oregon St.

There is no bike shop. The hardware stores in town have very basic bicycle spares.

Log on at the library (☎ 347-3221) in the City Hall complex, uphill from the visitor center on the left of Hwy 101.

Things to See & Do Explore the **Old Town** between 1st and 2nd Sts and Alabama and Fillmore Aves. Crafty, arty galleries such as **Gallery Gifts** at 210 2nd St, or sweet shops like **Bandon Sweets & Treats** at 255 2nd St are good diversions.

Taste and buy the wares at **Bandon Cheese Factory** (☎ 800-548-8961), 680 Hwy 101, while watching the cheese-making process.

Bandon Historical Society Museum, cnr Filmore Ave and Hwy 101, has many photos of the Bandon area, illustrating its Irish connection, plus industry and schools exhibits.

Tours of **Coquille River Lighthouse** (☎ 347-2209), 3.5mi west off Hwy 101 north of the Coquille River bridge, run daily from May to September.

View harbor seals and, in winter and spring, migrating whales at Coquille Point off SW 11th St. Fishing boats can be chartered at **Port O'Call** (☎ 347-2875 or ☎ 800-634-9080), 155 1st St.

Bandon Beach Riding Stables (☎ 347-3423), on Beach Loop Dr about 400yd south of the golf course, takes horse rides along the beach.

West Coast Game Park (☎ 347-3106), south of town on Hwy 101, is America's largest wild animal petting park.

Cranberry bog tours and tastings are available at Faber Farms (☎ 347-1166), 519 Morrison Rd. The annual Cranberry Festival is in early September.

Places to Stay & Eat Hiker/biker camping at ***Bullards Beach State Park***, west off Hwy 101 2.6mi north of town, costs $4 per person. Yurts can also be booked (☎ 347-2209).

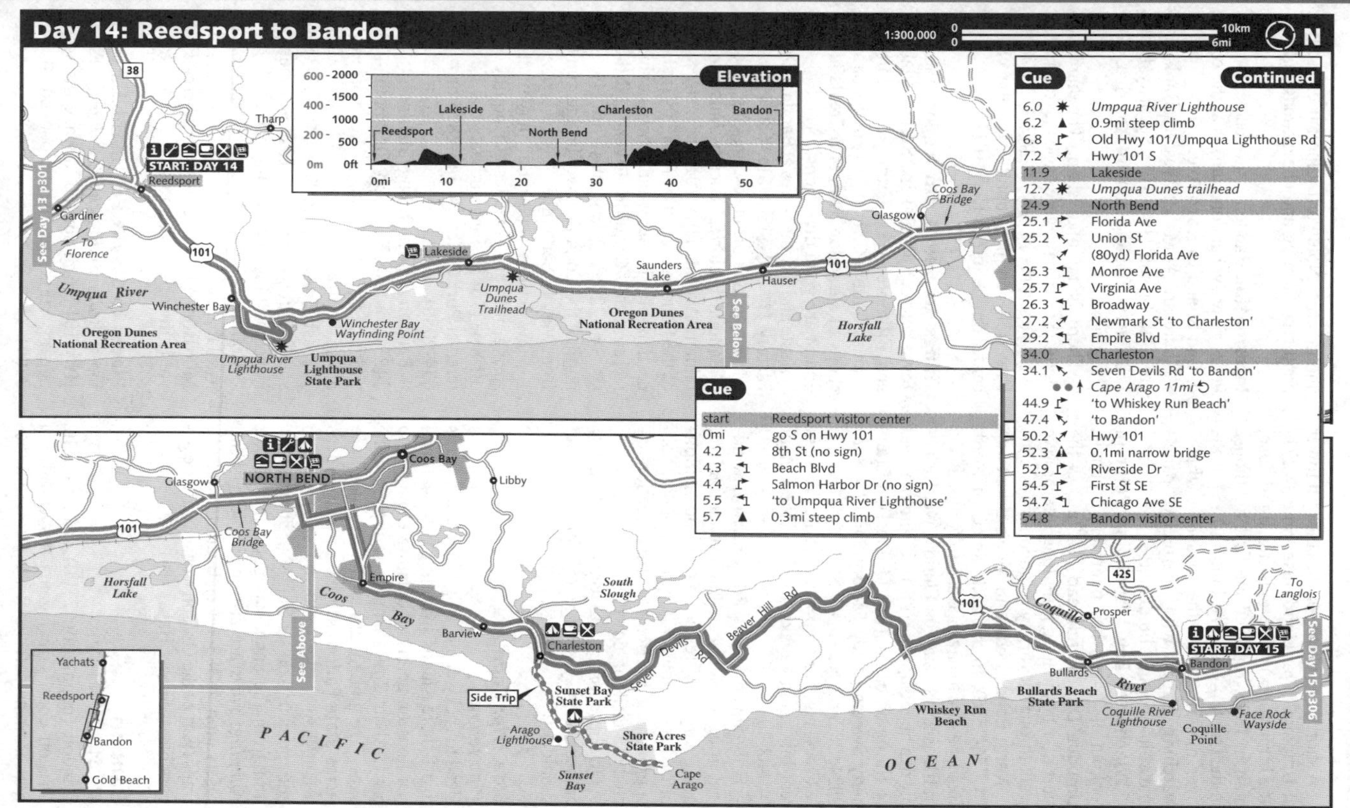
Day 14: Reedsport to Bandon
1:300,000
0
10km
0
6mi
N
Elevation
600 - 2000
400 - 1500
1000
200 - 500
0m 0ft
0mi 10 20 30 40 50
Reedsport
Lakeside
North Bend
Charleston
Bandon
Cue
start Reedsport visitor center
0mi go S on Hwy 101
4.2 8th St (no sign)
4.3 Beach Blvd
4.4 Salmon Harbor Dr (no sign)
5.5 'to Umpqua River Lighthouse'
5.7 0.3mi steep climb
Cue
Continued
6.0 Umpqua River Lighthouse
6.2 0.9mi steep climb
6.8 Old Hwy 101/Umpqua Lighthouse Rd
7.2 Hwy 101 S
11.9 Lakeside
12.7 Umpqua Dunes trailhead
24.9 North Bend
25.1 Florida Ave
25.2 Union St
(80yd) Florida Ave
25.3 Monroe Ave
25.7 Virginia Ave
26.3 Broadway
27.2 Newmark St 'to Charleston'
29.2 Empire Blvd
34.0 Charleston
34.1 Seven Devils Rd 'to Bandon'
Cape Arago 11mi
44.9 'to Whiskey Run Beach'
47.4 'to Bandon'
50.2 Hwy 101
52.3 0.1mi narrow bridge
52.9 Riverside Dr
54.5 First St SE
54.7 Chicago Ave SE
54.8 Bandon visitor center
See Day 13 p301
38
Tharp
START: DAY 14
Reedsport
Gardiner
To Florence
101
Umpqua River
Winchester Bay
Oregon Dunes National Recreation Area
Umpqua River Lighthouse
Umpqua Lighthouse State Park
Winchester Bay Wayfinding Point
Lakeside
Umpqua Dunes Trailhead
Saunders Lake
Hauser
See Below
Glasgow
Coos Bay Bridge
Horsfall Lake
NORTH BEND
Coos Bay
Libby
Empire
Coos Bay
Barview
South Slough
Charleston
See Above
Side Trip
Sunset Bay State Park
Arago Lighthouse
Sunset Bay
Shore Acres State Park
Cape Arago
Seven Devils Rd
Beaver Hill Rd
PACIFIC OCEAN
Whiskey Run Beach
Bullards Beach State Park
Bullards
Coquille River
Coquille River Lighthouse
Coquille Point
425
Prosper
To Langlois
START: DAY 15
Bandon
Face Rock Wayside
See Day 15 p306
Yachats
Gold Beach

The small ***Inn at Old Town*** *(☎ 347-5900 or ☎ 887-884-3466, Hwy 101)*, in the center of town, has rooms with kitchenettes, and some with jacuzzis, from $45. ***Driftwood Motel*** *(☎ 347-9022 or ☎ 888-374-3893, 460 Hwy 101)*, near the visitor center, has doubles from $60.

Cliff-hanging ***Table Rock Motel*** *(☎ 347-2700, 840 Beach Loop Dr)* has doubles from $45. Nearby ***Best Western Inn at Face Rock*** *(☎ 347-9441 or ☎ 800-638-3092, 3225 Beach Loop Dr)* has an equally dramatic location. Basic doubles are $105; rooms with ocean view, jacuzzi, balcony and fireplace are $205.

Luxurious ***Bandon Beach House B&B*** *(☎ 347-1196, ⓔ beachhouse@harborside.com, 2866 Beach Loop Dr)* charges $180 for large ocean-view rooms with king-size bed, private bathroom and gourmet breakfast.

Price 'n' Pride supermarket *(cnr Hwy 101 & 10th St)* is open 24 hours. ***Bandon Gourmet Bakery*** *(92 2nd St)* has artisan breads, woodfired pizza, desserts and handmade chocolate. Get inexpensive ice creams, as well as cheese, at the ***Bandon Cheese Factory***.

Bandon Fish Market *(Fruit St)*, in Old Town, serves reasonable fish and chips with coleslaw from $6. ***Jack's Pizza*** *(☎ 347-3911, 490 Hwy 101)* specializes in homemade pizza plus oven-baked sandwiches, hamburgers and chicken. Pricey ***Harp's on the Bay*** *(☎ 347-9057)*, also in Old Town, has a view of the Coquille River and lighthouse, and serves seafood, steaks, homemade pasta and soup. ***Lord Bennett's at the Sunset*** *(☎ 347-3663, 1695 Beach Loop Dr)* serves superb seafood and prime steaks with fabulous views.

Day 15: Bandon to Gold Beach

5–9¼ hours, 57.5mi

Hwy 101 stays a mile or two inland until Port Orford (27.8mi) before returning to hug the coast. Sea stacks, capes, beaches and spray are in abundance. There are two notable hills en route. A third steep hill is in the side trip at Port Orford. The road reaches a high point of 325ft at 19.7mi after a near imperceptible rise. ***Food*** is available at Langlois (15.3mi), Sixes (23.1mi), Port Orford (27.8mi) and Nesika Beach (49mi).

The strange bowling-green-like areas beside the route are cranberry bogs. The fruit grows in acidic, sandy soil, and is worth $15 million per year to Bandon's economy.

At **Face Rock Wayside** (2mi), the big rock amid the offshore sea stacks resembles the profile of a face. It is said to be that of a Native American princess, uplifted to the sky. The rest of her body is underwater.

A side trip at 27.8mi to the old **Port Orford Coast Guard station** (☎ 332-2352, ⓦ www.portorfordlifeboatstation.org) is recommended. Buy lunch in town before turning right at the sign off Hwy 101 where it bends sharply to the left. It's a steep climb to the station, listed on the National Register of Historic Places. There are picnic tables, walking trails to Port Orford Heads, and a museum (open weekends 1–4pm). Established in 1934 as one of the first coast guard stations, and the southernmost, on the Oregon coast, it was decommissioned in 1970. Its tower was an important navigational aid on the coast and the station a fortress against Japanese aggression in WWII.

Humbug Mtn State Park (34.4mi), on the left of the highway, is literally in the shadow of that mountain. Hiker/biker campsites are available ($4 per person).

After 51mi, the route diverges to the Old Coast Rd, a narrow, potholed but traffic-free remnant of bitumen on the edge of the continent, passing cool forest and open fields. Returning to Hwy 101, cross historic Rogue River Bridge at 55.4mi.

Gold Beach

☎ 541

Named for the oceanfront mines that yielded gold in the 1850s, Gold Beach lies near the mouth of the wild Rogue River. It is flanked by miles of gray-sand beaches popular with kite fliers and beachcombers searching for agate, shells and driftwood.

Information The Gold Beach Chamber of Commerce (☎ 247-7526 or ☎ 800-525-2334, ⓦ www.goldbeach.org), 29279 Ellensburg Ave, shares premises with the ranger office (☎ 247-6651), which has hiking information.

Klamath First Federal Bank, 29804 Ellensburg Ave, has an ATM. Dan's Ace Hardware (☎ 247-6822), 29733 Ellensburg Ave, sells basic bike spares. Internet access is available at Bookworm Bookshop (☎ 247-9033), 29401 Ellensburg Ave, and at the library (☎ 247-7246), corner Caughell & Colvin Sts.

Day 15: Bandon to Gold Beach

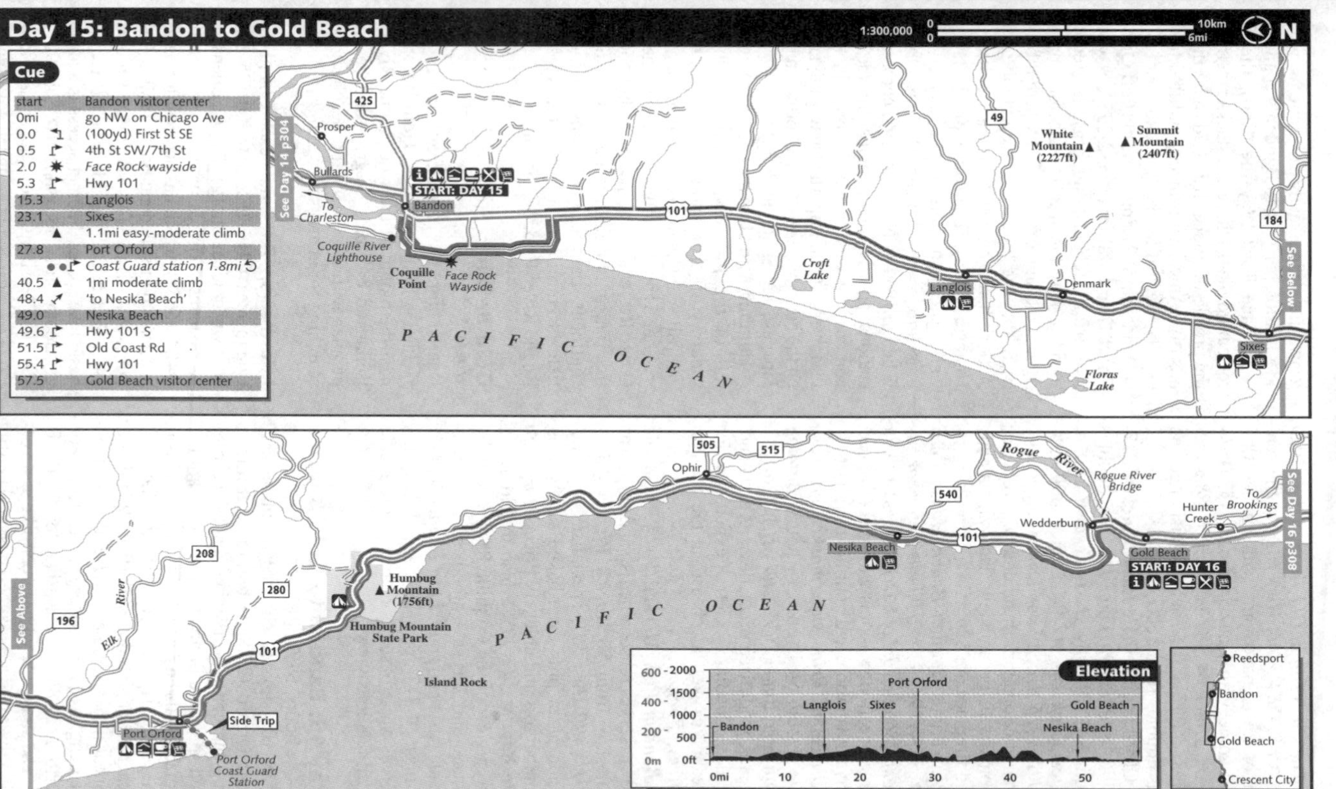

Cue

start		Bandon visitor center
0mi		go NW on Chicago Ave
0.0	↰	(100yd) First St SE
0.5	↱	4th St SW/7th St
2.0	✷	*Face Rock wayside*
5.3	↱	Hwy 101
15.3		Langlois
23.1		Sixes
	▲	1.1mi easy-moderate climb
27.8		Port Orford
	••↱	*Coast Guard station 1.8mi* ↺
40.5	▲	1mi moderate climb
48.4	↗	'to Nesika Beach'
49.0		Nesika Beach
49.6	↱	Hwy 101 S
51.5	↱	Old Coast Rd
55.4	↱	Hwy 101
57.5		Gold Beach visitor center

Things to See & Do The **Curry County Historical Museum** (☎ 247-6113), 29410 Ellensburg Ave, displays pioneer and Native American artifacts.

For **fishing** on the Rogue River, get tackle and information at the Rogue Outdoor Store (☎ 247-7142), 29865 Ellensburg Ave.

Jerry's Rogue Jets (☎ 800-451-3645) and Rogue River Mail Boats (☎ 800-458-3511) offer fantastic **wildlife viewing** opportunities (May–Oct); book ahead.

Places to Stay & Eat The ***Nesika Beach RV Park*** *(☎ 247-6077, 32887 Nesika Rd)*, on the Day 15 route, charges $14 a double for tent sites. ***Huntley Park Campground*** *(☎ 670-7691, 96847 Jerry's Flat Rd)*, 7mi from town on the south bank of Rogue River, has sites among myrtles for $8 a double.

City Center Motel *(☎ 247-6675, 94200 Harlow St)* has cramped, gloomy doubles for $45. ***Ireland's Rustic Lodges*** *(☎ 247-7718, 29330 Ellensburg Ave)* has doubles from $55. Oceanfront ***Sand 'n Sea Motel*** *(☎ 247-6658 or ☎ 800-808-7263, 1040 Ellensburg Ave)* charges $60. ***Shore Cliff Inn*** *(☎ 247-7091, 29346 Ellensburg Ave)* has similar rooms for $50. All charge more for ocean views.

Ray's Food Place *(cnr 6th St & Ellensburg Ave)* is good for supplies. ***Grant's Pancake, Omelette & Steakhouse*** *(☎ 247-7208, Jerry's Flat Rd)*, about 0.5mi east of Hwy 101, serves meals all day, with mains from $8. ***Port Hole Cafe*** *(29975 Harbor Way)* serves home-cooked meals, including seafood mains ($15). ***The Chowderhead*** *(☎ 247-0588, 29430 Ellensburg Ave)* is a seafood restaurant with mains from $14.

Day 16: Gold Beach to Crescent City

5–9 hours, 55.8mi

A moderately hilly day follows Hwy 101 along the shoreline all the way to the California state line. Views are dominated by sea stacks, many with special names and their own viewpoints. After Brookings (26.1mi), the only ***services*** are at Smith River (41.9mi).

An **historical marker** (5.2mi) commemorates the naming of Cape San Sebastian by Spaniard Sebastian Vizciano in 1603.A **viewpoint** at 7mi reveals an amazing number of sea stacks and offshore rocks battered by the ocean. **Arch Rock Viewpoint** (14.7mi) reveals yet more geomorphologic wonders.

Within **Samuel H Boardman State Park** is a picnic area (15.3mi), **Spruce Island Viewpoint** (15.5mi) and the **Natural Bridges Cove Viewpoint trail** (16.4mi). It's worth the 650yd return walk on a precipitous track to get up close (but not too personal – no fences) with these natural wonders. There are three natural bridges with blow holes and surging currents.

Thomas Creek Bridge (18.2mi) is the highest in Oregon, with its road surface about 345ft above sea level.

Lone Ranch Beach (23mi) has picnic facilities while ***Harris Beach State Park*** (26.1mi) has camping. Opposite the entrance to the park is Brookings' Oregon State Welcome Center (☎ 541-469-4117). The town has an excellent bike shop, Escape Hatch (☎ 541-469-2914), at 642 Railroad Ave.

Cross the state line into California at 34.2mi.

Crescent City

☎ 707

Founded in 1853 on a crescent-shaped bay as a port and supply center for inland gold mines, Crescent City has grown (not without drama) to a population of 8800. More than half the town was destroyed by a tsunami in 1964 (see the boxed text, p45). The city, like much of the nearby coast, is often cloaked with fog in summer and old and wet in winter, with up to 100 inches of rain falling annually. Fishing, tourism and the Pelican Bay prison are economic mainstays.

Information The Chamber of Commerce (☎ 464-3174 or ☎ 800-343-8300) is at 1001 Front St. The National Parks Center (☎ 464-6101, ext 5064), corner 2nd and K Sts, has details of nearby parks, campgrounds and redwood forests.

Six Rivers National Bank is at 1492 Northcrest Dr. Tri Counties Bank is at 936 3rd St. The supermarkets have ATMs.

Escape Hatch Sport & Cycle (☎ 464-2614), 960 3rd St, is closed Sunday.

Log on at Del Norte County Library (☎ 464-9793), 190 Price Mall, opposite the Chamber of Commerce.

Things to See & Do The **Del Norte Historical Society Museum** (☎ 464-3922), 577 H St, has a fine collection of Tolowa and Yurok artifacts and exhibits on the 1964 tsunami.

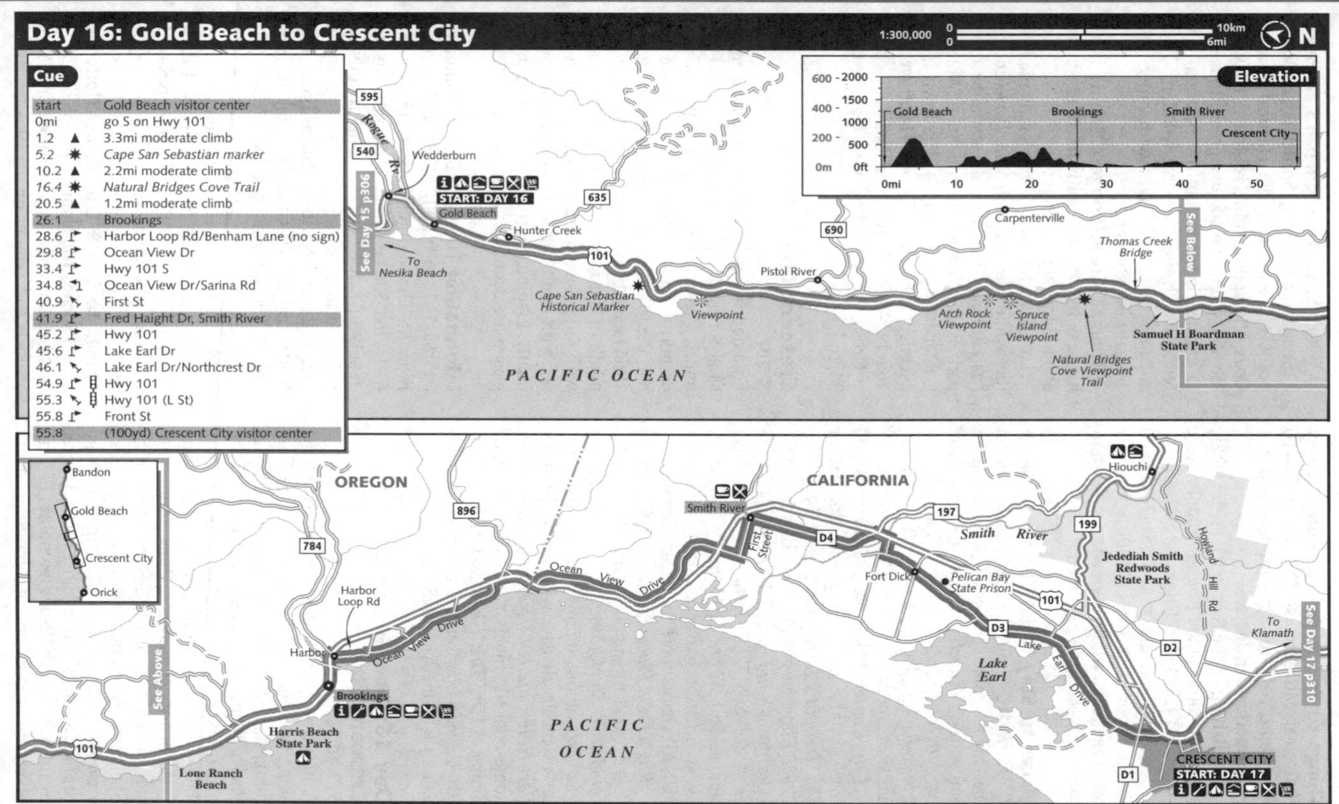

Day 16: Gold Beach to Crescent City

Cue

start		Gold Beach visitor center
0mi		go S on Hwy 101
1.2	▲	3.3mi moderate climb
5.2	✷	*Cape San Sebastian marker*
10.2	▲	2.2mi moderate climb
16.4	✷	*Natural Bridges Cove Trail*
20.5	▲	1.2mi moderate climb
26.1		Brookings
28.6	↱	Harbor Loop Rd/Benham Lane (no sign)
29.8	↱	Ocean View Dr
33.4	↱	Hwy 101 S
34.8	↰	Ocean View Dr/Sarina Rd
40.9	↘	First St
41.9	↱	Fred Haight Dr, Smith River
45.2	↱	Hwy 101
45.6	↱	Lake Earl Dr
46.1	↘	Lake Earl Dr/Northcrest Dr
54.9	↱ 🚦	Hwy 101
55.3	↘ 🚦	Hwy 101 (L St)
55.8	↱	Front St
55.8		(100yd) Crescent City visitor center

Ocean World (☎ 464-4900), 304 Hwy 101, offers submarine guided tours, shark petting tanks, a sea lion show and a gift shop.

Battery Point Lighthouse (☎ 464-3089), at the south end of A St, is accessible at low tide and opens as a museum (Apr–Sept).

The **waterfront park** behind the Chamber of Commerce is an attractive place to relax, listen to the seashore sounds, picnic or visit **North Coast Marine Mammal Center** (☎ 465-6265). The center rescues injured seals, which can be seen in pens beside the souvenir shop.

To view magnificent redwoods, take a 22mi ride through the **Jedediah Smith Redwoods State Park**. Follow the Day 17 route (but use the Day 16 map!), turning left onto Elk Valley Rd at the 0.4mi mark. After about 1mi, follow a bike route sign right onto Howland Hill Rd which soon begins a very steep climb, then descends unsealed through a grove of huge redwoods. This forest was used as a backdrop in a scene of the Star Wars movie *Return of the Jedi*. About 0.5mi after the sealed road begins again there is a covered wooden bridge. Beyond it, turn left onto S Fork Rd and again at Hwy 199 after the 1956 Neil S Christensen Memorial Bridge. There is an impressive view into the Smith River gorge from the span. Turn left onto Hwy 101 to return to Crescent City.

Crescent City's Great Tsunami

On 28 March, 1964, most of downtown Crescent City was destroyed by a tsunami (often incorrectly called a 'tidal wave') created by an earthquake measuring 8.5 on the Richter scale, centered on the north shore of Prince William Sound, Alaska.

Four waves – each higher than the last – reached Crescent City, starting a few hours after the earthquake, at 3.36am. The swells were so huge that they didn't crest and break like ordinary waves, but seemed to raise the level of the ocean. After the third wave, which almost came up to the town, residents thought the danger was over. But as it receded it sucked the entire bay empty, leaving boats that had been anchored offshore sitting in the mud.

When the fourth wave surged in, the frigid waters rose all the way up to 5th St, knocking buildings off their foundations, carrying away cars, trucks; anything not bolted down, and even a lot of things that were. Many residents stayed in their houses as they floated off their foundations. Twenty-nine blocks of the town were destroyed, and more than 300 buildings were damaged or displaced. Five bulk gasoline storage tanks exploded; 11 people were killed and three were never found.

Nancy Keller

Places to Stay & Eat Tent sites at ***KOA Redwoods*** *(☎ 464-5744 or ☎ 800-562-5754, Hwy 101)*, 5mi north of town, cost $19; Cabins sleeping four cost $36. ***Village Camper Inn RV Park*** *(☎ 464-3544, 1543 Parkway Dr)*, about 1mi north of town, has hiker/biker sites for $6 per person.

HI Redwood National Park Hostel *(☎ 482-8265, ⓔ redwoodhostel@mail.telis.org, 14480 Hwy 101)* is on the Day 17 route at 13.7mi, on the left after a screaming descent. It has beds from $15.

Penny Saver Inn *(☎ 464-3142, 665 L St)* has a pool and dreary but functional doubles for $49. ***Best Value Inn*** *(☎ 464-4141, 440 Hwy 101)* charges from $52. ***Super 8 Motel*** *(☎ 464-4111, 685 Hwy 101)* has rooms from $70, some of which face away from the noisy highway.

Battery Point Beach House (☎ *800-722-6587,* ⓔ *patt@wardlaw.com, 286 Wendell St)* is a self-contained house available for $150 per night (three-night minimum).

Supermarkets include ***Ray's Food Place*** *(625 M St)* and ***Safeway*** *(475 M St)*. ***Continental Bakery*** *(503 L St)* serves deli items, sandwiches, soup, coffee and drinks for breakfast and lunch.

The Apple Peddler *(☎ 464-5630, 308 Hwy 101 S)* is an excellent, 24-hour family restaurant. Meal-sized nachos are $6; chicken and fish mains start at $9.

Thai House *(☎ 464-2427, 105 N St)* has fish and rice specials for $11. ***Toreros Famosos*** *(☎ 464-5712, 400 Hwy 101 N)* is a family Mexican restaurant with large portions from $9.

Day 17: Crescent City to Orick

3½–6¼ hours, 39mi

One of the most awe-inspiring days of this ride starts with solid climbing through Del Norte Coast Redwoods State Park. A dark forest of some of the world's tallest trees engulfs the road as it winds up for almost 7mi to more than 1150ft before emerging on

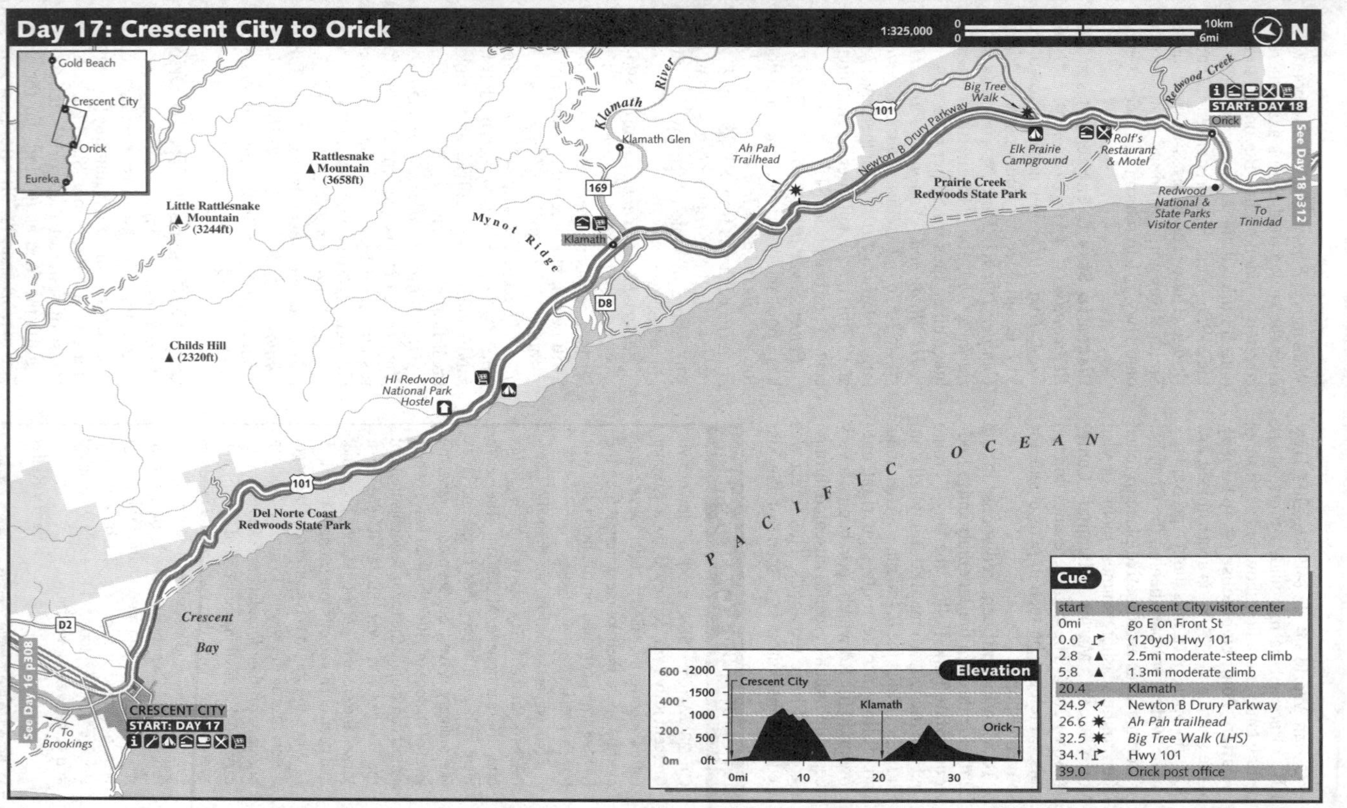
Day 17: Crescent City to Orick
1:325,000
0 10km
0 6mi
N
Gold Beach
Crescent City
Orick
Eureka
Rattlesnake Mountain (3658ft)
Little Rattlesnake Mountain (3244ft)
Childs Hill (2320ft)
Klamath River
Klamath Glen
169
Mynot Ridge
Klamath
D8
Ah Pah Trailhead
101
Newton B Drury Parkway
Big Tree Walk
Elk Prairie Campground
Rolf's Restaurant & Motel
Prairie Creek Redwoods State Park
Redwood Creek
START: DAY 18
Orick
See Day 18 p312
Redwood National & State Parks Visitor Center
To Trinidad
HI Redwood National Park Hostel
Del Norte Coast Redwoods State Park
PACIFIC OCEAN
Crescent Bay
D2
See Day 16 p308
To Brookings
CRESCENT CITY
START: DAY 17
Elevation
600 - 2000
1500
400 - 1000
200 - 500
0m 0ft
Crescent City
Klamath
Orick
0mi 10 20 30
Cue
start Crescent City visitor center
0mi go E on Front St
0.0 (120yd) Hwy 101
2.8 2.5mi moderate-steep climb
5.8 1.3mi moderate climb
20.4 Klamath
24.9 Newton B Drury Parkway
26.6 Ah Pah trailhead
32.5 Big Tree Walk (LHS)
34.1 Hwy 101
39.0 Orick post office

the edge of a precipice. Here, a sea stack-dotted view opens, seemingly to the whole California coast. The plummet back to sea level is followed by another climb after Klamath (20.4mi) to about 800ft.

There is a ***store*** on the left and a ***campground*** on the right at 16mi. Klamath's ***store*** is the last place to get supplies before ***Elk Prairie campground*** (33mi).

Along the beautiful, forested, hilly Newton B Drury Scenic Parkway, the 400yd **Ah Pah interpretive trail** (26.6mi) gives an insight into environmental rehabilitation. Walk the course of a former logging road, built in the 1940s, to see how its removal in 1995 has reduced erosion, protected water quality and encouraged forest regeneration.

At 32.5mi, the 200yd **Big Tree Walk** (LHS) visits one of the true giants of the forest. ***Rolf's Restaurant & Motel*** (see Places to Stay & Eat for Orick) is at 36.4mi.

Orick

☎ 707

Despite its location near fabulous redwood forest, this tiny service town is quite unattractive. A strip of derelict buildings and kitsch wood-carving factories leads into a down-at-heel commercial area. The town is bisected by Redwood Creek.

Redwood National and State Parks visitor center (☎ 822-7611, ext 5265) is beside the beach 2mi southwest of town. Orick Market has an ATM.

Things to See & Do Orick's only real attraction is its position as a base for exploration of the redwoods. If desperate, check out the **Curiosity Shoppe** at the north end of town with its redwood windmills and the chainsaw sculptures opposite.

Places to Stay & Eat The best accommodations are north of town, closer to the forests. The ***Elk Prairie campground*** in Prairie Creek Redwoods State Park has excellent hiker/biker camping ($3 per person, coin-operated showers), 6mi north of Orick. ***Rolf's Restaurant & Motel*** *(☎ 488-3841, Hwy 101; closed Nov–Mar)*, 2.6mi north of town, is legendary, attracting travelers from far and wide. Motel rooms cost $46 a double. The restaurant, operated by a German chef and his family, serves an eclectic menu incorporating elk, buffalo and wild boar plus a variety of German dishes. Portions are generous and reasonably priced. Breakfast is especially recommended – fill to near bursting for around $8.

Palm Motel *(☎ 488-3381, 21130 Hwy 101)*, north of the bridge, has an indoor pool and rooms for $40. ***Palm Cafe***, next door, serves breakfast, lunch and dinner until 8pm daily.

Orick Market, next to the post office, has basic foodstuffs. South of the bridge, ***Snack Shack*** serves takeaways.

Day 18: Orick to Eureka

4–7½ hours, 46mi

Today's route reaches no dizzying heights – the maximum is around 400ft at 14.0mi – though three moderate climbs arise in the first 14mi. The rest of the route is near flat at sea level. By contrast to the almost claustrophobic forested ride of the previous day, the route is largely through towns or open spaces dominated by agriculture, with more superb coastal scenery. After Trinidad (20.3mi), services are nearby but frequently off the route as it skirts the centers of busy McKinleyville and Arcata (35.4mi). Each has a bicycle shop – try McKinleyville Sporting Goods (☎ 839-9445), 1977 Central Ave; or Arcata's Life Cycle (☎ 822-7755), 1593 G St.

In the first 10mi or so, the road undulates with a narrow and/or rough shoulder but with fine views of beaches, lagoons and bird-thronged lakes. Along undulating Patricks Point Rd (14.4mi), there are camping and motel options. Sea lions populate the offshore stacks.

From 29.1mi, the Hammond Trail and Fischer Ave follow the route of an old railway line. Where Fischer Ave dives down a hill, the railway used to continue on a massive trestle of foot-square redwood beams to the old box-girder Mad River bridge. When the trestle was dismantled about 1965, the beams were taken to Disneyland to build one of the rides there. Traverse flat grazing land here – give way to cows coming home for milking – to cross the Mad River bridge. Continue along the level bayshore on busy but wide-shouldered Hwy 101 into Eureka.

The cue sheet describes the least complicated route to Eureka's visitor center but it can be a very busy and unpleasant route at peak times. An alternative is to turn right at the start of Eureka's built-up area (about

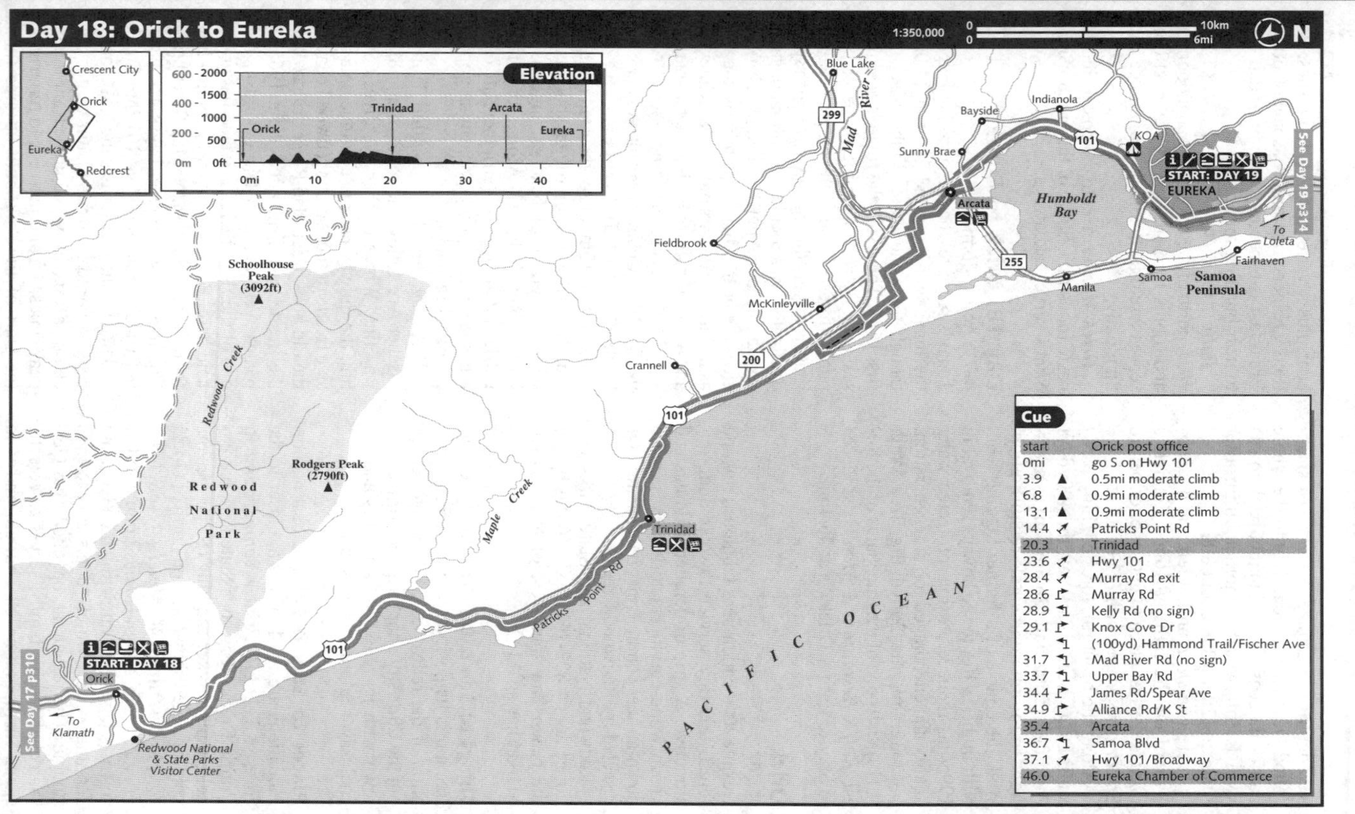
Day 18: Orick to Eureka
1:350,000
0 10km
0 6mi
N
Crescent City
Orick
Eureka
Redcrest
Elevation
600 - 2000
400 - 1500
1000
200 - 500
0m 0ft
0mi
10
20
30
40
Orick
Trinidad
Arcata
Eureka
Blue Lake
Mad River
299
Bayside
Indianola
Sunny Brae
101
KOA
START: DAY 19
EUREKA
See Day 19 p314
Arcata
Humboldt Bay
To Loleta
Fairhaven
Fieldbrook
255
Manila
Samoa
Samoa Peninsula
Schoolhouse Peak (3092ft)
McKinleyville
200
Crannell
Redwood Creek
101
Rodgers Peak (2790ft)
Redwood National Park
Maple Creek
Trinidad
Patricks Point Rd
PACIFIC OCEAN
101
START: DAY 18
Orick
See Day 17 p310
To Klamath
Redwood National & State Parks Visitor Center
Cue
start Orick post office
0mi go S on Hwy 101
3.9 ▲ 0.5mi moderate climb
6.8 ▲ 0.9mi moderate climb
13.1 ▲ 0.9mi moderate climb
14.4 Patricks Point Rd
20.3 Trinidad
23.6 Hwy 101
28.4 Murray Rd exit
28.6 Murray Rd
28.9 Kelly Rd (no sign)
29.1 Knox Cove Dr
(100yd) Hammond Trail/Fischer Ave
31.7 Mad River Rd (no sign)
33.7 Upper Bay Rd
34.4 James Rd/Spear Ave
34.9 Alliance Rd/K St
35.4 Arcata
36.7 Samoa Blvd
37.1 Hwy 101/Broadway
46.0 Eureka Chamber of Commerce

43mi) onto X St and follow roads close to the waterfront. Turn left onto 1st St, left again onto T St, again onto Waterfront Dr and again on L St, then right to 2nd St and again at Commercial St. Turn left onto Waterfront Dr, left at Del Norte St, right after 100yd to Felt St, which becomes Hawthorn St, reaching the visitor center after 3.2mi at the corner of Hwy 101 (Broadway).

Eureka

☎ 707

With nearly 28,000 people, Eureka is the largest town on California's far north coast. It hugs the shore of long, narrow Humboldt Bay, the state's largest bay and seaport north of San Francisco. Arriving via Hwy 101, a cyclist's first impression is likely to be unfavorable – thundering traffic bisects a tacky commercial strip. Yet, two blocks west, the placid old-town contains beautiful Victorian homes and a refurbished commercial area with good restaurants and attractions.

Information Eureka–Humboldt County visitor center (☎ 442-3738 or ☎ 800-356-6381, e eurekacc@northcoast.com) is at the corner of Broadway and Hawthorn St. It has a free leaflet on the trails of Humboldt County, including mountain-bike routes, and sells the colorful *Humboldt Bay Area Bike Map* ($2.95).

Six Rivers National Bank has branches at 402 F St and 800 W Harris St. Humboldt Bank is at 701 5th St and 2861 E St. US Bank is at 735 5th St.

Henderson Center Bicycles (☎ 443-9861; closed Sat) is at 2811 F St; Sport & Cycle (☎ 444-9274) is at 1621 Broadway.

The public library (☎ 269-1900), 1313 3rd St, has Internet access.

Things to See & Do Eureka's number one attraction is its old-town Victorian architecture. Most famous is the ornate **Carson Mansion**, at the east end of 2nd St, built by lumber baron William Carson in the 1880s. Said to have taken 100 men a full year to construct, it is now occupied by a private club and is not open for inspection. The pink house opposite was built as a wedding gift for Carson's son.

Antique shops cluster in the old-town between E and G Sts. An antique mall (☎ 445-8835), 533 F St, houses 25 dealers.

Humboldt Bay Maritime Museum (☎ 444-9440; open Tues–Sat afternoons), 423 1st St, features ship-building tools, the history of coastal shipwrecks and lighthouses. It was set to move locations; check with the visitor center.

Blue Ox Millworks (☎ 444-3437), at the foot of X St, is a working Victorian sawmill featuring antique machinery.

Hum-Boats (☎ 443-5157), at the bay end of F St, offers **kayak** and **sailboat rentals**, **ecotours** and a **water taxi service**.

Take a delightful **cruise** on Humboldt Bay in the 1910-built MV *Madaket* (☎ 445-1910), the oldest passenger vessel in continuous use in the USA.

Places to Stay & Eat Nearest camping is about 4mi northeast of town at ***KOA*** *(☎ 822-4243)*. Hiker/biker sites cost $15 for two. Follow signs east off Hwy 101.

Most motels are on or near noisy Hwy 101, which splits into southbound 4th St and northbound 5th St in the built-up area. ***Super 8*** *(☎ 443-3193, 1304 4th St)* charges $54, including continental breakfast and use of a pool. ***Motel 6*** *(☎ 445-9631 or ☎ 800-466-8356, 1934 Broadway)*, near the visitor center, charges $55 for small but well-equipped modern rooms, some of which are away from the road. Ritzy ***Holiday Inn Express*** *(☎ 442-3261, 2223 4th St)* and ***Red Lion Hotel*** *(☎ 445-0844, 1929 4th St)* have restaurants and doubles for $75 and $89 respectively. More basic but noisier, ***Fireside Inn*** *(☎ 443-6312, 1716 5th St)* and ***Econo Lodge*** *(☎ 443-8041, 1630 4th St)* charge $45 and $52 respectively.

The ***farmers market*** (10am–1pm Tues) is in the old-town. Markets include ***Pearson's Groceries*** *(241 F St)* and ***Safeway*** *(cnr W Harris & Fairfield Sts)*, 0.1mi north of the Day 19 route.

For gourmet coffee, pastries and snacks, try ***Humboldt Bay Coffee Co*** *(211 F St)*. ***Marie Callender's Restaurant & Bakery*** *(☎ 268-8255, 3502 Broadway)* is famous for its pies, serving breakfast, lunch and dinner daily.

For traditional Italian food, try ***Gabriel's*** *(☎ 445-0100, 216 E St)* in old-town. It caters to vegetarians. ***The Vista*** *(☎ 443-1491, 91 Commercial St)* is a restaurant/pub with menus for vegetarians and kids. It serves shellfish, wine and microbrews from

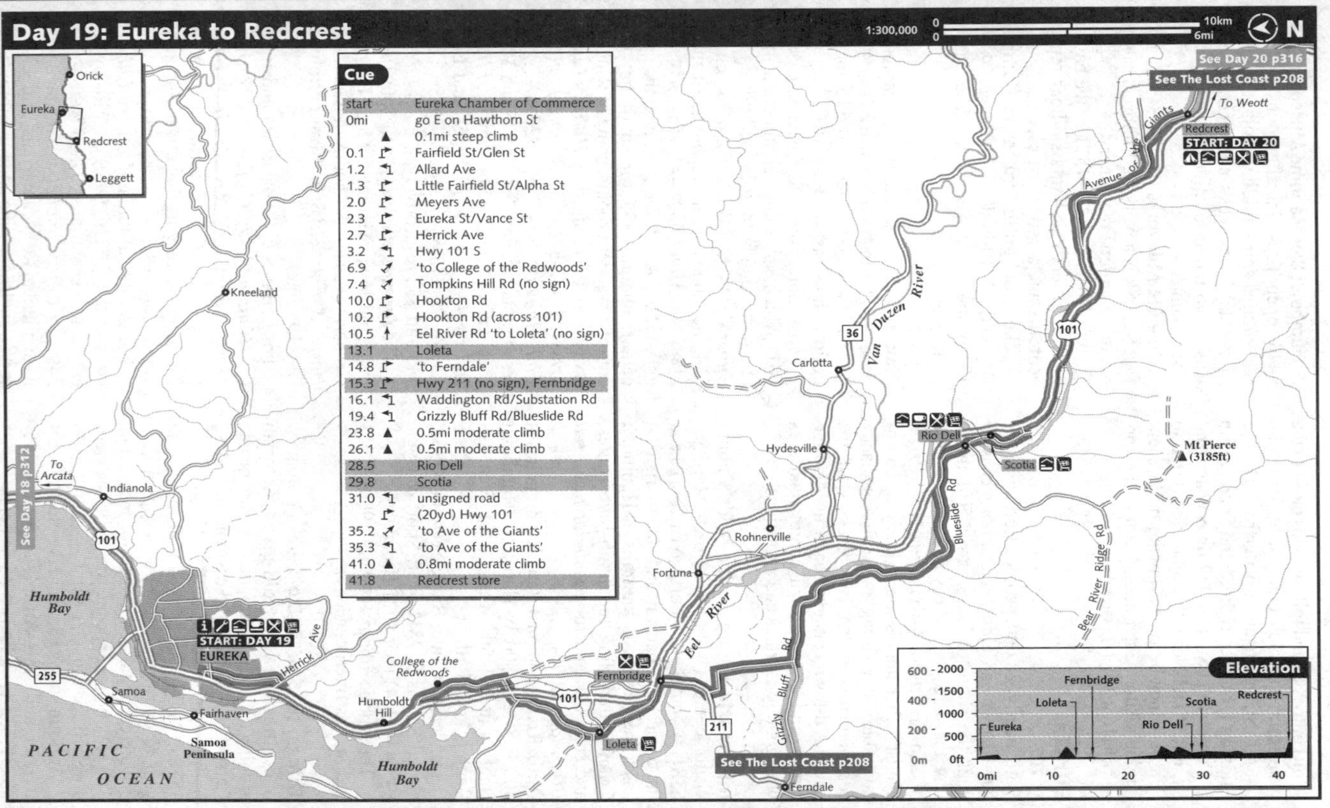

Cue		
start		Eureka Chamber of Commerce
0mi		go E on Hawthorn St
	▲	0.1mi steep climb
0.1		Fairfield St/Glen St
1.2		Allard Ave
1.3		Little Fairfield St/Alpha St
2.0		Meyers Ave
2.3		Eureka St/Vance St
2.7		Herrick Ave
3.2		Hwy 101 S
6.9		'to College of the Redwoods'
7.4		Tompkins Hill Rd (no sign)
10.0		Hookton Rd
10.2		Hookton Rd (across 101)
10.5		Eel River Rd 'to Loleta' (no sign)
13.1		Loleta
14.8		'to Ferndale'
15.3		Hwy 211 (no sign), Fernbridge
16.1		Waddington Rd/Substation Rd
19.4		Grizzly Bluff Rd/Blueslide Rd
23.8	▲	0.5mi moderate climb
26.1	▲	0.5mi moderate climb
28.5		Rio Dell
29.8		Scotia
31.0		unsigned road
		(20yd) Hwy 101
35.2		'to Ave of the Giants'
35.3		'to Ave of the Giants'
41.0	▲	0.8mi moderate climb
41.8		Redcrest store

5pm. ***Eureka Seafood Grotto*** *(☎ 443-1943, cnr 6th St & Broadway)* serves good clam chowder and fish and chips.

One of the most unusual eating houses in the area is ***Samoa Cookhouse*** *(☎ 442-1659)*, 'last surviving cookhouse in the West'. Cross the Humboldt Bay Bridge and follow the signs on Samoa Peninsula. Open for breakfast, lunch and dinner, it offers an all-you-can-eat fixed menu for $12.

Day 19: Eureka to Redcrest

3¾–6¾ hours, 41.8mi

Another memorable day's ride veers inland to go through majestic redwood forest along the 32mi Avenue of the Giants. After a short steep pinch to begin, gentle gradients predominate as the route winds inland along the valley of the Eel River (the third-largest river system in California with 3448mi of streams). Undulations increase towards Redcrest which, at 350ft, is the high point of the day. Several towns have ***food stores*** and other services. In Rio Dell (28.5mi), the Shell service station has an ATM.

Attractive wooden buildings dominate Scotia (29.8mi), a company town where the Pacific Lumber mill is the main employer. The ***inn*** is expensive. For cheaper motels try Rio Dell on the other side of Eel River.

Pick up an *Avenue of the Giants Auto Tour* brochure in the box at the north 'gate'. Words are inadequate to describe the feeling of riding between the massive ancient redwoods along the meandering Avenue of the Giants. Pictures don't do the forest justice either, and photography is hindered by the lack of light penetrating the high canopy. It is worth walking the frequent **pine-needle-carpeted tracks** on either side of the road – soak up the atmosphere of one of earth's true natural wonders. It is frightening to think how close the world came to the complete loss of the tallest trees on the planet, but for the work of the San Francisco–based Save-the-Redwoods League (☎ 415-362-2352, W www.savetheredwoods.org).

Redcrest

☎ 707

There's not a lot to Redcrest besides its small business area but its forest location is peacefully beautiful. Ask at the resort or general store for information. The nearest ATM is at the service station in Rio Dell (Day 19).

Things to See & Do Visit the **Eternal Tree House**, behind the cafe. A room has been hollowed out inside a living redwood. There's a gift shop nearby. **Stream fishing** for trout is popular on the Eel River (May–Nov). Use the Auto Tour brochure (see Day 19) to further explore **Humboldt Redwoods State Park**.

Places to Stay & Eat The ***Redcrest Resort*** *(☎ 722-4208, Avenue of the Giants)* offers all the accommodations in town. Tent sites are $16, motel units are $45, and self-contained one- or two-bedroom cottages are $49. An unusual option, suitable for families, is a tepee for $20 a night.

Redcrest General Store *(26452 Avenue of the Giants)* is on the opposite side, barely 100yd from the Resort (open to 7pm, 6pm Sun). The ***Eternal Tree House Cafe*** *(☎ 722-4247)*, across the road from Redcrest Resort, serves home-cooked light meals.

Day 20: Redcrest to Leggett

5–9 hours, 55.8mi

Continue on the awe-inspiring Avenue of the Giants for about 25mi before merging onto Hwy 101. A solid 2mi uphill to 650ft before Garberville (31.5mi) is the most notable climb on a moderately hilly day. It is advisable to stock up at Garberville, the only town on the route before Fort Bragg (end of Day 21) that has a good ***supermarket*** and banks.

Dyerville Overlook (4.2mi), at the confluence of the Eel and South Fork Rivers, offers views of a vast, damp Tolkienesque forest, often wreathed in mist.

Weott (6.8mi) is pretty much a ghost town – it has a post office and a gift shop but nowhere to buy food. Hiker/biker ***camping*** is to the right at the north end town sign (but hot showers are at the ***Burlington campground***, 1.6mi south).

Hobbiton (24.1mi) exploits the Tolkien theme – for a fee, visitors can walk through a village populated by *Lord of the Rings* characters. The nearby 'chimney tree', a live but hollow redwood, can be inspected free.

About 0.3mi beyond the ***Cooks Valley store***, there is the option of exiting right to the old road parallel to Hwy 101. It is slightly longer but has gentler grades and carries virtually no traffic. It returns to Hwy 101 after about 7mi.

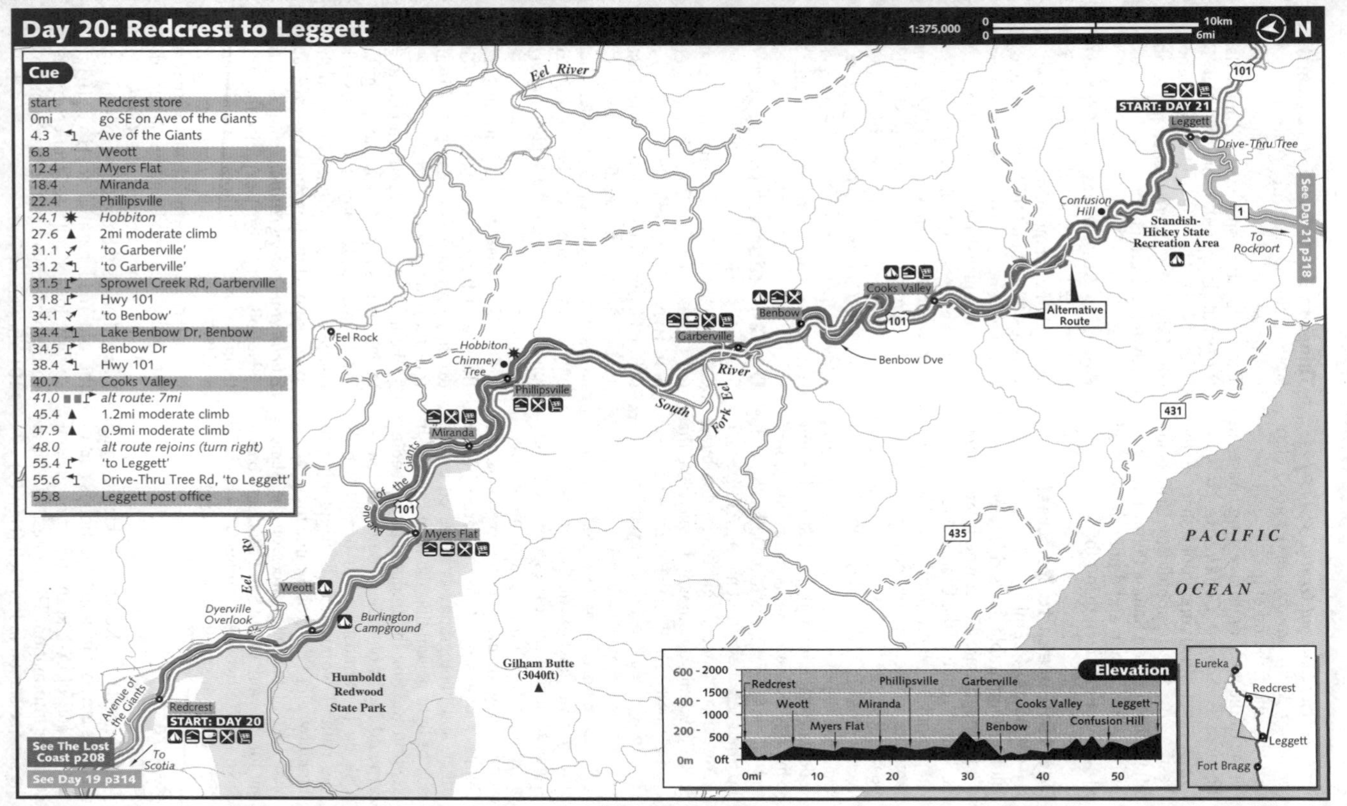

Day 20: Redcrest to Leggett

Cue		
start		Redcrest store
0mi		go SE on Ave of the Giants
4.3	↰	Ave of the Giants
6.8		Weott
12.4		Myers Flat
18.4		Miranda
22.4		Phillipsville
24.1	✱	*Hobbiton*
27.6	▲	2mi moderate climb
31.1	↗	'to Garberville'
31.2	↰	'to Garberville'
31.5	↱	Sprowel Creek Rd, Garberville
31.8	↱	Hwy 101
34.1	↗	'to Benbow'
34.4	↰	Lake Benbow Dr, Benbow
34.5	↱	Benbow Dr
38.4	↰	Hwy 101
40.7		Cooks Valley
41.0	↱	*alt route: 7mi*
45.4	▲	1.2mi moderate climb
47.9	▲	0.9mi moderate climb
48.0		*alt route rejoins (turn right)*
55.4	↱	'to Leggett'
55.6	↰	Drive-Thru Tree Rd, 'to Leggett'
55.8		Leggett post office

Leggett

☎ 707

Like Redcrest, quiet, low-key Leggett is a convenient staging point at the southern end of the ancient redwood forests. It has very limited services and attractions.

Ask for general information at the Chevron service station next to the post office.

Things to See & Do The **Chandelier Drive-Thru Tree Park** (☎ 925-6363), 0.5mi south of the post office, has a giant redwood, the Chandelier Tree, with a large square hole allowing cars to drive through. People actually pay $3 to do this ($1 for cyclists). The surrounding area has 200 acres of virgin redwood forest with picnic areas and nature walks.

Places to Stay & Eat Amid the redwoods north of Leggett, the ***Standish-Hickey State Recreation Area*** *(☎ 800-444-7275, Hwy 101)* has three campgrounds with sites for $16, plus swimming holes and fishing opportunities in the Eel River.

Opposite Confusion Hill on Hwy 101, ***Redwoods River Resort*** *(☎ 925-6249)* also has campsites ($17) plus cabins from $30 and lodge rooms from $60.

Leggett's only motel, ***Stonegate Villas*** *(☎ 925-6226)*, has small, modern, tastefully decorated rooms *without TV* – books and magazines are supplied instead – for $45 a double. It's 2.4mi along Drive-Thru Tree Rd (Hwy 271) south of town.

Leggett Market, at the north end of the business strip, has basic items. ***Cafe Paradiso*** *(☎ 925-1433, Drive-Thru Tree Rd)* serves meals from 8am to 7pm daily.

Day 21: Leggett to Fort Bragg

4¾–7 hours, 43.4mi

One of the hilliest and most isolated days of the whole ride offers a near-wilderness experience. For much of the ride, you could be alone thousands of miles from civilization, except for occasional other vehicles. Forests and sea, mountains and cliffs dominate the route. The zenith of the day's ride is also that for the whole trip, around 1500ft at 5.4mi. Only Westport (27.5mi) and Cleone (39.8mi) have ***food stores*** en route.

Almost immediately, the route begins the 4.6mi climb of the infamous (but overhyped) Leggett Hill. The climb is steady but not difficult (about a 950ft gain, averaging 4%) and generally cool as the road winds up through superb conifer forest. The more serious climb of 1.9mi, starting after nonexistent Rockport (17.8mi), gains about 700ft, averaging 7%. On a good day there are views across the tree-tops to the Pacific Ocean. It's something of a mystery, as well as a nuisance, that this lovely, winding road has loaded log trucks traveling in *both* directions.

After descending to the coast, the road runs right along the very edge of the continent below steep bluffs and above black-sand beaches. It often looks in danger of disappearing altogether in the next storm. In fact, Hwy 1 suffers frequent closures due to landslips and it's not unusual for short sections to be reduced to one lane after the seaward half of the road has fallen into the water. Devegetated patches on the slope above the road mark landslips. Unfortunately, weeds such as pampas grass quickly invade, outgrowing and replacing the native scrub.

South of Westport, the highway is very undulating and winding. After Ten Mile River, the road trends inland and the coastal plain widens. Cattle graze in large fields. Groves of eucalypts grow along the roadside. These huge, fragrant Australian natives, used for windbreaks, have become another weed in much of California.

Hwy 1 into Fort Bragg is narrow, hilly and busy. A quiet detour from Cleone avoids most of the worst. Turn right 0.1mi south of Cleone store onto Mill Creek Dr. After 0.7mi, pass under an embankment and climb the gravel track next to it to access the Ten Mile Trail, an old 'haul road' on top. This continues south, traffic-free, through conifer forest until an exit to a parking lot 2.7mi from Cleone. Return to the highway for the final 1mi. The Pudding Creek trestle south of the gate is scheduled for repair in 2002–03 allowing access into Fort Bragg. Then, according to the Ten Mile Coastal Trail Foundation, it will be possible to cycle between Fort Bragg and the Ten Mile River (about 7mi) without riding on Hwy 1.

Fort Bragg

☎ 707

The town takes its name from the fort established here in 1857, named for Colonel Braxton Bragg, a Mexican War veteran. In 1885, a lumber company was established on

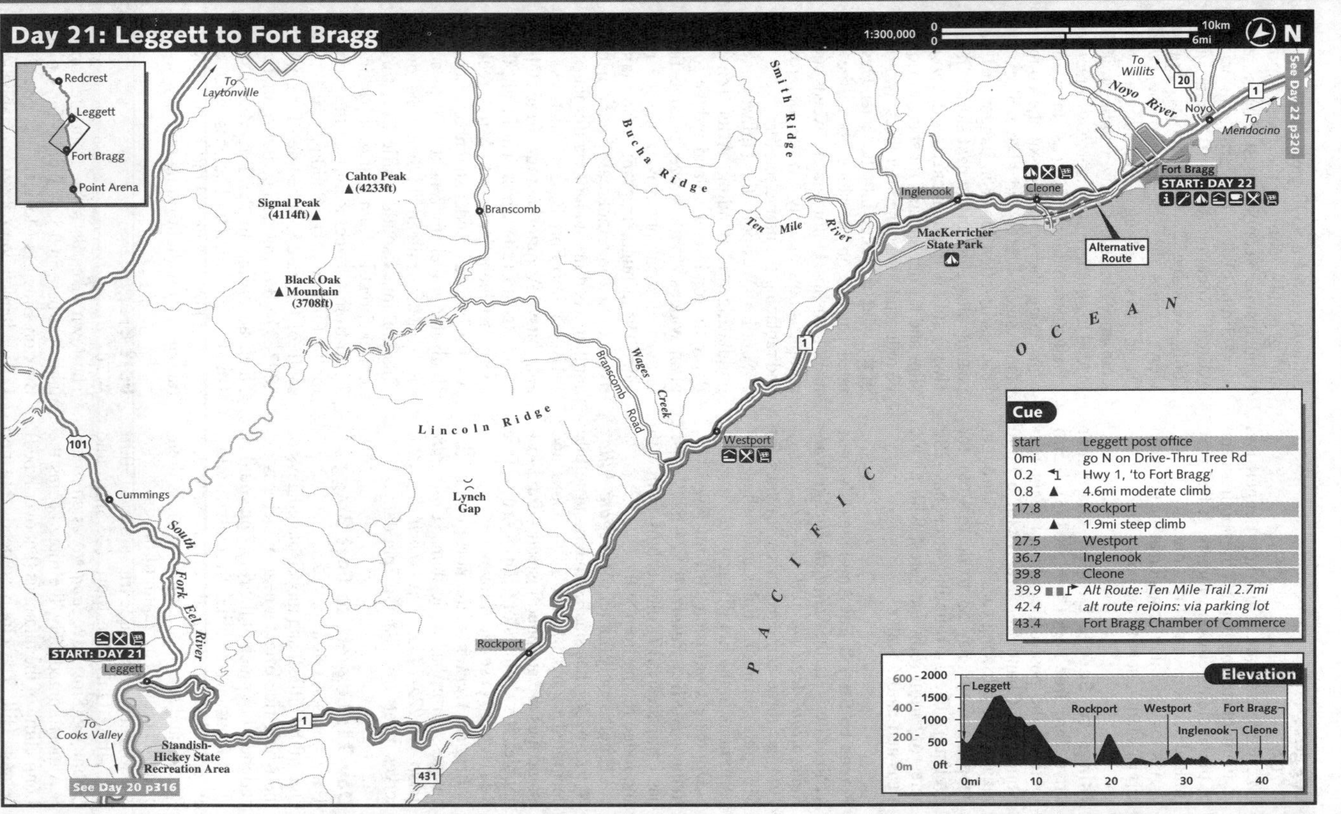

Day 21: Leggett to Fort Bragg
1:300,000
0 10km
0 6mi
N
Redcrest
Leggett
Fort Bragg
Point Arena
To Laytonville
Cahto Peak (4233ft)
Signal Peak (4114ft)
Branscomb
Black Oak Mountain (3708ft)
Bucha Ridge
Smith Ridge
Ten Mile River
To Willits
Noyo River
Noyo
To Mendocino
See Day 22 p320
Inglenook
Cleone
Fort Bragg
START: DAY 22
MacKerricher State Park
Alternative Route
Branscomb Road
Wages Creek
Lincoln Ridge
Westport
P A C I F I C O C E A N
Cummings
South Fork Eel River
Lynch Gap
Rockport
START: DAY 21
Leggett
To Cooks Valley
Standish-Hickey State Recreation Area
See Day 20 p316
1
20
101
431
Cue
start Leggett post office
0mi go N on Drive-Thru Tree Rd
0.2 Hwy 1, 'to Fort Bragg'
0.8 4.6mi moderate climb
17.8 Rockport
1.9mi steep climb
27.5 Westport
36.7 Inglenook
39.8 Cleone
39.9 Alt Route: Ten Mile Trail 2.7mi
42.4 alt route rejoins: via parking lot
43.4 Fort Bragg Chamber of Commerce
Elevation
600 - 2000
1500
400 - 1000
200 - 500
0m 0ft
Leggett
Rockport
Westport
Fort Bragg
Inglenook
Cleone
0mi 10 20 30 40

the abandoned fort site and, in the same year, the California Western Railroad, or Skunk Train, was established to get the big redwood logs to the coast. Fort Bragg is now a lively but not overly touristed destination.

Information With abundant information, the chamber of commerce (☎ 961-6300 or ☎ 800-726-2780, Ⓦ www.mendocinocoast.com) is at 332 N Main St. Bank of America and Washington Mutual are both on corners at N Main and Alder Sts. Inside Safeway, Wells Fargo Bank has an ATM.

Fort Bragg Cyclery (☎ 964-3509), 579 S Franklin St, is closed Sunday. Mendocino's & Bicycles Too (☎ 937-4330) is at 44850 Comptche-Ukiah Rd.

Log on at Mendocino County Library (☎ 961-6300), 490 Laurel St; or Computer Solutions (☎ 964-7861), 434 Franklin St.

Things to See & Do The handsome **Guest House Museum** (☎ 961-2840), 343 N Main St, was built in 1892. It holds historical photos and relics of the town's logging history (closed Mon).

The **Mendocino Coast Botanical Gardens** (☎ 964-4352), 2mi south of town, cover 47 acres between the highway and the coastal bluffs.

Fort Bragg's premier tourist attraction, the **Skunk Train** (☎ 964-6371 or ☎ 800-777-5865) makes daily runs to Willits, a journey of about 40mi over redwood-forested mountains. The station is a block west of Main St at the foot of Laurel St.

Fort Bragg Depot (☎ 964-4367), at 401 N Main St, has steam locomotives on display, coffee, food and gift shops.

Places to Stay & Eat Camp at ***MacKerricher Beach State Park***, west of Hwy 1 about 3.5mi north of town. Hiker/biker camping costs $3 per person with coin-operated showers.

The cheapest accommodations are probably at ***Driftwood Motel*** *(☎ 964-4061, 820 N Main St)* with quiet rooms set back from the street and color TV for $40. ***Colombi Motel*** *(☎ 964-8015, 647 E Oak St)* has clean rooms in a quiet location for $45.

Hi Seas Inn *(☎ 964-5929 or ☎ 800-990-7327, 1201 N Main St)* is right on the ocean edge, with doubles for $89/99 weekday/weekend. Also in a spectacular location, luxurious ***Ocean View Lodge*** *(☎ 964-1951 or ☎ 800-643-5482, 1141 N Main St)* charges $155/255 for rooms with king-size beds/spa and fireplace.

The superb ***Weller House Inn*** *(☎ 964-4415 or ☎ 877-893-5537, Ⓔ innkeeper@wellerhouse.com, 524 Stewart St)* is Fort Bragg's most luxurious B&B, charging $95 to $165. This includes a full breakfast served in the ballroom and a wine get-together at 5pm. Its reconstructed water tower, the tallest point in town, has a hot tub at the top.

Safeway is at 660 S Main St. A ***farmers market*** *(☎ 937-4336)* sells fresh produce (Wed 3.30–6pm, May–Oct).

For breakfast and lunch, try ***Eggheads Restaurant*** *(☎ 964-5005, 326 N Main St)*, specializing in crepes, omelettes, Benedicts and salads. Two doors north, ***Main St Diner*** *(☎ 964-7910)* has a selection of vegetarian dishes from $8. ***Headlands Coffeehouse*** *(☎ 964-1987, 120 E Laurel St)* serves waffles, pastries and *panini*, and has live entertainment each evening.

D'Aurelio & Sons *(☎ 964-4227, 438 S Franklin St)* serves reasonably priced home-made pizza and Italian dinners. ***Cafe Prima*** *(☎ 964-0563, 124 E Laurel St)* offers familiar as well as exotic cuisine, including Swahili dishes from the Kenyan chef.

Day 22: Fort Bragg to Point Arena

4–7¼ hours, 44.4mi

Another constantly undulating day has three notable climbs, all short (one steep, two moderate), each reaching just 300ft. The ride is all along Hwy 1 very close to yet more spectacular coastline. ***Food*** is available at Mendocino, a side trip at 9.5mi, as well as at Albion (16.5mi), Elk (25.5mi) and Manchester (39mi).

The trestle bridge (16.3mi) near Albion is an impressive sight. A ***motel***, ***campground*** and ***store*** are nearby.

Take extra care on the road around Elk, which is narrow with minimal shoulder. It often clings to the very edge of the cliff with only a rickety picket fence to keep cyclists from a watery grave.

Side Trip: Mendocino

2mi

It's worth a detour down to trendy 'Mendo', if only to visit its bakeries and sample their

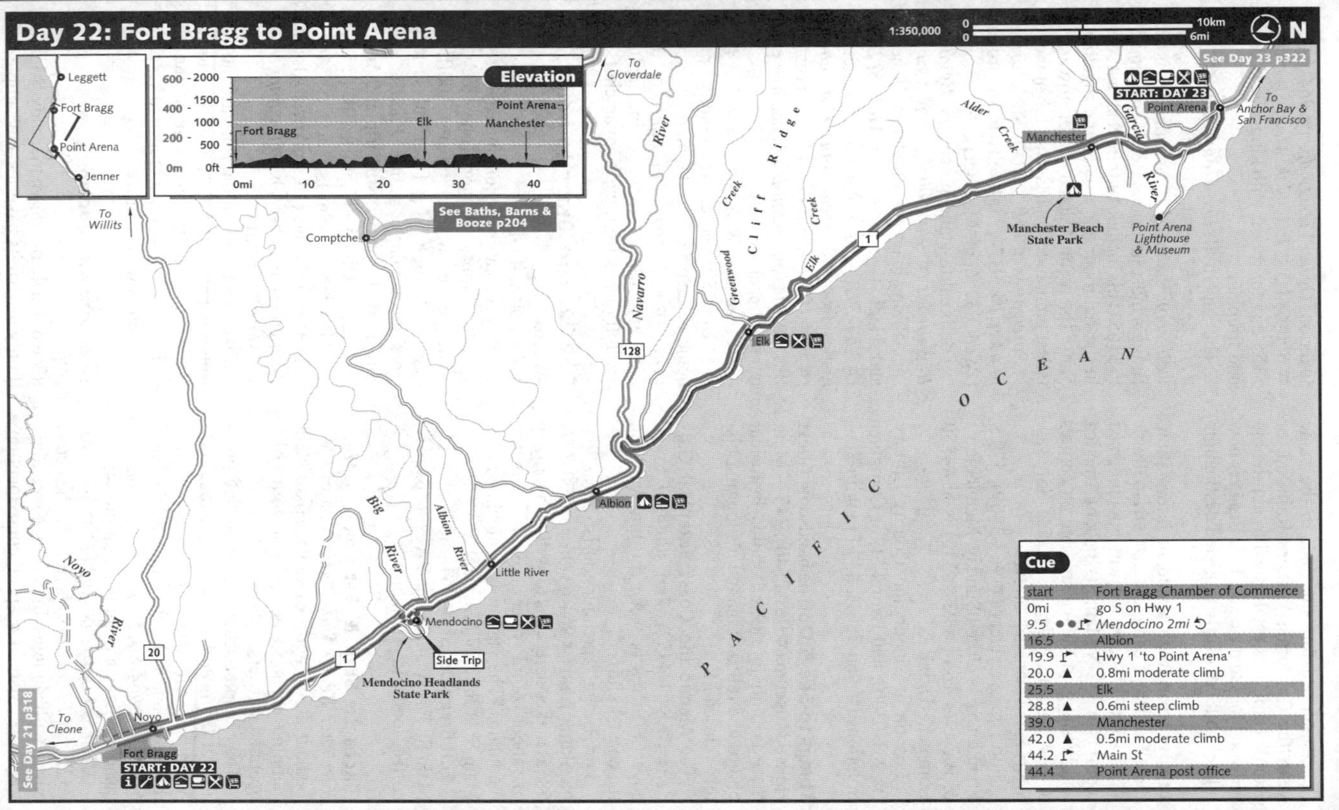

start	Fort Bragg Chamber of Commerce
0mi	go S on Hwy 1
9.5	*Mendocino 2mi*
16.5	Albion
19.9	Hwy 1 'to Point Arena'
20.0 ▲	0.8mi moderate climb
25.5	Elk
28.8 ▲	0.6mi steep climb
39.0	Manchester
42.0 ▲	0.5mi moderate climb
44.2	Main St
44.4	Point Arena post office

wares. There's also Mendocino Headlands State Park, a museum and an arts center.

Well-preserved, Victorian-era wooden buildings make interesting streetscapes. The entire town is on the National Register of Historic Places, and overlooks the ocean with waves crashing on rocky headlands. To avoid the return climb, veer left at the bottom of the hill in town to rejoin the highway at the route's 10.2mi point.

Point Arena

☎ 707

A small fishing town of 420 people, Point Arena takes its name from the nearby windswept point where a lighthouse has stood for more than a century. Many among the population are 'refugees' who moved from San Francisco in the 1970s, seeking an alternative lifestyle.

Information Contact Point Arena Merchants Association (☎ 888-842-8800) at PO Box 493, Point Arena, CA 95468. West America Bank, 204 Main St, has an ATM. Use the Internet at Coast Community Library (☎ 882-3114), 280 Main St.

Things to See & Do The historic **Point Arena Lighthouse & Museum** (☎ 882-2777) is about 2mi north of town and another 2mi west of the highway, on a side road.

Ride to the **wharf**, 1mi along Iversen Rd at the foot of the hill in town. Check out the convoluted bedding planes of the upthrust rocks forming the cliffs.

The town has a number of interesting Victorian weatherboard buildings, which can be viewed from the street. **Iversen House**, on Iversen Rd near Hwy 1, dates from 1870.

Mendocino, Star of the Silver Screen

Though Mendocino is only a tiny town, more than 60 films for TV and the silver screen have been shot here, starting with *The Promise*, a 1916 silent film. Some of the better-known motion pictures filmed here include *East of Eden* (1954), starring James Dean; *Same Time, Next Year* (1978); the *Murder, She Wrote* TV series (1984–88); *Dying Young* (1990); *Forever Young* (1992); and *The Majestic* (2001), starring Jim Carrey.

Places to Stay & Eat To the right of the Day 22 route at 38.2mi, ***Manchester Beach State Park*** is about 1mi along unsigned Kinney Rd. Hiker/biker sites ($3 per person) have water and toilets but no showers. Closer to the highway on the same road, ***Manchester Beach KOA*** (*☎ 882-2375 or ☎ 800-562-4188, e mendokoa@mcn.org*) charges $8 for hikers/bikers (including showers). Cabins cost $44. The nearest store is at Manchester.

At the northern entrance to Point Arena, ***Rollerville Junction RV Park*** *(☎ 882-2440, e pbellew@mcn.org)* has a store. Hiker/biker camping costs $12 per person. Cabins are $44 per double plus $5 for each extra adult – own bedding required.

In town, the ***Sea Shell Inn*** *(☎ 882-2000 or ☎ 877-733-7435, 135 Main St)* has modern, quiet doubles for $50.

About 1mi west of town at the wharf, ***Coast Guard House Historic Inn*** *(☎ 882-2442)* has rooms from $125 to $185. ***Wharf Master's Inn*** *(☎ 882-3171 or ☎ 800-932-4031)*, a restored 1862 Victorian house once home to the wharf master, has rooms starting at $120.

The town ***grocery*** and ***deli*** is at 185 Main St. Nearby is the renowned ***bakery*** *(213 Main St)*. A couple of doors uphill, ***Holy Grounds*** *(☎ 882-3502)* serves juices, coffee, sandwiches, bagels and light meals.

In contrast to the counter-culture cafes downtown, ***Pirates Cove Cafe*** *(☎ 882-2360, 405 School St)*, up the hill, appears decidedly right-wing with National Rifle Association propaganda and militaristic decor. The proprietor, also a cartoonist penning 'Friendly Folks' cards (w www.mcn.org/h/rtanis), serves good, traditional breakfasts, lunches and dinners.

Downtown, try ***El Burrito*** *(☎ 882-2910, cnr Main & Mill Sts)* for organic Mexican lunch and dinner.

Day 23: Point Arena to Jenner

4½–8¼ hours, 51.6mi

Begin the day on a narrow, undulating and shoulderless road through grazing fields. There are only two notable hills; the first is immediately out of town and the second (43.2mi) reaches the day's peak of 600ft. ***Food stores*** are at Anchor Bay (10.6mi), Gualala (13.6mi), Ocean Cove (35mi) and Fort Ross (38.6mi). Gualala's hardware store (☎ 884-3503) stocks very basic bike spares.

Day 23: Point Arena to Jenner

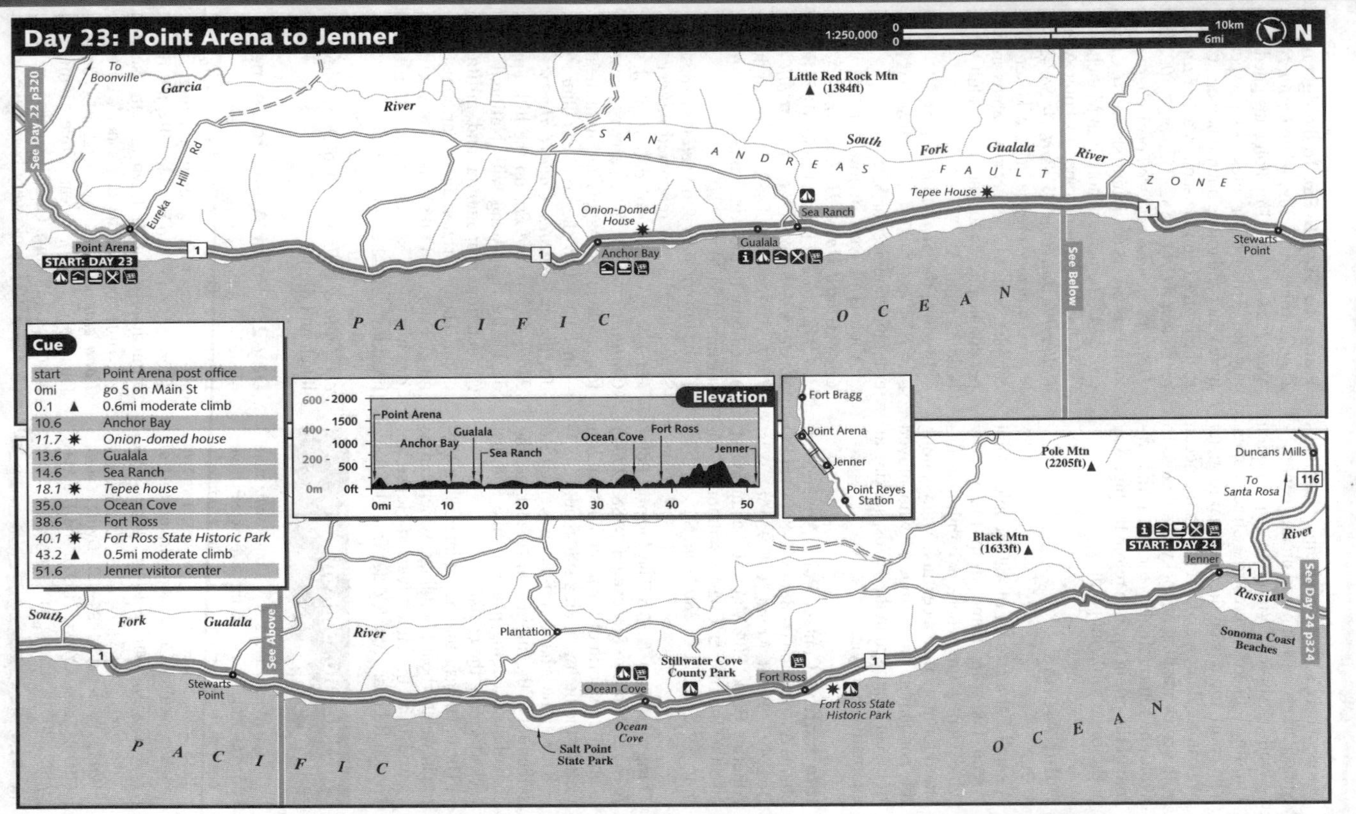

Cue

start		Point Arena post office
0mi		go S on Main St
0.1	▲	0.6mi moderate climb
10.6		Anchor Bay
11.7	✱	*Onion-domed house*
13.6		Gualala
14.6		Sea Ranch
18.1	✱	*Tepee house*
35.0		Ocean Cove
38.6		Fort Ross
40.1	✱	*Fort Ross State Historic Park*
43.2	▲	0.5mi moderate climb
51.6		Jenner visitor center

The road is often on the very edge of the cliff. Thick eucalypt groves dominate the vegetation around the 30mi point, where the traffic can be heavy on the still-narrow, winding road. After 40mi, constant undulations and longish climbs are tiring but the coastline is spectacular. There is little habitation along the coast between Ocean Cove and Jenner. Watch for cattle wandering on the road.

Interesting examples of Californian architecture are visible beside the route. On the left opposite Pirates Dr (11.7mi), note the house with the **onion-domed towers**, which would not be out of place in downtown Moscow. At 18.1mi, opposite a sign announcing Bosuns Beach, glance left at the swooping lines of the **tepee-inspired wooden house** in the treeline.

Stillwater Cove County Park campground (36.2mi) is a useful intermediate facility. Hiker/biker sites cost $3 per person. Buy food at the Ocean Cove store 1.2mi north.

Fort Ross State Historic Park (☎ 847-3286; 40.1mi) has a reconstruction of a Russian fort – once the southernmost American outpost of the 19th-century Russian fur trade – and a primitive ***campground*** (41.8mi).

Jenner

☎ 707

A tiny resort town, Jenner perches on the hills at the estuary of Russian River. Highway turnouts north of town offer views of the **harbor seal colony** at the river mouth. Pups are born March through August.

Jenner visitor center (☎ 865-9433) is tucked away on the water's edge opposite the service station. The service station store has an ATM.

Check out the visitor center's displays about the estuary, and spot the birds and mammals that frequent it.

Places to Stay & Eat The RV park at the south end of the Russian River Bridge no longer allows tenting. The nearest attractive camping option before town is at Stillwater Cove (see Day 23), otherwise continue 9.3mi to Bodega Dunes (see Day 24).

River's End (☎ *865-2484, 11048 Hwy 1)* has doubles from $75 and cabins with fireplaces for $120. Its restaurant serves *haute cuisine* with sumptuous dishes such as pheasant breast ($27) and filo vegetables ($16). ***Jenner Inn*** (☎ *865-2377 or* ☎ *800-732-2377,* ⓔ *innkeeper@jennerinn.com, Hwy 1)*, in the center of town, has private cottages from $88 to $258 with a two-night minimum. It serves breakfast to guests, has a wine bar and art gallery, and offers yoga classes and massage.

The service station ***store*** has an uninspiring range of food for self-caterers. ***Seagull Gifts & Deli*** (☎ *865-2594)*, next to the visitor center, serves snacks, coffee and takeaways, and has shadeless outdoor tables. ***Sizzling Tandoor Restaurant*** (☎ *865-0625, 9960 Hwy 1)*, 1.3mi south of town, serves curries ($12–16) and vegetarian specials ($9); closed Tuesday.

Day 24: Jenner to Point Reyes Station

3¾–6¾ hours, 42.5mi

Another day entirely on Hwy 1, passing the Sonoma Coast Beaches before briefly detouring inland. It has few notable hills but almost constant tiring undulations. Returning to the coast at Tomales Bay, the route runs straight along the San Andreas Fault Zone. The prominent Point Reyes National Seashore across the narrow bay is part of a different crustal plate, moving northwest relative to the rest of North America. Two moderate hills book-end the day while a third rises in the middle with a 0.4mi steep pinch on top as a *coup de grâce*. This reaches the day's high point of almost 300ft. ***Food*** is available at several towns.

Bodega Dunes campground (9.3mi) has hiker/biker sites ($3 per person) and coin-operated showers.

Around the 28mi mark, the road overlooks the marsh flats of the Point Reyes National Seashore, home to many wading birds. However, with so many feral eucalypts around, this could be Australia.

Point Reyes Station

☎ 415

With a gas station, a saloon, art galleries, restaurants and tourist shops, Point Reyes Station (PRS), population 675, is the hub of West Marin. One-horse Olema, 2.3mi southeast, claims the honor of being the epicenter of San Francisco's Great 1906 Quake. Today it has camping, motel and food services.

Information There is no visitor center at PRS but Bear Valley visitor center (☎ 464-5100) at Olema has displays and information

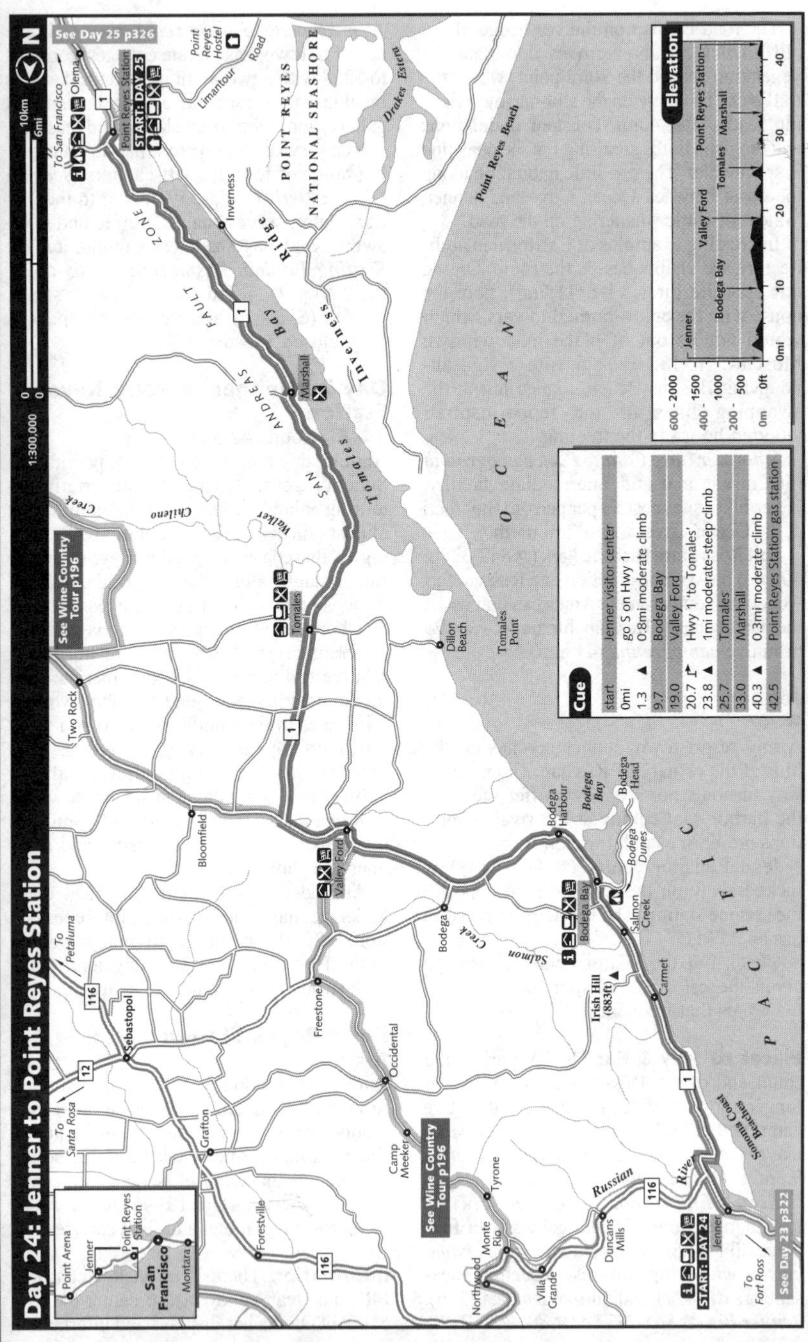
Day 24: Jenner to Point Reyes Station
1:300,000
0 10km
0 6mi
N
See Day 25 p326
See Day 23 p322
See Wine Country Tour p196
See Wine Country Tour p196
START: DAY 24
START: DAY 25
Point Arena
Jenner
Point Reyes Station
San Francisco
Montara
Point Reyes Hostel
Limantour Road
Olema
To San Francisco
Drakes Estero
POINT REYES NATIONAL SEASHORE
Point Reyes Beach
Inverness
Inverness Ridge
SAN ANDREAS FAULT ZONE
Tomales Bay
Marshall
Walker
Chileno Creek
Tomales
Dillon Beach
Tomales Point
Two Rock
Bloomfield
Valley Ford
Bodega Harbour
Bodega Bay
Bodega Head
Bodega Dunes
Bodega
Salmon Creek
Carmet
Irish Hill (883ft)
Freestone
Occidental
Camp Meeker
Tyrone
Monte Rio
Northwood
Villa Grande
Duncans Mills
Russian River
Sonoma Coast Beaches
To Fort Ross
To Petaluma
To Santa Rosa
Sebastopol
Grafton
Forestville
PACIFIC OCEAN
Cue
start Jenner visitor center
0mi go S on Hwy 1
1.3 ▲ 0.8mi moderate climb
9.7 Bodega Bay
19.0 Valley Ford
20.7 ↱ Hwy 1 'to Tomales'
23.8 ▲ 1mi moderate-steep climb
25.7 Tomales
33.0 Marshall
40.3 ▲ 0.3mi moderate climb
42.5 Point Reyes Station gas station
Elevation
600 - 2000
400 - 1500
1000
200 - 500
0m 0ft
0mi 10 20 30 40
Jenner
Bodega Bay
Valley Ford
Tomales
Marshall
Point Reyes Station

about Point Reyes National Seashore and the San Andreas Fault.

Bank of Petaluma is at 11400 Hwy 1, PRS. Outside Olema's post office, in the shopping center near the campground, is an ATM.

The Internet is available at PRS library (☎ 663-8375), 11431 Hwy 1, Suite 7.

There are several bike shops along the route from Fairfax (Day 25).

Things to See & Do From Bear Valley visitor center there are lots of **hiking trails** on the National Seashore. The shortest – a circuit of about 0.6mi that starts from the picnic area across the road – is the fascinating **Earthquake Trail** along a section of the San Andreas Fault. The amount the earth can move during a quake is graphically illustrated by the gap in a once-continuous fence across the fault line.

Browse through PRS's galleries such as **William Lester Gallery** (☎ 663-9365; open Thurs–Mon), 11101 Hwy 1, displaying the artist's paintings; **Black Mtn Weavers** (☎ 663-9130) at 11245 Hwy 1, showing the textiles and clothing designs of 15 local artists; and, next door, **Zuma Ethnic Arts & Crafts** (☎ 663-1748).

Five Brooks Ranch (☎ 663-1570), 3mi south of Olema on Hwy 1, hires horses. It has 50mi of bridle trails through woods to the seashore.

For **kayak rentals**, phone ☎ 663-1743.

Places to Stay & Eat Huge ***Olema Ranch Campground*** *(☎ 663-8001 or ☎ 800-655-2267)*, 2.3mi past PRS, has very ordinary, tired facilities and is expensive at $20 per site. ***Samuel P Taylor State Park***, over Bolinas Ridge 7.5mi along the Day 25 route, has hiker/biker camping ($3 per person, coin showers) amid redwood groves.

The only cheap indoor option is the ***Point Reyes Hostel*** *(☎ 663-8811, 1390 Limantour Rd)* in the National Seashore. Beds cost $13 to $15, including use of a family room and kitchen.

Nonsmoking ***Point Reyes Seashore Lodge*** *(☎ 663-9000 or ☎ 800-404-5634; W www.pointreyesseashore.com; 10021 Hwy 1, Olema)* is in a beautiful spot and charges $125 to $295 for doubles, including a breakfast of fruit, cereal and pastries.

For details of small inns and cottages, check the Web site W www.ptreyes.com (☎ 663-1872 or ☎ 800-539-1872) or log on to W www.coastallodging.com.

An English Oak B&B *(☎ 663-1777; e sharyn@anenglishoak.com; cnr Bear Valley Rd & Hwy 1, Olema)* has rooms from $92/120 weekday/weekend and a private cottage, sleeping up to six, for $120/160 per double ($15 per additional person). Cyclists get a 10% discount.

Palace Market *(Hwy 1)*, opposite 3rd St, sells groceries. ***West Marin Neighborhood Deli & Cafe*** *(☎ 663-8464, Hwy 1)* is one of several businesses in downtown PRS serving takeaway sandwiches, pizza and snacks.

Point Reyes Oyster Company *(☎ 663-8373, 11101 Hwy 1)* sells organically grown premium shellfish on weekends. ***Point Reyes Villa*** *(☎ 663-5482, 10905 Hwy 1)* serves Italian and American cuisine, including veal, steak, seafood, chicken, pasta and pizza. Mexican ***Taqueria La Quinta*** *(☎ 663-8868, cnr Hwy 1 & 3rd St)* serves homemade tortillas, tamales, salsas and chili.

A five-minute walk south of Olema Ranch, ***Olema Farm House Restaurant & Bar*** *(☎ 663-1264; 10005 Hwy 1, Olema)* specializes in fresh oysters, steaks and outdoor dining. Next door, the ***Olema Liquor & Deli*** is open daily for grocery items, drinks and ice cream.

Day 25: Point Reyes Station to Montara

5¼–9¼ hours, 57.7mi

Traveling through San Francisco, this day features a number of taxing hills and traffic is much heavier. From Lagunitas (10.1mi) the route becomes increasingly urban and navigation is complicated by the many busy roads. Crossing the Golden Gate Bridge is a highlight. If you're keen to check out the great city, see San Francisco (pp183–88) for information about accommodations and other services.

The route tops 600ft on the steep climb up Bolinas Ridge (3.3mi) but only reaches its highest point for the day (665ft) in the hilly suburbs south of San Francisco (46.8mi). After a descent to sea level, there's a final 1mi-long moderate-to-steep gradient into Montara. Plenty of services line the route from Lagunitas to the Golden Gate, but few are close by in the built-up area south.

After the Bolinas Ridge climb, an alternative bikepath can be used to avoid rough,

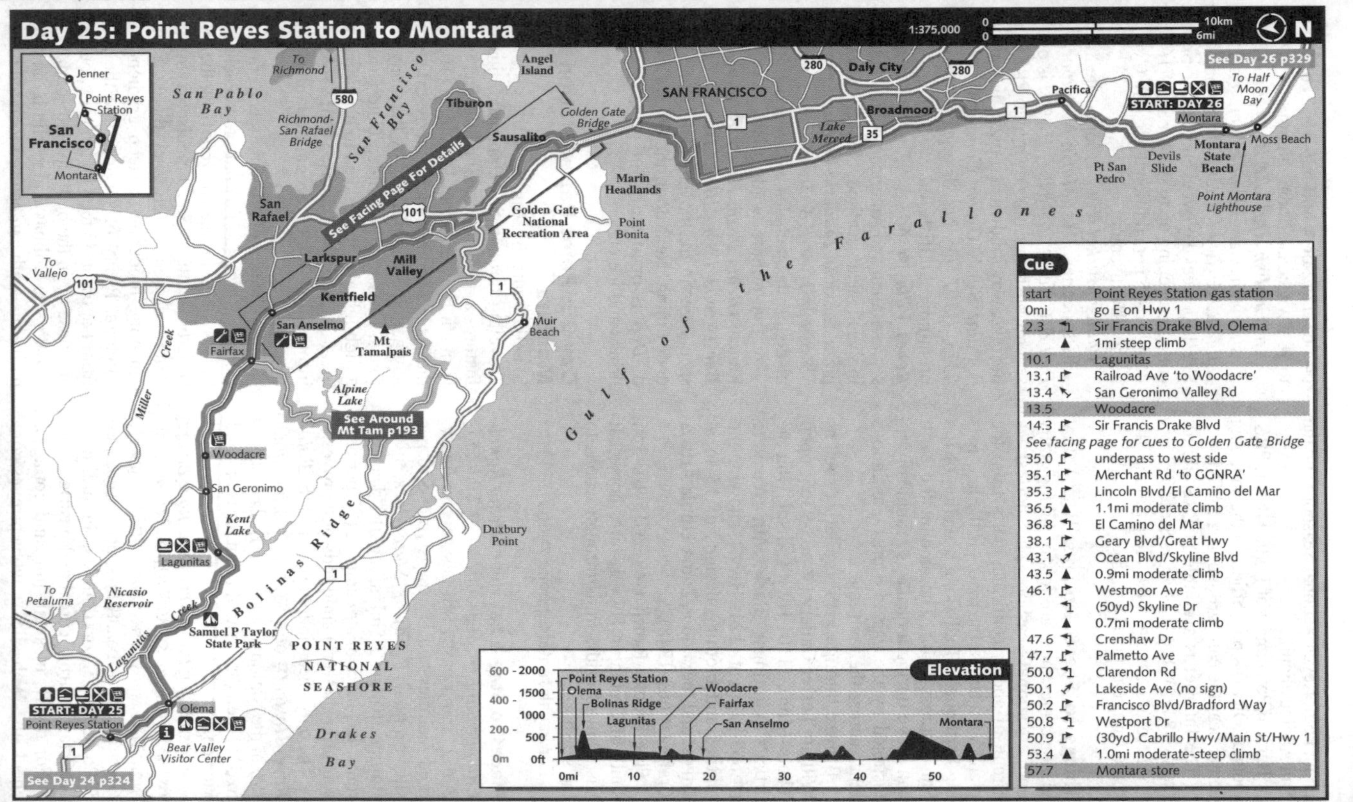

start	Point Reyes Station gas station
0mi	go E on Hwy 1
2.3	Sir Francis Drake Blvd, Olema
▲	1mi steep climb
10.1	Lagunitas
13.1	Railroad Ave 'to Woodacre'
13.4	San Geronimo Valley Rd
13.5	Woodacre
14.3	Sir Francis Drake Blvd
See facing page for cues to Golden Gate Bridge	
35.0	underpass to west side
35.1	Merchant Rd 'to GGNRA'
35.3	Lincoln Blvd/El Camino del Mar
36.5 ▲	1.1mi moderate climb
36.8	El Camino del Mar
38.1	Geary Blvd/Great Hwy
43.1	Ocean Blvd/Skyline Blvd
43.5 ▲	0.9mi moderate climb
46.1	Westmoor Ave
	(50yd) Skyline Dr
▲	0.7mi moderate climb
47.6	Crenshaw Dr
47.7	Palmetto Ave
50.0	Clarendon Rd
50.1	Lakeside Ave (no sign)
50.2	Francisco Blvd/Bradford Way
50.8	Westport Dr
50.9	(30yd) Cabrillo Hwy/Main St/Hwy 1
53.4 ▲	1.0mi moderate-steep climb
57.7	Montara store

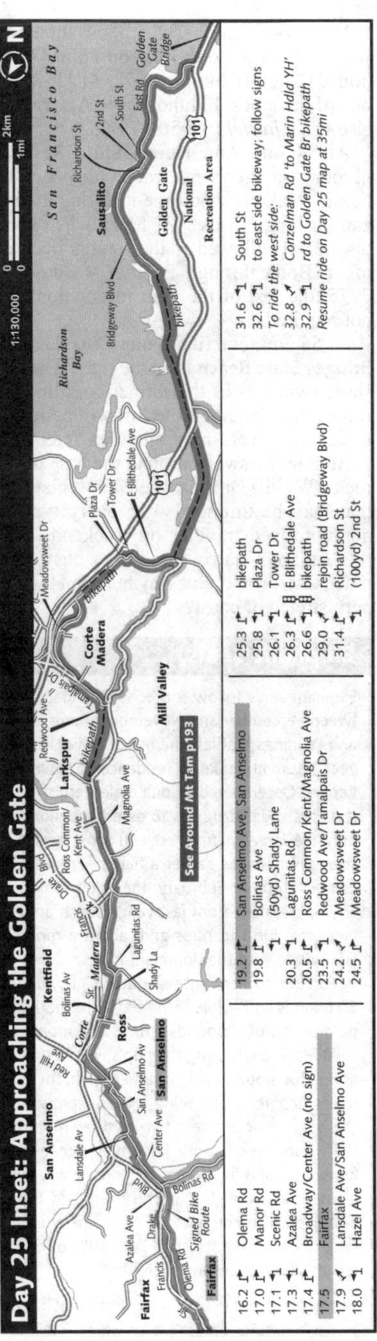

narrow, often busy Sir Francis Drake Blvd, which winds through redwoods. Brake hard on the descent to react to the bike route sign in time.

The route uses a signed bike route from 17mi and a couple of bikepaths: one at 25.3mi next to Hwy 101; another at 26.6mi that joins Bridgeway Blvd on the approach to Golden Gate Bridge. To ride on the east side of the bridge, simply follow the signs. The west side bikepath closes to cyclists at 3.30pm on weekdays; on weekends and holidays, the it's open to cyclists from early morning, closing from 10pm to 5am. When it is closed, cyclists must use the east side, which we recommend taking anyway.

The route's wealthy suburban streets southwest of the bridge offer panoramas back to the Golden Gate and across to Marin Headlands. Number 540 El Camino del Mar (36.8mi) is actor Robin Williams' house.

The urban sprawl gradually thins on the run south from Daly City with the route again clinging to the coast.

Montara

☎ 650

A small, laid-back tourist town (population 2500) with most services, Montara lies within sight of the infamous Devils Slide area of Hwy 1. This unstable cliff area often unleashes mud and boulders following winter storms, cutting the highway.

Information About 7mi south at Half Moon Bay, Coastside Chamber of Commerce (☎ 726-8380, W www.halfmoonbaychamber.org) is at 520 Kelly St.

Montara's Neighborhood Grocery Market has an ATM.

Half Moon Bay has two bike shops: Bicyclery (☎ 726-6000) at 101 Main St; and Bike Works (☎ 726-6708) at 20 Stone Pine Rd.

Internet access is available at Half Moon Bay Library (☎ 726-2316) at 620 Correas St.

Things to See & Do Trails climb from the Martini Creek parking lot, north of town, into **McNee Ranch State Park** where there are many hiking trails.

Check out the **Point Montara lighthouse**, which started as a fog station in 1875 after two steamers wrecked on the ledge offshore.

Montara State Beach is popular for swimming.

The Half Moon Bay area has many **biking trails** for riders of all levels – from the paved, flat, coastside trail along the ocean bluffs, to mountain biking through redwood groves on winding, steep, usually one-lane mountain roads. Ask the visitor center for details.

Places to Stay & Eat For hiker/biker camping, ***Half Moon Bay State Beach***, *(☎ 726-8820)* is 7.4mi south of Montara and 0.3mi along Kelly Ave. The cost is $3 per person, with cold-water showers.

The only cheap option in town, the spectacularly located ***Point Montara Lighthouse Hostel*** *(☎ 728-7177)* is adjacent the lighthouse. Beds are $13/16 for members/nonmembers; reservations recommended.

Farallone Inn *(☎ 728-8200, 1410 Main St)* is a B&B charging $110 during the week and $165 on weekends.

At El Granada, 3.4mi south of Montara, ***Harbor View Inn*** *(☎ 726-2329, 51 Ave Alhambra)* has doubles starting at $126.

The ***Neighborhood Grocery Market & Gas Station***, next door to Farallone Inn, sells food every day.

A small cafe with patio seating, ***Coastal Affair*** *(☎ 728-5229, 8455 Cabrillo Hwy)* serves Montarans with bakery items and coffee. ***Cafe Gibraltar*** *(☎ 728-9030, 171 7th St)* is open until 9pm. ***The Chart House*** *(☎ 728-7366, 8150 N Cabrillo Hwy)* is right on the beach and serves steaks, seafood and salads with views.

About 1mi south of town at Moss Beach, ***Pizzeria del Sol*** *(☎ 728-5151)* serves breakfast, lunch and dinner. Across the road, ***El Gran Amigo*** *(☎ 728-3815, 2448 Cabrillo Hwy)* does authentic Mexican food to eat-in or take away.

Day 26: Montara to Santa Cruz

5¼–9½ hours, 58.6mi

This ride is pretty much all level or gently undulating; only one serious hill rears its head (15.5mi). The route reaches its day maximum of 500ft about 0.5mi after this grade eases. The wide-shouldered Hwy 1 can be busy and is quite commercialized early. The sea is out of sight between El Granada (3.4mi) and San Gregorio State Beach (19mi). Beyond, the route enters a beautiful, uninhabited area of cliffs covered with windswept coastal heath. Davenport (44.8mi) has the only ***food store*** between Half Moon Bay and Santa Cruz.

Numerous state beaches flank the highway all the way to the **Pigeon Point Lighthouse** (28.2mi), built in 1872. At 115ft, it's one of the tallest lighthouses in America. It also has a ***hostel*** (☎ 650-879-0633).

At 34.7mi, **Año Nuevo State Reserve** harbors an elephant seal colony on the beach. Peak viewing time is during mating and birthing (15 Dec–31 Mar), when visitors are only allowed on the popular licensed tours. Book through Parknet ☎ 800-444-7275, the rest of the year reservations are not required.

At 54.3mi, entering Santa Cruz, **Natural Bridges State Beach** is on the right. The offshore remnants of the former coastline are roosts for innumerable brown pelicans. Lucky observers may spot sea otters cavorting in the swells around the base of the rocks. W Cliff Dr is paralleled by a bikepath that may be thronged with every type of nonmotorized traveler on weekends. The road, though narrow and also busy, is a much faster route. But why hurry on this superb stretch of coast?

Elephant Seals

Elephant seals follow a precise calendar: between September and November young seals and yearlings that left the beach earlier in the year, return and take up residence. In November and December, the adult males return and start the ritual struggles to assert superiority; only the largest, strongest and most aggressive 'alpha' males gather a harem. From December through February, the adult females arrive, pregnant from last year's beach activities, give birth to pups and, about a month later, mate with the dominant males.

At birth an elephant seal pup weighs about 80 pounds and, while being fed by its mother, puts on about 7 pounds a day. One month's solid feeding will bring the pup's weight up to about 300 pounds but, around March, the females depart, abandoning their offspring on the beach. For the next two to three months the young seals, now known as weaners, lounge around in groups, or pods, gradually learning to swim, first in the rivers and tidal pools, then in the sea. In April, the young seals depart, having lost 20% to 30% of their weight during this prolonged fast.

Scott McNeely

Day 26: Montara to Santa Cruz

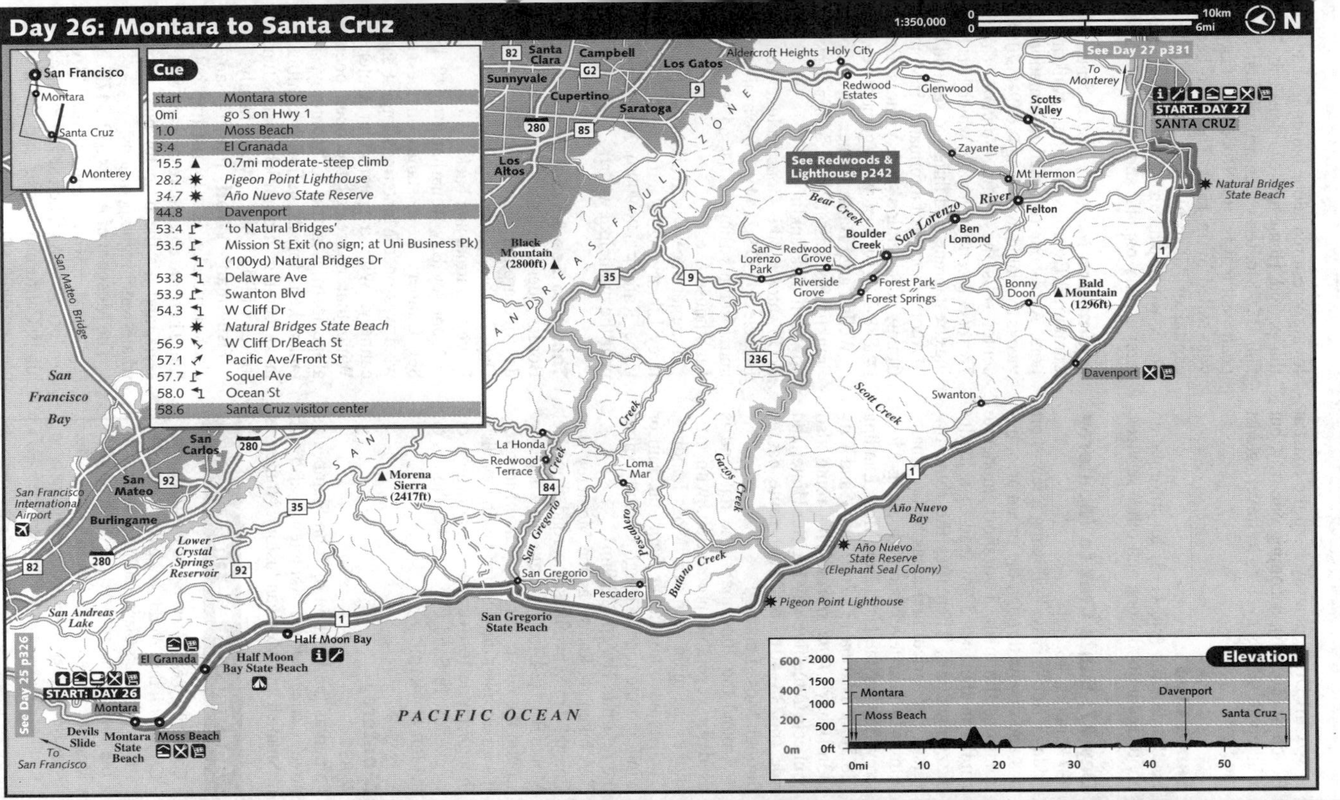

Cue

start		Montara store
0mi		go S on Hwy 1
1.0		Moss Beach
3.4		El Granada
15.5	▲	0.7mi moderate-steep climb
28.2	✷	*Pigeon Point Lighthouse*
34.7	✷	*Año Nuevo State Reserve*
44.8		Davenport
53.4	↱	'to Natural Bridges'
53.5	↱	Mission St Exit (no sign; at Uni Business Pk)
	↰	(100yd) Natural Bridges Dr
53.8	↰	Delaware Ave
53.9	↱	Swanton Blvd
54.3	↰	W Cliff Dr
	✷	*Natural Bridges State Beach*
56.9	↘	W Cliff Dr/Beach St
57.1	↗	Pacific Ave/Front St
57.7	↱	Soquel Ave
58.0	↰	Ocean St
58.6		Santa Cruz visitor center

W Cliff Dr veers away from the coast at Beach St (56.9mi), becoming one way, but a bikepath allows cyclists to travel against the flow.

Santa Cruz

See Santa Cruz (pp241–3) for information about accommodations and other services.

Day 27: Santa Cruz to Monterey

4–7¾ hours, 46.2mi

Today's ride is easy. Following a few short ups and downs through the urban area, undulations diminish. Two short, moderate climbs in the first 22mi lead to a hardly dizzying 205ft. Thereafter the route traverses flat agricultural areas before finally joining a near-level bikepath along Monterey Bay for the last 12mi. Moss Landing (28.5mi), Marina (37.2mi) and Sand City (43mi) have ***food stores***. This route also connects to the five-day Big Sur Hinterland ride (pp233–40); its Day 1 route passes through Moss Landing.

Around the 20mi mark, the flat land is used for vegetable production, with artichokes the main crop near Moss Landing. Cyclists have no shelter from sun, rain or wind and the road is rough in parts before the return to Hwy 1 (23.9mi).

A bikepath, known as the Monterey Bay Coastal Trail, parallels the road from Del Monte Blvd (34.4mi) virtually the whole way around the curve of the bay into Monterey. It's an excellent facility for touring cyclists, though prone to over-pedestrianization on weekends. In Sand City, a bike shop is on the left at 44.1mi.

Monterey

☎ 831

Famed as the location of John Steinbeck's novel *Cannery Row*, Monterey is also rich in Spanish and Mexican history. Numerous lovingly restored adobe buildings date from this period. Home to the Ohlone tribe since 500 BC, Monterey Peninsula's first European visitor was Juan Rodríguez Cabrillo who sailed by in 1542. The town became capital of Alta California after Mexico's break with Spain in 1821. Modern Monterey is very popular and heavily touristed.

Information Monterey visitor center, 401 Camino El Estero, serves only walk-in visitors. A 24-hour recorded information service is available by calling ☎ 649-1770. The center sells the useful *Monterey County Travel & Meeting Planner*, which lists lodgings, restaurants and things to see and do.

Another source of information is Monterey County Convention and Visitors Bureau (☎ 888-221-1010, Ⓦ www.gomonterey.org).

Wells Fargo Bank, corner Alvarado and Franklin Sts, has an ATM; other banks are downhill on Franklin St.

Downtown bike shops include Aquarian Bicycles (☎ 375-2144), 486 Washington St, and Joselyn's Bicycles (☎ 649-8520), 638 Lighthouse Ave.

Internet access is available at the Monterey Library, 625 Pacific St, and Karaoke Cyber Kafe (☎ 648-9090), 256 Figueroa St, near the municipal wharf.

Things to See & Do Although Border to Border riders will do this anyway, a good day ride around Monterey is to follow the Day 28 route along spectacular **17-Mile Drive** to Carmel and back.

Monterey Bay Aquarium (☎ 648-4800), 886 Cannery Row, stands on the site of what was once Monterey's largest sardine cannery. With a spectacular Outer Bay Wing that re-creates the open ocean, it alone justifies a trip to Monterey. Touch tanks, kelp forests, jellyfish exhibits and tanks teeming with sunfish, sharks, tuna and turtles will delight the whole family.

Fisherman's Wharf, like its San Francisco namesake, is a tourist trap but good fun. There are colorful restaurants and noisy seals, and it's the base for boat trips and whale-watching expeditions.

The **Museum of Art** (☎ 372-5477), voted 'best small town museum in the USA', has two locations. A branch at 559 Pacific St exhibits Californian artists and has a superb photographic collection (open Wed–Sun).

And You Can Eat Them

Castroville, near Monterey, is the 'Artichoke Capital of the World'. A giant artichoke stands outside its Giant Artichoke Restaurant. The town holds an Artichoke Festival mid-May. The first Artichoke Queen back in 1948, Miss Norma Jean Baker, achieved more fame in other endeavors as Marilyn Monroe.

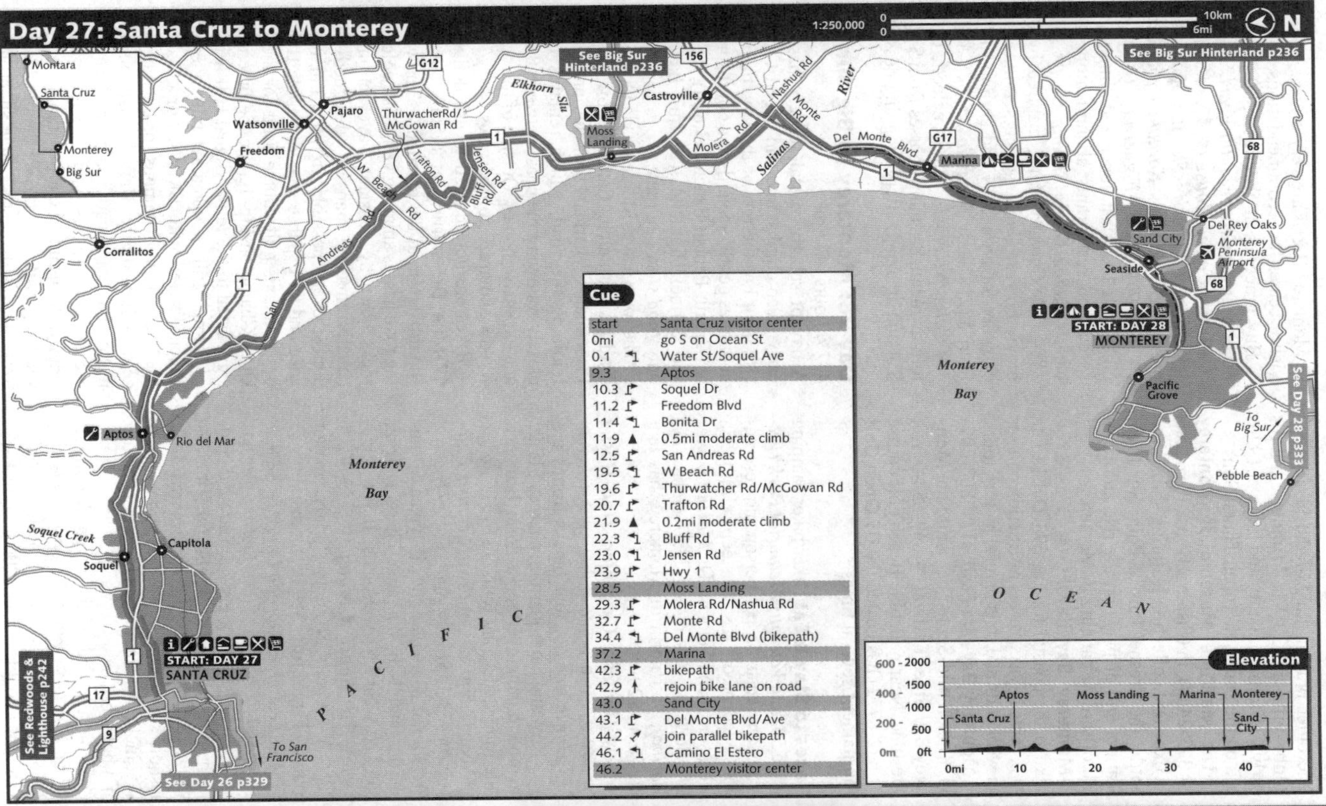

Cue		
start		Santa Cruz visitor center
0mi		go S on Ocean St
0.1	↰	Water St/Soquel Ave
9.3		Aptos
10.3	↱	Soquel Dr
11.2	↱	Freedom Blvd
11.4	↰	Bonita Dr
11.9	▲	0.5mi moderate climb
12.5	↱	San Andreas Rd
19.5	↰	W Beach Rd
19.6	↱	Thurwatcher Rd/McGowan Rd
20.7	↱	Trafton Rd
21.9	▲	0.2mi moderate climb
22.3	↰	Bluff Rd
23.0	↰	Jensen Rd
23.9	↱	Hwy 1
28.5		Moss Landing
29.3	↱	Molera Rd/Nashua Rd
32.7	↱	Monte Rd
34.4	↰	Del Monte Blvd (bikepath)
37.2		Marina
42.3	↱	bikepath
42.9	↑	rejoin bike lane on road
43.0		Sand City
43.1	↱	Del Monte Blvd/Ave
44.2	↗	join parallel bikepath
46.1	↰	Camino El Estero
46.2		Monterey visitor center

The other branch, La Mirada, in an early adobe villa at 720 Via Mirada, explores early Californian history and looks at 1920s life on the peninsula (open Thurs–Sun).

The **Maritime Museum of Monterey** (☎ 373-2469), in Customs House Plaza, has an excellent collection featuring ships-in-a-bottle, the Fresnel lens of Point Sur Light Station, and displays on the rise and rapid fall of sardine canning in Monterey.

Monterey Bay Kayaks (☎ 373-8357), next to the coastal trail at 693 Del Monte Ave, rents kayaks, offers instruction courses on weekends and runs natural history tours.

Monterey Bay Jazz Festival (☎ 800-307-3378) is in mid-September while the **Monterey Bay Blues Festival** (☎ 649-6544) is in late June. Nearby Pebble Beach golf course (☎ 622-8772) has hosted the **US Open Golf Tournament** several times.

Places to Stay & Eat Hiker/biker camping at the 50-acre ***Veterans Memorial Park*** *(Veterans Dr)* costs $5 per person; no reservations accepted. It's a steep climb via Jefferson St and Veterans Dr. ***Marina Dunes RV Park*** *(☎ 384-6914; 3330 Dunes Dr, Marina)*, 9mi north of Monterey, has tent sites from $20.

New ***Monterey Carpenters Hall Hostel*** *(☎ 649-0375, ⓔ info@montereyhostel.com, 778 Hawthorne St)*, four blocks from Cannery Row and the Aquarium, charges $17/21 member/nonmember for a dorm bed. Private rooms, sleeping four, cost $51.

About 2.5mi east of town, ***Scottish Fairway*** *(☎ 373-5551 or ☎ 800-373-5571, cnr N Fremont St & Alcalde Ave)* is typical of numerous motels in this area, charging from $65/120 weekdays/weekends. It has large, rooms. The ***Super 8 Motel*** *(☎ 373-3081, 2050 N Fremont St)*, with slightly smaller rooms, charges from $59 in summer.

More central, ***El Dorado Inn*** *(☎ 373-2921 or ☎ 800-722-1836, 900 Munras Ave)* has basic, older-style rooms from around $50. With more charm, ***El Adobe Inn*** *(☎ 372-5409 or ☎ 800-433-4732, 936 Munras Ave)*, a short stroll from town, has rooms from $75, including continental breakfast and use of a hot tub.

At the top end of the range, ***Monterey Plaza Hotel*** *(☎ 646-1700 or ☎ 800-368-2468, 400 Cannery Row)*, built over the water, has doubles from $200 a night.

Monterey B&Bs are very pricey. Ask the visitor center for recommendations.

Buy groceries at ***Safeway*** *(570 Munras St)* or ***Sunrise Grocery*** *(400 Pearl St)*.

Plumes Coffee House *(☎ 373-4526, cnr Alvarado & Franklin Sts)* is popular for brews and light meals. ***Karaoke Cyber Kafe*** *(☎ 648-9090, 256 Figueroa St)* serves diner-style breakfast, lunch and dinner.

Seafood restaurants abound along the wharf. ***Bubba Gump Shrimp Co*** *(☎ 373-1884, 720 Cannery Row)*, inspired by the movie *Forrest Gump*, is fun, serving clam chowder for around $4 and shrimp dishes from $12. Classy ***Montrio*** *(☎ 648-8880, 414 Calle Principal)*, with its eclectic Californian menu, has main courses from $12 to $24 and amazing, artery-clogging desserts.

Day 28: Monterey to Big Sur

4–7¼ hours, 44.8mi

A day of superb coastal scenery has two early steep climbs, into and out of Carmel (16.3mi). For the rest of the day, the route undulates gently upwards to a 600ft summit at 32.7mi. Pebble Beach (13.6mi), Carmel and Carmel Highlands (21.3mi) have the only ***food stores*** en route.

The route leaves Monterey via the Coastal Trail bikepath along Cannery Row, passing Fisherman's Wharf and the aquarium, before rejoining the road, which remains level, closely following the coast between the sea and expensive homes. Outside of town, deer wander and graze golf fairways.

Bikes are not charged to use delightful **17-Mile Dr**, starting at 6.5mi, but you should sign in at the gatehouse. The winding road passes amazing yellowish volcanic rocks hewn by constant wave action and equally amazing mansions designed with almost every possible architectural influence and no expense spared. Pebble Beach has a famous **golf course** used for the US Open Championship. Ignore the bike route signposted to the left at Signal Hill Rd.

Carmel, full of upmarket boutiques, its streets littered with BMWs, Porsches and Mercedes, is most famous for once having actor Clint 'Dirty Harry' Eastwood as mayor. Its central park is a good place for a break, with toilets and a supermarket nearby. Prices may be lower, though, at the ***shopping mall*** (18.6mi) on the outskirts of town. This is the last sizeable supermarket

Day 28: Monterey to Big Sur

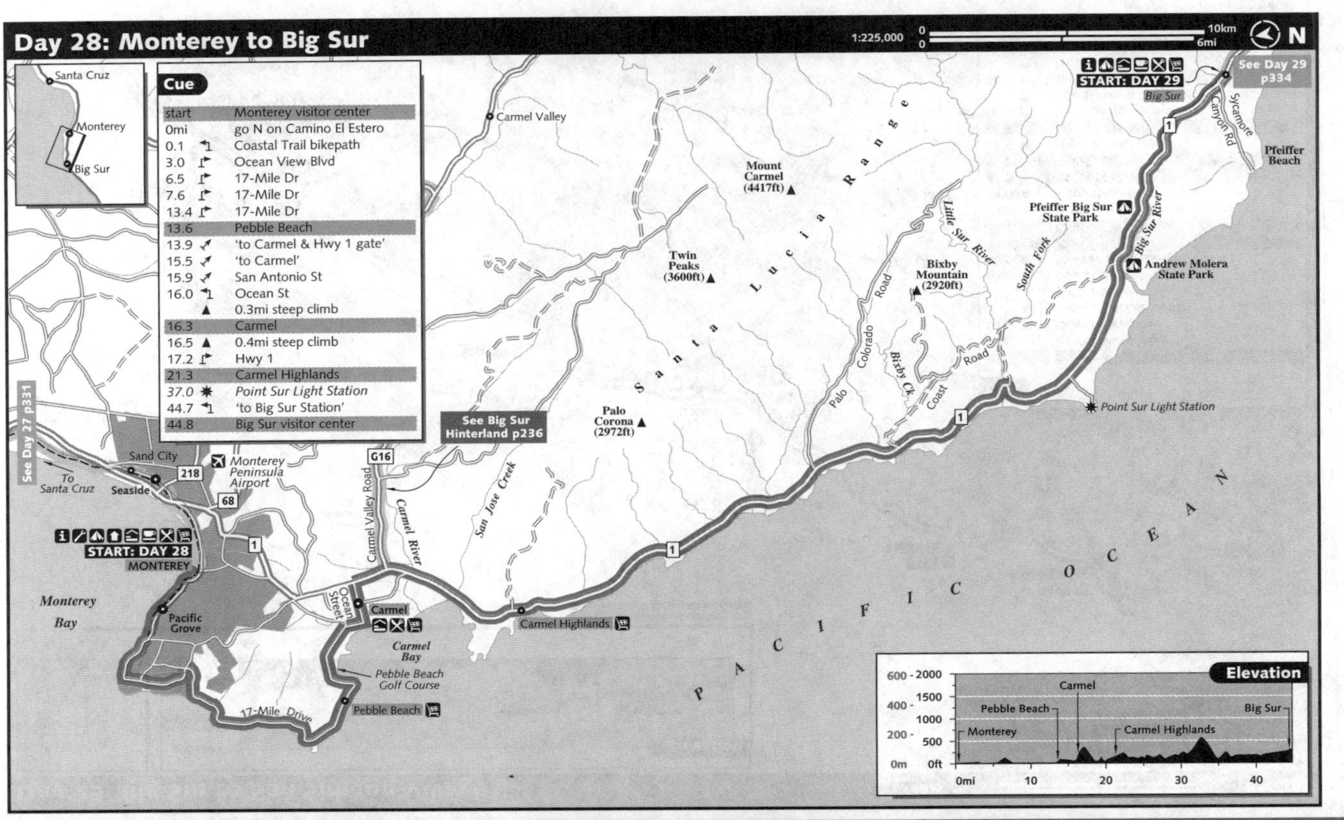

Cue

start		Monterey visitor center
0mi		go N on Camino El Estero
0.1	↰	Coastal Trail bikepath
3.0	↱	Ocean View Blvd
6.5	↱	17-Mile Dr
7.6	↱	17-Mile Dr
13.4	↱	17-Mile Dr
13.6		Pebble Beach
13.9	↗	'to Carmel & Hwy 1 gate'
15.5	↗	'to Carmel'
15.9	↗	San Antonio St
16.0	↰	Ocean St
	▲	0.3mi steep climb
16.3		Carmel
16.5	▲	0.4mi steep climb
17.2	↱	Hwy 1
21.3		Carmel Highlands
37.0	✸	*Point Sur Light Station*
44.7	↰	'to Big Sur Station'
44.8		Big Sur visitor center

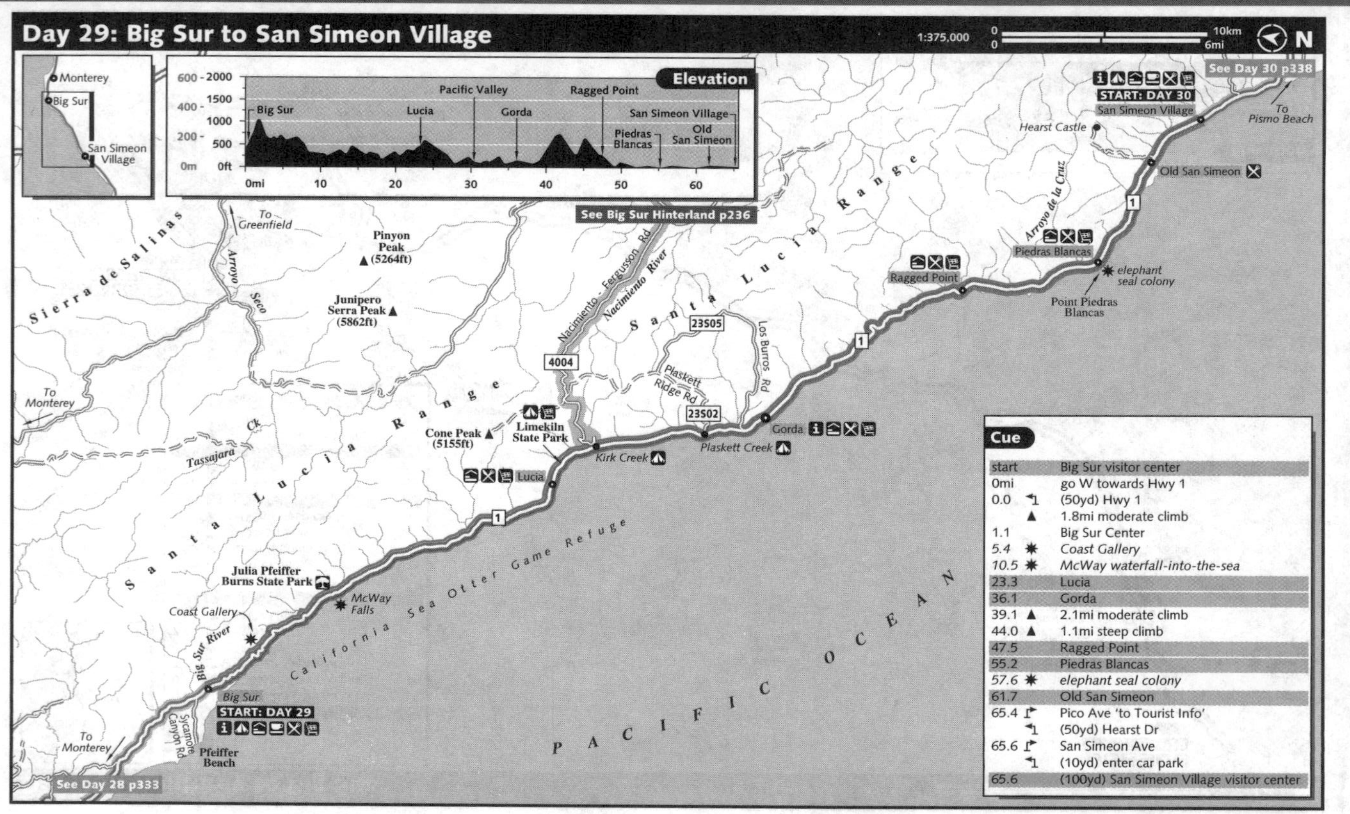
Day 29: Big Sur to San Simeon Village
1:375,000
0 10km
0 6mi
N
Monterey
Big Sur
San Simeon Village
Elevation
Big Sur
Lucia
Pacific Valley
Gorda
Ragged Point
Piedras Blancas
San Simeon Village
Old San Simeon
0mi 10 20 30 40 50 60
0m 200 400 600
0ft 500 1000 1500 2000
See Big Sur Hinterland p236
See Day 28 p333
See Day 30 p338
To Pismo Beach
To Monterey
To Greenfield
START: DAY 29
START: DAY 30
Big Sur
Pfeiffer Beach
Sycamore Canyon Rd
Big Sur River
Coast Gallery
Julia Pfeiffer Burns State Park
McWay Falls
California Sea Otter Game Refuge
Tassajara Ck
Arroyo Seco
Sierra de Salinas
Santa Lucia Range
Pinyon Peak (5264ft)
Junipero Serra Peak (5862ft)
Cone Peak (5155ft)
Limekiln State Park
Lucia
Nacimiento - Fergusson Rd
Nacimiento River
4004
23S05
23S02
Kirk Creek
Plaskett Ridge Rd
Plaskett Creek
Los Burros Rd
Gorda
Ragged Point
Piedras Blancas
Point Piedras Blancas
elephant seal colony
Arroyo de la Cruz
Hearst Castle
San Simeon Village
Old San Simeon
PACIFIC OCEAN
Cue
start Big Sur visitor center
0mi go W towards Hwy 1
0.0 (50yd) Hwy 1
1.8mi moderate climb
1.1 Big Sur Center
5.4 Coast Gallery
10.5 McWay waterfall-into-the-sea
23.3 Lucia
36.1 Gorda
39.1 2.1mi moderate climb
44.0 1.1mi steep climb
47.5 Ragged Point
55.2 Piedras Blancas
57.6 elephant seal colony
61.7 Old San Simeon
65.4 Pico Ave 'to Tourist Info'
(50yd) Hearst Dr
65.6 San Simeon Ave
(10yd) enter car park
65.6 (100yd) San Simeon Village visitor center

until Morro Bay (Day 30). About 10mi past Carmel, the highway returns to spectacular coastline and traffic is lighter.

At 37mi, views extend to the 1899 **Point Sur Light Station**, perched 360ft above the surf. This is the only complete turn-of-the-(20th)-century light station open to the public in California. Organized tour groups are permitted for three-hour tours ($5) incorporating the history and wildlife of the area. No reservations are accepted; visitors meet on the west side of Hwy 1 about 400yd north of Point Sur naval facility. Phone ☎ 831-625-4419 for the current schedule.

The short access road to ***Andrew Molera State Park campground*** leaves the highway to the right at 39.8mi. Toilets and water are the only facilities but a bonus for cyclists is that RVs are not permitted.

Big Sur

See Big Sur (pp239–40) for information about accommodations and other services.

Day 29: Big Sur to San Simeon Village

5¾–10½ hours, 65.6mi

A long hard day starts with a climb to more than 1000ft altitude then a cliff-hanging ride winding around headlands with stupendous coastal views north and south. Two more moderate-to-steep climbs totaling 3.2mi, starting at 39.1mi and 44mi, each take the road from close to sea level back to 700ft. There are frequent turnouts for vistas, usually light traffic and, on good days, a brisk northerly tailwind. This virtually uninhabited coastline has limited services. The **Coast Gallery** (5.4mi on the left) features the work of well-known artists and has a cafe, while Lucia (23.3mi), Gorda (36.1mi), Ragged Point (47.5mi) and Piedras Blancas (55.2mi) each has a ***store*** and/or ***restaurant***.

Below the road on the right in Julia Pfeiffer Burns State Park (10.5mi), you'll see the 80ft **McWay Falls**, California's only waterfall running into the sea.

Limekiln State Park (25.3mi), accessed via a steep downhill road on the left, has hiker/biker sites ($10), showers and a ***store***, which is much better stocked than the one at Lucia. Los Padres National Forest has a campground, ***Kirk Creek*** (27.3mi), where hiker/biker sites cost $5 per person. Offshore is the California Sea Otter Game Refuge. ***Plaskett Creek campground*** is on the left at 32.4mi.

Gorda Springs Resort (☎ 805-927-3918), at Gorda, has expensive motel rooms for $135/200 weekdays/Friday and Saturday and

The Man & His Castle

After inheriting the family fortune upon his mother's death in 1919, newspaper publisher William Randolph Hearst (1863–1951) picked San Simeon (where he had spent many summers as a boy) as the site of his new private home, La Cuesta Encantada (the Enchanted Hill), now known as Hearst Castle.

The castle was designed by renowned architect Julia Morgan. Though originally a reasonably sized project, it grew to accommodate Hearst's expansive interest in art and in Hollywood actor Marion Davies. As Hearst purchased cathedral ceilings, refectory tables, Grecian urns and Roman columns, Davies invited Hollywood's elite to spend weekends at 'the ranch', playing tennis, swimming, watching movies in a full-scale theater and driving through the zoo and gardens stocked with exotic animals and plants.

When Hearst died, the enormous project was still unfinished, but photos and reports from his last years reveal a man – surrounded by his wealth and the accolades of Hollywood's beautiful and talented – who seemed, in spite of his bizarre excesses, oddly contented with what he had done.

HAYDEN FOELL

Marisa Gierlich

cabins from $200/225. Its ***Whale Watcher Cafe*** serves good breakfasts, lunches and dinners but is also expensive. The resort store operates as an information center.

Point Piedras Blancas elephant seal colony (57.6mi) is right beside the road. You are likely to hear it, or smell it if the wind is right, before you see it. Interpretive panels give information on the life cycle of these huge marine mammals. Nearby at 55.2mi, ***Piedras Blancas Motel*** *(☎ 805-927-4202)* can be useful if time or light runs out. Ordinary doubles cost from $70/120 weekday/weekend in August (about $40 less in a low-season month such as October). The adjacent cafe serves basic snacks and light meals.

San Simeon Village

☎ 805

This rather characterless mile of motels and restaurants is south of the original San Simeon, which began as an 1850s whaling station. In 1865, George Hearst bought 45,000 acres of land and established a beachside settlement on the west side of Hwy 1, across from today's entrance to Hearst Castle, which was built from the 1920s to the 1940s. The Hearst Corporation still owns most of the land south to the northern edge of the modern village.

Information San Simeon Chamber of Commerce (☎ 927-3500 or ☎ 800-342-5613), at 9255 Hearst Dr, can offer tourist information.

San Simeon Restaurant, Bar & Grill has an ATM.

Cambria Bicycle Outfitter is about 6mi southeast, just off the Day 30 route.

Internet access is available at West Cambria Library, 900 E Main St.

Things to See & Do Tours of **Hearst Castle** (☎ 800-444-4445) are *the* attraction. There are four different tours, each costing $14. They start with a bus trip from the castle visitor center at the bottom of the hill, 3mi northeast of San Simeon Village. The visitor center has a food service, gift shops, a free exhibit on Hearst and his castle as well as the **National Geographic Theater** (☎ 927-6811), which shows an entertaining 40-minute film on Hearst's life (see the boxed text 'The Man & His Castle, p335) and the construction of the castle on a five-story-high screen ($7).

Within San Simeon State Park, the **Santa Rosa Creek Natural Preserve** provides habitat for the endangered tidewater goby (a fish); the **San Simeon Natural Preserve** is a popular spot for migrating monarch butterflies; and the **Panu Cultural Preserve** protects the site of archaeological finds dating back 6000 years. A 3.3mi trail leads through the park.

Moonstone Beach Dr, 2.3mi southeast on the Day 30 route, has a mile-long trail from which harbor seals can be spotted at low tide. The striped cows grazing on the left at the outskirts of town (0.5mi) are actually zebras.

Places to Stay & Eat Close to the road 1.3mi southeast of town, ***San Simeon State Park*** has hiker/biker camping for $3 per person, with coin showers.

San Simeon Motel 6 *(☎ 927-8691* or *☎ 800-466-8356, 9070 Castillo Dr)* charges $40 for one or two people.

Silver Surf Motel *(☎ 927-4661 or ☎ 800-621-3999, 9390 Castillo Dr)* has a pool, spa and laundry, and charges $69/89 weekday/weekend. ***San Simeon Lodge*** *(☎ 927-4601, 9520 Castillo Dr)* has doubles for $75/115.

More expensive motels are on the ocean side of Hwy 1. ***Best Western Cavalier Oceanfront Resort*** *(☎ 927-4688 or ☎ 800-826-8168, 9415 Hearst Dr)* charges $83 to $154 for a double. The upmarket ***Cavalier Restaurant*** *(☎ 927-3276)* is next door.

About 2.7mi southeast of town on the Day 30 route is a strip of expensive oceanview lodges. ***Sea Otter Inn*** *(☎ 927-5888 or ☎ 800-965-8347, 6656 Moonstone Beach Dr)*, charging $100/130, 'is one of the cheapest', according to its manager.

San Simeon Deli, at the northwestern end of Castillo Dr, sells groceries, sandwiches and deli items.

Carriage Restaurant *(☎ 927-8607, 9290 Castillo Dr)* is popular with cyclists. A stack of its delicious fluffy buttermilk pancakes makes a very satisfying breakfast for $5. Dinner main courses cost around $9. ***San Simeon Restaurant, Bar & Grill*** *(☎ 927-4604, 9520 Castillo Dr)* serves breakfast, lunch and dinner. Fish and chips cost from $7.

Day 30: San Simeon Village to Pismo Beach

4¾–8½ hours, 53.2mi

The day's ride is entirely without significant hills but, as the route penetrates Southern

California, urban development and its associated traffic increase. Most of the route from near Cambria (4.5mi) to Cayucos (18.5mi), and again from Morro Bay (24.1mi), is away from sight of the sea. Cayucos, Morro Bay and San Luis Obispo (41.8mi) have ***food stores***.

At 4.5mi on the left, Cambria Dr leads (off the route) into Cambria, a town with many good restaurants, accommodations, banks, a farmers' market (2.30–5pm Fri) and an excellent bike shop: Cambria Bicycle Outfitter (☎ 927-5510), 2164 Center St.

Beyond Cambria, Hwy 1 rolls gently through grazing lands with constant traffic but a wide shoulder. There are views to the bare, rugged granite peaks behind Morro Bay and, later, to Morro Rock.

Along Los Osos Valley Rd (33.9mi), vegetable crops are planted in alternating rows of red and green, making a spectacular sight as the beds rise up the hillside.

The route goes through the center of busy San Luis Obispo (usually abbreviated to SLO and referred to as SloTown by residents); see pp219–21 for information about accommodations and other services. The SLO Roller Coaster ride (pp227–9) is a day ride here and two other rides are based in the SLO County (Pozo Saloon Stagger, pp229–30, and Epicenter Century, pp230–3). At 45.4 mi, the route skirts SLO airport.

Pismo Beach

☎ 805

A lively tourist town bordering 10mi of broad beaches, Pismo Beach has been famed since the late 19th century for tasty clams, and may be remembered by cartoon fans as Bugs Bunny's failed holiday destination after he neglected to take that 'left at Albuquerque'. Although the beaches are now pretty well clammed out, the town still celebrates a Clam Festival, attracting thousands of people in mid-October with an arts and crafts fair, music and food booths.

Information The Chamber of Commerce (☎ 773-4382 or ☎ 800-443-7778, W www.pismochamber.com) is at 581 Dolliver St. Take the free SLO County bike map.

Mid State Bank is at 801 Price St and Los Padres Bank is at 831 Oak Park Blvd. The 7-Eleven, corner S Dolliver and Cypress Sts, has an ATM.

The nearest bike shops are in adjoining Grover Beach: Grand Cyclery (☎ 481-3292), at 983 Grand Ave; and Switchbax Bikes (☎ 473-8324), 1343 Grand Ave.

Things to See & Do While chances of success are small, **clamming** is simple and fun. A sensitive foot twisted into the sand to ankle level is all the equipment needed, though to keep a clam (minimum size: 4½ inches) finders need a California fishing license (available at sport shops and liquor stores).

From late November to March, **monarch butterflies** cluster in the tops of eucalyptus and pine trees in North Beach Campground. Contact ☎ 489-2684 for guided walks.

Pismo Dunes Preserve, an extensive network of dunes at Oceano, includes a primitive campground and, somewhat ironically, a **Vehicular Recreation Area**, where hordes of noisy ATVs tear up the landscape.

Places to Stay & Eat Quiet hiker/biker camping ($3 per person) is available in the dunes at ***Oceano Memorial Campground***, 2.4mi south of the visitor center. It's entered opposite the Oceano Memorial County Park.

Despite dozens of motels, Pismo Beach rooms can be scarce and prices sky-high between May and September and during Clam Festival. Close to the beach, ***Surf Inn*** *(☎ 773-2070, 250 Main St)* has doubles from $50 to $80. ***Dolphin Cove Lodge*** *(☎ 773-4706, 170 Main St)* is a friendly, nonsmoking motel where ocean-view rooms cost $70 to $100 year-round. Upmarket, nonsmoking ***Beachcomber Inn*** *(☎ 773-5505, 541 Cypress St)* has well-appointed cottage-style rooms from $100 to $150.

Ask the Chamber of Commerce for a list of B&Bs in town.

Scolari's Food Court, in the Pismo Coast Shopping Plaza on Five Cities Dr, is a supermarket with bakery and deli sections.

Several good chowder houses are on Pomeroy St. ***Splash Cafe*** *(☎ 773-4653, 197 Pomeroy St)*, serving rich and chunky clam chowder, has queues down the street on busy weekends. Across the street, ***Black Pearl Coffeehouse*** *(☎ 773-6631)* has java, bakery items and a young clientele. Popular ***Guiseppe's*** *(☎ 773-2870, 891 Price St)* serves lunch and dinner of southern Italian specialties, wood-fired pizzas, home-made bread, pasta and seafood. For good fish and

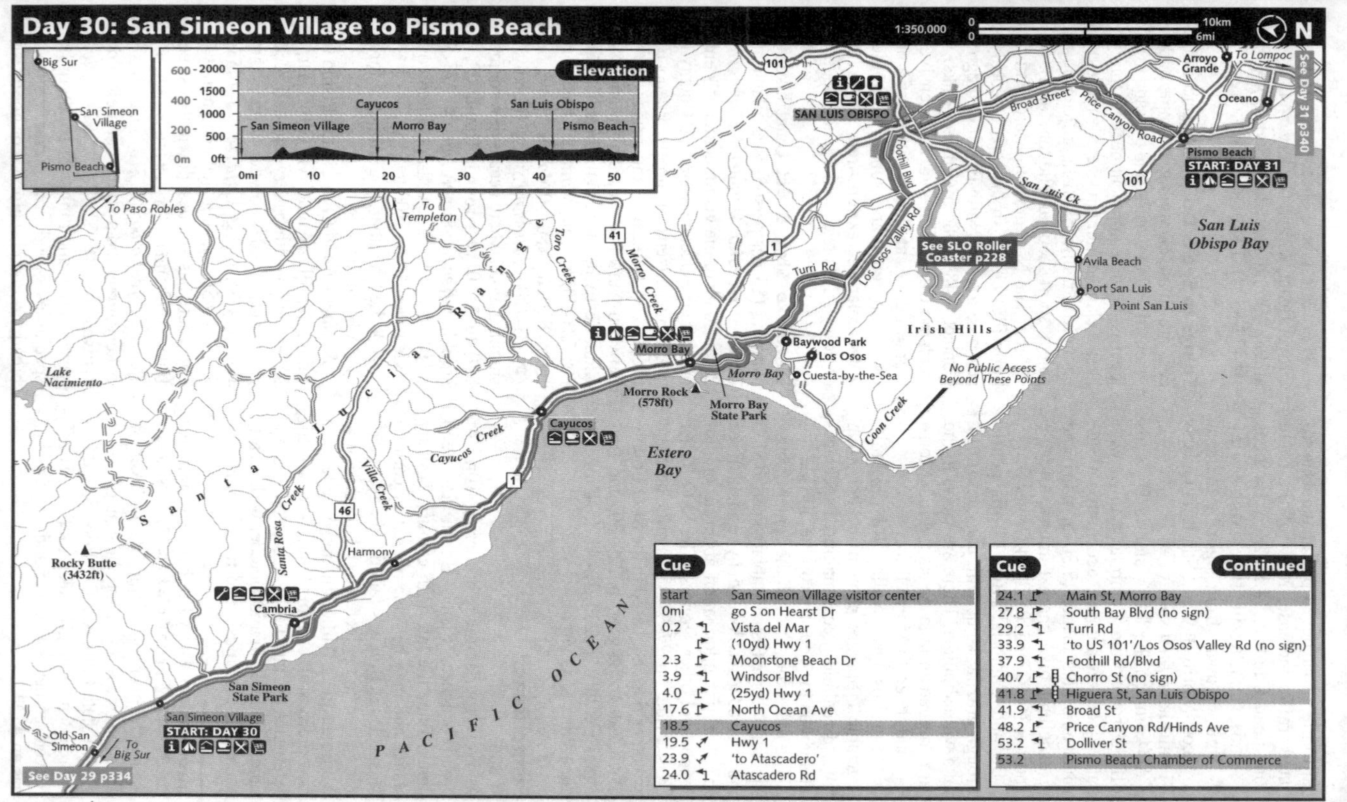
Day 30: San Simeon Village to Pismo Beach
1:350,000
0 10km
0 6mi
N
Big Sur
San Simeon Village
Pismo Beach
Elevation
600 - 2000
1500
400 - 1000
200 - 500
0m 0ft
0mi 10 20 30 40 50
San Simeon Village
Cayucos
Morro Bay
San Luis Obispo
Pismo Beach
To Paso Robles
To Templeton
Lake Nacimiento
Rocky Butte (3432ft)
Santa Lucia Range
Toro Creek
Morro Creek
Cayucos Creek
Villa Creek
Santa Rosa Creek
Harmony
Cambria
San Simeon State Park
Old San Simeon
To Big Sur
San Simeon Village
START: DAY 30
See Day 29 p334
Cayucos
Morro Bay
Morro Rock (578ft)
Morro Bay State Park
Estero Bay
PACIFIC OCEAN
Baywood Park
Los Osos
Cuesta-by-the-Sea
Turri Rd
Los Osos Valley Rd
Foothill Blvd
Irish Hills
Coon Creek
No Public Access Beyond These Points
See SLO Roller Coaster p228
SAN LUIS OBISPO
Broad Street
Price Canyon Road
San Luis Ck
Avila Beach
Port San Luis
Point San Luis
San Luis Obispo Bay
Arroyo Grande
To Lompoc
Oceano
Pismo Beach
START: DAY 31
See Day 31 p340
Cue
start San Simeon Village visitor center
0mi go S on Hearst Dr
0.2 Vista del Mar
(10yd) Hwy 1
2.3 Moonstone Beach Dr
3.9 Windsor Blvd
4.0 (25yd) Hwy 1
17.6 North Ocean Ave
18.5 Cayucos
19.5 Hwy 1
23.9 'to Atascadero'
24.0 Atascadero Rd
Cue Continued
24.1 Main St, Morro Bay
27.8 South Bay Blvd (no sign)
29.2 Turri Rd
33.9 'to US 101'/Los Osos Valley Rd (no sign)
37.9 Foothill Rd/Blvd
40.7 Chorro St (no sign)
41.8 Higuera St, San Luis Obispo
41.9 Broad St
48.2 Price Canyon Rd/Hinds Ave
53.2 Dolliver St
53.2 Pismo Beach Chamber of Commerce

chips at reasonable prices, try ***Pismo Fish & Chips & Seafood Restaurant*** *(☎ 773-2853, 505 Cypress St)*, family-run at the same location for more than 30 years.

Near Oceano Campground, ***Arnie's Deli*** *(☎ 473-2000; 307 Pier Ave, Oceano)* also serves award-winning chowder.

Day 31: Pismo Beach to Lompoc

4–7 hours, 43.9mi

The majority of this day's ride is entirely out of sight of sea and lacks any serious climbing. The last 10mi make up for it with a 2.3mi, sometimes steep ascent to just above 1000ft at 36.7mi. Happily, this means the ride ends with a marvelous downhill. The big climb comes as the route crosses the Purisima Hills, skirting Vandenberg Air Force Base (VAFB) and its Missile Test Center. Guadalupe (15.8mi) has the last ***food store*** en route.

For 10mi through Pismo Beach and its surrounding towns, suburban strip development dominates, then agricultural and industrial areas, and finally development thins out into semi-rural residential areas. Seemingly ubiquitous eucalypts line the roads until the 12mi mark, when the route enters exposed agricultural flats.

The land is used for cattle grazing beside the freeway section of Hwy 1 starting at 26.3mi. Crops again dominate with the turn onto rougher Harris Grade Rd (33.4mi). The climb is through hills covered in scrubby vegetation, which gives no shade. From the crest there are panoramic views of Lompoc.

An historical marker commemorates the original **La Purísima Mission site** (38.7mi). Established in 1787, the mission was damaged by a quake in 1812 and abandoned in 1834. State and National Park services have undertaken a restoration project (see Things to See & Do for Lompoc).

Lompoc

☎ 805

Lompoc (pronounced 'Lom-poke'), with 41,500 people, is the largest town along Hwy 1 between Pismo Beach and Santa Barbara. A quiet military town with wide, shady streets, it is surrounded by hills that become a mosaic of wildflowers in spring.

Information Lompoc Valley Chamber of Commerce (☎ 736-4567; closed weekends) is in an attractively restored 1891 building at 111 S I St. The building is made of 'chalk rock', extraction of which is a town industry.

Washington Mutual Bank is at 1508 N H St. Albertsons supermarket has a Wells Fargo Bank with an ATM.

Bicycle Connection (☎ 736-4849), 223 W Ocean Ave, is open every day.

Log on at Lompoc Public Library (☎ 736-3477, ext 11 to book; open every afternoon), 501 E North Ave.

Things to See & Do The Chamber of Commerce has a map locating **murals** around town. One of the biggest is on the side of the Chamber itself. The Art Alley across the road displays works of more than 300 professional and amateur artists from the region. Another brochure maps a heritage walk of Lompoc's old-town.

Lompoc Museum (☎ 736-3888; closed Mon), in a neoclassical villa at 200 S H St, has Chumash and regional artifacts.

Mission La Purísima Concepción (☎ 733-3713), on Hwy 246 about 3mi northeast of the town center, is one of two missions run by the State Park Service. The reconstructed mission buildings are decorated as they were during the mission period, its fields support livestock and the gardens are planted with medicinal plants once used by the Chumash tribe. About 15mi of hiking and horse trails surround the mission, and there's a museum and a bookstore.

VAFB is one of the USA's most important military and aerospace installations. The **Western Spaceport Museum and Science Center** (☎ 736-6381) coordinates free (weekly) 2½-hour tours of the base. Reserve at least a week ahead. Non-US citizens need a passport.

Lompoc airport (☎ 740-0290), on the northern edge of town, has **glider rides** and aerobatic instruction.

Places to Stay & Eat With hiker/biker sites for $4 per person, ***River Park RV Campground*** *(☎ 875-8009, 125 W Walnut Ave)* has cold showers only.

Motel 6 *(☎ 735-7631 or ☎ 800-466-8356, 1521 N H St)* has small doubles for $40. ***Lompoc Motel*** *(☎ 736-7517, 528 N H St)* has ordinary but largish rooms for $70 a double (less than half that Nov–Mar). ***Quality Inn*** *(☎ 735-8555, 1621 N H St)* has doubles for

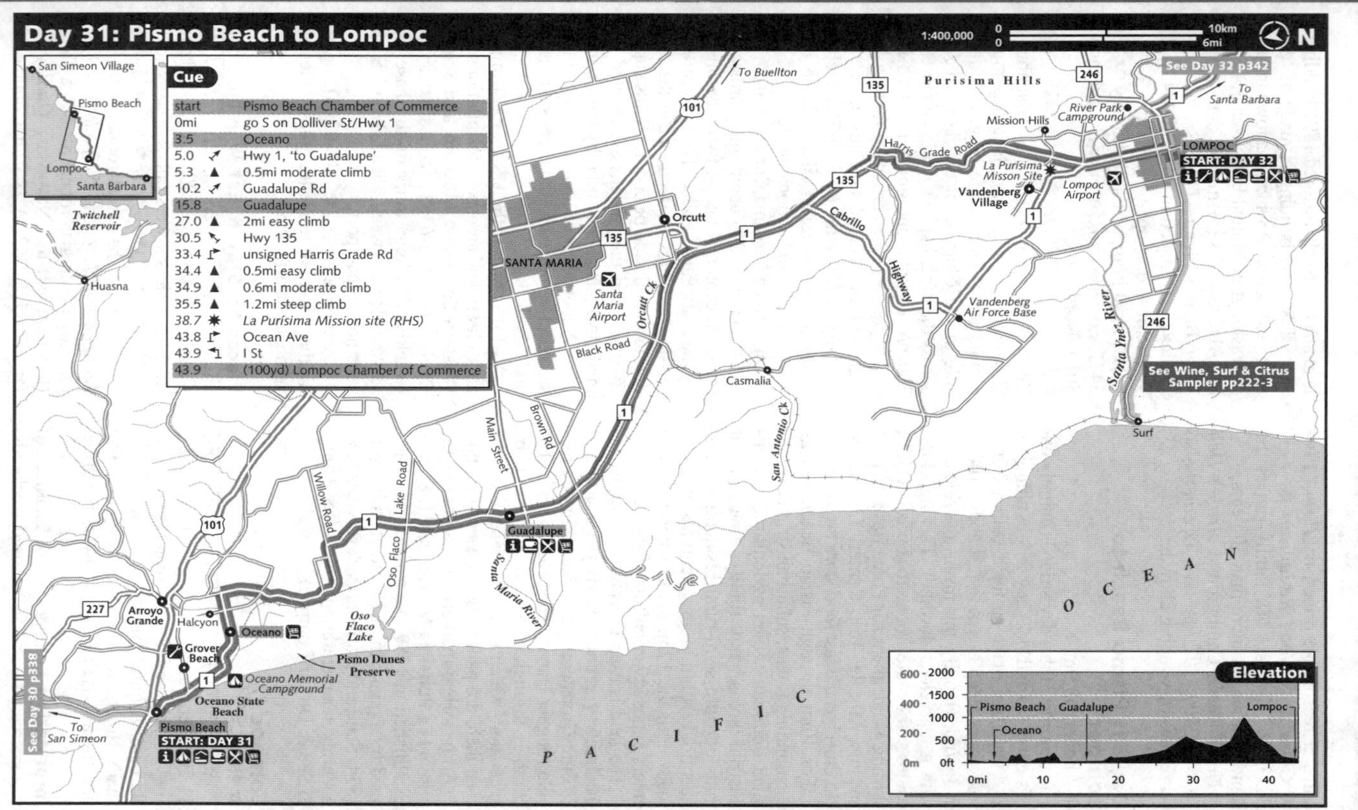
Day 31: Pismo Beach to Lompoc
1:400,000
0 10km
0 6mi
N
Cue
start Pismo Beach Chamber of Commerce
0mi go S on Dolliver St/Hwy 1
3.5 Oceano
5.0 Hwy 1, 'to Guadalupe'
5.3 0.5mi moderate climb
10.2 Guadalupe Rd
15.8 Guadalupe
27.0 2mi easy climb
30.5 Hwy 135
33.4 unsigned Harris Grade Rd
34.4 0.5mi easy climb
34.9 0.6mi moderate climb
35.5 1.2mi steep climb
38.7 La Purísima Mission site (RHS)
43.8 Ocean Ave
43.9 I St
43.9 (100yd) Lompoc Chamber of Commerce
San Simeon Village
Pismo Beach
Lompoc
Santa Barbara
Twitchell Reservoir
Huasna
To Buellton
Purisima Hills
See Day 32 p342
To Santa Barbara
River Park Campground
Mission Hills
Harris Grade Road
La Purísima Misson Site
Vandenberg Village
Lompoc Airport
LOMPOC
START: DAY 32
Orcutt
SANTA MARIA
Santa Maria Airport
Orcutt Ck
Cabrillo
Highway
Vandenberg Air Force Base
Santa Ynez River
See Wine, Surf & Citrus Sampler pp222-3
Black Road
Casmalia
Surf
San Antonio Ck
Main Street
Brown Rd
Willow Road
Lake Road
Oso Flaco
Guadalupe
Santa Maria River
Arroyo Grande
Halcyon
Oceano
Oso Flaco Lake
Grover Beach
Pismo Dunes Preserve
Oceano Memorial Campground
Oceano State Beach
Pismo Beach
START: DAY 31
See Day 30 p338
To San Simeon
PACIFIC OCEAN
Elevation
600 - 2000
1500
400 - 1000
200 - 500
0m 0ft
Pismo Beach
Oceano
Guadalupe
Lompoc
0mi 10 20 30 40

$79 to $99 all year. ***Redwood Inn Motor Lodge*** *(☎ 735-3737, 1200 N H St)* charges $55/80 weekday/weekend.

A ***farmers market*** *(cnr Cypress & I Sts)* is held from 2 to 7pm Friday. In the shopping mall behind Washington Mutual on H St is a huge ***Albertsons supermarket***, open until midnight. In the mall, ***Country Waffles*** serves breakfast until 3pm daily. The plazas on Central Ave have pizza and taco restaurants and a ***Vons supermarket***.

There's a vast selection of cafes and restaurants on H St, Constellation Rd and Ocean Ave. Opposite Quality Inn on H St are chain fast-food stores ***Pizza Hut*** and ***Taco Bell***. ***Lompoc Burgers*** *(☎ 740-1488, 600 N H St)* serves them charbroiled – burger, fries and a drink costs under $4. Salads and fish dinners are available.

Fat Cat's Restaurant *(☎ 736-8099, 124 E Ocean Ave)*, ***International House-Pancakes*** *(☎ 736-8231, 1140 N H St)*, ***Oki Sushi*** *(☎ 735-7170, 1206 W Ocean Ave)*, ***Saletti's Italian Restaurant*** *(☎ 736-2050, 812 N H St)* and ***Thai Cuisine*** *(☎ 736-7450, 920 N I St)* illustrate the range of cuisines available and are all worth a try.

Day 32: Lompoc to Santa Barbara

4¾–8¾ hours, 54.4mi

Today's section is undulating but the climbs are easy. The high point is about 1065ft, at 16.3mi, reached at the end of a long but gradual rise. Scenery is of rolling hills and wide open rangelands before the return to the coast, after which the now busy, wide-shouldered Hwy 101 is hemmed into a narrow corridor between the ocean and the Santa Ynez Mtns. No food is available en route before Goleta (43mi). For a longer (three to four days), more scenic route, substitute this day with the Wine, Surf & Citrus Sampler ride (pp221–7).

The ride leaves Lompoc on Hwy 1, gently rising through the chaparral-covered Santa Rosa Hills. A wide shoulder and usually light traffic make for pleasant cycling conditions.

The route joins Hwy 101, passing a large highway rest area with picnic tables and phones. It reaches the coast at Gaviota Beach State Park (21.4mi). The nearby 'town' of Gaviota (22.5mi) has no services unless bulk oil refinery product is needed. Offshore, numerous oil platforms dot the horizon.

Beyond Gaviota, Hwy 101 rolls between rounded granite hills and the blue Pacific. At 26.8mi, a vista point on the right gives access to an **old highway bridge**, open to walkers and cyclists only (if riding across, beware the gaps in the bitumen at joints). A number of state beaches with campgrounds line the coast.

After the Hollister Ave exit (40.5mi), beyond which cyclists are banned from the freeway section of Hwy 101, the ride is through a built-up area. Goleta, part of Santa Barbara's urban sprawl, has shopping malls but little else to tempt touring cyclists.

Santa Barbara

See Santa Barbara (pp218–9) for information about accommodations and other services.

Day 33: Santa Barbara to Port Hueneme

3½–6½ hours, 40.3mi

This short day has no hill of note other than a moderate grade on Ortega Hill Rd (5mi). Food is available at Carpinteria (11mi), Ventura (26.9mi) and Oxnard Shores shopping mall (35mi).

Carpinteria ('the carpenter's shop') was named in 1769 when Spanish explorers observed the indigenous people building wooden canoes here. A short way beyond the town, at 13.8mi, cyclists are somewhat confusingly directed to exit Hwy 101. However, the route immediately re-enters the highway via an on-ramp.

Another confusing junction is at 24.4mi; do not divert along the exit to Emma Wood State Beach! It is not obvious but the shoulder bike lane continues on Hwy 101 in the direction signposted 'to Freeway Only'. The route then veers right onto a separate bikepath 0.3mi farther and becomes W Main St at 26.8mi.

The approach to Port Hueneme is very busy – a parallel bikepath starting at Ventura Rd (38.1mi) offers relief, running beside the naval base.

Port Hueneme

☎ 805

The seaside community of Port Hueneme (pronounced 'wy-nee-mee') has 21,000 people. It is an enclave surrounded by Oxnard and dominated by the navy base, which occupies much of the port's deep water.

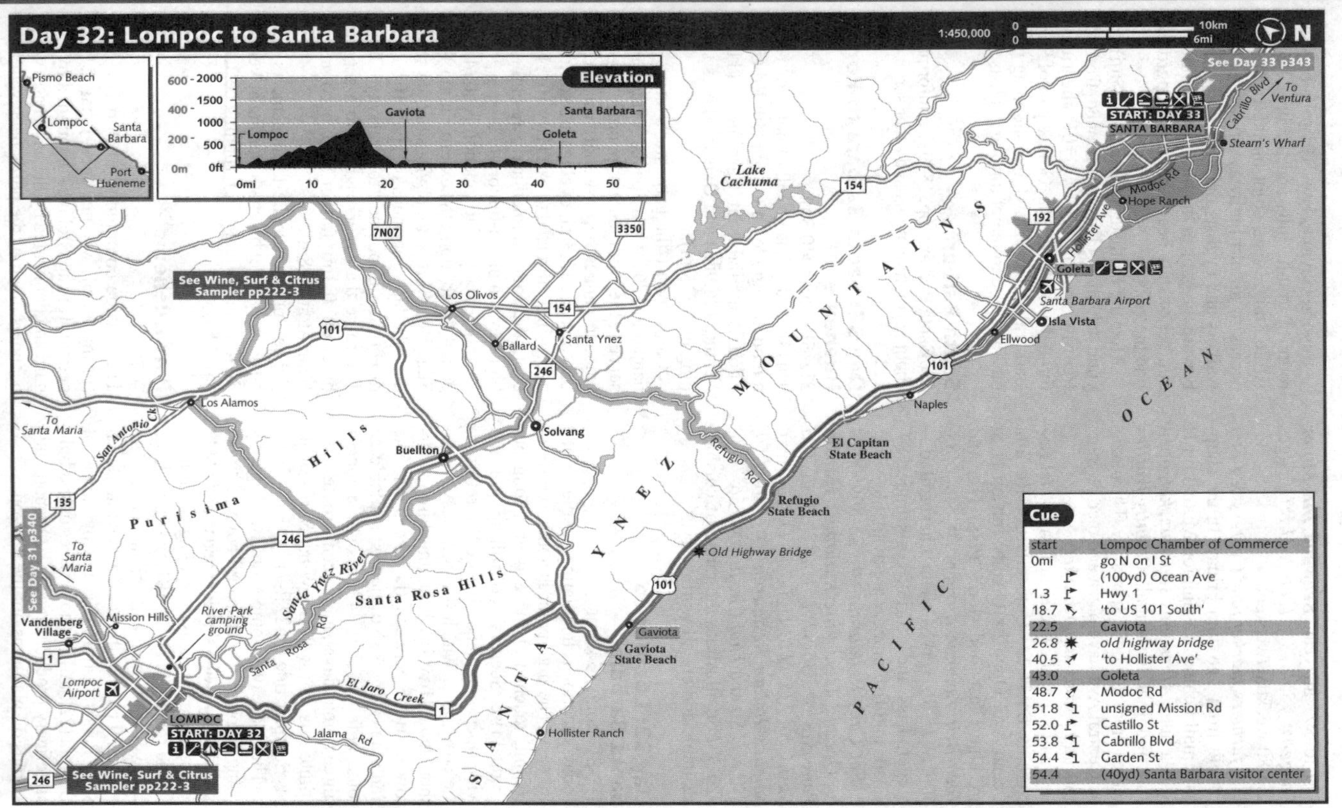

Day 32: Lompoc to Santa Barbara
1:450,000
0 10km
0 6mi
N
See Day 33 p343
See Day 31 p340
See Wine, Surf & Citrus Sampler pp222-3
See Wine, Surf & Citrus Sampler pp222-3
START: DAY 32
LOMPOC
START: DAY 33
SANTA BARBARA
Elevation
600 - 2000
1500
400 - 1000
200 - 500
0m 0ft
0mi 10 20 30 40 50
Lompoc
Gaviota
Goleta
Santa Barbara
Pismo Beach
Lompoc
Santa Barbara
Port Hueneme
Cue
start Lompoc Chamber of Commerce
0mi go N on I St
(100yd) Ocean Ave
1.3 Hwy 1
18.7 'to US 101 South'
22.5 Gaviota
26.8 old highway bridge
40.5 'to Hollister Ave'
43.0 Goleta
48.7 Modoc Rd
51.8 unsigned Mission Rd
52.0 Castillo St
53.8 Cabrillo Blvd
54.4 Garden St
54.4 (40yd) Santa Barbara visitor center
PACIFIC OCEAN
SANTA YNEZ MOUNTAINS
Santa Rosa Hills
Purisima Hills
Lake Cachuma
Solvang
Buellton
Los Olivos
Ballard
Santa Ynez
Los Alamos
Vandenberg Village
Mission Hills
Lompoc Airport
River Park camping ground
Santa Ynez River
Santa Rosa Rd
Jalama Rd
El Jaro Creek
San Antonio Ck
Hollister Ranch
Gaviota
Gaviota State Beach
Old Highway Bridge
Refugio Rd
Refugio State Beach
El Capitan State Beach
Naples
Ellwood
Isla Vista
Goleta
Santa Barbara Airport
Hollister Ave
Modoc Rd
Hope Ranch
Stearn's Wharf
Cabrillo Blvd
To Ventura
To Santa Maria
To Santa Maria
101
154
246
192
1
135
3350
7N07

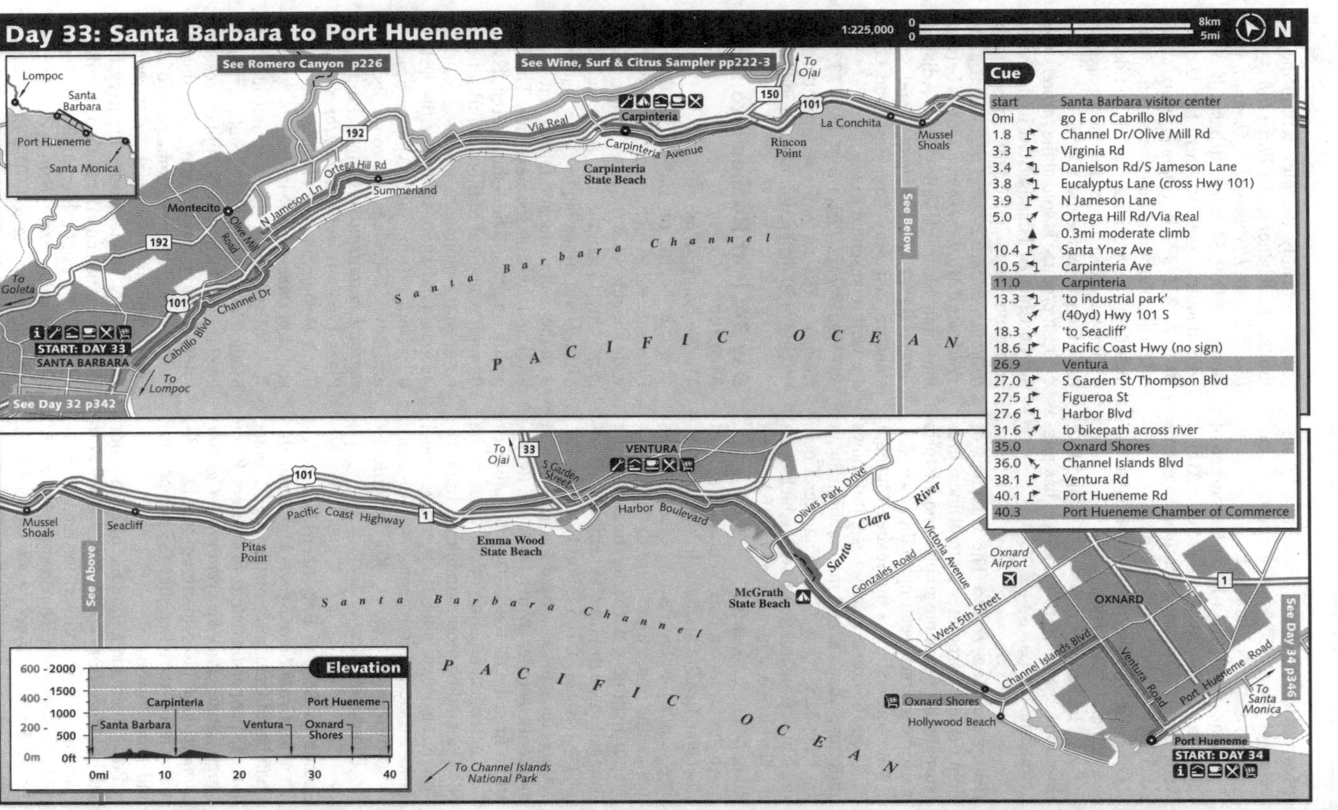
Day 33: Santa Barbara to Port Hueneme
1:225,000
0 8km
0 5mi
N
See Romero Canyon p226
See Wine, Surf & Citrus Sampler pp222-3
Lompoc
Santa Barbara
Port Hueneme
Santa Monica
To Goleta
START: DAY 33
SANTA BARBARA
To Lompoc
See Day 32 p342
Montecito
Olive Mill Road
N Jameson Ln
Ortega Hill Rd
Summerland
Channel Dr
Cabrillo Blvd
Via Real
Carpinteria
Carpinteria Avenue
Carpinteria State Beach
To Ojai
Rincon Point
La Conchita
Mussel Shoals
See Below
Santa Barbara Channel
PACIFIC OCEAN
Cue
start Santa Barbara visitor center
0mi go E on Cabrillo Blvd
1.8 Channel Dr/Olive Mill Rd
3.3 Virginia Rd
3.4 Danielson Rd/S Jameson Lane
3.8 Eucalyptus Lane (cross Hwy 101)
3.9 N Jameson Lane
5.0 Ortega Hill Rd/Via Real
0.3mi moderate climb
10.4 Santa Ynez Ave
10.5 Carpinteria Ave
11.0 Carpinteria
13.3 'to industrial park'
(40yd) Hwy 101 S
18.3 'to Seacliff'
18.6 Pacific Coast Hwy (no sign)
26.9 Ventura
27.0 S Garden St/Thompson Blvd
27.5 Figueroa St
27.6 Harbor Blvd
31.6 to bikepath across river
35.0 Oxnard Shores
36.0 Channel Islands Blvd
38.1 Ventura Rd
40.1 Port Hueneme Rd
40.3 Port Hueneme Chamber of Commerce
Mussel Shoals
See Above
Seacliff
Pitas Point
Pacific Coast Highway
Emma Wood State Beach
To Ojai
S Garden Street
VENTURA
Harbor Boulevard
Olivas Park Drive
Santa Clara River
Gonzales Road
Victoria Avenue
Oxnard Airport
McGrath State Beach
West 5th Street
OXNARD
Channel Islands Blvd
Ventura Road
Port Hueneme Road
To Santa Monica
See Day 34 p346
Oxnard Shores
Hollywood Beach
Port Hueneme
START: DAY 34
To Channel Islands National Park
Elevation
600 - 2000
400 - 1500
1000
200 - 500
0m 0ft
Santa Barbara
Carpinteria
Ventura
Oxnard Shores
Port Hueneme
0mi 10 20 30 40

Information Visit the Chamber of Commerce (☎ 488-2023, Ⓦ www.huenemechamber.com) at 220 N Market St.

A Bank of America is on the corner of Channel Islands Blvd and Victoria Ave. A Wells Fargo ATM is in a booth on Hueneme Rd, 100yd west of Ventura Rd.

Open Air Bicycles (☎ 985-5045) is at 437 W Channel Islands Blvd.

Port Hueneme Library (☎ 486-5460; closed Fri & Sun), 510 Park Ave, has public Internet access.

Things to See & Do The Chamber of Commerce incorporates a small local **museum** featuring photographs and historic maritime artifacts relating to the town.

More interesting is the **Seabee Museum** (☎ 982-5165) on the navy base. It displays uniforms, weapons and memorabilia about the legendary Navy Civil Engineer Corps and Naval Construction Force, which operate worldwide. Entry (free) is off Ventura Rd opposite Sunkist St.

At the south end of Ventura Rd, Port Hueneme Beach Park has a **fishing pier** jutting 1240ft into the Pacific. Coastal views include the port's lighthouse to the west.

Sportfishing and **charter boats** can be arranged through Port Hueneme Sportfishing (☎ 488-2212), 105 E Port Hueneme Rd.

Port Hueneme is a base for activities in the **Santa Monica Mtns National Recreation Area** to the east. The Chamber of Commerce has a listing of activities in the NRA, including **mountain biking**. Information is also available from the National Parks Service visitor center (☎ 370-2300, Ⓦ www.nps.gov/samo/), 401 W Hillcrest Dr, Thousand Oaks.

Places to Stay & Eat Hiker/biker camping at ***McGrath State Beach***, 8mi before the Chamber of Commerce on the Day 33 route, costs $3 per person with coin showers. Point Mugu State Park's ***Sycamore Canyon campground*** (13.5mi along the Day 34 route) has hiker/biker sites ($3 per person) and coin showers.

Port Hueneme's motels offer a poor choice. ***Marv-Inn*** *(☎ 488-7067, 645 E Port Hueneme Rd)* was closed for renovation at the time of research. The dreary, inaccurately named ***Surfside Motel*** *(☎ 488-3686, 615 E Port Hueneme Rd)*, with basic doubles for $50, is probably the pick within the city limits. Much better is ***Del Playa Inn*** *(☎ 488-0977; 711 W Hueneme Rd, Oxnard)*, 0.7mi along the Day 34 route. It has a pool and quiet doubles from $50. ***Casa Via Mar Inn*** *(☎ 984-6222, 377 W. Channel Islands Blvd)* offers doubles with king-size beds from $67, including hot breakfast, coffee and donuts, VCR with free movies, free newspaper and use of a pool and tennis courts.

Fresh produce is sold at the ***farmers market*** on Channel Islands Blvd in the harbor area (Sun 10am–2pm). ***Von's supermarket*** *(Channel Islands Blvd)* is near Victoria Ave. ***Tradewind Market*** *(Ventura Rd)* is between Park and Pleasant Valley Rds. Adjacent, ***Ann's Bakery & Mexican Food*** serves standard takeaway fare. Fast-food chains are well represented in town.

Three Rockys Pizzeria *(☎ 488-7777, 307 Hueneme Rd)* is a family restaurant proudly serving '150 different kinds of food'.

Day 34: Port Hueneme to Santa Monica

4¼–7½ hours, 47mi

The ride begins on flat, fairly dull Port Hueneme Rd, which, although busy, has a wide shoulder as it traverses an agricultural area. Ahead loom the craggy Santa Monica Mtns. Undulations begin at the 26mi point with the road rising and falling between sea level and 200ft in the next 7mi. The busy, undulating and wide-shouldered Hwy 1 through strung-out Malibu (35mi) squeezes between the mountains and the ocean. The steepest (and shortest) hill is the last, the 0.1mi pinch from Santa Monica beach up into town. Services en route include a ***seafood restaurant*** (16.7mi); Point Dune Plaza (26.4mi), with ***food stores*** and the Cycle Design bike shop (☎ 310-589-2048); and ***supermarkets*** at Malibu.

A **'Missile Park'** (6.1mi), outside Point Mugu Naval Air Warfare Station, proudly displays products of US military research. Interpretive panels among the dummy-guided missiles and decommissioned jet aircraft emphasize how many different and increasingly efficient ways the navy has to blow things up and kill people or, in military parlance, 'to establish credible deterrence'.

Leo Carillo State Beach campground (18.7mi) is on the left. At 24mi, there's a ***supermarket*** and ***restaurants*** at a mall on the outskirts of Malibu. ***Malibu Beach RV Park campground*** is on the left at 30.6mi.

At 42.7mi the busy road becomes very unpleasant when its shoulder disappears. Turn into a parking lot opposite Temescal Canyon Rd to join a beachfront bikepath. The popular bikepath goes under Santa Monica Pier before an exit leads to the city streets.

Santa Monica

☎ 310

With its early-20th-century pleasure pier, parks overlooking the Pacific Ocean and a colorful Main St district, Santa Monica is an '8-sq-mi urban village', and one of the more agreeable parts of greater Los Angeles (LA).

Information The Santa Monica visitor center (☎ 393-7593, W www.santamonica.com), 1400 Ocean Ave, is in a small kiosk. Ask for a copy of the *Santa Monica Bike Map.*

California Federal Bank, corner 5th St and Santa Monica Blvd, has Citibank opposite.

Supergo bike shop (☎ 451-9977, ext 2), corner Broadway and 5th St, has a service department at 1445 5th St, the rear of the green building next door. Also in town is Helen's Cycles (☎ 829-1836), corner Broadway and 26th St.

Access the Internet at the public library, corner Santa Monica Blvd and 6th St.

Things to See & Do Walk out onto 1600ft **Santa Monica Pier**, the oldest surviving pleasure pier on the west coast. At the seaward end, an historical display documents the pier's origin in 1908 and its subsequent tribulations. It offers fine coastal views, especially at dusk. The amusement park area has rides and sideshows.

Blazing Saddles (☎ 393-9778), on the pier, rents bikes. Route maps are available for five different rides near town. The hardest and best go into the Santa Monica Mtns.

UCLA Ocean Discovery Center (☎ 393-6149) conducts **fish feeding** on weekends at 3pm under the carousel at the pier. The Center, with touch tanks and aquariums, opens to the public on weekends.

In a house built in 1894, **California Heritage Museum** (☎ 392-8537), 2612 Main St, has period rooms with changing exhibits and photographic displays.

The fascinating **Museum of Flying** (☎ 392-8822), 2772 Donald Douglas Loop N at the Santa Monica Municipal Airport – enter off Ocean Park Ave – is housed in an enormous hangar. Three floors exhibit legendary aircraft such as the WWII Mitsubishi Zero and P-51 Mustang, WWI Fokker and a replica of *Voyager*, the first aircraft to fly nonstop around the world (closed Mon & Tues).

Places to Stay & Eat The closest camping to Santa Monica is ***Malibu Beach RV Park*** *(☎ 456-6052 or ☎ 800-622-6052, 25801 Pacific Coast Hwy)* with tent sites for around $20.

Busy, impersonal ***Santa Monica International AYH Hostel*** *(☎ 393-9913 or ☎ 800-909-4776, ext 05; 1436 2nd St)* has beds in 10-bunk rooms for $22/25 members/nonmembers. Four-bed private rooms are available from $60.

Motels are not cheap in trendy Santa Monica. ***Sea Shore Motel*** *(☎ 392-2787, 2637 Main St)* has rooms from $70 and suites sleeping up to four for $100. ***Hotel Shangri-La*** *(☎ 394-2791 or ☎ 800-345-7829, 1301 Ocean Ave)* is in a swank 1939 Art Deco building. Rooms furnished with retro-style furniture, some with kitchenettes and ocean views, cost from $145. ***Hotel Carmel*** *(☎ 451-2469 or ☎ 800-445-8695, 201 Broadway)* has renovated rooms ($100–200). Top end ***Georgian Hotel*** *(☎ 395-9945 or ☎ 800-538-8147)*, with its blue geometric facade, is an eye-catching Art Deco landmark. Standard rooms cost $210 to $500 a night.

Fresh produce is sold at a ***farmers market*** on the 3rd St promenade (Wed 9am–2pm, Sat 8.30am–1pm). Phone ☎ 458-8712 for other locations.

Many restaurants and bars are on the 3rd St promenade. Elsewhere, ***Real Food Daily*** *(☎ 451-7544, 514 Santa Monica Blvd)* is very popular for its organic, vegetarian dishes ($9–13). Next door, ***Golden China Restaurant*** *(☎ 393-9695)* serves Mandarin cuisine daily with 'Healthy Menus' from $9 to $13.

Crocodile Cafe *(☎ 394-4783, cnr Santa Monica Blvd & Ocean Ave)* serves meal-size salads and California cuisine from $10. Get a big ice-cream cone for dessert at the ***ice creamery*** next door.

A restaurant that gets great word-of-mouth recommendation is ***Ocean Avenue Seafood*** *(☎ 394-5669, 1401 Ocean Ave)*. Try the sampler of oysters from different parts of the USA or the salmon served on a cedar plank.

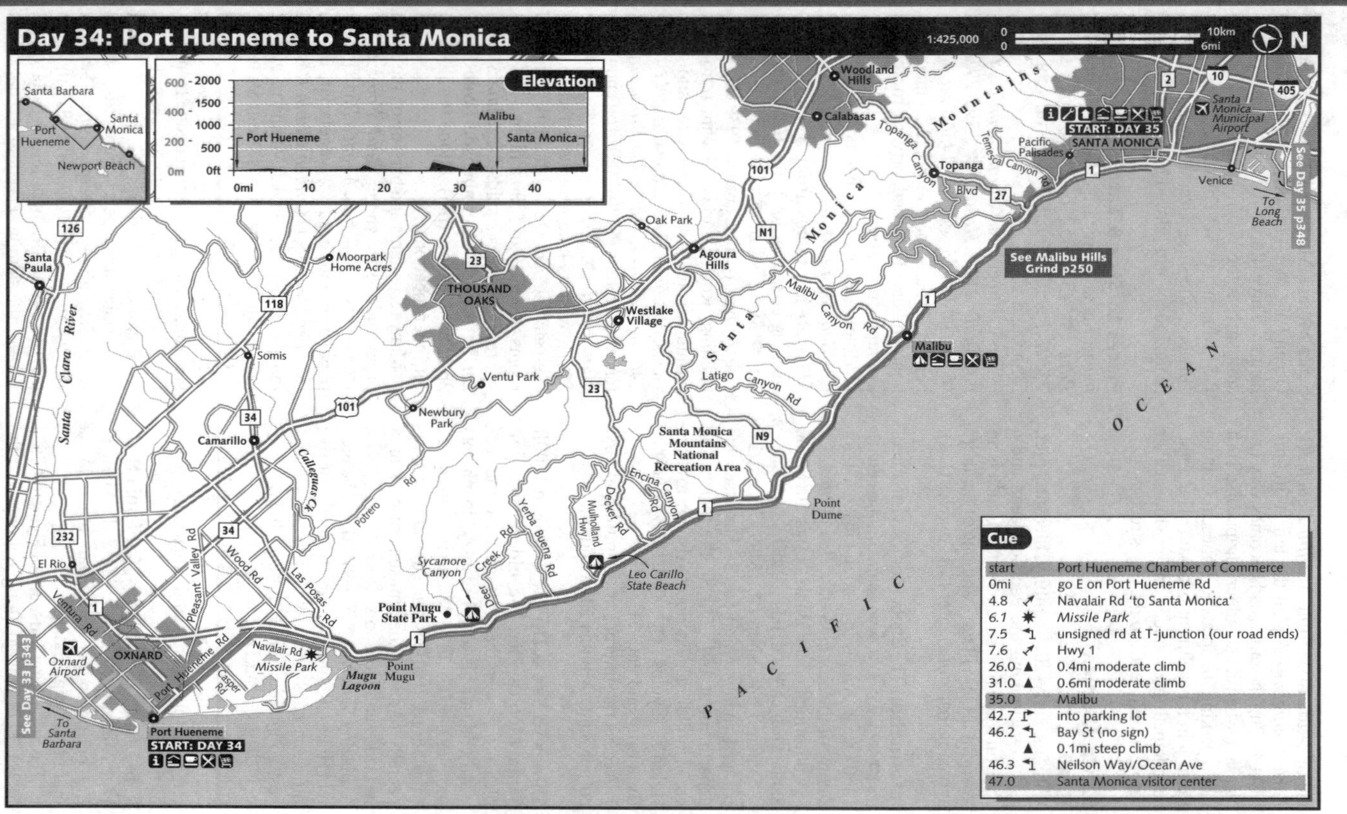
Day 34: Port Hueneme to Santa Monica
1:425,000
0 10km
0 6mi
N
Santa Barbara
Port Hueneme
Santa Monica
Newport Beach
Elevation
600 - 2000
1500
400 - 1000
200 - 500
0m 0ft
0mi 10 20 30 40
Port Hueneme
Malibu
Santa Monica
See Day 35 p348
See Day 33 p343
See Malibu Hills Grind p250
START: DAY 35
SANTA MONICA
START: DAY 34
Port Hueneme
Cue
start Port Hueneme Chamber of Commerce
0mi go E on Port Hueneme Rd
4.8 Navalair Rd 'to Santa Monica'
6.1 Missile Park
7.5 unsigned rd at T-junction (our road ends)
7.6 Hwy 1
26.0 0.4mi moderate climb
31.0 0.6mi moderate climb
35.0 Malibu
42.7 into parking lot
46.2 Bay St (no sign)
0.1mi steep climb
46.3 Neilson Way/Ocean Ave
47.0 Santa Monica visitor center
PACIFIC OCEAN
Santa Monica Mountains
Santa Monica Mountains National Recreation Area
Malibu
Point Dume
Leo Carillo State Beach
Point Mugu State Park
Point Mugu
Mugu Lagoon
Missile Park
Navalair Rd
Casper Rd
Port Hueneme Rd
OXNARD
Oxnard Airport
Ventura Rd
El Rio
Santa Paula
Santa Clara River
Camarillo
Somis
Moorpark Home Acres
Newbury Park
THOUSAND OAKS
Ventu Park
Westlake Village
Oak Park
Agoura Hills
Calabasas
Woodland Hills
Topanga
Topanga Canyon Blvd
Temescal Canyon Rd
Pacific Palisades
Malibu Canyon Rd
Latigo Canyon Rd
Encina Canyon Rd
Decker Rd
Mulholland Hwy
Yerba Buena Rd
Deer Creek Rd
Sycamore Canyon
Potrero Rd
Las Posas Rd
Calleguas Ck
Wood Rd
Pleasant Valley Rd
Santa Monica Municipal Airport
Venice
To Long Beach
To Santa Barbara

Day 35: Santa Monica to Newport Beach

4¾–8½ hours, 53.7mi

A lot of the ride is on bikepaths, meandering along the beach at sea level. A couple of miles beyond Hermosa Beach (14.8mi), the route swings inland and into the pretty, suburban Palos Verdes hills. This is the only section with climbing. A short, very steep pinch from the beach is followed by moderate climbs to about 550ft. After descending again to sea level, the route remains flat for the rest of the day. Food is widely available on this mostly urban ride.

The bikepath route is often poorly signposted and confusing. Particular attention is necessary at the exit to Washington Blvd (3.3mi); the re-entry opposite Mildred Ave (4.1mi); and the crossing of Admiralty Way (4.8mi). From 6.1mi, the bikepath continues meandering through a virtual Sahara of sand, passing LA airport, followed by expensive beach houses and a forest of beach volleyball courts.

The pine- and eucalypt-shaded road through the rolling hills of Palos Verdes offers distant views of the suburban sprawl. It has plenty of traffic but a mostly good shoulder. Descending on Anaheim St, the route passes through gritty port and industrial areas – becoming flat and treeless with noisy traffic.

Newport Beach

☎ 949

The largest and most sophisticated of Orange County's beach towns, Newport (population 72,000) has a harbor clogged with pleasure craft and roads clogged with cars. The Pacific Coast Hwy (Hwy 1) passes through the section of town centered on harbor activity. Yacht clubs, boat dealerships and seafood restaurants cluster in buildings that once served as shipping warehouses for the Irvine Ranch, a large sheep-raising, tenant farming operation that was part of an original Spanish land grant on which the city of Irvine was built. The late film star John Wayne was a resident of Bayshore Dr. Harbor cruises pass his former home.

Information Newport Beach Conference and Visitors Bureau (☎ 722-1611 or ☎ 800-942-6278, Ⓦ www.newportbeach-cvb.com), 3300 W Coast Hwy, is open weekdays. The Channel Inn has tourist brochures and its enthusiastic proprietor can answer most questions. Get a free town map to aid navigation.

The *Newport Beach Bikeways Map* is available from City Hall (☎ 644-3309), 3300 Newport Blvd.

Wells Fargo Bank is 0.2mi south of the visitor center, corner Riverside Ave and Coast Hwy. Albertsons supermarket has an ATM.

Chicago Bike (☎ 650-4203), 4525 W Coast Hwy, should really be listed under Things to See & Do. It's truly a one-of-a-kind bike shop where every preconception and theory about cycling is challenged. Ask to see the collection of unusually spoked wheels and the owner may offer a look at his superbly outfitted, unconventionally geared touring bike. Ordinary bike shops in town include The Bike Doctor (☎ 673-3884), 3415 Newport Blvd, and Let it Roll II (☎ 675-3136), 3130 W Balboa Blvd, next door to Albertsons.

Log on at Newport Beach Library (☎ 717-3800), 1000 Avocado Ave, 0.1mi northeast of Coast Hwy.

Things to See & Do Back Bay, north and east of the Coast Hwy bridge, has wetlands with migratory birds, and a bike trail, entered off Jamboree Rd, from which to observe the natural surroundings of the **Newport Bay Ecological Preserve**.

Museums include the **Orange County Museum of Art** (☎ 759-1122), 850 San Clemente Dr, which has cutting-edge contemporary exhibits and a sculpture garden; and **Newport Harbor Nautical Museum** (☎ 673-7863), housed in a sternwheeler moored at 151 E Coast Hwy. It documents and preserves regional maritime heritage with models, photographs, paintings and memorabilia. Both are closed Monday.

Ferry services to **Santa Catalina Island**, 26mi offshore, and **harbor cruises** (☎ 673-5245) leave the 1905 **Balboa Pavilion**, Newport's most historic landmark. It's near the end of Main St on Balboa Peninsula. For a day ride there, see Catalina Island Crossing (pp253–6).

Paddle Power (☎ 675-1215), 1500 W Balboa Blvd, rents **kayaks**, **canoes** and **surf skis**. Around 31st St and Newport Blvd are a number of **brewpubs** and **live music** venues but the rowdiest nightlife is near Balboa Pier.

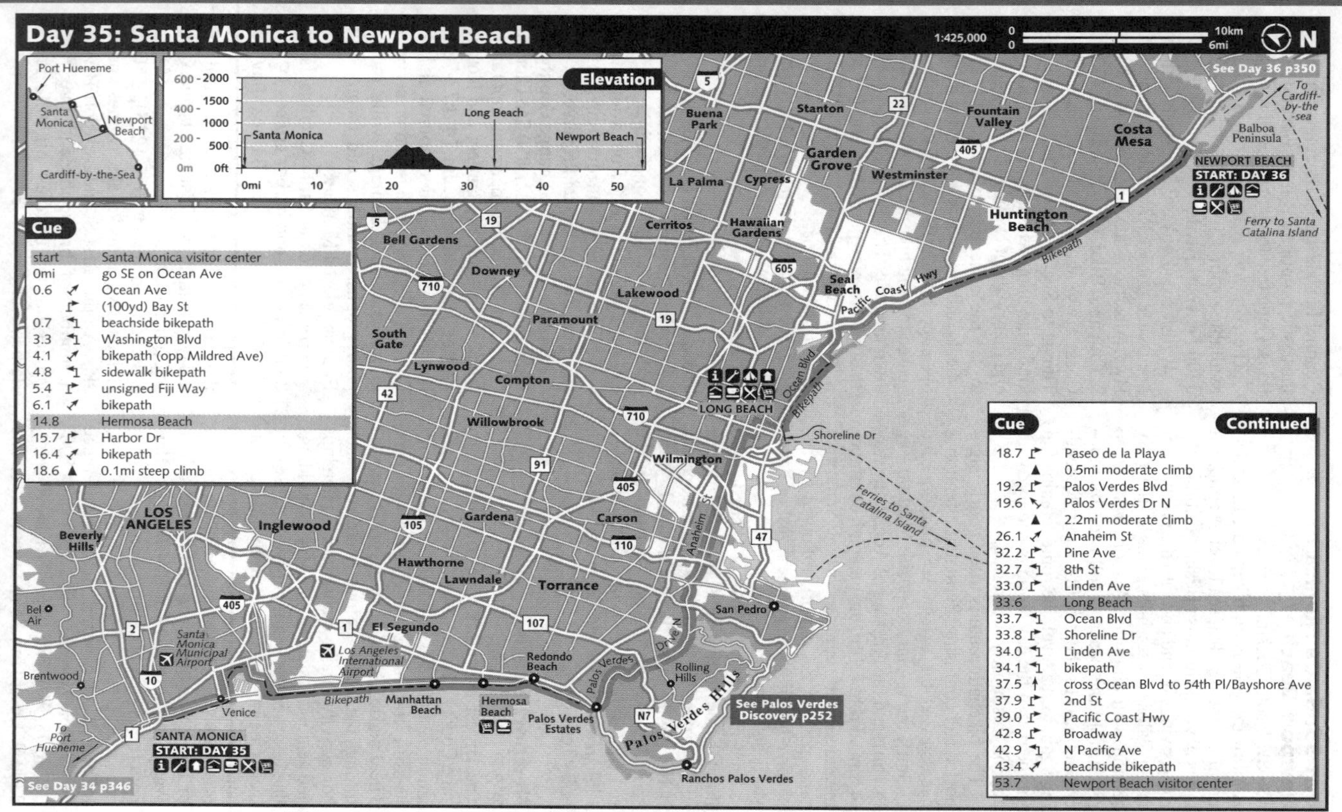
Day 35: Santa Monica to Newport Beach
1:425,000
0 10km
0 6mi
N
Port Hueneme
Santa Monica
Newport Beach
Cardiff-by-the-Sea
Elevation
600 - 2000
400 - 1500
1000
200 - 500
0m 0ft
0mi 10 20 30 40 50
Santa Monica
Long Beach
Newport Beach
Cue
start Santa Monica visitor center
0mi go SE on Ocean Ave
0.6 Ocean Ave
(100yd) Bay St
0.7 beachside bikepath
3.3 Washington Blvd
4.1 bikepath (opp Mildred Ave)
4.8 sidewalk bikepath
5.4 unsigned Fiji Way
6.1 bikepath
14.8 Hermosa Beach
15.7 Harbor Dr
16.4 bikepath
18.6 ▲ 0.1mi steep climb
Cue Continued
18.7 Paseo de la Playa
▲ 0.5mi moderate climb
19.2 Palos Verdes Blvd
19.6 Palos Verdes Dr N
▲ 2.2mi moderate climb
26.1 Anaheim St
32.2 Pine Ave
32.7 8th St
33.0 Linden Ave
33.6 Long Beach
33.7 Ocean Blvd
33.8 Shoreline Dr
34.0 Linden Ave
34.1 bikepath
37.5 cross Ocean Blvd to 54th Pl/Bayshore Ave
37.9 2nd St
39.0 Pacific Coast Hwy
42.8 Broadway
42.9 N Pacific Ave
43.4 beachside bikepath
53.7 Newport Beach visitor center
See Day 34 p346
See Day 36 p350
SANTA MONICA
START: DAY 35
NEWPORT BEACH
START: DAY 36
LONG BEACH
See Palos Verdes Discovery p252
To Port Hueneme
To Cardiff-by-the-sea
Ferry to Santa Catalina Island
Ferries to Santa Catalina Island
Bel Air
Brentwood
Beverly Hills
LOS ANGELES
Santa Monica Municipal Airport
Venice
Inglewood
Los Angeles International Airport
Bikepath
El Segundo
Manhattan Beach
Hermosa Beach
Redondo Beach
Palos Verdes Estates
Palos Verdes Drive N
Rolling Hills
Palos Verdes Hills
Ranchos Palos Verdes
San Pedro
Hawthorne
Lawndale
Gardena
Torrance
Carson
Wilmington
Anaheim St
South Gate
Lynwood
Compton
Willowbrook
Bell Gardens
Downey
Paramount
Lakewood
Cerritos
Hawaiian Gardens
La Palma
Buena Park
Cypress
Stanton
Garden Grove
Westminster
Seal Beach
Fountain Valley
Huntington Beach
Costa Mesa
Balboa Peninsula
Ocean Blvd
Shoreline Dr
Pacific Coast Hwy
Bikepath

The **Balboa Fun Zone**, on the north side towards the end of the peninsula, built in 1936, has fairly tacky arcade games, tourist shops, restaurants and a vertically challenged Ferris wheel.

Places to Stay & Eat Don't expect bargain lodgings in this town. Two locations permit tent camping in the area. ***Crystal Cove State Park*** *(☎ 494-3539, 8471 Pacific Coast Hwy)* is about 5.9mi south between Corona del Mar and Laguna Beach. It has sites along coastal bluffs and in a chaparral canyon inland of the highway. It offers primitive camping (no showers) at $7 per site. In town, ***Newport Dunes Aquatic Park*** *(☎ 729-3863)* is on the bay side of Backbay Dr (turn east off E Coast Hwy at Jamboree Rd south of the visitor center). Primarily a resort for RVs, it charges $31 to $50 per site.

The best-value low-end motel, ***Newport Channel Inn*** *(☎ 642-3030 or ☎ 800-255-8614, 6030 W Coast Hwy)* has large rooms for $79/99 weekday/weekend. Charming ***Balboa Inn*** *(☎ 675-3412 or ☎ 877-225-2629, 105 Main St)* has standard rooms for $139/169.

Luxury Italian-themed ***Portofino Beach Hotel*** *(☎ 673-7030 or ☎ 800-571-8749, 2306 W Oceanfront)* has suites from $159/179 to $279/339, with fireplaces, marble bathtubs and views of nearby Newport Pier.

Albertsons supermarket *(32nd St)*, near Balboa Blvd, opens daily. A daily ***fishermans market*** (7–10am) is at the Newport Pier, along McFadden St off Balboa Blvd.

Among innumerable eating places, every taste is catered for. West of the visitor center, ***Thai Wave*** *(☎ 645-3057, 211 62nd St)* has dinner specials from $8 and vegetarian dishes. ***Spaghetti Bender*** *(☎ 631-8646)*, adjacent to Channel Inn, serves big plates of pasta for $6 and is open for dinner every day. Casual ***Cappy's Cafe*** *(☎ 646-4202)*, on the east side of Channel Inn, opens at 6am daily for breakfast and lunch. It's popular among locals for dinner (Wed only), with steaks ($11) and roast chicken ($9).

Along Restaurant Row, east of the visitor center on the south side of W Coast Hwy, the ***Rusty Pelican*** *(☎ 642-3431, 2735 W Coast Hwy)* gets local recommendation for its seafood, prime rib, chicken and pasta.

Hard Rock Cafe *(☎ 640-8844, 451 Newport Center Dr)* is open every day until late.

Day 36: Newport Beach to Cardiff-by-the-Sea

5½–10 hours, 62.4mi

This longish ride uses several bikepaths and has no long climbs. A couple of gentle undulations take the route over the seaward side of the San Joaquin Hills to Laguna Beach (11mi). A few more hills, of mainly nuisance value, arise through San Clemente (23.1mi), one-time hideaway for President Richard Nixon.

Navigation is simple until San Clemente. From here the route follows a convoluted but quiet series of latin-named suburban streets, returning to bikepath at 27.2mi – the San Clemente Coastal Bike Trail.

San Onofre nuclear generating station is at 30mi, 1mi before San Onofre State Beach. Exiting the park, the flat old road, closed to motor vehicles, crosses a scrub-covered plain between the I-5 freeway/railway and the ocean. The route traverses the Camp Pendleton Marine Corps base from 38.2mi to 47mi before returning to the simple navigation and heavier traffic of the highway for the rest of the day.

Cardiff-by-the-Sea

☎ 760

Shortened to a less mouthfilling 'Cardiff' by most, this laid-back collection of restaurants, surf shops and New Age–style businesses attracts a young crowd. The town dates from 1875 when the Mackinnon family homesteaded on the north shore of San Elijo Lagoon.

Information Cardiff Chamber of Commerce (☎ 436-0431, W www.cardiffbythesea.org) is in the 'Towne Center' shops, 2051 San Elijo Ave (open Mon & Fri 10am–3pm and, depending on volunteer staff, Tues–Thurs 10am–2pm). An ATM is inside Seaside Market.

Encinitas, 2.4mi north on the Day 36 route, has El Camino Bike Shop (☎ 436-2340), 121 N El Camino Real, and Dan's Coast Cyclery (☎ 753-5867), 565 S Coast Hwy.

The town's branch of San Diego County Library (☎ 753-4027; closed Sun & Mon), 2027 San Elijo Ave, has Internet access.

Things to See & Do The **San Elijo Lagoon Ecological Reserve**, south of town, is

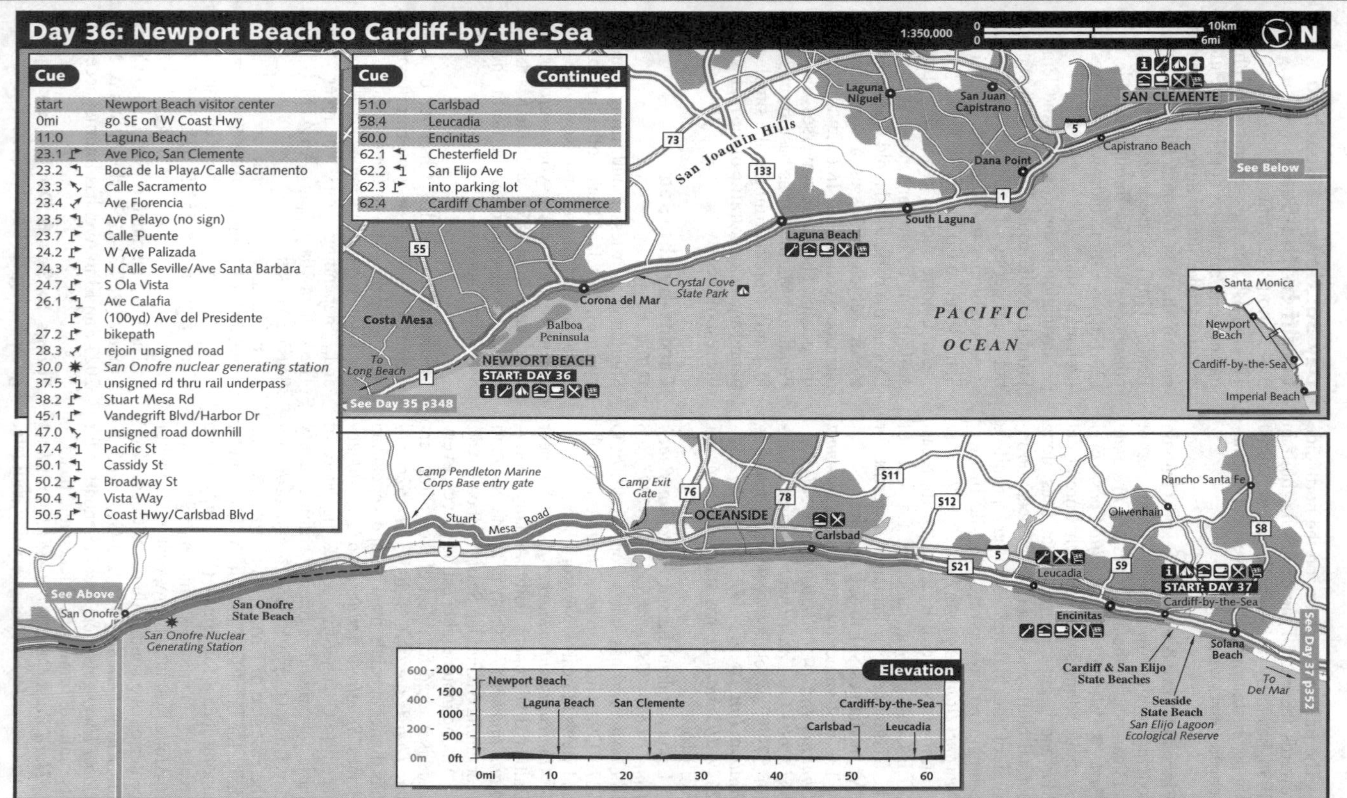

Day 36: Newport Beach to Cardiff-by-the-Sea

Cue	
start	Newport Beach visitor center
0mi	go SE on W Coast Hwy
11.0	Laguna Beach
23.1	Ave Pico, San Clemente
23.2	Boca de la Playa/Calle Sacramento
23.3	Calle Sacramento
23.4	Ave Florencia
23.5	Ave Pelayo (no sign)
23.7	Calle Puente
24.2	W Ave Palizada
24.3	N Calle Seville/Ave Santa Barbara
24.7	S Ola Vista
26.1	Ave Calafia
	(100yd) Ave del Presidente
27.2	bikepath
28.3	rejoin unsigned road
30.0	*San Onofre nuclear generating station*
37.5	unsigned rd thru rail underpass
38.2	Stuart Mesa Rd
45.1	Vandegrift Blvd/Harbor Dr
47.0	unsigned road downhill
47.4	Pacific St
50.1	Cassidy St
50.2	Broadway St
50.4	Vista Way
50.5	Coast Hwy/Carlsbad Blvd

Cue	Continued
51.0	Carlsbad
58.4	Leucadia
60.0	Encinitas
62.1	Chesterfield Dr
62.2	San Elijo Ave
62.3	into parking lot
62.4	Cardiff Chamber of Commerce

important to migratory waterfowl on the Pacific flyway. Over the years, 40% of North America's bird species have been observed on the lagoon. The 1000-acre reserve was dedicated in 1983 to preserve the lagoon's natural values. Walking trails, accessed behind Seaside State Beach, follow its southern shore.

Beach activities and **surfing** are popular at Cardiff and San Elijo state beaches. Hire equipment at 101 Board Sports (☎ 942-2088), 828 N Coast Hwy, Encinitas.

One fascinating activity is watching the elegant **California brown pelicans** 'surfing'. A squadron of these large birds, in line-astern formation, can often be seen gliding along the breakers, mere inches above the swell. When the lead bird reaches the break, it banks sharply and peels off over the crest, gliding out to the next incoming wave to repeat the process. The following birds do the same, in a remarkable display of precision flying.

Places to Stay & Eat Hiker/biker *camping* on the cliff opposite town in San Elijo State Beach costs $3 per person with coin showers.

Indoor accommodations are expensive in town. ***Country Side Inn*** *(☎ 944-0277 or ☎ 800-322-9993, 1661 Villa Cardiff Dr)* charges $98 per double in summer, including a buffet breakfast. ***Cardiff-by-the-Sea Lodge*** *(☎ 944-6474, 142 Chesterfield Dr)* charges from $126.

North in Encinitas, family-oriented ***Moonlight Beach Motel*** *(☎ 753-0623 or ☎ 800-323-1259, 233 2nd St)* charges $76/80 weekday/weekend. ***Encinitas Lodge*** *(☎ 944-0301 or ☎ 800-566-6654, 186 N Coast Hwy)* has double rooms for $79. ***Leucadia Beach Motel*** *(☎ 943-7461, 1322 N Coast Hwy)*, between Carlsbad and Encinitas, has doubles for $50/60 without/with air-con.

Seaside Market in the Towne Centre plaza is open daily. Tempting smells waft from ***VG Donuts & Bakery*** *(106 Aberdeen Dr)*, open at 5am. Adjacent ***Jay's Gourmet*** *(☎ 634-3353)* sells inexpensive salads and pizza. ***Ki's Kitchen*** *(☎ 436-5236, 2591 S Coast Hwy)* is recommended for economical vegetarian lunches with nice views. ***Las Olas*** *(☎ 942-1860, 2655 S Coast Hwy)*, down the hill and across from Cardiff State Beach, serves authentic Mexican, including grilled fish tacos and mango margaritas (open breakfast, lunch & dinner). ***Vigilucci's*** *(☎ 942-7332, 1933 San Elijo Ave)* is a casual, moderately priced Italian place. Upmarket eateries include ***Charlies by the Sea*** *(☎ 942-3100, 2526 S Coast Hwy)* and ***Chart House*** *(☎ 436-4044, 2588 S Coast Hwy)*, both on the water.

Day 37: Cardiff-by-the-Sea to Imperial Beach

5–8 hours, 38.8mi

This epic journey's final day is mostly urban and has one significant hill. A 2.7mi easy-to-moderate climb from sea level at 6.8mi to 435ft near La Jolla. After the hill it returns to sea level in San Diego (28.3mi). Ritzy Del Mar (4.5mi), La Jolla (9.5mi), Pacific Beach (19mi), San Diego and Coronado (28.4mi) all have food and other services.

Entering San Diego, at 25mi, a parallel bikeway beckons, offering relief from traffic on N Harbor Dr. However, it is quite confusing to navigate and considerably longer.

From downtown San Diego, a ferry (☎ 619-435-8895) makes a 15-minute crossing of San Diego Bay to Coronado. This 'island' connects to the rest of the continent at Imperial Beach via the narrow Silver Strand spit, as well as by an elevated toll bridge to the city. The ferry departs San Diego on the hour daily from 9am until 9pm ($2.50 per trip, including bike).

Finish in Imperial Beach or take the side trip to continue to the Mexico border.

Side Trip: International Border

19mi return

Completion of the Border to Border epic is nigh! It's but a short, one-hill ride to Border Field State Park, lying within a whisker of the archetypal border town, Tijuana, Mexico. The only barrier to visiting Mexico is the tall, razor-wire-crowned international boundary fence, which marches out of the sea and across shaved hills deep into the heart of the continent. Beside an Italian-marble monument, placed in 1851 to commemorate the frontier treaty, a US Border Patrol truck faces the sea, engine constantly running, its driver on alert for any unauthorised incursion from the south. Through the chainlink, Tijuana's imposing Bullring-by-the-Sea is visible, looming over the broad, dusty streets of an alien land. To the hazy north along a crescent of sand, tall buildings of downtown San Diego scrape the sky.

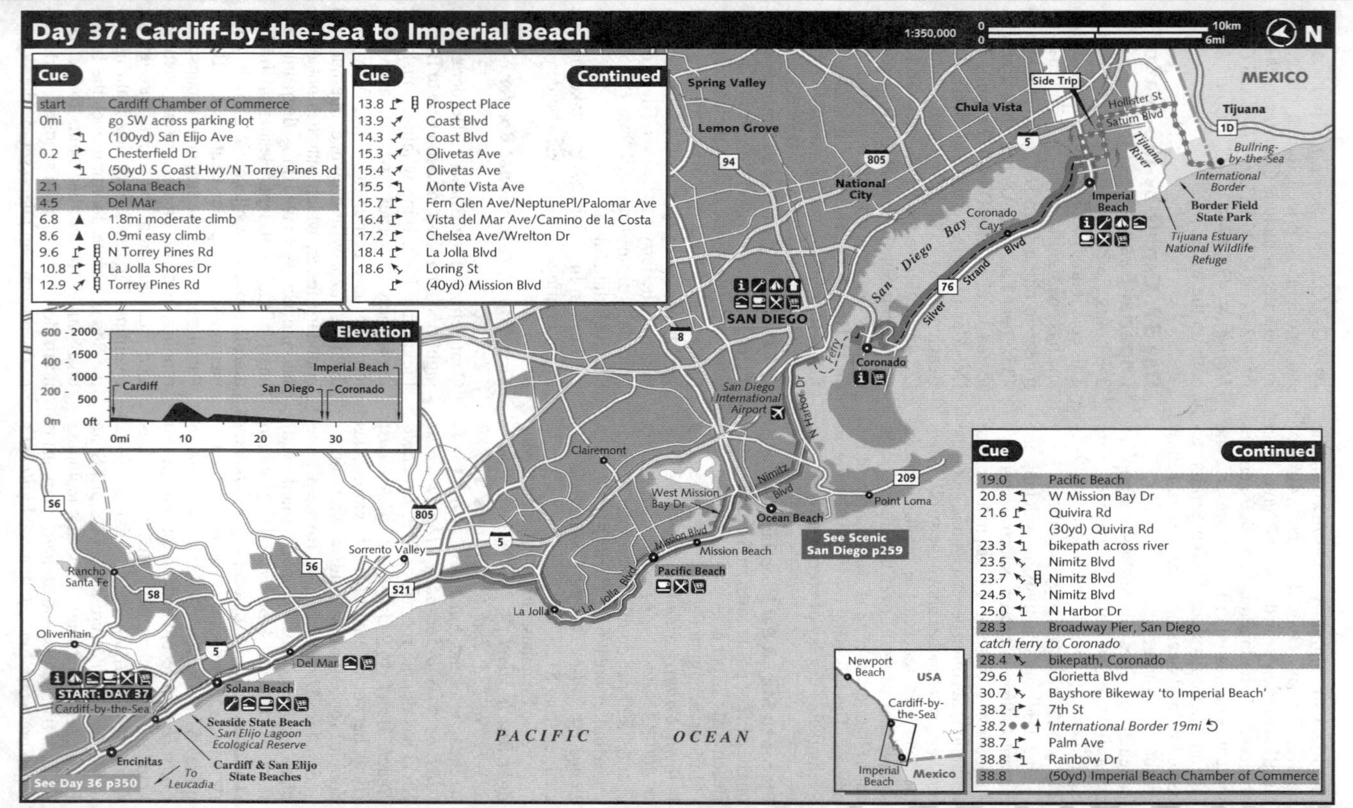

Day 37: Cardiff-by-the-Sea to Imperial Beach
1:350,000
0
0
10km
6mi
N
Cue
start Cardiff Chamber of Commerce
0mi go SW across parking lot
(100yd) San Elijo Ave
0.2 Chesterfield Dr
(50yd) S Coast Hwy/N Torrey Pines Rd
2.1 Solana Beach
4.5 Del Mar
6.8 1.8mi moderate climb
8.6 0.9mi easy climb
9.6 N Torrey Pines Rd
10.8 La Jolla Shores Dr
12.9 Torrey Pines Rd
Cue Continued
13.8 Prospect Place
13.9 Coast Blvd
14.3 Coast Blvd
15.3 Olivetas Ave
15.4 Olivetas Ave
15.5 Monte Vista Ave
15.7 Fern Glen Ave/NeptunePl/Palomar Ave
16.4 Vista del Mar Ave/Camino de la Costa
17.2 Chelsea Ave/Wrelton Dr
18.4 La Jolla Blvd
18.6 Loring St
(40yd) Mission Blvd
Elevation
600 - 2000
1500
400 -
1000
200 -
500
0m
0ft
Cardiff
San Diego
Coronado
Imperial Beach
0mi
10
20
30
Cue Continued
19.0 Pacific Beach
20.8 W Mission Bay Dr
21.6 Quivira Rd
(30yd) Quivira Rd
23.3 bikepath across river
23.5 Nimitz Blvd
23.7 Nimitz Blvd
24.5 Nimitz Blvd
25.0 N Harbor Dr
28.3 Broadway Pier, San Diego
catch ferry to Coronado
28.4 bikepath, Coronado
29.6 Glorietta Blvd
30.7 Bayshore Bikeway 'to Imperial Beach'
38.2 7th St
38.2 International Border 19mi
38.7 Palm Ave
38.8 Rainbow Dr
38.8 (50yd) Imperial Beach Chamber of Commerce
Spring Valley
Lemon Grove
Chula Vista
National City
SAN DIEGO
MEXICO
Tijuana
Side Trip
Hollister St
Saturn Blvd
Tijuana River
Bullring-by-the-Sea
International Border
Border Field State Park
Tijuana Estuary National Wildlife Refuge
Imperial Beach
Coronado Cays
San Diego Bay
Silver Strand Blvd
Coronado
Ferry
San Diego International Airport
N Harbor Dr
Nimitz Blvd
Point Loma
Ocean Beach
See Scenic San Diego p259
West Mission Bay Dr
Mission Blvd
Mission Beach
Pacific Beach
Clairemont
La Jolla
La Jolla Blvd
Sorrento Valley
Rancho Santa Fe
Olivenhain
Del Mar
Solana Beach
START: DAY 37
Cardiff-by-the-Sea
Seaside State Beach
San Elijo Lagoon Ecological Reserve
Cardiff & San Elijo State Beaches
Encinitas
To Leucadia
See Day 36 p350
PACIFIC OCEAN
Newport Beach
USA
Cardiff-by-the-Sea
Imperial Beach
Mexico
94
805
5
76
8
209
S6
56
S8
S21
1D

To head straight to the border on entering town (38.2mi), continue about another 0.8mi on the bikepath, which emerges onto 13th St. Ride south on 13th St for about 0.7mi. (Or, from the Chamber of Commerce, head 0.9mi east along Palm Ave to turn right at 13th St.) Make a left at the traffic lights onto Imperial Beach Blvd then, after 1.3mi, a right onto Hollister St. After another 2.2mi, turn right onto Monument Rd and pedal 3.4mi to Border Field State Park's entry booth. Here, follow the unnamed sandy road to the left for a final 0.8mi, climbing briefly to a headland and the parking-lot-at-the-end-of-the-USA. A fine view of the Pacific unfolds but, unfortunately, there is nowhere to buy food or drink and no facilities other than toilets.

You've made it! Retrace the outward route but turn right at Saturn Blvd to avoid one-way streets. A left onto Palm Ave will lead you to the Chamber of Commerce downtown.

Imperial Beach

☎ 619

The most southwesterly city in the USA, Imperial Beach is right on the Mexican border. Its most prominent landmark, the near-1500-ft-long pier, juts from the beach restaurant precinct. The other landmark visible is the Bullring-by-the-Sea in Tijuana, directly across the border from Border Field State Park. Imperial Beach hosts the US Open Sandcastle contest each July. Its oceanfront can sometimes be closed to swimming because of pollution from the Tijuana River, a problem the international Border Environment Cooperation Commission is attempting to solve.

Information Imperial Beach Chamber of Commerce (☎ 424-3151, ⓔ ibcofc@aol.com; 9am–5pm weekdays) is in the shopping center on the corner of Rainbow and Palm Sts. Enter off Rainbow St opposite Citrus Ave.

Union Bank of California, corner Palm Ave and 9th St, and Federal Credit Union, corner Palm Ave and Delaware St, have ATMs, as does the 7-Eleven store, corner Carolina St and Palm Ave.

Saltwater Magic Cycle & Sport (☎ 423-7873; closed Mon) is at 226 Palm Ave, near the beach.

The library, corner Imperial Beach Blvd and 8th St, has Internet access.

Things to See & Do To truthfully boast you've pedaled from Border to Border, do the **Day 37 side trip**.

The walking trails of **Tijuana Estuary National Wildlife Refuge**, off 3rd St, offer excellent wildlife watching. The visitor center (☎ 575-3613; closed holidays) is on Caspian Way. The refuge is an important rest area for migratory birds on the Pacific flyway. Of the 370 species of birds that visit the area, only 50 species remain year-round.

Wander out on the **pier** after inspecting the colorful, postmodern **sculpture** 'Surfhenge' at its landward end.

Places to Stay & Eat The ***San Diego Metro KOA*** *(☎ 800-762-5267; 111 N Second Ave, Chula Vista)* is about 3mi away via the bikepath from the north end of Saturn Ave. Tent sites cost $26 per double. Cabins cost $41 with one double bed.

The cheapest motel is ***El Camino*** *(☎ 424-3555, 550 Hwy 75)*, where dimly lit, older-style rooms cost $40 all year (including tax; credit cards not accepted). ***Silverado Motel*** *(☎ 575-1414, 1722 Palm Ave)* charges from $40. More salubrious places include ***Seacoast Inn*** *(☎ 424-5183 or ☎ 800-732-2627, 800 Seacoast Dr)* with doubles from $76 and the ***Hawaiian Gardens Suite Hotel*** *(☎ 429-5303 or ☎ 800-334-3071, 1031 Imperial Beach Blvd)*, charging $89 all year.

Wally's IGA Market is in the Imperial Shopping Center near Delaware St on Palm Ave (Hwy 75). ***Seacoast Natural Foods***, in the shops around the visitor center, sells fruit and vegetables and health foods until 8pm.

Next door to the visitor center, ***Silver Sea Chinese Seafood Restaurant*** *(☎ 575-8785)* opens for lunch and dinner, serving Szechuan Mandarin cuisine. Across the parking lot, ***Sushi Sushi*** *(☎ 429-5955)* continues the fish theme and has interesting ice-cream desserts (closed Sun).
Beach Club Grille *(☎ 628-0777, 710 Seacoast Dr)* offers inexpensive family dining. Salads start at $6 and Greek dishes such as gyros and spanakopita cost $4 to $8. ***The Tin Fish***, at the end of the pier, serves all meals (until 8pm), with reasonable portions of fish and chips from $8 and mixed seafood dishes from $10.

Glossary

AAA – American Automobile Association, also called 'Triple A' or the 'Auto Club'
Amtrak – national, government-owned passenger railroad company
Angeleno – a resident of Los Angeles
ATM – Automated Teller Machine; electronic means for extracting cash from banks
ATV – all-terrain vehicle; *4WD*

brewpub – a pub that brews and sells its own beer
BLM – Bureau of Land Management; government agency that controls large areas of public land

caldera – a very large crater that has resulted from a volcanic explosion or the collapse of a volcanic cone; Crater Lake in Oregon is an example of the latter
chamber of commerce – association of local businesses that commonly provides a tourist information service; does not provide information about nonmembers
cot – camp bed (babies sleep in cribs)
creek – small stream

drugstore – pharmacy
DUI – driving under the influence of alcohol and/or drugs

entree – the main course of a meal

4WD – four-wheel-drive vehicle; *ATV*

gallery – a shop where artwork is sold; institutions that exhibit an art collection are usually called museums

HI-AYH – Hostelling International-American Youth Hostels; hostels affiliated with Hostelling International, which is managed by the International Youth Hostel Federation
hiker/biker site – campsite specifically for hikers and cyclists, not available to travelers with motor vehicles, often nonreservable

jog – two turns close together (dogleg)

KOA – Kampgrounds of America; a private RV-oriented organization that provides campgrounds with substantial amenities

microbrewery – small brewery making specialty beer in limited quantities

national monument – a place of historic, scenic or scientific interest set aside for preservation
National Recreation Area – a term used to describe NPS areas of considerable scenic or ecological importance that have been modified by human activity, such as by major dam projects
National Register of Historic Places or **National Historic District** – a listing of historic buildings that is determined by the NPS and based on nominations from property owners and local authorities; buildings and districts must have played a significant role in the development of a community
NPS – National Park Service; division of the Department of the Interior that administers US national parks and monuments

old-growth forest – forest more than 200 years old and never altered by humans
overlook – a lookout (above a scenic feature)

podunk town – small, unimportant and isolated town
powwow – a Native American social ceremony conducted by a shaman; the gathering or fair usually includes competitive dancing

rotary – *traffic circle, roundabout*
roundabout – *rotary, traffic circle*
RV – recreational vehicle, also known as a motor home or camper

sea stack – hard volcanic coastal rock formations originally covered with softer sedimentary rock that has since eroded away
single-track – off-road trail only wide enough for a bike

traffic circle – *rotary, roundabout*

yurt – a circular canvas or wooden tent or building available at some State Park campgrounds, especially in Oregon

This Book

Marisa Gierlich was the coordinating author of *Cycling USA – West Coast*; she wrote the introductory chapters, the Northern California chapter and the Los Angeles Region section of the Southern California chapter. Katherine Widing wrote the Washington chapter; Tullan Spitz wrote the Oregon chapter; and Gregor Clark wrote the Central California and Southern California chapters, as well as the Sierra Nevada section of the Northern California chapter. Neil Irvine wrote the West Coast chapter.

The Your Bicycle chapter was written by Darren Elder, with contributions by Nicola Wells, Neil Irvine and Sally Dillon; the Health & Safety chapter was written by Marisa Gierlich, Dr Isabelle Young and Kevin Tabotta. Material from Lonely Planet's *Pacific Northwest* and *California & Nevada* guides was used for parts of this book.

FROM THE PUBLISHER

Cycling USA – West Coast is the seventh in Lonely Planet's new series of cycling guides. The series was developed by the On the Edge Unit in Melbourne and the Cycling Crew are: Andrew Smith, Angie Phelan, John Shippick, Marg Toohey, Michael Blore, Sally Dillon, Sonya Brooke and Darren Elder.

Marg and Sonya coordinated the editing and mapping/design, respectively, of this book. Marg was assisted by Angie, Andrew Bain, Janet Brunckhorst, Sally and Thalia Kalkipsakis. In mapping, Sonya was assisted by Andrew, Eoin Dunlevy, Jarrad Needham, John, and guidance came from Michael. Glenn van der Knijff saved the day with layout checks.

Thanks to Annie Horner, Matt King, Phil Weymouth and Brett Pascoe for helping with illustrations and images, and to Fiona Siseman for handling publishing admin. The cover was designed by Vince Patton.

A big thankyou to Darren Elder for his guidance and enthusiasm for the series – we miss you and wish you all the best now you've swapped your seat in the office for the high seas.

Lake Washington Circuit

See pp110–13

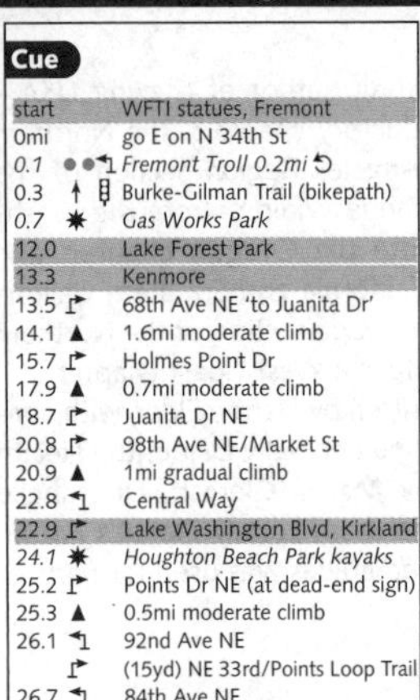

Cue

mi		cue
start		WFTI statues, Fremont
0mi		go E on N 34th St
0.1	●●↰	*Fremont Troll 0.2mi* ↺
0.3	↑	Burke-Gilman Trail (bikepath)
0.7	✷	*Gas Works Park*
12.0		Lake Forest Park
13.3		Kenmore
13.5	↱	68th Ave NE 'to Juanita Dr'
14.1	▲	1.6mi moderate climb
15.7	↱	Holmes Point Dr
17.9	▲	0.7mi moderate climb
18.7	↱	Juanita Dr NE
20.8	↱	98th Ave NE/Market St
20.9	▲	1mi gradual climb
22.8	↰	Central Way
22.9	↱	Lake Washington Blvd, Kirkland
24.1	✷	*Houghton Beach Park kayaks*
25.2	↱	Points Dr NE (at dead-end sign)
25.3	▲	0.5mi moderate climb
26.1	↰	92nd Ave NE
	↱	(15yd) NE 33rd/Points Loop Trail
26.7	↰	84th Ave NE
28.4	↰	Overlake Dr W/Overlake Dr E
29.3	↑	NE Lake Washington Blvd
30.1		Bellevue
30.2	↱	101st Ave SE
30.5	↰	100th Ave SE
	▲	0.2mi steep climb
30.7	↰	SE 8th St
31.0	↱	104th Ave SE (unsigned)/106th Ave SE
32.8	↰	bikepath to I-90
32.9	↱	I-90 bikepath
35.8	↱	'to Seattle'
36.0	✷	*I-90 floating bridge*
37.7	↱	bikepath
	↰	(15yd) S Irving St 'to Lake Wash. Blvd'
37.8	↱	Lake Washington Blvd S
38.5	↰	Lake Washington Blvd E
38.9	↰	Lake Washington Blvd E 'to UW'
40.3	▲	0.3mi gradual climb
41.1	↱	Arboretum Dr E
42.1	↰	E Foster Island Rd
42.3	↱	Lake Washington Blvd E
42.7	↱	'to Historical Museum' 24th Ave E
42.9	↰	E Shelby St
	✷	*Museum of History & Industry*
43.0	↱	Montlake Blvd
43.2	↰	'to UW & Burke-Gilman Trail'
	↗	sidewalk
43.3	↖	'to UW & Burke-Gilman Trail'
43.4	↰	bikepath 'to Gas Works Park'
45.9		WFTI statues, Fremont

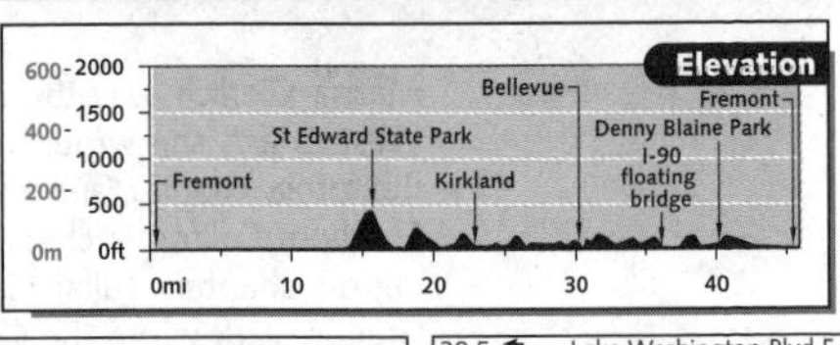

Bainbridge Island Circuit

See pp113–14

Cue

mi		cue
start		Chamber of Commerce, Winslow
0mi		go NE on W Winslow Way
0.1	↰	Ferncliff Ave NE/Lofgren Rd NE
2.1	↱	Moran Rd NE
2.5	↱	Manitou Beach Dr
3.3	↑	Manitou Beach Dr
4.1	↱	Sunrise Dr NE 'to State Park'
6.7	✷	*Fay Bainbridge State Park*
6.8	↰	Lafayette Ave
7.4	↰	Euclid Ave
7.8	↰	Phelps Rd NE
8.0	✷	*Frog Rock*
8.2	↱	Hidden Cove Rd
10.1	↰	Manzanita Rd/Bergman Rd
11.4	↱	Peterson Hill Rd NE
11.6	▲	0.2mi hard climb
11.9	↱	Miller Rd
12.4	↱	NE Arrow Point Dr
12.5	△	0.3mi steep descent
12.8	▲	0.3mi steep climb
13.2	↱	NE Arrow Point Rd
13.5	↰	Frey Ave
13.8	↰	Battle Point Rd
15.1	↰	Battle Point Rd
15.8	↱	Miller Rd NE 'to Lynwood Center'
16.2		Island Center
18.1	↱	Lynwood Center Rd
19.0	●●↱	*Point White Vistas 4.6mi* ↺
19.2		Lynwood Center
19.8	↖	NE Oddfellow Rd
	●●↱	*Fort Ward State Park 2.7mi* ↺
20.4	↗	NE Blakely Ave
21.0	↖	NE Halls Hill Rd/Rockaway Beach Rd NE
	▲	0.3mi moderate climb
21.7	△	0.2mi steep descent
22.9	↑	Eagle Harbor Dr NE
25.5	↱	NE Wyatt Way
	▲	0.1mi moderate climb
25.9	▲	0.3mi gradual climb
26.3	↱	Madison Ave NE
26.6	↰	Winslow Way
26.9		Chamber of Commerce, Winslow

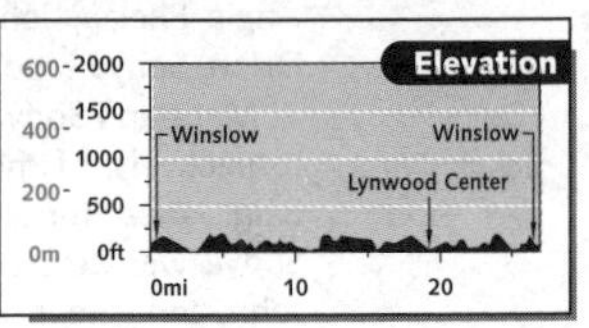

Mt Rainier Magnificence

See pp114–20

Day 1

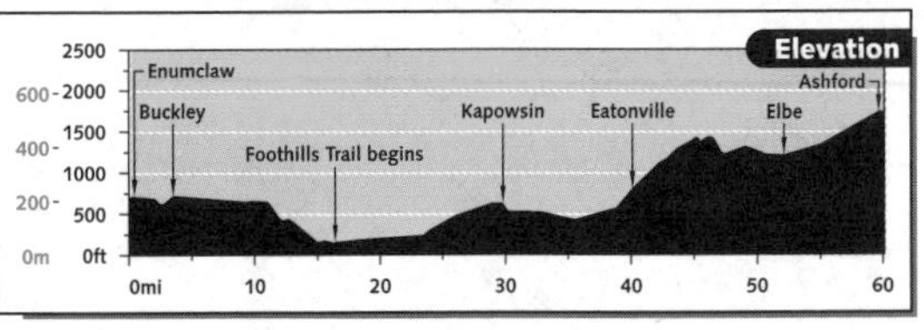

Mt Rainier Magnificence (continued)

See pp114–20

Day 1 (continued)

Cue

start	Enumclaw Chamber of Commerce
0mi	go SW on Cole St
0.4	Hwy 410 W
3.2	A St
	(100yd) River Ave
3.3	*museum*
3.5	Buckley
3.9	'to Hwy 410 West'
4.0	112th St E
9.3	214th Ave E
9.8	120th Ave E
10.8	198th Ave E
11.1	Rhodes Lake Rd
13.6	McCutcheon Rd E
14.9	128th St E (cross river)
15.6	Hwy 162
16.2	Foothills Trail bikepath
19.0	Foothills Trail bikepath
19.2	Orting
19.4	Bridge St
19.5	Harman Way S/Hwy 162 S
20.5	Orville Rd E 'to Electron'
23.4	0.5mi gradual climb
29.8	Orville Rd E, Kapowsin
38.8	Hwy 161/Washington Ave
38.9	1mi moderate climb
40.0	Center St E/Alder Cutoff Rd
40.1	Eatonville
40.3	3mi moderate climb
47.3	Hwy 7/Hwy 706
51.8	cross railway tracks
52.1	Elbe
52.5	cross railway tracks
55.0	*Spirits of Iron*
60.1	Ashford General Store

Day 2

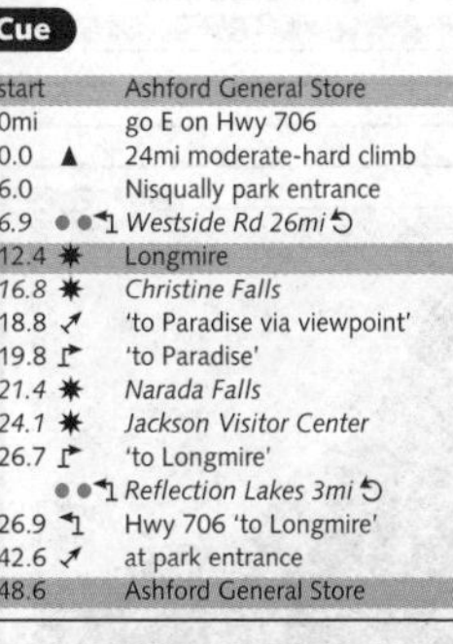

Cue

start	Ashford General Store
0mi	go E on Hwy 706
0.0	24mi moderate-hard climb
6.0	Nisqually park entrance
6.9	*Westside Rd 26mi*
12.4	Longmire
16.8	*Christine Falls*
18.8	'to Paradise via viewpoint'
19.8	'to Paradise'
21.4	*Narada Falls*
24.1	*Jackson Visitor Center*
26.7	'to Longmire'
	Reflection Lakes 3mi
26.9	Hwy 706 'to Longmire'
42.6	at park entrance
48.6	Ashford General Store

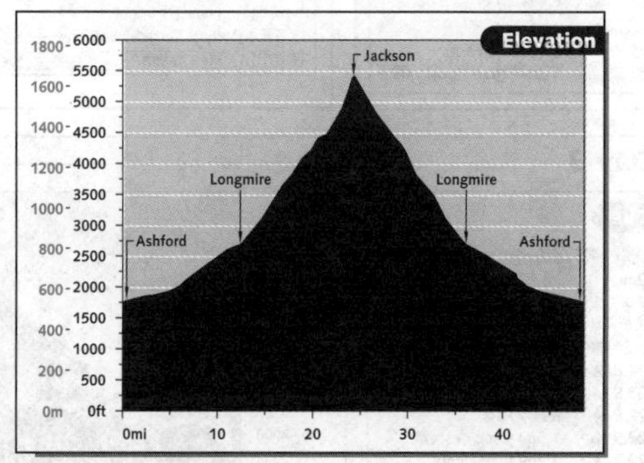

Day 3

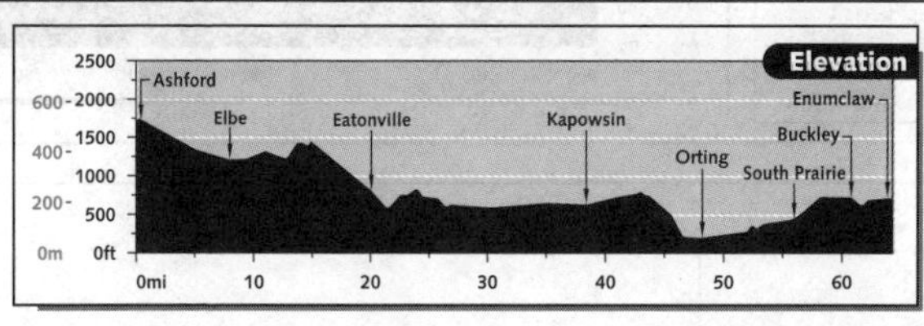

Cue

start	Ashford General Store
retrace Day 1 route to Eatonville	
20.0	Eatonville
20.1	Washington St/Hwy 161
21.5	1.1mi gradual climb
23.1	E'ville Cutoff Rd 'to Tacoma'
	Dogwood Park
25.8	*Northwest Trek 6.2mi*
26.8	Pulford Rd/78th Ave E
28.8	340th St E
30.3	Hwy 7
31.5	320th St E
33.1	Lebor Devore Rd E
34.1	Webster Rd E
34.4	304th/Kapowsin Hwy
38.4	Kapowsin
	Orting-Kapowsin Hwy
42.6	0.5mi gradual climb
45.4	1.2mi steep descent
48.2	bikepath/Calistoga St, Orting
52.0	S Prairie-Carbon River Rd E
55.5	Meeks Ave
55.6	SW 3rd St
55.8	Emery Ave
56.0	Hwy 162, South Prairie
56.2	2mi gradual climb
58.2	Mundy Loss Rd (unsigned)
59.2	112th St E
60.3	at Hwy 410 'to Hwy 165'
60.4	S River Ave
60.8	Buckley
61.1	A St
61.2	Hwy 410
63.9	Cole St 'to city center'
64.3	Enumclaw Chamber of Commerce

North Cascades Contrasts

See pp120–31

Day 1

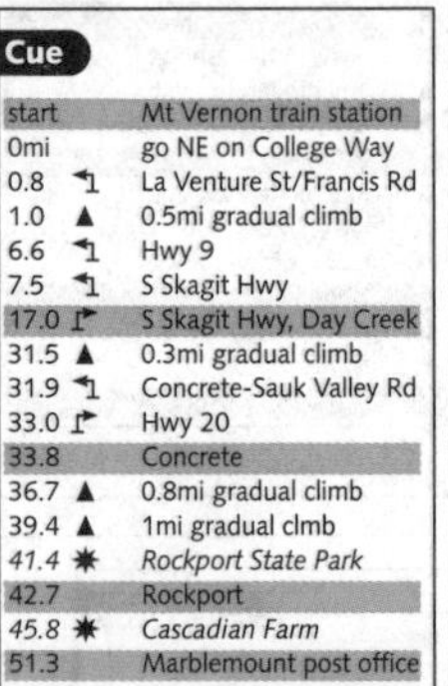

Cue

start	Mt Vernon train station
0mi	go NE on College Way
0.8	La Venture St/Francis Rd
1.0 ▲	0.5mi gradual climb
6.6	Hwy 9
7.5	S Skagit Hwy
17.0	S Skagit Hwy, Day Creek
31.5 ▲	0.3mi gradual climb
31.9	Concrete-Sauk Valley Rd
33.0	Hwy 20
33.8	Concrete
36.7 ▲	0.8mi gradual climb
39.4 ▲	1mi gradual clmb
41.4	*Rockport State Park*
42.7	Rockport
45.8	*Cascadian Farm*
51.3	Marblemount post office

Day 2

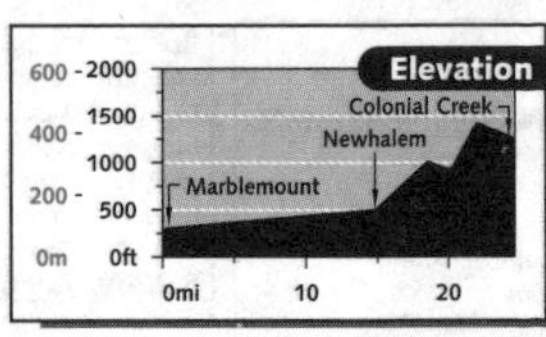

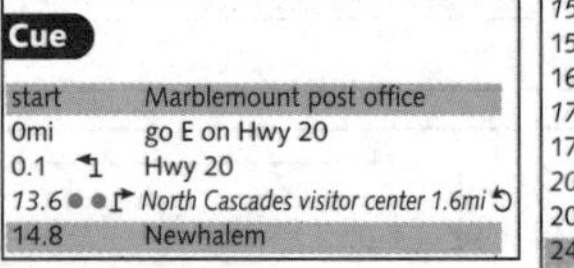

Cue

start	Marblemount post office
0mi	go E on Hwy 20
0.1	Hwy 20
13.6	*North Cascades visitor center 1.6mi*
14.8	Newhalem

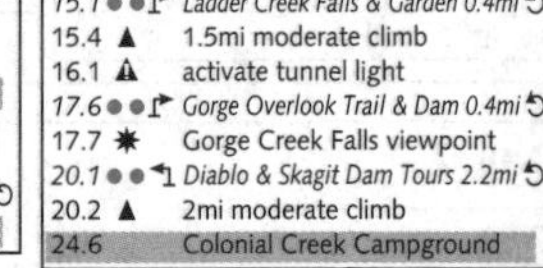

15.1	*Ladder Creek Falls & Garden 0.4mi*
15.4 ▲	1.5mi moderate climb
16.1	activate tunnel light
17.6	*Gorge Overlook Trail & Dam 0.4mi*
17.7	Gorge Creek Falls viewpoint
20.1	*Diablo & Skagit Dam Tours 2.2mi*
20.2 ▲	2mi moderate climb
24.6	Colonial Creek Campground

Day 3

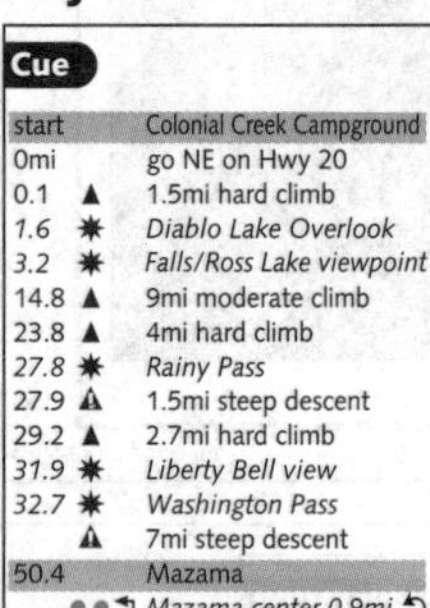

Cue

start	Colonial Creek Campground
0mi	go NE on Hwy 20
0.1 ▲	1.5mi hard climb
1.6	*Diablo Lake Overlook*
3.2	*Falls/Ross Lake viewpoint*
14.8 ▲	9mi moderate climb
23.8 ▲	4mi hard climb
27.8	*Rainy Pass*
27.9	1.5mi steep descent
29.2 ▲	2.7mi hard climb
31.9	*Liberty Bell view*
32.7	*Washington Pass*
	7mi steep descent
50.4	Mazama
	Mazama center 0.9mi
63.9	Winthrop visitor center

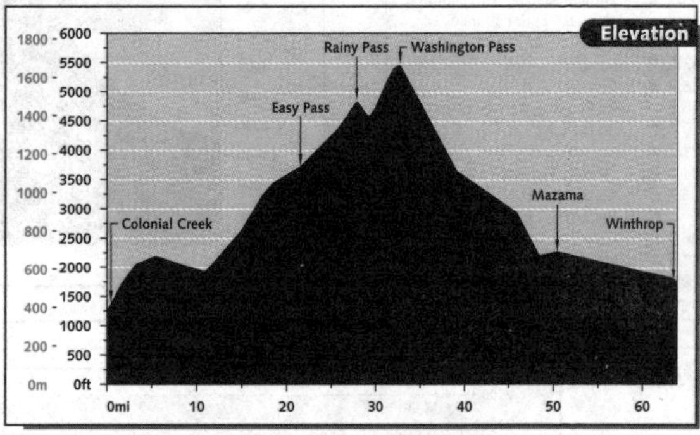

Day 4

Cue

start	Winthrop visitor center
0mi	go E on Hwy 20/Riverside Rd
0.4	Twisp-Winthrop Eastside Rd
0.6	Twisp-Winthrop Eastside Rd
9.6	Hwy 20
	Twisp 1.8mi
11.4	Hwy 153 'to Carlton'
19.8	Carlton
31.5	Methow
41.1	*Alta Lake State Park 4mi*
42.3	*fruit stand*
42.7	Hwy 97
51.9	Antoine Creek Rd/Apple Acres Rd
52.0 ▲	1.2mi hard climb
58.7	Hwy 97 (Alt) 'to Chelan'
62.4	Woodin Ave
62.7	Columbia St
62.7	(100yd) Chelan visitor center

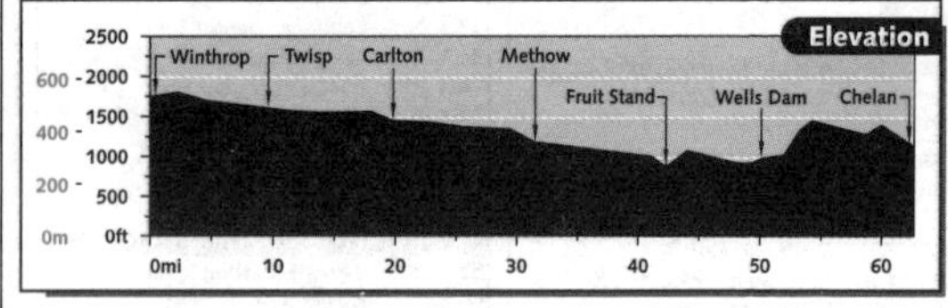

North Cascades Contrasts (continued)

See pp120–31

Day 5

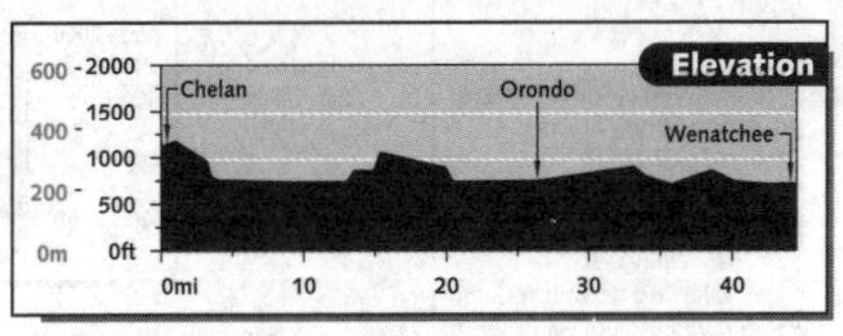

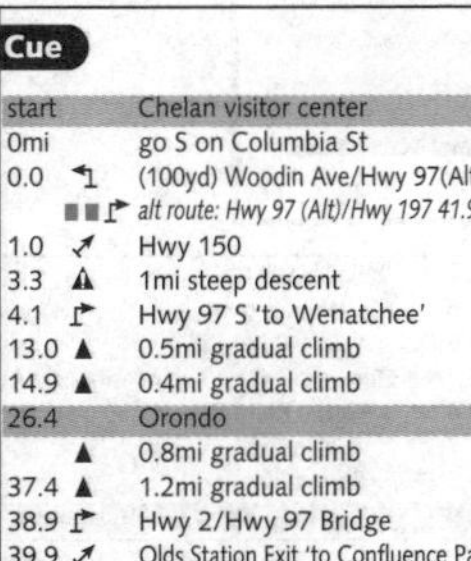

Cue

start	Chelan visitor center
0mi	go S on Columbia St
0.0	(100yd) Woodin Ave/Hwy 97(Alt)N
	alt route: Hwy 97 (Alt)/Hwy 197 41.9mi
1.0	Hwy 150
3.3	1mi steep descent
4.1	Hwy 97 S 'to Wenatchee'
13.0	0.5mi gradual climb
14.9	0.4mi gradual climb
26.4	Orondo
	0.8mi gradual climb
37.4	1.2mi gradual climb
38.9	Hwy 2/Hwy 97 Bridge
39.9	Olds Station Exit 'to Confluence Park'
40.2	Hwy 97(Alt)/Euclid Ave
	alt route rejoins: continue
40.4	*Apple Visitor Center*
40.6	Euclid Ave
40.7	'to Confluence State Park'
41.1	enter Confluence State Park
41.3	Apple Capital bikepath
41.5	cross on footbridge
42.2	Hawley St
42.5	Apple Capital bikepath
42.6	Apple Capital bikepath
43.9	5th St (at {Bronze Man} statue)
44.1	Wenatchee Ave
44.5	Wenatchee visitor center

Lopez Island

See pp134–6

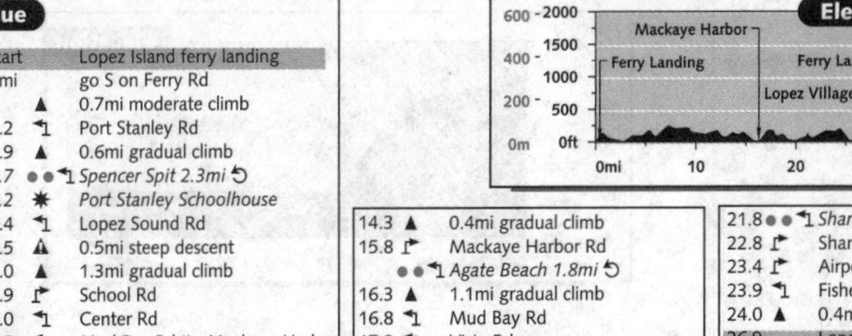

Cue

start	Lopez Island ferry landing
0mi	go S on Ferry Rd
	0.7mi moderate climb
1.2	Port Stanley Rd
2.9	0.6mi gradual climb
3.7	*Spencer Spit 2.3mi*
4.2	*Port Stanley Schoolhouse*
5.4	Lopez Sound Rd
5.5	0.5mi steep descent
6.0	1.3mi gradual climb
6.9	School Rd
8.0	Center Rd
9.5	Mud Bay Rd 'to Mackaye Harbor'
11.3	0.2mi gradual climb
13.1	0.6mi gradual climb
13.8	Aleck Bay Rd
	Sperry Peninsula 3.4mi RTN>
14.3	Aleck Bay Rd
14.3	0.4mi gradual climb
15.8	Mackaye Harbor Rd
	Agate Beach 1.8mi
16.3	1.1mi gradual climb
16.8	Mud Bay Rd
17.9	Vista Rd
19.2	Richardson Rd
19.9	Davis Bay Rd/Burt Rd
20.2	0.5mi gradual climb
21.0	0.2mi gradual climb
21.8	Shark Reef Rd

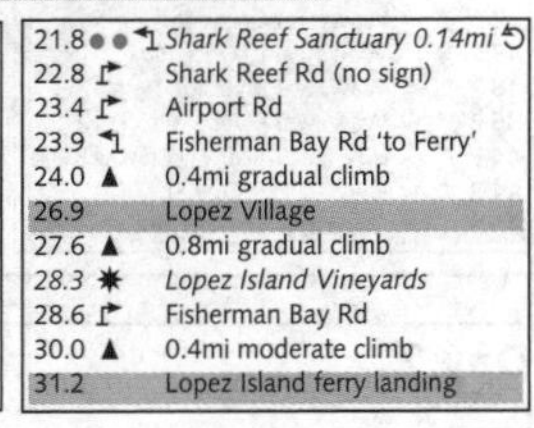

21.8	*Shark Reef Sanctuary 0.14mi*
22.8	Shark Reef Rd (no sign)
23.4	Airport Rd
23.9	Fisherman Bay Rd 'to Ferry'
24.0	0.4mi gradual climb
26.9	Lopez Village
27.6	0.8mi gradual climb
28.3	*Lopez Island Vineyards*
28.6	Fisherman Bay Rd
30.0	0.4mi moderate climb
31.2	Lopez Island ferry landing

Orcas Island

See pp136–7

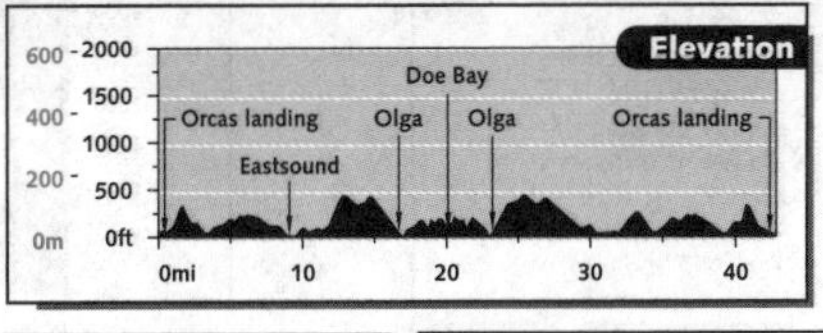

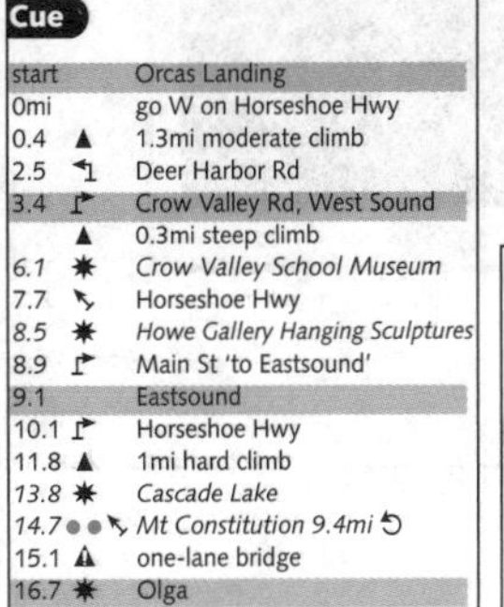

Cue

start	Orcas Landing
0mi	go W on Horseshoe Hwy
0.4	1.3mi moderate climb
2.5	Deer Harbor Rd
3.4	Crow Valley Rd, West Sound
	0.3mi steep climb
6.1	*Crow Valley School Museum*
7.7	Horseshoe Hwy
8.5	*Howe Gallery Hanging Sculptures*
8.9	Main St 'to Eastsound'
9.1	Eastsound
10.1	Horseshoe Hwy
11.8	1mi hard climb
13.8	*Cascade Lake*
14.7	*Mt Constitution 9.4mi*
15.1	one-lane bridge
16.7	Olga
	Point Lawrence Rd 'to Doe Bay'
17.0	1mi moderate climb
17.3	Point Lawrence Rd
18.7	0.2mi gradual climb
19.2	0.5mi gradual climb
19.8	0.3mi steep descent
20.1	Doe Bay
	retrace outward route to Terrill Beach Rd
30.1	Terrill Beach Rd
30.5	Mt Baker Rd
31.8	Lovers Lane
32.0	Enchanted Forest Rd
	0.3mi steep climb
32.3	1mi gradual climb
34.4	West Beach Rd
	West Beach 0.5mi
34.6	*Orcas Island Pottery}*
34.7	0.7mi gradual climb
35.7	Crow Valley Rd
39.3	Deer Harbor Rd, West Sound
	Deer Harbor 8mi
39.4	0.6mi moderate climb
40.2	Horseshoe Hwy
40.4	0.7mi gradual climb
42.8	Orcas Landing

San Juan Island

See pp138–9

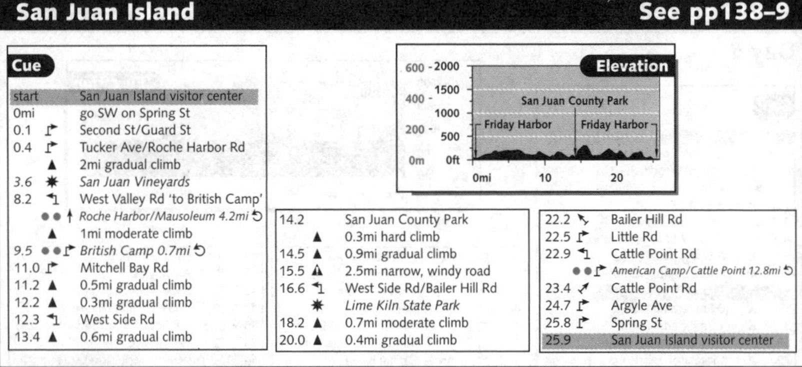

Cue

start		San Juan Island visitor center
0mi		go SW on Spring St
0.1	↱	Second St/Guard St
0.4	↱	Tucker Ave/Roche Harbor Rd
	▲	2mi gradual climb
3.6	✷	*San Juan Vineyards*
8.2	↰	West Valley Rd 'to British Camp'
	●● ↑	*Roche Harbor/Mausoleum 4.2mi* ⟲
	▲	1mi moderate climb
9.5	●● ↱	*British Camp 0.7mi* ⟲
11.0	↱	Mitchell Bay Rd
11.2	▲	0.5mi gradual climb
12.2	▲	0.3mi gradual climb
12.3	↰	West Side Rd
13.4	▲	0.6mi gradual climb
14.2		San Juan County Park
	▲	0.3mi hard climb
14.5	▲	0.9mi gradual climb
15.5	⚠	2.5mi narrow, windy road
16.6	↰	West Side Rd/Bailer Hill Rd
	✷	*Lime Kiln State Park*
18.2	▲	0.7mi moderate climb
20.0	▲	0.4mi gradual climb
22.2	↖	Bailer Hill Rd
22.5	↱	Little Rd
22.9	↰	Cattle Point Rd
	●● ↱	*American Camp/Cattle Point 12.8mi* ⟲
23.4	↗	Cattle Point Rd
24.7	↱	Argyle Ave
25.8	↱	Spring St
25.9		San Juan Island visitor center

Snake & Spiral Circuit

See pp142–6

Day 1

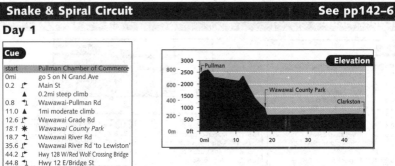

Cue

start		Pullman Chamber of Commerce
0mi		go S on N Grand Ave
0.2	↱	Main St
	▲	0.2mi steep climb
0.8	↰	Wawawai-Pullman Rd
11.0	▲	1mi moderate climb
12.6	↱	Wawawai Grade Rd
18.1	✷	*Wawawai County Park*
18.7	↰	Wawawai River Rd
35.6	↱	Wawawai River Rd 'to Lewiston'
44.2	↱	Hwy 128 W/Red Wolf Crossing Bridge
44.8	↰	Hwy 12 E/Bridge St
45.9		Clarkston Chamber of Commerce

Elevation

Pullman — Wawawai County Park — Clarkston

Day 2

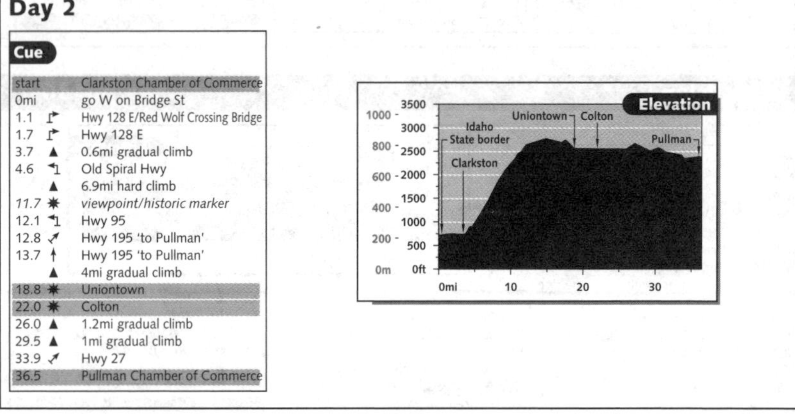

Cue

start		Clarkston Chamber of Commerce
0mi		go W on Bridge St
1.1	↱	Hwy 128 E/Red Wolf Crossing Bridge
1.7	↱	Hwy 128 E
3.7	▲	0.6mi gradual climb
4.6	↰	Old Spiral Hwy
	▲	6.9mi hard climb
11.7	✷	*viewpoint/historic marker*
12.1	↰	Hwy 95
12.8	↗	Hwy 195 'to Pullman'
13.7	↑	Hwy 195 'to Pullman'
	▲	4mi gradual climb
18.8	✷	Uniontown
22.0	✷	Colton
26.0	▲	1.2mi gradual climb
29.5	▲	1mi gradual climb
33.9	↗	Hwy 27
36.5		Pullman Chamber of Commerce

Snake & Spiral Circuit (continued)

See pp142–6

Day 3

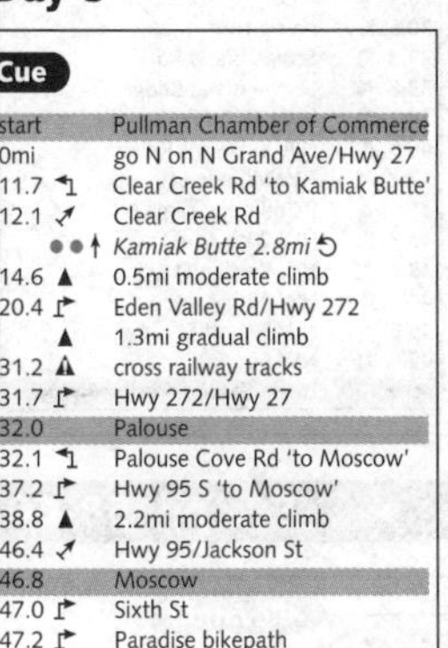

Cue

start	Pullman Chamber of Commerce
0mi	go N on N Grand Ave/Hwy 27
11.7	Clear Creek Rd 'to Kamiak Butte'
12.1	Clear Creek Rd
	Kamiak Butte 2.8mi
14.6	0.5mi moderate climb
20.4	Eden Valley Rd/Hwy 272
	1.3mi gradual climb
31.2	cross railway tracks
31.7	Hwy 272/Hwy 27
32.0	Palouse
32.1	Palouse Cove Rd 'to Moscow'
37.2	Hwy 95 S 'to Moscow'
38.8	2.2mi moderate climb
46.4	Hwy 95/Jackson St
46.8	Moscow
47.0	Sixth St
47.2	Paradise bikepath

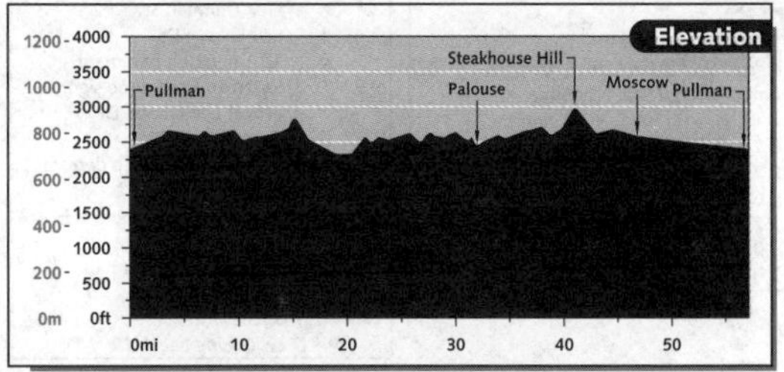

47.6	Third St (cross Line St)
48.3	Perimeter Dr
	(20yds) Chipman Trail bikepath
49.0	*Appaloosa Horse Museum (RHS)*
55.5	Bishop St
55.6	Palouse River Trail bikepath

55.8	bikepath (after bridge)
56.2	cross Riverview St
56.4	Spring St
56.6	Main St
56.9	N Grand Ave
57.1	Pullman Chamber of Commerce

Forest & Island Jaunt

See pp157–8

Cue

start	Union Station, Portland
0mi	go S on NW 6th Ave
	(110yd) NW Irving St
0.1	NW Broadway
0.2	NW Glisan St
0.6	NW 14th Ave
1.2	NW Raleigh St
1.9	NW 24th Ave
2.0	NW Thurman St
3.1	NW Thurman St
3.4	Leif Erikson Dr
	12.1mi rough pavement
9.9	Saltzman Fire Rd (no sign)
	(16yd) Leif Erikson Dr
15.2	Germantown Rd
	1.3mi twisting steep descent
16.5	NW Bridge Ave
16.6	Hwy 30 'to Scappoose & St Helens'
20.4	Sauvie Island Bridge
20.7	U-turn through car park
	cycle under bridge
27.2	Reeder Rd
	swimming beach 10mi
28.4	*dike*
30.5	no sign
31.8	Sauvie Island Rd
33.8	Sauvie Island Bridge
34.1	Hwy 30 'to Portland'
40.9	NW St Helens Rd
42.7	NW Vaughn St
	0.2mi steep climb
43.3	NW 24th Ave
43.6	NW Raleigh St
44.3	NW 13th Ave
45.0	NW Everett St
45.6	NW 6th Ave
45.9	Union Station, Portland

Columbia River Gorge

See pp158–60

Day 1

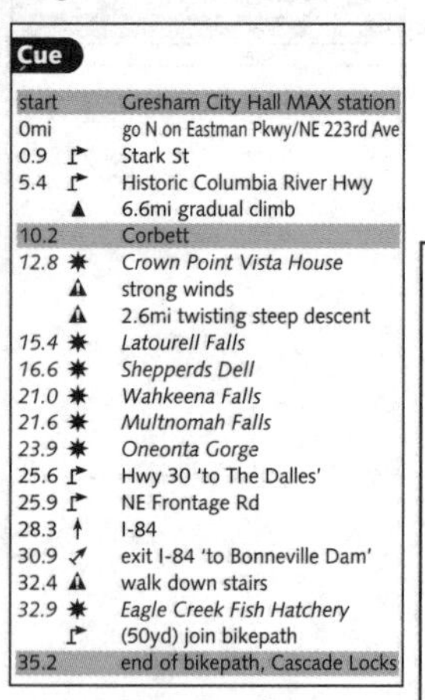

Cue

start	Gresham City Hall MAX station
0mi	go N on Eastman Pkwy/NE 223rd Ave
0.9	Stark St
5.4	Historic Columbia River Hwy
	6.6mi gradual climb
10.2	Corbett
12.8	*Crown Point Vista House*
	strong winds
	2.6mi twisting steep descent
15.4	*Latourell Falls*
16.6	*Shepperds Dell*
21.0	*Wahkeena Falls*
21.6	*Multnomah Falls*
23.9	*Oneonta Gorge*
25.6	Hwy 30 'to The Dalles'
25.9	NE Frontage Rd
28.3	I-84
30.9	exit I-84 'to Bonneville Dam'
32.4	walk down stairs
32.9	*Eagle Creek Fish Hatchery*
	(50yd) join bikepath
35.2	end of bikepath, Cascade Locks

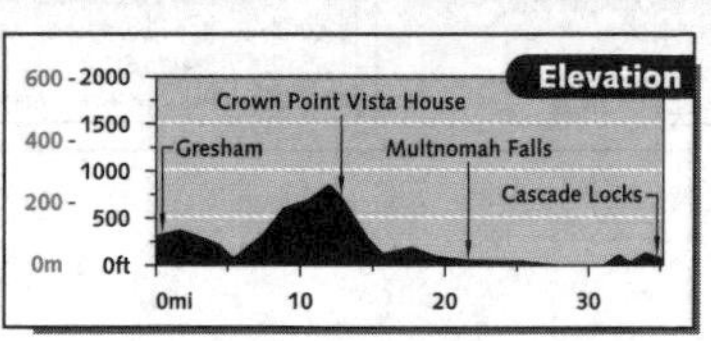

Day 2

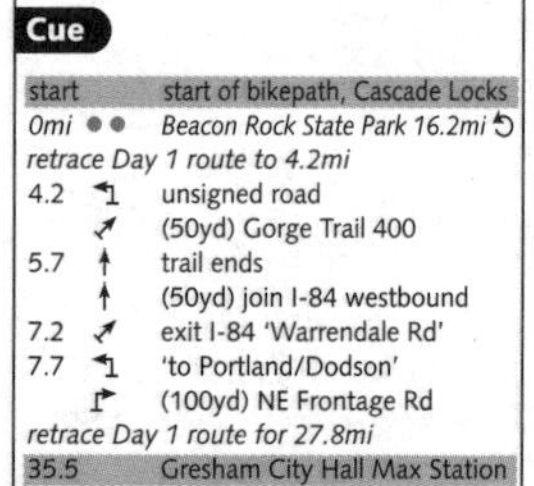

Cue

start	start of bikepath, Cascade Locks
0mi	*Beacon Rock State Park 16.2mi*
retrace Day 1 route to 4.2mi	
4.2	unsigned road
	(50yd) Gorge Trail 400
5.7	trail ends
	(50yd) join I-84 westbound
7.2	exit I-84 'Warrendale Rd'
7.7	'to Portland/Dodson'
	(100yd) NE Frontage Rd
retrace Day 1 route for 27.8mi	
35.5	Gresham City Hall Max Station

Willamette Valley Ramble

See pp160–4

Day 1

Cue

start	Lane County Courthouse, Eugene
0mi	go N on Oak St
0.2	E 5th Ave
0.4	High St/Cheshire Ave
0.8	join multi-use path
2.9	Stephens Dr
	(100yd) bikepath
4.0	Copping St
4.3	Owosso Dr
4.7	River Rd
14.0	Lovelake Rd
17.0	Hwy 99 (no sign)
17.2	Noraton Rd
20.0	Old River Rd 'to Monroe/Ingram'
23.3	W Ingram Island Rd 'to Monroe'
23.5	Hwy 99 (no sign) 'to Monroe'
26.1	Coon Rd, Monroe
	1.6mi moderate climb
27.7	Kyle Rd 'to Alpine'
29.1	Alpine Rd 'to Alpine'
30.8	Alpine
30.9	Bellfountain Rd
33.5	Bellfountain
	Bellfountain Park 2mi
	2.1mi moderate climb
37.5	*National Wildlife Refuge (RHS)*
41.3	*Tyee Winery 1.9mi*
42.5	Llewelyn Rd
44.0	Fern Rd
44.0	*Bellfountain Cellars 3.6mi*
49.1	Applegate St, Philomath
49.9	cross footbridge
50.3	bikepath 'bike route'
52.0	cross road
	(15yd) bikepath
52.2	bikepath beside SW 53rd
53.7	Campus Way multi-use path
54.3	*Irish Covered Bridge*
54.9	Campus Way (path ends)
55.8	14th St
	(100yd) Monroe Way
56.4	3rd St
56.7	NW Tyler Ave
56.8	NW 2nd St
56.8	(50yd) Chamber of Commerce, Corvallis

Willamette Valley Ramble (continued)

See pp160–4

Day 2

Cue

start		Chamber of Commerce, Corvallis
0mi		go S on NW 2nd St
	↰	(200yd) NW Van Buren Ave/East Hwy 34
1.4	↱	Peoria Rd 'to Harrisburg'
23.9	↑	Hwy 99 E, Harrisburg
24.5	↰	La Salle
24.8	↱	6th/Coburg Rd
24.7	↘	Coburg Rd
36.4	↗	Willamette St/Coburg Rd, Coburg
40.7	↱	Crescent Ave
42.3	🚦 ↑	cross N Delta Hwy, bikepath
43.3	↰	cross Willamette River
43.4	↘	bikepath
43.6	↰	Copping St
43.9	↑	bikepath
44.9	↑	Stephens Dr
	↰	(100yd) bikepath
47.0	↗	bikepath
	↑	(100yd) High St/Cheshire Ave (no sign)
	●●↱	*Skinner Butte 1.8mi* ↺
47.2	↱	E 3rd Ave
47.3	↰	Pearl St
47.7	↱	E 8th Ave
47.8		Lane County Courthouse, Eugene

Lava & Lakes Circuit

See pp164–9

Day 1

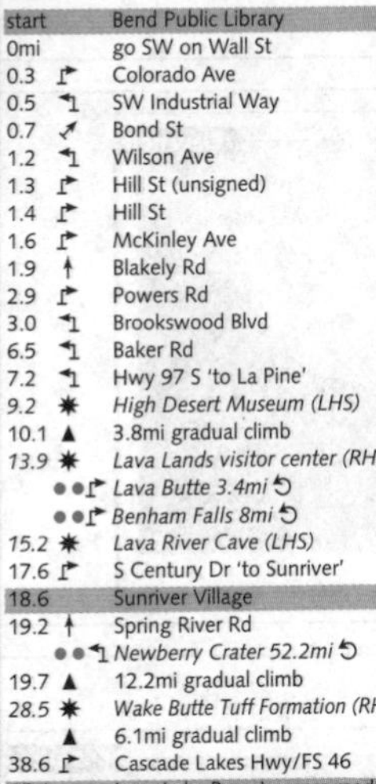

Cue

start		Bend Public Library
0mi		go SW on Wall St
0.3	↱	Colorado Ave
0.5	↰	SW Industrial Way
0.7	↗	Bond St
1.2	↰	Wilson Ave
1.3	↱	Hill St (unsigned)
1.4	↱	Hill St
1.6	↱	McKinley Ave
1.9	↑	Blakely Rd
2.9	↱	Powers Rd
3.0	↰	Brookswood Blvd
6.5	↰	Baker Rd
7.2	↰	Hwy 97 S 'to La Pine'
9.2	✱	*High Desert Museum (LHS)*
10.1	▲	3.8mi gradual climb
13.9	✱	*Lava Lands visitor center (RHS)*
	●●↱	*Lava Butte 3.4mi* ↺
	●●↱	*Benham Falls 8mi* ↺
15.2	✱	*Lava River Cave (LHS)*
17.6	↱	S Century Dr 'to Sunriver'
18.6		Sunriver Village
19.2	↑	Spring River Rd
	●●↰	*Newberry Crater 52.2mi* ↺
19.7	▲	12.2mi gradual climb
28.5	✱	*Wake Butte Tuff Formation (RHS)*
	▲	6.1mi gradual climb
38.6	↱	Cascade Lakes Hwy/FS 46
45.4		Lava Lake Resort access road

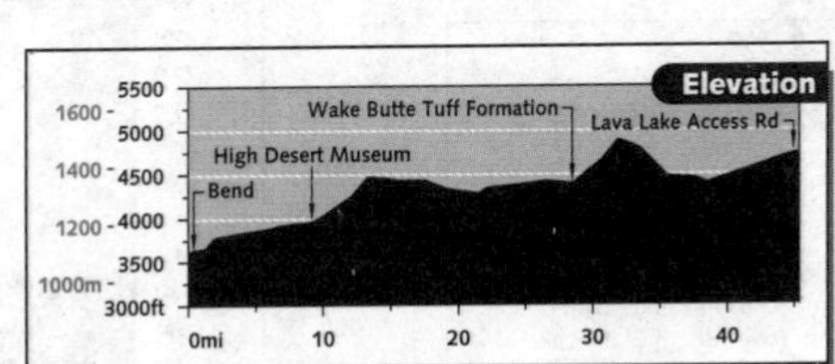

Day 2

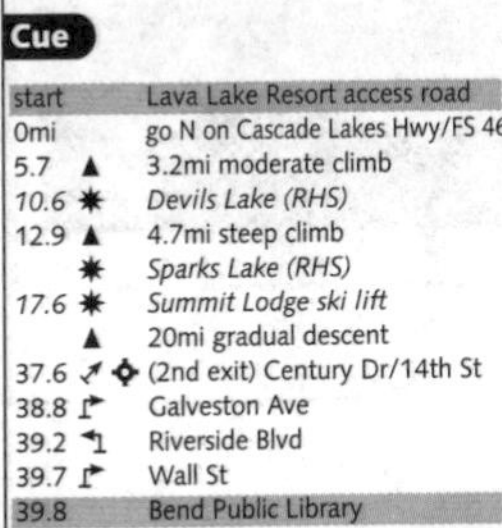

Cue

start		Lava Lake Resort access road
0mi		go N on Cascade Lakes Hwy/FS 46
5.7	▲	3.2mi moderate climb
10.6	✱	*Devils Lake (RHS)*
12.9	▲	4.7mi steep climb
	✱	*Sparks Lake (RHS)*
17.6	✱	*Summit Lodge ski lift*
	▲	20mi gradual descent
37.6	↗ ✪	(2nd exit) Century Dr/14th St
38.8	↱	Galveston Ave
39.2	↰	Riverside Blvd
39.7	↱	Wall St
39.8		Bend Public Library

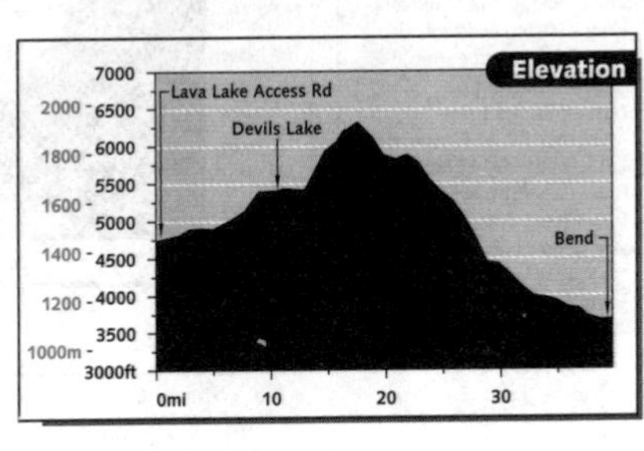

CUES & ELEVATION PROFILES OREGON

Southern Oregon Extravaganza

See pp169–75

Day 1

Cue

start	Klamath Falls chamber of commerce
0mi	go NW on 6th St
0.2	Main St
0.9	Hwy 97 ramp
	(16yd) Conger Ave
1.2	Conger Ave
1.4	California Ave
2.1	Delta St
	(100yd) Siskiyou St
2.4	Oregon Ave
2.9	Nevada Ave
3.1	Lakeshore Dr
7.7	Hwy 140
14.1	3.3mi moderate climb
17.4	2.1mi steep descent
27.2	Rocky Point Rd
30.0	'to Rocky Point Resort'
30.2	Rocky Point Resort

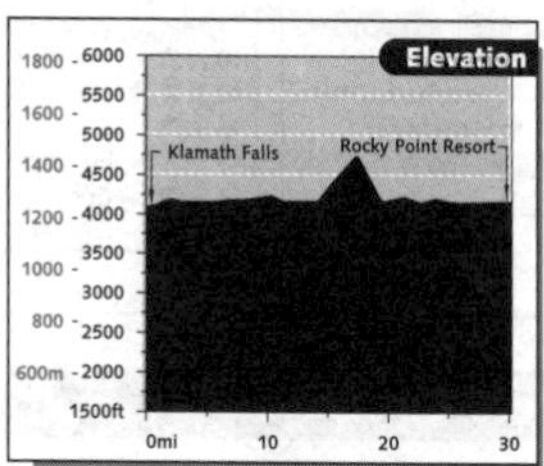

Day 2

Cue

start	Rocky Point Resort
0mi	go N on Rocky Point Rd
0.2	'to Westside Rd'
0.4	Westside Rd
19.8	Weed Rd 'to Crater Lake & Ft Klamath'
21.7	Hwy 62, Fort Klamath
29.0	9.6mi moderate-hard climb
38.6	Hwy 138 'to Crater Lake'
	(100yd) ranger kiosk
40.3	5.4mi steep climb
42.7	*Steel Visitor Center (LHS)*
45.5	*Rim Drive 32.6mi*
45.9	Crater Lake Lodge, Rim Village

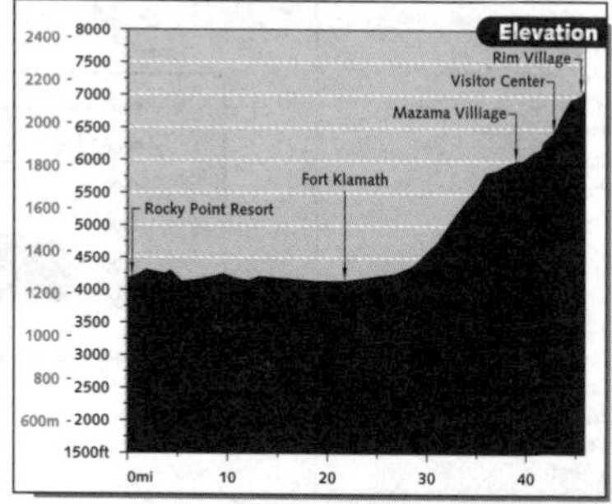

Day 3

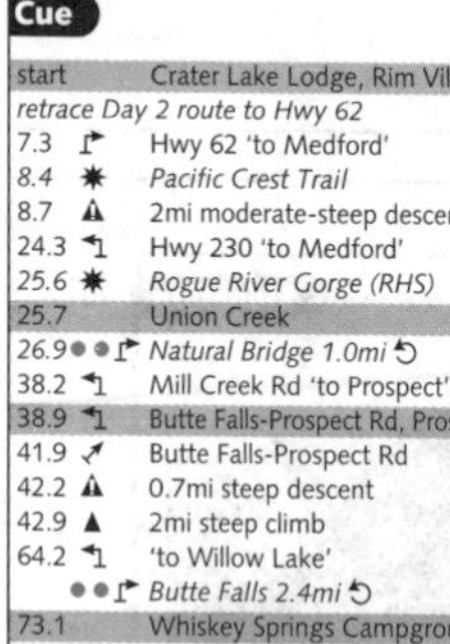

Cue

start	Crater Lake Lodge, Rim Village
retrace Day 2 route to Hwy 62	
7.3	Hwy 62 'to Medford'
8.4	*Pacific Crest Trail*
8.7	2mi moderate-steep descent
24.3	Hwy 230 'to Medford'
25.6	*Rogue River Gorge (RHS)*
25.7	Union Creek
26.9	*Natural Bridge 1.0mi*
38.2	Mill Creek Rd 'to Prospect'
38.9	Butte Falls-Prospect Rd, Prospect
41.9	Butte Falls-Prospect Rd
42.2	0.7mi steep descent
42.9	2mi steep climb
64.2	'to Willow Lake'
	Butte Falls 2.4mi
73.1	Whiskey Springs Campground

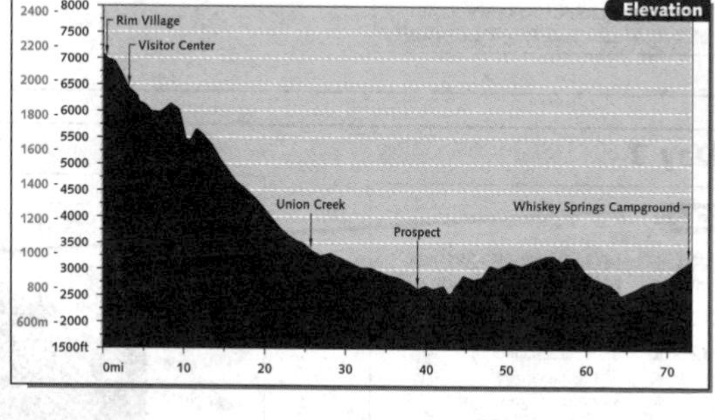

Southern Oregon Extravaganza (continued)

See pp169–75

Day 4

Cue

start		Whiskey Springs Campground
0mi		go S on Butte Falls-Prospect Rd
1.5	▲	7.2mi steep climb
9.6	↱	Hwy 140 'to Medford'
9.8	↰	USFS Rd 37/Big Elk Rd
11.0	✱	*Brown Mountain Lava Field*
18.7	↱	Dead Indian Memorial Hwy
22.3	▲	5.4mi moderate climb
27.7	⚠	12mi twisting steep descent
36.1	⚠	cattle grid
40.7	↱	Hwy 66 'to Ashland'
41.0	↗	East Main St 'bike route'
41.6	✱	*Ashland Vineyards (RHS)*
43.9	↱	Lithia Way
44.4	↘	'to city center'
	↰	(10yd) N Main St
44.5		Ashland visitor center

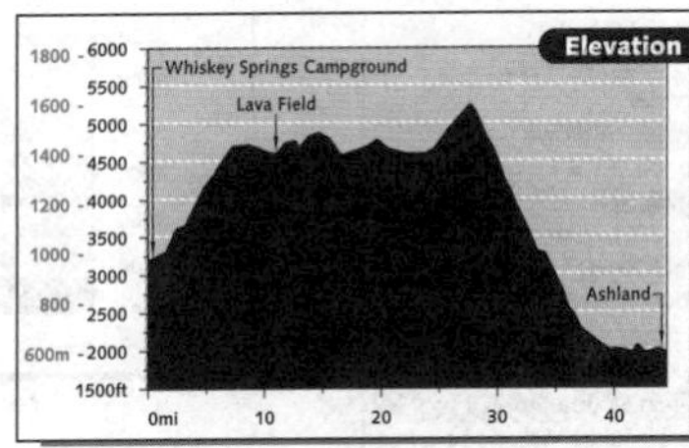

Wild West Roundup

See pp175–80

Day 1

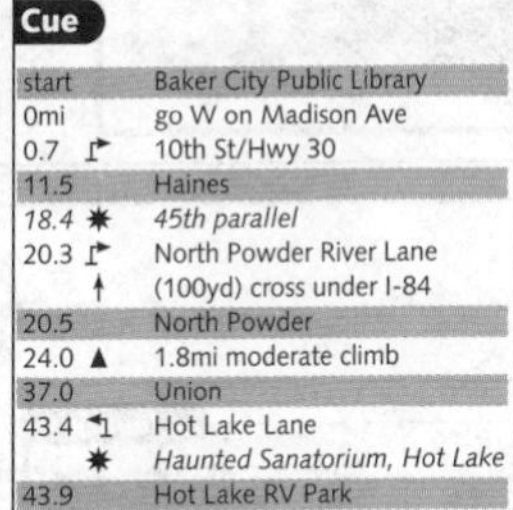

Cue

start		Baker City Public Library
0mi		go W on Madison Ave
0.7	↱	10th St/Hwy 30
11.5		Haines
18.4	✱	*45th parallel*
20.3	↱	North Powder River Lane
	↑	(100yd) cross under I-84
20.5		North Powder
24.0	▲	1.8mi moderate climb
37.0		Union
43.4	↰	Hot Lake Lane
	✱	*Haunted Sanatorium, Hot Lake*
43.9		Hot Lake RV Park

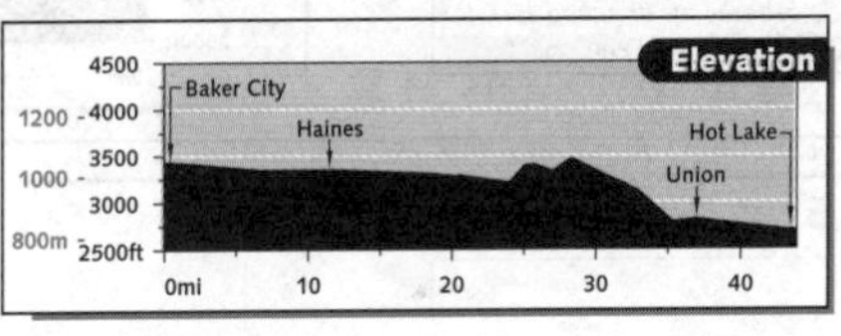

Day 2

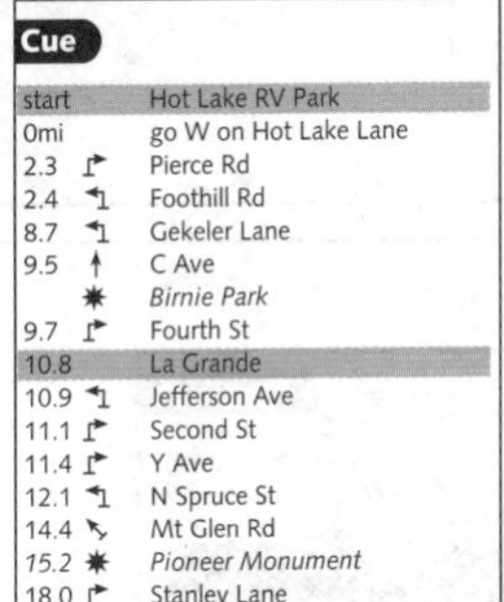

Cue

start		Hot Lake RV Park
0mi		go W on Hot Lake Lane
2.3	↱	Pierce Rd
2.4	↰	Foothill Rd
8.7	↰	Gekeler Lane
9.5	↑	C Ave
	✱	*Birnie Park*
9.7	↱	Fourth St
10.8		La Grande
10.9	↰	Jefferson Ave
11.1	↱	Second St
11.4	↱	Y Ave
12.1	↰	N Spruce St
14.4	↘	Mt Glen Rd
15.2	✱	*Pioneer Monument*
18.0	↱	Stanley Lane

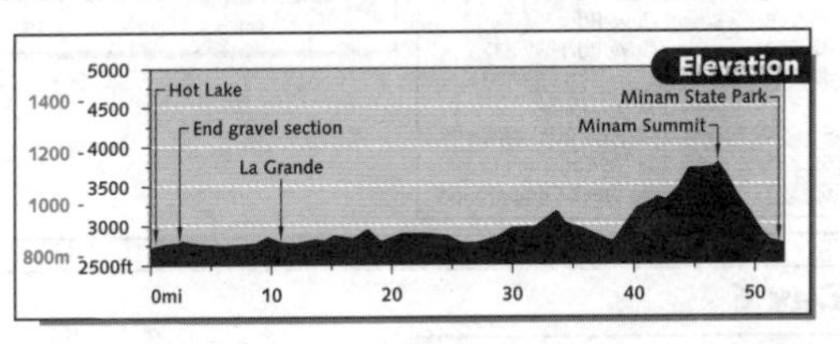

19.1	↰	Hunter Rd
24.7	↗	McKenzie Lane
27.0	↰	Summerville Rd, Summerville
29.9	↗	Summerville Rd
31.8	▲	1.9mi moderate hill
34.4	↱	Rte 204 'to Elgin'
35.8	✱	*Boise Cascade Mill*

38.0	↰	Hwy 82, Elgin
	↱	(50yd) Hwy 82
38.3	▲	8.6mi moderate climb
46.9		Minam Summit
	⚠	5mi twisting steep descent
51.9	↰	unsigned park access road
52.4		Minam State Park

Wild West Roundup (continued)

See pp175–80

Day 3

Cue

start	Minam State Park
0mi	go S on access road
0.5	Hwy 82
14.1	Hwy 82, Wallowa
14.6	Hwy 82
22.6	Lostine
22.8	Hwy 82 'to Enterprise & Joseph'
32.9	Enterprise
33.3	N River St/Hwy 82
33.8	Hurricane Creek Rd
39.2	Airport Rd
41.5	N Main St, Joseph
42.1	Lakeside Rd 'to Wallowa Lake Park'
43.0 ✱	*Chief Joseph Cemetery (RHS)*
47.7	Wallowa Lake State Park

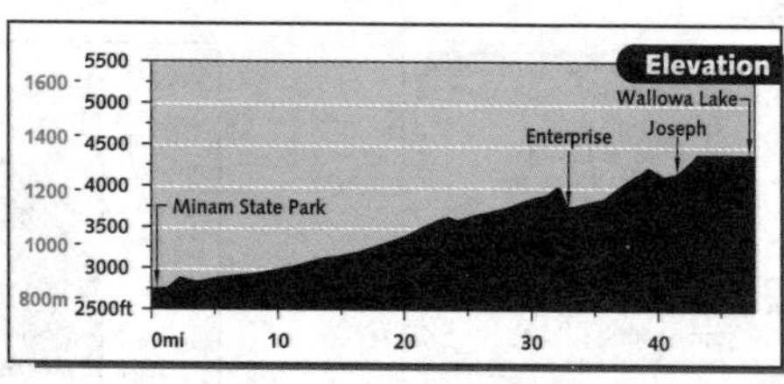

Day 4

Cue

start	Wallowa Lake State Park
0mi	go N on Lakeside Rd
retrace Day 3 route to 6.2mi	
6.2	Hwy 82
11.9	*retrace Day 3 route to 45.7mi*
45.7	Minam State Park

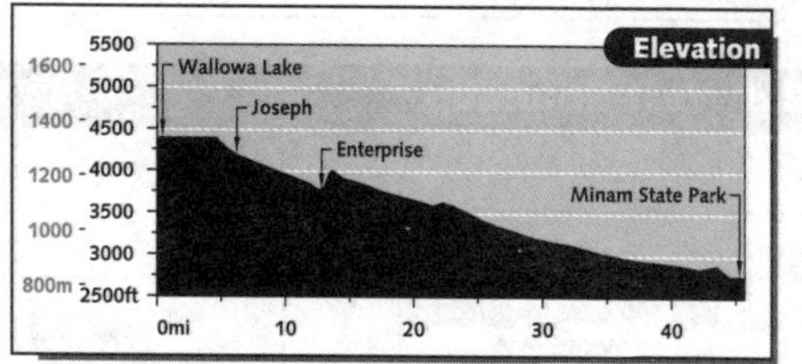

Day 5

Cue

start	Minam State Park
0mi	go S on park access road
0.5	Hwy 82
retrace Day 2 route to Elgin	
14.4	Hwy 82, Elgin
22.5	Imbler
27.7	Market Lane
38.1	Lower Cove Rd
42.5	Lower Cove Rd/Hwy 237
42.7	Cove
51.3	Hwy 237 'to Union'
51.6	Hwy 237/Hwy 203, Union
52.2	Hwy 203 'to Catherine Creek'
60.7	Catherine Creek Campground

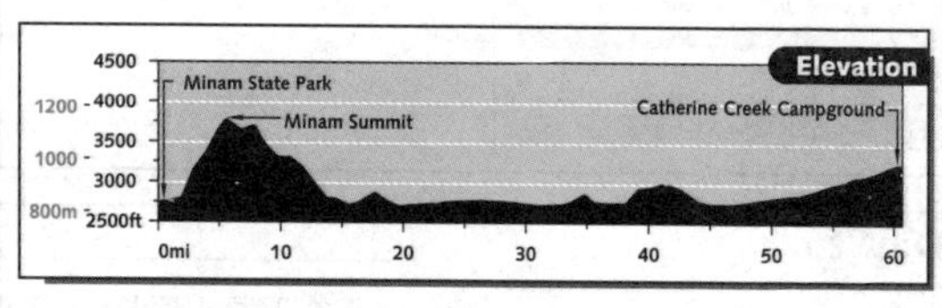

Day 6

Cue

start	Catherine Creek Campground
0mi	go S on Hwy 203
1.9 ▲	4.4 moderate climb
12.8	Hwy 203
13.5	Hwy 203 'to Baker City'
21.6 ▲	1.6mi moderate climb
32.1	Old Trail Rd
37.1	N Cedar St
38.2	Campbell St
38.5	Resort St
38.6	Baker City Public Library

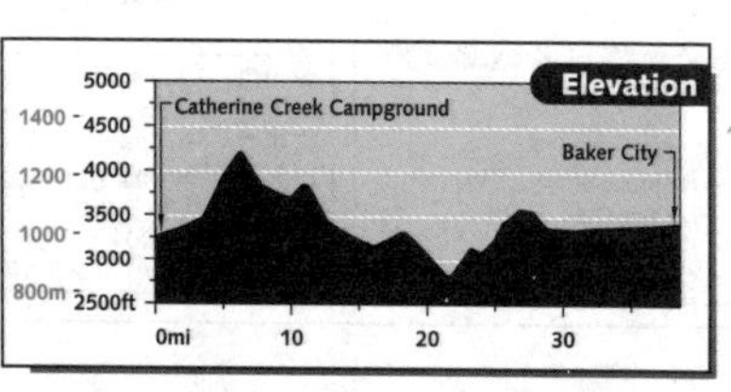

San Francisco Orientation

See pp188–92

Cue

start	Ferry Building, World Trade Center
0mi	go W on The Embarcadero
1.3	*Pier 39, Fisherman's Wharf*
1.7	Taylor St
	(17yd) Jefferson St
2.1	*Aquatic Park*
2.4	uphill on McDowell Ave
2.6	downhill through Marina Green
2.8	Laguna St
2.8	(2yd) Marina
4.9	Mason St
	(2yd) Crissy Field Ave
5.1	Lincoln Blvd
5.3	steep shoulder
7.0	25th Ave
	(10yd) Scenic
7.1	26th Ave
7.1	Scenic
7.3	uphill
7.4	El Camino Del Mar
8.1	*Palace of Legion of Honor*
8.1	Legion of Honor Dr
8.6	Clement St
9.4	El Camino Del Mar
9.5	Point Lobos Ave
9.8	*Cliff House; Great Hwy begins*
13.7	Skyline Blvd
14.2	John Muir Dr
15.5	Lake Merced Blvd
17.5	Sunset Blvd
19.9	follow path under overpass
20.0	*Golden Gate Park*
	Martin Luther King Jr Blvd
21.3	Transverse Dr (unsigned)
21.7	John F Kennedy Dr
23.1	Stanyan St
23.2	Haight St
24.0	Divisadero St
24.2	Castro St
24.8	18th St
25.3	*Mission Dolores Park*
25.7	Mission St
26.2	14th St
26.4	Folsom St
27.7	4th St
28.3	King St
28.5	*Pac Bell Park*
29.8	Ferry Building, World Trade Center

Around Mt Tam

See pp192–3

Cue

start	GG Ferry Terminal, Larkspur
0mi	go W on Sir Francis Drake Blvd
0.2	bikepath, 'Downtown Larkspur'
0.9	South Eliseo Dr
1.6	Bon Air
1.8	Magnolia Ave
2.6	Kent Ave
3.5	Lagunitas Rd
3.6	Shady Lane
4.2	Bolinas Ave
4.8	San Anselmo
5.1	San Anselmo
6.5	Bolinas Rd, Fairfax
10.2	*Pine Mtn Loop trailhead*
14.4	Alpine Lake Dam
	3.1mi hard climb
16.9	Ridgecrest Blvd
20.6	Pan Toll Rd/Panoramic Hwy
	East Peak parking lot 2.4mi
22.0	Pan Toll Rd 'to Mill Valley'
26.6	Sequoia Valley Rd
28.1	Molino Ave
	4mi steep descent
28.5	Montford Ave
28.6	Linden Lane
28.7	Miller Ave, Mill Valley
29.2	Camino Alto
32.2	Redwood Ave
	(10yd) Montecito Dr, bikepath
33.2	Bon Air
33.4	South Eliseo Dr
34.0	bikepath
35.1	GG Ferry Terminal, Larkspur

Wine Country Tour

See pp194–202

Day 1

Cue

start	Walnut Park, Petaluma
0mi	go N on Fourth St
0.3	Western Ave
2.1	Chileno Valley Rd
6.0	Chileno Valley Rd
15.6	Tomales-Petaluma Rd 'to Petaluma'
17.6	Valley Ford Rd, 'to Bodega Bay'
27.5	Valley Ford
28.1	Valley Ford-Freestone Rd
30.6	Bodega Hwy
32.1	Bohemian Hwy, Freestone
35.7	Occidental
40.6	Main St
41.8	Monte Rio
41.9	Bohemian Hwy
42.0	Hwy 116
45.9	Guerneville main intersection

Day 2

Cue

start	Guerneville main intersection
0mi	go E on Hwy 116/River Rd
1.6	Rio Nido
2.8	*Korbel Champagne Cellars*
5.2	Westside Rd, 'to Healdsburg'
9.8	*Davis Bynum Winery*
11.6	*Rochioli Vineyards & Winery*
11.8	*Hop Kiln Winery*
14.8	*Rabbit Ridge*
16.4	Mill Creek Rd enters on LHS
16.9	W Dry Creek Rd
22.3	*Quivira Vineyards*
25.8	Yoakim Bridge Rd
26.4	Dry Creek Rd
33.8	US 101
34.1	Healdsburg Ave
34.6	Healdsburg Plaza

Day 3

Cue

start	Healdsburg Plaza
0mi	go N on Healdsburg Ave
1.3	Alexander Valley Rd
6.6	*Alexander Valley Vineyards*
7.0	*Field Stone Winery*
7.2	Chalk Hill Rd
8.5	*Macama Historical Bridge*
11.6	8mi twisting steep descent
13.0	*Chalk Hill Winery*
15.3	Faught Rd
18.1	Old Redwood Hwy, Larkfield
19.2	Mark West Springs Rd
19.8	1.8mi moderate climb
25.9	Franz Valley Rd
26.0	1.1mi steep climb
29.1	Franz Valley School Rd
31.1	0.5mi hard climb
35.5	Petrified Forest Rd
36.1	Hwy 128/Foothill Blvd
37.0	Lincoln Ave/Hwy 29
37.0	Calistoga main intersection

Wine Country Tour (continued)

See pp194–202

Day 4

Cue

start	Calistoga main intersection
0mi	go E on Lincoln Ave/Hwy 29
0.7	Hwy 29
2.1	Old Toll Rd
3.2	2mi hard climb
4.3	Hwy 29 (no sign)
6.8	*Robert Louis Stevenson Park*
	3.2mi twisting descent
15.5	Middletown
16.0	Hwy 175 (no sign)
16.1	Barnes St
17.6	Harbin Springs Rd
19.9	Harbin Hot Springs

Day 5

Cue

start	Harbin Hot Springs
0mi	go S on Harbin Springs Rd
3.8	Hwy 175/Main St
3.9	Hwy 29, Middletown
4.5	Butts Canyon Rd to 'Guenoc Valley'
10.3	*Guenoc Winery*
15.8	1mi gradual climb
21.1	*Litto's Hubcap Ranch*
21.3	*Pope Valley Winery*
21.6	Ink Grade
	4.1mi steep climb
25.9	White Cottage Rd
27.0	cross College Ave
29.6	cross Deer Park Rd
29.7	4.3mi twisting steep descent
32.8	Howell Mtn Rd
34.0	Silverado Trail/Pope St bridge (jog)
34.8	Edwards St
35.0	Hunt Ave
35.1	cnr Hunt Ave & Hwy 29, St Helena

Day 6

Cue

start	cnr Hunt Ave & Hwy 29, St Helena
0mi	go N on Hwy 29/Main St
1.0	*Beringer Vineyards*
3.1	*Bale Grist Mill State Historic Park*
4.8	*Bothe-Napa Valley State Park*
7.1	Dunaweal Lane
7.7	*Clos Pegase*
7.8	*Sterling Vineyards*
8.0	Silverado Trail (no sign)
19.7	Hwy 128, to 'Rutherford'
21.0	Conn Creek Rd
21.1	*Caymus*
22.1	Skellenger Lane
23.0	Silverado Trail
27.3	*Silverado Vineyards*
28.3	*Stag's Leap*
34.4	Trancas/Hwy 121
34.6	Silverado Trail/ Hwy 121
36.6	3rd St
37.0	Soscol Ave
37.2	Pearl St
37.4	Napa transit center

Baths, Barns & Booze

See pp202–6

Day 1

Cue

start	Ukiah bus stop/airport
0mi	go N on S State St
0.6	Talmage Rd
0.9	cross Hwy 101
2.3	Talmage
2.7	East Side Rd
15.7	Hwy 175
16.1	*Fetzer Vineyards*
	Hwy 175
17.0	Hopland
	Hwy 101
17.2	Mountain House Rd
18.1	8.3mi moderate climb
26.4	Hwy 128
33.6	Yorkville
34.5	*Yorkville Vineyards & Cellars*
38.7	*Martz Vineyards*
41.5	0.9 moderate climb
46.0	Otto's Ice Cream, Boonville

Day 2

Cue

start	Otto's Ice Cream, Boonville
0mi	go NW on Hwy 128
5.4	Indian Creek Campground
6.0	Philo
8.3	*Gowan's Oak Tree*
10.6	*Husch Vineyards (LHS)*
	Roederer Estates (RHS)
13.1	Navarro
16.3	*Navarro River Redwoods*
17.5	Flynn Creek Rd
21.1	1.7mi easy climb
23.7	1.6mi twisting descent
26.1	Comptche
	Comptche-Ukiah Rd
27.7	2.2mi hard climb
34.6	1.5mi twisitng descent
42.2	*Montgomery Woods*
42.9	Orr Hot Springs

Day 3

Cue

start	Orr Hot Springs
0mi	go SW on Orr Springs Rd
0.0	4.3mi hard climb
7.1	3.5mi twisting steep descent
12.1	N State St
15.4	Ukiah bus stop/airport

The Lost Coast

See pp206–11

Day 1

Cue

start		Ferndale library
0mi		go S on Main St
0.2	↰	Ocean Ave
8.3	▲	500yd moderate climb
10.6	▲	500yd moderate climb
13.0		Rio Dell
14.3		Scotia
15.5	↰	unsigned road
	↱	(20yd) Hwy 101
19.7	↗	'to Ave of the Giants'
19.8	↰	'to Ave of the Giants'
25.5	▲	800yd moderate climb
26.3		Redcrest
30.6	↰	Ave of the Giants
33.1		Weott
34.8		H Redwoods Park Headquarters

Day 2

Cue

start		H Redwoods Park Headquarters
retrace Day 1 route for 4.3mi		
4.3	↰	Bull Creek Rd, 'Honeydew'
8.7	✷	*Rockefeller Forest*
9.3		Albee Creek campground
19.2	▲	1.7mi hard climb
20.9		Panther Gap
	⚠	4.5mi twisting steep descent
25.7	↱	Mattole Rd, Honeydew
35.5		AW Way County Park

Day 3

Cue

start		AW Way County Park
0mi		go N on Mattole Rd
5.5	↗	Lighthouse Rd to 'Petrolia'
6.4	↰	Mattole Rd, Petrolia
	●● ↑	*to hiking trails 6mi* ↺
6.5	↱	Front St, 'to Ferndale'
17.6	▲	2.3mi hard climb
19.9	⚠	1.4mi twisting steep descent
21.6		Capetown
21.8	▲	2.4mi hard climb
29.0	⚠	6.7mi twisting descent
35.7	↱	Ocean Ave (no sign)
35.8	↰	Main St
36.0		Ferndale library

Yosemite's Western Gateway

See pp211–15

Cue

start		Yosemite Bug Hostel, Midpines
0mi		go N on Hwy 140
	⚠	2.6mi steep winding descent
2.6	✷	*Briceburg Info Center*
17.0	↰	Foresta Rd
19.4	↱	El Portal Rd, El Portal
19.5	↰	Hwy 140
21.0	▲	2mi steep climb
	⚠	narrow road for 8mi
23.0		Yosemite NP entrance
	▲	6mi moderate climb
28.5	↗	cross river, join Southside Dr
33.2	↘	to join bikepath
33.6	↰	bikepath towards bridge
33.9	↰	bikepath paralleling Northside Dr
34.1	↰	across Northside Dr
34.3		Yosemite Lodge

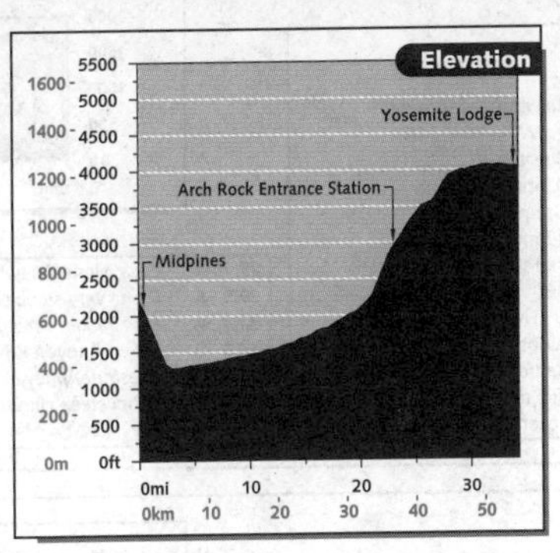

Wine, Surf & Citrus Sampler

See pp221–7

Day 1

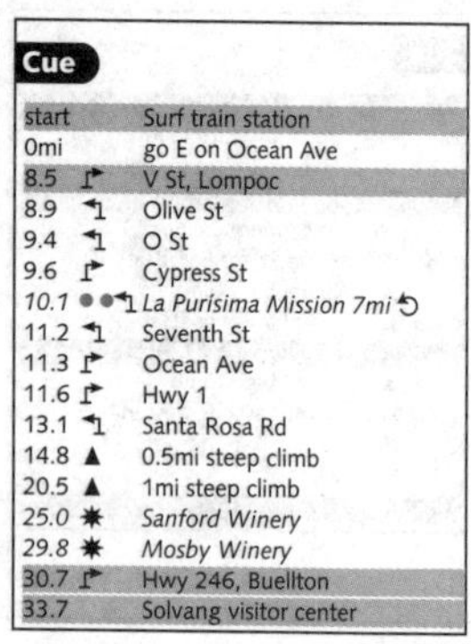

Cue

start	Surf train station
0mi	go E on Ocean Ave
8.5	V St, Lompoc
8.9	Olive St
9.4	O St
9.6	Cypress St
10.1	*La Purísima Mission 7mi*
11.2	Seventh St
11.3	Ocean Ave
11.6	Hwy 1
13.1	Santa Rosa Rd
14.8	0.5mi steep climb
20.5	1mi steep climb
25.0	*Sanford Winery*
29.8	*Mosby Winery*
30.7	Hwy 246, Buellton
33.7	Solvang visitor center

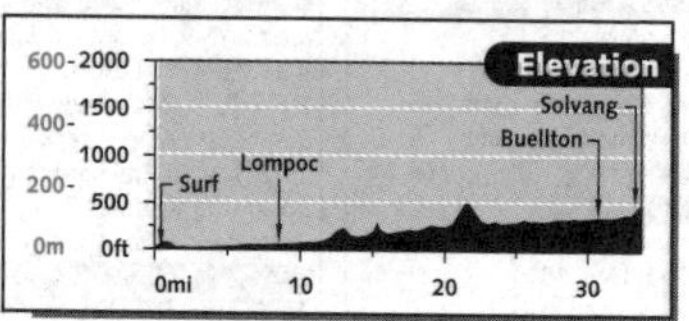

Day 2

Cue

start	Solvang visitor center
0mi	go W on Hwy 246
3.0	Buellton
7.0	0.5mi steep climb
9.2	Drum Canyon Rd
13.8	1.5mi steep climb
15.3	1mi steep, rough descent
18.5	Bell St, Los Alamos
19.0	US Hwy 101
21.3	Alisos Canyon Rd
23.0	*Bedford Thompson Winery*
24.1	3mi moderate climb
27.8	Foxen Canyon Rd
29.1	*Zaca Mesa Vineyard*
29.5	0.6mi very steep climb
32.3	*Fess Parker Vineyard*
33.8	Foxen Canyon Rd
	Firestone Vineyard 1mi
34.3	0.7mi steep climb
38.2	Hwy 154

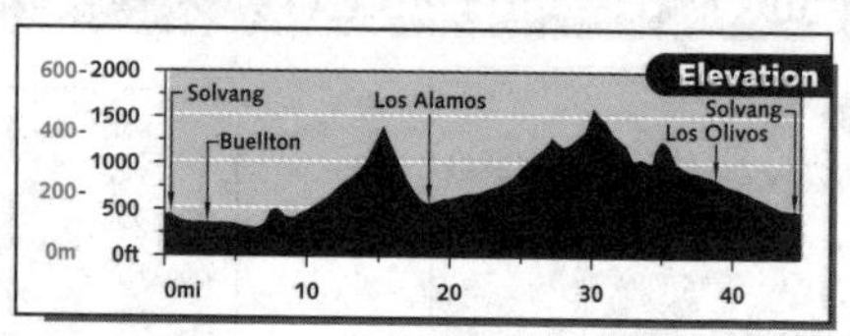

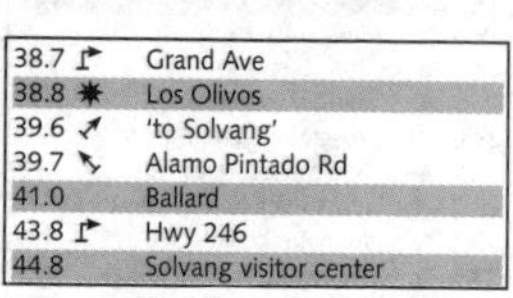

38.7	Grand Ave
38.8	Los Olivos
39.6	'to Solvang'
39.7	Alamo Pintado Rd
41.0	Ballard
43.8	Hwy 246
44.8	Solvang visitor center

Day 3

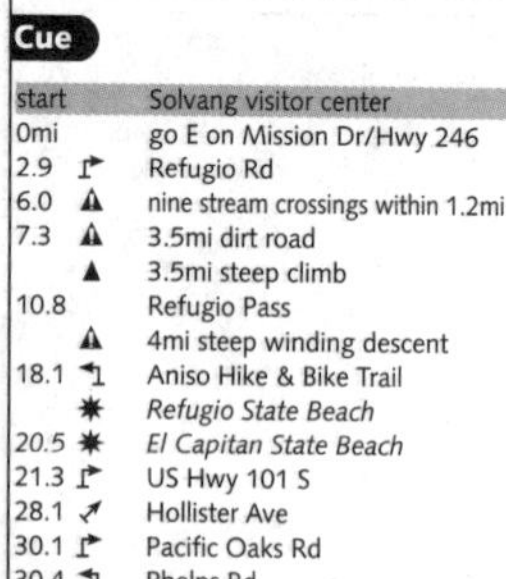

Cue

start	Solvang visitor center
0mi	go E on Mission Dr/Hwy 246
2.9	Refugio Rd
6.0	nine stream crossings within 1.2mi
7.3	3.5mi dirt road
	3.5mi steep climb
10.8	Refugio Pass
	4mi steep winding descent
18.1	Aniso Hike & Bike Trail
	Refugio State Beach
20.5	*El Capitan State Beach*
21.3	US Hwy 101 S
28.1	Hollister Ave
30.1	Pacific Oaks Rd
30.4	Phelps Rd
30.9	Storke Rd
31.3	Coast Route bikepath
33.8	*Goleta Beach County Park*
37.7	Nueces Dr/Coast Route bikepath
38.5	Modoc Rd/Coast Route bikepath
39.3	Modoc Rd/Crosstown Route
41.4	Mission St

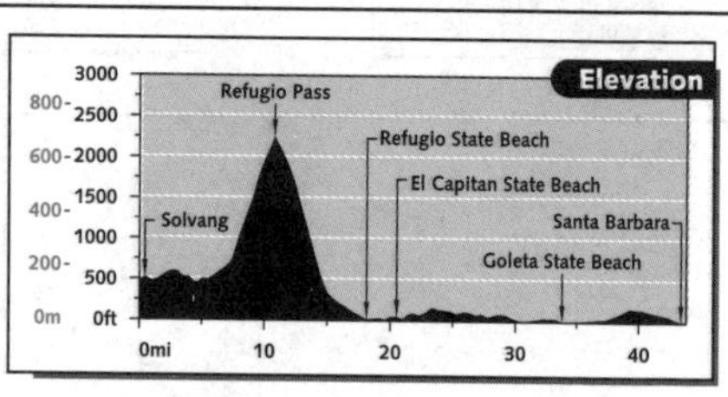

41.5	San Pascual St
41.9	Arrellaga St
	(50yd) Dutton Ave
42.1	Micheltorena St
42.3	Castillo St
43.5	Montecito St
43.8	Santa Barbara train station

Wine, Surf & Citrus Sampler (continued)

See pp221–7

Day 4

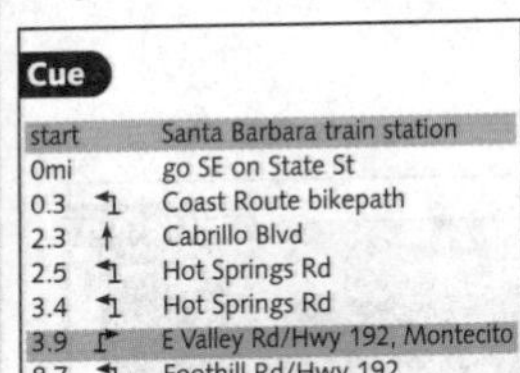

Cue

start	Santa Barbara train station
0mi	go SE on State St
0.3	Coast Route bikepath
2.3	Cabrillo Blvd
2.5	Hot Springs Rd
3.4	Hot Springs Rd
3.9	E Valley Rd/Hwy 192, Montecito
8.7	Foothill Rd/Hwy 192
10.2	Foothill Rd/Hwy 192
13.1	Foothill Rd/Hwy 192
15.0	Gobernador Canyon Rd
16.0 ▲	0.5mi steep climb
17.8	Hwy 150
18.0 ▲	2.5mi steep climb
22.2 ▲	1mi steep climb
29.5	Lake Casitas Recreation Area
32.5	Ojai Valley Bikepath
34.5	cross Hwy 150 (stay on bikepath)
35.5	bikepath 'to downtown'
35.7	E Ojai Ave
35.8	Ojai visitor center

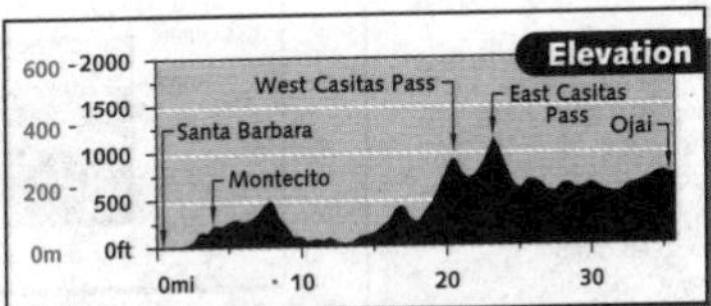

SLO Roller Coaster

See pp227–9

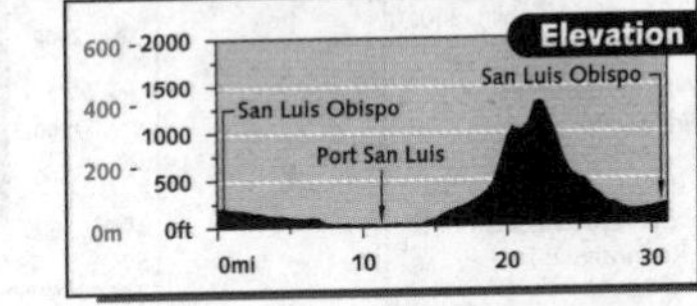

Cue

start	San Luis Obispo visitor center
0mi	go SE on Chorro St
0.1	Higuera St
0.7	S Higuera St
4.5	Ontario Rd
7.3	Bob Jones Bike Trail
8.3	bikepath crosses San Luis Bay Dr
9.6	Avila Beach Dr
11.3	Port San Luis
retrace outward route to San Luis Bay Dr	
14.3	San Luis Bay Dr
14.8	See Canyon Rd
18.8 ▲	1.5mi steep climb
20.4 ⚠	1.1mi dirt road
21.5 ▲	0.4mi steep climb
21.9 ⚠	1.1mi dirt road
22.5 ⚠	2mi steep descent
24.0 ⚠	1mi dirt road

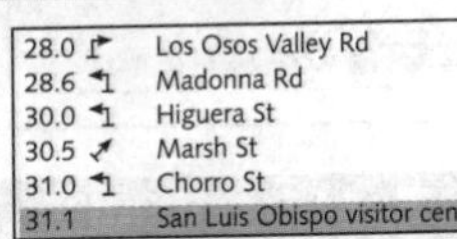

28.0	Los Osos Valley Rd
28.6	Madonna Rd
30.0	Higuera St
30.5	Marsh St
31.0	Chorro St
31.1	San Luis Obispo visitor center

Pozo Saloon Stagger

See pp229–30

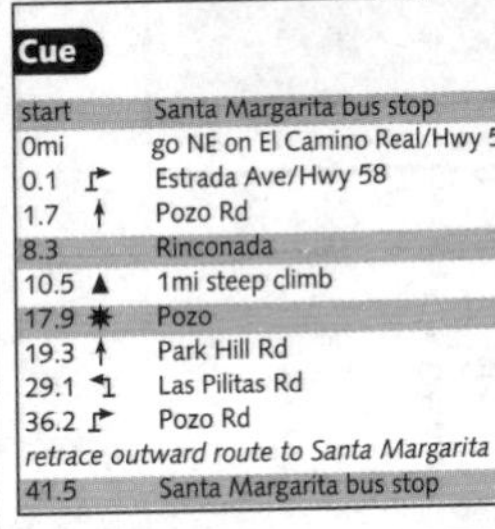

Cue

start	Santa Margarita bus stop
0mi	go NE on El Camino Real/Hwy 58
0.1	Estrada Ave/Hwy 58
1.7	Pozo Rd
8.3	Rinconada
10.5 ▲	1mi steep climb
17.9 ✱	Pozo
19.3	Park Hill Rd
29.1	Las Pilitas Rd
36.2	Pozo Rd
retrace outward route to Santa Margarita	
41.5	Santa Margarita bus stop

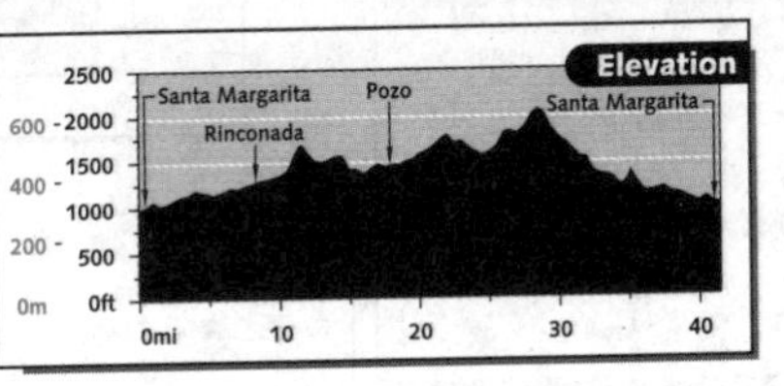

Epicenter Century

See pp230–3

Day 1

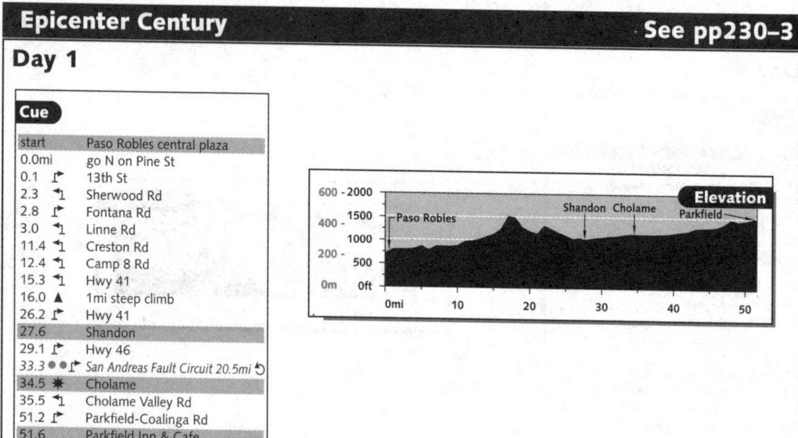

Cue

start		Paso Robles central plaza
0.0mi		go N on Pine St
0.1	↱	13th St
2.3	↰	Sherwood Rd
2.8	↱	Fontana Rd
3.0	↰	Linne Rd
11.4	↰	Creston Rd
12.4	↰	Camp 8 Rd
15.3	↰	Hwy 41
16.0	▲	1mi steep climb
26.2	↱	Hwy 41
27.6		Shandon
29.1	↱	Hwy 46
33.3	●●↱	*San Andreas Fault Circuit 20.5mi* ⟲
34.5	✱	Cholame
35.5	↰	Cholame Valley Rd
51.2	↱	Parkfield-Coalinga Rd
51.6		Parkfield Inn & Cafe

Day 2

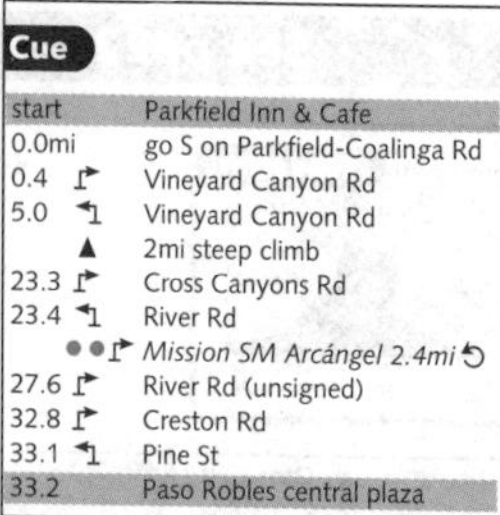

Cue

start		Parkfield Inn & Cafe
0.0mi		go S on Parkfield-Coalinga Rd
0.4	↱	Vineyard Canyon Rd
5.0	↰	Vineyard Canyon Rd
	▲	2mi steep climb
23.3	↱	Cross Canyons Rd
23.4	↰	River Rd
	●●↱	*Mission SM Arcángel 2.4mi* ⟲
27.6	↱	River Rd (unsigned)
32.8	↱	Creston Rd
33.1	↰	Pine St
33.2		Paso Robles central plaza

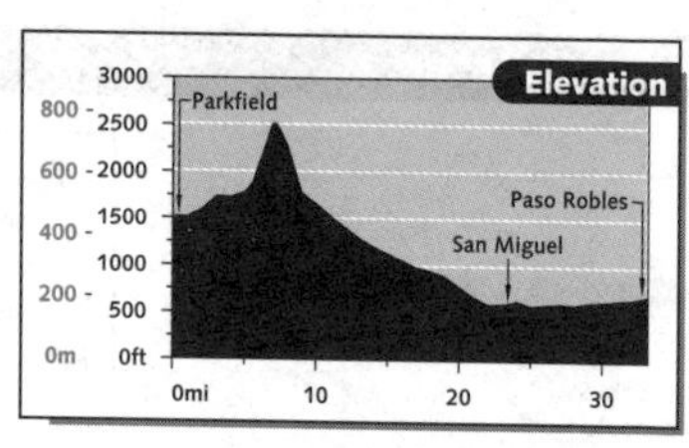

Big Sur Hinterland

See pp233–40

Day 1

Cue

start		Salinas train station
0mi		go SW on Station Place
0.1	↱	W Market St/Hwy 183
2.8	↰	McFadden Rd
5.0	↱	Cooper Rd
5.5	↘	Nashua Rd
12.3	↰	Hwy 1
13.1	↘	Moss Landing Rd, Moss Landing
13.9	↰	Hwy 1
14.2	↱	Dolan Rd
17.5	↰	Russo Rd
17.9	↰	Elkhorn Rd
18.5		Elkhorn
19.7	✱	*Elkhorn Slough Estuarine Reserve*
22.3	✱	*Kirby Park Public Access*
24.7	↰	Elkhorn Rd/County Highway G12
25.1	↱	Garin Rd
26.7	↱	Lewis Rd
26.9	↰	Vega Rd
29.2	↰	San Miguel Canyon Rd
29.8	↱	San Juan Rd/County Highway G11
32.0	↰	Aromas Rd
32.7	↱	Blohm Rd, Aromas
33.2	↱	Carpinteria Rd
33.5	↰	Carr Ave
	▲	1.3mi steep climb
35.1	↱	Anzar Rd
39.5	↱	San Juan Hwy
41.6	↱	Monterey St
41.7	↰	Second St
42.0		San Juan Bautista central plaza

Elevation: 600 - 2000; 400 - 1500; 1000; 200 - 500; 0m 0ft; Salinas; Moss Landing; Elkhorn; San Juan Bautista; Aromas; 0mi; 10; 20; 30; 40

Big Sur Hinterland (continued)

See pp233–40

Day 2

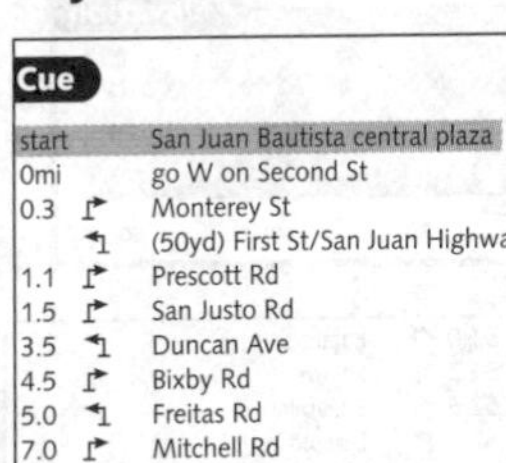

Cue

start		San Juan Bautista central plaza
0mi		go W on Second St
0.3	↱	Monterey St
	↰	(50yd) First St/San Juan Highway
1.1	↱	Prescott Rd
1.5	↱	San Justo Rd
3.5	↰	Duncan Ave
4.5	↱	Bixby Rd
5.0	↰	Freitas Rd
7.0	↱	Mitchell Rd
7.5	↑	Union Rd (cross Hwy 156)
11.4	↰	San Benito St

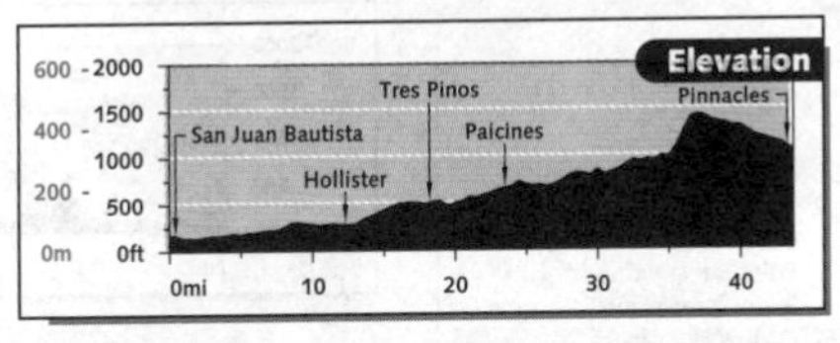

12.3	↱	Nash Rd, Hollister
12.9	↱	Airline Highway/Hwy 25
18.2		Tres Pinos
23.5		Paicines
24.4	↱	Cienega Rd

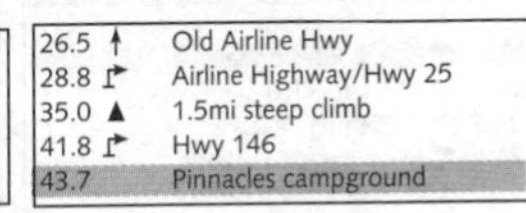

26.5	↑	Old Airline Hwy
28.8	↱	Airline Highway/Hwy 25
35.0	▲	1.5mi steep climb
41.8	↱	Hwy 146
43.7		Pinnacles campground

Day 3

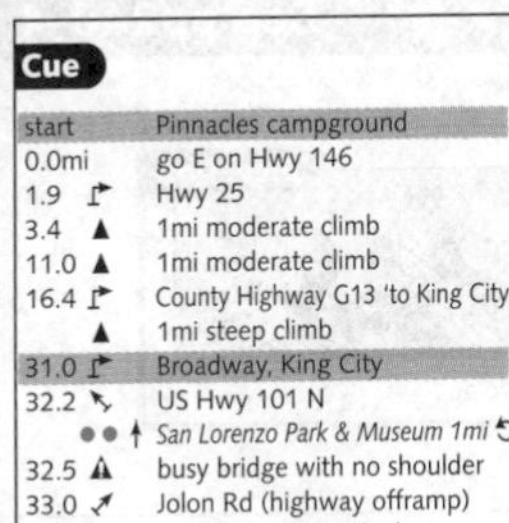

Cue

start		Pinnacles campground
0.0mi		go E on Hwy 146
1.9	↱	Hwy 25
3.4	▲	1mi moderate climb
11.0	▲	1mi moderate climb
16.4	↱	County Highway G13 'to King City'
	▲	1mi steep climb
31.0	↱	Broadway, King City
32.2	↘	US Hwy 101 N
	●● ↑	*San Lorenzo Park & Museum 1mi* ↺
32.5	⚠	busy bridge with no shoulder
33.0	↗	Jolon Rd (highway offramp)
42.5	▲	1.2mi very steep climb
51.3	✱	*Old Jolon Townsite (LHS)*
51.5	↱	Mission Rd
56.4	↱	'to the Hacienda'
56.7		Hacienda Guest Lodge, Jolon

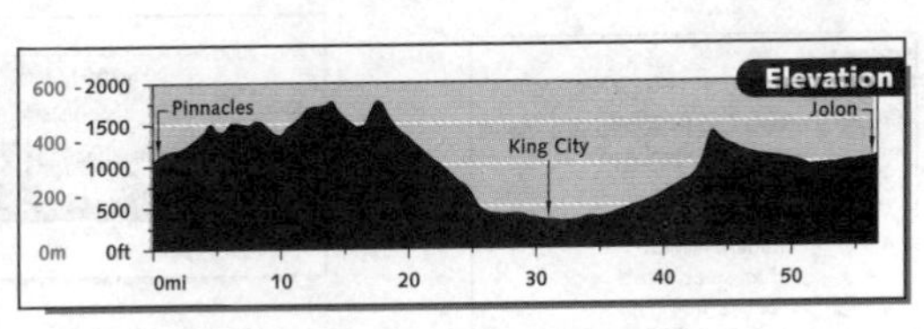

Day 4

Cue

start		Hacienda Guest Lodge, Jolon
retrace Day 3 route to Mission Rd		
0.2	↰	Mission Rd
0.3	↗	Nacimiento-Fergusson Rd (no sign)
1.9	⚠	single-lane bridge
4.0	▲	1mi steep climb
12.7		Ponderosa campground
16.3	▲	3mi steep climb
19.3		Nacimiento Summit
	⚠	7mi steep winding descent
26.4	↱	Hwy 1
26.5		Kirk Creek campground

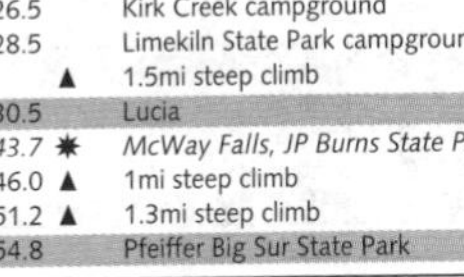

28.5		Limekiln State Park campground
	▲	1.5mi steep climb
30.5		Lucia
43.7	✱	*McWay Falls, JP Burns State Park*
46.0	▲	1mi steep climb
51.2	▲	1.3mi steep climb
54.8		Pfeiffer Big Sur State Park

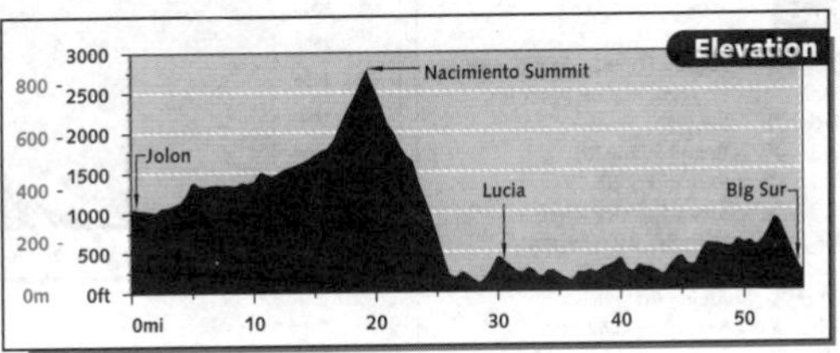

Big Sur Hinterland (continued)

See pp233–40

Day 5

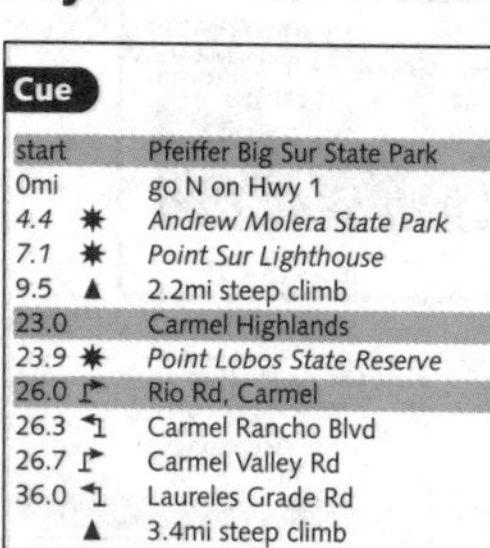

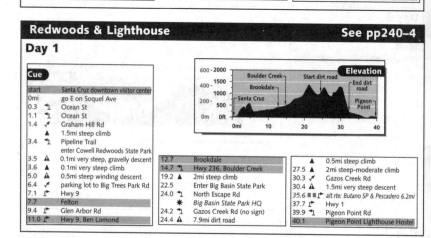

Cue		
start		Pfeiffer Big Sur State Park
0mi		go N on Hwy 1
4.4	✱	*Andrew Molera State Park*
7.1	✱	*Point Sur Lighthouse*
9.5	▲	2.2mi steep climb
23.0		Carmel Highlands
23.9	✱	*Point Lobos State Reserve*
26.0	↱	Rio Rd, Carmel
26.3	↰	Carmel Rancho Blvd
26.7	↱	Carmel Valley Rd
36.0	↰	Laureles Grade Rd
	▲	3.4mi steep climb
41.8	↱	Hwy 68

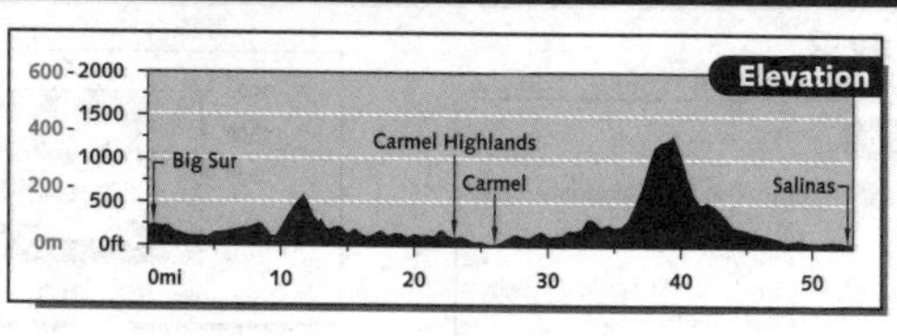

46.2	↗	Portola Dr offramp
46.4	↰	'to Portola Dr'
46.7	↱	Portola Dr
48.0	↱	'to Freeway'
48.2	↱	River Rd
48.3	↰	Hwy 68
50.9	↱	Blanco Rd

51.0	↰	Pajaro St
51.2	↰	Pajaro St
52.6	↰	E Gabilan St
52.8	↱	Lincoln Av
53.0	↱	W Market St
	↰	(10yd) Station Pl
53.1		Salinas train station

Redwoods & Lighthouse

See pp240–4

Day 1

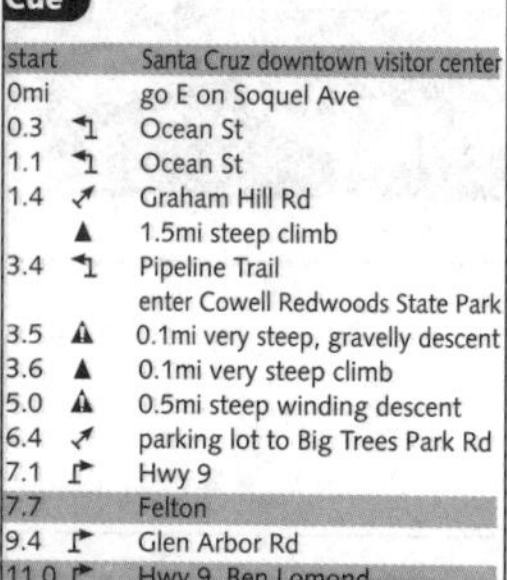

Cue		
start		Santa Cruz downtown visitor center
0mi		go E on Soquel Ave
0.3	↰	Ocean St
1.1	↰	Ocean St
1.4	↗	Graham Hill Rd
	▲	1.5mi steep climb
3.4	↰	Pipeline Trail
		enter Cowell Redwoods State Park
3.5	⚠	0.1mi very steep, gravelly descent
3.6	▲	0.1mi very steep climb
5.0	⚠	0.5mi steep winding descent
6.4	↗	parking lot to Big Trees Park Rd
7.1	↱	Hwy 9
7.7		Felton
9.4	↱	Glen Arbor Rd
11.0	↱	Hwy 9, Ben Lomond

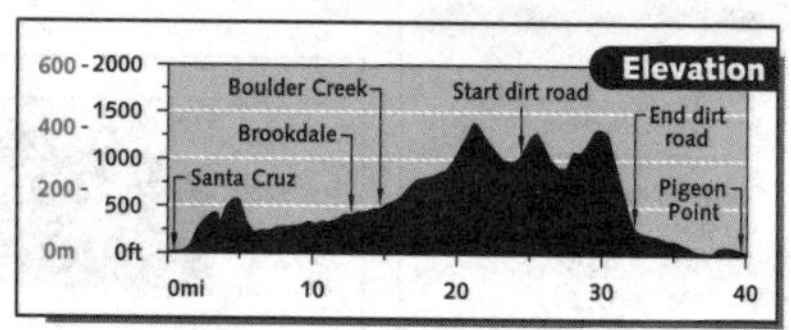

12.7		Brookdale
14.7	↰	Hwy 236, Boulder Creek
19.2	▲	2mi steep climb
22.5		Enter Big Basin State Park
24.0	↰	North Escape Rd
	✱	*Big Basin State Park HQ*
24.2	↰	Gazos Creek Rd (no sign)
24.4	⚠	7.9mi dirt road

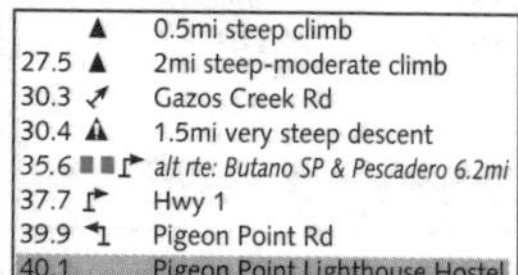

	▲	0.5mi steep climb
27.5	▲	2mi steep-moderate climb
30.3	↗	Gazos Creek Rd
30.4	⚠	1.5mi very steep descent
35.6	■■↱	*alt rte: Butano SP & Pescadero 6.2mi*
37.7	↱	Hwy 1
39.9	↰	Pigeon Point Rd
40.1		Pigeon Point Lighthouse Hostel

Day 2

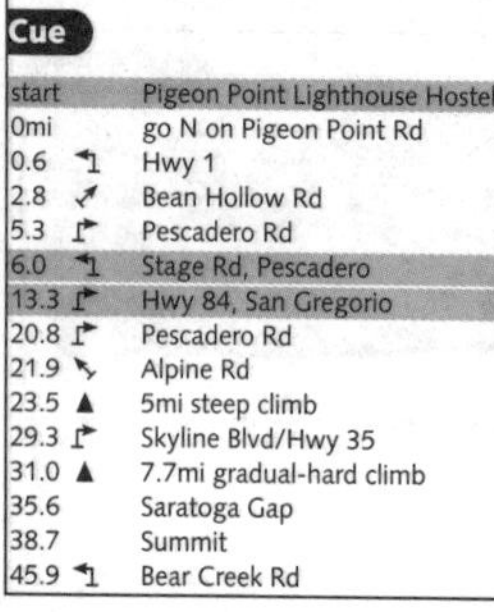

Cue		
start		Pigeon Point Lighthouse Hostel
0mi		go N on Pigeon Point Rd
0.6	↰	Hwy 1
2.8	↗	Bean Hollow Rd
5.3	↱	Pescadero Rd
6.0	↰	Stage Rd, Pescadero
13.3	↱	Hwy 84, San Gregorio
20.8	↱	Pescadero Rd
21.9	↘	Alpine Rd
23.5	▲	5mi steep climb
29.3	↱	Skyline Blvd/Hwy 35
31.0	▲	7.7mi gradual-hard climb
35.6		Saratoga Gap
38.7		Summit
45.9	↰	Bear Creek Rd

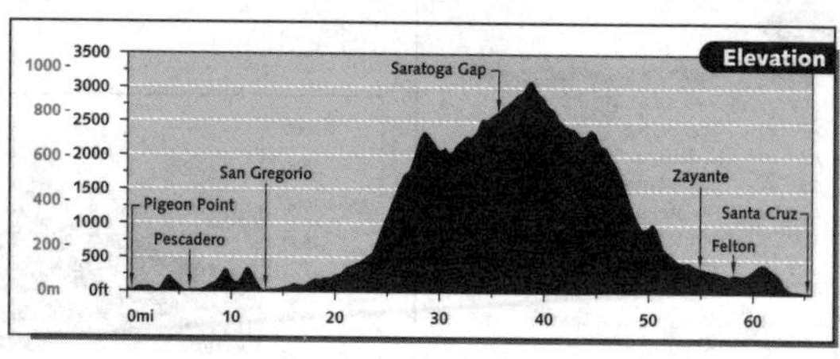

46.5	↱	Summit Rd
46.7	↱	Upper Zayante Rd
46.9	⚠	2.5mi steep winding descent
54.9		Zayante
57.7	↱	Graham Hill Rd

58.1	↰	Hwy 9, Felton
65.3	↗	River St
65.4	↰	Front St
65.6	↱	Soquel Ave
65.7		Santa Cruz downtown visitor center

Malibu Hills Grind

See pp249–51

Cue

start	Santa Monica Pier
0mi	go N on South Bay Bike Trail
3.4	leave bikepath
	(15yd) Pacific Coast Highway
4.6	*Gladstone's 4 Fish*
6.1	Topanga Cyn Blvd (Hwy 27)
9.9	Fernwood Pacific Dr
	2.7mi hard climb
12.6	Saddle Peak Rd
15.9	Schueren Rd
16.3	4.7mi twisting steep descent
17.7	Rambla Pacifico
18.4	Las Flores Cyn Rd
21.0	Enter Malibu
21.8	Pacific Coast Hwy
27.7	parking lot
	(15yd) South Bay Bike Trail
31.1	Santa Monica Pier

Palos Verdes Discovery

See pp251–3

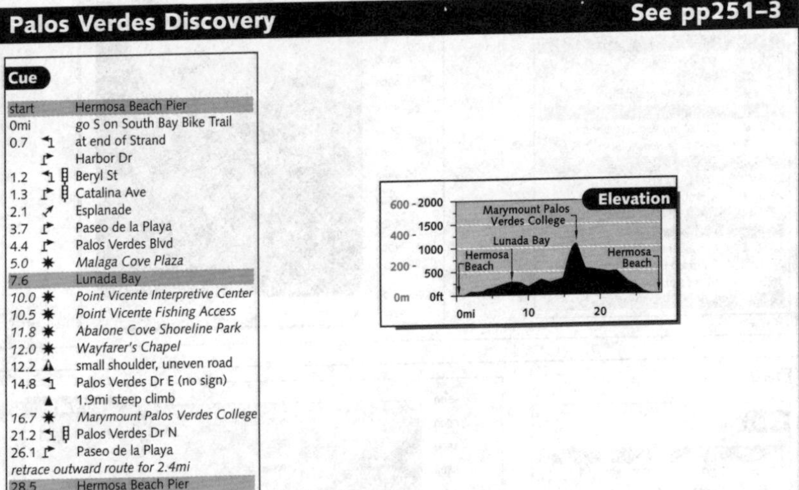

Cue

start	Hermosa Beach Pier
0mi	go S on South Bay Bike Trail
0.7	at end of Strand
	Harbor Dr
1.2	Beryl St
1.3	Catalina Ave
2.1	Esplanade
3.7	Paseo de la Playa
4.4	Palos Verdes Blvd
5.0	*Malaga Cove Plaza*
7.6	Lunada Bay
10.0	*Point Vicente Interpretive Center*
10.5	*Point Vicente Fishing Access*
11.8	*Abalone Cove Shoreline Park*
12.0	*Wayfarer's Chapel*
12.2	small shoulder, uneven road
14.8	Palos Verdes Dr E (no sign)
	1.9mi steep climb
16.7	*Marymount Palos Verdes College*
21.2	Palos Verdes Dr N
26.1	Paseo de la Playa
retrace outward route for 2.4mi	
28.5	Hermosa Beach Pier

Catalina Island Crossing

See pp253–6

Cue

start	Isthmus Pier, Two Harbors
0mi	go S on Two Harbors Road
	13mi dirt road
	2.3mi steep climb
4.5	1.5mi steep descent
6.2	*Little Harbor Beach & Campground*
7.0	1mi steep climb
8.5	0.5mi steep climb
9.5	*Escondido Ranch*
	3mi steep climb
13.0	*Airport-in-the-Sky*
19.8	3mi steep descent
23.0	Green Pier, Avalon

Mountain to Desert Descent

See pp260–4

Day 1

Cue

start	Julian visitor center
0mi	go S on Main St
0.2	Hwy 79
	3mi moderate climb
9.0	Cuyamaca
11.2	2mi steep winding descent
14.3	*Cuyamaca Rancho State Park HQ*
20.5	Descanso
20.6	Old Hwy 80
21.5	1.5mi steep climb
23.0	Guatay
25.7	Pine Valley
26.0	8.5mi steep climb
27.1	Sunrise Hwy/County Hwy S1
36.5	Burnt Rancheria Campground
36.9	Laguna Mtn Store, Mt Laguna

Day 2

Cue

start	Laguna Mountain Store, Mt Laguna
0mi	go N on County Hwy S1
14.2	Hwy 79
20.0	Hwy 78, Julian
26.7	Banner
31.5	*Butterfield Stage Rte 44.4mi*
38.6	County Hwy S3/Yaqui Pass Rd
39.0	Tamarisk Grove Campground
	1.6mi steep climb
40.6	Yaqui Pass
45.4	Deep Well Track
45.7	Borrego Springs Rd
50.9	W Palm Canyon Dr
52.8	Park visitor center, Borrego Springs

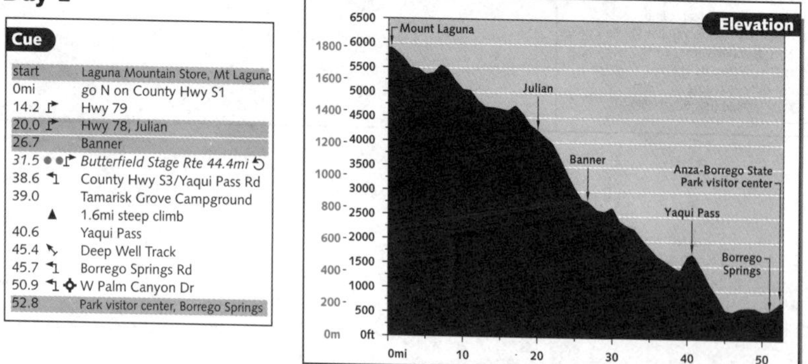

Index

Abbreviations

NP – National Park
NRA – National Recreation Area
NWR – National Wildlife Refuge
SP – State Park
SR – State Reserve
See parks & reserves for these and other wilderness areas.

Text

For a listing of rides, see the Table of Rides (pp4–5)

Bold indicates maps.
For a listing of rides, see the Table of Rides (pp4–5).

Bold indicates maps.
For a listing of rides, see the Table of Rides (pp4–5).

Bold indicates maps.
For a listing of rides, see the Table of Rides (pp4–5).

R

S

lonely planet
Los Angeles

lonely planet
California
& Nevada

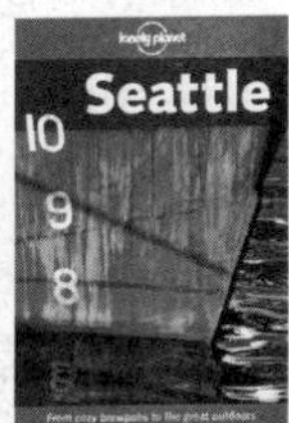
lonely planet
Seattle

lonely planet
Pacific Northwest

lonely planet
San Diego
& Tijuana

lonely planet
San Francisco

lonely planet
USA

lonely planet
Hiking in the
USA

lonely planet
Hiking in the
SIERRA NEVADA

lonely planet
Diving & Snorkeling
Monterey Peninsula
& Northern California

Lonely Planet
UNPACKED
Again
tony wheeler

lonely planet
USA
PHRASEBOOK

ABOUT LONELY PLANET GUIDEBOOKS

Lonely Planet published its first book in 1973 in response to the numerous 'How did you do it?' questions Maureen and Tony Wheeler were asked after driving, busing, hitching, sailing and railing their way from England to Australia.

Written at a kitchen table and hand collated, trimmed and stapled, *Across Asia on the Cheap* became an instant local bestseller, inspiring thoughts of another book.

Eighteen months in South-East Asia resulted in their second guide, *South-East Asia on a shoestring*, which they put together in a backstreet Chinese hotel in Singapore in 1975. The 'yellow bible', as it quickly became known to backpackers around the world, soon became the guide to the region. It has sold well over half a million copies and is now in its 10th edition.

Today an international company with offices in Melbourne (Australia), Oakland (USA), London (UK) and Paris (France), Lonely Planet has an ever-growing list of books and other products, including: travel guides, walking guides, city maps, travel atlases, phrasebooks, diving guides, wildlife guides, healthy travel guides, restaurant guides, world food guides, first time travel guides, condensed guides, travel literature, pictorial books and, of course, cycling guides. Many of these are also published in French and various other languages.

In addition to the books, there are also videos and Lonely Planet's award winning Web site.

Some things haven't changed. The main aim is still to help make it possible for adventurous travelers to get out there – to explore and better understand the world.

At Lonely Planet we believe travellers can make a positive contribution to the countries they visit – if they respect their host communities and spend their money wisely. Since 1986 a percentage of the income from each book has been donated to aid projects and human rights campaigns.

Lonely Planet gathers information for everyone who's curious about the planet – and especially for those who explore it first-hand. Through guidebooks, phrasebooks, activity guides, maps, literature, newsletters, image library, TV series and Web site we act as an information exchange for a worldwide community of travellers.

LONELY PLANET OFFICES

Australia
Locked Bag 1, Footscray, Victoria 3011
☎ 03 8379 8000 fax 03 8379 8111
e talk2us@lonelyplanet.com.au

USA
150 Linden St, Oakland, CA 94607
☎ 510 893 8555 or ☎ 800 275 8555 (toll free)
fax 510 893 8572
e info@lonelyplanet.com

UK
10a Spring Place, London NW5 3BH
☎ 020 7428 4800 fax 020 7428 4828
e go@lonelyplanet.co.uk

France
1 rue du Dahomey, 75011 Paris
☎ 01 55 25 33 00 fax 01 55 25 33 01
e bip@lonelyplanet.fr
w www.lonelyplanet.fr

World Wide Web: w www.lonelyplanet.com *or* AOL keyword: lp
Lonely Planet Images: e lpi@lonelyplanet.com.au